# JOHN MAJOR
## THE AUTOBIOGRAPHY

JOHN MAJOR has been Conservative Member of Parliament for Huntingdon since 1979. He served as Foreign Secretary and Chancellor of the Exchequer before succeeding Margaret Thatcher as leader of the Conservative Party and Prime Minister in November 1990. He was to hold both positions until May 1997, winning a remarkable victory in the 1992 general election.

John Major and his wife Norma live in London and Huntingdon. They have two children, Elizabeth and James.

# JOHN MAJOR

## THE AUTOBIOGRAPHY

HarperCollins*Publishers*

HarperCollins*Publishers*
77–85 Fulham Palace Road,
Hammersmith, London w6 8jb

The HarperCollins website address is:
www.**fire**and**water**.com

This paperback edition 2000
1 3 5 7 9 8 6 4 2

First published in Great Britain by
HarperCollins*Publishers* 1999

ISBN 0 00 653074 5

Set in Linotype Minion with Photina display by
Rowland Phototypesetting Limited,
Bury St Edmunds, Suffolk

Printed and bound in Great Britain by
Clays Ltd, St Ives plc

To Norma, Elizabeth and James

# CONTENTS

CONTENTS

# ILLUSTRATIONS

Aged about nine months. *(Personal collection)*
At Cheam Common Infants School, aged about six. *(Mirror Group Newspapers)*
Aged eight. *(Personal collection)*
My parents, Tom and Gwen. *(Personal collection)*
Aged about ten. *(Personal collection)*
Rutlish School colts cricket team, 1958. *(Rex Features)*
Our wedding reception, 3 October 1970. *(Personal collection)*
Speaking in Lambeth Council Chamber, 1970. *(Personal collection)*
Newly elected Member for Huntingdonshire: May 1979. *(Rex Features)*
In the garden at Hemingford Grey with Norma, Dee, James and Elizabeth. *(Rex Features)*
In the garden with James and Elizabeth. *(Rex Features)*
My first meeting with George Bush as Foreign Secretary. *(Official White House photograph)*
My speech as Chancellor to the 1990 Conservative Party Conference. *(Press Association/Topham)*
In the garden at Finings, 1990. *(Srdja Djukanovic/Camera Press)*
Launching the campaign for the Conservative Party leadership: November 1990. *(Richard Smith/Katz Pictures)*
The Gulf War. Meeting soldiers from the 3rd Battalion of the Desert Rats in eastern Saudi Arabia: 8 January 1991. *(David Giles/PA News)*
With Nelson Mandela in London: April 1991. *(Glynn Griffiths/The Independent)*
With François Mitterrand and George Bush: London, July 1991. *(Associated Press)*
On a visit to George Bush at Kennebunkport: August 1991. *(Associated Press)*

With HM the Queen at Balmoral: September 1991. *(Personal collection)*
The First Waltz at the 1991 party conference. *( John Downing/Daily Express)*
With Australian Prime Minister Bob Hawke at a charity cricket match: Harare, October 1991. *(Frank Spooner Pictures)*
The Maastricht summit: December 1991. *(Pierre Ache/Katz Pictures)*
On the soapbox in Luton during the 1992 general election campaign. *(Adam Butler/PA News)*

In Tamworth during the campaign. *(John Voos/The Independent)*

With Chris Patten at a Central Office press conference. *(Adam Butler/PA News)*

Arriving at Central Office after winning the 1992 general election. *(Mark Stewart/Camera Press)*

Waving to supporters with Norma and Chris Patten after the election victory. *(Mark Stewart/Camera Press)*

With Helmut Kohl: Birmingham summit, October 1992. *(M. Cleaver/Associated Press/Topham)*

At Dublin Castle during the Downing Street Declaration negotiations: December 1993. *(Adam Butler/Press Association/Topham)*

With British troops at Gough Barracks, Armagh. *(PA News)*

Press conference at Chequers with Bill Clinton: June 1994. *(PA News)*

Taking the salute with Helmut Kohl. *(Personal collection)*

In the Cabinet Room with children from Birmingham Children's Hospital. *(Rebecca Naden/PA News)*

Cabinet meeting: July 1994. *(Adam Butler/PA News)*


With HM Queen Elizabeth the Queen Mother during the VE-Day fiftieth anniversary ceremony. *(Brendan Beirne/Rex Features)*

With HM the Queen: 7 May 1995. *(Alpha)*

Announcing my resignation as leader of the Conservative Party: 22 June 1995. *(Stefan Rousseau/Press Association/Topham)*

Constituency visit to Ailwyn Community School: 23 June 1995 *(Stephen Daniels)*

John Redwood declares his candidature for the party leadership. *(Rex Features)*

Restored to the leadership: 4 July 1995. *(Tony Harris/PA News)*

The Cabinet meets in the garden of Number 10 after the leadership election. *(Alpha)*

Launching my 'Sport – Raising the Game' policy at Millwall Football Club: July 1995. *(Tom Smith/Daily Express)*

With Paddy Ashdown and Tony Blair: August 1995. *(Neil Munns/Press Association/Topham)*

With Bill and Hillary Clinton at Number 10: November 1995 *(Michael Stephens/PA News)*

Addressing British troops in Bosnia-Herzegovina: May 1996. *(S.T.R. Stringer/Associated Press)*

The opening session of the G7 Summit in Lyon: June 1996. *(O.E. Stringer/Associated Press)*

The Three Tenors visit Number 10: July 1996. *(Neil Munns/Associated Press)*

Relaxing at Chequers: June 1996. *(Simon Walker/Times Newspapers)*

# ACKNOWLEDGEMENTS

So many people helped with this book. Many are in the Civil Service and must remain anonymous, but they know who they are, and they have my profound thanks.

In the early stages of the enterprise, Matthew Parris asked me who was doing my research. When I told him that I intended to do it myself, Matthew recommended that Julian Glover should join me. Julian made a massive contribution to the finished text. He delved, researched, suggested, edited and wrote drafts, and was indispensable. I owe him a special debt – and Matthew too, both for his recommendation and for the generous interest and stream of suggestions which helped improve the narrative.

A number of former public servants can be thanked by name. They include Lord Butler of Brockwell, Lord Burns of Pitshanger, Lord Wright of Richmond Upon-Thames, Lord Craig of Radley, Sir Rodric Braithwaite, Sir Peter Middleton, Sir Crispin Tickell and Sir Charles Powell, all of whom searched their own memories and made helpful suggestions. Sir Richard Wilson, the Cabinet Secretary, permitted me the use of an office to store and study the many confidential files so swiftly located for me by his Private Office and the Duty Clerks at Number 10.

The staff of the House of Commons Library coped magnificently with many requests for information. I am most grateful for their professionalism. I would also like to thank the London Library for their assistance.

In writing this book I spoke to many former colleagues in government. There are too many to list in full, but among those I must thank are colleagues now in the House of Lords: Tristan Garel-Jones, Douglas Hurd, Ian Lang, Paddy Mayhew, Tony Newton and Richard Ryder; as well as Ken Clarke MP, Michael Heseltine MP, Virginia Bottomley MP, Michael Howard MP, Francis Maude MP, David Davis MP and Sir Alastair Goodlad, all of whom helped to clarify episodes left obscure in official documentation. Other former colleagues, Lord McColl of Dulwich, Sir Robert Atkins MEP, Sir Graham Bright and Sir John Ward, gave me access to contemporary notes, as did other former and present members of the Commons who wish to remain anonymous.

Both the former heads of my Policy Unit, Baroness Hogg of Kettlesthorpe and Lord Blackwell, were immensely generous in providing information and checking recollections. I received substantial help on domestic issues from a former member of my Downing Street staff, Nick True. Among my political staff, Howell James checked memories and dug out hidden files, and Jonathan Hill and George Bridges each lent me their special skills.

I owe a special debt to Vernon Bogdanor, Professor of Government at Oxford University, who generously read much of the book for historical accuracy and made numerous invaluable suggestions for additions and – occasionally – deletions. I greatly appreciated his wise advice. Sir Martin Gilbert, the eminent biographer of Winston Churchill, offered early guidance and has kindly agreed to hold documentation made available to me that will, I think, assist future historians to understand the motives of many who play a part in this narrative. Dr Anthony Seldon, who wrote such a comprehensive biography of my life, was always ready with advice when I sought it.

Gabriel Fawcett helped enormously with research and in the preparation of drafts on foreign affairs.

Many friends searched their memories for me – Olive Baddeley, Emily Blatch, Peter Brown, Peter Golds, Jean Lucas, Derek Oakley, Andrew Thomson, Barbara Wallis – all of them friends for all seasons.

My publishers, HarperCollins, have been steady throughout. Eddie Bell maintained a quiet confidence that I would deliver the manuscript on time, and my publisher Michael Fishwick and my editor Robert Lacey made sure that I did. Michael returned to the charge on numerous occasions to draw out more of the story. With the able assistance of Robert and of Rivers Scott he tightened and reshaped the text. My thanks are also due to Melanie Haselden for tracking down many of the illustrations.

Finally I must pay tribute to those who had to cope with me as I wrote. All the members of my office contributed. Arabella Warburton, my Private Secretary, was a tower of strength, drawing on her own memories of my time at Number 10, contributing ideas, choosing photographs and organising my life and schedule across several continents. With tremendous efficiency, Lorne Roper-Caldbeck undertook the coordination of the book, typing almost all the manuscript and enduring my handwriting without complaint. Caroline Sheffield also typed some early chapters. Victoria Panton and Anne Lakeman kept my office running as we worked. My Constituency Secretary Gina Hearn shouldered a great deal of work to release me to write, and contributed her own political recollections. All took with equanimity the inevitable dramas of writing a book. They will all be relieved, I am sure, that it is now done.

So too will my family. The reconstruction of my father's life and times and my early life owes much to the research of my brother Terry, and the formidable memory of my sister Pat and half-sister Kathleen, who I learned of only recently. My children Elizabeth and James were unfailingly eager for me to set out the story they had seen from a family perspective. Above all, I wish to thank Norma, who has researched, typed, edited, encouraged and lived with this manuscript for two years. It is true to say that without her there would have been less of a story to tell. I hope that she will now return to her own writing, and that in some way I can repay the love and support she has given me during the highs and lows of political life. I am not sure that will ever be possible, but I will try.

I hope this book will bring enjoyment and fresh insight to those who read it. The opinions expressed and any errors of fact or omission are, of course, entirely my own responsibility.

JOHN MAJOR
*Huntingdon*
*September 1999*

# FOREWORD

SINCE I LEFT 10 Downing Street, I have often thought – why politics?

From politicians themselves the standard response is a burning ambition to improve the lot of the poor, say, or the disabled, or to 'change things for the better'.

There is truth in these claims – they are not to be disparaged. But the answer is too often calculated to win approval, too self-serving, and almost always incomplete. Motives for entering politics are much more complex. Mine certainly were.

Politics attracted me from an early age. I longed to be involved, and loathed the thought that I would have no part in making the decisions that would shape my life and times. The thought of a run-of-the-mill job did not appeal; I wanted excitement and the stimulus of the unexpected – although, I was to learn, one can overdose on that. I did believe in public service and public obligation, and if I'd had a double first I would have been attracted to a career in the Civil Service. But I had no wish to be a second-rank civil servant, and my background and lack of paper qualifications would more or less have dictated that fate, irrespective of any talent I might have shown. Being insufficiently educated to advise ministers, I decided early on to be a minister myself, and to harness others' learning to my native good sense.

*Fame is the Spur*, wrote Howard Spring. He was right. Political life is stimulated by ambition, and providing ambition is not obsessive, I see nothing wrong in that. Even in these cynical days it is something to be a Member of Parliament, with those precious initials after your name.

I was attracted to the Conservative Party because it did not draw its language from the dark emotions of envy or resentment. It cared for the weak, the poor and the old, but unlike the Labour Party it did not demand a lifetime of adherence to a class struggle. It saw people as individuals, not as political troops. The Conservatism of Harold Macmillan, Iain Macleod and Rab Butler understood and spoke the language of compassion. Compassion is a virtue the best of the Conservative Party has long lived by, and without which it would never have become the broad-based, tolerant party I joined. The tone of Conservatism that appealed to me did not cultivate the envy of the few in order to improve the condition of the many. It argued for the opportunity to build security and ownership and wealth – and it showed the practical way to do so. It was not hidebound by ideology. This philosophy made me a Conservative from the first moment I truly thought about politics.

The life of politics is like no other. It has many joys and excitements, and I would not have missed them. But there is a price to be paid for the fame and the fun, and too often it is paid by family and friends. Politics at the top is all-consuming. Every interest is swept up and subordinated to its demands. I tried to guard against this by living parallel lives – politics and private life – which I did my best to prevent merging. In this I was largely successful, preserving my personal friendships and interests, and, I hope, providing a sense of balance for the life after high office.

However, private interests cannot be wholly hidden. Appearances at Lords and The Oval made my love of cricket apparent. Some knew of my affection for soccer, but few of my love of rugby, the cinema, theatre, music, gardening and, above all, books. I did not draw attention to them; I kept them, as far as possible, in the secluded area of my life. While part of me longed for the political limelight, another part demanded privacy.

And for very good reason. Even as my political profile rose and I became ever more public property, I knew this would not last for ever. Senior politicians spend only a limited time in the sun, and I did not want to leave the front line of politics as a husk, bereft of everything but a backward glance to memories of my political noontide. I knew that becoming prime minister at the age of forty-seven would mean being ex-prime minister within two Parliaments, unless something extraordinary were to happen. I intended from the outset to be prepared for the day I left office, since, following it, there would still be a lot of life to be lived.

Twenty years in Parliament, so far, has left me with a high regard for most parliamentarians. There are always a few charlatans in the Commons, concerned for self rather than country or party, and a few rent-a-quotes, avid above all for publicity. They strut the stage for a while, but are soon recognised for what they are. This shallow minority has inspired among the public an incomplete view of political life.

Government has changed over the decades. In the middle of the abdication crisis of 1936, Stanley Baldwin spent a month and a half at Aix-les-Bains, phoning Number 10 twice a week for news. Churchill's ill-health during his last years as prime minister went unreported, and was unknown to most voters. In 1959–60 Harold Macmillan toured Africa for weeks, leaving Rab Butler in charge at home. None of that would be possible today. The prime minister's instant reactions are demanded daily, and his press secretary provides them. The reporting of politics changed too, as the battle for newspaper circulation grew ever more intense. In the 1980s even *The Times* and the *Daily Telegraph* largely stopped verbatim reports of proceedings in Parliament, replacing them with columns by sketch writers. Caricature can illuminate and entertain, but the absence of proper reporting is a loss. I hope that one day it may return.

Even among lobby correspondents, the emphasis changed. There is more pressure to come up with sensational stories, less hesitancy to print speculative ones. In all this, there has grown up an unscrupulousness, a willingness to give credence to rumour, a refusal to correct or apologise, an amnesia about last week's splash or leading article. 'Government to do X', the headlines shriek. The government patiently explains that it never had any intention of doing any such thing. The next morning, the headlines read 'Government retreats on X'. No doubt this sells newspapers. But it also sells their readers short.

Television has brought immediacy to political events and much greater awareness of them. It has introduced modern politicians to the electorate, warts and all, in a way their predecessors never were. In 1989 I voted against letting the cameras into the Commons, but I now believe I was wrong to do so. Television has also introduced the electorate to their politicians. Even as the voters' interest in politicians wanes, politicians themselves are absorbed by what people want and feel and do. Up to a point, this is a healthy development.

Television has great power, but its emphasis on brevity does distort. Politics is complex, and reports too often oversimplify. I commented once that an hour-long address on education would earn me one minute on prime-time television news. This would be accompanied by one minute from the Labour leader, who had not read or heard the speech, and one minute from the Liberal leader, who had not understood it. This was a parody, but one with a lot of truth in it. It is equally true that the crude picture of public opinion which the media offers MPs can oversimplify horribly.

At the top level of politics, the words of politicians are pored over to extract every possible nuance beyond their straightforward meaning. An industry has grown up of pundits who interpret what politicians may mean by what they say, and they are assisted by 'friends' of the politicians ever eager to explain. Too often these Chinese whispers mean the end product is unrecognisable, but, in an age where perception is all, what was meant becomes less important than what is reported.

The effect of all this has been to add immeasurably to the electorate's cynicism about politics. I recognised this as prime minister, but I could not break free from it. I regret that. I longed to move away from 'politician-speak', but feared misinterpretation. I should have been bolder: it is appalling that we sometimes inflict such nonsense on the electorate as 'the government's position is clear' (when it isn't); 'we have exciting new plans' (when we don't); and 'we want a better future for our people' (which we do, but how patronising that expression is. They are not *our* people. They do not *belong* to any political party. They are individuals who are worth more than those who patronise them).

In our age of 'spin' the electorate is thrown an increasing volume of pap. Every day it becomes harder to obtain widespread currency for ideas or beliefs without retreating into soundbite or cliché. I would not have recognised a 'soundbite' if it gripped me by the windpipe. I only hope my meaning sometimes, if fitfully, transcended my words.

As a young MP I did not court journalists, but as I rose through ministerial ranks, I came to know a few of them. Some I trusted, others not, and I kept well clear of those with a reputation for political fiction. Generally in the early years I had a friendly, perhaps even an over-generous, press, and no personal reason to mistrust them.

After I became prime minister this was to change; and so swift had been my climb up the greasy pole that I was unprepared for the onslaught. Party leaders are treated differently, prime ministers even more so. They are praised to excess or damned to perdition, sometimes both at the same time. I cannot claim to have enjoyed this, because no one could. I have yet to meet a politician with a hide like a rhinoceros. Those legendary thick-skinned beasts are said to exist, but if they are not extinct, or mythical, they are very rare. I learned to disregard the more obvious untruths and absurdities in the media, but yes, they stung, and those who say they do not deceive themselves.

But politics offers many rewards to offset these pinpricks. It is exhilarating to be at the centre of great events. It is satisfying to unravel a problem that seems insoluble. It is rewarding to help people who look to you for assistance. There are friendships that flourish amidst the rivalries as colleagues jostle for the same prizes. Cabals, gangs and partnerships are formed. The shared intentions, the hard work, the planning, the plotting, the highs and lows of joint campaigns create bonds that can be unbreakable and shared experiences that will never be forgotten. Nor is this surprising. Politics is about ideas, convictions, passions and ambitions, and MPs have these in abundance. It would be extraordinary if this did not lead to vivid exchanges and lasting relationships of friendship or, sometimes, enmity.

I found this especially true in the Whips' Office, where there is one collective mind – the Office view arrived at after discussion – and one objective, which is to protect and advance the interests of the government. Nothing leaks from the whips. I often thought of their office as the most secure place in Western Europe.

Of course there are regrets. I shall regret always that I rarely found my own authentic voice in politics. I was too conservative, too conventional. Too safe, too often. Too defensive. Too reactive. Later, too often on the back foot. I inherited a sick economy and passed on a sound one. But one abiding regret for me is that, in between, I did not have the resources to put in place the educational and social changes about which I cared so much; I made only a beginning, and it was not enough.

I do not regret breaking the cycle of inflation. Or beginning the peace process in Northern Ireland. Or the health and education reforms. Or introducing a national lottery which would fund the arts, sport, heritage and charities more generously than ever before. I am proud to have introduced public-sector reform to protect the consumer and, by winning the 1992 election, to have enshrined the reforms of the preceding thirteen years, and forced Labour to accept what hitherto had been anathema to them. I was pleased to keep Britain in Europe and to prevent the Conservative Party from splitting. To do so I took a lot of criticism that the old pro-European Harold Macmillan would have understood. Selwyn Lloyd, once Macmillan's foreign secretary, recalled him saying on his sickbed in 1963 that 'Balfour had been bitterly criticised for not having a view on Protection and Free

Trade. Balfour had said the important thing was to preserve the unity of the Conservative Party. He had been abused for that. But who argues now about protection and free trade? When was the last time the conventional arguments were exchanged? 1923? Whereas the preservation of great national institutions had been the right policy. Lloyd George might have been clear-cut on policy, but he destroyed the Liberal Party.' The day may come when a similar judgement is made on the single currency.

When I talked of a classless society I wanted to say that the people who pushed wheelbarrows when I mixed cement for a living were human beings worthy of respect. They are as much in 'God's lively image' as a nobleman with sixteen quarterings. I was in earnest about classlessness. I wanted to say that the subtle calibrations of scorn in which this country rejoices, the endless puttings down and belittlings, so instinctive that we do not notice ourselves doing them, are awful. They are so awful they stop us seeing men and women whole.

Class distinction is to me exactly the same as racial distinction. The utter repulsiveness of racial prejudice is something that I have sensed since I was a child. I loathe the language of contempt or hatred. I expect always to be colour-blind and class-blind, and not to spurn or despise anyone on those grounds. Contempt is first cousin to hatred. It is best replaced by understanding.

What I believe in – and I make no apology for being unscientific about it – is a rough-and-ready decency. I should have advocated it more often and made a virtue of it. But to many politicians and onlookers today a rough-and-ready decency is not enough. They demand an ideology, intellectual mentors, a political template by which to judge every circumstance. I reject that. Most people simply do not think in that way. Of course there must be broad principles and recognised values to underpin political decisions, but to believe that decisions can only be in the national interest if they conform to the ideology of some guru must surely be nonsense. Let us have convictions by all means, but not the sort of convictions that are the flip-side of bigotry. A politician's responsibility should above all be a readiness to do what is best in all the circumstances to deal with the issue at hand.

My politics was quiet politics. I disliked brash populism. I distrusted bitter conflict. I was at ease with the knitting-up of conciliation. It may have been boring to some, it may have been seen as grey, but it had its points. In *Can You Forgive Her?*, the first of Anthony Trollope's great political novels about the Palliser family, an aspirant candidate muses upon the duties of being an MP. He is duly elected, and serves his party and his country well. His name, I recall, was John Grey. And perhaps I should have reminded my critics of what the Impressionist painter Camille Pissarro wrote in a letter to his son Lucien, also a painter: 'Never forget to make proper use of the whole dazzling range of greys.' Hallelujah.

This book is not a history of our time. It is a personal odyssey that covers successes and failures but which ended in a crushing rebuff on May Day 1997. We – I – made mistakes. We paid for them. But we had successes too. On the day I became prime minister interest rates were 14 per cent, inflation 9.7 per cent, and unemployment 1.75 million, on its way to three million. When I left Number 10, interest rates were 6 per cent, inflation 2.6 per cent, and unemployment 1.6 million and falling. It was the healthiest economy any government had handed to its successors for generations. How we lost, despite this economic turnaround, is part of this story. In it I will not concede possession of the recent past to the mythographers of left or right who have every self-interest in retouching the history we made. For New Labour a Year Zero view of politics conveniently covers up the follies and errors of Labour's past and denies the advances of good Conservative government.

Nor do I concede the Year Zero philosophy of some on the right. Conservatism was not discovered only in the 1980s, nor was it lost in the 1990s. Such a view is absurd. The 1980s were indeed great years of achievement and I was proud to have been a small part of them. But a proper respect for those achievements is not enhanced by rewriting history and denying the successes that preceded them, or those that have followed. Continuity matters to Conservatives. Some ideologues on the right forget that.

My great predecessor as Member of Parliament for Huntingdon, Oliver Cromwell, cautioned the painter Lely as he began a portrait of him: 'Remark all these roughnesses, pimples, warts, and everything as you see me, otherwise I will never pay a farthing for it.' He wanted an accurate portrait. So do I, and I have tried to achieve one. Politics, like life, is not all black and white. Sometimes it is grey, and in this story I have tried to colour in all its shades.

# CHAPTER ONE

## The Search for Tom Major

I KNEW VERY LITTLE ABOUT my antecedents until I began writing this book. The search for my family provided many surprises.

As a boy, I soaked up the atmosphere of my parents' unconventional life. When my father, Tom, was old and ill he would entertain me for hours with stories of the extraordinary things he had done. He painted vivid pictures of his boyhood in nineteenth-century America and of his own father, a master builder. He spoke of his years in show business and brought great entertainers like Harry Houdini and Marie Lloyd to life for me. He had a tireless fund of evocative stories and a formidable memory that stretched back well into the last century. He was a wonderful raconteur and I learned to be a good listener at his bedside.

No doubt my father could embroider for effect, but I never knew him to lie. Much was left out, as I was to discover, but whenever he exaggerated or embellished my mother hurried in to try to damp the story down. I grew up with his tales and accepted them without question, though his wayward life left little evidence for us to confirm what he said. After I joined the Cabinet in 1987 and the press began to delve into my past, an impression was sometimes given that I was withholding information. Not at all. I knew so little myself. But at that time my family, too, began to delve. The burden initially fell on my brother Terry. Later, when I started this book, we worked together. We had to piece together a life without documents that had begun 120 years before. It was a fascinating adventure. In the search for Tom Major, we unearthed a remarkable, idiosyncratic life.

His roots lay in the West Midlands. My great-great grandfather, Joseph Ball, was a prosperous Willenhall locksmith; his son, John Ball, born at the end of the Napoleonic Wars, was licensee of the Bridge Tavern, just outside

Walsall. It still exists today. John and his wife Caroline had six children, of whom the second, Abraham Ball, born in January 1848, was my grandfather. He married a young Irish girl, Sarah Anne Marrah; illiterate, my grandmother signed my father's birth certificate with an 'X'. I never met her, of course, but I still have a photograph, taken not long before she died in 1919, of her feeding chickens at my father's house in Shropshire. She looks a formidable lady, a not improbable mother of an adventurous and restless son. And my father certainly was that.

He was born in 1879, and christened Abraham Thomas Ball. But he was always known as Tom, and never Abraham. 'Major' was the stage name he adopted as a young man. Had he not done so, I would have been John Ball, sharing the name of the leader of the Peasants' Revolt against the poll tax.

Tom was Abraham and Sarah's only natural child, and I had always believed he had been brought up alone. He was not. In one of the many surprises I had while researching this book, I learned of an older adopted son, Alfred, born to a destitute bridle-bit maker. My grandparents, his neighbours, took Alfred in, and it was only when he married that he learned he was adopted. My father never spoke of him to me.

Brought up as brothers, Tom and Alfred did not spend long in the Midlands. When my father was about five my grandparents emigrated to America, and settled in Pittsburgh. They must have hoped for a better life. They sailed on the SS *Indiana* from Liverpool to Philadelphia, and were appalled by conditions on board. The *Indiana* was a primitive two-masted steamship belonging to the American Line, built for stability rather than speed or comfort. The journey took three weeks; poorer migrants, travelling as deck passengers, were fed, so my father told me, with salted herrings from a barrel – much like sea lions in a zoo. He was lucky, and travelled in better circumstances. In America, my grandfather soon found work as a master bricklayer, building blast furnaces for the Andrew Carnegie Steel Works in Philadelphia.

I know little about my family's time across the Atlantic. No photographs or records survive. If they wrote or received letters, they are lost. But Abraham apparently prospered, and my father had a happy and comfortable American upbringing. Perhaps something of his classless, independent background was to rub off on me.

My father often spoke of living in Fall Hollow, in the foothills of the

Allegheny Mountains in Pennsylvania. He used to tell me he had found Indian arrowheads in the woods behind his house. I could find no place named 'Fall Hollow'. Panic. Was his – and my – story true? Terry, with the aid of the *Pittsburgh Post Gazette* came to the rescue. Fall Hollow, near Braddock, did once exist, just as my father said.

I would know more if I still had the dented travelling trunk in which he kept old documents and cuttings about his time in America and his work as a trapeze artist. The trunk ended up in a dusty alcove in the cellar at 80 Burton Road, Brixton, my parents' last home, and was left there when my sister Pat and her husband Peter moved out. I remember investigating it as a child. I saw the oversize evening suit and top hat my father wore in his publicity postcards, photographs (including one of him wearing his trapeze costume), and scores for a music-hall band.

The new owners of the bungalow in Worcester Park, Surrey, where I lived as a boy, found a number of remarkable items from my father's life in their loft: a make-up box, a clown suit, shoes, wigs and scores of sheets of old music-hall songs, many signed by the composers. It was the residue of a music-hall life on the move.

My father began his career as a performer in America. He used to say that as a child he joined a local fife-and-drum band in Pennsylvania, became skilled at twirling a baton, and twice performed as a young drum major in front of President Grover Cleveland. I cannot prove this, but I do remember my mother swinging a baton of her own on our lawn at home (to the astonishment of our neighbours – it was not the sort of thing one did in Worcester Park) and telling me Father had taught her, so there is some circumstantial support for the story.

Soon my father was performing in the circus ring. He taught himself acrobatics in the cellar of his father's building workshop, and by the age of eight, he claimed, he was the top man in a four-man pyramid. As a teenager, he said, he performed on the flying trapeze without a safety net – to attract a larger crowd and earn a bigger fee.

I can't be certain exactly when or why my grandparents returned to England but by 1896, when Tom was seventeen, he and Alfred and their father were back in the West Midlands. The two young men were active members of the Walsall Swimming Club, and in the late 1890s their names appear repeatedly in local newspaper reports of swimming galas, taking part in an odd array of events, from canoe races in comic costume and aquatic 'Derbys' (with the swimmer as a horse carrying a 'jockey'), to life-saving exhibitions, swimming races in fancy dress (Tom winning a prize as a 'new woman' in bloomers) and water-polo matches.

By the turn of the century, press mentions of my father cease. He may have moved away from Walsall; certainly less-newsworthy things now occupied his time. One of them became a family secret, unmentioned, something which again I did not discover until I was researching this book. As well as an adopted uncle, I had another brother.

In July 1901 a young dancer, Mary Moss, married to a musician named James Moss, gave birth to a son in Wigan. They called him Tom and registered his birth on 25 July, but the details they gave were untrue: the baby's father was not James Moss but my father, Tom – then a twenty-two-year-old bachelor. James Moss brought the boy up as his own; indeed he may never have known he was not the father. But Tom Major did not lose touch with his son, and the child – my half-brother – was to enter my life many years later in Brixton, in circumstances no one could have imagined.

It is not hard to guess how my father met Mary and James Moss, for he was now a professional stage performer. The first of his variety shows that I can trace was 'The Encore', put on at the Grand Theatre, Stockton-on-Tees, in August 1902. Tom Major appeared on the bill as part of a double act, 'Drum and Major', with his future wife, Kitty.

Five years my father's senior, Kitty was already married to a masseur, David Grant, when they met. The appeal of a life with a masseur must have worn off, for she soon formed a permanent professional partnership with my father which took her away from her husband, and she married Tom after Grant's death, in 1910.

Kitty and Tom – 'Drum and Major' – were in regular work. September 1902 saw them on stage in Portsmouth; December took them to Hastings; and in the first half of 1903 they appeared in turn at Camberwell, Birmingham, Middlesbrough, Bolton, Manchester, Birkenhead, Plymouth, Stockton and Wolverhampton. Only political party leaders perform in a more bewildering succession of venues.

It was a peripatetic existence, but they must have loved travelling because they did not stay long in Britain. In July 1903 the pair sailed from Southampton, and did not return for almost a year. An advertisement in the *Stage* announced that they were 'Touring in South America'; which was brave of them, since neither spoke Spanish. While they were there, I learned from my father, they spent time on a cattle ranch in Argentina. He used to tell me tales of the gauchos and their way of life. He also claimed that in Buenos Aires he had worked in a millionaires' club, looking out for card-sharpers and winning back their gains. As an old man he was still an avid card-player.

And he crossed the River Plate – at least according to family legend – stumbling into a civil war in Uruguay, and was forced to enlist briefly in a local militia. Perhaps the name 'Major' confused someone. Tom used to recount how he had a white band pinned to his arm and had been ordered to march a group of undesirables out of town. He claimed that the white band denoted his status as an officer, but in fact, as my brother has subsequently discovered, at the time of his visit Uruguay was hotly divided between two political clans, the Blancos and the Colorados – the Whites and the Reds. Even a small piece of clothing of either colour committed you to one side or the other. Probably inadvertently, my father had joined the rebellious Blancos in their failed challenge to the Colorado party.

Their revolutionary phase behind them, Tom and Kitty returned to England in April 1904 to a thriving career. A fortnight after docking they were on stage in Blackpool, and they toured the country continually until the outbreak of war in 1914. They must have appeared in almost every big theatre in Britain, but life was not easy for music-hall performers. Contracts were cancelled without notice; shows were moved from theatre to theatre without compensation; and some theatres demanded that artistes play daily matinees but take payment only for evening shows. Individually, most performers were at the mercy of management. Collectively they believed they could protect themselves, and decided to do so.

A conference was called of leading stage figures, which Tom and Kitty attended, and on 18 February 1906 the Variety Artistes Federation was formed at the Vaudeville Club in London. Everyone present joined that same evening, and queued to pay the subscription of two shillings and sixpence. Tom and Kitty were Founder Members Numbers 97 and 98; my sister Pat still has our father's white-and-green membership badge. I cannot recall, however, mentioning to the Huntingdonshire Conservative selection committee that my father was a pioneer trade unionist.

By 1914 Tom and Kitty were running a successful touring company. Tom had developed a heart condition which disqualified him from active service in the First World War, but they continued to appear on stage, their entertainments doubling as recruiting drives. My family still has an autograph book in which Tom collected the signatures of soldiers in the audience who had been decorated for their valour.

The end of the war saw the music-hall business return to normal. Throughout 1920 and 1921 Tom and Kitty travelled Britain, never stopping anywhere for more than a month, performing sketches and revues such as 'Stop Press', 'Ginger', 'Fantasy' and 'After the Overture'.

And now, as I found out to my astonishment while researching this book, a surprise half-sister joins the family troupe. At about this time my father had an affair with one Alice Maude Frankland. She became pregnant, and a daughter, Kathleen, my father's second child, was born in October 1923. Alice soon disappeared from the scene, but Tom and Kitty adopted Kathleen just a month after her birth. While they criss-crossed the country with their shows, the baby was boarded with a foster-couple. In about 1927 or 1928, they decided to bring her home. 'The Majors want to take Kath away,' her foster-parents were told – a heartbreaking moment. Sense prevailed, and Kathleen stayed where she was, though my father continued to provide financial support.

I have yet to reach 1930 in my family's story, and already we have stumbled across an unrelated 'uncle', a wayward father, illiteracy, adultery, remarriage and two previously unknown half-siblings. Childhood memories have left me with a rock-solid respect for the traditional basics of family life and family duty; but if, unlike some Conservative colleagues and supporters, I have always taken with a pinch of salt the myth of a past golden age of conventional families, splendid education and national virtue, then I, and millions of my compatriots, have reason to. Life in Britain has never been simple, and never will be.

Kathleen was not to enter my life until after I had left Downing Street. Although she always knew of my family, I was not aware of her, and she was startled when in 1990 her half-brother became prime minister. She could have sold her story to the press for a small fortune. Instead, she kept the secret. Only after the 1997 general election did I learn that I had a half-sister, alive, well and living in England.

It was lucky for young Kathleen that she stayed with her foster-family, for a catastrophe would soon cost Kitty her life. While she was rehearsing on stage, a steel girder from the safety curtain came loose, fell, and struck her on the head. She was terribly injured, and though she lingered on for months with her mind impaired, she died in June 1928, perhaps mercifully for so vibrant a woman, and was buried at Prees Cemetery in Shropshire. Kitty and my father had been together for over twenty-five years. When she died my father was deluged with sympathetic letters, from everyone from theatre managers to call-boys. She was much loved.

After the accident Kitty had been comforted and nursed by a young dancer who had joined my father's show six years earlier, at the age of seventeen. She was one half of 'Glade and Glen', a speciality act – and a cheeky, teasing, self-willed girl, often in trouble for misbehaviour and pranks. But she charmed her way out of every scrape, and had been a favourite of Kitty's. A year after Kitty's death, she married her boss, Tom, twenty-six years her senior, and cared for him for the rest of his life. Her name was Gwen, and she was my mother.

Gwen's past held surprises for me, too. In 1991, one of my constituents with an interest in family history wrote a letter to me in which he suggested that I might have shared more than my job with Margaret Thatcher. My mother's family had roots in the Boston district of Lincolnshire, not far from Margaret Thatcher's home town of Grantham, and research suggests that it is likely – though not certain – that through my mother Margaret Thatcher and I have common ancestors in eighteenth-century Lincolnshire.

As the 1920s ended and music halls gave way to cinemas, my father left show business. It was the right decision, for his profession was dying, but it must have hurt. His 1929 marriage certificate shows his occupation as 'builder', but I have no reason to believe he ever was one – though he may have financed the building of bungalows. Certainly he was soon in a different trade, modelling animals and garden ornaments. My parents moved from Shropshire to a bungalow in Worcester Park, and children soon came along. A son, Thomas Aston, was born in 1929, but sadly lived only a few days. Then came Pat, born in 1930, and Terry, in 1932.

In the course of his life, my father once told me, he had made and lost fortunes several times over. What he meant by a fortune I don't know, but for him the 1930s were good times. He became the first car-owner in the area; Pat and Terry were sent to fee-paying schools; and my mother had domestic help while she worked to build up my father's business. All this changed with the outbreak of the Second World War. My father was sixty. His workforce joined the services and, as he had foreseen, the market for his ornaments collapsed. The car went. Pat and Terry were withdrawn from their private schools. Pat, the more academic of the two, won a scholarship to Nonsuch Grammar School for Girls, but Terry went to the local state school. My father became a Senior Air Raid Warden, and my mother began work in the local library, supplementing the family income by giving dancing lessons at home.

She had hoped for another child, but did not expect one. In late 1942 she began to suffer persistent heartburn and went to her doctor, a salty-tongued medic with a sharp bedside manner. 'Don't be bloody silly, woman,' he boomed at her. 'You're pregnant.' It was not an easy pregnancy, and my birth was dramatic. My mother collapsed in the kitchen with double pneumonia and pleurisy, and was rushed to St Helier Hospital, Carshalton, where she nearly died. I was born a few hours later, on 29 March 1943. Within days I, too, was perilously ill with a virulent infection. I only just survived, and to this day bear scarred ankles from the many blood transfusions.

My mother returned to her job in the library, taking me with her in my pram. When a German flying bomb landed in a nearby street, it killed ten people and shattered hundreds of windows. Glass splinters fell into my cot which, mercifully, was empty. Forty-seven years later I was to hear the sound of breaking glass when the IRA launched a mortar at Downing Street. For my mother, the flying bomb was too much. The family moved to Saham Toney in Norfolk for the rest of the war, returning to Worcester Park in 1945.

My first memories are of a small bungalow with four rooms, a bathroom and a kitchen. Our garden was long and narrow, dotted with sheds in which my father worked. We had a lawn just large enough for ball games, and two ponds: one shallow with a few goldfish, the other a deep iron tank sunk into the ground. There were rockeries, fruit trees to plunder and larger trees to climb.

Money, though, was an irregular commodity. Mostly we were comfortable but not well-off. Our neighbours were friendly and we were relaxed and at ease in our community, but I soon realised my parents were more exotic than those of my friends. For a start they were much older – when I was born my father was nearly sixty-four and my mother a few weeks short of thirty-eight. Gwen, clad in straight-up-and-down 1930s sports garb, raised eyebrows even from friendly neighbours by exercising and throwing her Indian clubs in the garden. My father, in the early days, could be spotted with his batons, as could Pat, doing acrobatics. When I think of this scene, I'm reminded of the families of circus performers described by Dickens in *Hard Times*:

> The father of one of the families was in the habit of balancing the father of another of the families on the top of a great pole; the father of a third family often made a pyramid of both those fathers ... all the fathers could dance upon rolling casks, stand upon bottles, catch knives and balls, twirl hand-basins, ride upon anything, jump over everything, and stick at nothing. All the mothers could (and did) dance, upon the slack wire and the tight rope, and perform rapid acts on barebacked steeds; none of them were at all particular in respect of showing their legs ...
>
> They all assumed to be mighty rakish and knowing, they were not very tidy in their private dresses, they were not at all orderly in their domestic arrangements, and the combined literature of the whole company would have produced but a poor letter on any subject. Yet there was a remarkable gentleness and childishness about these people, a special inaptitude for any kind of sharp practice, and an untiring readiness to help and pity one another, deserving, often of as much respect, and always as much generous construction, as the everyday virtues of any class of people in the world.

I remember my father as a stern old man, but kind. My mother idolised him and cared for him in every way. She must have known of his earlier dalliances, but nothing was ever said, at least not in our hearing. Our father's word was law, and he never had to raise his voice to keep order. In his prime he had been a truly striking figure, 'a great and stylish Edwardian actor,' one biographer of mine has written, 'over six feet tall, athletic in build and expansive in his gestures.' Now ill and prematurely aged, he was still master in his house.

But it was my mother who brought up the family and ran the home. My father made the decisions. She carried them out. She was a Peter Pan figure who never quite grew up. The sprite of mischief was always with her. Loving and beloved, she was a magnet for lame ducks. I remember sitting at the table about to eat my lunch when a cold and hungry gypsy knocked at the door. He was invited in and my mother served him my meal, leaving me hungry. She did not ask me to do the washing up – she would not have considered that fair. But neither did she ask the gypsy to do it.

Gwen had a straightforward philosophy. Share what you've got. Be polite to others. Think of their feelings. Make allowances for them. Stand up for yourself but don't cause unnecessary offence. Don't show your own feelings. It was a simple code. She believed it and she lived it.

At the age of five I went to Cheam Common Infants' School, which was around half a mile from our home in Longfellow Road, graduating to the Junior School in the autumn of 1950. I was taken to school at first, but it was an easy journey, and I was soon walking there and back on my own.

Sometimes I was given small amounts of pocket money on a rather haphazard basis – or earned it by doing small tasks. With this I often bought presents for my mother. My father did not approve. 'That is not why we give him the money,' I overheard him say to my mother. 'Why does he do it?' He was angry and I didn't understand why. His view was that they had given me some of the little they had, and he did not think I should spend it on them. But I often did. I liked giving presents and my mother loved receiving them.

I liked receiving presents too, and except for one occasion when there was no money, Christmas and birthdays always brought something. Footballs, Meccano sets, pens and pencils for school, and classic books: *Ivanhoe*, *Quentin Durward*, *The Black Arrow*, *Tom Brown's Schooldays*, *20,000 Leagues Under the Sea*, *Knights of the Round Table*, the *Greyfriars* stories – all of these and many more were favourites. Thus began my lifelong love affair with books.

Books introduced me to a world I'd never known, and people I would never meet. My parents encouraged me to read, although my father was too active and physical a man to be a great reader himself. He had too much else to do. But later, after he began to lose his sight, he derived great pleasure from the 'talking books' sent to him by the Nuffield Centre for the Blind, which came in large pouches and were fragile records like the old 78s of the time. They kept introspection at bay when his dreams crumbled. I would sit with him and listen to them for hour upon hour. We often talked of books. The authors he remembered from his youth were Rider Haggard, Jack London and Arthur Conan Doyle – and not only, he said, for the Sherlock Holmes stories.

'Have you ever read *The White Company*?' he asked. I hadn't, and nor did I until the 1990s, when Stephen Wall, my Private Secretary at the Foreign Office and later at Number 10, and subsequently our Ambassador to the European Union, gave me his own precious copy.

My mother didn't read much. She was too busy running the family, cosseting my father and helping lame ducks. I don't think my brother Terry was much of a reader either, but I could be wrong, because he has surprised me all my life. I'm never quite sure what he'll do next – and neither, I suspect, is he. He seems to enjoy allowing the world to underestimate him while he chuckles at it.

My sister Pat did read – a lot. Academically, she was the clever one of the family, and an astute judge of character. After I became prime minister she would phone me up and say, 'Don't trust him. He's up to no good.' She was almost always right.

For me, books were an escape and an education. Some became lifelong friends. *Fame is the Spur*, *A Horseman Riding By*, *How Green was my Valley*, Trollope – *Phineas Finn* and *Phineas Redux* were never far from hand. Biographies and histories joined Agatha Christie, Neville Cardus, Thomas Costain and many more, not forgetting Mrs Henry Wood's *East Lynne*. I loved Jane Austen and Dickens – especially *The Pickwick Papers*, *A Tale of Two Cities* and *Great Expectations*.

I learned that there is as much to be learned from durable, well-written bestsellers as from more serious offerings. For me, these books were more than mere entertainment. They became companions and tutors, cherished friends to be picked up again and again, the true furniture of the mind. I did try more heavyweight reading when I began studying in my late teens. I read Kafka and Voltaire, Spinoza on ethics and Aristotle on politics. I even read Nietzsche, to try to see why his writings had become textbooks of the Nazis. I dipped into Colette, Hardy and Voltaire, and added them to my collection. Most of these books remain on my shelves today.

I can remember none of my friends from primary school, but I cannot have been unpopular for I was elected captain of the football team. We won most of our games and were good enough to reach the final of a local schools' knockout competition, but lost 2–1 after I gave away a silly goal. I was inconsolable. I also learned to play cricket. Once I was given out lbw first ball, when I knew I had hit the ball smack in the middle of the bat.

'But I hit it,' I protested, confident that my explanation would persuade the umpire to put right his mistaken decision. It didn't. 'You're out,' he said, waving his hand in dismissal. 'Now off you go.' It was the first time I realised that adults were fallible and that, if on shaky ground, they could become even more assertive than if they were right.

I had a few fights at school, mostly with boys who were throwing their weight around, and it led to trouble. I was winning one when a teacher dragged me away from the scrap, slapping me painfully around my head and shoulders and visibly losing his self-control. I was contemptuous of him from then on. I thought he was unjust. But I wasn't a natural trouble-maker. I worked quite hard and was as keen to please as most small boys. When we were asked to produce a painting for an exhibition I misunderstood and took in one that my elder sister, Pat, an excellent artist, had painted. I was mortified to overhear a teacher saying I had brought in a painting, but 'his sister did it'. I felt like a cheat and slunk away.

At home I had pets. I bred mice and sold them to friends, with a slice of fruitcake thrown in as an inducement to buy. My white doe angora rabbit, Frisky, was given an assignation with a blue bevan buck rabbit owned by a friend. We watched and waited with interest, and were not disappointed. A litter was produced, though not all survived. We had a dog, too, a white bull terrier called Butch. He was a wonderful companion and curled up on my bed each night, before returning to the lounge as soon as he thought I was asleep.

I pause, writing this. Everyone must have such stories from childhood. But perhaps it is worth illustrating that prime ministers are no different. From the pages of some politicians' memoirs the statesman seems to spring perfectly formed, almost from the cot, without all the trivial things that matter so much to a child. But some of the memories which writing this has brought back are every bit as strong and as moving to me as the headlines about my life which were to come.

Outside school my fun was largely self-created, apart from visits to Saturday-morning cinema, where the films always ended on a dramatic note to encourage you to return the following week. It was my sister Pat who encouraged my interest in cricket. She took me to the local sports club to see Worcester Park play. We studied books on how to bat and bowl, and I spent hours practising when I could find no one to play with me, chalking up stumps on the garage door to bowl at. In the winter I turned the garage into a goal against which I dribbled a football, shot and took penalties without number. If other boys were around I would play with them. When they were not, I was quite content to play alone.

I also ran. Longfellow Road abutted on to Green Lane, and formed a block about half a mile long. I ran around it for hour upon hour and raced against anyone and everyone – and always myself. I ran so much that an interfering neighbour told my mother I would injure myself, and for a while running was forbidden.

A brook ran along Green Lane and I used to jump across it to climb the trees on the far side. Once I fell out of one and returned home covered in blood – but I soon recovered. Worcester Park then was less built-up than it is now, and there were open hayfields and hedgerows full of birds' nests behind Longfellow Road. I brought home eggs that didn't hatch and ducklings that didn't survive, and learned that nature was best left to her own devices.

At home we talked of many things, but never politics or religion. I know from my brother and sister that my father was much against the socialists, and Mr Attlee was never forgiven for defeating Mr Churchill in the 1945 general election. My parents were believers, I'm sure, and their values were more Christian than those of many people who call themselves such; but going to church in their Sunday best and looking pious was not for them.

'She's got religion,' Mother would say disapprovingly of a neighbour, as though it were measles; and we kept clear for fear of catching it. So we never went to church on Sunday. Perhaps my parents had got out of the habit when they were travelling the country, though my mother, despite her open heart, had a puritanical side – probably, in part at least, because of my father's earlier philandering. Yet her God was a forgiving God, and I imbibed her values, although I always had a yen to take church more seriously than my parents did. That yen was largely unfulfilled. The Church appealed to me, but it never reached out to me.

I learned Christian values by example, but in no other way. And though I was baptised into the Church of England I was never confirmed – and had I been in later life, when I had become a public figure, I worried that it would lead to comment about my motives. For my parents the Church was something rather quaint, an honoured but distant institution that other people attended but we did not – except, of course, for fêtes and jumble sales. Chance and circumstance left me a believer at a distance; but a believer nonetheless.

In the 1950s the eleven plus examinations determined whether or not you went to grammar school. The names of the successful candidates were announced by the teacher in class, and as he intoned 'John' I felt my back being patted by the boy behind me. But the teacher went on to say 'John Hunt'. I thought I'd failed, and I remember the huge relief when my name was finally called out. So I left Cheam Common School in 1954 and went to Rutlish, a grammar school about three miles away in Merton. It was our first choice, and I looked forward to going. I liked the uniform, and the school played rugby, which I felt sure I would enjoy. They also played cricket, and set aside one term a year for athletics, which was unusual at the time.

Passing the examination to Rutlish led to furious rows with my parents. My birth certificate records me simply as 'John Major', although at the font my godmother, a librarian friend of my mother's with the unlikely name of Miss Fink, slipped in a 'Roy', to my father's fury. He hated the name, and wasn't too fond of Miss Fink, an exotic lady who had painted fingernails and who smoked Passing Cloud cigarettes. But my father had used two names in his life. Although he was christened 'Abraham Thomas Ball', he used 'Tom Major' as his stage name and generally thereafter. My elder brother Terry had been registered with 'Terry' and 'Major' as his Christian names and 'Ball' as his surname. Pat was the only one of us to be both christened and registered as 'Major-Ball'. Now, as I prepared to go to Rutlish, my parents decided to inflict this hybrid name on me. I bitterly objected. It was not my name, and, even worse, it was bound to cause trouble at school.

My mother and father thought it would put me more in tune with the school. I disagreed. My parents were usually kind and biddable, but on this occasion they were intransigent. In battles like this in the 1950s the adults won. And so – in the only cruel act of theirs I ever knew – I became John Major-Ball.

I have often wondered how much this decision affected my attitude to school. A great deal, I think. I got it all out of proportion. It meant I approached Rutlish with a wary unease. I believed I would have to excel at sport and be prepared to use my fists to earn the respect of my peers. Forty years later that may seem an odd judgement, but it was all too real for an eleven-year-old boy mortally embarrassed at sailing under false colours.

At the time my parents were under great strain. My father's health was poor and his eyesight was failing. I remember him falling off a stool in the kitchen when I came into the room as he was putting in a lightbulb, and from that day on I watched him deteriorate. Irrationally, but in the way a small boy can, I felt personally responsible for this. My mother's health was also worsening, with asthma and bronchitis her constant companions.

My father's garden-ornaments business was in difficulties, too. In 1950 or 1951 he made plans to sell it, pay off his debts and emigrate with us to Canada. His failing eyesight, spotted by a wary doctor at his second medical interview for Canada, put paid to this scheme. In urgent need of capital, he entered into a business deal with a widowed lady. She wanted a job for her sister's boyfriend and invested £3,000 to install him as my father's partner. The boyfriend began to learn the business, but disliked it. Soon he began to dislike the widow's sister too, and they fell out and parted company.

The widow demanded her money back. In his typical my-word-is-my-bond manner, my father hadn't bothered to legally formalise the deal. Nor did he have the money. He'd spent it. And he was unable to take the matter to court. He was not fit enough, financially or physically, and his case was weak. Why had an experienced man of the world like my father not legalised the deal? He was advised that the episode could be presented as one of a designing businessman out to fleece an innocent widow.

My sister, then only twenty-four, took over, negotiating with the widow and agreeing to repay the money over time, in a vain effort to save our father from having to sell the house. But the debt was many times my sister's annual salary, and my parents were faced with the loss of all they had. This must have been shattering for them and, I am sure now, explains my parents' impatience with my protests about changing my name. A few months after I went to Rutlish my father sold our bungalow in Worcester Park for £2,150. My parents seemed to age before my eyes.

We moved to a new home in Brixton in May 1955, when I was twelve. It was a sad comedown, part of the top floor of a four-storey Victorian building in Coldharbour Lane. We had two rooms for the five of us, plus Butch and a pet budgerigar. Dad, Terry and I slept in one room, and Mum and Pat in the other. This second room was used as a dining room and lounge during the day. We shared a cooker on the landing with the other top-floor tenant, a middle-aged bachelor. The lavatory, two floors below, was used by all the tenants. There was no bathroom. We washed at the sink or in a tub.

The house was home over the years to a rich collection of characters. The floor below us was occupied from time to time by three Irish boys who returned home to Ireland whenever taxes were due to be paid. They were huge fun. They played football with me in the street, and one of them, Christie, suggested Pat should run away with him. Another, Michael, actually proposed to her one morning as she left for work, but she wasn't really listening – a most convenient gift she has always had. Only later did she realise what he had said. It hardly mattered. She was convinced that they would end up with eleven children each. And anyway, she was determined to marry her long-term boyfriend Peter, which she eventually did.

Other tenants included a middle-aged cat-burglar. He was charming and lived with a beautiful girl of about nineteen, who disappeared when he was sent to jail. She used to walk around in her underwear, which was something of a novelty in the 1950s but added pleasurably to my education. The cat-burglar gave me his bets to place on racehorses with a local bookie who operated illegally in the tunnel at Loughborough Junction station. Once he offered me half a crown to see if there were any policemen around before he went out of the house, since he was anxious not to meet any. I agreed to scout for him, but high-mindedly refused to take the money. It probably wasn't his anyway.

Two other tenants were a Jamaican and his white girlfriend, an unusual liaison for the era, even though there was already heavy West Indian immigration into Brixton by then. He, too, was eventually jailed – for stabbing a policeman.

Life in the flat was very cramped. My father distrusted electricity, and would turn off the radio if there was lightning, or if water was dripping in the room from the ceiling. On wet weekends there was not much to do. I played Subbuteo for hours, running my own imaginary football leagues. Sometimes I would walk down the road to a large bakery and buy bread direct from the ovens. The smell was heaven and the bread warm and tasty.

Very occasionally I would stride up Denmark Hill to Dulwich Village and walk around, looking at smart houses with a warm glow through their curtains. I still remember looking through one window at the comfort inside, and seeing two young children playing board games with their mother. Such a life seemed very different from mine.

One winter evening on such a prowl, when I was thirteen, I was set upon by a gang of boys, and the word 'Mark' was cut into my thigh with a razor-blade. I told only my sister, who tended the wound with iodine, and kept my secret. I did not want my parents to know about the incident, and they never did. The branding has long since gone.

I was mystified by our relationship with our landlords. The house was owned by Tom, a man about twenty years younger than my father, and his wife Ann, always known as Nan, a tall, handsome woman with long blonde hair who had three children, Carole, Tom Junior and Nicholas. It was clear that they were not strangers to my parents, and they had offered us a roof when we needed it. When I asked my mother about Tom and Nan she became evasive. It was clear that my questions were unwelcome. She never answered them properly.

Tom was 'Uncle' Tom and Nan was 'Auntie', a common way for children to address adults those days. They occupied the ground floor and the basement. Their daughter Carole moved out soon after we arrived, and Nicholas was much younger than me, but Tom Junior was my age, and we became firm friends. Later in life he went to work in America, and for years we lost touch, but during the 1992 election he reappeared, unannounced and unexpected, and worked for me throughout the campaign.

Like my parents, Uncle Tom had been on the stage. He was a singer with a magnificent voice and the portly build of the classic tenor. For years he appeared with his sister, Jill Summers, who in her later years achieved fame as Phyllis Pease in *Coronation Street*. He had toured the halls – sometimes under the stage name of Signor Bassani – and had rarely been short of work.

Tom's last job in the theatre was to understudy Harry Secombe as Mr Pickwick in the West End. Alas, not for the first time, he drank too much, fell down some stairs and was sacked. He never sang professionally again, although he did sing at home, his voice beautiful and effortlessly wide-ranging. These were unforgettable evenings in Brixton.

It dawned on me that it was not chance that had brought our family to Brixton, but blood ties. Tom's surname was 'Moss', and though that meant nothing to me at the time, I had a hunch about his background. Now I have been able to confirm it. 'Uncle' Tom was the baby registered by the musician James Moss and his young wife Mary back in 1901. He was my half-brother. I would have thought it indelicate to put any such suspicion to my parents, and they would certainly have thought the enquiry unpardonable. I was sure I was right, and so were Pat and Terry. The reason we were living there was no longer such a mystery.

My memories of our six years or so at Coldharbour Lane are patchy. Certainly there was never much money in the household. Often the larder was bare until Terry received payment in advance from one of my father's most regular customers, the marvellous Mr Spiers of Margate, for garden ornaments he had not yet made. And, although I did not know it at the time, Aunt Nan often came to the rescue with loans.

For a while Terry lived in the garage he was working in, because there was so little room at home and he did not wish to spend hard-earned money on lodgings. That stopped as soon as my mother found out. Pat repeatedly put off her marriage to Peter as she and Terry worked to support the family, keep me at school and repay my father's debts. They were determined that my father should not go bankrupt.

The indignity of our situation affected my parents deeply, although they lived through setback and disaster without ever referring to their distress or ill-health. Not for nothing had they spent years in the theatre. They could act. But my mother was ageing fast, and my father retreated ever more into the past. They were never crabby or miserable, but fought adversity in their own way, laughing joyfully at minor triumphs, apparently certain that things would get better; outwardly optimistic and forever hoping for a future that for them, alas, would never come.

They were stoical in the face of all adversity. As my father became more blind, I became his eyes. I would take his arm when he went to collect his pension. In Coldharbour Lane that meant negotiating several flights of stairs, some steep outside stone steps from the door to the pavement and 150 yards of road to the post office. I learned to watch out for uneven paving stones, unleashed dogs, traffic turning into side roads and all the hazards whose avoidance is routine to the fully-sighted. It was good training for a future Minister for the Disabled.

Too stiff and proud to acknowledge ill-fortune, my father saw his troubles, his health, his blindness, as temporary setbacks from which he would somehow emerge triumphant. My mother, seemingly impervious to every blow, brushed them away as of no consequence, defended and cared for my father and was always unvanquished before a sea of troubles. If I found her with wet eyes often enough, I never found her without hope. If the rain came through the ceiling, as it did – well, the water could be mopped up and the ceiling repaired. If the bills piled up, they'd be paid eventually – no one could doubt that. If their health worsened, it would surely improve. There was always tomorrow, full of wonderful possibilities.

Especially, they thought, for me. I was to achieve what they had not. I was to put right what was wrong. My mother was confident of that. And since I had stayed at Rutlish after we moved to Coldharbour Lane, they were sure I had the best possible start. I knew that this confidence, too, was ill-founded, but I never told them.

Living in Brixton meant I had one and a half hours' travelling each way six days a week, since Rutlish had Saturday-morning school. I travelled by train from Loughborough Junction, first to Merton South and later, when I moved to the third year, which had different classrooms, to Wimbledon Chase. It was on these journeys that I picked up an addiction to morning newspapers – the *Daily Express* in those days – which I would not break until halfway through my tenure of Downing Street.

I would turn first to the sports pages – it was the time of Surrey's great run of seven County Cricket championships in a row, from 1952 to 1958 – and then to the news. I still remember my incredulity at the trial and execution for murder in July 1955 of Ruth Ellis, the last woman to be hanged in Britain. I could not believe her death penalty would not be commuted, and the experience turned me into a lifelong opponent of capital punishment. I remember, too, the dreadful Munich air disaster of February 1958, in which so many wonderful Manchester United footballers died, and the long saga of whether their manager Matt Busby would recover from his injuries. I remember them better than I remember Rutlish.

Our school uniform was expensive and could only be bought from one shop, Ely's in Wimbledon. My first blazer and cap were new, but as I grew, later uniforms were second-hand. Fortunately Rutlish jumble sales were a source of larger blazers, with the embossed buttons from the outgrown blazer carefully preserved and saved, since they cost two shillings and sixpence each from Ely's. Whenever my mother bought a jumble-sale blazer she ordered me to stay out of sight – she didn't want anyone to know for whom it was intended. She always bought them too large for me, in the belief that they would last longer as I grew. She must have thought nobody would notice.

She was wrong. Once, when I had lost two buttons from my sleeve, Mr Winsor, the school secretary, called me to see him, and offered me five shillings from the school fund to replace them. It was a sensitive and kind act, and I thanked him for it. But I couldn't accept, and my parents would have been horrified had I done so. They would have made me take the money back, which would have been even more shaming. In any event I felt abashed at the well-intended gesture and humiliated at the need for it.

Rutlish and I were not getting on. Some masters, like Bobby Oulton, the deputy head, and Harry Hathaway, who taught maths, remain clear memories, but most have long since been pushed from my mind; although we were not mortal enemies, we were certainly not good friends. I avoided after-school activities because it took too long to travel home. The Combined Cadet Force did not appeal to me – even apart from the cost of the uniform. And the lure of wearing a boater in the upper forms was certainly resistible. It all seemed rather pretentious to me.

My name did lead to squalls at school, though fewer than I had feared. A scrap or two and an early aptitude for rugby soon enabled me to settle well enough among my fellow pupils, and in my first year I was even appointed captain of rugby and told to pick teams for trial games. This was such a welcome task that it took precedence over all academic work. Mr Blenkinsop, the headmaster, was unimpressed when I ignored his valuable Latin tuition to concentrate on rugby trials, but he was too wise to take the responsibility away from me. Anyway, he had probably given up trying to teach me Latin.

Rutlish introduced me to foreign languages and the sciences (all draughty laboratories and odd smells), but the acquaintance was only casual. History and English were more bearable. Such homework as was necessary I did on the train, where an empty carriage provided a better opportunity than two crowded rooms in Brixton.

At school I did as little work as possible. I thought of the place as a penance to be endured. I kept myself to myself and cooperated only so as to keep out of trouble. I just didn't engage. I never took school interests home or bothered my parents with talk of extra-curricular outings or holidays; I knew they could not afford them.

At about this time, I discovered I was short-sighted. I could read comfortably and play games without difficulty, but – sitting at the back of the class to keep out of harm's way – I could not easily see the blackboard. In the days of blackboard teaching this was a real problem. No one noticed.

It has been said that I was bullied at school. That is not true: I was too good at sport to be a likely candidate for bullying. I was a member of the cricket and rugby teams for my house, and enjoyed my happiest hours playing those games. It was the best part of school. I even won a certificate from the *Evening Standard* for taking seven wickets for nine runs against Royal Masonic – including a hat trick. I once won a bet with my team-mate, Tony Weymouth, by hitting a cricket ball through a school window. It wasn't the window I was aiming for, but it was thought good enough.

Sport was a large part of my out-of-school life as well, and I formed a lasting attachment to Surrey County Cricket Club and Chelsea Football Club. I saw Chelsea play for the first time in 1955, the year they won the championship. They beat Wolves 1–0 with a Peter Sillett penalty, and I was hooked for life. I have spent many happy afternoons at Stamford Bridge, and many frustrating ones as well, as Chelsea demonstrated their legendary unpredictability. I can still smell the cheroot smoke and roasted peanuts of a sunny Easter afternoon in the sixties when they beat Everton 6–2, and Jimmy Greaves scored five goals. Such a result had rarity value, quite apart from the odours of the day. Supporting Chelsea over the years has been a rollercoaster ride, but it has been a great aid in developing a philosophical view of life.

Individual sports have never had the appeal for me of team games – except for athletics. I still remember the wonderful evening Chris Chataway, the great English middle distance runner, beat Vladimir Kutz, the seemingly invincible Russian champion. 'Chataway went thataway!' chanted the delirious crowd, and so he had.

But cricket is my first love. Clement Attlee once referred to cricket as 'a religion and W.G. [Grace] next to a deity'. He put an old fashioned tickertape machine into Downing Street so he could keep up to date with the cricket scores, and it was still there in my time.

Playing cricket gave me some of the happiest moments of my life – not that I was ever very good, but then many of those who love the game are indifferent performers. I had my moments, though they were pitifully few. My seven for nine at school was my zenith, although seventy-seven not out (against poor bowling and fielding in Nigeria) is another cherished memory.

Our home in Brixton was less than a mile from The Oval, home of Surrey. The great Surrey team of the fifties that won the County Championship for seven successive years was equipped for all conditions. They bowled Lock and Laker if the wicket took spin, Bedser if the ball would swing, and Loader if the wicket was quick. May, and later Barrington and Stewart, scored the runs, with Fletcher, Clark and Constable in support. Their fielding was superb. Lock was like a cheetah sighting prey in the leg trap, and Surridge took amazing catches with his telescopic arms – I used to believe he was the only man alive who could scratch his ankles while standing upright. It was a wonderful team of all the talents, and I never expect to see its equal.

I almost lived at The Oval during the school holidays. Armed with sandwiches and a soft drink I sat on the popular side in perfect contentment. If the weather was fine and the crowd large (as it often was) I would sit on the grass just outside the boundary rope, a delight long since forbidden by nannyish safety regulations. I suppose I was spoilt by the wonderful cricket I saw then, but those early days provided imperishable memories. The mind does play tricks, of course, but what I recall is that Surrey always seemed to win, and that in the early evening The Oval was always bathed in sunshine and shadow.

I was enraptured by the literature of cricket, which has a treasure trove no other game can match. For me Neville Cardus, C.L.R. James and E.W. Swanton stand before all other writers on the game. Cardus was the poet of cricket; his prose had a romance to it that swept the mundane aside. The first piece by Cardus I ever read was a pen-portrait of Denis Compton, in which he wrote of the infamous knee: 'the gods treated him churlishly. They crippled him almost beyond repair.' I never saw Compton again without that thought coming to mind.

I did suspect that Cardus stretched the truth a little as he fleshed out his affectionate portraits. Were cricketers really such characters, or was their charm enhanced in the poetic eye of a besotted beholder? Even if it was, it didn't diminish my enjoyment. Cardus, again on Compton, illustrated the point. He once asked two boys why they were not watching the cricket. 'Because there are no more Denis Comptons,' he reports them as saying. It is a marvellous tribute to the unique charm of Compton's batting, but would a small boy really have said that? I doubt it, but when I read it I loved it. And it *may* have been true.

C.L.R. James's masterpiece *Beyond a Boundary* sets out better than anyone before or since how cricket affects character and illustrates the better virtues; it undermined all my prejudices that such a lyrical love of the game should flow from the pen of a committed Marxist

Jim Swanton is the doyen of modern writers although, for reporting the game, he would give the palm to his good friend John Woodcock. Both men have seen much of the greatest cricket played in the last three-quarters of a century. Jonathan Aitken, a great admirer of Swanton, once gave me a set of all the Swanton books I did not already possess, and they are a prized part of my collection.

I have often sat watching cricket with Jim Swanton, and it is an education. His memory is phenomenal: he once said to me of Donald Bradman's 234 at Lords in 1930, which the Don thought was his greatest innings, 'He hit the first two balls he received for four; they went . . .' Jim stretched out his arm to point 'towards that advertisement hoarding over there.'

I have found that other old cricketers and cricket watchers have the facility for total recall as well. Alf Gover, the old Surrey and England fast bowler, brought to life a tour of India in the 1930s under the captaincy of Lord Tennyson. Alf was running up to bowl the first ball of the match when a vengeful curry from the night before began to make its presence known. Sensing disaster, he did not deliver the ball when he reached the wicket but, to general astonishment, sprinted past the stumps and straight off the pitch into the pavilion. A few minutes later, as he sat wretchedly in the washroom, Lord Tennyson knocked on the door. 'Alf,' he enquired, 'can we have the ball back please?'

It is difficult to capture the special fascination of cricket. It is unique. It has grace and charm and athleticism. It is unpredictable. It can change the mood of a spectator from lazy contentment to excitement within moments. A game can last up to five days, but the outcome may be uncertain until the end; changing weather conditions can up-end the state of a game. Above all, with occasional lapses, cricket is played with a generosity of spirit that is as refreshing as it is unfashionable. It is, I think, a very English game, that still encapsulates old values.

From the very start, cricket bred characters that the literature of the game has kept alive. Cricket lovers can talk for hours about the virtues of players they never saw, and the greatness of matches long ago. If I ever get to the Elysian Fields I intend to watch Trumper, and Grace, and Ranji, and so many others.

Cricketers are often very modest about their achievements, never realising the admiration they provoke among cricket lovers who do not have their skills. A few years ago, when Harold Larwood, the great old English fast bowler, was awarded his MBE, which was too little for all he did, and too late by several decades, I phoned him up in Australia, where he had lived for many years, to congratulate him. His granddaughter answered the phone but within moments the old man, now blind and frail, was speaking to me. I congratulated him and he thanked me for the award. And then he began to talk not of *his* exploits, but of his hero, Jack Hobbs, and innings he had played on sticky, treacherous wickets. Harold's memory was of seventy years earlier, but was as vivid to him as any contemporary event. This was no vainglory, just admiration of another man's great skill.

Nor is this bashfulness unique to Harold Larwood. I remember being with some former England and Australian international players discussing Bradman's last Test innings when, to general astonishment, he was bowled for nought second ball by Eric Hollies. Only later when I looked up the match in *Wisden*, the cricket lover's bible, did I recall that Arthur Morris, who had taken part in that conversation, scored 196 in that innings. Arthur had not mentioned it.

I would have loved to have been good enough to play cricket at the top level, but the basic skills were never there. I would have improved with practice, but never enough. It often seems to me that top-class sportsmen live their lives upside down. They are at their most famous when young, and end their playing careers at an age when most people in other professions are just beginning to reach positions of influence. Their reward though can be the bliss of fame and fortune and youth together, and the joy of doing something they love supremely well. It is an unbeatable combination, which is why few cricketers I have met ever regret their playing days, even if, for some, life must seem mundane ever after.

Politics is almost a mirror-image of cricket, in that fame and fortune often come with age, and it always surprises me that so few sportsmen carry their fame into public service. Chris Chataway did became a Conservative Minister, Sebastian Coe was a Member of Parliament while I was prime minister, and Colin Cowdrey serves in the House of Lords, but they are comparative rarities.

At school, I found that little was memorable in the classroom. If you worked hard at Rutlish you were encouraged. If you did not, you were ignored, unless you were disruptive; so I retreated to the shadows and stayed there, inconspicuous. Only once was there a price to be paid for not working. At about the age of thirteen or fourteen an opportunity arose for me to sit an entrance examination for Charterhouse. I was keen, but my school was not – only their top academic pupils would sit; they wanted no failures. Nor were my parents happy with the idea: what was wrong with Rutlish? And probably – though they never said so – they were worried about the extra cost a place at a leading public school would entail. I understood this, and the opportunity drifted away.

The years passed forgettably, and I have only sketchy recollections of them. GCE 'O' levels in 1959 approached without drama. My parents' struggle to hide their bad health and poor finances absorbed all their strength, and they did not push me at all. They assumed I would pass my exams as easily as my academic sister had passed her school certificate a decade before. But I had not worked, and I passed only three 'O' levels – History, English Language and English Literature.

Although this was self-inflicted failure, there was little reproach from my sick parents. They were, as ever, stoical, but I knew they were hurt and disappointed. They had hoped for so much, and I had achieved so little. I had let them down. And in their hurt I saw with sudden clarity the pleasure it would have brought them if I had produced the results for which they had hoped. It was a moment of deep shame.

I knew I would now have to work harder, but I saw no likelihood of doing this at Rutlish, and went to the headmaster to tell him I was leaving school. He seemed to bear my impending departure with fortitude, and did not object. Nor did he ask whether my parents approved – which was fortunate, since I had not informed them. When I told them later that the headmaster was content for me to leave they did not protest. They had too much else to worry them.

And so Rutlish and I parted around my sixteenth birthday, and I took stock. I had wasted my time at school, and had rarely been happy there. I left with no ambitions, other than a vague wish to go into politics. This had been heightened when I met our local Labour Member of Parliament,

Colonel Marcus Lipton, at a church fête. He had talked to me about politics and, seeing my interest, kindly arranged for me to hear a debate in the House of Commons (he probably did not imagine I would turn out to be a Tory).

I fell in love with the House of Commons the first time I saw it, sitting in the gallery watching the committee stage of the 1956 budget. Harold Macmillan, the Chancellor of the Exchequer, briefly came into the Chamber, and after that I knew I wanted to get into the House of Commons, and that I wanted to be chancellor. I could not bear to have other people telling me what would happen to my life – I wanted to make the decisions for myself. I came from a background where you were dependent so much on other people. I wanted to be self-dependent – not just within my own family, my own lifestyle, but self-dependent in helping to determine the sort of life I lived and the sort of country I lived in. That feeling is still there.

My ambition to enter Parliament never wavered, although at the time it seemed an impossible dream. I wrote around for a job, and found one as a clerk at an insurance-broking firm, Price Forbes, near London Bridge. When the interview ended I wasn't certain of the salary they had offered: was it £250 a year, or £150? Fortunately it was the higher sum, and I was launched into working life.

I bought a suit and opened a bank account. I paid one pound ten shillings a week into the family kitty, and the rest was taken up by travelling expenses, clothes and other routine expenditure. There was nothing left for frivolity. I sallied forth into the world as my father retreated from it.

I can see him now. Thick, overlong grey hair swept back, stern features, shirt and Fair Isle sweater under a tweed jacket, stepping out for the post office as fast as he could, without hesitation, using his walking stick to lever himself upright. He did not stroll – he marched. Near-blind he may have been, but he was devoid of self-pity. He taught me so much: not to be deterred by obstacles, not to give in to fate. For him, triumph and disaster were passing moments, to be enjoyed or endured. When they had gone, he moved on without regret. All this he taught me.

# CHAPTER TWO

## *From Brixton to Westminster*

T HE WORLD OF WORK was a new experience, but I soon realised that insurance broking was not life-enhancing. The rudiments of the profession, however, were simple enough, and I was prepared to accept the boredom of the routine, if there were opportunities to claw my way up the ladder to some serious responsibilities.

It was not to be. Several incidents pointed the way to a new career. When I overhead a senior manager extravagantly praise a thoroughly idle colleague because 'he comes from a good family', I wondered whether Price Forbes promoted on merit. If not, I had no chance. That day I was put under the tutelage of a man with a face like a fish and brilliantined blond hair. This was another mark against the company. Finally, on a day when I'd risen at 5 a.m. to study, far from being given worthwhile work to do, I was despatched to the store room to search for files, because 'You can climb like a monkey, I'm sure!' It was time to move on, and in any case a new opportunity beckoned, at the mouth-watering salary of £8 a week.

Terry was still making garden ornaments, but he needed capital. When one of his customers, a retired naval officer, Commander David, offered to buy the business, Terry accepted. Commander David wanted a second member of staff, and I joined Terry. I knew very little about garden ornaments, but Terry soon taught me.

In August 1959 we moved from Coldharbour Lane to a flat in a house on the Minet Estate at 80 Burton Road, Brixton. The only other tenants in the house, Bob and Enid, were a newly-married couple in their thirties. We had the basement, the ground floor and a bathroom on the first-floor landing. There was even a small front garden, and life was much improved. As ever, my mother attracted friends with the speed of light.

Working with Terry was fun. We left home early in the morning and cycled to Caldew Street, near Walworth Road, where we had a small work-shop. After two hours building up an appetite, a local transport café provided the best breakfasts I've ever had. I was the labourer and Terry the craftsman. Years later he wrote a book and, with tongue in cheek, described how garden ornaments were made. It amused the sneering classes no end that a future prime minister had made gnomes, but it was honest, manual work, and I have never been ashamed of it or regretted it.

In 1959 I joined the Young Conservatives after a plump young man named Neville Wallace knocked on my door one evening canvassing for members. My mother had already met Marion Standing, the Brixton Conservative agent, and was all in favour of my joining – but, as politics fascinated me, I needed no urging. It's entirely probable that my mother asked Marion Standing to send Neville around – but she never admitted it.

The Brixton YCs were then a merry and growing band, and as I had a few friends, I began to bring them in as new members. We took our politics seriously, and worked hard – but we played harder. One of the side effects of enjoying ourselves so much was that we found we had attracted to our number two members of the Dulwich Young Socialists. When this was discovered they admitted their (not very strong) allegiance to socialism, but charmed us by saying our social life was better. As one of them could drive and the other played the guitar quite well, no one cared very much.

We were a very mixed bunch. Tim Bidmead, who was addicted to Nat 'King' Cole's music; Maria, whose father spent the weekends fortifying himself for slating roofs throughout the week; Maureen the artist, who went to Liverpool Art College and married there; Sonia and Ann, two cousins; red-haired Jean, who married her boss; Derek Stone, Clive Jones, the two Alans, Penny, Malcolm, Delphine, Carol, Geoffrey, Margaret – and so many more. At the end of most evenings we adjourned to local pubs and plotted how to change the world. We didn't fancy being spoon-fed by the state and having our lives directed for us; we wanted doors to be opened so that we could make our own future. We were natural Conservatives.

It was Derek Stone who encouraged me to stand on a soapbox and speak to the passing public outside our association offices and in Brixton marketplace. Derek was married, a little older, and rather more worldly-wise than the rest of us. Engaging and fun, he played the devil's advocate. 'Go on, do it. Why not?' was his creed, and he lived it as well as preached it. He turned up one day with a microphone and a soapbox, and we were off and running. It was fun. No one paid much attention, but no one complained either. It was good training, and taught me a lot about the tolerance of the British.

We canvassed, enrolled new members, helped in political campaigns, held dances and tennis mornings, went on outings, published our own magazine, heckled local Labour MPs and thoroughly enjoyed ourselves. An elderly association member was scandalised when she found one of our members straining printers' ink through her stockings. Girls took off their stockings for one reason only, she thought. She was right: we needed the ink strained.

Meanwhile, in early 1960 Terry married his girlfriend Shirley – a marriage still going strong thirty-nine years later – and moved a few miles south to Thornton Heath; but we continued to work together. My mother's health was still poor, but she battled on. The YCs were wonderful to her. She loved them all, especially Derek Stone and Clive Jones, later to be my best man, and made our house an open house.

But my father's body was wearing out and he rarely left his bed, though his mind was clear and active to the very end. He died at home in bed at Burton Road, early in the morning of 27 March 1962. I was eighteen and he was eighty-three, and the bond between youth and age was very strong. He went as the sun rose. I was with him when he died. We knew he was dying and the family had been sitting up, in rota, overnight. I was sitting by his bed holding his hand. It was very peaceful. He was drowsy, half asleep and, I think, his mind had gone on ahead of his body. I did not know the exact moment he died. He was breathing so shallowly I wasn't sure. I felt the warmth leave his hand. For a man of the theatre, who loved the dramatic, it was a peaceful end. There was no collapse. No last words.

My father, the man who had given me life and love, was dead.

There were family tears and comforting words for my mother, who sat there with her cheeks wet, reliving a lifetime of memories. When I held her she clung on to me as though she would never let go. Then the dreadful rituals began. The doctor came to sign the death certificate. The vicar, J. Franklin Cheyne, a lovely old boy who had interviewed Dad for the parish magazine as 'one of the characters of the parish' only days earlier, came to offer solace. Neighbours came and went, the kettle boiled, tea was offered and the surreal atmosphere that follows death settled on the house.

I went for a walk, and to this day I do not know where I went. Life would not be the same, but there was much to do.

I found it hard to come to terms with the finality of death. Dad's death was the first time in my life that something had happened which I didn't believe I could put right in the future. It made a reality of what he had often said to me: make of life what you can, and take your chances, because they may never come again.

So far, I had not made much of my life. School – a failure; career – I had none; sport – not good enough; politics – I was only playing at it. I needed a career and qualifications.

I began studying more 'O' levels by correspondence course, and left my brother and Commander David to seek out something more promising to do. No sooner had I done so than Mother fell quite ill and, as Terry and Pat were earning more than I would be able to, it was economically sensible for me to be the one to stay at home and care for her.

This I did, but when she was well enough to be left, I found I couldn't get a job. I was unemployed – unemployable, I feared – from July to December 1963. Years later, when I was prime minister, some Labour Members of Parliament mistakenly claimed that I had never been unemployed. I think it was the *Daily Mail* which found corroborative evidence to prove that in fact I had. I was young and single, and had a brother and sister who were both in work, but I did get a glimpse of what it must be like as an adult with family responsibilities, unable to find a job. The Labour Party's intention was to suggest that Conservatives had no experience of unemployment, and didn't care about the unemployed. I should have taken more note of their tactics; Labour were to do this kind of thing again later, on a much wider front.

I found my situation degrading. I had ambition, but no prospects. I applied for jobs, signed on at the employment exchange, collected the dole, but could find nothing worthwhile. I was willing to lower my sights until I'd passed more examinations, but even that failed: I was turned down as a bus conductor because I was too tall. Eventually, just before Christmas 1963, I gratefully accepted a job offer from the London Electricity Board, and went to work at their offices at the Elephant and Castle.

It was a cheerful, happy place, with a cosmopolitan staff, but the routine was mind-numbing, and I was only to remain there for eighteen months.

I asked if I could work four days a week and study on the fifth (with an appropriate pay reduction), but this was refused. The LEB did not provide me with a career, but it was an important staging post in building up my self-belief that I could do better.

Politics continued to fascinate me, and in the spring of 1964, when I had just turned twenty-one, I contested my first election for Lambeth Council. Larkhall was a hopeless ward for the Conservatives, but I fought it as if it were a marginal, canvassing for support at every spare moment. I lost heavily – they might as well have counted my votes and weighed the Labour votes – but the experience whetted my appetite. The count at Lambeth Town Hall was hugely exciting, crammed with joyful people in red rosettes and resigned good losers in blue. Labour seemed impregnable in Lambeth in 1964, but that was soon to change. Not, however, at the general election in October that year, when Harold Wilson narrowly defeated Sir Alec Douglas-Home and Labour squeaked back into government after thirteen years in opposition. In Brixton, Marcus Lipton, the sitting Labour Member, comfortably saw off Ken Payne, the Conservative candidate. I worked hard for Ken, who warmly encouraged my own ambitions and offered to help me find a better job, but the result was never in doubt. Ken would have made a good Member of Parliament, but sadly he was never to get there, and comforted himself with a distinguished career in local government.

After my own diversion into local elections, I thought long and hard about my future. Politics beckoned more each day, but I knew that if I were to have a good chance of being selected as a Conservative candidate for Parliament, I had to obtain a professional qualification as well as a political profile. The profile was coming along quite nicely, but the career not at all. I could not now go to university, since I had no entry qualifications and no means of support even if I got there. I could not become articled to the law or chartered accountancy, since neither would provide any income for years.

It was going to have to be evening classes – which would wreck political activities – or a correspondence course which would wreck my sleep. That choice was easy. I could not give up politics. But what to study? Accountancy? Possibly. Insurance? No. Banking? Yes. I settled for banking, because it offered more choices of employment, the chance of travel, promotion (I hoped) on merit, and I could study at home.

I joined District Bank in May 1965, at the magnificent salary of £790 a year. I began studying immediately, rising each morning at 4.30 or 5 a.m., when the mind is uncluttered and the brain fresh. To this day I follow that pattern if I have something taxing to get through. For the first time in my life I enjoyed the process of learning, and I widened my reading as well. I studied in the morning, worked at the bank by day, enjoyed my politics in the evening, and read late into the night. Within sixteen months I comfortably passed the five papers of Part One of the Banking Diploma. It was tremendously exhilarating to feel I was getting somewhere.

I began to receive invitations to speak at Conservative meetings in and around London, and accepted every one I could. The audience was often small, but the experience was invaluable. The Young Conservatives in Lambeth used to play a game, challenging each other to speak for a minute on a subject suggested at random. I acquired habits then which remain with me still. I would go to the Minet Library in Brixton and research the subject, then scribble the facts I wanted to use on a piece of paper, jumbling them up in little circles until an argument developed in my mind.

I have always been able to soak up a lot of detail and recall it without difficulty – show me a page of figures and I can remember them. While I have never found it easy to win an unexpected argument, I discovered very early on that when I was buttressed by knowledge I didn't lose. I operate by knowing the facts better than the other person, so that I am confident in what I say. I felt uneasy with flowery froth and idle oratory. I couldn't deliver a speech that, when looked at in the cold light of early morning, meant nothing. I needed to have my feet on firmer ground. I can overcome this instinctive caution if I have direct contact with an audience, such as I got speaking on the soapbox or – on occasion – in the House of Commons. But often I needed to be provoked, to have my back against the wall, to give my best performances.

The hardest parts of a speech are the first and last paragraphs. When writing a speech you can start anywhere – even with the conclusion. I used to turn over the points I wanted to make until they formed a pattern, and then the rest would fall into place. That's why I find it hard to read speeches written by others. As those who have worked with me know, I could be hell to be with before a big speech, marching around and overreacting – mental preparation for the event. When I was prime minister my staff would often be in despair because they had produced a beautifully written speech that I would move all around because they weren't my words.

In the mid-1960s my sister Pat, her husband Peter and my mother left Burton Road and moved to Thornton Heath, within a few streets of where Terry and Shirley lived. I did not go with them. Some time earlier, at a church fête, I had met Jean Kierans, a teacher who lived opposite us in Burton Road. Jean was dark-haired, attractive and fun, and we had taken to one another immediately. My mother liked her – it was impossible not to – until it registered with her that Jean, despite her youthful looks, was twelve years older than me, was divorced, and had two young children, Siobhan and Kevin. My mother did not approve. Nevertheless, I moved in with Jean, who did all she could to earn my mother's approval, although it was a doomed enterprise from the start. She thought our age gap too wide, and never shifted her view. Jean encouraged my studying, and shared my politics.

In early 1966 I noticed an advertisement from the Standard Bank Group offering the chance of banking abroad, with large overseas allowances to supplement the salary. I applied, was accepted, and joined their home staff with the intention of applying for overseas service as soon as possible. I had not given up my political ambitions, but I saw the chance to travel, broaden my experience, save some money, improve my CV – and I had itchy feet. I was bored.

My chance to travel soon came. The Standard Bank of West Africa was one of the largest banks in Nigeria, and when fighting broke out in Biafra – a bitter and cruel conflict that was to become a full-scale war – they invited single men to volunteer for service there on a temporary basis. It was perfect. I applied immediately, and flew on secondment to Nigeria in December 1966.

I was lucky in my posting. I was sent to Jos, a plateau in the north of Nigeria, the scene of hard fighting some months earlier, but by then well away from the real privations of the war. Jos was thousands of feet above sea level, and had a glorious climate. I shared a flat with a Liverpudlian about my own age, Richard Cockeram, a member of the bank's permanent overseas staff. A young Hausa, Moses, was employed as steward/cook/valet and general factotum.

The Jos branch of the bank was managed by another Liverpudlian, Burt Butler, although much of the office revolved around a Ghanaian accountant, who reputedly had several wives. Certainly the wife who attended bank cocktail parties was not the same lady we met elsewhere. He helped me settle in, knew the routine of the office backwards, and let me master the extra responsibilities I was given.

Nigeria was a world away from all my previous experience. The glorious dawns, the high sky, the feeling of immense space, the remoteness, were all new to me. It was easy to see how Africa gained such a hold over people. The centre of social activity for the expatriate community was the Jos Club. It introduced me to curry (served with a vast array of side-plates of nuts and fruits), to outdoor film-shows beamed against white walls, to snooker, to lazy Sundays by the swimming pool, to a calmer, more comfortable and more reflective way of life than I had known. I enjoyed the privacy and peace, but perversely missed the bustle and speed of London life. Nigeria was an enjoyable interlude, but I was homesick within weeks.

Cameo memories of my time there are very strong. Reading *Papillon* and Michael Foot's biography of Nye Bevan, listening to the few records I could buy in Jos (most memorably Elvis Presley's *Blue Hawaii*), travelling to outlying branches of the bank in the cash wagon, getting to know the grave and respectful Nigerians and exchanging banter with the expatriate miners, bankers and administrators.

At Christmas, when I had been in Nigeria for less than three weeks, Richard asked Moses to buy a chicken from the market for our lunch. That morning we sat on the balcony of our flat like lords of the universe. But Moses didn't appear, and neither did the chicken.

We were not concerned. The power supply was unreliable and the stewards often shared kitchens – obviously Moses was working elsewhere. When lunchtime arrived, lunch did not. Richard, several Christmas drinks to the good, went to investigate. Moses appeared.

'Where's the chicken?' demanded Richard rather snappily.

'Downstairs, sah.'

'Downstairs? It must be ready by now. Bring it up.'

Moses looked doubtful. But off he went, and returned with a chicken which was far from oven-ready, chirpily looking around as Moses led it into the flat attached to a piece of string. It pecked around the tiled floor looking for seeds.

'Moses,' said an exasperated Richard, 'we wanted to eat it, not take it for walks.'

Moses protested: 'Sah, you did not tell me to kill it.' He picked the chicken up and reached for its neck as he tucked it under his arm: 'Shall I do it now?'

Richard blanched. Christmas lunch was very late that year, but we ate well on Boxing Day.

I disliked the institutional racism of colonial life, the lack of respect for the Nigerians, their low pay and poor prospects compared to the inflated pay of the expatriates. So much of the racism was just unthinking. The expatriates were not hostile to the Nigerians but they were careless of their feelings. It did not seem to occur to many of them that their Nigerian employees, whether bank staff or messengers or stewards, had their own responsibilities to their own families and, if they were listened to rather than talked at, they had their own ambitions as well.

My father, brought up in America in the latter part of the nineteenth century, often displayed the same attitude, whereas my mother, believing no one superior or inferior, had a wholly different view. She would go out of her way to befriend someone in a less fortunate position than herself. I sided with my mother, and it was one of the few subjects about which I ever argued with my father.

If the local staff were resentful of the incomers, as they occasionally were, it was unsurprising. I was saving £120 a month, a vast sum to me then, but more than a year's salary to most of the Nigerians. The expatriates were fiercely patriotic to the country they chose not to work in, and the greatest celebration during my time there was an impromptu party thrown by Scots working for the mining companies after Scotland beat England 3–2 at Wembley. Everyone got horribly drunk, including me, and it was not until I tried to stand up and kept hitting my head on the ceiling that I realised I had gone to sleep under a table. I was not alone – but then, I suppose, Scotland do not often beat England at Wembley.

I had hoped to stay in Nigeria for about a year and a half, but fate intervened after only five months when I was involved in a serious car accident. I cannot recall the prelude to the crash. I vaguely remember watching a film at the Jos Club while Richard was playing snooker. Other accounts – notably in Anthony Seldon's comprehensive and well-researched biography – suggest that I had attended a roving party for departing expatriates. What is certain is that Richard drove me home in his brand new Cortina, rather erratically – expatriates did not need driving tests in Nigeria at the time, he told me. I sat beside him, tired and sleepy, but certainly aware that he was not fully in control of the car.

I remember no more until I regained consciousness at the side of a road. We had crashed, and I could not move. Richard was sitting beside me on the grass, his head held in his hands, weeping and shocked. I tried to sit up – and couldn't. There was blood on my face and arms and spilled down the front of my shirt. My trousers were ripped to shreds and my left leg was grotesquely twisted. Even half-conscious, I realised my kneecap was smashed and my leg badly broken. 'I've done it this time,' I thought, and then lost consciousness. I don't know now long Richard and I were by the roadside, but he never spoke, and seemed to be in shock. I was in great pain.

Eventually a passing car stopped – hours later, I was told – and I was lifted gently into the back of a station wagon. My next memory is of lying on my back in an operating theatre, full of doctors and nurses in gowns and caps, with a blazing light shining in my face and my leg held aloft while plaster bandages were wrapped around it from toe to thigh.

I woke next morning in the Jos mission hospital, staffed by Nigerian Catholic nurses, to be told that my leg was broken in several places, the kneecap crushed beyond repair. 'Our X-ray equipment is very old, so we're not sure how bad the damage is,' they said. 'But we can't treat your knee. As soon as you're well enough to travel you must go home to England.' I was too ill to object, and the idea of home seemed very welcome.

But I could not leave immediately, for I was too ill to travel. Jos treated me as well as they could, but no one was sure how badly injured I was. I asked when I would be back on my feet, but there was no reassurance that I would ever walk normally again. When I called out in pain one night, a nurse who spoke no English brought me fresh, cool water and folded back the mosquito net, believing I was too hot. The mosquitoes fed well, but it was a small irritation compared to my other injuries.

When I was fit enough to fly home I travelled by light plane from Jos to Kano – my plastered leg propped up against bulging post-bags for comfort – and then onward to Heathrow sprawled over several seats and accompanied by a Barclays expatriate who was kind enough to travel with me. Mercifully I remember very little of the journey, but I was met by an ambulance, my mother, my sister and Jean.

I was taken to Mayday Hospital in Croydon. When I arrived I was very sick. I lay in bed in a corner, with pop music blaring as chattering nurses cleaned up the ward and changed the beds. Suddenly, the whole atmosphere changed. The Sister had arrived on the shift and seen what a poor state I was in. The noise ended, peace and silence reigned. I was washed, given painkillers and sleeping tablets, the bed was plumped up and thankful oblivion carried me off.

I have never forgotten that Sister, or the relief her discipline brought to the ward. While I was very ill she seemed always to be there; as I recovered, her attention moved on to more deserving cases. She was small, neat, utterly dispassionate, a thoroughgoing martinet, and if every sick person had her to hand they would be very lucky indeed.

My leg did not heal easily. I needed several more operations, without any real knowledge of my prospects of recovery. At times I lay in bed, dispirited, wondering if I would be a cripple for life. The reluctance of the nurses to talk about my injuries made me fear the worst. I realised that my rugby, soccer and cricket days were now over, but I accepted that cheerfully enough, hoping only that I would not lose my leg, and that I would be able to walk normally one day.

Standard Bank were wonderful. Members of their personnel department visited me regularly. I received increases in pay and bonuses; my job was kept open for the many months of my treatment and convalescence, and I could not have been better treated. I shall always be grateful to them.

As I began to feel better I returned to reading. I read everything Agatha Christie wrote – some good, some bad, some indifferent, all inventive – and became proficient at picking out her villains (years later when I saw *The Mousetrap* I soon guessed the guilty party). I read history, politics, Churchill on the Second World War, Neville Cardus on cricket, R.F. Delderfield, Howard Spring, books on banking – anything I could lay my hands on. My long months of convalescence were not wasted.

I left hospital in August 1967, painfully thin and still unwell. My leg was terribly wasted, and when the plaster-cast was removed it was appalling to look at as the scars continued their slow healing. Jean took me in, and I went back to live with her in Brixton. She nursed and cared for me as I began the long road to recovery. She had more warmth to offer than I deserved, and she rebuilt me mentally and physically. I was very fond of her. I loved being with her, but always – pushed to the back of my mind

– was our age difference, and the belief that this could not last. I was not sure it was fair of me to stay, but I was wrapped in such affection that I did.

When I was fit enough to care for myself I moved to a tiny flat owned by Pat and Ted Davies, two friends of Jean's, and returned to studying for my banking diploma. That September I passed Monetary Theory and Practice and returned to the bank – and to local politics in Lambeth. As my slow recovery continued I was approved, in October, as the Conservative candidate for Ferndale Ward in the local elections that were to be held the following May. It was another safe Labour fiefdom, or so it was thought: candidates for the wards we hoped to win had already been selected. Campaigning was a distraction from studying, but I structured the day to fit in both.

Before I was selected for Ferndale I addressed the Clapham YCs. Hobbling on crutches, I turned up at the Clapham Conservative headquarters, which was the wrong venue for the evening, as the senior association had their own meeting that night. I passed their guest on the stairs – a distinguished Queen's Counsel who would be speaking on law reform. We did not speak, but I was told he was Sir David Renton, the Member of Parliament for Huntingdonshire.

My mother was still worried about my health and my relationship with Jean, and in order to keep an eye on me, she accepted my invitation to come to a Brixton Conservative Supper Club. The guest speaker cancelled in mid-afternoon, and at two hours' notice I stood in for him. It was the first and only time my mother ever heard me speak to an audience.

I saw her sitting there, accepting the kind words from her neighbours, and I did not need to ask what was in her mind: if only Tom were here. If only . . . But he wasn't, sadly, and never could be now. But my mother nearly burst with pride, and the warm tears, so often near the surface in her gentle personality, flowed unstoppably. I felt very close to her that evening.

The pace of politics was beginning to accelerate. I drew on my experience, the people I had met and the things I had done, my work in banking and all I had done across Brixton and Lambeth, in getting myself known. To my advantage was the fact that I worked twice as hard as anyone else. I attended Young Conservative meetings and functions, canvassed, supported people in elections – I was just *there*. I was determined never to fail again through lack of effort, as I had at school. I was prepared to fail through lack of ability, through bad luck even, but never again through not having done what I was capable of.

That school failure haunted me, and I felt it very strongly. When I was making garden ornaments with Terry, I didn't see myself doing that for life. I looked around and thought, what skills do I have? What have I got to offer? I felt I had something, and decided I had better prove to other people that that was the case. That was why I started working so hard. Drive is as important in life as intellect.

I became a regular speaker for Conservative Central Office, was elected Treasurer of the Brixton Conservative Association, and gave evidence at a Central Office inquiry into a dispute with the formidably right-wing Association Chairman, an officer from Brixton Prison who had fallen out with our agent, Marion Standing, and wanted to have her removed. It was an unhappy incident, and I can't now remember the details, except that I was an ardent supporter of Mrs Standing. Although she came out of the inquiry well, she left the association soon after, as did the Chairman. In the midst of all this I continued to study.

I expected to lose in Ferndale Ward, but thought that contesting it would build up my curriculum vitae. I canvassed, hobbling around, and got a far better reception than I expected. Indeed, we were doing better across Lambeth than we had hoped. Barbara Wallis, one of our candidates in an unpromising ward in Vauxhall, reported a good doorstep reaction. So did Sir George Young in neighbouring Clapham. But I disregarded George's reports: George was 6'4" and canvassed with his Irish wolfhound, Cerberus, in tow. Cerberus looked even bigger than George: it was no surprise to me that everyone offered him support.

We were optimistic about gaining seats in the council elections. Harold Wilson's Labour government was very unpopular. It had devalued the pound the previous year and seemed unable to shrug off the difficulties it faced. Even so, winning Ferndale was not considered likely.

Then fate took a hand. On 20 April, three weeks before the local elections, Enoch Powell made his notorious 'Rivers of Blood' speech in Birmingham, warning of the dangers of immigration. It stirred emotions and fears, and turned a favourable Tory drift into an avalanche that changed the political landscape. Ted Heath sacked Enoch from the Shadow Cabinet. Quintin Hogg and Iain Macleod denounced him. But millions felt he had voiced their fears. The dockers marched in his support. There was political pandemonium – and everyone took sides.

I thought Powell was wrong and his speech inflammatory – Ted Heath was right to dismiss him, and I said so. But in Lambeth, Conservative politics was divided over his speech. Some council candidates, including my friend Clive Jones, strongly supported Enoch, and some issued 'We Back Enoch' leaflets as part of their election campaign. Barbara Wallis and another friend, Laurie Kennedy, opposed him. So did Bernard Perkins and Peter Cary, the two most senior local Conservative figures. Many white people in Brixton thought Powell was articulating their fears. The black residents felt threatened, though I did not know many of them to talk to about it. Those I did know shied away from speaking about Powell, because often they couldn't be certain if they were talking to someone who agreed with him or not.

I did not share the view that Powell was personally a racist, and I recognised that he was expressing genuine fears. But I was sure he was mistaken. Years later, in the Commons, when I came to know this strange and brilliant man, I saw at close quarters the spell he could weave. I did not often agree with him – he carried his arguments too much to extremes for my taste – but he was a remarkable parliamentarian. In 1968 he conjured powerful political magic. The Labour government slumped in the polls as Enoch caught the public mood. The local election results that year were catastrophic for Labour, and provided unimagined political riches for the Conservatives.

We won Lambeth in a landslide: fifty-seven of the sixty seats fell into our hands. The town hall count was alive with disbelief and excitement as seat after seat fell to the Tories. The new councillors were a mixed bunch. Reg Allnutt and Jean Langley, who joined me as the Ferndale victors, hadn't really expected to be elected, and were excited to make it, even if only by a handful of votes. Barbara Wallis, George Young, Clive Jones and many other friends romped home in other wards. They were political professionals. Barbara, short, red-haired, fiery for moderation (though in later years the moderation would slip), was later to become my constituency secretary in the Commons and at Downing Street. George Young served in my Cabinet. Clive Jones, amiable, large, a second son to my parents, was to be my best man and a friend for many years.

On the way home from the count I tried to wake up our Association

President, Mrs Evans, an elderly Welsh lady, to tell her the news. She was fast asleep, having gone to bed expecting to lose, as usual, and did not answer her bell. Undaunted, I was hoisted up a lamp-post with my damaged leg held gingerly to one side as I lobbed pebbles at her window. Suddenly, my companions fell very silent and I became conscious of another figure standing on the pavement. It was a policeman. 'And what are you up to?' he asked, reasonably enough. We explained our election win. He walked off shaking his head at the lunatic behaviour of the sort of young people who went in for politics, and Mrs Evans slept on.

There were one or two squalls as I settled in on the council. Bernard Perkins and Peter Cary made it clear that the new Conservative council would have no part in anti-black propaganda. I strongly agreed with this and fought my own battle against constituency activists who had opposing views. A few weeks after my election the Town Clerk, John Fishwick, gently took me to one side to query my eligibility to have stood as a councillor in Lambeth. I was living between three flats at the time, but the address on my nomination form was for a fourth address, at which I had never lived. Mr Fishwick had discovered this and was puzzled.

In fact, I did have a residency qualification for Lambeth. I was still living partly with Jean and should properly have registered as a Lambeth elector from her address – but, for reasons of discretion, I did not wish to do so. In order to ensure a residency qualification I had taken two rooms in nearby Templar Street, but had not been able to move in by the October deadline for inclusion on the electoral register. As a council candidate this left me in a dilemma, so I registered with the address of an old friend of my mother, Mrs Olifent, also in Templar Street, opposite the rooms I had rented. John Fishwick was highly amused, and I heard no more about this innocent deception until *Panorama* unearthed it – only partly accurately and to the great distress of Mrs Olifent, who was tearful and upset at the repeated questioning – twenty-five years later.

The greatest problem in Lambeth, then as now, was poor housing. Much of Streatham and Norwood was attractive, and small parts of Kennington were already being gentrified. But Clapham was declining, and large parts of Brixton were slums, overcrowded and insanitary. They were breeding grounds for discontent and misery. The 'swinging sixties' did not swing in Lambeth. Land prices were soaring, and owner-occupation was dying. The population was growing, and so were council costs. Many immigrants, mostly from the West Indies, who had come to England in search of a better life, found themselves unemployed, without hope, living in deprived and miserable conditions as fear of real conflict rose around them. In the midst of this powder-keg, Enoch Powell's speech reverberated – reassuring the whites that their private fears were not overlooked, and terrifying the black population.

Lambeth was overwhelmed. The solution to the housing problem was to build more houses. Yet even as that was done, it created other problems. Remaining streets of owner-occupation disappeared. The population mix narrowed ever more to those in need. The pressure on education and other services rose. High expenditure forced up local rates and forced out small local businesses, thus worsening unemployment. A cycle of deprivation faced Lambeth.

And yet, somehow, Brixton battled on. Tenant groups, church groups, all manner of special-interest groups tried to improve local conditions; if this sometimes led them into conflict with a local authority that would not meet all their demands, that was unsurprising. Yet despite its problems, Brixton was always vigorous and vital. Brixton market was its epicentre: cosmopolitan, bustling, bursting with stalls and traders shouting their bargains, music overlaying the chatter, the scent of spices mingling with hot dogs and South London and Caribbean accents on every side.

The dominant figure on Lambeth Council was Bernard Perkins, the leader of the Conservatives, who knew local government inside out. By profession, he was a senior local government officer in next-door Wandsworth. He devoted all his free time to Lambeth. He was supported by Peter Cary, the deputy leader – a Nigel Lawson-like figure who was a specialist in housing. I was lucky. Bernard appointed me to the Finance and Housing Committees. I could have asked for no more, and threw myself into the necessary learning curve.

Politics began to take over more of my life. I left work each day and headed either for the Conservative Association, where I remained Treasurer, or the town hall for committees and other meetings. If I had none of my own to attend I listened in on others to learn all that was going on. My early-morning banking studies had to share the time with preparation for council meetings. I continued to pass the examinations, but my progress was slower than before.

At the end of 1968 the Brixton Association agreed with neighbouring

Clapham and Vauxhall to link together as the North Lambeth Conservative Group, and to appoint Jean Lucas, the formidably efficient agent for Clapham, as joint agent. Jean was to become, and remain, a great friend and ally. She gave me tremendous encouragement as I agonised over whether I would ever achieve my ambition of being elected to Parliament, and was to play a crucial role in bringing that about. Jean had a trainee agent with her, Peter Golds, whom I knew. He too would more than once play a crucial role in my future.

In January 1969 I became Peter Cary's deputy as Vice Chairman of the Housing Committee, and two months later, Vice Chairman of the Brixton Conservative Association. Lambeth Council was well served with officers. John Fishwick was an old-fashioned Town Clerk. Ted Hollamby was an enthusiastic Director of Planning, impatient to demolish the slums and build decent houses. He would drive around the borough waving his arms to point out monstrosities, apparently oblivious of the need to keep some control of the steering wheel.

The prince among them was Harry Simpson, the Director of Housing. Harry had begun his working life, aged fifteen, with the London County Council, and became a rent collector. He rose to be one of the most respected housing administrators in the country, and after leaving Lambeth, became Director of the Northern Ireland Housing Authority and, at the end of his career, of the Greater London Council (GLC).

I learned a great deal from this amazing man, and it was his drive and Bernard Perkins's leadership that earned Lambeth a high reputation in local government circles. Before and after meetings I would join Harry in his office and we talked housing – often late into the night. He was the best tutor there could be, both in housing and in the decent, civilised conduct of public affairs.

I also took an interest in my own housing, and bought my first home: a two-bedroom flat in Primrose Court, Streatham. It cost £5,600, and I was a reluctant purchaser, persuaded to buy by a fellow councillor, Geoff Murray, who already had a flat there. My hesitation was simply because I was too busy to buy, but he chipped away at me until I agreed. Later, a third Lambeth councillor, John Steele, also moved there, and Primrose Court became an annexe to the town hall – and my flat was often crowded with younger members of the council. I remained friendly with Jean, but our relationship had cooled.

That year I visited Russia, where Lambeth was twinned with the Moscow suburb of Moskvoretsky. Only the year before Russia had invaded Czechoslovakia to snuff out the Prague Spring of Alexander Dubček, and I was interested to see for myself what our Cold War enemy was really like at close quarters.

The visit was a mass of contradictions. The Mayor of Moskvoretsky, a man called Chilikin, exercised his power ruthlessly, not least in his responsibility for housing. 'It's cold in winter without a flat,' he told me, smiling, and I did not think he was joking. We were entertained royally, and I saw my first opera, *Queen of Spades*, at the Bolshoi Theatre and my first ballet, *Swan Lake*, at the Palace of Congresses, with Natalia Bessmertnova dancing the lead. I preferred the ballet, little knowing that I would soon meet someone who would introduce me more comprehensively to the delights of opera. The Russian system delivered political power with age, and Chilikin was fascinated that I was thirty years younger than the rest of our delegation. After the ballet he plied me with drinks until the early hours of the morning to see if I could stand the pace. As my father's remedy for toothache for young children had been neat whisky (it took away the toothache but left a sore head and a sleepy child), I was well able to cope. Chilikin was impressed.

But I was not impressed with the new buildings he showed me. If this was communism, it was appalling. Hospitals had electrical wiring sticking out of the walls; houses and flats were built to a very low standard, with no attempt at landscaping to produce an attractive environment. Only mud and rubble lay between the housing blocks. It was a lesson in what to avoid, but a later study trip to Finland, where the quality of building was very high, left no room for complacency about what we were doing in Lambeth.

That year Lambeth faced a dustmen's strike over 'totting', a practice in which the dustmen ransacked the bins to identify items for resale. We had negotiated the end of totting, but the dustmen went on strike to reclaim the right. We resisted. The strike continued, and the outlook for public health and cleanliness was grim. The Conservative councillors, with voluntary help, decided to collect the rubbish themselves, and commandeered the dustcarts. It was strike-breaking in a unique way. Almost every councillor helped. The action created headlines around the world, but they concentrated mostly on Sir George Young and his wife Aurelia, also a Lambeth councillor. George is a baronet, and the sight of him and Aurelia driving the dustcart and collecting bins was irresistible: 'My old man's a dustcart, Bart,' chortled the press. But the councillors' response was successful: a settlement was agreed, and Lambeth faced no more industrial action during the Conservative years.

In February 1970 I became Chairman of Housing, and the following month Chairman of Brixton Conservative Association as we began to prepare for the GLC elections on 9 April, and the expected general election. I had been asked whether I wished to contest the GLC elections for Hammersmith and Lambeth, but decided I had my hands full.

The GLC elections were held that year on a borough-wide basis, with four candidates being elected from Lambeth. One of the Conservative candidates was Diana Geddes, who on polling day was working out of our Brixton Road headquarters. Peter Golds brought a friend with him to help bring in the votes. I saw them as they arrived. She was slender, a little above average height, with mid-brown hair, shining brown eyes and a beautiful, curving, glamorous smile. Dressed in a beige checked suit, fawn blouse and white, knee-length boots, she was stunningly attractive.

'Hi,' said Peter. 'This is Norma. She's come to help.'

She was Norma Johnson, 'mad on opera', said Peter, adding that she'd been known to sleep outside Covent Garden all night to get tickets for Joan Sutherland. Within minutes I discovered she was a teacher with her own Mini, her own flat – temporarily living at home because she'd rented it out – not very political, but Conservative, and that she also designed and made clothes.

The demands of election day drove us apart. Norma and Peter went out in her Mini to collect and deliver voters to the polling station. I canvassed, cajoled workers, kept in touch with candidates, filled in wherever necessary and arranged for Norma to attend the count at Lambeth Town Hall. Although the Conservatives won control of the GLC that night, we did not win the seats in Lambeth. But I had found Norma.

A few days later she phoned. She was having a party – would I like to come? Parties weren't much my scene then, and I wanted Norma alone, not in a crowd. I declined, pleading another engagement. She phoned again several days later. She 'happened to have a spare ticket for a gala at Covent Garden'. Was I interested? I was.

The gala was a tribute to Sir David Webster, the retiring administrator at Covent Garden. It was a long programme and it overran. The opera house was hot and oppressive, and the music too somnolent for someone who had been reading council papers until 2 a.m. and writing banking essays from six in the morning. As Joan Sutherland closed the gala singing the mad scene from *Lucia di Lammermoor*, I fell asleep.

I knew from the moment we met that I wanted to marry Norma. Ten days later we were engaged. Norma was an only child. Her mother, Dee, had been widowed as a twenty-two-year-old in 1945 when her husband Norman – who served in the Royal Artillery throughout the war – had died in a motorcycle accident days after it ended. Four months earlier Dee had lost her baby son, Colin, at only six days old, and with Norman's death she and three-year-old Norma were on their own. When life treated Dee harshly she fought back. For much of her life she held down two or three jobs at the same time to ensure that she and Norma lacked nothing. Norma went to boarding school from the age of four, and had grown up very independent and practical.

My mother was back in hospital with yet another bronchial and chest infection, and I took Norma to see her. For once there was no caution, no holding back, no reservations. She was as certain as I was that this was the right girl.

Meanwhile, in Brixton, a mini-crisis was brewing. The Conservative candidate for the general election was James Harkess, personally charming but strongly right-wing, with Powellite views on race that he expressed vigorously and openly. He and I were never going to agree. He saw the problems of immigration. I saw people trying to better their lifestyle. Nor did it seem to me that implying that half of his electorate were unwelcome in the constituency was a vote-winning platform.

At the AGM of the association Harkess made a wild speech that was strongly anti-immigrant. I was appalled at his intolerance, and embarrassed too, especially as we had a new West Indian member present, who must have been mortified. I replied angrily from the chair, rebutting Harkess's remarks, and the atmosphere turned sulphurous. I knew that relations between us were soured beyond repair. The ramifications were considerable. Jean Lucas, the group agent for Lambeth, strongly backed me, as did Lady Colman, President of the association, and widow of the former Conservative Member for the seat who had been defeated in 1945. Others in the association felt the same.

Gradually it became apparent that the consensus was that James Harkess's views would damage race relations in Brixton, and with them the Conservative cause. I took soundings, and spoke to Harkess about our concerns, but did not receive any positive response. Finally I went ahead with a motion for the executive to consider selecting a new candidate. It would certainly have been approved, and I had Diana Geddes in mind as his replacement. Then Harold Wilson called the general election, and the meeting to discuss whether the candidate should be replaced instead endorsed him, dutifully and without enthusiasm.

It was an odd election campaign, in blazing weather. Opinion polls gave Labour a huge lead, but they proved inaccurate. When the votes were counted the swing to the Conservatives across the country was apparent from the first result. By the end of the night, to everyone's surprise but his own, Ted Heath was prime minister with a comfortable majority.

There was never any doubt that Colonel Marcus Lipton, the Labour candidate, who was an excellent constituency MP, would be comfortably re-elected in Brixton. In nearby marginal Clapham, Bill Shelton, the Conservative candidate, comfortably took the seat vacated by its Labour MP, Mrs Margaret MacKay, from the recently adopted Dr David Pitt, a black Labour candidate, but without raising the race issue. The swing in Clapham showed what a potent force that issue was, and how inflammatory it could have been in Brixton. We had been fortunate. Labour's huge opinion poll lead and Marcus Lipton's long incumbency as the Member meant that James Harkess was considered to have no chance of winning. Passions were stilled by the certainty of his defeat, and he soon moved on from Brixton. Clive Jones lost in neighbouring Vauxhall. On Lambeth Council, the Conservatives were aware that we were probably only short-term tenants at the local level, and that Labour was likely to regain control at the next council elections in 1971. Too many of our majorities were tiny for us not to realise that even a small swing of the political compass would have a serious impact.

We thought our best chance was to mount a real attack on poor housing conditions, and set to it with a will. Bernard Perkins as leader and Peter Cary as Chairman of Finance gave me their full backing as we set about the task. We continued our building and slum-clearance programme. We drew up schemes to sell council houses and to build houses for sale in an attempt to revive owner-occupation and encourage skills and employment in Lambeth. We established registration schemes to tackle overcrowding. We set up arrangements with Peterborough New Town for families to move there into jobs and good housing (I little knew that eight years later many of them would become my constituents in Huntingdon). We encouraged ministerial visits so that we could show the new government our problems as we sought more help and finance.

I remember showing Peter Walker, the new Environment Secretary, the squalor of life in the Geneva Drive–Somerleyton Road area of Brixton, where there was mass overcrowding in dilapidated homes with poor facilities. We met one West Indian on the third-floor landing of one of these monstrosities.

'Where do you live?' I asked him for the Minister's benefit.

'Here,' he said, puzzled.

'No,' I pressed him, 'which room?'

'I don't have a room,' he replied. 'I live here.'

And he did, on the landing.

It was problems like that that encouraged us to open the first Housing Advice Centre in London. The concept was simple. Anyone with a housing problem, of any sort, could go to the Advice Centre for help and advice, free of charge. Soon it was so popular it was packed.

There was another aspect of life in Lambeth that struck me forcibly. Some people in need were aggressive; but very few. Most were frightened of bureaucracy, of government, of their powers to tax, to put up rents, to give or withhold planning consent and, above all, to house them in council flats or not. Moreover, councillors and council officials were too often hidden away. To the public they could be anonymous figures, but nonetheless figures whose decisions could blight or improve their lives. This was particularly true of the decisions to rehouse following slum clearance and new building, and the often artificial restrictions on council tenants even if they were rehoused. At tenants' meetings the resentments voiced against these anonymous figures were fierce.

I decided to take the Housing Advice Centre on tour, with the main council officials accompanying councillors at public meetings, to face the people directly, answer their questions and explain our policies. There was, at first, a lot of resistance to this revolutionary idea, but with strong backing from Bernard Perkins and – among the officers – Harry Simpson, it was soon agreed. The meetings were a huge success, often attracting audiences of many hundreds that overflowed the halls we had booked. I chaired the meetings, with the Chairman of Planning and Social Services invariably in attendance as well as the local councillors for the ward. More importantly to the public, the Directors of Housing and Planning were there, with other officers, and especially the Lettings Officer, who allocated council houses and flats.

These meetings were generally good-natured, but with the occasional rowdy and angry intervention. I loved them, and thought they were a valuable safety valve. I regretted then — and still do — the fact that such meetings were not a regular practice for all councils. I believe they should be.

Some incidents still stick in the mind. Once, a man held up a rat he'd found in his house. What was I going to do about it? he demanded. I asked where he lived. He told me, and after a whispered consultation I was able to tell him that he lived over the border in Southwark. It was a Southwark rat – and he should take it to Alderman Ron Brown, brother of the former deputy leader of the Labour Party George Brown, and a leading member of Southwark Council. For my pains, he threw the rat at me – happily he was a very poor shot.

At a meeting in Kennington a young, strikingly attractive woman dressed from top to toe in shiny black leather rose to ask a question. The audience looked at her with more than passing interest.

'I am the wife of the Vicar of . . .' she began, but got no further, as the unlikelihood of this registered and the hall erupted in raucous amusement. We did get her question eventually, but I can't recall what it was. Later she became a Labour councillor.

At the end of these meetings I would hang around, usually with Harry Simpson, who had given me a lift to the hall, to gauge reaction. Even those members of the public who hadn't liked the answers they'd received enjoyed the meetings. It was politics made real, and not hidden away in committee rooms. These meetings made a profound impression on me: politics seemed so far removed from electors, and they rarely expected to meet the decision-takers. They were accustomed to poor service, remote officials and a system run for government and not for the public. I promised myself that, if I ever had the chance, I would try to open up government and make it more accountable.

I spent every spare moment I could with Norma. She learned about politics, while I began to understand opera. Norma's mother Dee set herself to planning a big wedding. Then, in mid-September, just over two weeks before the wedding, the phone rang at four o'clock in the morning. I picked it up with foreboding. It was my brother Terry, very upset.

'Mum's dead,' he said, 'a few minutes ago. In Mayday.'

I had not expected this. My mother's ill-health had been a constant feature of my life ever since I was a child, but she always battled through. She had been determined to come out of hospital for my wedding. Now she would not, and my heart broke for her. She had lost her last fight with just sixteen days to go.

I lay in bed after Terry's call, reliving memories of the woman whose fondest hopes had always been for others: firstly my father, and then her children. As the youngest, more hopes had been poured into me, and I had always taken it so much for granted. The smallest gesture cheered and lifted her; the greatest blow would never crush her. My father may have dominated our family, but my mother was its heart. When she died, lame ducks lost a saint. Strangers found in her an instant friendliness. An hour's acquaintance made a friend for ever. All her life she had been gregarious and, even in her last illness, had become so friendly with everyone at the local corner shop that it closed on the day of her funeral. She was open-hearted and open-handed. But her generosity of spirit was to her family and those in need. She could be an implacable foe when she chose, but in those near to her she inspired the same love she gave so generously. A few days after her death, Mum was cremated at Streatham Vale crematorium, and her ashes were laid beside Dad's.

I wondered whether we should postpone the wedding, but I knew that my mother would have thoroughly disapproved of such a gesture. Besides, Pat and Terry insisted that we go ahead. The day before the wedding I slipped and fell in a corridor in Lambeth Town Hall, when my suspect left knee gave way. It swelled up like a balloon, and Clive Jones helped me home, where I lay in the bath with an ice-pack wrapped around my knee.

'Eat your heart out, young Lochinvar,' grinned Clive as he sipped a whisky beside the bath. 'I suppose you could always hop down the aisle.'

Saturday, 3 October 1970 was crisp, clear and sunny, and in the morning I could hobble pretty well. My main worry was that the wretched knee would collapse under me as Norma and I walked back down the aisle. But the whole day went perfectly. Norma was acceptably late, and looked lovely.

St Matthew's Church in Brixton was packed. Clive had the ring. June Bronhill – the petite and lovely Australian soprano who had sung Lucia at Covent Garden and starred as Elizabeth Barrett Browning in the West End production of Ronald Millar's *Robert and Elizabeth* – sang 'Ave Maria', and her wonderful voice echoed around the church. Norma had known June for years, made dresses for her, lived with her as temporary nanny to her daughter, Biddy, and they were close friends. I clutched Norma's arm as we walked back down the aisle, and we made it safely to the door. 'I thought *you* were supposed to support *her*,' was Clive's comment.

After a honeymoon in Ibiza we returned to Primrose Court, and Norma turned it from a bachelor flat into a home. Writing in the late nineties, it is hard to remember how life was in 1970. Our combined income was around £3,000 a year, and £8 a week sufficed for the housekeeping. But week by week our flat took on a new face. Corners were filled, rooms were painted, books and records appeared, and astonished friends marvelled at the transformation of my spartan pad.

Life and politics resumed in Lambeth. In January 1971 I was shortlisted for the vacant parliamentary candidacy at Norwood, but this was Bernard Perkins's fortress, and he was selected. We prepared for the council elections in May, and I was selected for Thornton Ward in Clapham, which was thought to be a much safer bet than Ferndale. On 28 March, the day before my twenty-eighth birthday, Norma told me she was pregnant, and in May, despite all our efforts, the Conservatives were soundly defeated in Lambeth as Labour regained its fiefdom. Ken Livingstone succeeded me as Housing Chairman, and Tony Banks also became a councillor.

I barely knew either of them before they were elected, although Ken's emergence as a Labour council candidate caused quite a stir in Norwood, where his mother was an active member of the Conservative Association. Both of them were already identifiably the characters who later became so well known, and Tony Banks was soon involved in controversy as allegedly the moving spirit behind an attempt to ban the Queen's portrait from the council chamber. (After the 1997 general election he was photographed taking the loyal oath with his fingers crossed behind his back.)

Moving to Thornton Ward did me no good at all: I lost by 411 votes. I was disappointed by the reversal of our fortunes in Lambeth because we were generally thought to have done a good job. Years later Ken Livingstone was very flattering about what our Conservative council had achieved. But there was still so much more to do. I was philosophical about my own defeat. The role of councillor in opposition did not appeal very much.

I decided it was time to try to move onto the national stage. To do so I needed to pass the selection procedure to get on the Conservative Central Office list of approved candidates. Jill Knight, the MP for Edgbaston, who lived in Lambeth and had heard me speak, sponsored my application, and by early June it had been submitted. Then fate, in the shape of Peter Golds, intervened.

Peter was a firm believer that I should be in Parliament. He had mentioned this to a fellow agent, Tony Dey, and took me to see Tony and Bob Bell, the affable President of the St Pancras North Association. It was suggested that I apply for the seat. No one was remotely bothered that I was not an approved candidate. St Pancras North was a safe Labour seat, with Jock Stallard as a well-established local Member. There was little chance of winning, but it was perfect for me: a London constituency, convenient to where I lived and worked, affordable, even on my average income, and the best I could hope for aged twenty-eight.

I had continued studying, and in September 1971 I finally sat and passed the Accountancy and Practice of Banking papers that completed my Banking Diploma. It had taken me six years to pass ten examinations, all of them at the first attempt, as politics, Nigeria, recovery from the car accident and marriage had competed for the limited hours of every day. I was delighted to have passed, even though the qualification was less a tool for a banking career than an element of building up the necessary curriculum vitae for politics. I applied for the vacancy at St Pancras North, was invited for interview with thirty others, and was shortlisted with only one rival.

That summer Norma and I enjoyed a glorious holiday in an old chantry with a secluded garden. We lazed through the long summer days and planned the future. Norma's pregnancy was nearing full term. She had never been fitter or happier, and she bloomed with health. It was fortunate that she did so, because Elizabeth was in no hurry to make her first entrance. Then, early one November evening, she finally announced her impending arrival.

I saw both my children being born, and am glad I did so. In 1971, when Elizabeth was born, it was quite revolutionary to allow fathers to be present, but King's College Hospital in Camberwell had no qualms about it at all.

Elizabeth was a full-term baby, but her birth was interminable. After fifteen hours I was sent away to lie down – 'This is all very tiring, dear,' said the nurse. A few hours later the doctors took me aside and told me Norma needed an epidural. The risks were explained to us, but Norma agreed, and after thirty hours, in the early hours of 13 November 1971, a plump and chubby Elizabeth bounced across the delivery table and lustily announced that a new force had arrived.

There are some moments in your life when every second is implanted indelibly in your mind. Perhaps most parents feel this at the birth of their child. I certainly did. And when I held Elizabeth for the first time I knew my life was changed. She was warm and comfortable, vulnerable and dependent. Here was a baby who – whatever else happened – would for ever be loved, and who one day, I hoped, would tell her grandchildren about Norma and me.

It was after 2 a.m. when I left the hospital to walk home, for the buses had stopped and there were no taxis around at that time. I didn't so much walk as float. Anyone about the streets that November night would have wondered, who was this lunatic who ran, walked, skipped, turned round in circles, hopped, stepped, jumped up and down and cheerily sang to himself out of sheer exhilaration?

I planned the future and, more immediately, wondered how early I could phone Dee, Norma's mother, with the news. I needn't have worried about that. As I stepped into our flat the phone rang. It was Dee. She was very agitated. 'She's had the baby, hasn't she?' she said. 'I know she has. I haven't been able to sleep. Is she all right?'

I told her. She sighed and hung up without a word. Moments later she phoned back.

'Sorry,' she said. 'I was so relieved. I knew, just knew she was having the baby. Now tell me all about it.'

So I did. And if the world ever contained a more relieved and pleased grandparent – well, I can't imagine her.

At first Elizabeth was going to be called Jane. But that didn't last. When I visited Norma in hospital the following day she was cuddling a plump and contented baby.

'I don't think Jane is right,' said Norma. 'She looks like an Elizabeth.' And so Elizabeth she became.

Later that month I was selected as the prospective parliamentary candidate for St Pancras North after addressing the interview panel and answering their questions. I had received an enthusiastic response, and was told I had won comfortably. 'Some voted for you and quite a few for Elizabeth,' as Joan Couzens, soon to be my press officer, put it. Joan was one of a number of characters in the association, and certainly the most vivid. She loathed the Labour Party she saw in London, which brought out in her some outrageously right-wing instincts which were held in check by her common sense. She enjoyed flirting with them, however, and often wrote me draft press releases in poetry, based on her instincts, not her common sense, which we both knew could never be used, but which gave us great fun. She was a fine artist as well, and she and her husband Bertie became firm friends.

St Pancras North may have been unpromising political territory for the Conservatives, but my three years as its candidate, which embraced both the February and October general elections of 1974, taught me a huge amount about the party and the volunteers who ran it at local level.

Tony Dey, the agent, was laconic and efficient. Bob Bell, the President, and his wife Edith, Francis Klein, the Chairman, Dennis Friis, Roland Walker and so many others worked tirelessly for little political reward other than to uphold Conservative principles. They weren't ideological warriors. They believed in the Conservative cause. They grumbled sometimes about some of the leaders and some of the policy, but they loyally battled on.

I worked hard for them in St Pancras. Between my adoption as prospective candidate and the February 1974 election I worked the seat as if it were a marginal, visiting it nearly every evening and every weekend. Margaret Jay, who succeeded Tony Dey as my agent, worked me hard – and herself as well. Norma joined me whenever she could. It was hard work but it was a lot of fun too, although it became harder as Ted Heath's government ran into difficulties.

Ted had been elected on a strong centre-right platform, but events had forced him off it. Trade union power forced up wages and prices and brought about an incomes policy that upset many in the party and even caused discontented murmurings amongst the St Pancras North loyalists. Ted took Britain into the Common Market, an inevitable, correct and courageous decision, but one that was very controversial, too.

Then came the miners' strike over a pay claim that would have given some miners up to a 50 per cent rise. The National Coal Board had offered 13 per cent, which was rejected, and an overtime ban began. The miners were led by Joe Gormley, a traditional Labour figure, but not a militant. His interest was in the miners' well-being and not in attacking the Conservative government. Other miners' leaders, though, such as Mick McGahey and Arthur Scargill, did see the chance of confrontation and bringing down the government.

The strike worsened. Implacable positions were taken and Ted Heath was forced into a box. Many Conservatives, mostly but not exclusively on the right, wanted to 'take on' the miners. 'Who governs the country?' they asked. Others recognised the sympathy and respect in which the miners were widely held by the British people. Some of their leaders might be militant, but the British sense of fair play knew that the miners did a job that few would care to do. The public admired the miners and liked the common sense they often heard from rank-and-file NUM members. But they did not like the militants.

Crisis beckoned, and the three-day week was imposed from 31 December 1973 as stocks of coal fell. Pressure mounted. Ted Heath had a dilemma. If he negotiated a settlement because of the economic effect the strike was having, he would be accused of weakness, especially from within the Conservative Party. If the strikes continued the economy would suffer, and gradually public opinion would turn against the government. The third choice, a huge gamble, was a general election to reinforce the government's authority. Little thought was given to what would happen if the government was re-elected, but the strike itself went on.

Ted Heath went for broke and called the election on the theme of 'Who Governs Britain?' At the time I was delighted, and the early opinion polls were favourable, as was reaction on the doorstep, even in St Pancras North. But a one-issue election is dangerous. Midway through the campaign complex evidence on miners' pay suggested that they were earning even less than the NUM had declared. Harold Wilson claimed an election had been called over an 'arithmetical error'. Sympathy swelled for the miners.

The public mood changed. Unhappy Tories voted Liberal, and Labour crept home as the largest party. Ted Heath was out and Harold Wilson, to his surprise and everyone else's, was back in Downing Street, at the head of a minority administration. One bright spot was that George Young was elected to Parliament with a small majority at Ealing, Acton. In St Pancras North Jock Stallard was alarmed by the strength of support I had in some streets, but overall he won comfortably.

A second general election later that year was inevitable. The St Pancras North Conservative Association generously told me I could seek a better seat with their blessing, but could recontest St Pancras if I failed to find one. I did not try very hard, although I was shortlisted for marginal Paddington, where I was narrowly defeated by Mark Wolfson, later MP for Sevenoaks. I also applied for Portsmouth North, where I was assailed with questions about flogging and hanging, which the questioner favoured – whether sequentially or alternatively I wasn't sure – and I didn't. That was the end of Portsmouth North, who picked a well-known businessman, John Ward, who would later become my PPS when I was prime minister.

After this setback, I decided to stay in St Pancras North, and contested it again in the second general election of the year in October. The constituency was of little interest nationally, and the only publicity we received was for my new agent, Sue Winter, the youngest in the country and very pretty. It made no difference. Again I lost, after a rather bitter campaign and an unpleasant count, with jeering Labour activists. Jock Stallard's majority increased. Labour gained seats nationally, and had a very narrow overall majority of only three seats. Soon they would need to rely on Liberal support to stay in government.

By now Norma and I had sold our flat in Primrose Court and bought a modern end-of-terrace house, West Oak, in The Avenue, Beckenham. Elizabeth was growing, and we needed more space. West Oak was a small estate in lovely wooded grounds, full of mostly young married couples, and we were very happy there. Among our neighbours were David Rodgers, a former aide to Iain Macleod, and his wife Erica, who had been National Vice Chairman of the Young Conservatives.

Norma was pregnant again, and James was born in January 1975. I was again present at the birth, and he arrived much more speedily and with much less drama than Elizabeth. We had no difficulty over his name: he was James, if a boy, from long before he was born. He was a fit, contented baby from the very start.

Politics moved on, and in February 1975 Margaret Thatcher defeated Ted Heath to become leader of the Conservative Party. I had never met her, and little guessed how much our paths would cross in the future.

No one expected another early general election – public and politicians were battle-weary – but as seats were advertised or fell vacant I applied for them. I received rejection after rejection without interview, and was puzzled and despondent. It was Jean Lucas, by then the agent for Putney, who solved the puzzle after I applied for the vacant candidacy there. She telephoned and asked whether my biography needed to be jazzed up, and then noticed that the biography sent to Putney by Central Office was not mine. She made enquiries. The answer was comical. There were two John Majors. One, me, on the approved candidates list for Parliament, and the other on the list of would-be candidates for the GLC. Someone at Central Office had transposed the biographies, and was sending out my namesake's – which was pretty thin – to all the seats for which I had applied. Unsurprisingly, I had not been invited for interview.

After Jean's intervention I was invited to Putney, interviewed and short-listed. I was led to believe I was the front-runner and likely to be adopted. But, as their selection process rumbled on, a by-election was called at Conservative-held Carshalton, and I was interviewed and reached the last eight. I withdrew from Putney, and an unknown barrister was chosen: his name was David Mellor. 'He is very clever and one day will make a real name for himself,' predicted Jean Lucas.

At Carshalton I was preceded for interview by a confident young man carrying a briefcase with the initials 'N.F.' prominently displayed. I asked who he was, and was told his name was Nigel Forman. I had a premonition that he would be selected; he was, and comfortably won the ensuing by-election.

I continued to apply for a seat. Sevenoaks did not interview me. At Ruislip Northwood I disagreed sharply with a member of the selection committee over housing and was not invited for further interview. At Dorset South I reached the second round of interviews and was waiting with the others for my ordeal when I saw the selection committee rise respectfully as a well-built young man with dark hair entered the room. One of the other candidates scowled: 'That's Lord Cranborne – he owns the constituency.' That was not quite true, although he certainly owned a lot of land. He was selected, and twenty years later I was to appoint him to my Cabinet as leader of the Lords, and he was to run a crucial campaign for me to save my premiership. Self-evidently, Robert had great ability, so perhaps owning the constituency didn't matter.

After the two general elections I contested, Standard Bank had realised I was set on a political career, but remained supportive. Roy Mortimer, one of the senior executives, and Peter Graham, the managing director, were unfailingly helpful, even though they knew the bank was second in my working affections. By 1976, Tony Barber, who had been Chancellor of the Exchequer in Ted Heath's government, was chairman of the bank, and took me with him as his personal assistant to the International Monetary Fund Conference in Manila. That was the year sterling hit trouble and Denis Healey had to turn back from Heathrow Airport to deal with the crisis.

As a result, Tony Barber, his predecessor, was bombarded with press and interviews at Manila, and I dealt with many of them on his behalf; it was my first exposure to high-profile politics, and it lived up to my expectations. I worked eighteen hours a day but it whetted my appetite for the drama of politics. I returned home even more eager for a political career.

When a vacancy for the Huntingdonshire constituency was circulated to all approved candidates I applied immediately, but was not hopeful. It was a rural seat with a large Conservative majority, and it seemed an unlikely home. Norma disagreed. 'It is for you,' she insisted. She knew the area because she had been sent to stay with her great aunt in nearby Bourn for summer after summer during her childhood, while her mother Dee continued to work through most of the school holidays. She was confident about Huntingdonshire from the start.

About three hundred candidates applied, including Peter Brooke, Chris Patten, Michael Howard and Peter Lilley, so I knew the competition would be tough. I contacted Andrew Thomson, the agent, and he generously answered all my questions about the association and the constituency.

The first interview merely involved the candidate giving a twenty-minute speech on a Saturday morning, followed by questions. It went well enough, and Andrew Thomson phoned me the next morning to tell me I had reached the last eighteen. Another interview followed, which went better, but against stiffer opposition I was not certain of progressing further. I followed Peter Lilley, and after I had finished, found him sitting on a bench at Huntingdon station waiting for the train to London.

'It was fine,' he said, responding to my enquiry, 'but you never can tell.' But I thought he looked despondent. Months later Peter was given a lift by a young agent, and was speculating ruefully on why I had been selected for Huntingdonshire. Who was I, he asked, and what had I done to earn such a gilt-edged seat? He seemed aggrieved. The young agent thought Peter was criticising me, and read him a lecture on my virtues. It was Peter Golds – my first trainee agent in Brixton.

After a third interview I was shortlisted. As Huntingdonshire was such a secure seat there was some interest in the final contestants. 'Crossbencher', the political column of the *Sunday Express*, said I hadn't a chance of selection. Given Crossbencher's forecasting record, this was good news. That same morning the phone rang. It was a member of the selection committee, Anne Foard.

'I shouldn't be phoning,' she said, 'but I am – so this must be private.' She then gave me advice. Be yourself. Show humour. Bear in mind that half the constituency, and the electorate, are big-city overspill. 'Oh,' she said, 'and by the way, the district council meet on Wednesday. It would be good for you to be there to listen. And to be seen.'

It was wise advice. Andrew Thomson had already said pretty much the same thing. Being used to the political activity of Lambeth, Huntingdon District Council was a pleasant surprise. I was almost the only spectator, and the object of as much interest, nudging and winking, as the agenda. And the debate puzzled me. It was fierce, and all about 'local pyromaniacs trying to burn down our county', as one councillor put it, to the accompaniment of much support. It seemed like a serious crime wave. Then sturdy, outdoor figures with weatherbeaten faces defended the pyromania, and the truth dawned: they were talking about stubble-burning. It was urban man against rural, and a real eye-opener into the issues that stirred the community. That visit to Huntingdon was one of the best investments in time I ever made.

On the way to the final selection meeting I was preparing myself mentally for another disappointment. I couldn't get my head around the fact that I might be selected for one of the safest seats in England. Norma had no such inhibitions. She was confident we would win. As our second-hand Austin 1300 estate chugged towards Huntingdon she asked me if I had remembered that 'Friday is an anniversary'. I hadn't, but it was.

'It's five years to the day that you were selected as the candidate for St Pancras North,' said Norma. 'Tonight you must do it again.'

I am superstitious, and that seemed a good omen. The selection meeting was in the Commemoration Hall, Huntingdon, and the final opposition was tough. I learned later that Jock Bruce-Gardyne, formerly MP for Angus, had under-performed, having a foul cold. Lord Douro was thought to have had one piece of good news already that week, having become engaged to the Kaiser's granddaughter. Alan Haselhurst, later Deputy Speaker, spoke brilliantly, and was the runaway favourite when I spoke, last of the four. It went well, and, the ordeal over, Norma and I returned to the holding room and then to the local pub to consider our chances as the balloting got under way.

The Commemoration Hall as we returned was a scene of pandemonium. A decision had obviously been made. Wild applause and cheering could be heard, and as we hurried to the holding room I peered through the glass windows in the door of the main hall and saw Anne Foard, my telephone confidante of Sunday, standing on a chair whooping, with her hands clapping above her head.

Moments later Archie Gray, the Chairman of the association, entered the holding room. We all stood, tense and expectant.

'You've all done magnificently,' he said. 'It was hard to choose, but Mr Major has been selected.' Smiling, he walked over and shook my hand. As he did so I knew the course of my life had been determined.

From the start Huntingdonshire fitted me like a glove, although a few of the older members were startled to have a candidate from Brixton and an agent from Glasgow. They soon mellowed. Norma and I immediately decided to move to the constituency and put West Oak on the market. Unfortunately for us, subsidence of a neighbouring house in our terrace reduced its value and made it more difficult to sell. It took months, and throughout that time I commuted between my home in Beckenham, my job in the City and the constituency in Huntingdon. We found a lovely house in St Neots but, to my fury, we were gazumped by a partner in one of the local estate agents. Eventually we found a conventional four-bedroomed detached house in the beautiful village of Hemingford Grey, and moved in just before Christmas 1977.

By this time I was already getting to know the huge constituency and its rich variety of interests. From the outset, I was treated as the Member-in-waiting and not the candidate. It was assumed that I would win, though 'not by as many as Sir David', as I was regularly informed, though never by Sir David. He saw the constituency changing, and had no fears for the majority. Sir David Renton, QC, KBE, MP was an immense support. He had been elected in 1945, still in uniform, as Major Renton, and he and his wife Paddy were as firmly entrenched in Huntingdonshire as any Member could be.

David and Paddy had a handicapped daughter, Davina, and both worked tirelessly for charities, especially the National Society for Mentally Handicapped Children. David began to involve Norma in this work, and her association with Mencap, as it became, was to grow through the years. I began to get used to mentally handicapped adults, whose minds had not aged with their bodies, holding Norma's hand or cuddling her with all the affection of children. We came to understand how so many volunteers work so devotedly for this cause, and years later we were able to put the famous addresses of 10 Downing Street and Chequers to good use in raising funds for this and other charities.

David and Paddy Renton were kindness itself, and there was never the slightest friction between us. They entertained us at their home, supported us throughout the constituency and eased us into the mainstream of Huntingdon life. I shall always be grateful to them and hope, one day, to be as gracious to my successor as David was to me.

And this support mattered. A long incumbency attracts a great deal of loyalty, and if Sir David had muttered uncomplimentary remarks, or hinted at criticisms, even in private, they would have been voiced abroad and caused difficulties. It is human nature to cast doubt over one's successor to bolster one's own sense of experienced superiority, but David never did so. Over the years I found in him a wise adviser and a political friend and confidant whom I could trust completely and who never let me down. In 1998, in his ninetieth year, David, now Lord Renton, was still active in the House of Lords, and I had the pleasure of speaking at several of the events to mark his landmark birthday. On one occasion Margaret Thatcher and I both spoke at Lincoln's Inn. Margaret, as Margaret Roberts, had sought, and received, David's help as a young barrister.

David's *joie de vivre* never dimmed. In his eighties I called on him one Sunday lunchtime to find him in tennis shorts shaking his head sadly.

'I've been playing with Jeffrey Archer,' he said, 'and, you know, his game's going off. And he's so young.' Jeffrey was in his late forties.

Other senior members of the Huntingdonshire Conservative Association welcomed us warmly. Maurice and Doris Twydell and Tony Finch-Knightley introduced us to 'old' Huntingdon, while Mike and Beryl Robertson – the best judges of how the vote was going locally – did the same for us in the overspill estates.

Archie Gray, a retired naval commander, was chairman, and his writ ran. But, like so many Conservative associations, Huntingdonshire was largely an amazonian enterprise. Many of the guiding forces were women. The President, Mrs Jo Johnson, was a Scot, one of many active in the association. Jo was one of the wisest ladies I ever knew, and a huge support. She was no fair-weather friend. Nor was Emily Blatch, later Baroness Blatch and a senior member of my government, or Olive Macaulay, whom I later gave away in her marriage to Eric Baddeley. As for Anne Foard, she placed a bet at a hundred to one that I would be Chancellor of the Exchequer within ten calendar years of my election to Parliament – and she won.

The farmers were prominent in the constituency. Roger Juggins took me in hand and explained farming. The Juggins family had been in Stukeley for centuries, and had a political commitment to match the Cecils or the Churchills. Ted Smith added to my farming education, as did Joe Pickard, who once remarked, 'They tell us you know nothing about farming, but Sir David tells us you're all right.' Sir David said I was all right! I needed no other endorsement for the farming community.

Old Mr Skinner introduced me to pigs. He loved his pigs, and no luxury was too good for them. With the wind behind them the pigs could make their presence known over a wide area, but no one complained. They all liked Mr Skinner and his pig farm was state-of-the-art.

The non-farmers were just as helpful. Mike Bloomfield, Ivor Ross Roberts and Mike Harford, all successful businessmen, introduced me to the business community and, like many others in Huntingdon, became firm friends.

Andrew Thomson, my agent, was another Scot. Sometimes controversial, he was determined to bring in the new voters in the overspill areas outside Huntingdon and Peterborough, and worked me mercilessly to do so. Meet people. Meet people. Meet people. That was his motto. And it worked. I knew the constituency and it came to know me, and it was a happy relationship. Some MPs see their constituency only as a vehicle to get into Parliament, and something of a cross to be borne. I was lucky. I never did. From the very first, Huntingdon became a home, the source of many friends and a political fortress.

I left nothing to chance. Over the months I came to know Rotary Clubs, business groups, charities, schools, tenant groups, sports clubs and everything else that was active in the constituency. I knew the election could come at any time. Jim Callaghan, the Prime Minister, had formed a Lib–Lab pact to stay in government, but it looked very fragile. Each morning as I commuted from Huntingdon to King's Cross I wondered how long they'd last. And returning home each evening I hoped it wouldn't be long.

But stagger on they did. And on. And on. An election looked inevitable in October 1978 when Jim Callaghan announced that he was making a prime ministerial broadcast, but all he said of note was that there would be no election until the spring. After two years' hard slog as the prospective candidate for Huntingdonshire, and seven years since my first candidacy at St Pancras North, a further delay was dispiriting. A long, hard winter lay ahead, but it was longer and harder for the Labour government as the Winter of Discontent set in.

Eventually, a dramatic defeat by one vote on a Confidence Motion brought down the Callaghan government on 28 March, and the following day the election was called. It was the best birthday present I ever received.

The Huntingdonshire machine swung into action. It was a Rolls-Royce operation compared to anything I had experienced before. By day I canvassed, visited pubs and clubs, market squares, railway stations and retirement homes, gave interviews and filled every moment with activity. Each evening I held three public meetings at 7 p.m., 8 p.m. and 9 p.m. in different villages. Almost all were packed out, with standing room only, and the reception was almost always very friendly. There was little opposition, but I was leaving nothing to chance. The Liberal candidate was Major Dennis Rowe, a well-known local figure, and the Labour candidate a young man named Julian Fulbrook. Years later, in the Blair campaign of 1997, I saw Fulbrook trotted out to praise Labour as if he was a neutral who had fallen in love with the New Labour Party. The age of the spin doctor had arrived.

A few hecklers followed me around. One, a Labour supporter, was a persistent nuisance, and one evening I responded pretty sharply to his comments. He rose from his seat, snorted disapproval and stalked out in high dudgeon. Unfortunately for him he was so intent on registering his disgust that he walked into the broom cupboard rather than out into the night air. The audience watched fascinated, then burst into laughter and applause as he emerged. Red-faced and embarrassed, he slunk out and did not reappear. I missed him – he had provided many a light-hearted moment during the campaign.

Election day, 3 May 1979, dawned crisp and bright. It looked as though we were set to win nationally, although, curious to relate today, many wondered if Britain really would elect a woman as prime minister. But I was confident locally, and Andrew Thomson was super-confident. I drove around the huge constituency with Archie Gray, starting in the south and visiting polling stations and committee rooms. Norma and Andrew Thomson performed a similar odyssey, starting from the north. We planned to meet in the middle.

As Archie and I reached the village of Brampton, I was astounded to see long queues of RAF personnel from the local air station patiently waiting to vote. Archie purred. 'Look at that. They're not going to put a Labour government back in office. You're going to win, my boy.' So saying, he produced a bottle of champagne.

'A little early,' he went on, 'but we have something to celebrate.'

We pulled into a layby and cheerily drank half the bottle. Thus fortified we pressed on.

At each committee room the mood was buoyant. A high turnout, a Conservative lead and, in some areas, very little sign of opposition. It was a joyous day of pleasurable anticipation and growing excitement. As the polls closed I went to the club at 'The Views', the association headquarters, where Emily Blatch had some more news.

'I've done a straw poll,' she said, 'outside a few polling stations. Based on that, you've romped home. I think you've won by twenty thousand!'

Everyone chortled. Good news probably, was the consensus, but not *that* good.

Because Huntingdonshire was such a large rural seat it did not count the vote until the next day, so Norma and I sat in front of the television as the national drama unfolded. It was soon apparent that there was a swing to the Conservatives. Many who were to become good friends were elected. Robert Atkins won Preston North, John Watson was in at Skipton, Chris Patten at Bath, Matthew Parris at West Derbyshire, Nick Lyell at Hemel Hempstead, Graham Bright at Luton – and then Brian Mawhinney won back Peterborough from Labour. From that moment I had no doubts. If marginal Peterborough was comfortably won, how could neighbouring Huntingdonshire be lost? At 5 a.m., with the certainty of a Conservative government and the happy anticipation of supporting it in the House of Commons, I went to bed.

The count at St Ives was well under way when I arrived the following morning, and the result was soon clear. There was one glorious moment:

as I looked at the line of tables holding counted votes for each party, the 'Votes for Major' tables stretched way ahead. A huge pile of freshly counted votes appeared, and I waited for them to be added to my opponents' totals – but they weren't. They were all Conservative votes, and more tables were levered into place to hold them. Emily Blatch had been right, and the result far exceeded our expectations. The candidates were bussed back to Huntingdon, where the result was traditionally announced by the High Sheriff from the balcony of the courthouse overlooking the packed market square. I had polled over forty thousand votes, and had a majority of 21,563. At last I was a Member of Parliament.

Later that afternoon, after much celebrating in the Conservative Club, Norma and I went home in delight, to find our front doorstep festooned with cards, flowers, chocolates and champagne. I had found my political home.

# CHAPTER THREE

## Into the Commons

WHEN I WALKED INTO the Commons as an MP for the first time on 9 May 1979 it was still the magical place I remembered from my first visit as a thirteen-year-old. I had promised myself then that I would go again when I could enter as a matter of right. Now, one hundred years after my father's birth, I could, and I knew how my parents would have felt had they been with me as I arrived.

I have never lost my awe for the institution of Parliament or the majesty of the building. It has history in every nook and cranny, and the shades of the past can easily be conjured up even though its purpose is to prepare the future. The place half glances over its shoulder at what has been. I believe the aura of the Commons, of itself, can influence policy, tugging at the imagination of Members. Would a glass-and-steel legislature have summoned the same emotions, for instance, over 'sovereignty'?

As I walked through the Members' Entrance for the first day of the new Parliament the policeman on duty greeted me with a cheery 'Good morning, Mr Major. Congratulations.' Since I was but one of many anonymous new Members, I was astonished that he had done his homework so speedily. I soon learned that this was a matter of pride among the police, staff and attendants at the Commons.

The new Conservative intake in 1979 was large in number and, we were assured flatteringly, one of the most talented for many elections. Many of its members would find their way to high office. Chris Patten, John Patten, William Waldegrave, David Mellor, Ian Lang, Robert Cranborne, Stephen Dorrell, Douglas Hogg and Brian Mawhinney would all reach the Cabinet. Nick Lyell, Tristan Garel-Jones, Robert Atkins, Richard Needham and many others served in senior posts. Graham Bright and John Ward both served as my Parliamentary Private Secretary during my time at Number 10. Others like Matthew Parris and John Watson had great talent but would leave the House for careers in journalism and business.

The new Members soon formed their own alliances. Within weeks, like-minded Conservative colleagues set up dining clubs. The Blue Chips included those new MPs with most experience of the inner ring of government, often gained through working at Central Office or as a front-bench aide – Waldegrave, Patten and Patten, Cranborne and Garel-Jones foremost among them. It was the praetorian guard of the 1979 intake, with a healthy hint of one-nation scepticism about the instincts of Britain's new Prime Minister. Most of us, of course, hardly knew Margaret Thatcher. I had met her for the first time at the Berwick and East Lothian by-election in 1978, when I visited the constituency to help the Conservative candidate Margaret Marshall, an old friend from Lambeth days. We thought we would win the seat, but Mrs Thatcher arrived for a day, sniffed the political air, and privately doubted we would make it. She was spot on. It seemed that our new prime minister had an acute political nose.

I was to join the Blue Chips after the 1983 election, but at first I gravitated to the Guy Fawkes Club. Perhaps more workaday than the Blue Chips, it had its share of future stars, among them Stephen Dorrell, David Mellor, Graham Bright and Brian Mawhinney. We had asked each other what we hoped to achieve in Parliament, and I had answered without hesitation: 'Chancellor.' 'PPS to the prime minister,' said another member, Graham Bright, just as wet behind the ears as I was. In October 1990 Graham, the loyal and down-to-earth MP for Luton South, became my PPS at the Treasury, and he moved with me to Number 10 when I became prime minister a few weeks later.

A number of my new colleagues had built reputations for themselves before entering the Commons, and were widely expected to gain early promotion. Others chose the tortoise's strategy, and set out painstakingly to learn the way Parliament worked. The Chamber of the Commons is the display cabinet for talent for the world at large, but committees and back-bench groups are where worth is often recognised by the cognoscenti within Parliament, and especially by the all-seeing Whips' Office, who hold Members' fates in their hand as surely as any prime minister.

Some colleagues found their feet in Parliament before others had found the washroom. I had been in the House for only a few days when I walked across the Central Lobby to turn into the corridor that leads to the

Members' Lobby and the Chamber. As I did so a figure emerged from the shadows. It was Tristan Garel-Jones.

He clasped my arm: 'I'm worried about the government,' he said.

Tristan was the first rebel of our intake. He voted and spoke against the government over its handling of independence for the Banaban Islands, situated in the South Pacific and soon to be part of the minuscule state of Kiribati. This minor rebellion was led by Sir Bernard Braine, a senior Member who was anti-abortion, anti-drink and pro-island. He impressed us new boys by his fiery sense of injustice, and a passion that was easily aroused and easily stilled. His indignation could be Vesuvial, and to witness an eruption for the first time was awesome, even if the frequency of subsequent eruptions diminished their excitement. Bernard's constituency of Essex South-East (subsequently renamed Castle Point) included Canvey Island, but he had a bee in his bonnet about all islands – he loved them like a father. In 1979 his affections had settled on the distant and unfortunate Banabans, and he drew new Members to his cause. He was persuasive – 'Don Quixote de la Essex', someone called him – and Tristan signed up as his Sancho Panza, though I doubt he could have found the Banabans on a map.

Tristan was not the only Blue Chip to share Bernard's passion for islands. Jocelyn Cadbury, the newly-elected MP for Birmingham Northfield and a specialist in the cultural history of Polynesia, also threw himself into the battle. A shy, sensitive, painfully principled man, a few years later he took refuge in a better world by his own hand. I cannot remember what happened to the Banabans, but I will not forget Jocelyn's fate. I heard of his death with dismay early one evening at a garden party in Huntingdon. Later, when the Blue Chips had their portrait painted by Rose Cecil, Robert Cranborne's sister, we asked her to include Jocelyn. He is there in a portrait on the wall, poised ethereally on the fringes of the picture, remembered fondly by his parliamentary friends.

A new Parliament meant elections for the 1922 Committee, the representative body of all Conservative backbenchers. I knew few of the candidates. Nor did many of the other new Members. But we quickly began to learn parliamentary ways. We received notes from every candidate inviting support. Cabals were formed for and against – the political instinct to be part of a tribe was very strong. The Smoking Room was full of partisans. The bars abounded with rumour and gossip. Sir Edward du Cann's Rolls-Royce was reported in action, drawing up in Westminster side-streets beside new

Members and offering them a lift to the Commons. One more carload. A few more votes. It was good-humoured and clubbable, and we all loved being part of it. I voted for Sir Edward (without the incentive of a lift in his Rolls), and found him to be one of the best chairmen of a meeting I ever saw. He did attract stories, though.

'What time is it, Ted?' he was once asked. 'Dear boy –' peering at his watch '– what time would you like it to be?'

Another colleague told me how, crying into his brandy in the Smoking Room because his local newspaper had attacked him, he had sighed to Sir Edward, 'I suppose after years in this place you get used to being attacked.'

Sir Edward patted his arm: '*Nice* people never do.'

These were jolly elections, with a drink in the Smoking Room often making the bargain between candidate and elector. Mr Pickwick, with his experience at Eatanswill, would have felt very much at home.

I settled down, decided to listen and learn before committing myself to a maiden speech, and was elected Joint Secretary to the Conservative Backbench Environment Group, with John Heddle, the new Member for Lichfield, as my partner. I shared a large office with other Members including John Carlisle, who was to become a persistent and outspoken opponent in later years, and who took pleasure in offending every politically-correct code that existed. John Butcher, an opponent also on some issues, but more thoughtfully and less vociferously, was another companion of those early days.

Huntingdonshire was a huge constituency that generated a large postbag which increased every year as I became established there. My secretarial problems were soon solved. One day a small figure with fiery red hair bounded up to me outside the Commons post office.

'I always said I'd come and work for you if you got elected. So here I am!' she declared. It was Barbara Wallis, my former colleague from Lambeth days.

'I thought you worked for Chris Patten at the Conservative Research Department,' I said.

'I did,' said Barbara, 'but that's then, and now's now. I've come to work for you. I know you've got no one. These are my terms.'

So began a happy working relationship that was to last until Barbara retired, thirteen years later, having spent two years with me at Number 10.

And even then she only left after identifying her successor, Gina Hearn, who remains with me still, offering the same high-quality service.

Barbara was indomitable. No MP was a hero to her, and she was something of a legend among the members of the Secretaries' Council, the Westminster secretaries' 'trade union'. She was astute politically, having served on Lambeth Council with me and twice contested the parliamentary constituency of Feltham, and had forceful political views that veered from very liberal to intensely crusty Conservative. She was loyal and fearsomely efficient; the constituency purred at the ultra-smooth service she provided, and I basked in the credit that was largely due to her own efficiency. Yet later, when everyone else urged me to run for the leadership of the party after Margaret Thatcher resigned, Barbara dissented. 'It's too early,' was her view. I entered the contest anyway, and Barbara joined the team, worked day and night, and was ever-present in those dramatic few days.

Not every new MP takes cheerfully to the place. Some never do. With my unusual background (for a Conservative MP) and lack of practised gentlemen's-club ways, you might suppose that at first I felt ill at ease. Not so. As a new backbencher I was as happy as Bunter in a bakery. In the early days I was not among those who dined eagerly with members of the Cabinet and other senior figures in the party. I attended a drinks and question session one evening with the Chancellor of the Exchequer Geoffrey Howe, and saw the danger of such occasions. Some new colleagues had views, and brought them forward. 'Why are the government . . . ?' 'Should not the government . . . ?' 'It is surely clear that we should . . .' They sounded to me like talking press releases culled from the *Campaign Guide to the Election*. Geoffrey gently explained the political realities of life, and left some of the more assertive questioners looking rather callow. Others, saying nothing, gave the impression of being tongue-tied or (depending upon their demeanour) wise. I decided that short, pithy questions were the best option and stuck to those. Having now spent many years on the other side of the desk at such meetings, I'm sure that early judgement was right. As Kenneth Baker once put it, in a slightly different context, the line between sycophancy and rebellion is difficult to tread. I watched others carefully, and noted what worked and what did not; I saw the mistakes some made by self-promotion and an eagerness to lend a glib line to every passing newspaper hack.

I made my maiden speech in mid-June in a debate on Geoffrey Howe's first budget. The Chamber had barely sixty Members in it when I rose to speak, but that did not diminish my nervousness. I was well-prepared, but even so, looking up, I was pleased to see the familiar face of Canon Ronald Jennings, a constituent from St Ives, sitting in the Public Gallery for the debate. He smiled down with a clerical benevolence that I took as a very good sign.

It was an unremarkable first speech: the traditional tour of the constituency, a mention of Oliver Cromwell, Huntingdon's most famous son, a complaint about the government grant to Cambridgeshire, broad support for the budget. Soon it was over and, if I had not distinguished myself especially, I had not disgraced myself either. It is a tradition in the Commons that maiden speeches are greeted with acclaim provided the first-time orator manages to string together a few sentences. I received, therefore, ludicrously complimentary hand-written congratulatory notes from colleagues (as did most others, I later found to my dismay), and went home content that a hurdle had been overcome and that I could now widen my horizons as a new Member. The induction was over – now the real work could begin.

The Commons is not easily impressed with new Members, but it remembers foolishness for a long time. And so I was cautious and well-prepared whenever I spoke. New Members need issues to make their mark, and I was soon to have one. In 1980 it was announced that the United States was to station sixty-four Cruise missiles at RAF Molesworth, in my constituency, and this began to attract anti-nuclear protesters in large numbers. My constituents, familiar with RAF bases at Brampton and Wyton and American servicemen at Alconbury, were unperturbed by the imminent arrival of the missiles, but they became very anxious as the peace protesters grew in number and their level of activity increased. As one robust Molesworth resident, Stephen Hill, put it: 'The peace movement will cause more disturbance to our peaceful environment than the missiles will.' In August 1983 2,500 CND protesters occupied part of the base to protest against the plans, and in October they planted wheat, destined for famine relief in Eritrea, on four acres of the base.

As the protesters began to establish a permanent 'peace camp' on the perimeter of Molesworth, local villagers and their neighbours in Brington and Bythorn set up their own 'Ratepayers Against Molesworth Settlement' organisation. Local feelings grew heated, and I spoke at public meetings called by parish councillors at nearby Brington School, at which resentment of the intruders was expressed in lively fashion. Ratepayers' groups even hired a light aircraft to fly over the base pulling a banner saying 'CND Go Home'.

Some of the protesters were on Church land, and Bill Westwood, the Bishop of Peterborough, came to see me in the Commons. When he left, nearly three hours later, I tossed an empty bottle of Glenfiddich in the wastepaper basket and knew I had found an ally. He became a firm friend, was one of the best pastoral bishops I've ever come across, was revered in Peterborough, and later became a familiar voice through his regular contributions to 'Thought for the Day' on Radio 4's *Today* programme.

Molesworth brought me into contact with Michael Heseltine for the first time. Already a big beast of the Commons, in the government when I was still a councillor, he was defence secretary, and was taking the battle to the anti-nuclear protesters. He willingly met me, alone and with delegations, to discuss how to deal with the problem of the 'peace camp' and the three hundred or so campers who were, by 1983, causing real bitterness in Huntingdonshire. Betty Steel, a local farmer's wife, spoke for many: 'We value our village, houses, our way of life, and do not look forward to having them devalued, destroyed or disrupted by invasions.'

Nor did I. Nor did Michael Heseltine, who wanted the Cruise missiles safely installed. On 6 February 1984, in a massive overnight operation, police and Ministry of Defence officers evicted the protesters as 1,500 Royal Engineers from seven squadrons built a seven-mile perimeter fence around the base. It was a huge operation and brilliantly executed. The next morning, Michael visited Molesworth to inspect the work. It began to rain and a concerned officer handed him a flak jacket to protect him: the pictures of a flak-jacketed Heseltine greatly multiplied the already large press coverage.

My own constituency Member's role in all this called for no great courage. I was very lucky that my first big issue concerned something in which I personally believed, on which I could support the government, which was popular locally and which brought me into contact with Cabinet ministers, and in a positive way.

During my first two years in the Commons I prepared many speeches but delivered only a few. One of the frustrations of being a new backbencher of the majority party is that competition to speak is very heavy, and the Speaker will call you only rarely. The government whips too, anxious to expedite the business and being more interested in your vote than your views, encourage short speeches or, better, no speeches at all.

In 1981 I was invited to become Parliamentary Private Secretary to Patrick Mayhew and Timothy Raison, the two Ministers of State at the Home Office. Paddy approached me early one evening after a vote and offered me the job. He seemed somewhat embarrassed: 'I hope it's not too much of a bore,' he said, 'but we'd like to have you. It's lots of work and no pay. What do you think?'

I thought, 'Yes, please,' and nearly bit his hand off. I was lucky in this first job. Paddy Mayhew was later to become one of my closest parliamentary colleagues, particularly during his time at the Northern Ireland Office. Tim Raison was a reserved intellectual who had strayed into politics and loved it. They both had the solid, common-sense instincts of traditional Tories, with a fine distaste for ideology.

The role of the parliamentary private secretary can be boring – acting as an unpaid Commons caddie, arranging drinks with the minister, being his eyes and ears in the House – but it is often the first step on the ladder. And it does give the opportunity to see government from the inside, albeit peripherally, and to attend ministerial meetings. When the chemistry works, the PPS can often influence the decisions of his minister. At that time neither Paddy nor I could have guessed how closely we would work together years later on the problem of Northern Ireland.

Being a parliamentary private secretary opened up new avenues to me. I attended regular 'Prayer Meetings' at the Home Office chaired by Willie Whitelaw, then Home Secretary and the acknowledged deputy to Margaret Thatcher. The first morning I attended such a meeting I joined the little throng of Home Office ministers and PPSs outside the Home Secretary's office as we waited to be summoned. Finally, in we went, and at the far end of a large room there was Willie, a huge man, rising from his seat as we trooped in. He singled me out although we had barely exchanged a word before that morning.

'Welcome,' he boomed. 'Come in. Come and sit down. So pleased you've joined us. Very good news. Yes, very good news indeed. Yes, very!'

If I was good enough for Paddy Mayhew and Tim Raison, I was good enough for him. Willie's welcome made it seem that my arrival as the most junior (unpaid) member of the government was vital to its future well-being. He had a gift for inclusion and for inspiring loyalty. And for being loyal himself, for, despite having been defeated by Margaret Thatcher in the battle to succeed Ted Heath, he had been her most loyal lieutenant and remained so whenever she was in difficulty.

Willie was unique. One morning in July 1982 the Prayer Meeting gathered in sombre mood. An intruder, Michael Fagan, had somehow forced his way into the Queen's bedroom at Buckingham Palace, which was an appalling breach of security. The Queen had handled the matter with aplomb, but that did not ease Willie's position as Home Secretary.

'I shall have to resign,' he announced. 'I should like to know what my colleagues think.'

We demurred: 'No, no, no, Home Secretary, you mustn't'. Paddy Mayhew led the charge and, in due seniority, we all told Willie that on no account should he go. He listened gravely. We finished. There was a long silence.

'I'm very grateful,' said Willie. 'I will accept the views of colleagues.'

It was a professional performance. Willie Whitelaw had the great gift of leaving you uncertain as to his motives. Had he really been considering resignation? Or was he testing the ground to see if it was secure enough for him to remain in office? I never knew – and that was part of his skill. In any event, to our great relief, Willie did not resign.

However, he didn't always 'accept the views of colleagues'. The Conservative Backbench Committee on Home Affairs was often a bugbear to him. He met them regularly, groaning resignedly, 'Let them in, are the drinks ready?' Once they were in he listened to them, encouraged them, flattered them, but rarely changed his intended course of action. The following morning the Prayer Meeting would discuss their demands.

'My colleagues,' Willie would say of the committee, 'think I should . . .'

He would pause. Sometimes he would ask for views. When he did not, we waited to hear how he would deal with such and such a tricky demand.

'Well,' Willie would say. 'If that's what my colleagues think . . .' Pause again. 'Then,' he would conclude triumphantly, 'then that's what they think.' That was it. We moved on.

Behind this bluff act was a sharp and shrewd political calculator of a brain. Willie was never a detail man, but his instinct was superb. He sniffed the political wind and knew which way it was blowing.

In early 1982 Tony Marlow, the MP for Northampton North, asked me if I wished to join a tour of the Middle East to learn more about the Arab–Israeli conflict. Tony had already made a reputation as a parliamentary-thug-in-waiting, and was a fierce Palestinian partisan. He had 'reckless' and 'trouble' stamped through him like 'Brighton' through a stick of rock, but I accepted his invitation when he explained it was a large, all-party delegation. The trip was packed with incident.

I was fast asleep in our hotel in Beirut one night when we were suddenly told that Yasser Arafat, the leader of the PLO, would see us. We piled into cars and were driven to meet him. He was a small man, unshaven and soft-spoken, dressed in combat uniform and poised over a large map on a table. Coffee was served and Arafat spoke and invited questions. The meeting was memorable, not least because, for the first time, I was meeting someone generally considered in the UK to be a terrorist.

A hunchbacked secretary brought in a tray of tea in glass cups. He stumbled, and the tea spilled forward, spreading across the unfurled map Arafat was using to illustrate Palestinian land claims. Gently and systematically he began to mop up the tea as he was peppered with questions. Two Labour members of our group, Peter Snape and Dale Campbell-Savours, were pointed, even aggressive: when would the Palestinians recognise Israel? Arafat was unperturbed, and replied coolly to the effect that even if he knew, which he did not, he would hardly announce this to a random group of British backbench MPs. Richard Needham, a Tory, intervened, and said that he understood that Arafat was cross, but that meetings such as this did make an impact – even on him, a half-Jewish, half-Irish Earl.

Arafat blinked and looked at him: 'How do I address a half-Jewish, half-Irish Earl?' he enquired.

The irrepressible Snape could not resist it: 'Kneeling,' he said. 'Kneeling.'

The room froze, but Arafat chortled and the rest of the meeting passed harmoniously.

A day or so later, we were driving towards Bethlehem when for some reason our convoy stopped. As it did so an Arab youth appeared on the brow of a hill just behind us and hurled a large rock through the air. I was talking to Ken Weetch, the Labour Member for Ipswich, when it hurtled between us at head height and crashed into the car. Not knowing what was happening we turned around, and as we did so gunshots rang out. An Israeli patrol was heading towards us and firing at the rock-thrower. We were caught in the crossfire. I threw myself to the ground beneath the car. Richard Needham and Dale Campbell-Savours crouched down on the back seat while Peter Snape also threw himself underneath the car and (entirely by chance, he claimed) found himself beside one of our attractive guides. It was a scary few moments, and only by good fortune were by-elections avoided.

The consensus was that the Palestinian boy was a clot, and the Israelis had overreacted. Richard Needham, a brilliant mimic, and Snape, ever ready for a joke, exacted their revenge. As we passed through Israeli customs they became Oberleutnant Needham and his faithful batman, Corporal Snape, in heavy German accents. It took ages to get through customs, and we were lucky not to end up in jail.

On 2 April 1982, Argentine armed forces invaded the Falkland Islands and established military control. The Commons met the next day, a Saturday, in an angry mood, incensed at this national humiliation. We forget now that immediately after the invasion Margaret Thatcher had her back to the wall. As she left Number 10 for the emergency session of Parliament she received a hostile reception from the crowd gathered in Downing Street. Other ministers, too, were booed and hissed as they drove into the Commons.

It was the first time I had seen the power of this assembly when it was aroused. The atmosphere was electric. I had not foreseen this. The government was clearly in trouble, and my assumption had been that Conservative ranks would close firmly behind a still relatively new prime minister. I was surprised at the extent to which they did not. The collective mood was one of real anger that the Falklands had been invaded and that the government had been too ill-informed or impotent to prevent it. These backbenchers, I saw, had a mind of their own. It was a vivid illustration of how the collective will of Parliament can shape policy-making. No one seeing or feeling that mood at close quarters could have been in any doubt that if the government was to survive, it would have to act forcefully and speedily.

The Prime Minister announced the despatch of a Task Force to recover the islands – and it was as well that she did. Amid rumours that the Foreign Office had received the plans of the invasion days earlier, the Commons that morning resembled mob rule. Michael Foot, the leader of the opposition, demanded the government prove that it was not responsible for the betrayal of the Falkland Islands. Sir Edward du Cann, the Chairman of the 1922 Committee, was astounded that we were so woefully ill-prepared. Nigel Fisher, a senior Conservative, said ministers had much to answer for to the country. John Silkin, Labour's defence spokesman, told the Prime Minister, the Foreign Secretary and the Defence Secretary: 'The sooner you get out the better.'

After the debate, in private meetings, Conservative backbenchers savaged senior ministers. Some criticism, albeit Delphically-phrased, had been aired in the Chamber, but it paled into insignificance beside the strength of the comments in the Tea Room and in the backbench committees.

As I sat in the train returning to Huntingdon, I was not sure the government would survive. We were, in any event, very unpopular at the time, and I was certain there would be ministerial blood shed. The Foreign Office team of Peter Carrington, Humphrey Atkins and Richard Luce did resign, although John Nott, the Defence Secretary, had his offer of resignation refused by Mrs Thatcher. Peter Carrington and his team were not, of course, solely to blame, but they judged – correctly, I think – that ministerial heads were needed, and they offered their own.

If the Cabinet had not sent the Task Force, Margaret Thatcher would not have survived as prime minister. She took a great risk, requiring huge nerve, but the alternative was certain catastrophe. I overheard a washroom conversation in which two Cabinet ministers denounced the expedition as 'ludicrous' and 'a folly' due to the lack of air cover for the fleet. It gave me a glimpse of the tension that existed at the heart of government.

Out of the bleak scenario of early April Margaret Thatcher fashioned her greatest triumph, and the political terrain was bulldozed into a new landscape. During those few weeks the martial nature of the British nation made itself clear: huge crowds waved off the Navy from Portsmouth, and even larger numbers welcomed it back. Every development of the conflict was pored over, the final success brought forth a tremendous feeling of national pride, and the iconic stature of 'the Iron Lady' was assured.

In January 1983, announcing that he did not wish to contest the forthcoming election, John Nott resigned as defence secretary, and there was a small reshuffle in which I was appointed an assistant whip. It was almost the last job announced in the changes, and one of the most junior. But I was thankful. A number of the 1979 intake had already joined the government, John Patten, Donald Thompson, David Mellor, Tristan Garel-Jones, Ian Lang and William Waldegrave among them, and I was relieved not to be overlooked again. I accepted the invitation from a public phone booth at King's Cross station, en route to Huntingdon, responding to a message to phone Michael Jopling, the Chief Whip.

It was a modest promotion, and at first sight less exciting than being a departmental minister. I learned very quickly that this was an outsider's judgement; once in the Whips' Office I realised that it was one of the main engine-rooms of government. Norma was delighted – not least, I suspect, because I was so pleased. I told her all I knew about the Whips' Office. 'It sounds wonderful,' was her comment. 'But what exactly do whips do?'

The Whips' Office is unique, and joining it has a special cachet, as the appointment to it is not made by the prime minister but by the popular acclaim of fellow whips. One blackball excludes: the rationale for this is that the Office works so closely together that compatibility between the members is essential (whips watch one another's backs, while other politicians often go for each other's throats). The chief whip may, and often does, propose a shortlist of potential new whips, but the Office makes the final choice. In doing so it tries to balance political opinion across the party as well as ensuring that all parts of the country are represented.

The Whips' Office is singular in other respects as well. It exists to deliver the government's business, and will do so even if the collective view of the Office is that the legislation is unwise. But that collective view will be delivered forcibly to the prime minister by the chief whip, and to relevant ministers, who ignore it at their peril. The Whips' Office view is private and, to my certain knowledge, the most leak-free office in government. Ministers, even prime ministers, might be shocked by the robust opinions expressed in private about their policies, performance or personalities by the whips. The Office is nobody's patsy, as politicians with an arrogant streak have often learned. This is invaluable, because the whips know the collective view of the parliamentary party better by far than any minister, and are able to make that view known as policy is brought forward. The Office too, and the chief whip particularly, are crucial in advising the prime minister about the performance of ministers and backbenchers, which is vital in determining whether Members climb the parliamentary ladder to senior positions, slip from high office, or remain for ever on the back-benches waiting in hope.

I knew little of this when I joined Michael Jopling's team. Michael was crisp, rather soldierly, blunt and straightforward, and believed the Office owed the Prime Minister the unvarnished truth and a majority in the

Lobby. He delivered both. In many ways he was a traditional chief whip, understanding of occasional principled rebellion but wholly intolerant of rent-a-quote, persistent rebels. In private he was jovial and fun and (most unexpectedly) a motorcycle enthusiast, to be seen hurtling around the country in full black leathers with his red-haired wife, Gail, on the pillion. When he was displeased with the Office he did not hold back. 'I'm absolutely disgusted,' he'd say. In the background, my alert ear would catch Tristan Garel-Jones's comment on any disaster: 'Thank God it's only a game.'

Michael had old-fashioned virtues. A tale current among his colleagues was that when Matthew Parris made a speech at the Oxford Union which barely hid the fact that he was gay, Michael called him in. He wasn't sure how to deal with the problem of this contrary backbencher.

'Look, Matthew,' he began, 'there are some things one just doesn't say. I don't believe in God. But I've never felt a need to tell anyone about it. Even my wife doesn't know.'

A puzzled Matthew left, to have Michael's true meaning spelled out to him later.

The Whips' Office was a talented team. Michael Jopling's deputy was Tony Berry, who would be tragically murdered by the IRA's Brighton bomb in October 1984. The backbone of the Office was two old soldiers, Carol Mather and Bob Boscawen, both holders of the Military Cross with very distinguished war records. Both had been wounded in the war. Bob had been terribly burned facially and had been one of the 'guinea pigs' treated by the pioneering plastic surgeon Archibald McIndoe. With great courage he had entered public life and, with Carol, now held sway in the Whips' Office.

The Office included the occasional exotic. Spencer le Marchant conducted life and politics only over the finest champagne. His goal in life was to spread bubbling bonhomie to whomsoever he met: this pushed up the collective mess bill for the whips to alarming proportions. 'I'm entertaining for England,' an unabashed Spencer would say in answer to the occasional complaint about the bills. 'Your health. Can I pour you one?' The hospitality began at 10 a.m., the champagne being offered in splendid silver half-pint tankards. We signed the cheques as he sipped on, and ignored the overdraft.

Sometimes Spencer's high spirits took him too far. Once he devised a plan to stage a 'horse race' round the Members' Smoking Room, for which the 'horses' would be the younger Tory MPs (Spencer adopted Matthew

Parris, and intended to dress him in the yellow-and-green le Marchant racing colours). The 'course' would be once around the perimeter of the Smoking Room on the tables, chairs and sofas, without touching the floor. The race had to be called off when the *Evening Standard* got wind of it – this was a time when unemployment was high and climbing, and swathes of British manufacturing industry were facing ruin.

It was a team with exacting standards. One day Tristan Garel-Jones, then a junior whip, walked in wearing a Loden overcoat. He was already, in embryo, the irreverent Tristan who, to some members, was later to become the Machiavelli of the Office, rumoured to be in touch with every cabal. The Loden was a garment so favoured by Foreign Office mandarins that it had been christened 'the Single European Overcoat': Tristan's was a far from fetching olive green, the standard colour, and its appearance was not enhanced by his having neglected to put on any socks that morning. Carol looked him up and down in horror, gazed at Bob, then back at Tristan. He then announced: 'The last time I saw someone wearing a coat like that – I shot him.'

Tristan, outgunned by the old soldier, fled.

I had joined the Whips' Office in the run-up to the general election which Margaret Thatcher called for 9 June 1983. The result never seemed in doubt. Margaret's success in regaining the Falklands made her as unbeatable as the Labour Party were unelectable, with their preposterously left-wing manifesto. Gerald Kaufman, the cynical spirit of Labour's front bench, called it the longest suicide note in history, but it was worse than that. Moreover, the defection of a number of senior Labour figures to the Social Democratic Party produced an organic split in the left of politics that almost guaranteed an overwhelming Conservative victory. In the event the election was a walkover and Margaret increased her parliamentary majority from forty-four to 144. In Huntingdon (as the constituency was now called) I had no difficulty and was comfortably re-elected by 20,348 votes – over 62 per cent of those cast.

After the election my vague hopes that I might be appointed a parliamentary under-secretary (a junior, junior minister) came to naught. I remained an assistant whip in a Whips' Office changed by the appointment of John Wakeham as Chief Whip and John Cope as his deputy. The Office took on a different style. John Wakeham was subtle, reflective, a persuader, a fixer, fascinated by *why* something happened rather than simply *what* had happened. He was laid back, adept at delegation, and he played Mrs Thatcher like a master fisherman landing a prized salmon. He began, as a matter of policy, to bring some of the brightest young talents of the parliamentary party into the Office. He was ideal for the role.

The next two years as a whip taught me so much about how Parliament really worked, as I saw its dramas from the inside track. I learned about our colleagues and our opponents: their strengths, their weaknesses, their interests and sometimes their secrets. I came to know the team players and the loners; the able and the dotty.

The whips met daily in the House of Commons at 2.30 p.m., except on Wednesdays, when we gathered at 12 Downing Street, the Chief Whip's domain, for a longer meeting that usually began at 10.30 a.m. and ended at lunchtime. We planned parliamentary business, bullied and cajoled where necessary, and shared every piece of intelligence that came our way. We discussed the opportunities and pitfalls of the week ahead and made our dispositions. John Wakeham received all the Cabinet papers and made them available to any whip who wished to read them: I devoured everything of interest.

An awful incident occurred in the House one snowy night when I was sitting on the bench beside Michael Roberts, a junior Welsh minister, in a late-night debate. The Chamber was almost deserted. Suddenly, Michael stumbled over a phrase, repeated it haltingly, groaned, then collapsed to the floor beside me. I was with him in moments, but he was beyond all help. He had suffered a massive coronary and must have died before he hit the floor. The sitting was suspended, and Michael Jopling, the Chief Whip, pleaded with the Press and the Public Galleries for privacy 'at this difficult moment'. They left quietly and unprotesting, as shocked as we were. Gently, in an air of disbelief, Michael was taken out of the Chamber.

I remember driving home in the snow in the early hours of the morning and thinking of the tragedy of his death. Above all, it brought home to me the transitory nature of life and politics. Michael Roberts was not an old man – he was in his mid-fifties – but I knew that soon people would be talking about who would stand for his Cardiff seat in the by-election.

As I was given responsibility for managing the parliamentary business of first the Department of the Environment then the Northern Ireland Office, I became familiar with their policies and with the task of steering debates on the floor of the Chamber. I sat for weeks upon end, many hours at a time, on committees at which by tradition I was unable to speak, but was responsible for ensuring that the legislation progressed. I did deals with the opposition about when the committee sat, for how long, and when votes would be taken, and I sanctioned absence from the government side if the numbers present assured me that our majority was secure.

As an Environment whip I became involved in the abolition of the GLC, and in the annual fights over central government support for local authorities. These were often very bloody, as Members fought for cash for their political backyards. It was good preparation for the future. I also had a general responsibility for delivering the votes – and seeking the views – of Conservative MPs from East Anglia. They were a mixed bunch who were generally biddable and responsive to persuasion, but rarely to threats. Many of us coalesced into a group dubbed the 'East Anglian Mafia'; it would come to my aid in the very different circumstances of November 1990.

With our huge parliamentary majority it was easier to send a colleague home early than to persuade him to change his mind over an issue about which he felt strongly. One evening a Conservative backbencher, the maverick right-winger Peter Bruinvels, droned on for far too long in an almost empty Chamber. He ignored my pointed expressions to sit down. Fed up, I sent him a note: 'Do you have any children?' Puzzled, Bruinvels shook his head and carried on speaking. I sent a second note: 'Then why don't you go home and do something useful?'

He sat down.

In Huntingdon, Norma and I were looking for a larger house. For months it had been a fruitless search, but one Saturday she came home and told me she had seen a house that might be possible, although it was too big and too expensive. We decided to look at it together. It was called Finings. We drove through the gate and up a gravelled drive fringed with mature lime trees which ended in a turning circle, in the centre of which was a fifty-foot cedar. Built in 1938, the house, with wisteria climbing up its back wall, stood in two and a half acres of garden with a large lawn and a wide variety of trees and shrubs. Much of it was heavily overgrown, with an old orchard of trees long past fruiting. The garden was open to farmland on two sides and undeveloped land on the third. Although it was ringed with trees there was no fence and it was a haven for whole families of rabbits, which we thought picturesque until we saw the damage they could do. In the winter, when they were hungry, they would literally tear the bark off the trees. As we made our presence felt they retreated, but our battle to expel them was to be a long one.

The house had potential. It felt right. It had charm and grace and gave an impression of being much older than it was. We couldn't afford it, but we bought it. Selling the house in Hemingford Grey proved difficult, and for six months we took out a bridging loan which nearly crippled us financially. I've never regretted it.

On 3 October 1984, our fourteenth wedding anniversary, I became a senior whip with the grand title of 'Lord Commissioner of the Treasury'. This simply arose through Buggins's turn as whips left the Office and their juniors were automatically promoted, but I was delighted. I learned of my promotion as I returned from Latin America where, in the absence of a Foreign Office minister, I had been sent on a tour of Peru, Venezuela and Colombia. This was a fascinating visit with two highlights. The first was a visit to Machu Picchu, the lost city of the Incas, which had been stumbled on by an American professor in 1911. I was riveted by it. The second was one morning when I was asked to have coffee with a Roman Catholic priest in a shanty town outside Lima. As the clock struck eight, out of the miserable hovels, young children emerged clean and scrubbed and carrying satchels or bags. I stopped one and talked to him, with the priest as interpreter. The boy told me he wanted to be a brain surgeon. That, I thought, is ambition: I only wanted to be Chancellor of the Exchequer.

On the evening of 11 October 1984 I left the Grand Hotel in Brighton, where I had been staying for the Conservative Party Conference, to return early to Huntingdon. Five hours later, at 2.45 a.m., an IRA bomb ripped through the hotel. It was a calculated plan to murder the Prime Minister and her Cabinet, and five people were killed, including Tony Berry, and John Wakeham's wife Roberta. John Wakeham and Norman Tebbit and his wife Margaret were severely injured. It was a miracle that the carnage was not far worse.

The first I heard of the tragedy was at 5 a.m., when my brother Terry telephoned me to see if I was at Finings or still in Brighton. I turned on the television and, like most of the country, saw the awful pictures of Norman Tebbit, in agony, being lifted out of the rubble. John Wakeham's legs had been badly crushed, and during his long absence from Parliament his deputy John Cope took temporary charge of the Whips' Office. I offered, as a fellow East Anglian MP, to care for John Wakeham's Maldon constituency, which I did for many months until he was recovered.

As Treasury Whip, I was that bit closer to the chancellorship. The appointment turned out to be crucial to my future career – and, for reasons I will set out later, to Margaret Thatcher's. I began to see at close quarters the immense influence of the Treasury on every aspect of government. I enjoyed working for Nigel Lawson, a radical chancellor, confident in his intellect and one of the main architects of the government's policy.

Nigel's morning meetings, known as 'Prayer Meetings', generally held in his study at Number 11, were a mixture of monologue and philosophical debate, but as a former whip he retained a fascination for Commons gossip. I was happy to keep him up to date. I rarely commented on his policies unless invited, although I had my views. Nigel would have listened, but done nothing. He knew what he wished to do, and his mind could not be changed.

My role as Treasury Whip led me into a serious row with the Prime Minister. Each summer, by tradition, the Whips' Office entertained her to dinner, and in June 1985 we met at Number 10. Unusually, House of Lords whips were invited too. Margaret Thatcher was never noted for her small-talk with colleagues, and the first two courses passed with only desultory exchanges. It was evident that she wished to turn to some serious political discussion, and John Wakeham said, 'The Treasury is at the heart of policy. I'll ask the Treasury Whip to begin.'

I regarded it as my role to tell the Prime Minister what the backbenchers were saying, and I did so. 'They don't like some of our policies,' I told her. 'They're worried that capital expenditure is being sacrificed to current spending.' I set out in detail the grumbles that every whip present knew were the views of the vast majority of our backbench colleagues.

Margaret did not like the message at all, and began to chew up the messenger. I thought her behaviour was utterly unreasonable, and repeated the message. She became more shrill in her criticisms. 'I'm astonished at what you're saying,' she snapped. I made it clear again that I was merely reporting the views of many Members, but she continued to attack me. I became increasingly annoyed, and said: 'That's what colleagues are saying, whether you like it or not – it's my job to tell you, and that's what I'm doing.' Her tirade continued. By now I was past caring about tact, shaking with anger, and nearly walked out. I repeated the message once more. It made no impression at all, and as she raged on the whips around me became very uncomfortable. I was almost beside myself with fury, and made no attempt to hide it. Even as I spoke, I thought I might be wrecking my career, but I was too angry to backtrack – which, in any event, would have been craven. I may not be promoted, I thought, but I'm not going to be humiliated.

Carol Mather intervened to support me. Margaret turned on him with an angry word. Bob Boscawen hastened to support Carol. He was met with a glare. I had no intention of backing down, and pitched in again. The meeting was dangerously close to collapsing in mutual recrimination. Jean Trumpington, one of the Lords whips, attempted to lower the temperature and had her head bitten off for her pains. It was an extraordinary performance by the Prime Minister, and I have never forgotten it. As we rose from the table for post-dinner drinks her husband Denis came up to me. 'She'll have enjoyed that,' he remarked, and drifted off happily, clutching a gin and tonic. John Cope sidled up and suggested I might make my peace with Margaret. 'I think,' I told him, 'that it's up to her. You'd better tell her that.'

The next day, to my astonishment, this extraordinary woman did just that. Since phrases like 'wets' and 'dries', 'one of them' or 'one of us', were already part of the Thatcher folklore, I assumed that after our argument I would be cast into outer darkness at the first opportunity. My career, I was sure, would be on hold if not on stop. But I was wrong.

In the late afternoon I was sitting as the Whip on Duty on the Treasury Bench in the Commons. Margaret swept in from behind the Speaker's Chair and sat beside me. She could not have been more charming. She mentioned some ideas I had previously put to her, so inconsequential I cannot now remember them, and said she wished to discuss them. Another whip was summoned to the bench, and an *ad hoc* discussion commenced in the Whips' Office, with the Prime Minister and me seated in armchairs. Without the fracas of the previous night being mentioned, peace was declared.

A few weeks later, in the autumn reshuffle, I was promoted to my first ministerial post in a department. Not for the first or the last time, Margaret Thatcher had surprised me.

# CHAPTER FOUR

## Climbing the Ladder

I N THE LATE SUMMER OF 1985 I was at home at Finings watching the death throes of the England–Australia Test at The Oval on television. I had hoped to be at the match, but the probability of a reshuffle, and whispers that I would be promoted, kept me by the phone. England's pace bowler Richard Ellison was mopping up the Australians as I awaited events. Norma was out, and James and Elizabeth were at school, so I was alone. And I had a dilemma.

I was horrified that I might be offered the job of Minister of Sport. I loved sport and politics, but they were separate parts of my life, and I had no wish to mix them. This was the first of two occasions in my career when I was to wonder whether or not to accept a promotion. I paced the room, and decided that I wanted a job in the mainstream of politics, or no job at all. If the Prime Minister offered me Sport I would say no, and ask to stay in the Whips' Office. I marshalled my arguments, knowing that she would not welcome such a response.

The telephone rang. It was Number 10. The Prime Minister wished to speak to me later – would I be around? 'Yes,' I said. And waited. And paced. England won the Test match. I continued to wait.

Finally the phone rang again. It was the Prime Minister. 'I'd like you to leave the Whips' Office and go to Social Security,' she said. 'It's where I started. It's a good place to be. Norman Fowler will be your Secretary of State – get in touch with him straight away. Good luck.' And that was it. I breathed a sigh of relief. I was a minister, and with a mainstream brief.

I did not know Norman Fowler well, but he was very welcoming at the department; although much later, when we knew each other far better, he admitted that he had had reservations about my appointment. He feared I was a 'Whips' nark' – put in place to keep tabs on the plans of the biggest-spending department of all. He had good grounds for this suspicion. I learned from officials that not long before I arrived, a garrulous junior minister had passed details of the ministry's plans for social security reform to Nigel Lawson.

No reservations were evident in Norman's welcome to me. From the start, he brought me into the core of the ministry's work, and we came to be firm friends. I enjoyed the department from the moment I set foot in it. My work as Parliamentary Under Secretary for Social Security was detailed and gruelling, and often very boring, with masses of routine letter-signing. Six or seven red boxes accompanied me home every weekend, and sometimes it took me until Sunday night to get through them all. But it gave me an insight into an area of policy that few people ever master. There was nothing abstract about the portfolio – since it embraced pensions, housing and social security benefits, every policy decision we took directly affected the quality of life of many very vulnerable people.

Norman Fowler headed the social security side of the department, with Tony Newton immediately below him as the Minister of State, responsible in particular for disabled people. I was junior to Tony. Jean Trumpington, one of the redoubtable characters of Parliament, was our Minister in the House of Lords, covering all aspects of the department's business.

I once asked Jean why she had chosen the title 'Trumpington'. 'Well, dear,' she said, 'as you know, people take a title from places they know well. I knew two villages very well: one was called Trumpington, and the other was Six Mile Bottom. Which one would you have chosen?' Jean's humour knew no bounds. The House of Lords loved her. So did we.

Norman Fowler had the great political gift of worrying away at a complex problem for days on end, to the total exclusion of all else, until the problem was solved. Making few mistakes, he was the epitome of 'a safe pair of hands' – although while he was avoiding one catastrophe, other decisions and problems piled up elsewhere that could have officials and junior ministers tearing their hair in frustration. But Norman proved his point. No other secretary of state successfully mastered this massive department – ultimately it was split in two – but he ran it with distinction for over five years. He was a far more formidable operator than many with higher public profiles, and he rarely lost an argument in Cabinet – or outside it.

Tony Newton, the Minister of State, was a fully-fledged human being with no sense of self at all; his thought was always for others. I once said that if a tramp stole his suit Tony would rush after him with a matching shirt. He saw every problem first from the human angle, although – if persuaded change was necessary – he would take through the most controversial legislation. He was the ultimate team player, trusted on all sides and a specialist in social security, whose knowledge matched that of many of the department's officials. Tony was later to be one of the most reliable and trusted ministers in my government.

We all worked in Alexander Fleming House, an appalling concrete-and-plate-glass building, full of airless corridors. Since it was two miles south of the Thames, at the Elephant and Castle, it was something of an outpost of Margaret Thatcher's empire. It was close by the London Electricity Board building where, more than twenty years earlier, I had been so pleased to find a job. That memory was a reminder to me of the hidden difficulties faced by the people affected by the department's decisions.

The eighties was a decade that gloried in thrusting self-reliance. Success was envied and aped. This stand-on-your-own-two-feet mentality drove Britain towards better things. It helped the nation regain its respect. But self-reliance can be taken too far, and a proper balance must be kept. Some people simply do not have the capacity to succeed, and others are trapped by circumstances. Many of these people were our clients in Social Security, and our policy was to target help to those most in need, and to enable as many as possible to cope on their own.

The department, when I arrived, was on the threshold of complex and (in the end) effective reforms to pension and social security benefits. The aim was to simplify the system and to ensure that benefits went to the people who actually needed them. A Bill had already been drafted before my promotion, but when Tony and I began to take the legislation through the Commons we very quickly realised that its later clauses, which dealt with social security, were deficient, and would not achieve their objectives. They could not be passed as they stood.

We hit on a solution. I would take the first twenty clauses, on pensions, through Commons committee stage on my own, while Tony and Norman rewrote the latter half of the Bill. The pension clauses were ferociously complex, and on Tuesdays and Thursdays, when the committee met, I was up by five in the morning to brief myself properly. The Bill undertook the liberalisation of the private pension market. This would make it easier for people to take their pension with them from one job to another without being penalised, and it also offered help to people to build up a personal pension plan of their own. Millions of individuals were to benefit, with the help of government support and generous tax relief. Over six million people were to take out personal pensions, with well over £200 billion held in them. The Bill was a tough baptism for a junior minister, but it enabled me to form an excellent working relationship with Tony and Norman, and speedily settled me into the department.

On social security, the Conservative government was viewed with suspicion by a Labour Party confident in its attacks on us. This confidence was not always matched by the ability of the party's front bench team, but nonetheless, the political battleground gave me a lot of experience at the dispatch box.

After late-night votes Tony Newton and I would often linger to chat over a drink. Like me, he was a politics addict who had learned his trade in the Whips' Office, and from the outset our relationship was easy. Tony was a habitual smoker – something of an embarrassment when he became Health Minister – and was forever harassed, because he took on more commitments than any mortal could easily handle. He offered help to others, but rarely asked for it himself, even when his need was evident. Once he lost two front teeth in an accident shortly before he was due to appear both in committee and on television. I offered to do the television interview for him. 'Really?' he said. 'Are you sure? I could do it.' But his gap-toothed grin suggested he knew it would not be wise.

Norman Fowler believed in giving his junior ministers every opportunity to improve their profile in the media, especially if the interviews were very early in the morning or very late at night, and he was unfailingly supportive if things went wrong. Each Monday all the department's ministers were expected to join him for lunch at a nearby pizza restaurant where, free of the office and officials, we could discuss the pure politics of what we were about. Since I saw a good deal of Norman and Tony I knew how their conversations would go, and since I loathe pizza I usually found a reason to miss the meal. It was some weeks before Norman realised why I was a permanent absentee, and the pizzas were replaced by salad lunches in the office. The lack of ministerial garlic in the afternoon was much welcomed by civil servants.

I was well served by my officials, in particular by my Private Secretary

Norman Cockett. Norman was bespectacled, with a full beard and a gentle good humour that took the sting out of every difficulty. He was never ruffled, the first of the many civil servants with whom I worked who were dedicated to public service. He put in the same killing hours as me. At his desk to brief me when I came into the office before breakfast, he was often still on hand when the House voted at 10 p.m., and sometimes did not leave for home until 2 a.m.

It was Norman Cockett who showed me the effects of our decisions at the sharp end. Our first visit was to a benefits office in my constituency, a gentle introduction. Our next trip was shocking. We arrived at an inner-London social security centre just before midday, and did not leave until 3.30. For all of that time there were never fewer than a hundred unhappy people queuing to see the handful of stressed clerks dealing with their enquiries, and there were only thirty seats in the room. The office, I learned, had a staff turnover of more than 100 per cent a year. It was a grim place.

The experience sowed some of the seeds in my mind of what would become the Citizen's Charter. I saw no reason why people should suffer such scandalously poor service, and the following afternoon I sat down with Norman Cockett and produced a note on my visit for Norman Fowler, proposing that we sorted out the London benefits system. It led to a scheme which greatly improved the distribution of benefits in the capital.

The post of parliamentary under secretary is really an apprenticeship: more senior positions beckon if the test is not flunked. Parliamentary under secretaries have the influence of access to more senior ministers, and take day-to-day decisions on how things are done, but policy is the prerogative of their more elevated colleagues. I was lucky at Social Security because very early on I appeared a lot in the Commons and helped to take through a significant piece of legislation. This gave me a profile I would not otherwise have received so early on, and is perhaps one reason my political career accelerated.

I began to receive invitations to political events all over the country. One in particular sticks in my mind. In spring 1986 Robert Cranborne, a fellow Blue Chip and the Member for Dorset South, asked me to join a handful of other MPs on a panel of speakers at a Conservative Party event in a small village in his constituency. With me were Tristan Garel-Jones, still in the Whips' Office; Virginia Bottomley, recently elected to the Commons and already Chris Patten's Parliamentary Private Secretary; and

Matthew Parris, who at an impending by-election would leave politics for journalism. We drove down to Dorset, and to pass the journey talked about the issues that might come up that night. Our conversation became light-hearted, and someone – I don't remember which of us – suggested that we each write down a 'frivolous fact', and attempt to introduce it in our replies later that evening. The idea began as a joke, but by the time we arrived at the village hall we had dared each other to go ahead.

Matthew spoke first, and crisply dropped his point – that Upper Volta had recently been renamed Burkina Faso, 'the country of wise men', into his reply to a question on women's rights. Virginia was convincing in bringing out the fact that 'frogs swallow with their eyes shut' into her answer. My turn came next – and, suppressing my mirth, I succeeded in including the point that Anne Boleyn had six fingers on one hand in my piece. But Tristan failed dismally. Almost in stitches, he just about managed to keep a straight face, but dared not bring in his silly fact – I think it was that 18 per cent of the British population regularly share a bath. The following morning at breakfast, we put a white feather on his plate.

Peter Bottomley, Virginia's husband, also an MP, and a Transport minister, joined us for dinner at Cranborne Lodge. We told him what we had been up to, and he was sorry to have missed the fun. He made up for it when answering Transport questions in the Commons a few days later. One MP raised the matter of traffic congestion in Mayfair. 'I have been down Park Lane on a bus,' Peter informed the House. 'I took a sandwich with me, and it was unfinished when I reached the other end. Unlike frogs, which eat with their eyes closed, I had mine open. Neither the bus nor the traffic was held up.'

He was asked another question. 'Like the first inhabitants of Burkina Faso,' he began his reply, 'the land of the wise men, otherwise known as Upper Volta, I might wonder whether it is right to take all those powers into my department's hands.'

His answer to a third question completed the set. 'We can do many things with statistics. We can say that Anne Boleyn had six fingers or that 18 per cent of people share their baths. However, it is more important to consider each bus lane to see whether it is worthwhile.'

Impressed by Peter's bravura performance, when I bumped into Tristan I teased him, 'Go and tell the Prime Minister.' He did, though he was concerned that she might not see the joke. We need not have worried. 'It's the only good thing I've ever heard about Peter,' she replied.

As the summer of 1986 advanced, rumour hinted that I might be promoted again in the forthcoming reshuffle. I realised this was a possibility, but thought it unlikely, given my slender experience and the usual prime ministerial practice of leaving beginners in their jobs a little longer than a year. Although I was ambitious, I did not wish to leave Social Security until I had learned all I could in my role there.

The fates, however, were generous. When the reshuffle came in September, Tony Newton was moved sideways within the department, becoming Minister of State for Health, and at Norman Fowler's request I was promoted to Tony's place as Minister of State for Social Security.

Responsibility for the disabled now fell to me. Since the late 1970s, Norma had been involved with the charity Mencap, and for my part I vividly remembered the difficulties my father had faced when he lost his sight. So this was a job I relished on both these counts, and in addition because it has engendered its own fraternity. My predecessors in the role, on both sides of the House, treated me as one of their own. I was fortunate too that my new deputy as parliamentary secretary was an old friend, Nick Lyell, who as a lawyer had a gift for detail, and with whom I worked very easily. My new Private Secretary, Colin Phillips, soon introduced me to the delights of a steak lunch at the nearby Horse and Groom pub, where we spent many a jolly hour and took quite a few decisions. I was not to know that such pleasures would soon be curtailed as my anonymity fell away.

The jump from parliamentary under secretary to full minister of state is a big one; it means you have entered the pool of ministers from which the Cabinet is chosen. I now attended far more of the Cabinet sub-committees that are the machinery of policy-making, and began to see government and its characters from the inside: who carried weight, who knew his or her brief, who was politically astute, and who had an overblown reputation. It soon became clear to me why rumours of reshuffle casualties were often so accurate – the Cabinet committees mercilessly exposed ministers who were not on top of their jobs or were out of sympathy with policy. Broad-brush answers or flip comments might suffice in the debating atmosphere of the Commons, but you had to be master of the detail to win your way in the committees.

Within days of my appointment I realised that I would be responsible for replying to a debate at the Conservative Party Conference the following month. Despite years of attendance, and many attempts to speak from the floor, I had never been called to do so. Now, though unknown nationally, I was to speak from the platform. In retrospect I can see now that the Social Security debate that year was not of great importance, and in any event, the only speeches that really mattered were those of Cabinet ministers. But it did not feel that way at the time, and I was extremely nervous.

I sat in my garden in the September sun composing a speech. Never had I found one so hard to write. I had little experience of big rallies, and social security does not readily lend itself to conference oratory. Soon the ground at my feet was littered with discarded texts. The speech passed off well enough on the day, however, and I earned a crouching ovation from the audience, many of whom were wondering who was on next, and whether the subject to follow would be more politically exciting. No conference speech ever gave me so much trouble as my debut, and I was mightily relieved when it was over without disaster.

When Parliament reassembled in November I began to get to know the many disabled lobby groups who worked with such dedication for their special interests. In most cases they were not the left-wing warriors I had expected to find, and although not many were obvious Tories, I enjoyed the relationships that were soon built up. I would have liked to have become closer to them, but their institutional role of lobbying the government made that more difficult than I had imagined.

Soon after I had been appointed the McColl Report landed on my desk. Ian McColl, a distinguished professor of surgery, had chaired a Committee of Inquiry into the service provided by the artificial limb and appliance centres. It was a high-powered committee including Brian Griffiths, soon to be appointed head of the Prime Minister's Policy Unit at Number 10, and Marmaduke ('Duke') Hussey, who had lost a leg at the Anzio beach-head in 1943 but had gone on to a distinguished career and was a former Chief Executive and Managing Director of Times Newspapers.

The report was fiercely critical of the services available to disabled people: wheelchair design was out of date; artificial limbs were poorly fitted; and the contract arrangements between the department and the near-monopoly suppliers were inadequate. As I had nearly lost a leg myself in Nigeria I was instinctively sympathetic to the disabled. I knew I was fortunate not to be in need of an artificial limb myself.

The department was disenchanted with the McColl Report, but I decided to implement it in full, and called in Professor McColl to discuss the way forward. I had not previously met the author of this rip-roaring critique of current policy, but he turned out to be a slender, sandy-haired individual of gentle disposition who was courteously but firmly determined to ensure his report was not shelved – as, he told me, he had been threatened it would be by an angry civil servant. His good nature soon overcame any residual resentment among the department's officials, and a Special Health Authority was set up with a wide-ranging brief to improve services for disabled people. I invited Lord Holderness – formerly Richard Wood, a Conservative MP and government minister who had lost both his legs to a bomb in Libya in 1943 – to chair the new authority, and he and his colleagues worked to such effect that services greatly improved.

Ian McColl, however, was not to drift out of my life. In 1989 Margaret Thatcher sent him to the House of Lords, and in the 1990s he became my Parliamentary Private Secretary in the Lords. He spent his early mornings operating at Guy's or St Thomas's Hospitals and then came on to Number 10, where he had become the doctor-in-residence as well as a political adviser, and one of the most popular figures in Downing Street.

My higher profile as a minister of state made me a bigger target for criticism, and on one issue, although for a few days only, I became Public Enemy Number One. January 1987 was bitterly cold. Heavy falls of snow covered the whole country, and there was genuine concern about how vulnerable people would keep warm. The previous summer the department had prepared a new scheme of cold weather payments to help the vulnerable when the temperature fell below a certain level, but with Arctic blizzards sweeping Britain, the system looked hopelessly bureaucratic. I was even accused of having personally devised a scheme that would never be triggered (although why anyone would have done that the critics never explained).

As I drove from Huntingdon to the Commons on icy roads and in grim weather, the radio news made it clear that the cold weather payments were *the* issue of the moment, and that the opposition's attack on what it called our 'heartless system' would be fierce. I had not realised, until I listened to Labour spokesmen, that by introducing a new scheme to help the old pay for their heating in cold weather we had been deliberately trying to freeze them to death. Labour, however, assured everyone that that was our intention. And they pinned the blame on me.

I had no authority to change the scheme and make early payments under it without both Treasury approval and extra funding – neither of which was forthcoming. The Treasury refused to yield, and an alarmed Margaret Thatcher – no doubt with an eye to Prime Minister's Questions, where uproar was guaranteed – summoned John MacGregor, the Chief Secretary to the Treasury, and myself to see her at Number 10 and thrash out our solution to this winter crisis. I pleaded for money, and John resisted. We were in the first-floor study, in which Margaret liked to work, and I looked through the window at the deep snow covering Horse Guards Parade. 'It must be very cold in a two-up, two-down semi with no heating,' I said. Mrs Thatcher turned to me sharply, then looked out, and I knew I had won.

The Treasury approved the expenditure, and I announced that one and a half million vulnerable people would receive a £5 payment towards their heating bills. The vulnerable were reassured, the Labour fox was shot, the Tories were delighted, and I ended my brief stint as a hate figure.

It was a timely introduction to the sort of political flash-fire that can so often cause trouble. The Treasury was not always all-powerful, and Margaret Thatcher was a good deal more alert to popular concerns than her detractors liked to suggest. I moved from villain to hero in a matter of hours, and within a short time revised the system of cold weather payments to make it a good deal more effective. That done, the weather improved, and the new system remained untested.

I enjoyed my two years at Social Security, and did not anticipate that they would soon come to an end. In early 1987, however, the Conservatives returned to the lead in the opinion polls, and all parties began to prepare themselves for a general election. After two successive election defeats Labour still looked unelectable, and we were generally confident of another win. As the election approached speculation grew, and I was tipped for all manner of jobs in the new Parliament.

I had a modest role in the preparations for the June election by helping the Treasury to 'cost' Labour's social security policies. The bulk of this work was done by Andrew Tyrie, then Nigel Lawson's special adviser, and after 1997 the Tory Member for Chichester. It was a brilliant success in undermining Labour's claim to be able to afford their programme without massive tax increases.

When the election was called, Peter Brown, my constituency agent in Huntingdon, had prepared yet again for me to fight the seat as though it was a marginal. I was committed to a busy programme, including three speeches each evening at different villages, as well as a string of question-and-answer sessions with special-interest groups. This was our normal practice. We expected to win the election in Huntingdon, but we never took it for granted and left nothing to chance, working hard for the biggest possible majority.

Our plans were complicated when I was invited to join a number of Central Office press conferences during the campaign. As these took place early in the morning, I would drive to London after my evening speeches and return to the constituency mid-morning. It was exhausting, and sleep was at a premium. But it was exhilarating to see the campaign from the centre. I was at the morning conference a week before polling day on 4 June, 'wobbly Thursday', when Margaret – tired and in pain from a tooth infection – was snappy and irritable, and everyone walked on eggshells to avoid provoking an explosion.

It was evident from the underlying atmosphere at Central Office that morning that the relationship between Norman Tebbit, as Party Chairman, and David Young, the Secretary of State for Employment and a leading figure in planning the campaign, was one of mutual distrust. But our private rolling daily opinion poll never blinked, and the election was won comfortably. Division of the anti-Conservative forces gave Mrs Thatcher a reduced, but still substantial majority of 102, although she received only 42 per cent of the poll. It was a stunning third election victory for her.

At Huntingdon I won with a record majority of over twenty-seven thousand, and more than two-thirds of the vote. It was now one of the safest Tory seats in the country. Norma and I returned to Finings to celebrate and ponder the next five years. Neither of us would then have believed that when the party was to defend its majority at the next general election, it would be doing so with me as prime minister.

# CHAPTER FIVE

## Into Cabinet

THE DAY AFTER the 1987 election came the startling news that Norman Tebbit was stepping down as party chairman. Although our campaign had been criticised as inept, and rumours abounded that Norman's relationship with the Prime Minister had deteriorated, this was still a shock. We had just won an election – albeit against an unelectable opposition – and Norman was popular in the party for his robust Conservatism and for the courage with which he had returned to front-line politics after the dreadful injuries he and his wife Margaret had suffered in the bombing of the Grand Hotel in Brighton. He and I were to have our differences in later years, but he was a loss to the government, and I was sorry to see him go. So, despite their reported disagreements, was the Prime Minister, who tried in vain to persuade him to stay.

I was asked to call on Margaret at Downing Street on the Saturday afternoon following the election. My days at Social Security were at an end. Another year, another job. But where next? A sideways move as a minister of state seemed unlikely, since a telephone call from Number 10 would have sufficed to tell me that. I considered the possibilities. I was sure that John Wakeham would be promoted to the Cabinet, leaving a vacancy as chief whip. John MacGregor, too, the Chief Secretary to the Treasury, was bound to be offered his own department. Either of those two vacancies seemed possible for me. As I drove to London, the lunchtime news listed the ministers believed to be leaving the Cabinet. It seemed the reshuffle was going to be a big one.

When I arrived at Number 10 I was shown into the small waiting room on the ground floor near the Cabinet Room. To my surprise the Transport Secretary John Moore was already waiting there, and within a few minutes we were joined by Norman Fowler, the Paymaster General Kenneth Clarke and John MacGregor. Then the Industry Secretary Paul Channon arrived.

One by one we were summoned to learn our fates. As John MacGregor preceded me, I guessed that I was to join the Cabinet as Chief Secretary to the Treasury. This proved to be right. When I was called in to see her the Prime Minister was warm and friendly. She spoke of the importance of the job, adding almost as an afterthought, 'The Queen is expecting you at the Palace this afternoon so you can join the Privy Council.' Although membership of the Privy Council is automatic upon joining the Cabinet it is a preferment of some significance. It is coveted more than any other recognition in the Commons, and I was delighted. As I left Number 10 with Norman Fowler (the new Employment Secretary) for the Privy Council the skies opened and the rain pelted down as we huddled under an umbrella. But nothing could have dampened our spirits that day, and the meeting of the Privy Council was a very jolly affair.

Later I learned that I had been right in my guesses about the two jobs that might have been offered to me. The Prime Minister's original intention, backed by William Whitelaw, was for me to become chief whip; but Nigel Lawson asked for me as chief secretary, and after a tussle he gained Willie's support and had his way. This meant that I would now join the Cabinet, whereas the chief whip attends Cabinet but is not a member of it.

It is tempting to reflect on how events might have turned out if I had become chief whip. An appointment to that post usually lasts for a whole Parliament. If that had been so in my case, I might never have been foreign secretary, chancellor or prime minister. Instead I would have been chief whip during Margaret's leadership contest against Michael Heseltine in 1990. I have often wondered if I would have been able to obtain for her the few extra votes that would have enabled her to win on the first ballot. She would then have remained prime minister until the next general election, when the electorate as a whole would have had the chance to judge the government. I believe we would probably have lost that election – but it would have been a more fitting end for a long-serving prime minister than removal by her own colleagues. Moreover, it would never have given rise to the bitterness that has scarred the Conservative Party ever since. Nor would Europe have become such a divisive issue.

But all that lay far ahead, and I was pleased at the job I had been given. The Treasury is the most powerful department in the government, since it not only determines macro-economic policy but controls the purse strings.

Macro-economic policy was the prerogative of the Chancellor, Nigel Lawson, but public spending was to be my responsibility as chief secretary.

The chief secretary has one of the lowest profiles of any Cabinet minister, but this is deceptive. For he is the most influential minister in determining the division of the total of public spending – who gets what. This gives him the power, if he wishes, to facilitate new policies or to hold them back. Thus, although the most junior member of the Cabinet, the chief secretary has an authority far greater than the casual observer ever realises. As prime minister I was always very careful who I appointed to the role, and watched very carefully what they did with it.

The Treasury had many of the best officials in Whitehall. My Private Secretary, which in Whitehall parlance means the head of my Private Office, was Jill Rutter, a Treasury high-flyer. She had an extremely sharp brain and an acid sense of humour that spared no one. She had a proper respect for ability at all levels – but none for seniority alone. Jill was fearless, and had a healthy disregard for conventional wisdom. She was a fierce protector of her turf and her minister. An added bonus for me was her love of cricket, for she was a long-standing member of Surrey County Cricket Club. Sometimes we would relax between meetings by catching up with a Test match on television or, since long hours were normal, watching the late-night highlights with other members of my Private Office before leaving the Treasury building.

The most important part of the chief secretary's year is the public expenditure survey, which begins in the summer when each secretary of state puts in a 'bid' for his department's financing for the next three years. These bids set out the ambitions of the department for the years ahead. Rather as the black widow spider dances an odd quadrille with its partner before finally mating, the public spending round has its own rituals. The bids often contain an unrealistic wish list, and are invariably padded so that the minister can be seen to make 'concessions' in head-to-head negotiation with the Treasury.

I arrived at the Treasury to find that the bids for the forthcoming years were very high: for the first year alone they amounted to £6 billion more than the sum previously allocated, which was quite unaffordable. In response – the first part of the ritual – I prepared a paper for Cabinet in late July that set maximum spending levels for the next three years. For the first year, over which the greatest battles are always fought, I recommended that we should hold spending to the level agreed by Cabinet the year before – although I proposed spending increases after that. The paper had three purposes: to gain the collective approval of the Cabinet for the sum total of expenditure that was affordable; to convince the markets that we had a sensible policy; and to emphasise that the Treasury was not an Aladdin's cave to be ransacked. I was firmly backed by the Prime Minister and the Chancellor, and – as I had done some private canvassing – I received support from other ministers.

More surprising was that some of the ministers who had asked me for the largest increases for their departments were strongly supportive of restricting total expenditure: that stern monetarist Nick Ridley, for one, clearly saw scope for cuts elsewhere, whilst being confident that his own budget at Environment required a great deal more money. Nick was not alone; he was merely the colleague whose bid was most obviously at odds with his own philosophy.

Throughout August, the Treasury raked through each department's bid, enabling me to identify the weak points to attack when I wrote to ministers challenging their assumptions and costings. All this is ritual foreplay to prepare the ground for the detailed one-to-one negotiations between the chief secretary and the spending ministers at which the expenditure levels are agreed. Every subheading of expenditure is pored over at these bilateral meetings, which drag on for many hours. Several meetings are usually necessary before a conclusion is reached. The bilaterals are revealing. They expose vividly the ability of ministers and their personal commitment to their programmes.

The process represents a sharp learning curve for the chief secretary, who has to be able to challenge not only the expenditure figures but also the policy of every department. This is gruelling, but it offers an insight into Whitehall that is unavailable to any other minister. Years later, as prime minister, the bank of knowledge I built up as chief secretary was immensely useful in giving me an understanding of what lay behind ministerial proposals. I often found that the most important point of policy-making was not what was proposed, but why.

Although my first few months as chief secretary were tough, I felt at home at the Treasury, and my two years in the job were amongst my most enjoyable in government. The amount of detail to be absorbed is formidable, but since I believe that every pound of taxpayers' money which is spent has to be justified I did not mind that at all. I found that I was easily able to absorb and recall at will a huge amount of detail about public spending, which gave me a tremendous advantage in negotiations with ministers. Nor did I find it difficult to predict accurately how colleagues would couch their arguments: I simply put myself inside their minds and considered what I would do in their place. The volume of work meant that I did not contribute much to macro-economic policy-making, but since Nigel Lawson listened to others only as a prelude to announcing what he had intended to do anyway, this did not much matter. I had no ideological baggage on economic and financial policy, and I admired Nigel's skills.

Nigel carried the role of chancellor with great self-assurance. He had reached the peak of his authority in government, and no trace of self-doubt ever crossed his mind. He often worked in his study at Number 11 Downing Street rather than at the Treasury, summoning officials and ministers when he needed them. When he did appear at the Treasury it was often for large meetings of all his ministers and senior officials. These he conducted like a professorial seminar. Nigel would pronounce. Comment would be invited. Nigel would adjudicate. Policy was decided. Government was made to seem very simple.

Nigel was supported by an impressive team of officials and ministers. Sir Peter Middleton, the Permanent Secretary, was a sharp Yorkshireman, level-headed and pugnacious to the extent of provoking an argument simply for the intellectual joy of having one. An intensely private man, he was a close friend of Nigel, and was very perceptive about events and people. Robin Butler, the Second Permanent Secretary in charge of public spending, had been Margaret Thatcher's Principal Private Secretary at Number 10, and knew the Whitehall machine and all its ways. No one was surprised when he leapfrogged over more senior colleagues to become Secretary to the Cabinet and Head of the Civil Service. He was easy-going, helpful and efficient – and one of the most competitive men I have ever met, a fine sportsman who excelled at rugby and cricket. The third of the main figures was Terry Burns, the Economic Adviser. Tousle-haired, youthful, genial and without pomposity or malice, Terry was a man of passionate interests. Life was never boring to him, and he never seemed downcast (except momentarily when his beloved Queen's Park Rangers were having a string of bad results). He had made his reputation as an economic forecaster for the London Business School.

Amongst the other ministers at the department, I had an amiable but wary relationship with Norman Lamont, the Financial Secretary to the Treasury. The Financial Secretary is number three at the Treasury, and after the election Norman must have hoped for promotion to chief secretary. If my appointment was a setback to him, he gave no outward sign of it, although our conversations were usually guarded. We did not share cheery confidences. The erudite Peter Brooke was the minister of state responsible for VAT and Europe. I had first met him in my days as parliamentary candidate for St Pancras North, and he was always ready with a good-humoured story. The final Commons minister, the Economic Secretary, was Peter Lilley. Previously Nigel's PPS, Peter was rather shy and withdrawn for a politician, but was highly intelligent, with a fine analytical mind, and sometimes surprisingly waspish. It was a talented team, all of whom were to reach the Cabinet. In the Lords, the able Simon Glenarthur had the difficult task, which he performed admirably, of speaking for all Treasury ministers. I often wished that he too had been in the Commons to supplement the talent available there.

In early September I began the detailed bilateral discussions with ministerial colleagues. The toughest negotiator of them all was Peter Walker, the Secretary of State for Wales. Peter believed in the virtues of public spending, and was determined to use it to the full in the Principality. His general air was of a man who did not care whether he remained in the Cabinet or not, and was not remotely interested in being a team player if that meant making concessions to an economic policy he distrusted.

As a negotiating tactic this was devastating. Peter simply asserted that his bids were the minimum necessary; he could not manage with less; the Prime Minister had promised him the money when she gave him a job he had not asked for; he did not much like the Treasury, because it got in the way of good policy; and so, like it or lump it, he expected us to cough up. Since (apart from his opinion of the Treasury) much of this was true, there was not much that could be done with Peter. It was perhaps fortunate for me that most of the Welsh budget was a fixed proportion of the sums available to English departments for the same responsibilities. Peter's bids, therefore, were only for small amounts – which made his approach even more infuriating, since in the midst of discussions for much larger sums, they were not worth the argument. He knew this, and his stubbornness was a deliberate tactic. His approach to the Treasury was best summed up by an annotation in my appointments diary which simply read: '3.30 Public Expenditure Settlement – Wales (Secretary of State, Dick Turpin).' Highway robbery was his forte.

Kenneth Baker, the Education Secretary, was the polar opposite of Peter. He would bound in full of enthusiasm, with lots of new ideas, all of which, he assured me, would be hugely popular with the electorate and would guarantee yet another election victory. Ken cared a lot about education, and in Cabinet committees he handled the Prime Minister on the subject better than anyone else I ever saw. As a former Education minister herself, she enjoyed picking holes in his plans, particularly when he was devising changes to the curriculum. It was a game they both enjoyed. 'That's absurd,' she would say. 'I know which official suggested that.' Ken would demur, deny that it was that official, make a joke of it, deflect her criticism, and gradually manoeuvre the Prime Minister into a position where he made tiny concessions to her, and she would have appeared graceless to seek more.

It was good spectator sport for the rest of the committee, and I admired the way he performed, but his technique was less effective where the issue was money and not ideas. When detailed questions on cost were put to Ken, he was often poorly briefed. His spending plans were grossly inflated, and it never took long to remove the padding. At the end of our negotiations Ken bounded out as cheerfully as he had come in, but with much less money than he had sought.

Kenneth Clarke, the Health Secretary, simply enjoyed a good argument. It was evident to me why Ken had chosen the law and then politics as a profession. Our meetings always took a long time as we argued points of detail, agreeing the facts but disagreeing about the conclusion. It was good-natured but very time-consuming. Eventually, when we had reached stalemate, I suggested we throw the officials out and do a deal between ourselves. Behind closed doors I told Ken that his bids were outrageous. Rather disarmingly he agreed, but added that if he had frankly admitted it, I would have asked for even more reductions. This, of course, was true. Having agreed that he was asking for too much and I was offering too little, we soon reached an acceptable compromise. We then sat chatting over a drink before re-admitting the officials and announcing the outcome.

The Home Secretary Douglas Hurd was a subtle negotiator who began his meeting with a rather discursive statement setting out all the desirable expenditure he had himself excluded from the bids before he submitted them. 'All very necessary,' he would say, 'and we'll have to do it one day, but' – and here he would shake his head sadly – 'I know there are many demands to be met.' It was a clever technique, designed to cut off many of the Treasury's traditional arguments. Douglas was reasonable in manner but tough on substance. He would lean back in his chair, his right ankle across his left knee and an agonised expression on his face if any reduction to his bids was suggested. All this talk of money was obviously distasteful to him. If the Treasury case was good enough he would gradually concede, but eventually he would begin jingling a large bunch of keys in an agitated fashion. The key-jingling was a sign that he had reached his bottom line. Jill Rutter once said to me that Douglas and I would never have finished a negotiation if he had left his keys at home.

The Scottish Secretary Malcolm Rifkind was always difficult, and usually threatened to resign unless he got a better settlement. I once asked him at the beginning of a meeting whether he wanted to threaten to resign now, or to wait until we had finished. 'I think I'll wait,' he grinned, knowing even then he would only settle at the last moment. Scotland was well served by a series of Scottish secretaries who turned public expenditure negotiations into an art form.

The public spending survey is always hard pounding, and I found it doubly so first time round. In my favour was a growing economy and buoyant revenue; working against me was a general election manifesto that enabled ministers to claim a mandate for specific expenditure. As the survey covered the first three years of the Parliament they tried to include every election promise they could identify, and usually overestimated the expenditure necessary to cover it.

I tried to reduce or eliminate bids by challenging the case made for them by the ministers facing me, although in doing so I was always acutely aware that they had to return to their departments and defend the deal they had accepted. I always left them with what we in the Treasury called a 'lollipop', even if we had denied many of their cherished schemes. I had no wish to undermine their credibility or that of the government.

One tale needs scotching. John Moore, who after the election had become Secretary of State for Health and Social Security, and I were said to be rivals, and it was widely believed in some quarters that I gave him a poor settlement in order to damage his political career. John was a former

Treasury minister convinced of the virtues of low spending, and rather quixotically he tried to match his policies to his philosophy. In pursuit of this admirable consistency he bid for too little money in the public expenditure settlement, rather than too much. This concern for prudent economics would cause him much difficulty – a rare and honest approach that earned him opprobrium.

Gradually the deals were reached. Some took a long time. George Younger, at Defence, conceded only after many meetings and a firm refusal on my part to meet his demands. He was a hard negotiator, and eventually accepted that if he pushed his case to an adjudication by the so-called 'Star Chamber' – which would determine the outcome if I could not reach an agreement with the minister concerned – he would get no more cash. George was a good defence secretary: he attacked in strength and retreated in good order.

In the 1987 spending survey all the deals were eventually reached in bilateral meetings, the first time for years that the 'Star Chamber' had not been called upon. The Treasury's spending target was met too, although I had agreed an extra £1 billion for capital spending and large increases for health, law and order, defence and education. Despite this, the level of expenditure fell to the lowest proportion of national income since the early 1970s. This outcome was widely praised.

In January 1988, Willie Whitelaw retired as deputy prime minister. He had become the public face of tolerant Conservatism, a wise counsellor, and a restraint upon Margaret. He was irreplaceable. I was given some of his responsibilities. One of them, 'helping with the presentation of public policy', simply amounted to ensuring that Bernard Ingham, the Prime Minister's pugnacious Press Secretary, was briefed on Cabinet discussions. I was also given the job of adjudicating in disputes between departments when they were in conflict. In practice I was rarely called upon, unless the dispute involved money. Nevertheless, these rather imprecise new responsibilities were widely publicised and speculated upon, and my profile began to rise.

The public finances were buoyant when Treasury ministers and senior officials met in January at Chevening, the foreign secretary's official country residence, lent for the occasion of the annual weekend discussion on the budget options. It was to prove a dramatic budget. Nigel was determined to take advantage of the excellent fiscal position to make deep cuts in income tax. He reduced the highest rate from 60 per cent to 40 per cent, the basic rate to the 25p target Geoffrey Howe had set years earlier, and increased personal tax allowances by twice the rate of inflation.

The 1988 budget would cast a long shadow. Against all tradition there were angry interruptions in the Commons when Nigel made his Budget Statement, and the House was suspended for a brief time. Labour – and many others – were shocked by what they perceived as the budget's recklessness. I did not agree with them at the time. Whilst Nigel had cut taxes – and therefore the government's income – the public expenditure survey had also cut spending as a proportion of national income. Like Nigel, I saw the tax cuts as a taxpayer's dividend earned by the growth of the economy and the restraint in public spending. Moreover, despite the income tax cuts, Nigel had delivered a balanced budget, and one that had been warmly received by the Prime Minister and the Cabinet that morning when he had set out his measures for them. Our backbenchers too were ecstatic.

But there was a shark in the water. The official Treasury statistics were wrong, and badly misled the forecasters into seriously underestimating the growth in the economy. These dangers became apparent within months of the budget when a boom began, and inflation started to climb. To curb it Nigel raised interest rates to 12 per cent, then 13 per cent, 14 per cent, and eventually 15 per cent, the level I was to inherit as Chancellor. As the boom grew – and with it spending power boosted by wage increases, overtime and tax cuts – the housing market went crazy. Prices rocketed as people scrambled to become home-owners. It seemed a one-way bet, and purchasers concerned themselves only with whether they could meet their mortgage repayments; it was taken for granted that the value of their houses would go on rising. When the economy fell off the cliff and boom turned to recession, made worse by an adverse world economy, the housing market stagnated, prices tumbled, and millions found themselves burdened with negative equity, owing more on their homes than they were worth. This problem was to paralyse the economy in the early nineties, when the public would yearn for a return to the boom years, with no recognition that it was the boom itself which had led to many of their problems.

Despite the role of the 1988 budget in feeding the boom-soon-to-be-recession, the tax changes Nigel introduced were right. They ended the unjustifiably high taxation of income that had hampered investment. Nigel saw that long-term advantage very clearly, but he did not foresee the short-term problems. I had no premonition of what lay ahead either, and I defended the budget with conviction. By the time the malign combination of inflation, high interest rates, rising unemployment and a collapse in growth was fully apparent, Nigel and Margaret were no longer in government.

As chief secretary I was conscripted onto a new committee chaired by the Prime Minister to consider the future of the National Health Service and how to finance it. Nigel Lawson, John Moore and Tony Newton were also members (Ken Clarke and David Mellor would replace the latter two after reshuffles). The case for reform of the NHS was strong. Despite increased funding year upon year, there were perennial dramas with health authorities running out of funds in the last few weeks of the financial year, and 1988 was no exception. Nigel and John Moore were both keen to be brave and do something to solve the problem, and after initial reluctance Margaret agreed. In his memoirs Nigel would reveal that he persuaded the Prime Minister of the need to review hospital services immediately after having briefed her on the large tax cuts he was planning in his 1988 budget. This was a typical Lawson tactic: offer the PM something she would be pleased about, and then seek approval for an action he favoured.

The review was long and detailed and recommended fundamental changes that I continue to believe were worthwhile, though they were widely attacked. To ensure that NHS facilities were used effectively and patients treated more speedily, we devised a system to enable money to follow the patient – often outside the immediate health area. We also proposed two areas of devolution: hospitals were permitted to become self-governing, and large GP practices were enabled to control their own budgets.

Although these schemes were permissive – no one would be forced to be part of them – the debate that followed, as so often with the NHS, was based more on emotion than logic. Some of the criticisms were ludicrous. Labour, on political auto-pilot, said we were trying to 'privatise' the health service – although this had never been discussed for a moment throughout all our detailed deliberations. They also attacked the 'internal market' we created, claiming that we were putting money before patients. Here they were wrong too: we were in fact putting patients first, by ensuring that money was allocated more efficiently to increase the sum total of health care. In due course we legislated to bring our reforms into operation, and they were effective until they were partly reversed by the Labour government after the 1997 election.

When the 1988 public expenditure survey began, bids were once again far too high, although a number of ministers had strong claims to extra funding. Douglas Hurd had a compelling case for increased police expenditure and capital for an enhanced prison-building programme. Kenneth Clarke, now at Health, had an irresistible case for preparing for the NHS reforms – which, since I had helped to negotiate them, diminished my arguments against his bids. Paul Channon, now at Transport, submitted a strong case for more investment in roads and nationalised industries. Others, too, argued their case forcefully – notably Nick Ridley, George Younger and, of course, Peter Walker.

By this time Jill Rutter, my Private Secretary, had been promoted. Her replacement, Carys Evans, had a different style but was just as effective. When Peter Walker played the 'Welsh' card yet again, I dictated him a note, and Carys translated it into Welsh before we dispatched it. We hoped there was a Welsh-speaker in Peter's office.

As usual, the public spending negotiations were protracted. In many cases they continued throughout the Party Conference at Brighton in October. I sat in my hotel bedroom as ministers trooped in and out, but decamped to a different hotel for especially long discussions with George Younger, who as ever fought politely but determinedly for every penny. Slowly I persuaded him that I could not meet his bids, but he ceded ground only after heavy bombardment.

Negotiations with Nick Ridley, the Environment Secretary, were strained. I thought Nick a clever but erratic man of much ability and an admirable contempt for presentational niceties. In some quarters he was widely liked and admired. His junior ministers and officials – even those who loathed his often uncompromising views – nearly always spoke warmly of him. Like many in the Commons I had been astonished when Nick was appointed to the Cabinet, but he had an original mind and was wonderfully politically incorrect. Face to face, I respected him, but I did not like what he said behind my back. I found this apparent animosity from someone who did not know me well puzzling.

Whenever we met for negotiations Nick took off his jacket, and even his red braces looked pugnacious. We tried to get on, but even where we agreed our reasons differed, and neither of us felt at ease with the other.

Only rarely in my life have I utterly failed to form a relationship with someone, but Nick and I were doomed. I don't apportion blame for this, I simply note it. Later, when I was appointed chancellor, I understood Nick's frustration: he clearly wanted the job himself, and must have thought himself better qualified. He was certainly closer to the Prime Minister than I was. He suffered, and his private frustrations were reported to me.

Nick and I only rarely clashed in Cabinet or in committees. But one exchange in Cabinet committee did not endear us to each other. It also gave an interesting insight into the Prime Minister's occasionally rather engaging innocence. David Mellor, then the Minister of Health, had rather conversationally raised the issue of single mothers. Nick suggested gruffly that they should be housed together in hostels so that they could be 'cared for' (and, the subliminal agenda went, watched). I thought this patrician approach to be so careless of people's individual circumstances that I said ironically, 'Why don't we put red lights outside the hostels too?' Nick grasped what I was on about and flushed with anger, but the Prime Minister, not understanding at all, warmly supported my 'proposal'. 'They'll know where to go, Nick,' she enthused. Irony was not Margaret's strong suit.

Not that Nick's hostility was directed solely at me. It extended to Cecil Parkinson (at that time the Energy Secretary) as well. In 1988 Nick and I reached a stand-off in pre-budget discussions, and I told him that I intended to refer his settlement to the Star Chamber. Since this was chaired by Cecil the prospect was not at all to Nick's taste, and he quickly settled his budget at Environment in a brief meeting with Nigel Lawson – as I had suspected he would. His dislike of Cecil probably cost his department quite a lot of money.

Cecil was not called into action, as for the second year running all the spending agreements were reached without resort to the Star Chamber. The plans I agreed included an extra £2.25 billion for capital spending in the first year and large increases for health, law and order, defence, roads and local authority spending. These increases were possible because of the falling burden of interest payments on government debt and savings on social security payments as unemployment fell. The books balanced without any increase in overall spending for the first year of the survey, and only modest increases for the following two years.

As 1988 ended I could look back on two successful public expenditure rounds. My satisfaction was soured only by the increasing signs of economic problems to come. During those two years I had been so preoccupied with Treasury responsibilities that I had turned down a number of opportunities to deliver the sort of philosophical lectures that identify politicians with a particular credo. At the time I had no hesitation in refusing them. I was busy, and believed there would be many future invitations and ample time ahead to set out my ideas. Had I realised how my career was about to accelerate I might have acted differently. As it was, I delivered only one speech, to the Audit Commission in mid-1989, in which I tried to indicate that at least one Conservative felt that the public services performed a valuable role. This was a slightly dissenting voice to come from the Treasury, and was a trailer for the public service reforms that I was later to introduce.

As chief secretary to the Treasury, I came to know Margaret Thatcher much better. Since my role was to restrain public spending we were generally on the same side in most arguments. But we did have one fierce row. Short's Brothers, a large aerospace company in Northern Ireland, was an important local employer in an area of massive unemployment. It had huge debts, and Tom King, the Northern Ireland Secretary, and I were keen to sell it to Bombardier, a Canadian aerospace company, in order to save jobs. They would not buy it without a substantial dowry, but to my astonishment Margaret objected to the terms of the deal I proposed. She summoned me to Downing Street, where in front of her Principal Private Secretary Andrew Turnbull we had a two-hour confrontation that began coolly, turned frosty, and ended in fierce rowing. I felt her attacks on me were unjust. I had concluded the two most successful public spending rounds for years, and was now accused of not being concerned about taxpayers' money. Neither of us gave any ground, and I returned to the Treasury determined to resign if I was overruled. The next day, Margaret asked for further figures to justify my case, and then accepted it. But it had been a close call.

Yet again, a reshuffle was about to show that Margaret did not bear grudges over fierce arguments.

# CHAPTER SIX

# 'What's the Capital of Colombia?'

I HAD BEEN WIDELY TIPPED for a move from the Treasury to my own department, but the promotion I was given surprised everyone – except me; the whips' mafia had worked with its customary effectiveness. Three days before the reshuffle I had been warned by Tristan Garel-Jones that the Prime Minister intended to appoint me foreign secretary. I scoffed, and told him to lie down with an aspirin until he felt better. But I was not confident he was wrong. It was the sort of thing the whips would know, and he seemed very certain. I spent an uncomfortable weekend brooding on the prospect.

Norma was horrified. Of all the jobs in government the Foreign Office was the one she least wanted me to have, and the one for which I was least prepared. Moreover, I enjoyed being chief secretary. I had been in the job for two years, and felt thoroughly on top of it. It was flattering to be tipped for promotion, but I would have preferred to consolidate my position at the Treasury. I knew also that such a dramatic promotion would explode for good the contemporary wisdom that I had no enemies in politics. I knew that success could breed resentment, and that I would also be a sitting duck for the fire any commentator, colleague or opponent might henceforth care to direct at me.

The reshuffle began on Monday, 24 July 1989. Whitehall is a veritable grapevine on such days, and I kept in touch with colleagues by phone. Peter Brooke was followed into Number 10 by Ken Baker – self-evidently a change of party chairman. John Gummer, Cecil Parkinson and Nick Ridley were followed by Chris Patten. Others were said to have gone in privately, through the Cabinet Office. It was a substantial reshuffle but appeared to be without a pattern. Something was wrong, but I did not know what. I sat in the Treasury wondering and waiting.

Since I had been promoted in three of the past four years, I was an aficionado of reshuffles. I knew they began with the most senior Cabinet appointments, which were usually finished by lunchtime. So I expected to hear in the morning if I was to be moved. Lunchtime came – and went. Geoffrey Howe hadn't been moved, and I hadn't been summoned. Two o'clock. Three o'clock. I had put a bottle of champagne in the fridge in the hope of remaining in the Treasury. As 3 o'clock passed I asked Carys Evans, my Private Secretary, to fetch it with some glasses. As it was opened, the phone rang.

Carys looked up. 'It's Charles Powell,' she said. 'Would you please go and see the PM?'

Mrs Thatcher was in her study with Andrew Turnbull, her Principal Private Secretary. She looked fresh, and there was a bloom on her cheeks that I had often seen before. It meant she was relaxed, not on guard, in company with which she was comfortable – and about to bestow a favour. Charles had been smiling too when he showed me upstairs. My heart sank.

'John,' she said, 'hold on to your seatbelt. You are the centrepiece of my changes. Geoffrey has moved on, and I want you to be foreign secretary.'

If I had not been prepared, I am not sure how I would have reacted. As it was, I demurred – for my sake and hers. I believed I owed it to her.

'Prime Minister, I'm very flattered. But is this a good idea?'

'I'm very sure it's a good idea. Why shouldn't it be?' She made some disparaging noises about the Foreign Office – not just in connection with its attitude towards Europe. 'I want someone there who thinks as I do.'

'Aren't there others better qualified?' I said. 'Douglas Hurd? Nigel Lawson?'

She waved a hand dismissively. No words were necessary.

I persisted. 'I'm not sure it's a good idea from your point of view. People will assume I'm there just to carry out your bidding. That won't be good for either of us. I won't be offended if you think again.'

She wasn't having it – and if I'd said no it would have seemed like funk. And how could one possibly turn down such a glittering prize so happily offered? It would certainly have been ungracious. She would have been embarrassed, disappointed and, I think, hurt. My resistance to the appointment melted. Clearly the matter was decided, and there was no alternative Cabinet job left. I remembered the old adage: You don't negotiate with prime ministers, you say 'yes' or you say 'no' and take the consequences. I thanked her. We chatted. And I left the room as foreign secretary.

In the corridor I met Charles. He was grinning. 'What's the capital of Colombia?'

'Bogotá,' I said. 'Bogotá, Charles. I've been there. Years ago.'

I returned to my office at the Treasury to find that the Whitehall bush telegraph had excelled itself. My Private Office and advisers had gathered and a globe of the world had been sellotaped to the top of a bottle of champagne.

The Treasury was agog with excitement, but the atmosphere in my office was part celebration and part wake. Nigel Lawson did not join us, and as I sipped my champagne my mind kept turning to him. How was he feeling? He and Geoffrey had confronted Margaret before Madrid, and Geoffrey had now been moved. And Nigel, who had been chancellor for six years – what would be his next move? The office of foreign secretary, which surely he might have coveted, had been denied him and given to one of his junior ministers.

I had little time to reflect on this. Soon Stephen Wall, who was to be my Principal Private Secretary at the Foreign Office, and Andrew Burns, the Chief Press Officer, came to see me to discuss the preliminary press handling of my appointment.

Afterwards, I returned to the Commons. I knew my appointment would be controversial. As I walked across New Palace Yard I met Norman Fowler, my old boss at the DHSS, and now a close friend.

'Well, what did you get?' he asked.

'Umm . . . foreign secretary,' I said. 'I'm a bit concerned about it.'

'Crikey,' said Norman, pushing his glasses up his nose. "Crik-ey!'

The following morning I left Durand Gardens at 7.30 as usual and arrived at the Foreign Office at 8 a.m. I hadn't told anyone I would arrive so early, and no one was there to meet me except a posse of press photographers. I posed for the inevitable first-day photographs until Sir Patrick Wright, the Permanent Secretary, appeared. He greeted me warmly, a little embarrassed at not having been there when I arrived, and in we went.

Cecil Parkinson said later that 'there was a feeling Margaret had overdone it' in appointing me foreign secretary. He was right. But what were her reasons? She'd already said to Willie Whitelaw that in the next generation I would be her successor. Was she now anticipating that day by putting me into a job from which I would be well placed to win any forthcoming leadership election? I cannot know what was really going on in her mind. Nevertheless, it was an extravagant gesture of support.

The move to the Foreign Office changed my life in ways that were not all welcome. I was now considered to be a target for terrorists, and for security reasons I had to move out of my flat in Durand Gardens – let to me by Stan Hurn, an old friend from banking days. But the real disruption was to my lifestyle at Finings, a sanctuary in good and bad days, that changed beyond recognition.

Overnight, security moved in. A caravan disfigured my garden to house a detachment of the Cambridgeshire constabulary, and my garage was surrendered to the same cause. Electronic devices invaded the house and garden like unwanted Daleks. Changes were made to the house and to the perimeter of the garden. An armoured car and protection officers accompanied me every day, and that most precious of gifts – freedom of movement – was gone.

No longer could I walk down the road alone or call in at a shop. I was always accompanied. In time I became accustomed to this, and the protection officers became part of an extended family. At the time, however, Norma and I were desolate at our loss of privacy. The first few weeks of adjustment were miserable.

The Foreign Office were shellshocked at losing Geoffrey after more than five years. And they didn't expect me as his replacement. Did I really know or care about foreign affairs? Was I to be Mrs Thatcher's hatchet-man at the Foreign Office? They had reason to fear so, since all they knew of me was that as chief secretary I had questioned the expenditure of their department, as of all others. It was not the best of introductions, but the officials were too professional to let it show.

Their fears about me soon went away when they realised I did not have a mandate to reverse our European policies, and when I negotiated a satisfactory public expenditure settlement. This was not difficult. I saw Norman Lamont, who had taken my place as chief secretary, alone. Norman knew that I had approved the Treasury's bottom line as chief secretary, and would remember it. Moreover, being familiar with the layout of Treasury expenditure briefs, I could read Norman's notes upside down as they lay in front of him. We soon reached an agreement. A very good one, too.

My new office was outrageously grand (the staff apologised that the foreign secretary's room was being redecorated, and would this do?). It was entirely suitable for impressing visitors, and equally unsuitable for serious work. I prefer a plain room to work in, with a large table on which to spread everything out comfortably, and with few distractions. My new office did not meet these specifications, so, except when receiving guests, I decamped to the anteroom next to the Private Office.

I also took an instant dislike to Carlton Gardens, the foreign secretary's gilded but somewhat faded London home. Geoffrey and Elspeth Howe were in no hurry to move out, and I was in no hurry to move in. I told them to take their time, and settled into a flat at the Foreign Office so I could work longer hours and keep a closer eye on everything that happened. This was thought rather eccentric.

Geoffrey was stunned, almost disbelieving, at what had happened. 'Incredible, bizarre, astounding,' was apparently his reaction. The party was equally astonished. When he first appeared in the Commons in his new role as Leader of the House he received a tumultuous reception. It went on and on, and was clearly *for* Geoffrey and *against* Margaret. It was a warning that should have been noticed.

Geoffrey, whatever his private feelings, went out of his way to help me settle in at the Foreign Office. We met for what was intended to be a briefing but turned out simply to be a friendly chat. It was an odd encounter: the man who had loved the job wishing good luck to the man who did not want it. But he was supportive in public and in private – the perfect predecessor. If he felt any rancour, it was not directed at me.

I found the Foreign Office a revelation. Patrick Wright, the genial Permanent Secretary, went out of his way to be helpful. The officials were very high-calibre, and so was my ministerial team, all of whom, except William Waldegrave, were new to the Foreign Office. And yet whole forests were felled to produce long, comprehensive, written briefings. The professionalism was impressive, but it seemed to me that even trivial matters were sent to the foreign secretary for his decision, or simply to keep him informed. The Foreign Office was far more hierarchical than the Treasury.

Within days of my arrival I decided to devolve decision-making. In this I had the energetic support of Stephen Wall, who was a tower of strength, and Patrick Wright. My ministers William Waldegrave, Francis Maude, Tim Sainsbury, Ivon Brabazon and my old friend Lynda Chalker were perfectly capable of taking decisions on all sorts of matters without reference upwards. William Waldegrave had a brilliant academic mind, and was often talked of as a future prime minister. He had a phenomenal breadth of knowledge, but his intellect was not invariably an asset: it did not always equip him to understand the hopes and fears of lesser minds. Francis Maude was another with a first-class brain. He doesn't just look at things, he looks behind them. With Francis, there was no doubt that he had the ambition to sustain his ability. Lynda Chalker, whom I'd known since she was seventeen, was to become something of a legendary figure in sub-Saharan Africa, where they adored her, and called her the Great White Mother. I remember her shaking her finger at Kenya's President Daniel arap Moi, who was towering above her, holding a fly whisk.

I wanted to clear the decks for the big issues – especially Europe – that I knew I would soon have to face. I soon realised that the Foreign Office was very bruised and hurt by the open contempt in which it believed the Prime Minister held it – too many of her private *bons mots* had been reported back. I thought it ironic that the Prime Minister who so admired many individuals in the department should be so suspicious of it as an institution.

But I also soon saw why Mrs Thatcher felt as she did. Papers would be prepared in support of a recommendation, setting out facts which it was thought the Prime Minister would like, but omitting others which it was thought she would not. Charles Powell would of course swiftly rumble this tactic and assume that the Foreign Office was trying to hoodwink him and his boss. I stepped in at once, and personally altered any papers I considered at fault in this respect. From then on there was far less trouble between the Foreign Office and Number 10.

Treasury briefs, which concern the hard facts of finance, came easily to me, since I have always had a facility for absorbing figures. Briefs at the Foreign Office were different. They were about themes, and were less precise than economic papers. I did not immediately find them as easy to absorb as those I had been used to. It was said subsequently that during my time at the Foreign Office I did not like handling several issues at once. This was absurd. I had done that at the Treasury as a matter of course, and would do so later as prime minister. What I did not like was being asked to approve documents twenty times a day without having the time to digest them and consider their impact on policy. I did not like receiving bits of paper with a few scraps of generalised information and a request for a decision. I would say repeatedly, 'I don't know the background to this. I'd like to know it before I agree anything.' I would then speak to the officials, however junior, who could brief me in full. I have never been happy with superficial explanations. I have never been prepared just to wave things through.

I soon began to acclimatise myself. I discovered, rather unexpectedly, that the skills I needed as foreign secretary were very similar to those I had honed at the Treasury: an ability to prevail in eyeball-to-eyeball confrontations without humiliating one's opponent; and to make a dispassionate judgement of what could be achieved in the long term.

As I settled into the job I became more enthusiastic about it. I was frustrated that routine meetings with ambassadors and high commissioners took up so much time, although I was frequently told that Geoffrey had loved them. Nor did I view all the invitations to banquets and similar functions with any real eagerness – the only thing I enjoyed less than banquets were G7 summits.

Policy, though, was a different matter. There was a large field to play on, and the prospect was one I relished. And foreign-policy decisions cast a long shadow. Within a day of arriving at the Foreign Office I had to advise the Overseas and Defence Committee of the Cabinet (OD) whether or not to permit the export of British Aerospace's Hawk aircraft to Iraq. It was an attractive and lucrative sale which would be worth £1 billion initially and up to £3 billion over time, with up to 230 sub-contractors benefiting.

The MoD were in favour of the sale, and although they fairly set out the objections to it, they believed it could be justified within the guidelines for arms sales. I did not. The trainer version of Hawk could easily be adapted to carry all kinds of weapons, including chemical weapons, and would have been a wicked instrument if used – as I feared it would have been – for internal repression of Iraq's Kurds. Nor was I alone in that fear. MPs including Labour's Ann Clwyd and Jeremy Corbyn had already focused attention on human rights in Iraq, and had been well justified in doing so. I was clear that we should not sell Hawk trainers to Iraq, and warned Number 10 of the line I would take at OD.

Mrs Thatcher opened the discussion, as was her wont. She supported the argument she knew I was going to put, and no one in Cabinet said a word against her. There was no need. My recommendation was clear, and the Prime Minister's support was absolute. Everyone agreed that the sale should not go ahead. The Cabinet were not in favour of tyrants, or of selling weapons of repression to them. It was ironic that later we were to be accused of exporting arms to Iraq, since when Cabinet had the opportunity to do so it had refused.

Other issues were pressing for solution worldwide. The Soviet empire was collapsing. We had to consider aid for the new non-Communist government in Poland. We needed to re-establish relations with Argentina after the Falklands War. The Commonwealth Conference lay ahead, with inevitable ructions about South Africa. The European Community was gearing up for more integration. The Vietnamese boat people – 150,000 of them crowded into camps in Hong Kong, and still arriving – were a human as well as an international problem. Meanwhile three British citizens – Terry Waite, John McCarthy and Jackie Mann – had already been held hostage in Lebanon for over two thousand days.

For myself, the most immediate concern was a twenty-nation peace conference convened to discuss Cambodia and due to open in Paris on 30 July, less than a week after I had taken up office. Its primary objective was to prevent the Khmer Rouge, responsible under their murderous leader Pol Pot for the slaughter of untold numbers of Cambodians, from wielding any further power. The British were peripheral players in this drama, and had limited expectations of the outcome. But the conference, which of course marked my debut on the international scene, was an excellent introduction to the diplomatic circuit. Diplomacy is the oil that smoothes the movement of states from incompatible positions towards compromise. It has its own language, its own nuance. Stamina and patience are essential. Realism and oratory are both in demand, though frequently also in conflict. It has a fascination all its own if you can develop a high threshold of tolerance for frustration and – sometimes – hypocrisy in a worthy cause.

An essential component of any gathering of foreign ministers is bilateral discussion – that is, a meeting confined to two principals accompanied only by their top aides. At Paris, with my 'L' plates still fresh, I had two of significance.

The first was with Jim Baker, the US Secretary of State and a close ally of President Bush. I had not met him before, and I wished to resolve a dispute that was poisoning the atmosphere between our two countries over the Vietnamese boat people. More than thirty-one thousand had arrived in Hong Kong within the year, and around three hundred a day were sailing into the colony. Genuine refugees were being found homes around the world, but economic migrants, who were not refugees, were the nub of the problem. Camps had been set up to house them, but the conditions were wretched and worsening. Hong Kong could not cope. An international conference in Geneva had agreed that non-refugees should be returned home, but ducked the question of what to do with those who refused to do so. The British government believed that if we could not persuade economic migrants to return to Vietnam voluntarily, we would have no practical alternative but to return them by force. Hong Kong was demanding action this day, but the US wanted us to hold off.

It was a difficult meeting. Jim Baker was forceful and direct by nature, and our disagreements were expressed in plain English. I liked his approach, which I learned was typical of his exchanges with us – and of ours with him. Britain and America's community of interests and outlook generally made it possible to bypass diplomatic niceties and speedily deal with substance, and to some extent this was so now. Not entirely, however. We ended the meeting better informed about each other's reservations, but neither of us had changed his policy.

In Paris I also inherited from Geoffrey's diary a controversial meeting with Qian Qichen, the Chinese Foreign Minister. This was the first contact between the British and the Chinese since the bloody events in Beijing's Tiananmen Square only a few weeks earlier, when hundreds of pro-democracy student demonstrators were mown down or crushed beneath the wheels of Chinese army tanks. The brutality of the Chinese government's repressive action had shocked the whole world, but in particular the vulnerable inhabitants of Hong Kong, who were due to see their territory revert to Chinese sovereignty on 1 July 1997. The instrument of the transfer was the Joint Declaration signed by Margaret Thatcher and Geoffrey Howe in September 1984, and the target of much criticism and misunderstanding since. In fact, they had been negotiating from a position of hopeless weakness, since Britain's ninety-nine-year lease on the New Territories would expire on the legal date anyway, and it was widely believed that it would not be possible for Hong Kong and the Kowloon peninsula to remain British without the New Territories on the Chinese mainland. The only point at issue was whether the handover would take place with an agreement or without one. Whether the traditional open way of life in Hong Kong would be allowed to continue was thus entirely dependent on the goodwill of the Chinese government. Before Tiananmen Square it was possible to be optimistic. After it, trust was shattered. A mood of near despair gripped the territory. Its stock exchange fell 30 per cent, and business investment was held back. Against this background I felt that to refuse to meet the Chinese might win plaudits from the unthinking, but would in fact be no more than a piece of public-relations posturing that would remove any leverage we had to help Hong Kong. So I met Qian Qichen.

I found him a modern diplomat. A plumpish man, twinkling, undemonstrative, reflective, but arguing from a strong brief, and very conscious that his policy was made in Beijing. He was quietly inflexible. He knew the strength of China's position in law over Hong Kong. Yet he also recognised the damage the Tiananmen Square massacre had done to his country abroad. Our meeting was civilised and relatively straightforward. Although sharp differences were registered between us, we readily identified a way ahead and established a dialogue that was to continue – albeit uncomfortably from time to time – right up to the handover in 1997. None of this, however, deflected the short-term criticism my decision to meet him provoked in the press.

What struck me at the time about this relatively unimportant episode was the extent to which governments must sometimes do good by stealth. If I had stated publicly some of my reasons for agreeing to the meeting, I would have raised more fears than I quelled. Would people have been reassured to hear me say that our anxiety to restore world confidence in Hong Kong was in order to stave off financial paralysis, or would it have helped to bring about precisely that paralysis? Similarly, if I had said I wished to prevent the Chinese army from misbehaving in Hong Kong as they had done in Tiananmen Square, would that have reassured Hong Kong's inhabitants, or the reverse? And would not such undiplomatic public musings have put at risk any worthwhile dialogue with China, as well as damaging British business interests? With these thoughts in my mind I returned from Paris and began to read myself seriously into my Foreign Office brief. I had no doubt that I could master the job of foreign secretary, but I was acutely aware of how poorly prepared by experience I was for this role. Once more I had a tremendous amount to learn.

As the summer parliamentary recess began I returned to Finings to pore over briefing papers, until Tristan Garel-Jones suggested I decamped with my family to his house in Spain, a beautiful property on the plain beneath the Gredos mountains which would provide perfect peace in lovely weather. 'It's very quiet,' said Tristan. 'You can sit in the shade and work and everyone else can get a suntan. I'm not going – it's too hot for me in August.' I accepted gladly, and went with Norma, Elizabeth and James, Robert Atkins, the MP for South Ribble, his wife Dulcie and their two children, and a suitcase full of briefings.

From dawn to dusk, interrupted only by meals, the occasional chat, cricket scores from home, early-evening gin and tonic, and Robert complaining about the heat (it was indeed *very* hot), I read and read and read. Never had I crammed so hard, as I absorbed the patterns of Britain's relations with – and interests in – every part of the world. Fortunately for me, I have always been a fast reader, taking in the words in chunks rather than lines; on an ordinary holiday I get through at least a novel a day. Now, as the complex jigsaw came together, I became more and more enthusiastic about the opportunity I had been given. I so enjoyed reading myself into the new subject that the days flew by, and the joy of learning, the sense that it had a real purpose and that it was widening my horizons, was so great that, for the only time in my life, I rather regretted not having gone to university. I think I would have enjoyed it.

Shortly after my return from Spain I joined the Prime Minister in a 'mini-summit' at Chequers with President Mitterrand of France and his Foreign Minister, Roland Dumas. My talks with Roland were a sideshow, but they highlighted disagreements between the UK and France over social policy and European monetary union (EMU) that were to grow over the years. The French favoured a European social policy. We did not. I believed that European involvement would increase regulation, drive up costs and raise unemployment. I also believed it was for the British Parliament to decide upon such issues in Britain. These became familiar themes for me in future years, but were never accepted by the French.

Further differences were also obvious over the Delors Report on how the European Community could move to economic and monetary union. The full implications of Delors were still being debated, but the thrust was clear, and was unwelcome to the British government on economic and political grounds. I told Dumas, 'Apart from the desirability of a single currency, the problems of persuading public and parliamentary opinion would be acute.' For good measure I added that a single central bank was alien to our tradition of having interest rates set by the chancellor of the exchequer.

But these differences were not matters for immediate decision, and the five hours of talks were a success both at my level and between the two heads of government. The Prime Minister and President Mitterrand were very different characters, and it was enlivening to watch them in tandem. Both were unmistakable representatives of their nations: François Mitterrand could only have been a Frenchman, and Margaret Thatcher an Englishwoman. For that reason it was a fascinating contrast. Each performed in turn while the other watched admiringly and waited to get back to centre stage. It was not so much a meeting as a flirtation, which they both clearly enjoyed. Mitterrand was supposed to have said that the Prime Minister had '*les yeux de Caligula et la bouche de Marilyn Monroe*'. Years later, when I put this to him, he denied it, but it seemed in character, and having seen them together at the time, brilliantly apt.

Where they disagreed they circled one another warily, but did not follow the disagreement to a conclusion. When the Prime Minister set out our objections to the Social Chapter she did so crisply, making it clear that she saw it as an attempt to drag industry's costs in other European countries up to German levels. When the President responded he went out of his way to say that, while he favoured the Charter, he did not have the same goals as Germany. Thus was confrontation between Britain and France avoided by a mutual expression of disapproval of the Germans. It was like watching two master chefs taking turns to carve up the same piece of meat. These exchanges served their purpose on the day, but only at a price. I was to learn later that Helmut Kohl was well aware of such exchanges, and that they caused real damage to our relationship with Germany.

Then came the conference season, always in autumn. The first to concern me was the UN General Assembly (UNGA) in September, then the Conservative Party Conference at Blackpool in October, and finally the Commonwealth Heads of Government Meeting (CHOGM – 'Chog-um' to everyone at the Foreign Office), held that year in the Malaysian capital Kuala Lumpur.

The UNGA is a massive foreign-policy jamboree where representatives from all over the world come together to express their views. Paradoxically, with few exceptions, their speeches are ignored by the world media, but for diplomats they set out in order of urgency each country's hopes and fears. My speech contained a good deal of standard foreign-policy fare – although I had to fight hard for tough passages on the internal situation in China – and also some personal matters that I felt were important. One concerned the drugs trade.

Years earlier, during my Latin American tour as a member of the Whips' Office, I had visited Colombia. Near the British Embassy in Bogotá I met some men in fatigues displaying weapons and devices for use against drugs traffickers. They turned out to be members of the British Army sent to help the Colombians in their fight against this lethal trade. I now offered to increase that help.

I also pleased the Africans with a lengthy passage on South Africa. 'Apartheid cannot survive and does not deserve to survive,' I said, 'It is not something to be tolerated or to be patient with. It is something to oppose constantly and comprehensively.' I not only believed this, I also thought it might sweeten the atmosphere at CHOGM the following month. I was wrong – it did not. But a scholarship scheme I announced for black South Africans was well received.

One of my earliest actions as foreign secretary had been to agree to open talks – led, on our side, by Sir Crispin Tickell, our Permanent Representative at the United Nations – with the Argentinians in Madrid. These had made some progress in re-establishing our still shaky relationship following the Falklands War, and I sought to carry it forward by meeting the Argentinian Foreign Minister during my time in New York. I also met Tariq Aziz, the Iraqi Foreign Minister, in an attempt to secure the release of a British citizen who had been jailed in Baghdad. Aziz attempted to link the case with that of an Iraqi in London who had been convicted of murder. I told him that British politicians could not – and would not – interfere with our legal system. He seemed pretty baffled by this. Years later Robin Cook, as Labour's shadow Foreign Secretary, mistakenly claimed that my meeting with Aziz had been 'secret'. This had the effect of suggesting that we had been discussing illegal arms sales. It took the officials on whom I was obliged to call most of a Saturday searching through files to provide the information to refute this mischief.

Other bilaterals left their own memories. While a further meeting with Qian Qichen had been unproductive but friendly, one with the Israeli Foreign Minister Moshe Arens was less friendly. I asked some questions about Israeli policy which offended him. 'I'm not in a court of law – I don't have to answer your questions,' he said. I wasn't seeking a row with him, and in fact spent much of my time later at Number 10 improving

Anglo–Israeli relationships. But this was a tricky start. The Hungarian Foreign Minister was amusing, with anecdote upon anecdote to show that the European Commission's bureaucracy was worse than the Russians'.

One meeting was unexpected. I had intended to invite the Egyptian Foreign Minister for a bilateral at the United Nations Plaza Hotel. Unfortunately one of our officials misread the telephone number in the Directory of Delegations, and invited the Foreign Minister of Ethiopia. As our relations with Ethiopia were decidedly chilly at the time, this gentleman was startled but accepted immediately. When he was met at the lift by Crispin Tickell and Stephen Wall, the penny dropped immediately. 'Oh God,' said Crispin. 'It's the Ethiopian. I know him. It's the wrong man.'

Our unwelcome guest was shuttled into a side room while I was given a quick primer on Ethiopia. He was then hustled in for a twenty-minute meeting from which he departed with a look of extreme bewilderment. A few years before, I am told, the Foreign Office summoned an equally bewildered East German Ambassador to a meeting, in place of his West German counterpart.

It was at the Conservative Party Conference in Blackpool in October that I emerged from relative obscurity as Chief Secretary of the Treasury to the full glare of my new position. This was not the first time I had addressed the conference, but it was my debut as a Cabinet minister. Anti-European feeling in the party was becoming stronger. One young girl got tremendous applause when she said that, at the age of nineteen, she knew more about what was good for the UK than a sixty-year-old fuddy-duddy like Jacques Delors. The pro-Europe former Home Secretary Leon Brittan, then Vice-Chairman of the European Commission, who was only half-attending on the platform, joined in the applause, but I don't think he can have heard her remarks. If the Prime Minister had announced that she was taking us out of the EEC the majority of those in the hall would have cheered her to the echo.

It was against this background that I put forward the government's European policy. Here is what I said, well before I was prime minister, and in view of all that has taken place since I make no apology for repeating it:

> I am not someone who believes in Europe right or wrong. We must judge it on its merits. But a clear-eyed look at Britain's national interest shows beyond doubt that we have benefited

> from Community membership ... Fifty years ago, Europe was
> full of young people with knapsacks going off to fight. Now it
> is full of young people with haversacks going off on holiday.
> That is a better Europe ...

Today, I would not change a word of that speech. Nor would I change
what I said about economic and monetary union.

> It means different things to different people ... So far, the
> discussion has centred on only one set of ideas. They would
> involve an end to national currencies, to independent national
> central banks and to national control over fiscal policy ... We
> can't accept these ideas but there are other ideas to discuss and
> we will put them forward.

We did, but alas, as time has shown, we were too late.

At CHOGM in Kuala Lumpur later that month, South Africa and the
question of sanctions were the main sources of conflict, as we knew they
would be. The UK opposed sanctions, believing them to be counter-
productive. Everyone else supported them. There was no natural meeting
point.

Margaret Thatcher tried to head off the expected trouble. She met Dr
Mahathir, the Malaysian Prime Minister and Chairman of the Conference,
on the eve of the first session, urging that South Africa should not dominate
the discussion. Her hopes, never strong, were not realised. Mahathir's
silence was more expressive than any reply.

On the first morning of conference, Margaret Thatcher – incensed at
remarks made by other heads of government about South Africa at the
formal opening – quoted Archbishop Desmond Tutu, a figure known
worldwide as an opponent of apartheid, on the perverse effect of sanctions.
It was an effective, almost irresistible, debating point, but it was very
provocative. Battle was joined. As the conference proceeded there was no
sign of a conciliatory mood on policy towards South Africa, and a drafting
committee of foreign ministers was set up to paper over our differences
and agree a communiqué.

It met on 20 October, and was fairly bloody. There was dispute on
nearly every sentence, and much of the discussion was emotional. I was
utterly isolated, and was fighting on two fronts: to keep out the prejudicial
wording proposed by others, and to retain the British view in the com-

muniqué against opposition from every other foreign minister. The meeting became very bad-tempered despite all that Joe Clark, the Foreign Minister of Canada and Chairman of the group, did to keep it in order. The disagreement with the African and Asian foreign ministers was blunt, but the clashes with Gareth Evans from Australia were altogether rougher. We had clashed pre-conference when he had tried to bounce me into a meeting with leaders of the African National Congress, when our policy at that time was not to meet them. I had declined, and he had been very sore about it. 'You've got your script, but you've turned up for the wrong bloody play,' he yelled at one point.

In the drafting group our positions on sanctions were diametrically opposed. As each line was fought over the atmosphere became more sulphurous, and it spread to involve the other participants. When I queried the title of the Southern African section of the communiqué ('Southern Africa – The Way Forward'), Gareth said, 'Oh, I suppose you want to call it "Southern Africa – The Way Backwards".' There was a lot more gratuitous and sometimes rather light-hearted abuse. At one stage Gareth was so infuriated by an amendment from the Zimbabwean Foreign Minister, Nathan Shamiyurira, that he threw his draft to the floor, exclaiming, 'It's not the f***ing Koran.' I swear the Muslims went pale. The Malaysian Foreign Minister drew the edge of his hand across his throat, and for a few moments I enjoyed the luxury of having some allies.

Eventually at 1 a.m., after sixteen hours of hand-to-hand verbal combat, a text was agreed in which, in four separate places, I set out Britain's disagreement with the majority view. Reasonably satisfied that it was the best we could have done, I went to bed; but not before a piece of foolishness I later regretted. Tired and weary, I was overheard saying that Gareth Evans's behaviour was 'an example of the Les Patterson school of diplomacy'. Inevitably this was picked up and heavily featured in Australia. The remark was unfair, because in fact Gareth had made many skilful drafting amendments that helped mask our conflicting positions.

Over breakfast the next morning with Patrick Wright, Patrick Fairweather, the Under-Secretary for Commonwealth Affairs, and Stephen Wall, I reviewed the outcome. I suggested that some of the black African states who benefited from trade with South Africa were being hypocritical in calling themselves the 'front-line states', and that we should tackle them about it. The two Patricks stared thoughtfully at their cornflakes. Stephen, who knew me better than them, simply remarked that if I did, 'they'll think you're completely loopy'. He did not believe in holding back if he saw trouble ahead.

That day the text hammered out by the foreign ministers was placed before the heads of government for agreement. Some members of the Commonwealth felt that it was not severe enough on South Africa, and said so, but Margaret Thatcher proposed that it should be adopted without amendment, and this duly took place.

These proceedings were my first direct experience of the unbridgeable gap between the UK and the rest of the Commonwealth over South Africa, and I found them very frustrating. I loathed apartheid, but did not believe sanctions were an effective way of hastening its end. I thought they were mere window-dressing – and harmful with it; they simply hurt the poorest black South Africans. 'I want to satisfy empty black African bellies in South Africa, not liberal consciences outside it,' I said at a press briefing.

The Prime Minister was a veteran of such disputes, and was increasingly fed up by them. She approved of my reservations on the agreed statement but, as I learned later, felt I had missed one – namely the statement that sanctions were not intended to be punitive. I had accepted this because I thought it was an important admission by the other Commonwealth states which we could use as an argument against any proposal from them for *comprehensive* sanctions. Margaret Thatcher did not know my reasoning, since she did not ask me about it. I did not know of her reservations, since she didn't tell me about them.

Neither did I know that she had asked Charles Powell to draft a second statement, making plain our views as distinct from our reservations about the majority view. I was content with that. Charles set to in robust fashion. The heads of government had retired to the island retreat of Langkawi – reports came back that Margaret spent her lunchtime feeding Benazir Bhutto's fifteen-month-old baby, while Denis complained of the cold (the temperature was over 100 degrees Fahrenheit) and repaired to the bar for comfort.

When we saw Charles's text, Stephen Wall added some preliminary sentences to stress areas in which the communiqué made progress, and on that basis I was content for it to go forward. I was unaware of the dispute that had taken place on Langkawi over the foreign ministers' draft, or that, in the words of Brian Mulroney, Prime Minister of Canada, our

Commonwealth partners had 'watered their wine' to accommodate Margaret Thatcher. Nor, in my innocence, did I realise the extent to which the issuing of a separate statement breached normal procedure. Even if I had, I would have seen no reason why we should not express our own view. I did, though, see the risk that the second statement would be seen as a rift between myself and the Prime Minister, and for that reason asked for it to be issued as a joint statement.

The statement provoked two huge rows. The first, soon disposed of, was in the Heads of Government Meeting. 'How could Mrs Thatcher sign an agreement at 5 p.m. and repudiate it at 6 p.m.?' was the charge. Our view was that we stood by the agreement, but had added to it the reasons for our open and stated dissent to part of it. In fact, this irritable but perfectly straightforward squabble between heads of government suited everyone, because it enabled all concerned to peddle their views to their own domestic audiences. They all saw the advantage of that, and did so with gusto.

The second row had wider domestic impact. I had briefed the British press in very upbeat fashion about the communiqué I had agreed. They were grumpy and disgruntled that a novice foreign secretary had robbed them of a spectacular row at a boring conference. Unfortunately Bernard Ingham's initial briefing of the press was done in a rush – like the rest of us, he was catching up with the new draft – and delivered with characteristic Inghamesque brutality. It involved him more or less reading out a confidential letter from Charles reporting on the discussion on Langkawi, and recording the Prime Minister saying she did not much like the foreign ministers' text.

This was taken as a criticism of me, and was manna from heaven for the press. Ever eager for drama, they presented it as Mrs Thatcher disowning my negotiations, slapping me down and embarrassing me. The new boy on the block was being put in his place. There was some flavour of this in questions put to me at my press conference, but since I knew the Prime Minister did not intend to undermine me I did not allow it to worry me.

As I flew home, a day earlier than Mrs Thatcher since I had questions to answer in the Commons, I reflected on my first three months as foreign secretary. I was tired but reasonably satisfied. I thought I had made some solid gains. I was now infinitely better informed on foreign policy. I was comfortable and confident with bilaterals, and prepared to take on all comers. I had re-established relations with China after Tiananmen Square and was moving towards doing so with Argentina. I had staked out a pragmatic position on Europe and was getting the measure of how the EEC worked. I had weathered difficult confrontations at the Commonwealth Conference and felt the substance had gone well.

When I arrived at the Spelthorne Suite at Heathrow, however, I realised I was being complacent. The press were playing up the supposed row at CHOGM for all it was worth and more; the damage being done was evident. I licked my wounds and prepared to be more careful the next time Margaret and I travelled abroad together.

But there was to be no next time. After ninety-four days my brief tenure as foreign secretary would come to an end.

# CHAPTER SEVEN

# An Ambition Fulfilled

O N 26 OCTOBER 1989, after the Prime Minister had delivered her Commons statement on the Kuala Lumpur conference, she turned to me on the front bench and invited me to join her for tea in her room behind the Speaker's Chair. I assumed she wanted to make peace after the fuss over the foreign ministers' communiqué. Though she never apologised, she could be extraordinarily friendly to colleagues to whom she had caused trouble, sometimes treating them to an informal chat about politics in the stream-of-consciousness way she so enjoyed when she was relaxing. This, however, was to be no such cosy occasion. She had a bombshell to drop.

We had no sooner settled on the sofas in her room than she said without preamble: 'Nigel is going to resign and I might want you as chancellor.'

This was startling news, with political implications which shocked me even as the drama stirred my blood. 'When?' I asked.

'Today,' she said.

So far so clear, but the question in my mind was 'Why?' The strains between the Prime Minister and her chancellor were well enough known. Equally, however, I had noted in Cabinet how she generally supported Nigel, and sometimes even deferred to him – behaviour so out of character that it was, perhaps, an attempt at peacemaking, though I had not viewed it as such. She certainly never treated him in the cavalier, intolerant and often discourteous style she displayed towards Geoffrey Howe – whose forbearance, in its own way, was as remarkable as her rudeness. In the Commons, where not long before she had described Nigel Lawson's position as 'unassailable', he was accepted as just that, a great figure in the party, one of the long marchers, a fully-paid-up member of the Radical Tendency, and the Chancellor who, a mere eighteen months earlier, had been practically walking on water. Almost nobody, therefore, believed he really would resign – the Prime Minister and myself included.

I learned later that Nigel had demanded that the Prime Minister sack Sir Alan Walters, her old mentor who had returned in May for a second term as her economic adviser. I had never met Walters, but I did know that he had long been undermining the Chancellor in private. His contempt for Nigel was undisguised, and was a common topic of conversation in both the City and Fleet Street. Now he had broken cover with an article in the *Financial Times* ridiculing as 'half-baked' a line of policy Nigel was known to favour and the Prime Minister to oppose, namely joining the European Exchange Rate Mechanism (ERM), which would keep the value of sterling within pre-agreed limits against other European currencies. It is true that the piece had originally appeared in an American journal eighteen months before, but this second airing was accompanied by a note making it clear that Walters had in no way changed his view.

This situation would have been impossible for any chancellor, and Nigel was taunted on account of it both in Parliament and outside. Who was the real chancellor, Lawson or Walters? Who had the Prime Minister's ear, Lawson or Walters? With whom did she agree? Sadly, the answer to that last question was evident. She agreed with Walters, and for a proud man like Nigel this was intolerable. He demanded that Walters be sent packing, and he was right to do so. But by bluntly stating 'He goes or I go,' he placed Margaret in an equally cruel impasse – even if, by appointing Walters, it was of her making. She agreed with Walters and not with her chancellor. She could not back away from that, nor did she wish to. If she sacked Walters it would be clear she had done so with a pistol at her head. She had relied on him far too long for his departure, if it occurred, to be seen as anything other than a climbdown. She remembered the Madrid summit of June 1989, when Nigel and Geoffrey Howe had combined to compel her to agree to join the ERM when certain conditions were met. To capitulate and sack Walters would have destroyed her authority.

All the elements of disaster were assembled, and there was no Willie Whitelaw to mediate. The Prime Minister and the Chancellor had dug themselves into positions which allowed no compromise. For the moment at least, Margaret Thatcher was still the stronger. She refused to dismiss her adviser, and in the afternoon of Thursday, 26 October Nigel Lawson resigned. Ironically, his resignation was swiftly followed by that of Alan Walters.

Recalling the period today, my lack of foreknowledge of these events strikes me as odd. The signals were there, if only we had decoded them. Perhaps I should have done. It was clear to all that Nigel was no longer working in harness with Margaret; by shadowing the exchange rate of the deutschmark and pressing, repeatedly, for our entry into the ERM, he was setting out his own economic stall in competition with his prime minister. Indeed, with Geoffrey Howe he had put his position on the line even before the Madrid summit. Their differences with the Prime Minister became all the greater as the economic clouds gathered in the first half of 1989.

This discontent intermittently boiled over in public. In June 1989, a month after Alan Walters's return to Number 10, Nigel announced in a television interview that the length of his stay at the Treasury – already, at six years, a near-record – 'is a matter partly for the Prime Minister and partly for me and it will be resolved in the fullness of time'. Pressed on whether he would stay in office if asked in the coming reshuffle, he could only reply, 'You'll have to wait and see.'

These were not the words of an 'unassailable' chancellor. Indeed, in the reshuffle that followed, Margaret gave thought to moving Nigel. Even so, I was not alone in my surprise at the events of October 1989. The Prime Minister was just as stunned. There had seemed to be no differences that could not and would not be best worked out with Nigel in the government rather than outside it. Only later, when I had experience of the chancellorship, did I realise just how difficult his position had been. His departure was particularly tragic because he and Margaret agreed on almost everything apart from the management of the pound. They had dominated the government machine and, when working together, had done much to restore the British economy to vitality.

Nigel is unlucky to be remembered as the author of an unsustainable boom, for his radical policies had, with his predecessor Geoffrey Howe, reshaped a ramshackle inheritance into a vigorous economy. His achievements in areas such as privatisation, tax reform and the Public Sector Borrowing Requirement (PSBR) laid some of the foundations for the steady recovery of the 1990s. And, like all the best chancellors, he resisted the temptation to panic in the face of cries from the opposition, the press, the backbenches and, at times, his own prime minister.

After Margaret's bombshell I returned to the Foreign Office and phoned Norma. She was at Finings preparing to go to a constituency event. 'Oh, no,' she said. 'Another upheaval just as we were beginning to enjoy our selves. But it is the job you always wanted.' And it was.

Stephen Wall, my Private Secretary, came in to see me. He knew I had been with the Prime Minister and sat down, pad in hand, for a read-out. I told him I might be leaving the Foreign Office, and he went white, believing the Kuala Lumpur row had escalated. Knowing how irritated I was by the criticism that I was only at the Foreign Office to do the Prime Minister's bidding, he feared the worst. When I explained what had happened he was relieved on my behalf, but also aghast at the political implications.

Stephen and I had worked well together, and our partnership was about to end. He would have a new foreign secretary – the third in under a hundred days. 'Careless,' I suggested, 'to lose two foreign secretaries in such a short time.'

He grinned but, being the excellent civil servant he was, he was already thinking ahead and calculating who my successor might be.

'Douglas would be the best choice,' I said.

'Is he going to be?' asked Stephen.

'I've no idea,' I replied, 'but I'll do all I can to see that he is.'

Stephen didn't comment. For nearly two hours we paced around, considering the options, and regretting what might have been with our plans for Foreign Office reform, reliving the events of the past three months and waiting to see if the phone would ring. It did.

When I arrived at Number 10, Margaret was in her study on the first floor, tense but composed. At times of crisis officials close to prime ministers throw a protective girdle around them. Margaret knew that a storm was brewing, and her remarks were already beginning to take on the character of the response she would make in public to Nigel's departure. This was a sure sign of preparation for battle. She often convinced herself in private in order to be convincing in public. She told me that Alan Walters would also be resigning, thus ensuring that I did not have to raise this sensitive matter.

I accepted the chancellorship, reflecting that in this same room, only a short time before, I had tried to talk Margaret out of appointing me foreign secretary. I had thought that promotion premature. Now, a mere ninety-four days later, I was again reluctant to accept a glittering prize. I remember thinking gloomily that few people could ever have felt as I did at both such moments. Yet again political Christmas had come early for me and I was to have the job I most coveted, but under the most unhappy circumstances. The Chancellor had resigned because, despite his persistence, he had been prevented from pursuing the economic policy he thought right for Britain. Indeed, it was the only coherent policy on offer. Despite carping at Nigel for wanting to join the ERM, Margaret had no alternative policy of her own to put in place. I was now stepping into the destabilising policy vacuum that had been created.

The Prime Minister and I discussed the politics of Nigel's resignation. 'It's unnecessary. He's being silly,' was the view she expressed, but I don't think she really believed it. Sometimes this remarkable woman could seem very vulnerable, and she did then. I thought she was close to tears at one moment, and briefly took her hand. I would have offered her any support she needed. She seemed to be trying to convince herself that he was resigning because the economy was going wrong and he didn't know what to do. That seemed to me highly improbable; Nigel Lawson was a battler, not a shirker. We talked briefly about the economy and inflation, but no mention was made by either of us of European monetary union or the ERM. It was not the moment.

As for myself, I had begun to enjoy the Foreign Office. Only later were malicious tongues to say that in fact I had loathed it. And yet here I was being moved before I had had a chance to make any mark on policy, or to leave any lasting legacy. Even worse, the fact that I was being moved so swiftly and in a crisis meant that the canard that I was the Prime Minister's alter ego would follow me from the Foreign Office to the Treasury. This was no good, either for me or the Prime Minister.

The offer of the chancellorship did put me in a position to argue for Douglas Hurd to succeed me at the Foreign Office, and I did so. I seem to recall the Prime Minister wistfully expressing a preference for Cecil Parkinson, but officials assure me that he had been ruled out of contention. Tom King also got a mention. In any event, she conceded readily that Douglas was the obvious choice. Allowing yourself to be persuaded to do something you intend to do anyway is a useful ploy if you want to win over the persuader. Margaret may have been playing that game – as prime ministers sometimes do – but whatever her motives, the right decision was made, and Douglas, formerly a career diplomat, aware of other countries' problems but no pushover, got the job for which he was so exceptionally well qualified.

Once Douglas's appointment was agreed, Kenneth Baker joined us and the Prime Minister briefed him on the changes. As chairman of the party he would have to bear the brunt of the inevitable media onslaught. He rallied quickly from the shock and was practical and supportive. Kenneth's great strength was his presentational skill. As he braced himself, I reflected that if the Prime Minister had sent Beelzebub himself to the Foreign Office, Ken, with a straight face, would have presented his appointment to the media as that of a man with a wide experience of dealing with problems in a warm climate. Ken, thank God, was without shame.

At the Treasury rumours that 'John M' was to be the new chancellor were causing confusion. Did the 'M' stand for Major, MacGregor, or Moore? No one knew, but bets were struck. At least they could console themselves with the knowledge that all three Ms had a Treasury background. A ripple was caused when rumour suggested, mistakenly, that the choice was John MacGregor.

When I arrived it was like a homecoming, with a warm welcome extended in an atmosphere of expectation. But this was a crisis, and preparations had to be made in case measures to deal with it were needed. Luckily, the Treasury enjoys a crisis, having had a good deal of experience of them. The immediate decisions were straightforward. I did not wish to change ministers and precipitate a wider reshuffle. I was keen to keep Andrew Tyrie, Warwick Lightfoot and Judith Chaplin, Nigel's special advisers, all of whom I knew well. They were a good mixture. Andrew – known as 'Fang' because he liked to get his teeth into issues – had a rigorous intellect and was relentless in pursuit of his preferred policy; Judith was more detached but equally hawkish; while Warwick was bouncy and an excellent technician. I was also delighted to have John Gieve, a Treasury high-flyer, as my Private Secretary.

It was clear that we needed to reassure the markets that policy would not change, and a statement was issued to make it clear. I decided not to raise interest rates, despite pressure from colleagues and officials to do so. I was told this would demonstrate 'firmness of purpose'. More cynical voices suggested, 'Put them up now and blame the crisis. Bring them down later and take the credit.' But such a move would have been wrong. It would have added to the political turmoil and harmed a business sector that was already crying out for lower interest rates.

I telephoned Nigel to express my regret that he had gone. It was a brief and friendly conversation, but uncomfortable for us both. He was a little withdrawn, obviously tired, and probably, though irrationally, hurt that the post he had held for so long should have been filled so swiftly – and by one of his former junior ministers. I too was embarrassed, believing (though Nigel never hinted at such a thought, and disliked travel) that he would have liked to be appointed foreign secretary instead of myself earlier in the year – and now here I was taking over as chancellor. But none of this surfaced as, with true English decorum, we both said what needed to be said. Nigel wished me well. I silently and sincerely hoped that the manner of his departure would not, in the end, mar his satisfaction in his achievements.

Yet this man, with whom I had enjoyed working, would inevitably be bruised and hurt. The parliamentary party would be split and angry at such a damaging public dispute, and would take sides. A great deal of trouble and unpleasantness would follow. It soon did, and we gravely underestimated its extent.

The following day I was due to speak at a party meeting in Northampton, and I knew that my remarks would set the tone for future policy. The economic inheritance was dismal. The late-1980s boom had ignited inflation, set us on the road to recession, and destroyed even the strategy by which the economy was managed. I decided to concentrate on the objectives of policy rather than the means of achieving them. The principal objective was the destruction of inflation, an insidious demon, always waiting in the wings, that I had every reason to loathe. Inflation is disastrous and morally corrosive, and it destroys lives. Those who can best protect themselves or even gain from it are often those who have most, and the losers are those who have least. It is a tax on the poor and a tax-free benefit for the rich. While my own family's financial hardships were brought about by other causes, I had had enough experience of inflation's effects on neighbours and friends to make my detestation of it personal as well as theoretical.

I woke early the following morning and began making notes for the speech. Base rate now stood at 15 per cent, and I knew that defeating inflation would be a long and painful haul. Time after time, rising prices had wrecked the economy and led to a slowdown in growth or a full-blown recession. And each time, the cries for help from business – and the instant demands of politics – had led government after government to engineer a premature reflation that had eased the pain in the short term but led to a repeat of the problems later on.

We had been down this dreary path often, and it was a route I was determined to avoid taking. This time we had to kill inflation even if the cost was high. It would be immoral to shirk the task, and we didn't. But the measures would hurt. Many businesses and individuals would suffer, and the government would certainly not have an early recovery in the polls.

I decided to signal my intentions unequivocally. 'If it isn't hurting, it isn't working' seemed to me to sum up what lay ahead, and I made that the theme of the speech. I also made it clear that I was in favour of a firm exchange rate for sterling, and did not agree with letting it fall. The ghost of Alan Walters had to be exorcised and the markets needed to know that I meant what I said about inflation.

My call to arms was well received by the audience in Northampton, and I drew from it in my first speech in the House as chancellor a few days later. I emphasised that we must eliminate inflation, and confirmed that I believed that membership of the ERM would help to achieve that. If the Prime Minister winced, it wasn't noticed by those in the Chamber. Nor had she cause to, for I confirmed the mantra of the Madrid conditions. I also paid a deserved tribute to Nigel.

Though my tribute was sincere, our instincts were not always the same. I was concerned about the trade gap and had said so in speaking as chief secretary, whereas Nigel wasn't. Nigel favoured an independent Bank of England, and I didn't. Nigel had been prepared to shadow the deutschmark, while I had become convinced that this gave us all the disadvantages of ERM membership without the advantages.

Nor were those the only differences. Nigel, I felt, underestimated the importance of manufacturing; I worried about its decline. Nigel had cut back capital allowances; I was prepared to look at paying some of them in the first year. On this last point I was later convinced that some of Nigel's policy was right and mine wrong. When I looked at the case for reshaping capital allowances I received a Lawsonian lecture from Judith Chaplin and Andrew Tyrie on the folly of this. To my regret they convinced me.

None of these differences diminished my admiration for Nigel as chancellor. He had misjudged inflation in the late 1980s because indicators such as soaring house prices were misread. As a result he left office with inflation rising sharply. Some of this was due to his unwillingness to let the exchange rate take the strain, or to compensate elsewhere. Even so, he did not deserve Nick Ridley's harsh judgement that 'He knew the economy was going badly wrong and he knew he was entirely and solely responsible.' Nigel, like the rest of us, underestimated the depth of the recession to come in Britain and internationally, and believed he could see it out. The argument that he 'got out just in time' only came to look plausible much later.

In the first few weeks of my chancellorship my approach to inflation was well received, but months later when the policy really got to grips with the beast it was thought to be callous. Everyone paid lip-service to the principle of cutting inflation, but the hard-edged policies to do so were another matter entirely. But to me, bringing down inflation was pivotal, my constant objective and not an optional extra – and later this was the primary reason for our entry into the ERM. Nigel Lawson had advocated entry as early as 1985, securing the support at the time of Geoffrey Howe, Willie Whitelaw, Leon Brittan and Norman Tebbit. But Margaret – reinforced by Alan Walters's arguments – said no.

Had there been another route open to us, endorsed, as ERM membership was, by business groups and commentators, I would have been delighted. But there was not. The ERM offered the lodestar we needed and, for all the finger-pointing after 'Black Wednesday' in 1992 (see Chapter 14), it worked. I disagree with those who say that inflation would have been tamed successfully by our interest-rate policy alone. But that lay ahead. Now, as chancellor, the problem before me was clear, even if the solution was not. Economic policy was falling apart and needed a new anchor.

Uncertainty over EMU and the ERM was rising, and so was the political temperature within the Conservative Party. The dispute over exchange-rate policy still had the potential to tear the government apart. Europe was a ticking time-bomb. Within days of my appointment as chancellor, Geoffrey Howe, the Deputy Prime Minister – in what Margaret Thatcher later described as a speech of 'calculated malice' – stressed that we should honour our obligations to Europe over the ERM. Yet another Cabinet split was signalled. Nigel's resignation speech attacked the Prime Minister's whole style of government, reflecting the quiet opinion of a growing number of Tories.

I was also confronted with more immediate problems. The Autumn Statement announcing public spending allocations was only weeks away. The budget would have to be framed in very constrained conditions, and no real work had yet been done on it. And the Community Charge was a millstone that could not be shed, so great was the Prime Minister's commitment to it. Like every minister I had to make a conscious effort to avoid infuriating Margaret by referring to it as the 'Poll Tax'. I didn't always succeed.

On the Sunday following Nigel's resignation the Prime Minister gave an unconvincing interview on *Walden*, the influential political programme hosted by Brian Walden, a former Labour MP. Nigel appeared on the programme a week later. They flatly contradicted one another while the Labour Party looked on in delight. As Margaret and Nigel set out their different interpretations of events it was an early illustration of the total disregard for the wider Conservative Party interest that was to become commonplace where European policy was concerned, and was to place the government on the rack.

In Cabinet one of my first tasks was to present a paper Nigel Lawson had prepared on 'competing currencies', which was an alternative to the Delors plan for EMU. Whereas the Delors plan was prescriptive and involved the arbitrary abolition of traditional currencies, Nigel's paper advocated a gradualist, market-led coordination of economic policies across Europe. It was ingenious and inventive – and Cabinet readily accepted it – but even at the time, I think, it was clear that it was never going to work, because in a competition between the pound and the deutschmark, the German currency, with its greater depth, liquidity and credibility, was always going to win.

The scheme received a mixed reception when I presented it at my first 'ECOFIN', the EU's regular monthly meeting of economic and finance ministers, on 13 November 1989. Unfortunately it came too late, and was seen in Europe as a wrecking tactic. The episode illustrated the alarm we felt over our European partners' continuing enthusiasm for a single European currency. EMU was revived in the mid-eighties by Hans-Dietrich Genscher, the German Foreign Minister, and his French counterpart, Roland Dumas.

It was then taken up by Jacques Delors, but would have got nowhere without strong German and French support. The 'competing currencies' proposal would not be the last time we tried to head off this Delors-inspired initiative, because of what we saw as its destructive power where our own economy was concerned. Nor was it the last time we were rebuffed.

Back in Britain, the party and the press were keen to learn what I intended to do. Their chance came two days later when, on 15 November, I delivered the Autumn Statement – my first substantial parliamentary appearance as chancellor since Nigel's resignation. The events of the previous month meant that rather more attention was paid to my performance than might normally have been the case, but at least the annual spending round, which culminated in the Statement, was a part of the Treasury's work I felt fully at home with. As chief secretary, I had worked with Nigel on his Statement. Now I delivered a package largely prepared by my successor in that job, Norman Lamont.

The forecasts in the Autumn Statement were the first acknowledgement that the economy was slowing down, and they attracted a good deal of attention. As it happened, the forecasts were wrong. It is notoriously difficult to make predictions when an economy is turning either to growth or recession, and most of the forecasts, although gloomier than many expected, were less gloomy than they should have been.

In the three weeks since my appointment I had had only a limited chance to put my mark on the Statement. But that didn't occur to many journalists, who told their readers that by boosting spending and predicting hard times ahead I had single-handedly broken with the Thatcher–Lawson tradition. In fact it was the economic situation which did the breaking, for most of the spending increases were involuntary, being required simply to keep services at their current level as demand grew. I had not gone off in a new direction, but simply responded to circumstances. Indeed, had Nigel not left, he would have delivered a Statement along similar lines. What's more, had he had his way on entry into the ERM when he first proposed it, the conditions I inherited might have been somewhat less dire.

The biggest increase in expenditure was on the NHS, and this was largely determined by the needs of the NHS reforms (see pages 107–8). Financing these reforms was later to be cited as an indication that I had uncorked public spending and thus inflation. In fact this expenditure helped to mitigate the effects of the subsequent recession. The further spirals in inflation resulted from the continuing fall in sterling and the inexorable upward rise in prices that was the legacy of the late-1980s boom.

At the time, the Autumn Statement was well received, politically and economically, but soon after it sterling again came under pressure as a result of political and economic events. A Conservative backbencher, Sir Anthony Meyer, roundly attacked Margaret Thatcher in the Queen's Speech debate after the State Opening of Parliament on 4 December. He announced the following day that if no one else challenged her leadership, then he would.

Tony Meyer was a loner, a fierce pro-European and a paternalist left-of-centre Tory. It was courageous of him to challenge a well-established prime minister with overwhelming parliamentary and national support, but everyone knew that his challenge would fail. And so it proved, as, after a cursory campaign, the Prime Minister romped home with 314 votes to thirty-three against, with twenty-four spoilt ballot papers and three abstentions. But the fact that there was a contest at all was significant. The challenge gave the markets a jolt, too. By late December sterling had fallen steadily to around DM2.72, thus damaging hopes of lower inflation and, as a result, of a reduction in interest rates.

The Autumn Statement was followed by renewed pressure for an increase in interest rates, which Norman Lamont, the Chief Secretary, supported. Economically, the case was finely balanced, but politically I thought there was no argument for it, and I refused. This was not because I subordinated interest-rate decisions to political considerations, but because given the mood in the markets and in Parliament an increase in rates would not have had the economic effects intended. It would add to the atmosphere of crisis, create political panic, ignite yet greater dissatisfaction in Parliament, and so rule out any good it might have done.

Margaret Thatcher knew that an increase would have been seen as the economic price to be paid for her political dispute with Nigel, so she naturally agreed with my decision wholeheartedly. In any event she wanted interest rates down, not up. It was ever thus in the latter years of her premiership – the anti-inflationary 'Iron Lady' is a myth.

Nonetheless, our working relationship at this time was very easy and relaxed. I was enjoying the Treasury and she was enjoying having a chancellor with whom she was comfortable. Our conversations were easy ones whereas hers and Nigel's were not. I was much more open with her than Nigel had been, and she was with me.

But there were differences of emphasis between us. While I thought membership of the Exchange Rate Mechanism would help our anti-inflation policy, Margaret shied away from it. Her instincts – and Alan Walters's arguments – had made her deeply hostile towards the ERM. Yet neither she nor anyone else was putting forward a serious alternative course of action, and I felt from the outset that she could be persuaded to enter if the decision to do so did not humiliate her.

EMU and the single currency were unpalatable to us both, and we agreed that we should oppose them, although we disagreed on how to do so. The Prime Minister simply wanted to say no. I knew this would be useless. It would not stop our partners going ahead, and would only deprive the UK of any influence over their plans. Margaret was dismissive, even scornful, of this argument. She did not grasp that I was not asking her to change her policy on the single currency – because I agreed with her on that – but to be more subtle in her opposition to it, and less dismissive of those colleagues who thought differently.

I saw also – though Margaret, I think, did not – the extent to which this policy dispute was hurting her with many in the party. It was not so much the policy itself as the dogmatic way she advocated it that was doing her such damage. She was in real danger. My pleas fell on deaf ears. She simply did not take the point. It was magnificent, but it was not politics, as events were to show within a year. In any event we did not begin to engage seriously on either the ERM or the single currency until the early spring of 1990.

Before that came my first budget. One of the attractions of being chancellor is the opportunity to deliver a budget. Iain Macleod once memorably remarked that 'Money is the root of all progress,' and he was right. For two years as chief secretary to the Treasury I had negotiated public spending allocations and learned that by releasing – or withholding – money it was possible to change political priorities. But in 1990 the options for making significant changes in the budget were grimly restricted. I was boxed in by the state of the economy.

This was brought home to me vividly in a letter I received from Nigel Lawson early in January 1990 offering some friendly advice for my first budget. The advice was good – even though it was uncomfortable. In essence, Nigel said: don't put up taxes and don't reduce them; don't believe the seductive line that higher taxes will deliver lower interest rates; don't reduce interest rates for some time; don't on any account increase the £30,000 limit for mortgage interest relief (a constant demand of Margaret Thatcher's); but perhaps raise motor car benefit scale rates and play around a little with indexation. All this was good economic advice, but not very exciting. I knew I would not be able to deliver the sort of radical budget I would have wished.

I began to examine the options within days of becoming chancellor. Whereas Nigel had been probably the most technically knowledgeable chancellor since Gladstone, he was not always sensitive to the frailties or needs of others. He did not know what it was like to run out of money on a Thursday evening, whereas I did. Nigel favoured the entrepreneurs who made the economy tick, and he had done much to benefit them. The Prime Minister favoured the hard-working strivers who were succeeding, and wished to help them to greater success. I wished to concentrate now on those who wanted to succeed, were prepared to work, but who were often trapped by circumstances from which they could not break out. They were my main concern, and I shall always regret that throughout my days of power the weakness of the economy – which our priority was to put back on an even keel – prevented me from doing more to help them.

The contribution I was able to make to them was to bring down the inflation by which they were being disproportionately hurt. In effect, this was just like reducing a pernicious and widely-based tax on the poor. But it was also, of course, removing a curse, not bringing a benefit, and had little political resonance. Worse still, the counter-inflationary measures we had to take inevitably hurt people, and often made us seem uncaring, and this, for me, was bitterly frustrating and galling.

I wished to bring a different emphasis to our tax and expenditure plans. Nigel's radical budget of 1988 had dramatically reduced direct income tax for the higher-paid. It now seemed right for me to concentrate most on those who had least. I began to consider what we might do over a longer time-scale. I envisaged tax cuts exclusively at the lower end, aiming initially at a 20p basic rate and a higher threshold of income before tax bit. I favoured tax incentives to encourage self-provision and a radical reform of National Insurance contributions, which I saw as a lop-sided tax that bore only a passing relationship to social security entitlements. This – and much more – was in my mind, but in the prevailing economic conditions it could not go into my budget.

I did ask the Treasury for an in-depth examination of 'a caring package for the budget', but nothing very exciting emerged. The tax options they proposed didn't help really low-income families, because they didn't pay tax anyway, and public expenditure measures could only be limited as our national accounts swung from an annual repayment of debt to a large annual borrowing requirement. It was obvious even before the Treasury ministers' and officials' annual early-January weekend meeting at Chevening that we had no cash for an interesting budget, and would need considerable ingenuity if we were to produce one.

Over Christmas at Finings I closeted myself away from the festivities with papers prepared for the pre-budget discussions at Chevening. When I was reading them on Boxing Day Elizabeth, whose eighteenth birthday we had celebrated the previous month, asked me what I was doing. I explained to her that the Chevening weekend had become something of an institution. 'So has Christmas,' she said. 'Put the papers away.'

The work over the early-January weekend at Chevening is intense, and so is the enjoyment. One traditional feature is the Ministers versus Mandarins snooker game, which in my year was won by Peter Middleton and Terry Burns against Norman Lamont and me. They had been practising at the Reform Club, which Norman and I thought was akin to cheating. 'They give us boxes to work on while they practise,' said Norman. Terry and Peter grinned: it was true.

Chevening itself was far from the house of my dreams. I found it austere and unwelcoming, unlike Chequers when I came to know it. Geoffrey Howe had loved it, and spent a great deal of time there. I went there as little as possible. Nevertheless, party games and leisurely strolls around the admittedly beautiful lake that lies to the rear of the house helped lighten our working weekend.

The economic situation was altogether less fun. In early 1990 we were coming out of a boom that had been unprecedented in scale, and driven by the private sector rather than by policy. Domestic consumer demand had far outstripped supply, and forecasts had failed to register the extent of it. Inflation had picked up despite a dramatic rise in interest rates and a tightening of fiscal policy. House prices had risen crazily following the stock market crash of 1987. Credit had risen and savings had fallen. Neither government nor private-sector forecasts had revealed the scale of what had happened. Forecasts were especially uncertain, and we were steering the economy in a fog. It was obvious that we would have to be cautious. The Chevening weekend illustrated that in spades.

Gradually, in meeting after meeting, a series of measures emerged. I knew that mine could not be a 'big' budget. The state of the economy meant that I was condemned, broadly speaking, to a fiscally neutral package. To enliven it I looked for some eye-catching innovations. Moreover, as this would be the first budget to be televised live, I wanted to present it in a way that would be understood as easily in the living room as in the foreign exchange dealers' room. My working instruction to officials was: 'We need to explain not only what we are doing but why, and also what we expect to come of it.' I wished the presentation to be human and colourful, but the budget's real importance lay in the substance, which the discussions at Chevening had largely preordained.

The physical compilation of a budget is daunting. Every day representations on what to do (or not do) come from a thousand sources. The Confederation of British Industry, the Institute of Directors, the Trades Union Congress, chambers of commerce, trade organisations, charities, banks, building societies and many others all want to have their say. So do Cabinet colleagues, all of whom make representations, some of them original, others no more than familiar and hoary perennials. The Health Department usually wants to put up tobacco duty; the Scottish Office to lower whisky duty; the Social Security Department to help the poor; the Department of Trade and Industry to help business; and so on. If there were a Ministry for Weather it would demand more sunshine each year.

On this occasion every representation was considered, though some were speedily discarded. The Financial Secretary Peter Lilley, the Economic Secretary Richard Ryder and the Paymaster General Malcolm Caithness sifted through a huge number of options and made recommendations.

As chancellor, I followed Nigel's habit of huge meetings at which all Treasury ministers, together with officials – including ones from Customs and Excise and Inland Revenue – pored over 'budget starters' to examine them from every perspective. Only the most rigorous proposals survived this scrutiny, unless they were firmly backed by ministers as politically necessary. If officials didn't like such propositions, they made their view clear. The ultimate dismissal is a smiling: 'Of course, Chancellor, if you think it's politically necessary . . .' This implies disownership of the proposal, but also surrender.

Officials delivered their advice. Ministers made their decisions. The essential balance between an independent civil service and an elected government was maintained. Gradually, a package emerged. It was workmanlike, with some original touches, but not particularly exciting. Our 'budget in a nutshell' description was 'a budget for savers'. We abolished Composite Rate Tax, an automatic levy on savings interest at source even when the saver's income was too low to be taxed. This was a long-overdue reform. We encouraged wider share ownership and introduced the concept of Tax Exempt Special Savings Accounts (thenceforth known as TESSAs – the acronym was already in Treasury use, and was picked up by Gus O'Donnell, my Press Officer). It was my idea that we should do something for people with no savings, and offer them a tax-free advantage for saving comparable to those given to Personal Equity Plans (PEPs) by Nigel Lawson to the relatively well-off. I was determined to offer small savers – who had gained little or nothing from previous budgets – a tax advantage of real substance. TESSAs were my answer. I wished to build a savings safety net, and planned for TESSAs to run initially for five years, with individuals able to invest up to £9,000 over that period. They were a huge and instant success, and in due course around £30 billion would be saved in them by millions of small savers.

Tax changes were limited. Many were simply indexed for inflation, but there were increases for cigarettes, spirits, company car users and leaded petrol. There were innovations to encourage share ownership, small- and medium-sized businesses, training and charitable donations.

I decided also to help football. In recent years there had been tragedies at Bradford City and at Hillsborough, Sheffield Wednesday's stadium, where inadequate safety measures had led to many avoidable deaths. This had registered deeply with a sports-loving nation. After an inquiry, Lord Justice Taylor had recommended some very expensive safety measures which only the top clubs could comfortably afford. I decided to cut Pools Duty by 2½ per cent for five years, provided the £100 million reduction in taxation was passed to the Football Trust for ground improvements. I wished to promote safety as well as more comfortable, less dilapidated grounds to attract families and deter hooligans. This populist measure was widely welcomed – though it only survived against much scepticism in the Treasury, offset by the support of the football enthusiast Terry Burns. Officials and advisers were worried that clubs were being given a tax advantage when they were able to spend millions of pounds on transfer fees. A proposed levy on these fees only fell after careful examination. When it was first suggested no one had any idea about the total value of transfers. Gus O'Donnell was dispatched to buy a copy of *Rothmans Football Year Book*, which listed all transfers, so that the Treasury could calculate how much the measure would raise. I shall remember for ever that Chris Waddle was transferred from Spurs to Marseilles for £4.5 million, whilst Gary Lineker joined Spurs from Barcelona for £1.5 million. Such is the diversity of information that can cross the desk of a chancellor.

Any chancellor is entitled to feel a twinge of nerves on budget morning as he emerges from Number 11 holding his red dispatch box aloft and makes for the House of Commons to deliver his statement, and as 3.30 p.m. approached I felt the adrenaline begin to pump. But, like all other chancellors, I had been well served by my officials. The final touches to my speech had been completed the night before; now it was printed and ready. I had finalised the text of my broadcast for later that evening – largely written by Anthony Jay, the co-author of the hugely successful television series *Yes, Minister* – and prepared what I would say at the meeting with backbenchers which takes place after the chancellor has concluded his statement. I checked through the briefings which would shortly be going out to the media, and finally, after lunch, walked around the Downing Street garden to clear my mind and rehearse the speech without the text to make sure I was familiar with it. The tipple in the glass by my side during my speech – the traditional chancellor's privilege – was Hine brandy and water; Hine has long been a favourite of mine.

The most popular measure in the budget was a proposal to limit the impact of the Poll Tax, which was becoming ever more loathed by the day. I announced a doubling of the level of savings that would be disregarded when calculating Poll Tax rebates, from £8,000 to £16,000. This was wildly cheered, but led immediately to a huge row. The Poll Tax had been introduced a year earlier in Scotland – at the request of Scottish ministers – and I had not backdated the rebate improvement. Scottish Labour backbenchers scented a grievance to be exploited, and created a huge fuss even as I spoke.

This was not quite unprecedented, but ran against Commons tradition, since budgets are usually received without interruption. Mine was not. Television had made its mark.

After I had sat down, the Scottish Secretary, Malcolm Rifkind, under pressure from the perennially hostile Scottish media, threatened to resign if he was placed in 'an impossible situation' by the rebate not being made retrospective. Since Nigel Lawson had resigned only months earlier, followed by the Employment Secretary Norman Fowler (to 'spend more time with his family'), the prospect of another resignation was far from attractive. The cost of the concession – £4 million – was tiny, but what the Prime Minister and I took amiss was that we felt we were being bounced. Malcolm got his money, the Scots gloated, and I wiped egg off my face. It had never occurred to me that such a complaint could carry such force – but my education in Scottish politics had barely begun.

Overall, the joy-through-austerity merchants in the City – and in the press – were disappointed. They had wanted a 'tough' budget, with no increase in personal tax allowances. I didn't agree, because I was too unsure of the economic forecasts and I feared that a tighter budget would lead towards recession. In retrospect, on this at least I was right and my critics wrong. However, the markets disagreed, and the pound fell on the exchanges. Nor did the Poll Tax assistance ease the anguish of electors. Two days after the budget we lost the Mid-Staffordshire by-election – held after the tragic death of John Heddle, who had entered Parliament on the same day as myself – with a massive 21 per cent swing against the government.

The EU's regular ECOFIN meetings brought me into close contact for the first time with the Irish Finance Minister Albert Reynolds, later Prime Minister of Ireland, to whom I took immediately. Norma and I had breakfast with Albert and his wife Kathleen at an informal ECOFIN at Ashford Castle in Ireland. It was the first time I spoke about the 'Irish Question' with the man with whom I was later to establish the Northern Ireland peace process. Pierre Bérégovoy, who was to become Prime Minister of France, also became a friend, but was by no means an easy touch. I remember giving him breakfast at our Washington Embassy to try to sell him our policy on the 'hard ecu' (European currency unit) as an alternative to an abrupt change to a single European currency. Pierre was impressed by our embassy – which he compared to a 'grand palace' – but less so by our policy.

Tragically, this engaging man later killed himself in sad circumstances.

I also saw the European bureaucracy at work, and witnessed the effectiveness of British representation. Our Permanent Representative at the EC was Sir David Hannay, a fiercely competitive diplomat, and visually almost the double of Nigel Hawthorne, Sir Humphrey Appleby in *Yes, Minister*. Sir David, however, was more formidable than Sir Humphrey, and the sight of him privately taking aside some hapless Euro-official to tell him the facts of political life was one of the delights of Brussels. I often averted my eyes from these occasions, since I hated the sight of blood.

I enjoyed the ECOFIN meetings. The atmosphere was far more workmanlike, and far more to my taste, than the Foreign Affairs Council, where pertinent observations were often loud with 'waffle'. The finance ministers also formed a bond, because, unlike foreign ministers, they were excluded from European summits, which they resented. Blame for this absurd ruling is largely to be laid at the door of President Mitterrand of France, who regarded money as merely a means to an end, and finance ministers as 'accountants'. This explained to me why financial realities were a second-order question for the European Council. At Maastricht we obtained agreement that finance ministers would attend when matters related to economic and monetary union were to be discussed. Ken Clarke's sharp elbows made full use of this gateway.

There were some clashes in ECOFIN that taught me much about the politics of the European Union. We won battles to restrain tax harmonisation of VAT and to establish the European Bank for Reconstruction and Development in London. This bank was designed to help send investment into Eastern Europe, and was the biggest European institution we had attracted to the UK. It got off to a shaky start under Jacques Attali, President Mitterrand's former advisor, but rapidly became established under his successor, Jacques de la Rosière.

At ECOFIN it became clear to me that our European partners were much more set on implementing the Delors Report on Economic and Monetary Union – and moving to a single currency – than I had realised. Whilst we regarded the move as a fanciful long-term ambition faced by enormous problems, they were regarding it as more or less a *fait accompli*. Criticising it was as heinous as spitting in church.

When Britain entered the European Community on 1 January 1973, support for a common currency was growing among member states. But that decade's rocky economic conditions ensured that no action was taken until 1978, when Roy Jenkins, then President of the European Commission, established the European Monetary System. From then on, monetary union was always a *formal* ambition of the Community, though one that many thought would never be realised. Britain's support for the scheme was half-hearted at best. Denis Healey and Jim Callaghan had stayed outside the EMS in 1978, and Margaret Thatcher showed no enthusiasm for it in the early 1980s.

But nor did she oppose it when she had the opportunity. In 1985 European heads of government unanimously agreed the Single European Act, the treaty which established the single market, the Community's great success story. It also committed Britain to 'progressive realisation of economic and monetary union', the first time this undertaking had been given so explicitly. Why Margaret Thatcher accepted this I have never understood. Whatever the answer, she made no attempt to secure an opt-out for the UK. But those words were important. Perhaps Margaret let them through because they appeared in the preamble to the treaty and she regarded monetary union as an unrealistic aspiration. That seems quite possible, but if so it was a bad misjudgement. I remember Nigel Lawson's concern about the preamble when I was a Treasury whip, and those words were hung around our necks throughout the Maastricht negotiations. We were told we were *politically* committed by the Act to the progressive realisation of EMU.

The next step to monetary union came three years after the Single European Act, when the Commission President, Jacques Delors, produced his full-blown road-map to monetary union. German reunification a year later moved the scheme to the centre of Euro-politics. In return for French backing for early reunification, then far from certain, the German Chancellor, Helmut Kohl, signed up to President Mitterrand's pet scheme for monetary union. Margaret Thatcher's hostility to early German reunification gave a tonic to the Franco–German alliance at precisely the point when we could have benefited from German doubts about the whole single currency project.

Because of this, it was unlikely that political opposition from the UK would stop the process. Whereas our influence on most matters carried weight, we were listened to politely on EMU and then ignored. Everyone knew Margaret's opinion. We were sidelined. We were not in the ERM.

We were not in favour of a single currency. We were out of the debate.

I began to look for a way to give us more influence, so that our warnings over a single currency should be considered. In early 1990 I learned from Nigel Wicks at the Treasury of an idea being worked up by a former Foreign Office official, Sir Michael Butler, who had retired and was now a director of Hambros Bank.

The inventor of the 'hard ecu' was Paul Richards from Samuel Montagu, and Michael Butler became its energetic publicist and promoter. Michael Palliser, the Chairman of Samuel Montagu, passed the idea to Peter Middleton, who asked Nigel Wicks to look at it. With the active assistance of Treasury officials, led by Nigel Wicks, Michael Butler sketched out a plan for a 'common currency' based on the ecu that would permit ecu notes to be put into circulation.

This had real attractions. A common currency could co-exist with existing currencies, and would not require their immediate abolition. It would give business and consumers a choice, and would let the market determine whether a single currency should evolve. The Delors scheme, by contrast, was prescriptive, and depended upon the abolition of the currency of every country which entered any new currency zone.

The hard ecu had many advantages. It was market-driven, which made it difficult for ideologically-inclined Conservatives to condemn it. It was not prescriptive. It was not Made in Europe. Whilst it might lead to a single currency this was not certain, and would depend on choice exercised by many people over a long period of time. It was imaginative, it was positive, and it would surprise our European partners if we proposed it. It would ease the divisions opening up in the Conservative Party. It would put Britain back in the debate and give us a voice that would be heard as we opposed the unquestioning approach of so many in Europe towards a single currency. All these attractions drew me to the scheme. I knew we needed to enter the crucial debate in Europe, and the hard ecu was a more substantial proposal than Nigel Lawson's 'competing currencies'. This was a scheme with real merit that could work.

The Prime Minister was flatly hostile to a single currency, and appeared to me to have no idea of how committed our partners were to it. She was confident it wouldn't work, and seemed to believe that if she asserted that it would fail, then fail it would. She did not see the need to confront their determination. When, in April, I suggested to her that we should agree to

EMU for our partners provided we had an opt-out mechanism to enable the UK to stay out if we wished, she was dismissive. She did not accept that we could not block EMU by using our power of veto because France, Germany and the others were prepared to proceed with a Treaty of Eleven, leaving the UK outside. Later she wrote that I 'had swallowed the slogans of the European lobby' and was 'intellectually drifting with the tide'. I was not. I was confronting reality, while she was letting it pass her by. To believe that the rest of Europe would dance to our tune was pure fantasy.

However, in June she agreed that I could float the hard ecu a few days before the EU summit in Dublin. I did so in a speech to an Anglo–German business dinner that I took over from Norman Lamont. I made it clear that 'in the long term if people and governments so choose it could develop into a single currency'. To illustrate the seriousness of our intent I dispatched officials and ministers to European capitals to argue our case in the same way as myself.

It all came to nothing. On the day following the launch the Prime Minister announced in the House that our proposal 'does not mean that we approve of a single currency'. This undercut it badly, since one attraction of the scheme was that if people chose, the hard ecu could lead to a single currency over time. Her comments made people believe that she saw it – quite wrongly so far as I was concerned – as a diversion or wrecking tactic. So, as a result of her statement, did our European partners. The French and Germans were particularly hostile, even though we heard persistent rumours that the Banque de France had suggested something similar to President Mitterrand, only for him to reject it.

As fas as the ERM was concerned, I was not, personally, a determined advocate in principle, but I believed its potential advantages were substantial. I considered, as Nigel Lawson had done, that our membership would stabilise the value of sterling and help bring down inflation. I thought this case was strengthened as I recalled our search for the Holy Grail of price stability over two decades or so through the maze of formal and informal prices and incomes policies, M0, M3, M4, exchange rate shadowing and more. I did not favour the ERM as part of the preparation for a single currency. Nor did I see it as a European plot to lead our virtuous UK policy off course. I was, no doubt, ideologically unsound in not automatically assuming that foreigners were up to no good, but such a thought never occurred to me. I was simply bent on eliminating the pernicious effects of rising prices. The record of the deutschmark and Germany in doing so was certainly one of which we would have been proud. Nor did I accept blindly that membership of the ERM was inevitable. One of my first acts as chancellor was to commission a paper on alternative approaches to the exchange rate. I had not gone native at the Foreign Office, as Margaret Thatcher later liked to claim, but I recognised that the pro-ERM tide was strong. Most political opinion favoured entry. So did economic commentators. So did business opinion. A poll of the corporate sector in *Financial Weekly* revealed that 97 per cent of executives wanted sterling to join the ERM, and 66 per cent did not care at what rate we went in.

As at home, so it was abroad. Both the Foreign Secretary Douglas Hurd and I were repeatedly pressed to join by our European partners. Their pleas echoed concern about the domination of the deutschmark. Bonn and Paris were seen as too close – 'two threats in a single skin', as one Italian minister put it to me – and sterling's entry into the ERM would weaken this domination. More true, however, was the fact that only Britain and France *in tandem* could counter-balance Germany, and although the French always chatted amicably with the British, they invariably ended up siding with Germany, largely because the Germans so often capitulated to French demands. Nevertheless, the European pressure for entry was there. I gradually warmed to membership because logic was pushing inexorably in that direction.

Meanwhile, the economy was slowing down, and our economic difficulties, together with European disputes and the Poll Tax, were sapping confidence in the government and the Prime Minister. The pound was almost continually under pressure as speculation ebbed and flowed in accordance with the likelihood or otherwise of our joining the ERM. We had no alternative anchor for economic policy. One after another, the possibilities had been knocked away. Following the boom of the late 1980s, the monetarist orthodoxy and the Medium Term Financial Strategy had lost credibility. The money-supply targets were no longer credible; we could hardly shadow the deutschmark as Nigel had done – even he had abandoned this approach. We examined credit controls only to confirm their uselessness. I considered giving the Bank of England independence over interest rate policy, as Nigel had wished to do, and as Gordon Brown has since done. I dismissed the idea because I believed the person responsible for monetary policy should be answerable for it in the House of Commons.

If we let the exchange rate float freely, it was clear that the value of the pound would fall and push up inflation. If that happened, our choices would be bleak. We could raise interest rates, or we could raise taxes. Neither appealed. We were dangerously fettered. I knew that we had to re-establish economic credibility if we were to bring down inflation – and win the next general election, which, as we were now in mid-term, was already on the horizon. The ERM, with its emphasis on exchange rate stability, was no panacea, but it looked to me like the best – if not the only – way forward. Each morning at Number 11, I woke up between 4 and 5 a.m. and lay awake wondering how sterling would perform that day. Each hour I received market reports. The foreign exchange screen became a focal point of the day. A pfennig up or down influenced thinking far too much. I knew this could not go on.

The Prime Minister was as frustrated as I was over rising inflation and sky-high interest rates. No prime minister likes these twin horrors, and Margaret Thatcher was no exception. She feared the impact they had on her natural constituency of homeowners and small businesses, but she had no policy to combat them. Perversely, she opposed policies necessary to bring inflation down – whether higher interest rates, or exchange rate management, or tax increases. She knew what she disliked, but had no coherent strategy for achieving what she wanted – a strong pound and low interest rates. This, however, was a horse and carriage that did not go well together. Economic management was adrift.

Margaret Thatcher was always a mixture of shrewd political calculation and emotional responses. When her political judgement was to the fore, she recognised that we might have little choice but to join the ERM. But when her emotions took over, she tried to delay our joining. As emotion battled with judgement, policy-making was often two steps forward and one back. It was very debilitating, and my year as chancellor was to be peppered with reassuring briefings and statements, confirming that the Prime Minister really did agree with her own government's policies. Her deepest hostility was to a single currency and the political implications of surrendering monetary authority. Her opposition to sharing authority in the ERM, though acute, was less, and could, I sensed, be overcome by her wish for a stable economic environment. But not easily – especially as the powerful voices of Nicholas Ridley and Alan Walters still urged her not to yield. She was also intransigent because she felt she had been bounced into a commitment to join the ERM by Geoffrey Howe and Nigel Lawson before the Madrid summit. She would never forgive this.

In early February 1990, Nick Ridley learned that I was warming to the ERM. He did not approve, and sought to buttress the Prime Minister's opposition. He put to her the argument that German reunification, which she strongly opposed but which was now a certainty, provided a good excuse for abandoning our undertaking to join the ERM. The Prime Minister was very fond of Nick and agreed with him that Germany was dangerously powerful, but she did not fall for his argument, and stuck to her existing position. Nor did she encourage him to hope that she would change her mind, although he went away with a sense that he could raise their shared doubts in Cabinet, but not in public, unless they were cleared directly with her.

By early March, when inflation had risen above 8 per cent, I was convinced that entry to the ERM was a sensible option. I asked for a checklist to be established of how close we were to the Madrid criteria for entry. I recognised that if we went in, we could not do so at the expense of the Prime Minister's credibility. We had to be able to argue that her conditions had been met. The March assessment of this was encouraging, but there was still a long way to go. I also commissioned papers on the risks of early entry, as well as the advantages. If we were to go in, I had to be convinced it was right, and that I could advocate entry to the Prime Minister, in good faith, and defend it with conviction.

Discussion about European policy came increasingly to dominate my discussions not only with Margaret, but with Douglas Hurd. My working relationship with Douglas had always been very easy. We had begun meeting regularly at Mijanou's restaurant in Ebury Street for lunch when he was home secretary and I was first at the Treasury as chief secretary. When Douglas became foreign secretary, we met at his official residence in Carlton Gardens for breakfast, where Judy Hurd would fend off the children while we talked.

Douglas looked instinctively towards improving our European relationships, rather than simply using them for domestic advantage. We both believed the Prime Minister needed to be coaxed, and not browbeaten. We knew she could not afford to lose another chancellor or a foreign secretary but we never considered playing that card. We wished to convince her of the merits of entry into the ERM, and we believed persuasion and logic would achieve what an ultimatum would not. Nevertheless, Nick Ridley, remembering the Howe–Lawson axis, was deeply suspicious of us, and thought that our breakfasts were 'mysterious'. The only real mystery was how we managed to do any work as Douglas's children got ready for school.

On 29 March 1990, my forty-seventh birthday, I set about the task of talking round the Prime Minister. I knew it would not be straightforward, but I now saw entry as inevitable. Douglas agreed with me that Margaret would have to be persuaded on economic grounds. With his wry sense of humour, he joked that Napoleon had conquered most of Europe, so getting the Prime Minister to enter a small part of it should not be too difficult.

My first discussion with her launched the process, but resulted in a stand-off. I was fortunate in that so far as the ERM was concerned, I was far closer to her thinking than Nigel Lawson had been. I argued that we should not publish a future date for joining, since that would put us at the complete mercy of the markets. I also argued that we should enter within wide bands for rate fluctuation, and not confined in a narrow straitjacket. She agreed. I also made it clear that the pound was very vulnerable, and that the foreign exchange markets were getting used to high interest rates to sustain it. This was dangerous, and had a real impact on Margaret, who wished to reduce interest rates as soon as possible.

At this meeting we also discussed the forthcoming Inter-Governmental Conference on EMU, due in December, at which many propositions unpalatable to Britain would be discussed. Our exclusion from the ERM was making us bystanders in this debate. The Prime Minister did not like this argument, not least because it was true. Yet it did register with her. I felt I was making more progress than I had expected, when she broke off the conversation, saying she did not have time to pursue it further that morning. This was not to be the last occasion on which she would shy away from the topic. At least she did not dismiss it out of hand. I said I would return to the matter.

At the Treasury, although I put work in hand on possible entry dates, officials were very sceptical about the likelihood of getting a political decision to go ahead. We began looking at specific dates for entry, on the assumption that it would need to be at a weekend, to enable the markets to absorb the change before trading began. This exercise narrowed the choices dramatically, but fortunately commentators did not realise how limited they were. Had they done so, the speculation about whether, and when, we would enter would have been even more frenetic. Even as it was, the press couldn't resist playing a guessing game.

The first window was April to July, which was unlikely, because we would not by then have met the Madrid conditions. More promising was early September to late October. November and December were unattractive, being too close to the Inter-Governmental Conference. Entry that late would have been seen by our European partners as a belated attempt to buy influence at the conference, and if that were the case it would fail. If we wanted influence – and we certainly needed it – entry would have to be earlier, because there would be a great deal of discussion on many of the most prickly decisions before the conference began.

On 17 April, at a seminar on the economy, Peter Middleton was invited to prepare a paper on the mechanics of entry into the ERM. I sent it to the Prime Minister a few days after the dreadful local election results across the country on 3 May had made it evident that our economic problems, together with disputes in the party over European policy, were eroding our political support. The case for entry was strengthening both politically and economically.

I met regularly with Robin Leigh-Pemberton, the Governor of the Bank of England, to discuss the issue. He was an engaging man with whom to do business, jovial, well-mannered, a great cricket-lover and as English as they come. On one occasion we chuckled over a newspaper cartoon of Margaret and myself rowing together down the river past a signpost to the European Monetary System, with Margaret intoning 'Out, out' with each stroke while I intoned 'In, in,' supported by Nigel Lawson and Robin, who was bouncing up and down on the bank. Robin and I tossed a coin to see which of us would buy the original of this brilliantly spot-on drawing. He won, but a copy still hangs on my wall. Robin and I were as one on the need to join the ERM, if not in the level of our enthusiasm. He believed in it as a matter of principle, I, as I have said, as an anti-inflationary weapon.

By early June, it was apparent that the exchange rate was being propped up by the markets through their firm belief that we would enter the ERM. Treasury officials advised me that in their view we could join at any time, provided we did so with the flexibility to move 6 per cent up or down from the central rate at entry. They added that whilst it would be better if we could enter while inflation was falling, this was not essential. But politically the matter was different. The Madrid conditions that Margaret Thatcher had set called for inflation to be falling; at the very least we needed to be sure inflation had peaked.

June was a crucial month. Treasury opinion was hardening in favour of early entry. The markets were restless and difficult, and good government required a decision. I asked Treasury ministers their views. No one argued for sterling to stay out, though Andrew Tyrie suggested I consider delaying membership.

I again minuted the Prime Minister on the 'windows for entry', and set out the reasons for an early decision. Somewhat tongue in cheek, I proposed 20 July as a possible early date. I knew she would balk at this, but hoped it would encourage her to accept September or October.

At our next bilateral, on 14 June, the Prime Minister said, in terms, for the first time, that she no longer had reservations about entry. But she did favour further delay. She wished to see inflation falling, and she was concerned about the impact of German monetary union. She told me she hoped also to take a 'bonus' on entry, of either a higher exchange rate or a cut in interest rates. I knew then that her mind was moving to the advantages we could obtain from entry, and how to justify it. I agreed to consider the timing again, and to report back to her.

When I had done so, I proposed entry in September, or – depending on how the economy performed – a little later. The question of entry was now when, not if.

On 2 July, I minuted the Prime Minister suggesting that we join before the Conservative Party Conference in October. It was evident that, without a decision, it would be politically difficult to get through the conference and other set-piece occasions like the Lord Mayor's Banquet, held in November. If there was still uncertainty, speculation would build up before each of these occasions, as the markets anticipated an announcement. We needed a definite decision – yes or no.

I was sure we should grasp the nettle and join. A positive decision to enter would enable us to use major speeches in the autumn to spell out the implications. Still the Prime Minister hesitated until her self-imposed Madrid conditions could more easily be said to be met. The July option, never my favourite, but possible, was lost.

On 4 July, American Independence Day, the Prime Minister agreed to consider specific dates for entry to the ERM. The two likeliest dates were 14 September and 5 October. To ensure that the rate of entry would put the squeeze on inflation, the Prime Minister asked me to consider the practicalities of only a 4 per cent band around the central rate, rather than the 6 per cent we had previously agreed. This was a bewildering change of tack by her, but one that would be worthwhile if it made entry possible. Business remained hugely enthusiastic about entry, and at a meeting with the CBI the Director-General Howard Davies said they were 'still firmly committed to entry and against unilateral devaluation'.

Even at this late stage, further alarms lay ahead. In July, Germany set a rate for monetary reunion of one ostmark to the deutschmark – a politically-driven and unrealistic rate which put pressure on interest rates across Europe. Then, in early August, Iraq invaded the neighbouring state of Kuwait. As a result the price of oil shot up, boosting the pound, which was seen in the City as a 'petro-currency' because of our North Sea oil reserves. This market movement did not reflect the real economy, and we risked excessive deflation as exports suffered. Worried by the Gulf crisis and a possible war involving Britain – and, I think, because she sensed a good case for further delaying a decision she knew was necessary but didn't relish – Margaret once again considered deferring ERM entry.

I wondered myself if this might be wise, but decided it was not. It seemed to me that much depended on how things turned out in the Gulf. If it became a long-drawn-out affair, then the case for early ERM entry was strong, since we would be better placed to handle turbulence within the protection of the mechanism than on our own. But if the war was to be short, then I felt we would be right to stay out until it ended. Margaret agreed: since there was no immediate solution in sight, the crisis in the Gulf would not stop us joining, and we were back on course. Even the publication of a new book by Alan Walters did not unsettle her unduly – somewhat to my surprise.

On 3 September, I summarised the position in a lengthy minute. ('It's the day war broke out,' my Private Office warned. 'Is it the right day to send that out?' I sent it.) Earlier in the summer we had worried that sterling might be too low at entry for membership of the ERM to be a disinflationary discipline. Later, we were concerned that entry would push up the exchange rate so much that we might have to reduce interest rates when to do so would be inappropriate on domestic grounds. This fear never surfaced publicly, but by early September we were considering an entry rate around DM3, with the full agreement of the Bank of England.

The Prime Minister and I met on 4 September. We agreed that, while we could not yet cut interest rates, we would soon be able to do so without damaging our counter-inflation policy. But we both saw the danger of cutting rates before ERM entry, because it would look as though we were massaging the exchange rate downwards. That was emphatically not what we wanted.

We were not yet sure when inflation would peak – the obvious peg for entry and, if appropriate, an interest rate cut. At this meeting the Prime Minister raised for the first time the possibility of simultaneous entry and a reduction in interest rates – adding, on her own behalf, sugar to a pill she knew was good for her but which she did not want to take. I did not demur at the time, because I did not want an argument that would distract her from thinking positively about entry. Afterwards, I realised that this was a mistake. In due course the Prime Minister would impose that interest rate cut, and it would be harmful.

The pace now began to quicken, and despite poor economic statistics in September we decided to press on. I noted in a meeting with Peter Middleton that there was a growing feeling that a recession was looming, and that therefore the pressure for interest rate reductions would grow. I wished for the discipline of the ERM to ensure that these were justified, and not snatched at for purely political reasons. The Bank of England also reported that the markets were more fractious and difficult to manage. Robin Leigh-Pemberton warned me that this would worsen in the run-up to the Inter-Governmental Conference in December.

On 11 September I reported to the Prime Minister that the markets were expecting entry, and that public opinion would welcome it. I added that a decision to delay would weaken the exchange rate, raise inflation and delay interest rate reductions. I set out yet again the pros and cons of the possible entry dates, noting that 5 October was the last opportunity before the party conference.

We met the next day. Margaret reiterated her wish for an interest rate reduction at the time of entry. She also felt we could not delay entry beyond December, and asked me to come forward with a firm proposal for a date. The long journey was nearly at an end.

At the Treasury I assembled key officials – Peter Middleton, Terry

Burns, Nigel Wicks, Michael Scholar and Paul Gray – and we set out a timetable for entry on 12 October, the day of the Prime Minister's conference speech, whilst being careful not to rule out the fifth. Two days later, officials advised me that inflation should peak in September (the announcement would be made in October) at 10.9 per cent, and that we could justify an interest rate cut within a fortnight of that. There were three possible timings for the cut: independently of entry and before it (which no one favoured); simultaneously (which the Prime Minister was determined upon); and post-entry (which the Bank and the Treasury favoured). Despite my knowledge of the Prime Minister's preference I thought post-entry was right, and recommended this to her.

The next day the same group of officials, with the addition of Eddie George, the Deputy Governor of the Bank of England (in the absence of Robin Leigh-Pemberton, who was abroad), assembled at Number 10. After a spirited discussion on the interest rate cut, which everyone else opposed, the Prime Minister's desire prevailed: no cut, no entry. We had no choice but to defer to her.

I still had three fears. First, that even at the last minute the Prime Minister might change her mind, or that some unexpected event would intervene. Unlikely, but possible. Second, that a week's delay after a firm decision to join might lead to a leak. The media were in pursuit of a date each day. Third, that entry on 12 October had one huge drawback. The Prime Minister's speech at the Conservative Party Conference always generated massive – and usually favourable – coverage. But if she sat down at 3.30 p.m. and I announced ERM entry at 4 o'clock, her speech would be wiped off the news. I suggested to the meeting that we should therefore examine entry the following day – 5 October. There was a pause. The advantage of not waiting a week was obvious. 'Do it,' said the Prime Minister. 'Do it tomorrow.'

At 5 p.m. we trooped back to the Treasury. At 7.15 we were back at Number 10. The text of the announcement was prepared. The detailed advice on timing for the next day was ready. The arrangements for the Monetary Committee were in hand. Media packages were being prepared. It was decided who had to be contacted. We did not seek to wreck the Labour leader Neil Kinnock's speech to his party conference, which was taking place the next day, but neither did we see any reason to delay on that account. We were ready to go. Eddie George went off to talk to

European Bank governors. Nigel Wicks spoke to Mario Sarcinelli, the Chairman of the Monetary Committee, who warmly welcomed the decision.

I phoned a delighted Robin Leigh-Pemberton and Karl Otto Pöhl, the President of the Bundesbank, who congratulated me on a 'brave and courageous decision'. He was very supportive, and made no adverse comments at all about the exchange rate at which we intended to enter.

At 4 p.m. on Friday, 5 October, after the close of the foreign exchange markets, I made the formal announcement of Britain's entry into the Exchange Rate Mechanism. The Prime Minister made a brief statement in Downing Street, saying: 'We have done it because the policy is right.'

The press widely welcomed the decision. 'The time was right,' said the *Financial Times*. 'Both politically and economically, entry is shrewdly-timed,' said the *Financial Times*. Most other papers also took an approving view:

> 'Major plays ERM ace – shares soar as government seize political
> and economic initiative' – *Independent*
> 'No soft option' – *Daily Telegraph*
> 'Thank God – now down to some strong discipline' – *Sunday
> Telegraph*
> 'Business hails Britain's entry into ERM' – *Sunday Times*
> 'Tories take ERM gamble. Shares rocket in market euphoria' –
> *Guardian*

Two years later, when we were swept out of the ERM by turbulent market conditions, some of these newspapers would take a very different line. Defenders of our entry could scarcely be found, while those who claimed to have warned of the inevitability of disaster bobbed up everywhere. It was the golden age of hindsight.

Neil Kinnock welcomed the decision as 'momentous', while John Smith, his shadow Chancellor, attacked the fact that the Madrid conditions were not met (humbug, since he didn't support them anyway), but heralded 'the potential benefit that a more stable exchange rate could bring to the process of Britain's much-needed economic recovery'. Labour supported the rate of entry, but seemed to forget this two years later, when we pulled out. John Smith, who had taunted the government for not entering, called the Tories 'the only architects, the sole constructors, of our present dismal situation'. It was not what he had said at the time. But there were some dissidents. My PPS, Tony Favell, who had first joined me at the DHSS, resigned in protest – an unexpected departure and no doubt a straw in the wind.

In the Commons I made a statement following entry, and opened a debate on the decision a few days later. In my statement I said: 'The mechanism has a proven record of success over recent years in producing greater stability of exchange rates and lower inflation. The government believes that Britain, too, will benefit from membership. The Exchange Rate Mechanism will reinforce our counter-inflationary policies, help to provide the stability and certainty that industry needs, and set the right framework for a resumption of soundly based and non-inflationary growth.' In winding up the later debate, Norman Lamont reinforced the fact that joining had become inevitable by saying it would have been 'sheer masochism' to wait any longer. He was right.

Whilst entry received overwhelming support, long-term European critics in the Conservative Party like John Biffen attacked the decision. Teddy Taylor raised questions about options to withdraw if necessary. Bill Cash said, 'Thus far and no farther.' Nick Budgen advocated a floating pound. Norman Tebbit, once in favour, now pronounced himself 'agnostic' on ERM entry. Later, 'agnostic' would seem a mild way to describe his opposition.

One commentator, the genial Bill Keegan of the *Observer* – who had been a constant thorn in Nigel Lawson's side – was very prescient. He said outright that we had entered at too high a rate. When we left the mechanism two years later he, at least, was one of the few entitled to say 'I told you so.' He did not set out, however, how we could have negotiated entry at a lower rate.

We entered the mechanism at the market rate – DM2.95 to the pound. There was no real option of much divergence from this, though it later became politically useful for critics to claim that there was. If we had sought to enter at a markedly lower rate we would have been rebuffed by our European partners. They would not have allowed us to gain a competitive advantage upon entry by an artificial devaluation. Even if we had got away with it, the upward pressures on the pound would have been dramatic and we would have had to cut interest rates substantially to resist them, long before it would have been economically safe to do so. Any suggestion that we could have entered at a significantly lower rate is utterly unrealistic. Nor was it proposed by anyone closely connected with the negotiations.

The Bundesbank favoured entry at the marginally lower rate of DM2.90, while others actually favoured a higher rate. The Banque de France wanted DM3.00. So did the CBI. And the Prime Minister and the Bank of England wanted a firm rate, so that interest rates could fall. DM2.95 was around the average rate for the previous decade, and, according to the OECD's calculation of the pound's 'purchasing power', actually a 17 per cent *under-valuation* of sterling's worth.

We did ruffle a few feathers by not 'negotiating' our entry rate with the Monetary Committee in Brussels. Mario Sarcinelli wanted us to say 'We are not going against the tide of the market,' rather than specify an entry rate. This might have been polite, but there was nothing to negotiate, because no real flexibility in our rate at entry was possible. Two years later, after our exit from the ERM, with inflation driven from the system, the pound found its value well within the original margins at which we had entered.

We didn't get it all right. The decision to cut interest rates at the time of entry was certainly a mistake. It was fiercely attacked by Nigel Lawson in the House and by commentators outside. 'For reasons best known to himself – one can guess at them –' said Nigel, 'my right honourable friend' – he meant me – 'did not address the possibility of joining the ERM before reducing interest rates ... This is not a small point because sadly the conjunction of the two has led to a degree of cynicism in the financial markets for which we will have to pay a price.' Ken Baker wrote that the cut in interest rates was Margaret's 'fig leaf' for entry, and there is some truth in this. It is, however, not the whole truth – she was desperately keen to see interest rates fall, and no one was prepared to give her a guarantee that they would do so shortly after entry. The Bank of England expressly refused to commit itself on this, so she took the comfortable option of a cut when she knew she could get it.

I was more concerned when the Prime Minister privately began telling colleagues critical of entry that we could easily realign, and that she wouldn't use significant reserves to defend the exchange rate. This was not credible: a realignment – in essence a devaluation – would not be easy to obtain, and we would have no choice but to use our foreign-exchange reserves to defend our exchange rate if it began to fall too far. The Prime Minister's remarks showed a startling lack of commitment (or understanding) of the system she had just agreed we should enter. It was not even consistent with her own objectives: she had urged a high rate of entry to curb inflation (and hasten cuts in interest rates). She could hardly therefore be a ready devaluer, cutting the value of sterling at the first hint of difficulty and undermining our anti-inflation policy. Nonetheless, her remarks did raise a doubt in my mind about whether she would stick with the policy when it began to hurt – which it was likely to do as it squeezed inflation out of the economy – or whether she would distance herself from it and let it be known that it had been forced upon her. I dismissed such thoughts, as the pound remained strong and my concerns seemed academic.

During the year there had been some pleasant interludes. In September I attended the Commonwealth Finance Ministers' meeting in Trinidad – my first visit to the West Indies. I took the opportunity to visit the Test cricket ground at Port of Spain. Alas, there was no play at the time, but as usual the sight of a cricket pitch put me in a very sunny mood. So did an enjoyable afternoon with David Saul, the Finance Minister of Bermuda, who introduced me to rum punch. 'The second one is better than the first,' he joked, and it certainly seemed so.

The main business of the meeting was for me to launch a debt initiative for the world's very poorest countries that I had been working on for nearly six months. Many of these countries were in dire poverty, and the rise in the price of oil as a result of Iraq's invasion of Kuwait had dealt them a further blow. I proposed a substantial package of relief: a rescheduling of the whole stock of debt; a doubling in the amount of relief from one-third to two-thirds; the capitalisation of interest due on the debt, with no further payment for five years; and an increase in the repayment period to twenty-five years.

The Commonwealth finance ministers were delighted, and the package was endorsed later by the IMF Conference in Washington and warmly welcomed by the Secretary General of the United Nations. The net effect was to write off over US$18 billion in debt from the poorest and most highly indebted countries at a UK 'cost' of US$900 million – which was, of course, largely nominal, as it was highly unlikely it would ever be repaid. Britain had a good record in debt relief. Nigel Lawson had set the trend some years earlier, and later Ken Clarke and Gordon Brown would bring forward further debt alleviation. I hope it gave them as much satisfaction as it gave me: these poor countries need help, and it is unforgivable to let them fall further and further behind the rest of the world.

Despite all the difficulties, political and economic, I was enjoying my time as chancellor. Against a challenging background of high inflation and interest rates, an uncertain pound and a static economy, I felt I had picked up the pieces which had been broken and scattered in October 1989, and had put together an effective economic policy.

I delivered my second Autumn Statement on 8 November 1990, though the event rather lost out, in terms of press coverage, to the guessing game underway about the Prime Minister's future. If the party was hoping for early tidings of economic spring, it was disappointed. I forecast slightly increased growth for the year ahead, though I suspected that recession might also be on the cards. But this was not certain, and no advantage could accrue to anyone from a forecast that could only make it more likely. Meanwhile the impact of rising unemployment and a slowing economy had pushed up expenditure on social security by £3 billion, while the voracious demands of the NHS reforms added a similar sum.

Twenty-five days after ERM entry Geoffrey Howe resigned from the Cabinet. The combination of dissatisfaction with the Poll Tax and widening splits in the Cabinet over European policy were about to create an explosion that would sweep Margaret Thatcher from Downing Street. By the end of the month I had succeeded her as prime minister.

# CHAPTER EIGHT

# An Empress Falls

Within the folklore of the Conservative Party a myth has taken root which so confounds reason and reality that psychoanalysts may understand it better than historians. Its grip has been so strong that a false history has arisen in some Conservative circles and in the media. The myth is that in a moment of inexplicable folly and conspiracy, even madness, Conservative MPs ejected a leader at the height of her powers, presiding over a healthy party, a quiescent nation and a benign set of outside circumstances. It really was not like that.

In the autumn of 1990 the British economy was in deep-seated trouble; huge internal disputes were raging over Europe; the Community Charge, known and hated by millions as the Poll Tax, had proved unworkable and hugely costly; the Prime Minister was barely on speaking terms with the Deputy Prime Minister; a long-standing chancellor had resigned over policy; the party was far behind Labour in the opinion polls; an election was due in eighteen months; and within the parliamentary Conservative Party a sense of exasperation with the leadership was palpable.

I became prime minister because Margaret Thatcher fell. And her downfall was precipitated by two items on this list of troubles: the Poll Tax and Europe. I believe she could have survived either on its own. When they came together, she was trapped.

From the Falklands War onwards Margaret Thatcher had enjoyed an extraordinary dominance in the Conservative Party. Like all prime ministers, she had members of her party who disliked her style and some of her policies, but their opposition was muted by her three successive general election victories against a weak and disoriented Labour Party. Their unease had been a side-issue in the heyday of Tory triumph and Labour woe. But from 1989, as trouble piled upon trouble, their reservations seemed more valid and their numbers grew. In Parliament, they were joined by Members from the loyalist centre-right of the party – worried by the impact of the Poll Tax – and by colleagues uneasy at the Prime Minister's stridency over European policy. This combination of concerns was the crucial change. Although many still venerated 'the Iron Lady', there was widespread dismay that, too often, she was wrongheaded, and a growing belief that her best days were over. These doubts about policy were reinforced by a dire opinion-poll position that suggested many Conservative seats would be lost at the forthcoming general election. Members' instinct for self-preservation added to the sea of troubles facing the Prime Minister.

But, as the affection for her was strong, opposition tended to be more in sorrow than in anger. 'If only she would listen,' was the constant refrain. 'Why doesn't she soften?' Had we but known it, this was the voice of a parliamentary party that did not like its unpopularity and was looking for a change. This sentiment did not make Margaret Thatcher's removal a certainty, but it made the once unthinkable much more possible.

The signs had been there for some time. The Prime Minister had overwhelmingly defeated Sir Anthony Meyer's token challenge for the leadership of the party in late 1989, but amidst the cheering most of us missed the significance of the result. A long-serving, hugely successful leader with three successive election victories behind her had been challenged – and sixty Conservative MPs had declined to support her.

Margaret's campaign had been organised by Ian Gow, Richard Ryder and Tristan Garel-Jones. After it was over Tristan told me that, apart from the sixty malcontents, a further hundred members of the parliamentary party had needed to be 'worked on' to keep them on-side. I suggested to Tristan that he should see the Prime Minister to ensure that she knew this. He delivered his message on the Sunday evening following her victory. In his usual colourful style, he told the Prime Minister that pro-European Members were deeply unhappy with the 'tone' of her policy, and that dissatisfaction with the Poll Tax was everywhere. 'Unless you're careful,' he warned her, 'they'll be back. Hezzie [Michael Heseltine] will run, and they'll kill you.' It was vintage Tristan. 'It will be the daylight assassination of the Prime Minister.'

Margaret Thatcher did not react against the messenger, as she sometimes did. She defended the Poll Tax, and lambasted the Europeans. Tristan simply repeated the message. 'I'm only the Deputy Chief Whip,' he

Aged about nine months.

At Cheam Common
Infants School c. 1949,
aged about six – on the
right in the front row.

In the garden at home in 1951, aged
eight, with our cat Saham.

*Above* My parents, Tom and Gwen, in 1951, with our dog Butch.

*Left c.* 1953, aged about ten.

*Below* The Rutlish School colts cricket team in 1958 – I am third from the left in the back row.

Wedding reception, Lambeth Town Hall. Norma and I were married in St Matthew's Church, Brixton on 3 October 1970.

*Right* Speaking in Lambeth Council Chamber, 1970.

*Below* Newly elected Member of Parliament for Huntingdonshire: May 1979.

In the garden at Hemingford Grey, our first home in the constituency, with Norma's mother Dee, James and Elizabeth: 1979.

In the garden at Hemingford Grey with James and Elizabeth: 1979.

As Foreign Secretary in September 1989, my first meeting with George Bush in the Oval Office with (visible left to right): my Private Secretary Stephen Wall, Permanent Secretary Patrick Wright, British Ambassador Antony Acland, US Secretary of State James Baker and the President's National Security Adviser, Brent Scowcroft.

Still on good terms with Margaret following the announcement of our entry into the ERM. My speech as Chancellor of the Exchequer to the Conservative Party Conference in Bournemouth: October 1990.

A favourite photograph by Srdja Djukanovic, taken in the garden at Finings: 1990.

Launching the campaign for the leadership of the Conservative Party following Margaret Thatcher's resignation in November 1990. Seated (left to right): Andrew Tyrie, self, Norman Lamont and Graham Bright.

The Gulf War. Meeting soldiers from the 3rd Battalion of the Desert Rats in eastern Saudi Arabia: 8 January 1991.

Nelson Mandela arrives at Number 10 for his first official visit to London: 24 April 1991.

*Above* Overcoming the
language barrier with
François Mitterrand
and George Bush
during the G7
economic summit at
Lancaster House,
London: July 1991.

*Left* Presidential tour of
the Maine coastline
during a three-day visit
to Kennebunkport, the
family home of George
and Barbara Bush:
28 August 1991.

said as he left. 'But I'm telling you – the daylight assassination of the PM.'

I was more aware of her danger in retrospect than at the time. As a former whip, I kept my network across the party, and I heard that there were rumbles. In fact it was worse than that: grumbling was maturing into strong opposition. As a new chancellor I had my hands full with the onset of recession and my first budget, and was having trouble trying to control public expenditure. We were new members of the ERM, and had to prepare for the economic impact of the Iraqi invasion of Kuwait. With these Treasury preoccupations, I was insulated from the scale of the growing distress in the Tea Room. Despite the political gossip that reached me, the Prime Minister had been so powerful for so long that I could not imagine her removal. I discounted much of what I heard as political froth.

The government had just announced its legislative programme in the Queen's Speech, and the Prime Minister, with the coming general election in mind, was in no doubt that she would be in office to carry it out. She too was preoccupied with the imminence of a war in the Gulf. Talk of a challenge to her leadership, at fever-pitch in the spring, had died away in May after Labour's opinion poll lead fell back, and Michael Heseltine had appeared to resolve the matter by announcing that he would not challenge her 'this side of an election'. Anyone who did so, he said, would fail.

I supported Margaret Thatcher as prime minister. I was pleased to serve in her government and I defended her with conviction when criticisms were brought to me. Still, in private, I was uneasy; uneasy at Margaret's increasingly autocratic approach. Her warrior characteristics were profoundly un-Conservative. In public, her utter certainties were off-putting. In private she was capable of changing her mind with bewildering speed until she had worked up her public position. Often this way of working served her well. But not always. There were occasions when arguments were put to her which were extremely good, but which ran into the slammed door of a closed mind. Too often, she conducted government by gut instinct; conviction, some said admiringly, but at any rate without mature, detached examination of the issues. She lost her political agility; the Poll Tax and crude anti-Europeanism were the policies that resulted.

It was the Poll Tax which sowed the seeds of her destruction. The theory of the tax was impeccable: everyone benefited from local government services, so everyone should contribute towards the cost of them. This had never been the case with domestic rates, where only a minority paid for local government. High-spending local authorities were insulated at the ballot box from the wrath of the few who had to pay by the many who did not. By giving every resident a financial stake in local government, it was hoped that voters would compel rotten boroughs to clean up their act.

Ken Baker, as Environment Secretary, had promised that the Poll Tax would cost many residents less than the rates. But as councils set their Community Charge levels, it became evident that average bills were going to be far higher than before. It was an extremely painful prospect. Tory MPs were coming back from their constituencies in despair, and even strong supporters of the reform were getting edgy.

The twists and turns as we dealt with the ravages of the tax dealt a body-blow to our reputation for efficiency. Some £1.5 billion of public money was lost setting up, administering and replacing the Poll Tax; the total transfer costs to the national taxpayer reached over £20 billion by 1993–94. The Poll Tax also left local government dependent on the Exchequer for 80 per cent of its finance. It was a wretched tale, and one in which, late in the day, I had a walk-on part. Eventually, although I played no glorious role in opposing the introduction of the tax, it was brought to an end under my leadership.

Why did Margaret press ahead with what turned out to be an act of political suicide? Even lemmings have their reasons. So did she, and they were compelling. In the outcry that followed the introduction of the Poll Tax, the unfairness of the old rating system was forgotten. It was riddled with anomalies: the elderly widow paying the same as four wage-earners next door was a much-quoted example. Conservative Members had bulging postbags denouncing the rates, and motions were tabled at every Conservative Party conference demanding their abolition.

Revaluation of rateable liability – which pushed up bills for millions – fanned the embers of this resentment into flame. It came first in Scotland in 1985, and brought public and political outcry, coupled with demands that the rating system should be abolished forthwith. In England, where the system was different, the impact of revaluation was likely to be even greater. The atmosphere of barely suppressed panic left no doubt that something had to be done, and quickly; fear of the impact of rating revaluation turned the Poll Tax from the inconceivable to the unavoidable.

So, in May 1985, when I was just a junior Treasury whip, Cabinet endorsed proposals from Kenneth Baker to replace the rates with a flat-level

Poll Tax; Nigel Lawson dissented and was overruled. Ken Baker was a red-hot presenter of a bad case. He was unmatched as a master of black propaganda, and he won many battles in Cabinet by handling Margaret Thatcher with sly skill.

Kenneth Baker's original plans were well received. His estimate for the level of the Poll Tax was an average of £30 a head in 1990, when the system would be only partly in operation, rising to a fully-fledged £250 in the year 2000. There would be a rebate system to help the least well-off. These low sums were hugely attractive; it was not until much later that we found out they were utterly unachievable. The non-domestic rate, which was a milch cow for many local authorities and was loathed by business, was to be abolished and replaced by a Uniform Business Rate, set nationally and indexed to inflation

It is ironic that the Poll Tax was introduced early into Scotland at the request of the Scots, shocked by the revaluation of their rates; later, its unpopularity – and the inaccurate claim that Scotland was being used as a laboratory to test the tax – was central to the argument for devolution. The Poll Tax cast a long shadow.  ·

After the 1987 election, the government introduced a Bill to apply the Poll Tax across the United Kingdom, with the exception of Northern Ireland. The whips calculated there were twenty-four outright opponents to the Bill on our backbenches, and a hundred doubters. Margaret Thatcher was undaunted: the 'wets', she thought, would be seen off again. But in a vote on an amendment to the legislation, tabled by Michael Mates in April 1988, sufficient Tories voted against or abstained for the government's majority to fall from eighty plus to twenty-five.

I entered the Poll Tax story as chief secretary to the Treasury after the 1987 general election. Within Cabinet, Nigel Lawson continued to oppose the whole idea, and to warn that the tax would be unworkable and politically catastrophic. Although I warmed to the intellectual rationale of the tax, I was persuaded by Nigel's warnings; and as chief secretary I was often deputed by him to argue the Treasury case in Cabinet committees. Even when I thought I had won the argument, I lost the decision. Defeated on substance, I remained involved in practical questions of implementation.

The Poll Tax brought dramatic changes in the burden of local taxation for millions of people. We faced a crucial decision: should we introduce these changes in one go, or phase them in gradually? Ken Baker had proposed a long period of phasing. Nick Ridley, his successor as Environment Secretary, was determined on a short period or, preferably, no transition at all. Nigel Lawson, so often Nick's ally, regarded this view as 'apolitical to the last degree'.

At first, phasing won. But Nick did not lie down. He never did. He launched an energetic lobbying campaign for a clean switch to the Poll Tax. At the party conference in October, speaker after speaker got up to demand the abolition of the rates, with no transition period. At the Treasury, we believed this show of impatience had been contrived by Nick to impress Margaret. When I suggested this to Nick he denied it strenuously: it was, he claimed, a spontaneous uprising by thinking Conservatives. If so, many of them were soon to think again.

Margaret, however, was impressed, and despite the clear opposition of the Treasury team the decision was taken to abolish the transition in all but a few councils. In June 1988 we abandoned dual running altogether. Nick Ridley had won.

The Poll Tax became law in July. The issue then lay fallow until, nearly a year later, we began to discuss how much taxpayer subsidy should accompany the new tax upon its introduction. After the Treasury and the Department of the Environment failed to settle on a figure, Margaret adjudicated and an increase of £2.6 billion was agreed. It was at this point that we really lost control. By now, the estimated average Poll Tax bill had risen to well over £300. Colleagues were aghast. Worse was to come. Inflation and wage costs had begun to rise, and local authorities were increasing their spending and blaming the new tax for the higher bills. By late autumn, headlines warned that Poll Tax bills could be even higher.

Margaret replaced Nick as environment secretary with the more voter-friendly Chris Patten in late July 1989. Chris warned her in private that the tax was a liability, and began the first of many reviews of it – but Margaret made it clear to him that 'review' did not mean replacement.

Slowly, the scale of the political problem became clear. Conservative Central Office found out that in ten marginal constituencies, 82 per cent of individuals would be out of pocket as a result of the change from rates – and that was on the heroically optimistic assumption that local authorities increased their spending by just 7 per cent. The rates system had been untenable, but the Poll Tax was turning out to be worse.

Things slid downhill fast. By January 1990, by which time I had succeeded Nigel as chancellor, the Poll Tax monster was rampaging vora-
ciously. As local authorities set their budgets in stormy town hall meetings,
headline Poll Tax levels averaged £360, with some much higher: my old
borough, Lambeth, set theirs at £560. In March we sustained a massive
by-election defeat in Mid Staffordshire. The press blamed the Poll Tax.
Our backbenchers blamed Margaret and Nick.

In late March, Margaret rang me in something of a state. She had
assumed, she said, that if local authorities put up spending, they would get
the blame for putting up taxes. Instead, the government was getting the
blame for changing to the Poll Tax. She was worried about the impact of
high bills on people of modest incomes ('our people', she said) just above
the cut-off for Community Charge benefit. She asked me to examine means
of exercising some sort of direct control over local spending which, with
a larger level of grant, might bring down the Poll Tax bills. I agreed to do
so.

Margaret was right: a radical rethink was necessary. But it was ironic
that she should advocate it, since the pain endured by people just above the
benefit level was the direct result of the hard-edged 'financial accountability'
which had always been proclaimed as the main advantage of the Poll Tax.

On 31 March, the day before the Community Charge came into effect
in England, political protest erupted into violence with rioting in Trafalgar
Square. Many of the demonstrators may have been of the 'rent-a-mob' type;
but many were not, and I was shocked that the British people, normally so
slow to anger, should have taken to the streets over the reform of local
government taxation. The event was unprecedented in post-war Britain,
and it was becoming clear that the Poll Tax was not so much an albatross
as a ticking time-bomb, ready to explode. The political consequences of
this riot were nothing in comparison to the fury that erupted from the
Tory shires when the first Poll Tax bills arrived. The local government
election results in May were dismal.

Sinking beneath a sea of angry correspondence, our backbenchers began
to panic. As the year wore on, the issue fuelled a whispering campaign
about Margaret's leadership. She was in a bind, and did not know how to
escape. Although she had executed more than a few U-turns in her time
– pretending they were no such thing – she had comprehensively boxed
herself in on the Poll Tax. The zeal with which she had advocated it

meant that its unpopularity was seen as a failure for her personally, and its progressive emasculation was viewed as a climbdown of the most wretched sort. The Empress was losing her clothes.

Throughout April and May 1990 argument raged between the Treasury, the Department of the Environment and Number 10. At first we believed we would have to legislate to control the amount local councils could spend. As chancellor with a budget to stick to I supported this idea, but as a former whip I had grave doubts, given the mood on our backbenches, whether any such legislation would pass the House. Then, in July, we struck lucky. Fresh legal advice suggested that if the government set a figure for what it considered to be 'excessive' spending, we would be able to use our existing powers to prevent local authorities from exceeding it.

After a good deal of haggling we announced that local authorities could increase the total level of their spending by up to 7 per cent on the year before. We increased grant provision to them by £3 billion – an amount that should, according to Department of Environment estimates at the time, have produced a Community Charge that averaged around £376. This was a generous settlement, but was nothing like enough to satisfy many of our colleagues. It was becoming clear that any average charge above £300 was unacceptable to them.

Margaret could go no further in easing the pain, or her policy would have faced ridicule. Still the backbenches wanted more. By the autumn it was obvious the tax had to go; but Margaret was not ready to remove it. The muttering grew louder. Then a second wave of discontent hit Margaret. It was Europe. This time something had to give. It was to be her.

There were many myths which came to surround the fall of Margaret Thatcher. One of them is that she was brought down by a cabal of pro-European 'wets' for pursuing a clear and forthright line against anything to do with a united Europe. But nothing with Margaret Thatcher was ever quite that straightforward. For most of her time in government, her actions showed the Prime Minister to be as much a pragmatist over Europe as she was a sceptic: she tested new ideas to destruction before she accepted them, but accept them she very often did. Though many thought her line on Europe too abrasive, few disagreed with the decisions she ultimately took. She was unpersuaded on the need for a single currency, but was prepared to accept, even welcome, integration on issues such as the single market. Overall, the Prime Minister was undeniably 'on board' the European train, even though she was uneasy about where it was heading and complained loudly at every stop.

The trouble was that there was another Margaret Thatcher, usually confined to private quarters, whose gut reaction was much more hostile to Europe. She bridled at the very mention of Brussels, and was thought by many to share the views on Germany which Nick Ridley was quoted expressing in a *Spectator* interview in July 1990, and which were so intemperate he was forced to leave the Cabinet; he resigned, it was said, but in fact he did so at Margaret's request conveyed through Charles Powell. He was effectively sacked. Nick was unlucky. He told me he had made his remarks privately after the end of the interview – but they were printed anyway, and they destroyed him. Margaret's view was equally direct: 'Never trust the Germans.' Two world wars, she thought, proved that the country was expansionist by instinct. Britain's role was to stop it. She organised a seminar on German reunification at Chequers, and voiced sentiments so hostile to Germany that they alarmed many of those who attended.

These two Margarets could co-exist. They did for most of her premiership, to great effect. But, after ten years in power, she began to lose the knack of keeping the two sides of her personality bolted together. It can be a terrible error to argue straight from your emotional bedrock, but the Prime Minister was beginning to do so; like a shorting circuit she flickered and crackled. Intermittently the lamp of European statesmanship still glowed; then – fssst! – and a shower of vivid commentary would light up the Margaret who attracted the last-ditch Englander. It cost her the trust of many in her party, but also gave her the devoted admiration of Members of Parliament she would never have put in her government.

It all came crashing down at the end of October 1990, when she answered questions in the House on her return from the Rome European Council. It was a summit meeting which need never have taken place, and at which she had been unexpectedly pushed on monetary union. A deal had been reached, and in the Commons the pragmatic prime minister who had achieved so much, the leader who recognised that we needed to take Britain into the ERM, was on display. 'Of course we wish to see both the United Kingdom and the European Community flourish, and the government and the country have done a great deal to ensure that the Community does flourish,' she soothed MPs at Prime Minister's Questions. 'I believe that solutions will be found which will enable the Community to go forward as Twelve,' she said a few minutes later in her subsequent statement on the Rome summit.

Then the other Margaret Thatcher was unleashed. Monetary union – which she had signed up to in the Single European Act – was nothing more than 'a back door to a federal Europe'. My own scheme for a hard ecu (which could have unified Conservative opinion because it would have let the market decide whether we ever entered the single currency) was brushed aside even though she had agreed it. 'In my view,' she suddenly told the House, 'the hard ecu would not become widely used throughout the Community.'

I nearly fell off the bench. With this single sentence she wrecked months of work and preparation. Europe had been suspicious that the hard ecu was simply a tactic to head off a single currency, and now the Prime Minister, in a matter of a few words, convinced them it was. Nor had she finished. She reached for her gun. 'The President of the Commission, Mr Delors, said at a press conference the other day that he wanted the European Parliament to be the democratic body of the Community, he wanted the Commission to be the Executive and he wanted the Council of Ministers to be the Senate. No. No. No.'

As I listened, astonished at her outburst, I understood where it came from. It was pure frustration. She had returned from the Rome Council bruised and bursting to speak. She had been stung by Geoffrey Howe's statement on the *Walden* programme that the hard ecu could in time become a single currency. Even so, she had still made a prepared statement in line with policy – as a prime minister must. Then, in response to a question, she lunged into that now-famous unscripted outburst. I heard our colleagues cheer, but knew there was trouble ahead. As I was to find, it is very easy in the cockpit of the House of Commons to overemphasise noisily for fear that somebody will interpret a soft answer as a prelude to a shifting position. That carries great risks.

The immediate effect was to dislodge Geoffrey Howe, who resigned the following day. Though the fire in Margaret's Commons stand was impressive as a display, she seemed, as Geoffrey wrote later, to be 'breaking ranks with her own party'. I heard of the resignation as I drove into the Commons in the early evening. There were not many Tories about, but small groups were gathered together in heated speculation. Geoffrey was the kind of figure every government needs if it is to thrive. What attracted him about politics was not the drama or the glamour, but the substantive building up of policy. His departure could not easily be explained away, and I thought our hopes of winning the next election were fading. But even then, I did not imagine that Geoffrey's resignation spelled the end for the Prime Minister. Neither did the next day's *Times*: it described her leadership as 'robust, undaunted and unchallenged'.

In fact we were in real trouble, and it was getting worse. The Chancellor had resigned; the Deputy Prime Minister had resigned. And these two senior colleagues were long marchers, architects of much of our programme and of the intellectual force behind Thatcherism. If they were disillusioned, what was happening to relationships between the most long-serving members of the government?

I would not have been surprised if Geoffrey had left the previous year, when he was removed from the Foreign Office to become Leader of the House and nominal Deputy Prime Minister: it was a blatant demotion. But he had stayed on, to be treated with increasing intolerance by the Prime Minister. Her general tone towards him was sharp, occasionally even cruel. If he felt aggrieved, he would have been justified in doing so.

His last Cabinet meeting, on the morning of his resignation, was the worst of all. Geoffrey and Margaret were sitting side by side, directly opposite me. They could barely bring themselves to look at one another. Geoffrey stared down at his papers, his lips pursed; Margaret had a disdainful air, her eyes glittering. When he looked down the long Cabinet table, she looked up it. When she put her head down to read her notes, he looked straight up. The body language said it all. This treatment of a senior colleague was embarrassing for the whole Cabinet. Few, if any, members would have stood it for long; and none without resentment. Geoffrey, who has a placid temperament, did not know how to deal with it. He was – in the face of this ill-mannered lady – too much of a gentleman.

Nigel was gone. Now Geoffrey was gone. Michael Heseltine was waiting. Michael had long been a vocal critic of Margaret's policies on Europe and the Poll Tax, and now believed himself vindicated on both. He felt, too, that he had been the victim of dirty work at the crossroads over the Westland Helicopters affair, which had led to his storming out of the Cabinet in 1986. Of all Margaret's colleagues, he was obviously the best-placed to challenge her. Michael was able. He was experienced. He was the best platform orator in the party. Temperamentally, he was the wolf that hunted alone, but he had a large body of supporters who were keen to hunt with him. Even some of his opponents thought he offered the party an election-winning personality. If Margaret were to face a contest, Michael was by far the most formidable opponent on offer.

At the time, I was no ally of his. Apart from his help to me over the peace camp at Molesworth in 1984, I knew little of him. He was friendly, but he moved in a different circle. I did not wish to see a challenge to the Prime Minister, and did not support Michael. My loyalties remained where they were. I was forty-seven and had the job in politics I had always coveted – Chancellor of the Exchequer. I hoped to remain chancellor until the general election. Thereafter, I assumed there were two possibilities. The first, which the opinion polls said was likely, was that we would lose to Labour, in which case I expected Margaret would retire soon after and we would elect a new leader of the party. I would not have been a candidate. I did not wish to be leader of the opposition. Opposing is a special art, and Michael Heseltine, Ken Clarke and Chris Patten were all more suited to it than myself. In such circumstances I would have wished to take a leading shadow portfolio, possibly returning to foreign affairs.

If, though, we won the general election, it would have been my wish to stay as chancellor for about a year and then move back to the Foreign Office or to the Home Office. And then, insofar as I thought of it at all, I expected Margaret to retire as prime minister during the course of that Parliament. Her departure from Downing Street before the election never crossed my mind as a serious proposition.

I was aware that some in the party saw me as Margaret's *long-term* successor. Soon after I became chancellor, Peter Morrison, the Prime Minister's patrician PPS, and Francis Maude, the ascetic Financial Secretary to the Treasury, came to see me to say they believed I was well-placed to be the next leader of the Conservative Party. Peter invited me to his house for drinks to tell me I should stand 'after she's gone'. Our conversation was private, but Peter was an intimate of the Prime Minister, and his message was clear enough. Whether or not Margaret knew what he was up to, he would not have said such things had he thought she might disapprove.

Peter Morrison was a classic Tory figure whose father had been Chairman of the 1922 Committee of Conservative backbenchers. Although a few months younger than me, he had been in the House since 1974, and was one of those MPs who do not seek office for themselves, thinking – rather modestly, in his case – that they are not fitted for it, but who want to see their party successful and in government. I was flattered by his confidence in my future. 'Maybe. It's a long time ahead,' was all I said. Nothing more. No plans were made, and nothing came of it.

Over the weekend after Geoffrey's resignation, Michael Heseltine sent a public letter critical of the leadership to his constituency chairman. It was a warning shot, hardly obscured by his statement early the next week: 'I think Mrs Thatcher will lead the Conservative Party into the next election and the Conservative Party will win it.'

Number 10 responded by encouraging an early date for any leadership contest, in order to 'flush out' any challengers. They dismissed Geoffrey's resignation as a conflict over style, not substance, another error of judgement which only served to further infuriate Geoffrey, leading him to retort in his resignation statement in the Commons: 'I must be the first minister in history to resign because he was in full agreement with government policy.' And Michael Heseltine was taunted in lobby briefings for the press that he should 'put up or shut up'.

But the backbench rats began to desert the Prime Minister. Tony Marlow, the populist MP for Northampton North, was the first off the ship, declaring that there would be 'a new prime minister by Christmas'. Even after all that had happened, this seemed a barmy remark. But Tony was always around the Commons, and he turned out to be more in touch with backbench opinion than anyone realised. The press began to sense drama. Malcontents stalked the parliamentary lobbies, and trouble mounted.

It was Geoffrey's devastating resignation speech on 13 November which brought all this to a head. In her memoirs, Margaret calls it 'poisonous'. But he was driven to it. As Chancellor of the Exchequer and Foreign Secretary, Geoffrey had been a perfect foil for Margaret's more strident tone. But just as in partnership she had relied on his strength of purpose, in battle she had ignored it at her peril. The iron had entered into his soul, and he responded accordingly. 'People throughout Europe see our Prime Minister finger-wagging, hear her passionate "No, No, No" much more than the content of carefully-worded formal texts,' he said. 'The task has become futile . . . of trying to pretend that there was a common policy when every step forward risked being subverted by some casual comment or impulsive answer.'

I felt a mixture of agreement and dismay as he addressed a Chamber listening intently to every nuance. When he spoke of the way in which the Prime Minister had destroyed the hard ecu I could only agree. Still, I had not expected Geoffrey to deliver a speech which would destroy her. Geoffrey's steel has always been underestimated due to his easy-going manner. Again it was Margaret Thatcher's folly that she ignored this side of his character. Quite simply, she had disregarded all his private arguments; this was his only chance to put the record straight publicly. That was what he was doing. As I looked around the House I could not see the faces of my colleagues behind me, but I could see the reaction of the Labour and Liberal Members across the floor of the House. Their pleasure at Margaret's discomfort turned to glee as, to follow Geoffrey's cricketing metaphor, ball after ball hit the stumps.

I was sitting on the front bench beside Margaret. It was a struggle to know how to react. She was tense from top to toe, and it would have been utterly unconvincing to turn to her with comforting words; we sat in silence, listening and, in my case, wondering what would happen next, and how we could cope with the fallout. What defence would we have to the charge that the two great architects of Thatcherism had both repudiated the Prime Minister? Bernard Ingham, Margaret's loyal spokesman, had insisted that Geoffrey's departure was merely over a matter of style. Geoffrey's resignation speech had shown all too clearly that it wasn't, and had made stark the division in the Conservative Party; the iceberg to which Nigel Lawson had alluded in his resignation speech, formerly nine-tenths hidden, had now emerged above the waves.

Afterwards, I spoke to Margaret in the Prime Minister's room behind the Speaker's Chair. She knew well enough the political damage Geoffrey's speech had done her, though not, I think, that it would precipitate a leadership election. It appeared to me that her principal concern was what the speech revealed about her fractured relationship with Geoffrey. I do not think she understood how it had come about, how hurt he must have been by the disdain that she had heaped upon him. We sat for a while, and I tried to put the best gloss I could upon what had happened. I could not pretend that it was anything but a serious setback, and I did not. I offered Margaret the hopeful analysis that the speech might be cathartic, causing her colleagues to rally round her. I suggested too that as she was beleaguered, a lot of sympathetic support might emerge.

It was not to be. Geoffrey's call in his resignation statement for 'others to consider their response' brought Michael Heseltine out into the open: 'I am persuaded that I would now have a better prospect of leading the Conservatives to a fourth election victory,' he announced the following morning from the steps of his home.

Douglas Hurd and I were immediately asked by Peter Morrison to propose and second the Prime Minister's nomination for the leadership contest which would now take place. I did so without reservation. It seemed natural to me that the Prime Minister should be backed by her Foreign Secretary and her Chancellor. Despite my concerns I believed Margaret had earned the right to contest the next election as prime minister, and to let the electorate judge her record as a whole. I thought it bad politics to attempt to remove a sitting prime minister, and in no circumstances would I have stood against her.

Those with more recent memories of leadership contests within the Conservative Party might find it surprising that, though a contest was actually under way, on this occasion the Cabinet thought it its duty to stand foursquare by the Prime Minister. But we did. I and, to the best of my knowledge, all my Cabinet colleagues but one, David Hunt, voted for her. We turned away those in the party – and there were more than a few – who urged us to stand against her. We told everyone who asked our advice to back her, and made it clear that we would be doing the same. And we meant it. I believed that if Margaret Thatcher were to be dismissed from office it should be by the British people as a whole.

At the end of the week, I issued a statement of support describing Margaret as 'one of this country's most successful peacetime prime ministers'. It was a true representation of my views, but incomplete since it excluded my concerns. Nonetheless I would have been willing to help further in her campaign, but there was no attempt to rope me in. Peter Morrison was confident the operation was under control.

It wasn't. At Number 10 there was no chain of command, no systematic canvassing and not enough recognition of the political danger. During the crucial final days of the contest the Prime Minister was in Paris, at the Conference on Security and Cooperation in Europe (CSCE) summit to mark the end of the Cold War. In retrospect it is probable that a hard-fought battle against Michael (who did more than fifty press and media interviews within a day of declaring his candidacy) would have flushed out the two missing votes which would have enabled Margaret to win on the first ballot. Even had it done so, she would have been mortally wounded. In the event, those closest to her left her behind 'like an old umbrella in a taxi', as Tristan Garel-Jones put it.

Nonetheless, Margaret was right to go to Paris. The presumption on all sides was that she was going to win. As the only other prime minister who has fought a leadership election while in office, I know it would have been undignified for her to rush around asking MPs for their support. Clearly a contest against Michael Heseltine was quite a different proposition from the fight with Tony Meyer a year previously, and the whips had warned her that he would get a substantial vote. Still, Margaret had led the party for almost sixteen years, and had won three general elections. Conservative MPs knew everything there was to know about her. If she had fought tooth-and-nail in Westminster, people might have put it around that she was being forced to do so because Heseltine was 'doing better than expected'. Far better, she must have thought, to appear as one of the victors of the Cold War among world leaders in Paris than to throw herself into the Tory scrum in Westminster.

I, though, was not on the pitch. On the morning of Saturday, 17 November, three days after Michael kicked off the contest, I entered the Herts and Essex hospital in Bishop's Stortford for an operation on my wisdom teeth that had been arranged weeks before. Though I was discharged the next day, I recuperated at Finings, and did not return to London until the following Thursday, by which time Margaret had decided to stand down.

When Michael announced his candidature, I did consider postponing the operation. I had been warned that I might be out of action for up to a week. The government was in crisis. The press in ferment. Should the chancellor be *hors de combat*? Jeffrey Archer, one of the Prime Minister's most energetic supporters, thought not. He called to see me at the Treasury and urged me to delay the operation. I declined: if I had done so, the impression that I expected the Prime Minister to lose and was preparing myself to stand in the second round of voting would have been overwhelming.

In the event, when Margaret had resigned and I did enter the contest, the rumour spread that my operation had been a ploy. David Davis, the MP for Haltemprice and Howden, picked up this mischief. It came, he thought, from an over-enthusiastic supporter of Douglas Hurd who was trying to damage my candidacy; it fell away swiftly, but it had entered the political bloodstream and was often to emerge, as though it were fact, in later years.

It was nonsense: I was in pain from an abscess under a wisdom tooth, and had been for a long time. The operation had been booked weeks earlier after Jenny Acland, wife of the British Ambassador in Washington, had rushed me to a dentist there for late-night emergency treatment. Norma was insistent that the operation should go ahead, and Graham Bright, my PPS, also urged me not to postpone it any longer.

'Don't worry,' he said. 'I'll report to you every day and let you know what's going on.'

'I don't want you running around organising things,' I said to him.

He followed my orders, but he kept tugging at the leash – 'You've got to stand' – and his certainty began to persuade me that I stood a chance should Margaret fall. People had said this sort of thing to me before, and had left me unconvinced. But now I began to wonder. The support did seem to be there. Shortly before my operation, Terence Higgins, the MP for Worthing and a senior figure in the Commons, had called on me at the Treasury and urged me to stand if the Prime Minister failed to survive. Since Terence was a former Treasury minister, a Privy Councillor, a leader of moderate Conservative opinion in the House and one of the great mandarins of the 1922 Committee, I took his words seriously. I had suspected I would be written off by senior figures in the party as too inexperienced, but Terence's advocacy was reassuring. I would make a credible candidate.

Still, I was not keen. Late on the afternoon of Thursday, 15 November, as I worked in my study at Number 11, a call came through. It was Tristan Garel-Jones, ringing from the Foreign Office. Tristan's reputation as a Machiavelli-in-waiting is so strong that it is easy to overlook the fact that in his personal behaviour he is very straightforward and rather old-fashioned. What he thinks, he says without frills, especially to his friends. And he did to me. 'I think you ought to know,' he said bluntly, 'Norman Lamont has canvassed me on your behalf, and I must say I think his behaviour is rather improper.'

I agreed. Norman was not acting with my encouragement, and I told him so. 'If he's doing that, it's not my wish,' I said. 'I intend to vote for the Prime Minister, and I shall tell others to do likewise.'

'Good,' said Tristan, and hung up.

We both knew, however, that this might not be the end of the matter. 'If anything goes wrong for her, all these people are going to line up in front of you,' Tristan warned. Like Graham Bright, he was aware – more aware than I was – how strong my potential support was in the centre-right heart of the party.

On Friday night I was driven up to my constituency, and the next morning I opened a fair in Huntingdon to raise money for Mencap, Norma's favourite charity. She could not abandon it in mid-morning, so it was Peter Brown, my agent, who drove me to the hospital. The operation, which took place almost immediately, was trouble-free.

In London, though, things were going badly wrong for the Prime Minister. As I recovered from the general anaesthetic in my hospital ward on Saturday evening, Norma and Elizabeth bustled in to see me. I remember nothing of our conversation, but Elizabeth is certain we talked about whether or not Margaret would make it through the first ballot, which would be held on Tuesday. She says I speculated about whether I should stand. If so, I suspect I was expecting a firm 'no' in response. I didn't get it. 'Go for it,' said Elizabeth. Norma agreed. There might not be another chance.

I woke on Sunday morning with a sore and tender mouth, but able to go home. It was painful to speak or eat, and I was fed a colourful mix of painkillers. At home, I flicked through the newspapers, which were filled with speculation about Douglas Hurd stepping forward as a replacement for the Prime Minister. In London – though I did not know it – MPs were talking up my chances as a candidate who could draw support from across the party. I was still groggy from the operation when Ian Lang called, offering his support. I thanked him, but insisted that I would only consider running if Margaret Thatcher withdrew from the contest. At that point I still thought she would win on the first round.

On Monday morning, Jeffrey Archer appeared at Finings full of gossip, with a huge pile of newspapers under his arm ('Support for Major as Alternative Choice', said *The Times* on its front page). Jeffrey is one of a kind, unsinkable in a way even that famous survivor of the *Titanic*, Molly Brown, would admire. He works incessantly for the Conservative Party, and understands it from the grassroots up. He wanted Margaret to survive, but his verdict on her chances was bleak, and, with Norma, we discussed what might follow the ballot to be held the next day.

'Do you realise we're sitting here talking about you becoming prime minister?' Norma said suddenly. Though I was still only half-alert, the thought sank in. It was tempting to play with – but unreal, I assumed. I still expected Margaret to scrape through. The phone rang and rang again as colleagues and journalists tried to sound me out and keep me up to date with the swirl of events back in London.

Many of them descended on Graham Bright as well. His message was consistent: 'John wants no canvassing. He wants no organisation. She hasn't gone.' He then went freelance. 'But what you can do is let me know of other people of the same mind.' On the phone, he told me there was a groundswell of support for me to stand.

Far from being grateful, I was suspicious. 'How do you know?' I asked. 'Have you been canvassing?'

He promised me he had not. 'But you know our colleagues,' he said. 'They're positioning themselves.' Even before the first ballot, many in the party were preparing to walk away from a prime minister they admired because they felt she might lose the next election. Politics is sometimes a despicable business.

I was in no state to talk to anybody for long, but the impression I gained was clear. There was no campaign running on my behalf. There was no plotting. All my friends (including some who ended up backing Douglas Hurd) were planning to vote for Margaret – as, with Graham Bright as my proxy, was I. But the certainty had gone out of her campaign. A second ballot was beginning to look more likely, and if it took place, it was questionable whether Margaret would win it. Douglas had already indicated that he would stand should she step down. It was clear that I was expected to do likewise.

The result of the first ballot came early on the evening of Tuesday, 20 November. Norma and I watched on television at home. The party's 372 Members of Parliament had voted 204–152 in Margaret Thatcher's favour, with sixteen abstentions. The Prime Minister had won 55 per cent of the vote (more than the 53 per cent she got when she won the leadership in 1975, and more than the 49.7 per cent I would get a week later); but under the party's idiosyncratic system she was two votes short of the total she needed to win on the first ballot.

I was taking in the implications of all this when the phone rang in my study. It was Douglas, calling from the British Embassy in Paris. He was, he said, about to speak to Margaret. I told him I would support the Prime Minister for as long as she chose to remain in the contest. Then, like millions across the country, I followed the drama on television, as Margaret emerged from the Embassy and announced that she intended to contest the next round.

Ian Lang called to suggest I put out a statement of support for the Prime Minister, as Douglas had already done. I did so – and asked him to keep in touch. That evening, after the results of the first ballot had been announced, Tristan Garel-Jones held an impromptu supper at his home in Catherine Place which was to be misrepresented later in folklore as an anti-Thatcher cabal. Graham Bright was invited, and telephoned me to ask whether he should go. 'No,' I said. 'No.' He did not attend.

The phone began ringing early on Wednesday morning, and did not stop all day. At a quarter to eight I was woken by Ian Lang, who let me know that Douglas Hurd was rumoured not to be keen to run, but that two-thirds of the Cabinet were sliding towards him. At about 10 o'clock I asked Olive Baddeley, the Chairman of my association, to come and see me at Finings. When she arrived the press were already parked outside my gates. She found me in the sitting room, being fed yet more painkillers by Norma.

I wanted Olive's views on what I should do if Margaret went. 'Should I stand?' I asked. 'What would the constituency feel about it?'

She told me that if I had sufficient support I should stand, and that Huntingdon would back me. Elizabeth popped her head in to add her backing. Olive took a tray of coffee out to the press, and told them that I wasn't coming out to speak, and they might as well go home. She stayed at Finings to field the phone calls that continued throughout the day. John Cole, the BBC's political correspondent, was one of the few calls I took, more to glean information from him than to give it. Ken Clarke, newly shuffled from the Department of Health to Education, told me that Douglas and I should both stand, and that he was going to tell Margaret to stand down. 'Don't do that, Ken,' I told him, twice, but he felt she would be badly beaten in a second contest. Francis Maude told me he had talked to Margaret and had gained the firm impression that she was going to stand down. He assured me I would find a great deal of support in the party if she did.

At midday, the Prime Minister returned from France and reaffirmed her decision to fight. But as the afternoon wore on, Michael Heseltine was wooing – and winning – many of the MPs who had given Margaret their vote the day before.

The Prime Minister then rang me at Finings. She was brisk. 'Douglas is going to nominate me and I want you to second me,' she burst out before I could say a word. Although the result of the first ballot had been worse than we had feared, she did not refer to it. Nor did she ask my view of her prospects and whether she should stand again. She simply assumed that she had my support. Her approach was a classic example of her management style. Taken aback, I paused before replying: 'If that is what you want, I will.'

In her memoirs, Margaret says that my 'hesitation was palpable'. It was, but not because I was thinking of my own position. I was very ready to second her, and had told Douglas so, but I would have liked to have discussed her prospects and her campaign strategy before she committed herself. I knew, for example, how Ken Clarke felt, and guessed that he was not alone. But Margaret was peremptory, and once again I despaired at her style even as I pledged my support.

The crunch for the Prime Minister came early that evening when she met the members of her Cabinet one by one. She hoped to secure their active support, and must have believed that, face to face, she would be successful in doing so. She was to be disappointed. 'Treachery with a smile on its face' was her description some years later. Only a few last-ditchers told her she had a chance of winning. The bulk of the Cabinet promised her their votes, but added that they believed she would lose, and that she should leave the contest to avoid humiliation. The executive of the 1922 Committee, too, called for a wider choice of candidates that day – political code for their belief that Margaret could not win a second ballot.

In the early evening, Ian Lang called once more. 'The Prime Minister is mortally wounded,' he said. 'But the end could be messy.' He reported strong resentment against Heseltine; not all those who had voted for him wanted him to succeed. I told Ian that Graham Bright had let me know that he had already had calls from ninety-eight colleagues asking, in warm tones, what my intentions were. 'I'm not surprised,' replied Ian.

At about 8.30 that evening, Jeffrey Archer's driver arrived at Finings with the Prime Minister's nomination paper for the second round, already signed by Douglas Hurd. I scrawled my signature beneath his. By then I knew it was becoming less likely that the document would ever be used.

Was I prepared to stand? At Graham Bright's suggestion Norma typed out a second document as a fail-safe, advising Cranley Onslow, the Chairman of the 1922 Committee, that I was prepared to let my name go forward. I was reluctant to entrust this document to anyone, even Graham, while the Prime Minister remained in the contest. I asked Jeffrey's driver to wait for a while, and he did – for two hours, eating dinner – until Peter Morrison telephoned and told me it was almost certain the Prime Minister would withdraw from the contest the next morning. I signed the paper, then sealed it in an envelope for the chauffeur to give to Graham Bright and no one else. Under no circumstances, I insisted to Graham, was it to be used if Margaret did not withdraw. Jeffrey Archer's car headed back to London.

I was apprehensive. I realised that within twenty-four hours I might be entering a contest that could make me prime minister. I thought it was too soon for me, but that it was becoming difficult to stand aside. I did not know if I could win, or would receive only a derisory vote. But events were developing their own momentum.

I went to bed believing that the Prime Minister would announce her resignation the next morning, and as I woke, Peter Morrison rang from Downing Street to confirm it. Nominations for the second round closed at midday. Norma and I set off for Westminster early on Thursday morning. As we travelled through East London we saw a banner hanging out of a window: 'She's Gone!' I turned on the radio to discover that the news was now public. Someone else would be prime minister within a week.

But who? Douglas Hurd and I were the obvious candidates to stand against Michael Heseltine, but I was as unwilling to fight Douglas as he was to stand against me. Both of us were prepared to withdraw our nomination in favour of the other if it became clear that one of us was most likely to win. On the previous Wednesday night a meeting had taken place in a room off one of the ministerial corridors in the Commons – though I knew nothing about it at the time. About twelve senior ministers attended. They considered the merits of settling on a single candidate if, as seemed inevitable, the Prime Minister withdrew. The idea attracted some in the room, but Richard Ryder shot it down. A nominated candidate would be seen as a Cabinet stitch-up, he argued. In its present mood the party would not wear it. That was the fact of the matter. Both Douglas and I, whatever we may have wished to do, were trapped by circumstances into opposing one another as candidates.

On Thursday morning Douglas submitted his nomination papers while MPs who wanted me to stand began to gather at the Treasury. But where was the candidate? I had no mobile phone and was out of contact, stuck in the London traffic. Might I miss the midday deadline for the submission of nominations? Graham Bright did not reveal that he had my signed consent tucked in his pocket.

With about half an hour to go to the close of nominations, I arrived at my desk. Norman Lamont came in to tell me I had many supporters. I demurred, and suggested that Douglas would be the best candidate. Norman shook his head vigorously. Suddenly the doors of my office burst open and supporters poured in – Michael Howard, John Gummer, Peter Lilley, David Davis and Francis Maude among them. Many were senior ministers who had come straight from Cabinet; others were colleagues from the Treasury. Some were rising stars, such as William Hague, then with only a year in Parliament behind him. I was astounded. In Huntingdon, I had heard my name was one of those being talked about at Westminster. I had no idea that I was likely to find such strong backing so quickly.

The depth of my support came for both positive and negative reasons. The positive reasons were that my reputation had risen in the year that I had been chancellor. Though the economic indicators were disturbing, I had taken steps against inflation and the recession, got the pound into the ERM and cut interest rates. The public expenditure round a few weeks before had won rave reviews and left the Labour Party with little to criticise. And my speech at the party conference in October had been well-received. The negative reason was that I was not Michael Heseltine, but was the person best placed to defeat him.

If a candidate from the right wing of the party had stepped forward, things might have been different. None did. There was no obvious figure to do so: Norman Tebbit, before he declared for me, was one of the few talked about as a possible contender. Although Norman had a formidable reputation and would have received the enthusiastic support of a minority, he could never have carried the centre or the left of the parliamentary party; and by then he knew it. I suspected he backed me because he feared that if he had stood himself, Michael Heseltine would have won.

I would have preferred more time in a senior Cabinet post before seeking the leadership, but with the Foreign Secretary already in the contest, and a challenger from outside the Cabinet, I could not credibly stand aside without giving the impression that I had no stomach for the top job. Unless I wished to be written off in the future as having shrunk from the challenge, I had little choice but to throw my hat into the ring, though I was still not enthusiastic in doing so.

What, in particular, gave me pause for thought was that some of those closest to me, Tristan Garel-Jones and Chris Patten among them, supported Douglas Hurd. I would have been happy to support Douglas, too, though I was fairly sure Michael Heseltine would beat him. My own team stretched right across the parliamentary party to include many whose views were well to the right of mine. Because Margaret favoured me in the campaign, many of her followers backed me. She and her allies, however, deceived themselves if they thought I would pursue unchanged policies. I did not aim to mislead anyone, and attempted to make my views clear, pressing for social reform, tax cuts for the less well-off and improved public services. 'We must help the disadvantaged,' I wrote in that Friday's *Sun*, which was hardly a clarion call to the right of the party.

As the clock ticked towards the close of nominations at midday, John Gummer and Norman Lamont signed my nomination and Graham Bright rushed off to deliver it to Cranley Onslow, Chairman of the 1922 Committee, who had the dubious privilege of supervising the contest. It was a close-run thing. In haste, Graham struggled to open the lattice doors of an ancient lift behind the Speaker's Chair in the Commons and dropped the vital paper. It fluttered to the edge of the shaft and nearly fell into it. Cranley had assumed that the two 'H's, Hurd and Heseltine, would be the only members to put their names forward, and Graham's last-minute arrival was a surprise to him. 'I do hope it doesn't all end in tears,' was Cranley's comment.

Politics is a cruel and brutal trade, and there was no time to mourn the political passing of the Prime Minister. The second ballot would be held on Tuesday, 27 November, a bare five days away, and I needed a campaign team, a headquarters, a strategy and a manifesto. William Hague suggested we take over a house in nearby Gayfere Street as a base. It was owned by a young aspirant parliamentary candidate, Alan Duncan, and

William Hague dashed from the Treasury with David Davis to shift furniture. I headed into the Members' Dining Room at the Commons for lunch, accompanied by Gillian Shephard, Robert Atkins and Ian Lang. I was nervous, and slightly pale, at this first public appearance in the House since Margaret's downfall.

The core of my campaign team swiftly came together. My Treasury colleague Norman Lamont assumed overall responsibility – not, I was told later, without a little dissent. Ian Lang, Michael Howard, Francis Maude and Richard Ryder joined him in driving things forward. Francis, with Robert Hayward, the psephologically-skilled MP for Kingswood, looked after the voting figures. Richard headed our media operation and used his contacts with the party in the country to bring the National Union and constituency chairmen behind my candidature. Ian Lang was a key member of my team from start to finish, as he would be on subsequent occasions. Always a rock of support, he was one of the first to speak to me after my tooth operation, and the first to congratulate me after the result. Graham Bright ran my diary.

They were determined that I should stand out from the other candidates. In the first round, Michael Heseltine had frequently been caught by the television cameras walking alone, leaving the impression that his leadership bid was something of a one-man band. I had supporters packed around me wherever I went. And my team took care to proclaim the fact that I more than anyone else had attracted support from all wings of the party.

One question needed an immediate answer. What did I propose to do about the Poll Tax? Michael Heseltine's promise to abolish it had won him many first-round votes. Temporarily freed from collective responsibility, the six or so senior ministers on my team put their views with force. Michael Howard, once the minister in charge of the tax, pressed for a fundamental review of the role and financing of local government, thus outbidding Heseltine. I was not prepared to commit myself to lifting the lid of Pandora's Box, and, with the backing of Ian Lang and my Treasury adviser Andrew Tyrie, set a more modest line. I would join Michael Heseltine in promising action, but would not commit myself to abolition until it had been proved the best option. We agreed that, if pressed, I should say, 'The principle that everybody should pay something is established. The principle of a flat-rate charge is not.' This stance laid the way for the successful introduction of the Council Tax before the 1992 election.

Another urgent concern was the media. David Mellor performed heroically on a string of back-to-back television programmes. His boisterous advocacy left the other candidates sagging. Gillian Shephard, one of the most televised faces in the parliamentary party, willingly undertook a string of interviews. Andrew Tyrie set to drafting newspaper articles. And my proposer and seconder, John Gummer and Norman Lamont, put out a text. 'John is the candidate most likely to unite the party, representing the next generation of Conservative leadership,' they wrote. 'We are enormously encouraged by the spontaneous groundswell of support he has received in all parts of the party.' It was true.

As nominations closed for the second ballot, I issued a joint statement with Douglas Hurd, making it clear that we wanted a good-humoured contest. We stuck by it. I spoke to Douglas regularly through the campaign – 'Give my best to Tristan,' he remembers me ending my calls – and although it arose from my advocacy of a classless society, I was as uneasy as Douglas when the media came to portray the contest, falsely, as a battle between 'landed toffs' and 'the boy from Brixton'.

With his eye on making the most of our turmoil, Neil Kinnock had called a debate on a motion of no confidence for Thursday, 22 November. Against expectations, the move backfired. I was on the front bench when Margaret Thatcher spoke, and her robust and remarkable performance was one of the best of her career. She put Labour to the sword, and many on the government benches must have wondered whether they had been right, after all, to deny their leader a win in the ballot two days earlier.

But there could be no going back. If my enthusiasm for the contest had been a little subdued at the start, it soon sharpened as my bandwagon began to roll. MPs from across the party came flooding to our support. It was hugely exciting, not least because it was so unexpected.

I like elections, and I began to enjoy myself. There were vast numbers of interviews to do, all with the same questions: Was I the political son of Margaret Thatcher? What would I do with the Poll Tax? Did I expect to win? My answers became polished, though I was still far from fighting fit after my operation only days before, and had to be stuffed with antibiotics and Paracetamol before every appearance.

Late on Thursday night I had passed Graham Bright. He was loitering at the near end of the 'no' lobby, catching MPs as they passed to defeat

Labour's no-confidence motion. 'How goes the battle?' I asked, clapping him on the shoulder.

'Not bad,' he said laconically. 'You've got a third of the parliamentary party so far.' I thought he was joking. He was not. Francis Maude confirmed the numbers.

Friday morning brought our official campaign launch, at the Treasury. It was pandemonium, a phalanx of photographers with blinding flashguns and bright video lights. The noise of cameras made it almost impossible to hear the questions, and the lobby correspondents we needed to reach were trapped at the back of the undersized room. I tried to persuade the photographers to take their shots and go away. 'We're not moving, mate,' one muttered, and he spoke for them all. I tried again, surrendered, gestured for quiet, and began.

My aim was to bring together a fractured party. 'I have always studiously avoided labels on the grounds that they are grotesquely misleading,' I said. On Europe I offered 'gradualism, practicalism and common sense'. On the Poll Tax, I said I was 'increasingly convinced that we will not be able to leave things as they are', but I did not commit myself to abolition. I pointed to 'a general need to improve educational standards' and offered a foretaste of the policies with which I hoped to improve results, diversify the control of schools, widen parental choice and improve the status of teachers. Most heartfelt was my suggestion that we undervalued 'blue collar' skills and needed to 'make changes that will produce across the whole of this country a genuinely classless society in which people can rise to whatever level their own abilities and their own good fortune may take them from wherever they started'. It was the first time I had used the phrase 'classless society' – a suggestion of Andrew Tyrie's, I think, but very much in tune with my instincts. It was a moderate, perhaps even centre-left, platform. No one could have been misled about where I stood.

I concluded with a cricketing reference: 'It has been a good day, so far, with one exception,' I said. 'I'm afraid England are all out for 194. Not a good score for them, but it would be a perfectly satisfactory score for me.'

As the journalists filed out of the room and on to Douglas Hurd's launch, I was worried that the event had been chaotic. Would it be reported as a disorganised disaster? It was not. It made excellent television, and Robin Oakley, the political correspondent of *The Times*, was overheard declaring that the launch was 'exceptionally good, with an American-style buzz'. That gave me great cheer. From then on I launched into the campaign, increasingly confident that I would get a respectable vote, and soon even daring to think I might win.

Although my vote was growing, my campaign team did not permit me to relax. At Gayfere Street, Francis Maude and Robert Hayward kept lists of MPs pledged to us. Francis showed some of them to me, but as the campaign wore on I began to suspect that he was doctoring the figures to make my position seem less secure, to ensure I kept on working. 'I think it's going to be better than this,' I said to him on more than one occasion – as, in the event, it was. Francis later assured me that the discrepancy was caused by his applying too big a 'discount' to the numbers – only about one MP in ten, it seemed, misled the candidates about their intentions. Francis's caution was justified, since in public the three candidates claimed to have the backing of a total of 450 MPs, whereas only 372 sat in the Commons as Conservatives.

All three of us bidding for the party leadership began to scramble for endorsements from significant figures in the party. By Monday I had the support of eight members of the Cabinet, including David Waddington, the Home Secretary, and Cecil Parkinson, then Transport Secretary. Nigel Lawson and Geoffrey Howe declared their support for Michael Heseltine. Geoffrey's decision was understandable and half-expected, but I was sorry that Nigel, with whom I had worked so closely and amicably at the Treasury, did not support me. In his memoirs, he says this is because I did not ask him, which is a fair comment, and I was possibly at fault for not doing so. But it did not prevent him having a humdinger of a row with Norman Lamont when the news of his support for Michael became public.

The press were broadly friendly, although I was disappointed that the *Daily Telegraph*, the premier Conservative paper, backed Douglas, with Charles Moore, then the associate editor, writing in support of him. Charles also interviewed me, in an encounter neither of us enjoyed. He was a fierce supporter of Margaret (later he was to become her official biographer), and seemed genuinely offended that I should dare to be a candidate to succeed her. It was clear from the outset that he and I were oil and water. My team were bitterly angry at the way he had conducted the interview, and I was never to enjoy support from his pen. The *Sunday Times* backed Michael Heseltine, but I secured the overwhelming endorsement of the tabloids.

The turning point in my campaign came on Sunday. The papers brought some stunning opinion polls in my favour, and an interview I did on the *Breakfast with Frost* programme that morning went remarkably well. I was relieved at that, because David Frost is a dangerous interviewer. He is relaxed and non-combative, and as a result he often draws the unwary onto dangerous territory. He has a gift of persuading people to drop their guard in a way more aggressive questioners never manage. This time I got my message across. 'What I wish to achieve, whether you call it Majorism or not, is a much greater degree of opportunity and choice,' I said. 'I know that is a slogan, but it is a crucially important slogan.' They were not the words of a dyed-in-the-wool Thatcherite. It was my reply to Frost's last question which caught the upbeat mood of my campaign. With Christmas approaching, he asked whether friends should send their cards to 10 or 11 Downing Street. 'They can be absolutely safe if they send them care of the Treasury, for the Prime Minister is First Lord of the Treasury,' I told him.

The same day, Norma and I took part in a wholly contrived photo-opportunity in St James's Park. Later, it was to be remembered because I was driven the few hundred yards from Gayfere Street in a Jaguar belonging to the lobbyist Ian Greer – though, at Richard Ryder's insistence, we had paid him for the use of it. I was astounded at the crowds of journalists attracted by the event. Not only the BBC, ITN and the British press seemed to be there, but journalists from around the world. 'Is there something I don't know?' I asked, after it was over.

'Of course,' said Graham Bright. 'You're going to be the next prime minister.'

Not all my campaigning was as enthusiastic. I was mortally embarrassed to be interviewed about my religious faith on Radio 4's *Sunday* programme. My religion is a private matter. I do not flaunt it. I am a believer in the message more than the rituals of the Church. I did not want to do the interview, but was told by my team that if I avoided it, the view would be put about – wrongly – that I was a non-believer. I found the questions too personal to answer without seeming sanctimonious, and turned my answers to substantive issues. It was a gentle interview and I was not pressed; but I was glad when it was over. I have always been wary of politicians who parade their faith, and prefer a little English reserve on the subject.

Nor did I enjoy telephoning MPs to ask for their support. I found it unappealing to intrude in such a way, though my campaign team again insisted it was necessary. On the first occasion, Norman Lamont dialled the number and passed the telephone to me. He had called Michael Jopling, Chief Whip when I had entered office as the most junior whip in the party. We had a perfectly courteous conversation, but I did not feel I could ask for a specific commitment, and Michael did not offer one.

Other moments of the campaign are still vivid. I recall seeing Robert Rhodes-James, the scholarly historian who sat for Cambridge, in the early evening on the day before the second ballot. He explained to me that he had promised to vote for Michael on the second ballot, but would reconsider his support should the contest run on to a third. In the Commons, the chancellor of the exchequer's office adjoins the prime minister's. And the walls are thick. While Robert and I were talking, an extraordinary tumult broke out next door. There was a voice raised in anger, presumably Margaret's, although one could not be certain. There were several men shouting. The uproar was such that Robert and I, looking bemusedly at each other, had to come closer to hear each other.

I recall, too, a tiny minority of colleagues who hoped to use the contest to strike bargains. I turned them all down, including one who turned up uninvited at Number 11 Downing Street with his wife and children in tow. As the man waited to see me, Graham Bright warned me that he had a shopping list of items he wanted me to agree to in return for his vote. He came in, and started running through the list, which included a bypass around part of his constituency and a new hospital. I let him know pretty sharply that that was not how I worked, but he seemed deaf to my comments. 'I'm a gentleman and you're a gentleman, so it's a deal,' he was still saying as he was ushered out. It took Graham Bright's forceful clarification – 'You won't get a bypass *and* you won't get a hospital . . .' – before he realised his tactics had failed to work.

Both the Heseltine and Hurd campaigns stopped work for the weekend, but my team pressed on regardless. On Sunday morning Norman Lamont announced outside 11 Downing Street that we now had 150 committed supporters. Inside, we met to review the media campaign; I was encouraged to see Gordon Reece, who had been Margaret Thatcher's media guru, join us.

Number 11 had been a hive of activity since nomination day, with up to a dozen colleagues there all the time. They needed feeding and watering, and there was no staff to help. Barbara Wallis, my Constituency Secretary, moved in and took over, while Norma returned to Huntingdon to honour constituency engagements. Barbara's husband, Derek Oakley, was dragged in, too. While Barbara was buried under letters and messages, Derek took to the kitchen and also acted as the in-house doctor. I was still swallowing pills and potions after my operation, and Derek followed me everywhere to ensure I took them – even, at one stage, leaving them on my pillow with a despairing note. Norman Lamont had an appalling cold, and could be seen going around the house clutching a bottle of cough mixture. Once he mislaid it, and went into the kitchen demanding to know where it was. The terse reply, 'Where you last left it, I don't doubt,' was not well received.

Number 11 was not used to weekend visitors, and our stock of food soon ran out. Ever-increasing numbers of people headed for the kitchen to be fed, and Derek and Alan Duncan, whose house in Gayfere Street was full of our campaign workers, raided Sainsbury's and returned laden with carrier bags. At times the kitchen resembled a sandwich bar at lunchtime, with Alan cheerfully coping with piles of dirty dishes. On Sunday, I asked Derek to prepare dinner for 7 p.m. for ten people. Then 7.30 for twelve, changed to 7.45 for fourteen. The chicken casserole stretched further, and tempers did as well, as dinner was delayed until 8 p.m. Norman Lamont got a very dusty response when he appeared in the kitchen again just before eight, searching once again for his cough mixture. The meal was supplemented with two huge cans of baked beans, ceremoniously borne into the dining room on a silver salver. 'My favourite dish,' cried David Mellor. Despite the unconventional menu, the dinner was a great success.

I spent much of the campaign working from Number 11, but the real donkey work was done at Gayfere Street. Ian Lang, Francis Maude (sitting in the basement clutching worry beads) and Richard Ryder were central to the whole operation. They worked almost around the clock – as did many young political advisers and staff from Central Office, who took unpaid leave or resigned from their jobs to work on the campaign. By Monday morning, the day before the ballot, I knew I was close to victory. I didn't need to be told the canvassing figures. I've always been very sensitive to body language, and colleagues in the House began to react to me differently. The moment I walked into the Members' Tea Room that day, the whispered conversations and the glancing looks told me everything.

At a small meeting at Number 11 we reviewed the campaign and agreed that overkill was now the problem, such was the enthusiasm. It was decided that each wavering MP should be approached by only one person; names and numbers were shared out.

As Tuesday dawned, our MPs prepared to vote in the second ballot and I thanked my team for a first-class campaign, the *Independent* published a poll suggesting I was the candidate most likely to attract voters back to the Conservative fold. It astonished me. I did not think the public knew me well enough to put me ahead of Michael, and I had not set out to court the press. Norman Lamont then ran through the latest estimate of my likely support: cross-checking with Douglas Hurd had now weeded out almost all the MPs who had promised their support to more than one candidate. Norman's prediction was 175 votes, just twelve short of an outright majority. I was confident I would do rather better than that.

I was still not fully fit and was very tired. The campaign had been exhilarating and adrenaline had kept me going, but I slept very little. I had a drink with Margaret Thatcher at Number 10 before voting, then returned to Number 11. I was confident I would win or, at worst, poll well enough to proceed to the next ballot, which would be between the two leading candidates; either way, more long days lay ahead. I decided to do something I had almost never done during the day and went to bed, where I fell asleep within moments. When I awoke it was after 5 o'clock, and the result was due in an hour. I bathed and dressed and prepared myself for whatever was to come.

In the main reception room at Number 11 there was a big crowd, a television – without a proper aerial, it hardly had a picture – and an air of great expectancy. Cranley Onslow declared the result, and as he began to speak I put my arms around Norma. He announced the figures – fifty-six for Douglas, 131 for Michael, and 185 for me. There was uproar.

By the rules, I was two votes short of an outright win. But I realised that I had effectively made it – even if there had to be another ballot, I would certainly get two more votes. 'We could have done it tonight,' I thought; then it occurred to me that if the contest did go to a third vote on Thursday, I would not have to do Prime Minister's Questions that week.

Would there have to be another round? As we watched television,

Michael Heseltine came out of his house to concede defeat. Both he and Douglas said they would urge their supporters to vote for me. It was over. Soon, Cranley Onslow arrived to confirm that he would not prolong the contest. I had done it. In a street not three miles from Coldharbour Lane, I had become prime minister.

It was quite a scene. Ian Lang, standing just behind me, offered instant congratulations. John Gummer had tears on his cheeks, and many others were not far behind. Francis Maude rushed up, seized my arm in delight, then dropped back as he realised I was no longer just another Cabinet minister. Through the door which connects Number 10 and Number 11 came Margaret and Andrew Turnbull, head of the Private Office at Number 10, with Denis and Mark Thatcher in tow. Margaret came over to me. 'Well done, John, well done,' she said. She went to Norma. 'It's what I've always wanted,' she told her.

In Downing Street, the press were waiting for me to appear. I had already run through what I wanted to say to them with Andrew Tyrie and Richard Ryder, and moved towards the door. 'I'll come out,' said Margaret. I should have agreed. I have often regretted that I did not. But my team were over-sensitive to the Labour line that I was the political 'son of Thatcher', and, nervous that she would be seen as pulling the strings, Norman Lamont peeled her away. 'Please let him have his moment,' he said. Margaret watched me speak to the press from an upstairs window in Downing Street. It made a famous photograph.

'It has been a very clean election and an election based on substance, not personalities,' I said into the microphones in the street. 'It is a very exciting thing to become leader of the Conservative Party, particularly to follow one of the most remarkable leaders the Conservative Party has had. We are going to unite totally and absolutely and we will win the next general election.'

Within minutes of the result, the Civil Service machine clicked into gear. Andrew Turnbull choreographed arrangements for Margaret Thatcher and then me to see the Queen the next morning. Meanwhile, Number 11 Downing Street became a centre of world attention. It is not equipped for such occasions. In the kitchen the secretarial staff, old friends like Peter Golds, my brother Terry, Barbara and Derek had gathered for coffee. Graham Bright was trying to make me toast – I had hardly eaten all day – when the phone rang: it was President Bush, calling from thirty thousand feet in Air Force One to congratulate me. Number 11 is a large house, and I was nowhere near a phone. There was confusion. My brother spoke to Air Force One from the kitchen as people scurried around trying to find me. George Bush kept cutting out as his satellite link failed. In the end, I had a friendly conversation with the President as Andrew Turnbull hovered at my shoulder, with people washing up glasses in the background, not knowing who I was speaking to. Only in our own extraordinary country could a change of prime minister happen this way.

That evening I went over to the House to vote. Normally, when there is a three-line whip, MPs rush through the division lobby like children at the end of the school day. But not tonight. When I entered the lobby there was a tremendous cheer. Against all tradition, I stood on the steps leading from the Chamber into the 'no' lobby and gave an impromptu speech. I said I intended to bring every section of the party together, and promised I would have a Cabinet that represented every part of the party. I voted, then went into the Chamber, where Neil Kinnock generously came over to shake hands and wish me luck. Afterwards, Michael Heseltine was to be found in the Smoking Room dispensing champagne to help the rapprochement.

'I shan't be pulling the levers there, but I shall be a very good back-seat driver,' Margaret announced, enthusiastically, to the press. The comment was not made with malice, but it had a malign effect. It implied that after she had left Downing Street she would be making decisions about how things were run – and that was never going to be the case. Her comment ensured that if I continued with policies she had advocated I would simply be regarded as the 'son of Thatcher'; while if I did not it would be said that I was 'wrecking her legacy'. That, of course, is exactly how it turned out. The comment forced a wedge between us that was to grow wider as month succeeded month.

The following morning Margaret took her departure from the Queen, and minutes later I drove up The Mall with Norma beside me to 'kiss hands' as prime minister. The phrase is traditional and outdated – the Queen's hand is not kissed. After a brief conversation the Queen invited me to form a government and, as I accepted, I became prime minister.

As I began the drive back down the Mall, I wondered about what I would say to the media waiting in Downing Street. On a scrap of paper I set out some of the things that I believed: my hopes of creating a nation at ease with itself. I wanted to put behind us the Poll Tax riots, the exclusion of so many minority groups and those left outside the race to prosperity that we had seen in the 1980s – perfidious thoughts, no doubt, but deeply felt.

'I don't promise you it will be easy, and I don't promise you it will be quick, but I believe it to be an immensely worthwhile job to do. Because it will be neither easy nor quick – if you will forgive me – I will go into Number 10 straight away and make a start right now.'

As I walked into Number 10 I was met by Sir Robin Butler, the Cabinet Secretary, and the staff, who were lined up from the front door down the long corridor which leads to the Cabinet Room; they greeted my entrance with applause. Andrew Turnbull escorted me into the Cabinet Room; Norma went upstairs to the flat. There were already decisions waiting which needed prime ministerial approval.

# CHAPTER NINE

# *Prime Minister*

M Y INHERITANCE WAS UNPROMISING. We were on the eve of a war. The economic bubble of the 1980s was bursting. Inflation was approaching double figures. Interest rates were at 14 per cent. Unemployment had begun to rise by fifty thousand a month. House prices were falling. The economy was in the first phase of acute recession. Ahead lay a collapse in growth, equity values, sales and confidence – all directly traceable to the size of the boom in the late 1980s, although for some our membership of the Exchange Rate Mechanism was to prove a convenient scapegoat.

Policy changes were inevitable. The Poll Tax was deeply unpopular and could not survive, although no alternative source of local taxation was in sight. The trauma of Margaret's dismissal from office was deep and painful. Some in the party wished to cling to her legacy, and others to move away from it. Myth and legend were already displacing reality about her time as prime minister.

Nowhere was this more evident than in the debate over European policy, where from the outset I was standing astride a deep and widening fissure in the party. As I considered how to handle this, the shadow of my nineteenth-century predecessor as Conservative prime minister Sir Robert Peel was forever at my side: in all my time at Downing Street he was never to leave it. In repealing the Corn Laws in 1846, Peel shattered and divided the Conservative Party between a minority of free-trade Peel-ites and the bulk of protectionist Tories. It was not fanciful to see the possibility of a similar smash-up in the modern party. Already the European issue had been significant in the resignations of Nigel Lawson and Geoffrey Howe and the defeat of Margaret Thatcher. More victims seemed likely, but I did not wish the Conservative Party itself to be among them. The immediate prospect on all sides was of a sea of troubles. A short premiership, lasting only until the next election, seemed likely.

And yet this was an incomplete picture. The country had been transformed for the better in the years since 1979. Trades union reforms had removed the stranglehold of militancy over our affairs. Supply-side economic changes had boosted the flexibility and well-being of the economy. Privatisation had broken down the monolith of public ownership, and once-derelict public services were now hugely competitive private companies. Private enterprise had won the battle against socialism. Personal wealth had boomed, with the ownership of homes, shares and savings greatly increased. These were all hard-won and benevolent legacies, of permanent benefit to the British economy. Moreover, the Labour Party was ill-prepared for government and seen to be so. The Liberal Democrats were mere onlookers in the real battle for power. If the Conservatives were unpopular, there was no enthusiasm for our main opponents. I believed the next election was winnable.

And I was sure of my priorities as I sat at the Cabinet table to set them down. They were a mixed bag. Inflation. Public services. Northern Ireland. Unemployment. Each of them mattered to me. Inflation had wrecked our economy too many times, and I was prepared to carry through the tough and unpopular measures already put in hand to prevent it doing so once more. Never again should we emerge from one recession by actions that merely sowed the seeds of the next.

I wished to improve the performance of public services. Where this could best be done in the private sector, I would privatise. Where not, I wished to devolve decision-making so as to cut bureaucracy and improve the image of the service and the morale of public servants. There should be no excuse for poor performance. The culture of the public sector needed changing, and I believed I knew how to do it.

The hatreds and feuds of Northern Ireland forced their way into the forefront of my mind. It seemed to me our nation had become so weary of this ever-present scar that people were now willing to accept that nothing could be done. I was not. I believed in the politics of reason, and was intent on working for a settlement that would end the violence, and – unless the people of the Province chose to leave it – keep Northern Ireland within the United Kingdom.

Unemployment was rising towards two million. The economic waste concerned me, but not as much as the social implications for individuals and their families. My own brief experience of being without a job as a teenager had shown me the despair of men and women who wished to work but could not do so. I saw no long-term solution in creating jobs artificially, although this could ameliorate hardship in the short term. I did believe in the job-creating capacity of an inflation-free environment and the virtues of an educational and social climate that cherished manual skills with the same warmth as academic ability. Policy here would be for the long term.

These priorities reflected my hopes for the future as well as my perceptions of the recent past. Millions had seen their lifestyle improve in the 1980s, but Labour were right to complain on behalf of those who had been left behind. I wished to reach out to people in need, to fashion Conservative policies that would help those who had had a rough beginning. I believed I was well placed to do so.

This prompted some talk of 'Majorism'. I discouraged it. The Conservative Party does not belong to any one individual. The 'ism' I wished to promote was a traditional Conservatism tempered with an understanding of and sympathy for life at many levels. In my first speech to the party as prime minister I had made that clear enough:

> We aim for a society of opportunity ... But amidst the in-
> evitable thrust of life it should be a compassionate society. Genu-
> inely compassionate – because some people do need a helping
> hand to enable them to enjoy a life full of choice and inde-
> pendence.

There was nothing novel about this theme: it had often enough been a Conservative cry. It was the sort of Conservatism, exemplified by Iain Macleod, that had attracted so many of my generation to the centre-right of politics.

I followed it up with the ambition to spread 'the power to choose, the right to own'. A huge amount had been achieved by Margaret Thatcher – low taxes and the sale of council houses being obvious examples – but I was alert to the danger that these advantages might exclude a large minority. I wanted to ensure that they were not left out of the new prosperity. 'I think the poorest he that is in England hath a life to live, as the greatest he,' said Lt Colonel Thomas Rainsborough, speaking during the Putney

Debates of 1647. I agreed with that three-hundred-year-old sentiment, which explains why I spoke of a 'classless society': not a society without difference, but one without barriers. 'What are our hopes?' I asked, in a speech accepting the leadership.

> Let me tell you mine. It is to build a truly open society – open because we believe that men and women should be able to go as far as their talent, ambition and effort take them. There should be no artificial barriers of background, religion or race. We aim for a society of opportunity where people can better themselves and their families by their own efforts – a Britain that puts people in control of their own lives, to exercise their own choices, in their own time, in their own way.

And I meant it. A year later I set it out once more as the general election campaign began:

> I want to bring into being a different kind of country, to bury forever old divisions in Britain between North and South, blue-collar and white-collar, polytechnic and university. They're old style, old hat.

That was the core of what I cared about. I wanted to win the general election in order to make those wishes reality.

Late on the night of my election to the leadership, I began to put together my first Cabinet. As we were quite near a general election, I did not want wholesale changes. Most of Margaret's ministers could stay in their jobs. But a new chancellor was obviously a necessity. There were four possibilities: Chris Patten and Ken Clarke were both front-rank politicians, but neither had any Treasury experience. Chris, in any event, I needed elsewhere. John MacGregor and Norman Lamont were both credible candidates. Of the two, Norman was currently in the Treasury as chief secretary, and so was more familiar with current policy.

Norman had earned promotion. If I moved him to the Department of Trade and Industry – which was my initial inclination – there would be a wholly new team in charge of economic policy at precisely the moment the country was heading into recession. Britain was also a new member of the ERM. It was not a time for a new chancellor who would have to learn the job as he went along. The case for a familiar face, known to the markets and the City, was very strong. Though other names were put to me – and differing views expressed about Norman by those I consulted – I was not convinced. After the turbulence of recent weeks we needed stability. So Norman Lamont became chancellor. This was a significant moment, and the most controversial appointment of my premiership. Many colleagues were critical at the time, which undoubtedly made Norman's job more difficult. He had to earn credibility rather than have it conferred on him by his new position, and in a recession this was difficult. The argument that he lacked economic ability was simply wrong. The concern about his political profile was more telling as the economic weather became heavy. His tenure was marked by controversy and was to end in anguish, but as I will set out elsewhere, he was a better chancellor than he was given credit for being, and part of his legacy was the excellent economy we would hand over to Tony Blair in 1997.

I asked Douglas Hurd to remain at the Foreign Office – a role to which, I thought, he seemed to have been born. Douglas moved through British politics with such consummate ease that it was hard for even close colleagues to know when he was truly engaged and when on auto-pilot. He had the mandarin's ability to slither out of any trap, and I had cause to thank him for it; but he was more than a turbo-charged civil servant, for he could speak with passion and to crowds. I trusted and admired Douglas, and I needed him. If I ever entertained the tiniest doubt about him, it arose from his very ability. He was so good at persuading people that all would be well, and that their fears were imaginary, that I sometimes wondered whether he persuaded himself of this too. At what point, I wondered, if the wagon careered out of control, would Douglas scream, 'Help! Stop!'? Later, I would find out.

I wondered about Margaret. Should I try to keep her in the Cabinet? I soon decided not. She had presided over Cabinet for so long that I could not see her in a subordinate position. Nor could I see her in a Cabinet many members of whom had felt she should step down. Although Sir Alec Douglas Home, who served as foreign secretary in Ted Heath's Cabinet after having been prime minister, offered a precedent of sorts, this could not apply to Margaret. They were two very different characters. In any event, what job could she take? She could not be chancellor or foreign secretary after the rows about Europe. I thought briefly of leader of the House, but ruled it out. That had been Geoffrey Howe's last post, and though there may be jobs for which she is less well-suited temperamentally,

I cannot think what they are. I wondered whether she would want to go to Washington, as ambassador. But she had offered that to Ted Heath in 1979, and it would have looked as though I was simply trying to shuffle her off the stage. I decided there was no credible job to offer her.

There was a question, too, over what to do with Michael Heseltine. Michael hoped to go to the Department of Trade and Industry. He had won substantial support in the leadership contest, and his appointment to a senior position was right in principle and necessary in practice. He would also be a huge asset in winning the election. I discussed the options with him, and discovered that he feared I would offer him the Home Office. 'I don't want it,' he said, pre-empting any offer. 'It's a graveyard.'

Michael and I did not really know one another. We had never worked or socialised together. As rivals in the recent leadership election, we were still reserved with one another and uncertain how our relationship would work. Michael was, in the best sense, a man for the crowds, an inspirer, a persuader. Despite enormous personal ambition, and a trace of the vanity which none of us lacks, he was also a man of beliefs – to which he stuck bravely. His language was powerful, his ideas big and his horizons large. He had an unerring feel for the grand gesture. He was an Old-Testament prophet of a politician, and a man of great passions: Europe, deregulation, urban regeneration, arboriculture, making money. When something was not a passion he could be shamelessly cynical about it, but where he had a passion he was formidable in advocating it, and obstinate in stopping anything that did not fit into his preconceptions. Faced with a problem, he would metaphorically wave the mace around to club his enemies – and he was one of the best orators of post-war politics.

In later years I was to find out that crises were meat and drink to Michael. He loved them. His colour rose and he quivered like a greyhound in the trap. I remember striding down a corridor, when there were some fifty disasters going on around us, and Michael smiling happily and saying, 'Isn't it fun?' The pace of events, the drama of politics, whether good or bad, filled him with excitement, and he loved it; this is the core of the Heseltine personality.

Another of Michael's qualities which I gradually came to recognise was that when the chips are down he is absolutely loyal, and 100 per cent supportive. Other people may have wanted to duck away from shot and shell, but Michael would get in and fight. In the darkest days, Michael was always great company, one of the few people I would choose to sit down and have a drink, and relax with. He's always been seen as one of the biggest beasts in the political jungle, but he's not an arrogant beast. As deputy prime minister he never failed me.

At this time, however, I knew none of this. Foremost in my mind was the knowledge that this was the man whose candidacy had brought down Margaret Thatcher, and my appointment had ended his hopes of the premiership he had so coveted. It was no wonder we eyed each other warily. There was one job Michael could not refuse, and I offered it to him: his old post at Environment, which would include responsibility for reshaping the Poll Tax. He smiled – wryly, I thought, as though appreciating a shrewd move in a game of chess – and accepted.

I walked with him to the front door of Number 10, and we shook hands on the doorstep; I hoped this public display would emphasise our unity to our colleagues. With some it did, but with others it backfired. Some MPs loyal to Margaret resented Michael's return to the Cabinet, and the first mutterings began to be heard that I might not follow the previous prime minister's path in all ways.

Other appointments soon fell into place. Ken Baker had been a loyal chairman of the party for Margaret, but had taken too many political blows in her cause to stay in the same post for me. He was political reflex made flesh, with an attractive liberality of mind. Ken became Home Secretary – he didn't think it a graveyard at all – although it was to prove his final Cabinet post. Chris Patten became Party Chairman. We had an election to win, and I wanted our most able and voter-friendly faces centre-stage. Chris had good relations with the media, a gift for attracting loyalty, knew Central Office, warts and all, was an old friend with whom I could work easily, and, above all, had an instinctive rapport with a large part of the electorate.

Ian Lang, a close ally, who in the 1960s had written scripts for the satirical programme *That Was The Week That Was*, became Secretary of State for Scotland. Ian was steady, shrewd, highly intelligent and blessed with an ordered mind. He was custom-made for the Cabinet, and in a less vulgar age he would have become prime minister. His evenness of tone and temper, old-fashioned tolerance and fastidious distrust of extreme positions led the unthinking to dismiss him as an unideological Tory 'wet'. But to know him as I came to was to know a hard-nosed and common-sense politician with a strong sense of right and wrong. Ian was a witty mimic, and a wise and loyal colleague. As chief secretary I brought in the sharp-tongued and abrasive David Mellor, whose forensic skills seemed ideal for the role of negotiator-in-chief on public spending. Richard Ryder, one of the best political noses in Westminster, became Chief Whip. I asked the solidly right-of-centre David Waddington to resign his Westminster seat and become Leader of the Lords, with the thought that he could become a general troubleshooter and adviser in the Whitelaw mould. This move was a mistake for both of us, as we lost the by-election in his seat, and David soon realised he would have preferred to stay in the Commons.

I promoted Malcolm Rifkind to replace Cecil Parkinson, who was retiring from the front bench, at Transport. Behind a thoughtful and civilised aspect, Malcolm was a deceptively ambitious man, shrewd, and not beyond placing a finger in the wind. He liked ideas, was confident enough intellectually to execute some fairly breathtaking U-turns, and was, for a Conservative, a daring philosopher. But anyone who thought his head was in the clouds, or who mistook his amiability for unworldliness, misread a clever minister with a sharp eye for evolving opinion.

I wanted to bring more than a few new faces to the Commons Dispatch Box, and to refresh the whole conduct of government. Nowhere was this more apparent than in Cabinet. At least one Cabinet minister has spoken of his sense of 'liberation' at the first Cabinet meeting under my leadership. Margaret had often introduced subjects in Cabinet by setting out her favoured solution: shameless, but effective. I, by contrast, preferred to let my views be known in private, see potential dissenters ahead of the meeting, encourage discussion, and sum up after it. A different approach, but, I believe, one that is equally effective. Margaret had been at her happiest confronting political dragons; I chose consensus in policy-making, if not always in policy. We were each a product of our times, our characters and our parliamentary positions. She followed a disastrous Labour decade, and was able to boldly attack her inheritance. I had to talk up my inheritance, while moving with the minimum of fuss to correct my own party's mistakes.

I was conscious of the privilege and history of the role of prime minister, but was not daunted by it. I knew the tasks that lay ahead, and was determined to pursue them. My more personal and private emotions are less easy to express. I did feel that there were things I could not do because of my perhaps old-fashioned view of how a prime minister should behave. Levity, I suspected, would be interpreted as shallowness. I fancied that letting my emotions show would put me at a disadvantage, more so as prime minister than in any other job. After the pomp and circumstance of the Thatcher years I was keen to present an antidote to that, to show people that it was possible to be prime minister without changing, without losing the interests that every other Briton had, without having no time for holidays, no time for sport, no time for anything but the higher things of life. I wanted to show that it was possible to be prime minister and remain a human being, just like the fifty-five million other human beings in the country, but with an exceptional job.

I felt, too, that with the power and influence my new position brought with it, my capacity to hurt people – by disregarding them, snubbing them, appearing to forget about them – would be very real; particularly people who were in no position to answer back. I went out of my way to ensure that this did not happen. In Downing Street and elsewhere I wanted people without power to be treated with the same courtesy as heads of governments. I thought they deserved it. So, in one sense, having power reminded me that it needed to be exercised in a way that did not make you different from other people. But I had no problem about exercising the power to order people to do things. It was a tool, a mechanism. Douglas Hurd said to me later that he felt I 'did not enjoy the job', and perhaps he was right. I was brought up to accept obligations as well as rights, and I felt this strongly as prime minister. I think I felt quite differently about power than any prime minister this century.

From the outset, I did what I have always done with every new job. I played the promotion down as of little consequence, and got on with the job. I remember that in the week I became prime minister I arrived home for the weekend, and Elizabeth teased, 'Anything happen this week?'

At Number 10, Robin Butler, the Cabinet Secretary, and Andrew Turnbull were familiar figures from my Treasury past. So was Gus O'Donnell, who joined me as press secretary, and the robustly right-wing Judith Chaplin, who came with me to run my Political Office. It was a wrench to leave Andrew Tyrie at the Treasury, but Judith brought a feminine instinct to offset an all-male Cabinet. She did not always share my views on policy, and as polling day approached in 1992 she had to devote much of her time to Newbury, where she was the prospective Conservative parliamentary candidate. As a consequence she sometimes missed policy discussions, which she found frustrating. Nonetheless I valued her often wise counsel, and was delighted at her subsequent electoral success.

Margaret's fall and my election had occurred so speedily that I had barely had time to consider how to structure a policy unit at Number 10, other than to decide that new faces and a fresh direction were needed. Chris Patten and I were discussing this in the study at Number 10 when, almost at the same moment, Sarah Hogg's name came into both our minds. I asked my private office to track her down. She appeared about an hour later, dressed in an evening gown, a refugee from the interval of a performance of Stephen Sondheim's *Into the Woods*, at which she had been helping entertain the President of Gambia with her husband Douglas, a junior minister at the Foreign Office who had entered Parliament on the same day as me. That evening she became Head of the Policy Unit, and she would be at my side for the next four years.

Sarah was born to the political purple. She was the daughter of John Boyd-Carpenter, a senior member of Harold Macmillan's government. Her sharp brain, often hidden behind an engaging giggle, had made her one of the most influential economic journalists in the country, and I had seen her skills at close quarters during my years at the Treasury. She was respected by civil service mandarins and by politicians – a double not easily achieved – and as a bonus, her long-standing friendship with Chris Patten meant that the crucial Number 10 Central Office relationship would be in secure hands.

Sarah's job was tough. At the most, we had eighteen months of our parliamentary term to go, and there was no certainty that we would win the election. I let it be known that I expected her to have full cooperation from both Central Office and the civil service, but she often had to cajole or bully to get it. Forceful and effective, she became a lightning conductor for controversy. Dubbed the 'Deputy Prime Minister', she took many blows intended for me. Sarah was the key figure in bringing together our 1992 election manifesto – a Herculean task in the face of eighteen years of entrenched interests – and, unbeknown to me at the time, shed many a quiet tear in frustration as she did so.

Sarah soon picked a top-notch team to help her. Nick True had been a special adviser at the Department of Social Security when I was a junior minister there, and later at the Treasury. He knew me well, and I was delighted when he joined the Policy Unit, where he distilled my thoughts into artful speeches. Over the years many of my best phrases were to come from his pen. Sarah invited Jonathan Hill, once an adviser to Ken Clarke, to join the Policy Unit as its specialist in housing and transport. Before long he was roaming across the full breadth of policy-making, with a talent for spotting trouble and stamping it out. He became a Number 10 fixture, moving from the Policy Unit to become my Political Secretary in 1992. He left the Political Office in 1994, but returned to help during the party leadership contest in 1995, and for a final spell in the 1997 general election campaign. The remaining two members of the Policy Unit were in place when I arrived: Carolyn Sinclair and John Mills. Both brought lively minds to bear on the issues which faced us.

I gave the Unit more attention than was customary in a prime minister, wandering informally up to its first-floor offices whenever I had a spare moment. This, I soon learned, was almost unheard of, but it soon became a familiar pattern. Our formal and informal discussions soon bore fruit. An early pacemaker in domestic reform was education. In the spring I told Young Conservatives: 'At the top of my personal agenda is education. It is the key to opening new paths for all sorts of people – not just the most gifted – and for doing so at every stage of their lives.'

Not having had much education myself, I was keen on it.

Ken Clarke, as boisterous at Education as he had been elsewhere, seized on this commitment. A theme that ran through our education policy was my innate distaste for the inverted snobbery which distorts so much of our nation's way of life. In May 1991 we launched a White Paper, one lasting impact of which was to abolish the false divide between polytechnics and universities. 'Only in Britain could it have been thought a defect to be too clever by half,' I noted. For the 1992 general election, we published a separate education manifesto to emphasise our commitment.

Another priority, less specific perhaps, was tolerance; a Conservative value which some Tories overlooked, and which I aimed to restore to the fold. Two swift acts set the course: I decided to unfreeze Child Benefit payments (this was achieved, at my request, in Norman Lamont's first budget), and to compensate haemophiliacs who had been infected with the HIV virus as a result of contaminated blood transfusions. Both of these decisions achieved a certain notoriety, and were seen by some as signs that I was breaking with what had gone before. This was a characteristically false history. The broad tradition of our party *was* tolerant. If a certain shrill and censorious tone had set in, it was that tone which broke faith with our past. My predecessor was not personally unsympathetic, but some, less tolerant than she, saw 'Thatcherism' as a vehicle for intolerance and, sometimes, prejudice.

More broadly, I hated prejudice of any kind. My background had left me with few hang-ups about race; neither did I see homosexuality as a social evil. Many people are gay, and I saw no reason to cast them into outer darkness for that reason. I took the symbolic step of asking the actor Ian McKellen, a leading campaigner on gay issues, to Number 10; this produced a tide of letters – mostly critical, a few laughably bigoted – and some muttered dissent on the backbenches. I was shocked at the attitude of mind that seemed to think I should not have spoken to McKellen. (By an accident of timing, my next visitor that day was the French Prime Minister Edith Cresson, who had famously said that half the Anglo-Saxon male population was homosexual. I did not ask her how she knew.)

I had met Ian McKellen at a dinner given by Mary Soames following a performance at the National Theatre, and found him a courageous advocate for the cause of equal treatment of gays before the law. I did not agree with him on every point – nor, I think, did he expect me to – but he had a case that deserved a hearing. With my encouragement, in February 1994 Parliament voted to lower the age of consent for gays from twenty one to eighteen (although not to sixteen, which McKellen wanted). By tradition this was a free vote, of course. But it is more than an ex-whip's cynicism to observe that free votes do not just happen.

One other area of discrimination stared out at me every day. There were no women in my first Cabinet, and one Conservative backbencher, Teresa Gorman, said what she thought about that very plainly. Teresa was an unusual mixture of right-wing Tory and feminist, and if the front bench in the Chamber had railings, she would have chained herself to them. I sympathised with her sentiments, but there was no obvious female candidate banging on the Cabinet door demanding entry. I decided not to cave in to tokenism or to Teresa's pleas. Instead, I put two of our most talented rising stars, Gillian Shephard and Virginia Bottomley, to join Lynda Chalker in senior positions just below Cabinet rank, so that I would have viable woman candidates in place for future Cabinet reshuffles.

In addition, I put Angela Rumbold in charge of a ministerial group on women's issues; and after lobbying from Elspeth Howe I took a personal role in the Opportunity 2000 campaign, which worked to improve employment prospects for women. Launching the scheme in October 1991, I argued that 'the change in the role of women is fundamentally right. Why should half of our population go through life like a hobbled horse in a steeplechase? The answer is that they shouldn't – and increasingly, they won't.' But in Parliament, then as now, there were too few Conservative women in senior positions.

Returning now, almost nine years on, to some of the ideas I developed as prime minister, I am struck by two things. One is regret at how many of these ambitions were lost after 1992, displaced by the constant battles within the party and by economic circumstances. The eighteen months leading up to the general election in April 1992 was the time of greatest promise for me in government. There was much I hoped to do after the election, but which, as things turned out, I would not achieve. I shall regret this all my days.

The second point strikes me just as strongly: New Labour owes me a great debt. Very many of the ideas put forward against us in the 1997 general election campaign were ones I myself had advocated five years earlier: choice, ownership, responsibility and opportunity. Tony Blair's mantra of 'education, education, education' in 1997 mirrored mine in 1992, and the overall priority of public spending I bequeathed to him – controlling total expenditure, but allocating more and more to education and health – carried on after 1 May 1997. The language of New Labour may have been first-rate, but it was second-hand. 'A hand up, not a hand out' came with deadening regularity from Tony Blair; it was a phrase I used many times in 1991 and in the election a year later. So was another Blairism: 'for the many, not the few'. Seven days after becoming prime minister I called for privileges 'once available for the few to be enjoyed by the many'. Imitation can be flattering, but New Labour's imitation, when we had lost the ear of the nation, became a steamroller that was to flatten us. But that lay five years ahead.

My effort to nudge Conservatism towards its compassionate roots was far more than a calculated remarketing of a brand whose image had become tarnished. I believed in it. But it had an unintended effect. Margaret Thatcher, who in the second ballot in November 1990 had been a keen supporter of my leadership ambitions, was quickly disillusioned with my actions in office. In my eagerness to build 'a nation at ease with itself', Margaret thought she detected a desire to undo her achievements, and, egged on by those who surrounded her, fretted semi-publicly about several of my early decisions.

I understood her pain at losing office better than she knew. I saw it etched on her face, and in her uneasy posture when she sat on the back-benches. It was evident in her body language when we met: she was uncertain how to react to someone who now held what she regarded as *her* job. The former easy, breezy familiarity had gone. Politics had dominated her life, and, no longer prime minister, she felt dispossessed, cheated and betrayed by those she had led. Cut loose from the Downing Street support mechanism, lesser men than those who had once advised her now poured poison in her ear – perhaps with the intention of cheering her up. The target was, inevitably – who else could it be? – her successor. In March 1991 the drip-feed had its effect, and she publicly attacked what she saw as my 'tendency to undermine' what she had done in office. I was, she said, 'giving more power to government'. The gap between us began to widen. The decisions that most upset her were inevitable ones: Michael Heseltine returning to the Cabinet; burying the Poll Tax; easing the impact of the economic difficulties.

Nevertheless, the charge that I was somehow 'betraying her legacy' was untrue. In economic policy, in further privatisation, in law and order, I was no counter-revolutionary. In these policies, I led the Thatcherite march onwards with conviction – for I believed in it. Yet for Margaret my rebalancing of social policy seemed to obscure all of this, above all because of the abolition of one of her most treasured policies: the Poll Tax. Yet it had to go. It would have been crackpot to keep it. The tax had proved a disaster: unfair, unworkable and unacceptable. When I became prime minister I had not committed myself to its abolition, though in my bones I knew it would have to go. During the leadership contest I had kept open the option of reform, aware that if I had brazenly advocated abolition, I had no alternative to put in its place.

In my first days as prime minister I pondered this dilemma. A decade on, it is easy to forget that the Poll Tax was one of those issues over which passions raged and intellects clashed, but at the time it was the most vital policy issue facing me as prime minister. This was partly because it was, at base, all about Margaret Thatcher and her legacy. The matter became ideological and, for some, deeply personal. Despite overwhelming back-bench horror at sky-high Poll Tax bills, there was no unanimity in the

Tory Party that the principle of a universal flat-rate tax was wrong. The logic that had driven its imposition – that everyone should pay something towards the cost of services that everyone used – remained as beguiling as ever. Starry-eyed devotees of Margaret Thatcher saw her legacy as a holy relic, and to them the abolition of a tax she insisted would work was a sacrilege. Even as I write, there are MPs at the dottier end of the Tory Party who believe the Poll Tax would have come good in the end. Some sensible colleagues, too, were dismayed by the thought of changing the system of local taxation yet again. Ian Lang, for one, shuddered at the memory of rates revaluation and the outcry it provoked in Scotland, and was wary of any return to a property-based tax.

It seemed to me that there were two separate questions: how to make the tax bearable in the short term, and what its fate should be in the long term. I determined to answer them in sequence. Time was not on my side, since the amount of money to be made available for local councils had to be settled by late January 1991. If we were parsimonious, Poll Tax bills would climb; if we were generous, public expenditure would soar. I needed time to overcome opposition to change within the party if I was not to reopen the still-raw wounds of Margaret's departure, but I knew I had to sort out or replace the tax before I could call a general election. To do so would mean devising a new scheme, mollifying the party, and getting legislation through the House. It was not going to be easy.

Within days of my becoming prime minister, Chris Patten broke the depressing news that typical Poll Tax bills in the year ahead were likely to be around £400, and could reach £420. As Margaret Thatcher's last environment secretary, he had coped with the logistics of the tax. Now, as my first party chairman, he was alarmed by its political implications. So was I. Chris argued that we had to offer more money to local councils, and compel them to pass on the benefits of this in the form of lower bills.

In early December the Cabinet endorsed a comprehensive review of the Poll Tax, but made no commitment to replace it. The obstacle that had defied generations of local-taxation reformers was still there: no better system stared us in the face. The political reality was inescapable: a universal flat-rate tax could only be sustainable at a level the poorest could bear. At such a level, it would raise very little and, in the case of benefit recipients, would be uneconomic to collect. Clearly, the Poll Tax had to go altogether.

It was a gloomy conclusion, but the right one. But abolition would take time while we decided what would replace the tax. I decided that, in the short term, the only sensible option was to cut bills dramatically by increasing the proportion of council spending funded by the taxpayer – a proposal dubbed 'Big Bertha' by Sarah Hogg, who drew it up. At my request, the Treasury costed it in December 1990. They concluded that it would cost an unaffordable £8 billion, and an alarmed Norman Lamont issued dire warnings about the economic consequences of such an increase in expenditure.

He was right, but that still left us in a near-impossible political position. The election was looming, and the press, the public and most of the party were demanding action. Ian Lang warned me that Scottish local authorities had to set charges by the end of January, and could not redetermine them after that date. So on 11 January we put 'Big Bertha' on hold and agreed a smaller £1.1 billion package of transitional relief, helping those most hit by the charge. This was a palliative, but no solution. Poll Tax levels remained well above £400, and in March we lost David Waddington's supposedly safe seat of Ribble Valley to the Liberal Democrats, in a by-election dubbed by them a 'referendum' on the Poll Tax.

I was spending much of my time – when not preoccupied with the Gulf crisis – chairing a Cabinet committee whose remit was to devise a replacement system of local taxation. Scheme after scheme was ruled out, and the solution seemed as elusive as the Holy Grail. On the day the IRA attacked Downing Street with three mortar rockets (see pages 237–8), Michael Heseltine was in the building discussing the abolition of the Poll Tax with Sarah Hogg. As the windows shattered and the explosion reverberated he looked across at Sarah and grinned, 'This is a more explosive issue than even I thought.' It was a very English comment from the Cabinet's pre-eminent Welshman; but, bombs or not, the work of replacing the Poll Tax went on.

Out of the profusion of Michael Heseltine's proposals (some of which were made in what the Policy Unit called his 'arm-waving mode'), Policy Unit papers and Cabinet committee discussions, a scheme emerged: a banded property tax with a discount for single-person households. By April we were able to present the package to the full Cabinet. But legislation would take time; meanwhile the running sore of the Poll Tax hurt as badly as ever. An alarmed Sarah Hogg rang me at Finings and we ran over the options; she persuaded me to resurrect 'Big Bertha'.

Two weeks before the budget, on Sunday, 3 March, I called Norman Lamont into the Cabinet Room and dropped the Big Bertha bombshell into his budget arithmetic. I did not permit debate. 'We must do it,' I told him, 'whatever else we do to compensate.' Norman looked aghast, as well he might, considering that his budget had just been completely up-ended. It was evident that cutting the Poll Tax to sane levels could only be funded by increases in central taxation. Norman had only days in which to decide where to raise the money. I disliked bouncing him in this way, but I had no choice: we had to respond to the ludicrously high levels reached by the Poll Tax.

I left for a visit to our troops in the Gulf, and on my return was given the news that Norman had – with some reluctance – signed up. To cut Poll Tax bills he proposed a compensating 2.5 per cent rise in VAT, replacing one tax with another, and not increasing the overall tax burden. People would not pay more, they would simply pay more fairly.

Norman delivered all his budget speeches with aplomb, and in 1991 he rather enjoyed pulling this oversized rabbit out of the hat at the end of what had otherwise been a low-key budget. It earned him great plaudits for his ingenuity. A month later, Michael Heseltine unveiled the Council Tax. In a vintage, mane-tossing Commons performance he shoved aside the greatest obstacle on the road to a fourth election win. From then on, with Poll Tax bills slashed and a replacement in sight, local-government finance faded as an issue. Since alternatives to the rates had been vainly sought by successive governments for many years, this was quite an achievement.

Abolishing one of Margaret's legacies without breaking up the parliamentary party had not been easy. It robbed us of the option of an early election, and fed charges from Labour that the new government was 'dithering' and 'indecisive'. These charges were given credence when, in the Commons, Nigel Lawson quoted Pierre Mendès-France's saying 'To govern is to choose.' It was a statement of fact, and Nigel later assured me he did not mean it as an attack on me, but with Labour's 'dithering' charges in vogue, it was interpreted as a ringing critique of my leadership. I was at a whips' reception in their domain at Number 12 Downing Street when reporters tackled me about what Nigel had said, and I responded irritably, which only stirred the pot. I would have been wiser to just brush it aside, since, considering the country was engaged in a sizeable land war overseas while the government wrestled with a replacement for the major source of local taxation at home, the criticism was rather absurd. But politically it stuck.

Only now, years later, is it possible to understand how much was lost because I came into Number 10 from *government*, without my own programme settled, rather than from *opposition*, where my priorities would have been prepared and ready for action. The speed at which the incoming Labour government was able to act in 1997 illustrates this point: their plans were ready to roll, giving an impression of dynamism even where many of the policies were, in my view, unwise.

I, by contrast, came into Number 10 after thirteen years of Conservative government, and inherited policies some of which I had the pain of changing against the opposition of much of my own party and the jeers of my opponents. I did not enjoy the luxury of working up my own programme at leisure. It had to be done at speed and amidst the frenzy of government. Nor, after the party had been so long in government, could I create the image of a new agenda with a series of philosophical speeches on the principles of Conservatism. Yet people demanded new ideas and new policies – and swiftly.

Our response was inevitably piecemeal. A new, more friendly, approach to Europe; a fresh education agenda focusing on vocational qualifications and training credits for post-school further education; an embryonic series of changes to improve public services; the replacement of the Poll Tax. All of these had to be welded to the continuation of existing policies and the struggle against a worsening recession. As I wrestled with these intractable problems I tried to rally the Conservative Party in the country, and prepare a fresh approach for the general election that could not be more than eighteen months away.

All this was a sufficient agenda, but it is not an exclusive list of the immediate demands which faced me. Within weeks of my election as prime minister we faced an unavoidable obligation that dwarfed all domestic concerns.

We went to war in the Gulf.

# CHAPTER TEN

## *The Gulf War*

O N 2 AUGUST 1990, Iraq invaded the neighbouring state of Kuwait, and set in train the events leading to the Gulf War. It was an unprovoked attack carried out with brutal efficiency and enforced by terror. There were hideous atrocities. Iraq's troops tortured and killed hundreds of Kuwaitis. Rape was commonplace. Thousands were taken prisoner, and many were mutilated. The population of Kuwait fell by two-thirds in five months. It was an attempt by a dictator to wipe an entire state off the map.

The immediate fear was that Iraq's leader Saddam Hussein would turn next on the Gulf states and the rich prize of Saudi Arabia. His interest clearly lay in grabbing the Middle East's oil reserves. Within days, the US and Britain began diplomatic and military moves to assemble a military coalition to oppose him, and British aircraft were sent to protect north-east Saudi Arabia. By late August the UN had imposed sanctions against Iraq, and had empowered armed forces to enforce them.

Margaret Thatcher had not been idle. She understood the strategic importance of the Gulf, and she loathed dictators. It was the first test of Western resolve in the post-Cold War epoch, and it was vital that Iraq should not be allowed to annex territory as and when it chose. In early September, Parliament was recalled for a two-day debate at the end of which military action, should it become necessary, was approved by an overwhelming majority of 437 to thirty-five. General Sir Peter de la Billière, a former commander of the SAS, was appointed commander of British Forces in the Gulf, and the 7th Armoured Brigade was dispatched to Saudi Arabia to reinforce a multinational force. Margaret Thatcher's final Cabinet after announcing her resignation was attended by the Chief of the Defence Staff, Sir David Craig, and a decision to commit sixteen thousand extra

British troops to the Gulf was approved, taking our total commitment to forty-five thousand servicemen. 'Operation Granby', as the British operation in the Gulf was known, was in full swing.

This was the situation I inherited. War was not yet inevitable, but was looking highly probable. On 30 November 1990, two days after I became prime minister, United Nations Security Council Resolution 678 set 15 January 1991 as the final date for the Iraqis to withdraw from Kuwait, and authorised the use of 'all necessary means' to compel them to go. 'All necessary means' meant war.

Margaret had already established the Overseas Defence (Gulf) – OD(G) – Cabinet committee to oversee the crisis; it first met under my leadership on Wednesday, 5 December. Douglas Hurd, the Foreign Secretary, and Tom King, Defence Secretary, were essential members, and were joined by John Wakeham, the Energy Secretary, and Patrick Mayhew, the Attorney General. Marshal of the Royal Air Force Sir David Craig, Chief of the Defence Staff and a distinguished airman with experience of inter-service command, joined us from the outset. As the Gulf was to be primarily an air war for most of its course, his experience and advice were invaluable.

We were supported by Sir Percy Cradock, my foreign policy adviser, with Cabinet Secretary Sir Robin Butler and Len Appleyard from the Cabinet Office. Charles Powell, my Foreign Affairs Private Secretary, and Gus O'Donnell, my Chief Press Secretary, were also vital members. They were a formidable team. Robin Butler and Gus O'Donnell I knew well from my days at the Treasury. Gus was charged with ensuring that our public briefing was thorough and accurate. Percy Cradock, our adviser on intelligence matters, was an intriguing character. He thrived on dry, intellectual vigour, had a contempt for sentiment, weighed his words carefully and, when he spoke, was worth listening to. As a former ambassador to both Beijing and the German Democratic Republic, he had much experience of totalitarian governments. Unfailingly courteous, he believed politicians were of different – and probably inferior – clay to diplomats, and that they needed wise counsel. This he provided in full and generous measure, and his advice throughout the crisis was invaluable.

Charles Powell was the London end of the crucial direct telephone link with the White House, through which so much vital information was to flow. Other ministers and officials attended as necessary. Inevitably dubbed 'the War Cabinet', it was to meet twenty-six times over the weeks ahead.

The inner group began to make preparations for conflict. Strategies and military objectives were agreed. Arrangements were made to bring home embassy staff and British citizens. Plans were prepared for sustaining national unity, a particular concern of Douglas Hurd's. Undesirable Iraqis were expelled, although we soon realised that some mistakes in identifying them were made, through either haste or excessive caution. We discussed all the information available about the strength and capabilities of the Iraqi armed forces. We considered the threat to Israel, and how it might respond if attacked. When Saddam Hussein threatened that Iraq would resort to terrorism as part of the Gulf conflict, we introduced measures across the Middle East and in the UK to protect assets and personnel at risk.

The provision of military equipment was put in hand, as also was legislation for the introduction of emergency powers. Arrangements were made for medical treatment in the field and for the transport home of an unknown number of casualties – perhaps amounting to tens of thousands. Doctors and nurses volunteered to go to the Gulf, and additional money for the NHS was agreed and hospital wards earmarked for the wounded, the burned or the gassed.

Amidst our preparations, two fears predominated. First, how good were Iraq's forces? We knew Iraq had a huge and formidably well-equipped army. Many of their troops had combat experience from the Iran–Iraq war, and their crack force, the Republican Guard, had a fearsome reputation. Percy Cradock, in particular, never tired of speculating about how good this force might be.

Second, and even more of a nagging worry, would Saddam Hussein dare to use chemical or biological weapons on the battlefield? General Colin Powell, Chairman of the US Joint Chiefs of Staff, had told me his 'greatest fear' was that Saddam would be stupid enough to use such weapons. We dared not rule out the use – even prior to the conflict – of chemical weapons as an instrument of terror in population centres in the UK, the US or any of the countries forming part of the allied force. It was the first time we had ever faced such a threat, and it underlined the vulnerability of Western societies. We knew the Iraqis had sophisticated biological and chemical weapons, but we *thought* they had no warheads capable of carrying them, and that they had not mastered airburst technology. This was reassuring, but less comforting was our knowledge that they had weaponised anthrax and plague agents (bubonic plague), probably in soft-skin air-delivered bombs or in airborne spray tanks. This was a terrifying prospect for our troops. Anthrax was fatal if inhaled into the lungs, whilst botulinus toxin (BTX) caused muscle paralysis leading to death from asphyxia. Although the plague spores developed by the Iraqis responded to antibiotics, they could lead to a form of pneumonia with a very high mortality rate. Against this background it was decided to vaccinate British troops (on a voluntary basis), although only after the most stringent medical tests on each batch of vaccine. The US acted similarly to protect their forces.

We made it clear that we would not tolerate any Iraqi use of chemical or biological weapons, whether against troops or as a weapon of terror against unprotected civilian populations. So did the US. In private, Saddam Hussein received an unmistakable warning about the immediate and cata- strophic consequences for Iraq of any such attacks on civilians. I hoped he would take notice, but was not confident. I knew that if he did use these diabolical weapons, we would have to escalate our response to bring the war to a speedy and conclusive end before too many of our troops were exposed to them.

Throughout December, diplomatic efforts to prevent war continued, but without much hope that they would be successful. Iraq lifted travel restrictions so that foreign citizens held in Baghdad could return home, but gave no indication of its intention to pull out of Kuwait. War moved closer, although the allied coalition still hoped Iraq would withdraw from Kuwait by 15 January. President Bush volunteered to send his Secretary of State, James Baker, to Baghdad, and invited the Iraqi Foreign Minister to Washington. On announcing this, Bush rang to reassure me that the US was not going 'wobbly'. It was a bitter-sweet comment in view of the wide public currency given to a remark Margaret Thatcher had allegedly made earlier: 'This is no time to go wobbly, George.' He wasn't, but he knew diplomatic niceties needed to be observed if military support was to stay solid.

In Britain, too, we hoped to avoid war. Douglas Hurd sent me a note suggesting we tell Saddam that if he withdrew from Kuwait he would not be 'thumped', and my military advisers sensed that on neither side of the Atlantic was anyone hell-bent on a military solution. Within the War Cabinet there were concerns about the impact on public opinion of a protracted air campaign.

I wanted to obtain the widest possible public and parliamentary support for the hazardous undertaking that lay ahead. This was going to be a different sort of war. It was not the Falklands. This was not our island home that had been invaded. Although the decision to commit our servicemen to the conflict to come had already been made I sought a cross-party consensus, and was determined to keep Neil Kinnock, as leader of the opposition, and Paddy Ashdown for the Liberal Democrats, fully briefed. This was not only prudent in parliamentary terms, but would ensure that our servicemen knew there was the maximum level of support for the task ahead of them. It also made clear to the Iraqis the depth of British feeling over their behaviour. Tom King and Douglas Hurd briefed other senior political figures to build the maximum consensus.

I spoke to Neil Kinnock in my room at the Commons one evening a week before Christmas and found him very supportive. After he left I reflected upon how frustrating the conflict must be for him. Before I became prime minister Labour were well ahead in the opinion polls, but my election had turned them around. Now, when he must have wished to sink his political teeth into a new prime minister, he was forced to support him. Nonetheless, despite a dissenting minority in his party, he did so, and rose enormously in my estimation. Neil Kinnock was an old-fashioned patriot. Paddy Ashdown, a former professional Marine, was equally steady and convinced of the need for our participation in the war. At no time did either of them seek party advantage out of the conflict. It could be said that since public support for our action was overwhelming, they had no alternative but to row in behind it. But I saw them face to face, and their support was not simply political self-interest. They thought our action was right – and they backed it.

When I visited the Ministry of Defence for a briefing, David Craig stressed to those attending the extreme secrecy of what we were about to hear. The same evening, an episode occurred which caused us huge embarrassment. Three briefcases containing top-level documents concerning our war plans, and a laptop computer used during my briefing earlier in the day were stolen from the locked boot of a service car en route to Strike Command HQ at Wycombe. Astonishingly, the staff officer and his driver had both left the vehicle to visit a car showroom, and the thief had struck in their short absence. This was catastrophic; we had no idea if the theft was mere opportunistic villainy or an intrepid Iraqi intelligence operation.

The papers were recovered quickly, but our efforts to find the laptop were unsuccessful. Had military plans been saved in it? Christmas came and went. We agreed that, as it appeared that the papers had not been compromised or revealed to the Iraqis, we would not inform the United States of the incident until more was known about the likely contents of the laptop. Then, on 29 December, we learned that the *Mail on Sunday* was about to print the story, and informed the US immediately. A few days later we heard from the thief, who told us where to recover the computer: in a carpark in St John's Wood. We found it with a message in a brown envelope signed 'Edward'; it said, in so many words, that we were jolly lucky that he was a patriotic thief. We felt there was no answer to that. The computer (with the presentation saved on the disk), was returned to the Ministry of Defence, where, I am told, it lingered for some days in the post room at the front desk without anyone realising that it was what everybody had been looking for.

Just before Christmas, accompanied by Norma, I flew to Washington to meet President Bush. I had to secure the confidence of the Americans, who were still rocked by Margaret's departure. Our talks were due to be held at Camp David, the President's country retreat, but bad weather prevented us flying there from the White House. Instead we travelled by car in murky light along snowy roads. Charles Powell and I joined the President and his National Security Adviser, Brent Scowcroft, for the journey, whilst Norma travelled separately with Barbara Bush and Sir Anthony Acland, our Ambassador to Washington, and his wife Jenny.

I had barely known George Bush before this meeting. Although we had met when I was foreign secretary, this was the first time we had engaged on serious matters. But it was very relaxed, almost as though we were old and familiar colleagues. Sometimes you meet someone and the relationship is very easy. That was certainly true for me with George Bush, and I think it was true for him too. There was no hesitation. No unease. No holding back. No probing to find out the other's position. After a few relaxed courtesies we turned to business, with Charles and Brent taking notes as the car, despite the icy conditions, hurtled along at a good seventy miles per hour. The President told me his preferred date for action was 16 January, the day after the UN-imposed deadline for Iraq to withdraw from Kuwait; any longer delay would enable Saddam Hussein to seek to recruit allies by claiming that we were afraid to engage him in battle. There was no advantage for us in delay. We both accepted that a military solution was the inevitable way forward. The plan was for massive air strikes to degrade Iraq's defences, and then a ground onslaught. Our Arab allies believed the war would be very brief – perhaps only days – but the US and the British military believed it would be longer, and we planned for that.

President Bush and I discussed risks and options. We considered how to handle partial Iraqi withdrawal – a manoeuvre sufficient to gain some international support but insufficient to free Kuwait. Neither of us relished a fudged solution. This was 'the most difficult option', said the President, but we speedily agreed that the terms of the UN Resolutions must be met in full. No fudge was acceptable. We were concerned also that Saddam would attack Israel, which would respond militarily and so widen the conflict. Diplomatic moves were agreed or discarded as the car sped on.

We examined the logistics of military action: how and when to consult our allies; how to secure surprise; how the experts viewed night-vision conditions for bombing; whether a formal 'declaration of war' was necessary; environmental concerns over bombing chemical and biological sites; how to handle public opinion and the press. Thankfully, our estimates of casualties were far higher than turned out to be the case. All this and much more, which we had been considering separately before our meeting, we were now able to discuss together. One and a half hours later, as we arrived at Camp David, the principal options for 'Desert Storm' had been set out and agreed.

The Gulf War was an American-led war, with the UK, an essential supporting force, accepting tactical command by the US, with General Norman Schwarzkopf the commander-in-chief of the coalition force. We had no difficulty with this concept. The cooperation at military level between our respective armed services was excellent. David Craig and General Colin Powell, Chairman of the Joint Chiefs of Staff, were in contact daily, as were many of the other key military figures. We shared America's wish to preserve peace in the Gulf region, where we had long-standing allies and significant economic interests. We knew the region well and never doubted the desirability of working with the United States, on this occasion, as so often, our foremost ally.

At the end of our car journey President Bush and I were more of one mind on how to proceed than I would have believed possible. As prime minister, presiding over a nation soon to be involved in a full-blown land war, all of this was a strange and unexpected concept. Only a few months before I had been at the Treasury, wrestling with the ERM. Not many years before that I had been preparing social security reform. I had been comprehensively briefed, and I was sure of the facts and had no doubt about our objectives. But as a non-soldier, I was uneasy at sending others to war even though I had no doubt it was right to do so.

George Bush did have experience of war, and a distinguished war record. But he was not martial by temperament. He did not glory in war or in the military might of the United States; he was a reluctant, but convinced warrior. This lack of vainglory enabled him to piece together an unlikely coalition that was wide enough to discourage Russia or China from doing more than muttering frustrated dissent from the sidelines. It was a first-class piece of diplomacy from a first-class president.

On the eve of the war George wrote a letter to his children George (now Governor of Texas), Jeb (now Governor of Florida), Neal, Marvin and Doro that laid bare the man I came to know:

> Every human life is precious. When the question is asked, 'How many are you willing to sacrifice?' – it tears at my heart. The answer is, of course, none, none at all. We have waited to give sanctions a chance, we have moved a tremendous force so as to reduce the risk to every American soldier if force is to be used; but the question of loss of life still lingers and plagues the heart.

The world is safer, and in good hands, when on the eve of war its leaders possess such sentiments.

At Camp David, a further plenary meeting was held to discuss non-Gulf matters. The General Agreement on Tariffs and Trade (GATT) negotiations, US–European relations, access to Heathrow for US airlines – all had an airing. But everyone's mind was really on the Gulf.

Work over, George and Barbara Bush gave us a delightful weekend, full of log fires, good food, Christmas songs from a small male-voice army choir, and the occasional film. The President was at ease in his mind about what he had to do, and I had not a shred of doubt in mine that he was right.

I returned from the US to spend Christmas quietly at Finings and to reflect on an astonishing year. Norma and I celebrated the New Year at Chequers with James and Elizabeth and some long-standing friends, but the impending Gulf War never quite left my mind. Charles Powell and David Craig apart, no one else in the UK knew that we would be at war within a fortnight. For a prime minister of five weeks, it was a daunting prospect.

Preparations rolled on. The Labour backbencher Tam Dalyell, an honest and courageous man whom I respect, demanded the recall of Parliament to debate the situation, but he did not have the support of the official opposition. Some senior MPs were uneasy. Ted Heath and Tony Benn had been to Baghdad to argue for the release of hostages; a mistake, I thought, and one for which they were vilified. Neither much cared: they thought they were right and they wished to avoid bloodshed. Denis Healey muttered about the risks of war, but overall parliamentary support remained firm – more so, in fact, than Congressional support in the United States, where views were more divided and the Democrat majority was still arguing in favour of long-term sanctions. Gerald Kaufman, Labour's foreign affairs spokesman, warned that his party would not support the early use of force, but this was not followed through, since it was said more to placate potential Labour rebels than to deter the government. In Moscow, President Gorbachev remained implacably opposed to the use of force, and phoned me to tell me so. President Bush instituted more diplomatic initiatives while making clear to the Iraqis that there was no compromise on offer, and that the UN Security Council Resolution must be obeyed in full.

I visited the Gulf in early January to meet our troops and our Arab allies. It does not matter how good the briefing is, how many experts are advising you, how many piles of paper you have on your desk. If you go out and look people in the eyes, you get a different perspective. It was a hectic and crowded tour. I arrived in Taif, Saudi Arabia, late on 6 January and met the Amir of Kuwait, the Crown Prince and the Prime Minister early the following morning. They were downbeat, and distressed by the rape of their country. It was apparent that they were fearful that Saddam would get away with only a partial withdrawal from Kuwait, but they perked up noticeably when I said that would not be allowed. They were also concerned that if the Iraqis withdrew without a conflict, Kuwait would be forever vulnerable to a hostile neighbour with its force and arms intact. This was undoubtedly true, and would promise a long nightmare for Kuwait. I became more convinced than ever that a military solution would be longer-lasting than any diplomatic outcome, however welcome its short-term effect.

After leaving the Amir, I flew to Riyadh to meet the British community.

During the afternoon I met British forces, and warned Peter de la Billière that 16 January was the likely day of attack. He was mightily relieved that the decision had been taken and that an inelegant fudge to avoid conflict was unlikely. The sheer scale of the preparations was hugely impressive, and morale very high.

At 10.30 that night I met King Fahd after a banquet attended by the Saudi royal family in full formal costume. Our meeting was enlivened by news of the alleged defection of six Iraqi helicopters, which had Prince Sultan, the Saudi Defence Minister, scampering in and out trying to find out what was happening.

As for our meeting, the outcome could not have been better. After the warmest possible messages to Margaret Thatcher, who was well known and admired in Saudi, the King confirmed that his armed forces would join the military action and that Saudi Arabia would meet many of the costs of the British forces stationed there. British–Saudi relations were strong, and the Gulf War was to bind us even more firmly.

The following day I toured units of the 1st Armoured Division in the desert between Jubail and the Kuwaiti border. I wanted to meet the soldiers and explain to them why I was asking them to put their lives at risk. I climbed up onto a Challenger tank and spoke to a vast array of fit young men eager to know what lay ahead. I set out in straightforward terms what was at stake and why we were involved. They listened. And they cheered. And then they crouched around me, talking and joking and very excited. 'How do you feel about it?' I asked one of them, somewhat hesitantly. 'It's why we joined,' he told me. 'It's our job.' I knew then we would have no problem with troop morale.

They were well led, too, by General Rupert Smith and his senior colleagues. I met him when I climbed out of my helicopter in the desert and was greeted by a youthful-looking officer who led me to the General's HQ, a newly erected tent, largely bare except for maps, trestle tables and a few chairs. The youthful officer turned out to be the General.

At the port of Jubail I met the Royal Navy contingent, and saw the unloading of a massive stockpile of equipment for the British forces before moving on to Dhahran to see the Tornado air crews and their support staff, many of whom were civilian British Aerospace employees. It had been a furiously hot day, but it was becoming cooler, and the atmosphere, as it often is in that part of the world, was very still. At Dhahran, as the sun began to set, I once more stood on a box as the air crews gathered around in a huge horseshoe shape, their chatter not hiding the tension felt by all. Many held conspicuous placards on long poles – 'Hi, Mum' and 'When can I go home?' among them. I spoke of what was at stake and why they were there, and took questions. Only one mattered, and it came immediately: 'Are we going to have to fight?'

'Yes,' I said, 'and soon – perhaps within days.' No one asked much after that, but as the impromptu meeting ended, the men crouched around, cheerful and boisterous as if on the eve of a great sporting event. 'Thank you for telling us,' they said. 'We didn't think you would.'

I also met the ebullient Sultan Qaboos of Oman, one of Britain's firmest allies; he was as supportive and his hospitality as warm as ever. The Sultan has a great gift for surprise. He did not discuss the immediate problems. He assumed, as a matter of fact, that there would be a war, that we would win it, but what then? . . . 'beyond the far Jebel', as he put it. I was fascinated that he was focusing on the aftermath of the war before a shot was fired. As we walked around the garden of his palace I learned that the Sultan always took the long view.

Flying home, I stopped off in Cairo to meet President Mubarak of Egypt. He was robust and deliciously indiscreet. A tough ex-air force commander, Mubarak has a penchant for historical reminiscence together with an inexhaustible supply of witty and pertinent anecdotes. When I saw him he was very bored with pacifist American Congressmen, who had been calling on him in droves. 'Time is running out,' he said, and his view was clear. 'Get on with it.' He had been a bulwark of the Arab alliance, and had written to Saddam Hussein months earlier to tell him: 'You are committing suicide.' He remained of that view. It was just what I hoped to hear from him, and as I flew home I was relieved that our Arab allies were not only on-side but were bullish and eager to settle the matter. Saddam had misjudged them. He believed that air strikes would cause an explosion of anti-American feeling across the Arab world and that, as this happened, the US would cave in and opt for dialogue rather than battle.

Back home, on a bitterly cold afternoon at Alconbury air base, I had a long meeting with US Secretary of State James Baker, a large part of which was taken up with examining the implications of ordering incendiary bombing of chemical and biological weapons establishments in Iraq. I was concerned about how we could attack their storage and manufacturing sites without releasing deadly toxins into the air. Jim shared this concern, and we pressed the military hard. Could it be done? Yes, they assured us, it could be done without collateral risk. I agreed that we should keep this option in our armoury.

As we moved towards war, I remained worried about a sham peace cobbled together on the wrong terms. President Gorbachev was still keen to avoid conflict, though he had not blocked the Security Council Resolution. He telephoned me several times to argue against a military solution, but had no compelling reasons or alternatives. These could have been very difficult calls, but they were not. Mikhail Gorbachev and Margaret Thatcher had enjoyed a lively and vigorous accord. They liked and admired one another in an attraction of opposites, and he readily accepted me as her successor. We had an easy relationship.

Gorbachev was a remarkable man, and quite unlike any of his predecessors. A year after the Gulf War I had a private dinner with him at Admiralty House, where we sat talking for hours as he set out his views on Mother Russia. He was a charmer with a self-deprecating wit, and one story remains with me still. There was, he told me, a food shortage in Russia, with long queues for bread. Cold and frustrated, one man burst out of the queue: 'It's all Gorbachev's fault – I'm going to kill Gorbachev.' And off he went, returning two days later. The queue had shuffled forward a little. 'Have you killed Gorbachev?' he was asked. 'No,' he replied. 'The queue to kill Gorbachev is far too long.' As Gorbachev told this story he beamed with delight. I cannot imagine Stalin telling such a story. Gorbachev was fun – even though we differed over the Gulf.

And our differences were serious. I was convinced there was no choice but to settle the issue by war. He hated the prospect. Iraq was a traditional friend of Russia, and a war with it affronted Russian public opinion, as well as Gorbachev's own feelings. It was also likely to damage Russia's financial interests in Iraq. Above all, it would hurt Gorbachev's domestic standing. Russia was a powerful nation, used to its word counting, and yet the President of Russia was unable to prevent this conflict. It was very difficult for Gorbachev. He wearily acquiesced to the necessity for war.

Two days before the UN deadline expired I met President Mitterrand in Paris. The Gulf occupied only a small part of our two-hour discussion, which was amiable and enjoyable, and the President made no mention of a diplomatic initiative that the French launched in New York a few hours later. Nor had he warned the Americans. I was furious, and said so. It seemed to me that this was grandstanding to preserve as far as possible France's long-term trading relationship with Iraq. Mitterrand was offended and wrote to me in protest. This *contretemps* left a sour taste, but a telephone conversation more or less patched things up. In any event there was no purpose in a row.

As time ran out, I invited the Archbishop of Canterbury, Robert Runcie, and Cardinal Basil Hume to the Cabinet Room to secure their support for an action that was now only a few days away. We sat down and, over tea, I told them that diplomacy had failed – including a last-minute mission by the UN Secretary General Javier Pérez de Cuellar to Baghdad – and that the Iraqis were not only refusing to withdraw from Kuwait but showed no recognition that invading a neighbouring country was wrong. There was no choice left but force, I told the Cardinal and the Archbishop. Nor was there any weakening of will on the part of our Arab allies to expel Iraq from Kuwait.

Both churchmen recognised that a military strike was becoming inevitable, but they were fearful of escalation and a large loss of life. This was a valid fear, since Iraq had claimed publicly to have a 'secret weapon' capable of inflicting hundreds of thousands of casualties on allied troops. The Iraqi defence newspaper boasted: 'Iraq's arsenal contains surprises which will astonish our enemies.' We thought this was bluff, but couldn't be sure. Both Archbishop Runcie and Cardinal Hume gave me their public and private support and, in so doing, their reassurance that this would be a just war. Although I have never paraded my religion, their backing was important to me. I would have been uneasy without it.

The following day, I opened a Commons debate on the Gulf. The debate was emotional and tense, and enlivened by anti-war demonstrators in the Gallery. As I spoke of the 'rock solid' determination of the allied forces, red powder was thrown down into the Chamber, splattering mainly Labour MPs such as the veteran left-winger Ron Leighton, but also the elegant Julian Critchley on the Conservative side. I continued speaking as Julian dusted off the mess with an expression of disgust on his face. At the end of the debate 534 MPs of all parties voted in favour of military action – some, it must be said, with misgivings – and fifty-five Labour Members voted against, including two junior opposition spokesmen, who resigned as front-benchers. It was as good an endorsement as I could have hoped for. None, however, knew how soon that action was to be.

As the Speaker announced the result, I left the Chamber to take a call in my room in the Commons from George Bush. He confirmed that military action would begin – as we had agreed before Christmas – just before midnight Greenwich Mean Time on the following day, 16 January. He asked permission for US aircraft to use Diego Garcia airfield, a British territory in the Indian Ocean, and I readily agreed.

I went to bed with mixed emotions. Anticipation, of course. Also, confidence that we had no choice and were right to act, and consciousness of all that needed to be done in the days to come. I was anxious about what lay ahead, but above all I wondered what would be in the minds of the young aircraft crews as, for the first time, they launched themselves into action. I found it hard to imagine, but my visit to them had convinced me that they were ready for the fight and would do their duty with distinction.

So tight was the security that not even the War Cabinet or close ministerial colleagues were told of the action until the last hours before it began; only Sir David Craig, the Chief of the Defence Staff, Sir Peter de la Billière, Tom King and Charles Powell had advance notice. Douglas Hurd was informed about an hour before the first bombs fell.

After Operation Desert Storm had begun, normal party political hostilities were more or less suspended. On the first night I stayed up in the flat at Number 10 until reports of the early attacks came in, dozing only fitfully and being woken from time to time when hand-written reports from Charles Powell supplying new information came in. Charles did not sleep at all.

At 7 o'clock the following morning the War Cabinet met to receive a report of the overnight action, after which I made a statement to the battery of journalists and TV cameramen. The day's schedule was crowded. There were senior politicians to be briefed, Prime Minister's Questions to be prepared for, a parliamentary statement and the text of my prime ministerial broadcast for that evening to be agreed. I also saw and briefed the Queen.

That day was my son James's sixteenth birthday. Many of the servicemen I had met in the Gulf were not much older. As I thought of them, I saw James. There is nothing impersonal about war. It is about sending young people out to fight, and perhaps to die, for a cause older men decide is worthwhile. In this war they were not fighting for home and hearth as in the two great wars of our century. Nor were they fighting for the recovery of a British possession as in the Falklands. They were fighting for something less tangible: the maintenance of international law. They were fighting to prevent a dictator extending his power, and perhaps, thereafter embroiling a large part of the world in a wider war.

The agony and fear of war is felt as much by the parents and loved ones of those in action as by the men and women themselves. The purpose of my prime ministerial broadcast was to explain to those at home, who had seen events unfolding on television in their living rooms, why we had become involved. My decision to make the broadcast was not a spontaneous one – as many thought – but had been agreed with Douglas Hurd at Chequers just after Christmas. More impromptu was my instinctive 'God bless' at the end of the broadcast, which was much commented upon at the time. It expressed how I felt having met so many of the young men whose lives were now at risk. It is what I would have said to James.

Throughout this period I stayed up until the early hours of the morning, slept briefly, and woke, as usual, about 6 a.m. Charles Powell, it seemed to me, rarely slept at all. Nevertheless, he was thriving, and I saw vividly why Margaret had valued him so much. I was lucky in my Private Office throughout my years in Downing Street, but Charles, with his supreme efficiency and astonishing stamina, was the first illustration I had of what excellent service I would receive.

During the war, many others put in equally long hours to ensure that political and military decisions could be taken with accurate information. In the Cabinet Office, the Assessment Staff met daily at 4 a.m. to assemble intelligence from all sources; the Joint Intelligence Committee met at 6 a.m. to produce a briefing for ministers, and other senior officials met at 8.30 a.m. to prepare an agenda for a ministers' meeting at 10 a.m. This activity in Whitehall was matched in the operational headquarters of each of the services.

There were four phases to the planned campaign. The first and second concentrated on attacking Iraq's air defences, airfields, communications and command-control bunkers. This was to be followed up with a third phase, weakening Saddam's ground forces by destroying tanks, artillery pieces, ammunition dumps and logistical links. Many essential bridges were to be destroyed to cut off Iraqi forces in the 'Kuwait Field of Operations' from the rest of the country. Finally, when our ground forces were ready and the first three phases had been judged successful, would be the land battle itself. Our assessment before we started was that the air campaign might run for two to six weeks and the ground battle for a further month or so, depending on how much of a fight the Iraqis put up. Overall, it was the most intensive and complex campaign mounted since World War II. It was a much bigger operation than most people in Britain realised.

The bombing raids in phases one and two generally began around midnight, and continued through the night. The 'Air Tasking Order' for each twenty-four-hour period ran to hundreds of closely-detailed pages, which each aircrew had to follow to the second. The whole purpose, which was most successfully achieved, was to so weaken and demoralise the Iraqis that the final push by our ground troops could meet all our objectives. The air campaign was brilliantly achieved in a mere hundred hours, with minimal casualties on our side. And this in spite of the urgent need only twenty-four hours into the offensive to divert around 25 per cent of our resources to dealing with Iraqi Scud missile attacks on Israel and Saudi Arabia.

As targets, we were faced with some of the largest airfields in the world – Tabil, for example, was larger than Heathrow – and they were well protected by surface-to-air missiles and anti-aircraft guns. The RAF took on some of the most hazardous tasks, bombing at low level. Six Tornado jets were lost, two in the first twenty-four hours, although fortunately seven of the twelve aircrew survived. We lost no Jaguars at all. Huge anger was aroused when captured British pilots were paraded before the camera as Iraqi propaganda. I had met some of them in Dhahran just a few days before, and felt their plight very personally.

Despite the Tornado losses, it was clear by 23 January that we had achieved air superiority. To reduce the risks to our aircraft we switched to operation at medium level, which was particularly successful once we brought in ageing Buccaneer planes to laser-mark targets for Tornadoes equipped with precision-guided bombs. British Tornadoes also used a highly sophisticated – and expensive – weapon, the JP 233, against airfield paved surfaces, to so damage them as to prevent Iraqi planes from taking off. We were surprised that the Iraqi air force showed few signs of wanting to retaliate; indeed, a considerable number of their fighter aircraft were flown unarmed to Iraq's former enemy Iran. Happily, they were impounded, but the reason for this exodus was far from clear, and we remained concerned that Saddam might be saving his air resources until we started our ground attack. In fact, he never did get his aircraft back.

One particular concern was to avoid causing damage to the Shiite holy shrines of Karbala and An-Najaf, which could inflame public opinion in the Arab world against the allied cause. We had regular photographs taken of them so we could show that they had not been damaged by us, and they survived the war unscathed.

As the war got under way I remained in close touch with senior political figures, especially Margaret Thatcher, who was avid for information and eager to give advice. She was following every development closely, and I realised how frustrating it was for her not to be involved. Accordingly, I instructed that she was to be kept fully informed of everything that was going on. I also arranged for Ted Heath, Neil Kinnock and Paddy Ashdown to be kept briefed, and met them myself to discuss our plans and seek their views.

I felt wholly at home with this consensual approach, and was well rewarded for it. Neil Kinnock's advice 'not to allow a pause in the bombing after a day or so', for fear that Saddam would stave off defeat and gain foreign sympathy, was accompanied by the merry observation, 'To be blunt, the best time to kick someone is when they're down.' It was good advice – and not only in war, I later reflected.

There were alarms during the air campaign. At 3 a.m. on 18 January, within twenty-four hours of our first bombardment, Charles Powell woke me up. One of the things we dreaded had taken place: Saddam Hussein had attacked Israel with Scud missiles. Brent Scowcroft had called Charles to say that the missiles were already in the air, but we did not know what the warheads contained: were they conventional explosives, or chemical or biological weapons? As it turned out, they were conventional weapons – to everyone's enormous relief. Even so, only a strong diplomatic effort persuaded the Israeli Cabinet to let the allies respond for them. Iraq, of course, wanted to draw Israel into the war in the hope of recapturing Arab support. This tactic failed, but the Scud missiles took on a huge importance, as they could reach as far west as Jerusalem and as far down the Gulf as Dhahran and Riyadh. Knocking them out became a vital objective, and some very brave soldiers from Special Forces joined with the RAF to take out Scud launching-sites in Iraq. Their stories cannot yet be told in detail – suffice it to say that some exceptional servicemen gave their lives in remarkable operations.

As January proceeded, daily reports marked the progress of the air bombardment. By 21 January seven thousand sorties had been flown, with significant impact on Iraq's air defences, command and control centres, chemical and biological weapon sites, airfields and targets in Baghdad itself. The RAF played a huge role behind the American lead. Tornado GR1s dropped thousand-pound bombs; Tornado F3s were on combat air patrol supported by tankers; Jaguars were in action, and Nimrod maritime patrol aircraft were on surveillance. At sea, British maritime forces had captured Iraqi mine-layers and mine-sweepers and were in control of the Gulf. But the Iraqi army was still active, if damaged, and its crack troops, the Republican Guard, were well protected by anti-aircraft and surface-to-air missiles. Even at the end of the month, when civilian and military communications had been terribly knocked about, they were still not broken. Iraq had a series of well-protected deep-trunk communication cables below ground, but our air superiority was now absolute.

The air war lasted five and a half weeks, and there was tremendous support for its prosecution from nearly everyone in Britain. Apart from a few backbenchers on the Labour side, the Commons was united. Both Neil Kinnock and Paddy Ashdown remained reassuring in public and offered positive suggestions in private. Many of our parliamentary exchanges at PMQs were orchestrated. This experience turned me away from many of the cruder forms of party political conflict, for which, in any event, I had never felt much attraction. Here was a nation working together. It was an enriching experience.

On 29–30 January Iraq launched five battalion-sized attacks on an uninhabited and undefended town eight miles inside Saudi Arabia. These were repulsed and badly mauled by a Saudi-led Arab force. Some five hundred Iraqis were taken prisoner, and the Saudis thought Iraq had been robbed of the will to fight. The trickle of Iraqi desertions began to grow, but their ground forces retained substantial combat ability. And Iraq was using other weapons – by 25 January it had released millions of barrels of oil into the Gulf, causing massive environmental damage.

On Thursday, 7 February I was chairing a meeting in the Cabinet Room at Number 10 on the war which had a heavy agenda, including the reconstruction of Kuwait, the cost of burden-sharing, and ceasefire terms. There was a full turnout of ministers and officials: the usual Gulf team of Douglas Hurd, Tom King, John Wakeham and Paddy Mayhew, with Robin Butler, David Craig, Percy Cradock, Charles Powell, Gus O'Donnell and Len Appleyard in attendance. We had just turned to a discussion of the possibility of Iraqi terrorism in London: the last word I uttered was 'bomb'.

Suddenly there was a tremendous explosion outside the Cabinet window opposite me and behind Paddy Mayhew's right shoulder. 'It's a mortar,' I heard Tom King shout. Charles Powell put his hand on my shoulder and pushed me under the Cabinet table as the windows buckled in and everyone took cover. What sounded like two further muffled explosions followed – and then silence. As we rose from under the table, the building still seemed to be shaking. I could hear shouts and sirens in the distance. 'I think we'd better start again somewhere else,' I said, and we made our way down to the secure Cobra Room, which lies below ground in Downing Street.

No one, mercifully, was hurt, although the intention of the bombers had clearly been to kill. Normally at that time the full Cabinet would have been in session, but it had been delayed that morning because of the need for a meeting on the Gulf. We did not know whether the attack was by the Iraqis or the IRA, although it soon became clear that it was the latter. They had launched three mortars from a stolen van parked in Whitehall near the Ministry of Defence, and had come very close to murdering the ministers and officials most closely involved in the political direction of the Gulf War. For us it had been a narrow escape; for the IRA another day at the office, with only the regret that they failed to register their kill.

I decided Cabinet should meet at 11 a.m. as planned, to avoid the IRA claiming a propaganda victory. In any event we had important domestic matters to discuss – most immediately the severe weather conditions across the country and the need to approve extra social security payments to pensioners so that they might keep warm. We agreed the announcements to be made before ministers were driven through the snow and back to their departments. Government went on.

But the war remained our constant preoccupation. In a defiant speech Saddam boasted that he had sixty divisions prepared for 'the mother of battles'. It was soon to come. On 23 February I told Margaret Thatcher, Neil Kinnock and Paddy Ashdown that the ground campaign would begin the next day.

The attack – by the United States on the first day and by the British on the second – was staggeringly successful. Saddam told his Republican Guards that the allies had been stopped in their tracks, but this was the reverse of the truth. The allies' superior force broke through Iraq's lines very speedily and in all sectors. US and Saudi forces made gains on the twenty-fourth, and on the following day a complete enemy battalion surrendered to British servicemen from the 1st Staffords.

From then on, we bounded forward. The number of Iraqi PoWs swiftly grew to twenty-five thousand, and the military gains were spectacular. But one awful accident occurred: a US A10 aircraft on close air-support mistakenly attacked two Warrior armoured vehicles of the 4th Armoured Brigade, killing nine men of the 3rd Royal Regiment of Fusiliers and leaving eleven more wounded. It was to be our biggest individual loss of the whole campaign. Men killed by their own side. 'Blue on blue', it is called – the ultimate futility of war. I thought this was a double horror for the families, who all their lives would recall the pointless way in which their loved ones had been killed. The Americans felt this deeply, and both President Bush and Colin Powell telephoned me to express their profound sorrow.

Alongside such tragedies there were comic incidents. A US Marine vehicle became stuck in the mud at the side of a road in the Euphrates Valley. An Iraqi tank crew pulled it back on the road, then, when the US troops appeared out of the vehicle, the Iraqis threw up their hands and surrendered. In this fashion the land war sped towards its end, with resistance crumbling and allied forces troubled about the 'turkey shoot' of young Iraqis unable to defend themselves. The military commanders recommended a ceasefire, and President Bush, followed by all the other political leaders on the allied side, agreed.

The announcement of the ceasefire, on 28 February, was a frustrating conclusion. Kuwait had been liberated, and the war aim met. Although one death is too many, British casualties – forty-seven killed in action and in non-combat accidents – were far below our most hopeful estimates. The Iraqi war machine had been crippled and Saddam Hussein humiliated. But although his regime had been severely weakened, it had not been destroyed. He remained, to bellow defiance at the rest of the world and to wreak vengeance upon his enemies at home – which he soon did.

Later on, the hindsight specialists were critical of this conclusion, strongly arguing that Saddam should have been destroyed, if necessary by allied forces entering Baghdad. But the military objectives, agreed with the US even before I became prime minister, were to evict Iraq's forces from Kuwait and to reduce the fighting capability of the Republican Guard to ensure that they could not re-invade Kuwait when the Western members of the coalition departed. I understand the frustration of the critics, since I shared it at the time – as did President Bush. But they were wrong; moreover, they would have had little support from either the heads of government, or the generals who had responsibility for prosecuting the war.

When the conflict began, it did so under international law. UN Security Council Resolutions set out the war aims, and on that basis the House of Commons and other political assemblies supported the liberation of Kuwait. In the UK, the Labour and Liberal Democrat parties had frequently urged full compliance with the Resolutions – and no more. The Resolutions did not support the destruction of the Iraqi regime, for the very good reason that no Arab nation would have joined the coalition against Iraq if they had. There was no Resolution empowering the allies to go into Baghdad and drag Saddam out by the heels. Nor should the allies have done so, even if it had been possible. If the nations who had gone to war on the basis of international law were themselves to break that law, what chance would there have been in future of order rather than chaos? What authority in the future would the great nations have had against law-breakers if they themselves broke the law and exceeded the United Nations mandate? They would never have been trusted again. No similar coalition could have been formed in the future. And even if they had tried to, would the allies have found Saddam? If they deposed him, would the allies have occupied and ruled Baghdad? What would have been the exit strategy?

The fact is that the coalition would not have held together if the allies had gone on to Baghdad. The Arab members would have withdrawn, and the old canards about Western imperialism would have been raised again. The Arab nations wished to see Kuwait free, and Saddam Hussein humbled, but they had always feared that the Western allies had a hidden agenda to destroy and dismember Iraq. That fear was ill-founded, of course, but it was deeply felt, and it would have seemed to be justified if the war had not ended with the eviction of Iraq from Kuwait. Moreover, the lack of trust engendered would have had incalculable long-term political and trade ramifications. Saddam would have rejoiced if, at the moment of his defeat, the Arab world had united against the West. So would the Soviet Union. We would have won the war and lost the peace.

As the military effort ended, we began again to work on an enormous flurry of UN Resolutions to enforce the ceasefire, create a framework to constrain Saddam Hussein, establish UN weapons control and force the neutralising of weapons of mass destruction. We were to learn, however, that Saddam's word, solemnly given, was rarely honoured.

Shortly after the end of the war, on my return from a brief visit to see President Gorbachev in Moscow, I stopped off in the Gulf to see the terrible devastation Saddam had left in his wake. Plumes of thick, polluting smoke blackened the sky from hundreds of oil wells wilfully set on fire by the retreating Iraqis. Huge oil-slicks disfigured the Gulf itself, and the scars of war and destruction were everywhere. It was a brutal piece of work designed to do the maximum economic damage. In Kuwait and Dhahran I met our troops and spoke to RAF Tornado F3 and ordnance squadrons, as well as British Aerospace personnel who had contributed to the war effort. Surrounded by troops, I was presented with a Chelsea football shirt and a captured AK47 rifle. Holding the gun, I joked, in a moment of prescience, 'This will be useful for Cabinet.' In due course it found a home in the Imperial War Museum. The Amir of Kuwait presented me with a magnificent ceremonial sword to mark the completion of Operation Desert Storm. It lay on a side-table in the Cabinet Room at Number 10 for the remainder of my premiership.

As I warmly congratulated the troops on the magnificent job they had done, I sensed that they were waiting for something else to be said – and I knew what it was. I teased them for a moment, and then uttered the most popular sentence I ever spoke as Prime Minister: 'I promise you – you will go home soon.' They raised the roof. It was the one thing they wanted to hear. War was all very well, but coming home after the war was what mattered.

When I met King Fahd, we had a very Saudi exchange. He apologised for being late. He was very late indeed – timekeeping was not among his many gifts. He had, he explained, been absorbed with work, but he had not wanted me to pass through Saudi Arabia without meeting him. Charmingly, he added that he considered London to be his home from home, and that I should think of Saudi Arabia in the same way. As he pointed out, he already owned a house in London, while I did not own one in Riyadh. I replied that I didn't own one in London either. Ever the gentleman, the King said I was welcome to a share of his London house. Fahd had been firm in his support throughout the war. He paid a handsome and genuine tribute to the courage and determination of the British troops, and I wished they could all have heard those quiet and courteous words of praise.

One painful aftermath of the Gulf drama was still to follow. Defeated in the war, Saddam Hussein's fury turned on his domestic opponents – the Kurds. Saddam was like a wounded animal: he had lost, but he had not been completely crushed. Genocide was in the man's mind, and it was certainly in the man's character. The Marsh Arabs in the south of Iraq and the Kurds in the north both rose against him, but were easily beaten back by far more numerous and better-equipped forces. Bloody and cruel reprisals began.

On 21 March I was sufficiently concerned at the plight of the Kurds to raise it myself at Cabinet. Over the Easter weekend I received reports of worsening conditions amounting to near-genocide, and the television pictures highlighted the appalling reality. Kurds were fleeing to the mountains in the north of Iraq with few, if any, possessions and no food in order to escape mass murder. It was potentially a humanitarian disaster.

I was clear that we should help. The Kurds should not be sacrificed to Saddam's cruelty. Margaret Thatcher felt the same way, and publicly demanded help for them without knowing that action was already in hand. John Weston, the Political Director at the Foreign Office, was well ahead with plans to be launched the following week at the EC Council at Luxembourg, where we knew the French, at least, would back us. Lynda Chalker, the Minister for Overseas Development, had already arranged air-drops of food and medicine and was actively involved in providing humanitarian assistance.

The essence of our plan was simple, although its implementation was less so. It was to mark out safe areas – safe havens, as they became known – in which the Kurds would be protected from attack and could be fed and housed in safety. This was too big and costly an exercise for the British alone, and I knew we would need American and European support. No one seemed keen to take the lead, so I determined to do so. It was a risky undertaking, and might well have failed; but the humanitarian need was so evident it was a risk I was prepared to take. For me, a failure would simply have been a political embarrassment; for the Kurds, it would have meant almost certain death for tens of thousands. I never had a shred of doubt that it was right to proceed.

Implementing the plan was complex, and would involve troops in new risks for an unknown period of time. Final details of our proposals were not agreed until the short flight from Northolt to Luxembourg on the morning of 8 April. I worked on them in the plane with Michael Jay, a senior Foreign Office official, and Stephen Wall, formerly my Principal Private Secretary at the Foreign Office, who had succeeded Charles Powell two and a half weeks earlier. (Charles had decided not to take up an ambassadorship, which surely he deserved, or return to the Foreign Office. The private sector beckoned, and the public service lost a remarkably able man.) As we left the plane, my draft speech was still not typed, but our plan was decided and our tactics were set.

Before the summit began I spoke to Jacques Santer, Prime Minister of Luxembourg and chairman of the meeting, and told him of the plan. I then received the support of Germany's Chancellor Helmut Kohl – 'Ja. Gut, John, sehr gut' – and of François Mitterrand – 'France will do her duty.' Thus armed, I was certain of the support of the EU, and received it in full measure. Apart from helping to ease the miserable plight of the Kurds, they were delighted with the novelty of endorsing a British proposal launched through the EU. Stephen Wall immediately phoned Brent Scowcroft in the White House to brief him, and the 'safe havens' policy took wings. Within minutes, our Ambassador at the UN, David Hannay, was gaining backing for the scheme in New York.

At first, the US was reluctant. Its war effort had been substantial, and our 'safe haven' proposals involved more troop commitment, more expense, and promised to be a long and difficult exercise. I spoke twice to President Bush, following which the Americans gave wholehearted approval and the plan took effect. The President sent five thousand troops, the largest contingent, I sent two thousand and President Mitterrand a thousand. Food, water, clothing and shelter were provided on a massive scale. Genocide was averted, and literally tens of thousands of lives were saved. So too, I think, was the reputation of the allies, which would surely have been harmed had we turned a blind eye.

As Saddam survived, some ask: did the Gulf War achieve anything?

Yes, it did. It freed Kuwait. It protected the rest of the Gulf from a threat that would have grown. It weakened a dictator. It put the world on notice of his potential to do harm. It set a pattern for peacekeeping and allowed the United Nations to begin a weapons inspection programme which has done much to limit Iraq's chemical and nuclear weapons capability. It reinforced the United States as the foremost military power in the world.

And, above all, although it may be unfashionable to think in such terms, it was morally the right thing to do: it gave a signal that the world expected certain standards in international behaviour and would act to enforce them.

# CHAPTER ELEVEN

## Raising the Standard

WHEN I BECAME PRIME MINISTER I was determined to correct two problems that stretched right across government. Both had long dismayed and angered me, and needed the unique influence of Number 10 to put right.

The first was the culture of public services in Britain. Many of the services important to people were provided by the state sector, and funded by taxation. Despite many excellent public servants the service offered was often patronising and arrogant. Some officials seemed to have the attitude that as the service was 'free', everyone should be grateful for whatever they received, even if it was sloppy. There was a mentality in parts of the public service that no one had responsibility to give better service to the public, unless, of course, they were bribed with more pay or shorter hours. Complaints were treated with an anonymity and disdain that would have fast brought a private company to its knees for lack of customers. Working methods were often slapdash and inefficient, because there was neither the stimulus of competition nor true accountability for performance. New ideas were seen as threats. Services were run carelessly, wastefully, arrogantly and, so it seemed to me, more for the convenience of the providers than the users, whether they were parents, pupils or patients.

I loathed this attitude. Far from being 'free', taxpayers paid in advance for public services through compulsory deduction of tax from their income or through taxes added to the cost of their purchases. I believed they deserved the same high-quality service they would have expected if they paid cash on the nail.

Yet, although the public were wearied with poor service, they seemed disinclined to complain. It seemed pointless: the monolith would not listen, and nothing would be done. This perception was frustrating for the users of public services, and bad for the services themselves. It lowered the esteem in which the public sector was held, and so, inevitably, the self-esteem of many dedicated public servants whose efforts merited respect and reward.

The second problem was political. Privatisation had brought huge improvements in the quality of service in the 1980s, as well as lower prices. Yet the public face of the Conservative Party carelessly, sometimes tactlessly, still allowed itself to be seen as not caring about improving the public sector. Many in powerful positions failed to acknowledge the work done by excellent teachers, nurses or transport workers. They too easily forgot how vital their skills were to the lives of nearly everyone in the country.

At worst, some of my colleagues seemed to view such services as the railways as pointless historical relics. They saw the National Health Service as an embarrassing problem, ever demanding money, not as the source of national pride it is and should be. Such views were politically self-defeating. They were also fatuous and absurd, since Conservative governments had presided over the NHS for the majority of its lifetime, funded it with larger sums year upon year, and helped build it up to one of the best public health services in the world. But the impression too often conveyed was that our support was grudging; and our policy of privatising some parts of the public sector led people to believe we were hostile to all of it.

Dealing with these two problems was the motivation behind the programme of action called the 'Citizen's Charter'. Of course I wanted to make the Conservative Party more popular, but that paled into insignificance against the prize of raising the quality and standing of public service as a whole.

Why did I care so much about this? For those cold and rational motives, certainly, but also for more personal and emotional reasons. My own life history was different from that of most of my predecessors at Number 10. My Conservatism came from what I saw, what I felt, and what I did, as well as what I read. It shaped what I wanted to do in office. When I was young my family had depended on public services. I have never forgotten – and never will – what the National Health Service meant to my parents, or the security it gave despite all the harsh blows that life dealt them.

Nor have I forgotten the care I received at a critical time, after my accident in Nigeria. These personal experiences left me with little tolerance for the lofty views of well-cosseted politicians, the metropolitan media or

Whitehall bureaucrats, who made little use of the public services in their own lives, and had no concept of their importance to others. They may have looked down on the public sector and despised it as second-rate, but many of them knew nothing of the people who worked there, or the manifold problems they faced.

In addition to improving the quality of public service, I wanted to raise the standing of those hundreds of thousands of people who work selflessly in all branches of them, and who take pride in what they do. I wanted to make them feel their work was valued. I planned to see good standards of service publicly recognised and rewarded – both in the honours list and through a new good-service award for public bodies, something that I eventually created in the Charter Mark.

On the other hand, life experience had not left me naively starry-eyed about the public services. As a young man without money or privilege behind me, I had also come up against the dark side of the coin. Telephones answered grudgingly or not at all. Booths closed while customers were waiting. Time pointlessly lost when appointments were not made or kept. Unacceptably long waiting times. Remote council offices where, after a long bus journey, there was no one available to see you who really knew about the issue. People left in the dark about why something was happening – or more often not happening. Anonymous voices and faces who refused to give you a contact name. Offices where correspondence or calls never seemed to be dealt with by the same person and you had to begin from first base, time after time after time. This was the weekly reality for millions of people in Britain up to the end of the 1980s. It was a problem worth tackling.

It is easy to be cynical about this – as some on both the right and left of politics were about the Charter – and to say, from the comfort of privilege and the cushion of an expense account, that these were trivial issues, or somehow evidence that I had a chip on my shoulder. I totally reject that. There are few people alive who have not faced such irritations, or worse. These inefficiencies are a drag on the economy as a whole. They waste time and money. They cause frustration and pain. My view was blunt: taxpayers paid for the public sector. They deserved a personal, prompt and quality service.

The conventional view of the political right in the 1980s was that this could only be done by privatisation. In some instances that was the right medicine, as was proved by the huge success of British Airways and British Telecom after they were sold. The lure of privatisation was increased by its success; it was copied around the world. It was an error of historic proportions for the Labour Party – from Michael Foot to Tony Blair – to have resisted, as they did, every single privatisation. To give one example: hundreds of millions of pounds more could have been raised in the market for improving our railways if Tony Blair and Clare Short had not raised the foolish, but in 1996 all too credible, spectre of renationalisation. Mr Blair now blithely tells us he never intended to carry out that threat; in effect that it was just so much more characteristic candyfloss to gull the Labour Party faithful. It did not seem so at the time.

Some areas would not readily, or perhaps ever, be privatised. I wanted to improve services in those areas; to rest our fortunes entirely on privatisation seemed to me to be too ideological, too lacking in vision or ambition. The services that could not and should not be privatised – chiefly schools and hospitals – were important to millions of daily lives. In order to achieve improvement in them I knew I would have to confront old attitudes both towards public services and inside them. The Tory right were not the only ones with an attitude problem. They believed the only good public service was a privatised one; but the vast majority of civil servants, even in the Treasury, seemed to believe the only way a service could be improved was to throw money at it.

I began to map out this territory publicly in 1989, when I was chief secretary to the Treasury. That June, in a lecture to the Audit Commission, I warned against denigration of the valuable inheritance of the public sector. I argued that we needed to improve its use of resources; measure its performance more rigorously; and make services act more responsively towards their users. Change to avoid decay was the implicit message.

Within weeks I had left the Treasury for the Foreign Office. Ninety-four days later I was back at the Treasury as chancellor, although the tumultuous pace of events over the next year left no opportunity to pursue this issue further. But the future of public service was high on my agenda in November 1990 when I entered Downing Street. I set out my priorities at my first two full meetings with my new Policy Unit in January 1991. I told them I felt we ought to have pressed on more boldly in the past with work on the privatisation of British Rail and British Coal, but that I had reservations in the case of the Royal Mail. I said that central and local government contracting-out ('contractorisation', in the mercifully short-lived jargon of the time) must be part of our armoury. I was also concerned that those parts of Whitehall which had been moved 'offshore' into agencies should continue to involve and embrace the private sector and its skills. I wanted to bring the discipline and effectiveness of the private sector into the public services.

But, as I told the Policy Unit, this was not enough. We needed to go further. We had to remove ideological uncertainty from areas of the public sector that I had no intention of permitting to be privatised, such as health and schools. And we had to find new ways of raising sharply the general quality of public service and of empowering the consumer, patients, parents and passengers alike. I instructed the Policy Unit to make this a priority for action. As it was still possible in early 1991 that we might face a general election later in the year, I was keen to clarify new ideas in domestic policy areas swiftly. Our fresh approach would need to deliver real, practical benefits, to capture the public imagination and shoot, if we could, the occasional Labour fox.

Already, I hoped that some of the ideas and decisions that would be forced by development of these policies would provide meat for our Manifesto and a domestic agenda for the next term. Sarah Hogg asked Nick True in the Unit to coordinate development of this policy strand. As Nick was also one of the principal figures working with me on significant speeches, we were able to use public speeches to test the water and to coax forward my sometimes unresponsive colleagues.

I was quite explicit about my intentions as early as 7 February 1991 in a speech to the Young Conservative Conference in Scarborough. I concentrated then on education, which I saw as the service most seriously in need of change. Our teachers and schools were saddled with a deposit of failed ideas and a complacent and bureaucratic department, which seemed to have a mania for expanding its authority and influence. Kenneth Clarke, the Secretary of State for Education, who was always prepared to cross the road to pick a fight, was just the man to get to grips with this. But I was already sure we needed to set up a strong external foil to the department. For that reason I issued an instruction in late January that I was to be fully consulted on the future of the Schools Inspectorate. We were not, of course, looking at schools alone. The target I set in the speech was 'an unending search for better quality in all our public services'. In private that search was already well under way.

Initial discussions, both in Number 10 and with other departments, showed that there was some useful work already being done, with Ken Clarke being particularly creative. On the other hand, there was an almost audible dragging of feet in many departments, partly because of a lack of creative energy at the top, and partly because of that inevitable playing for time that occurs when an election is in sight, particularly one where the Civil Service believes that control of government is likely to change.

I decided to force the pace a little. The tactic was to say more in public, and then to bring together key ministerial colleagues to probe their ideas. In fields where the introduction of true competition and choice was impractical, I was certain that publishing the performances of different schools, hospitals, local authorities or transport services would act as a kind of surrogate competition to raise standards. Those bodies which were seen to be underperforming would come under pressure to explain why, and to improve. If we could at the same time, as I intended, also devolve more management responsibility to the local service level, then local governors, teachers, managers, train operators and others would have the opportunity to improve standards as well as the incentive to do so. An information revolution would be just as effective a way of doing this as the left-wing device of regulation by state, quango or local education authority. It would provide greater freedom, allow variety and experiment, and bring real satisfaction when success was achieved.

The public sector had suffered for years because it was too secretive and too ready to cover up substandard performance. I had concluded already that it was essential to separate powers between those who provided services and those who checked on them. I intended to open up the public sector to proper scrutiny and accountability. We needed to switch the focus from a naïve weighing of the gold in the bucket to a serious appraisal of what quality of service was delivered to the public and with what value for money. We had to end the excessive focus on financial *inputs* rather than service *output*. I knew that if I could achieve this it would be a huge gain – for taxpayers and service users alike. It was absurd that ministers were rated (in Whitehall and up and down the country) on their effectiveness in screwing money out of the Treasury, not on saving public money or raising service standards. It was a false measure, and I was out to break down this mentality. This was not easy, since an increasingly sceptical Treasury, so often an ally of efficiency, soon began to show signs of thinking that talk of better public services was evidence of a seriously demented prime minister planning to spend, spend, spend.

As part of the information revolution, we decided that standards for every service should be published, both as a benchmark for improvement and to show the public what they could expect. So too, and in clear, comprehensive detail, should results. I wanted to see reports on performance placed in public libraries and in newspapers. These would show, on a range of key measurements, how local services were doing. Relative success would be a source of pride. I intended also to provide incentives for good performance, through more performance-related pay. Relative weakness would be a point of pressure on failing management to upgrade standards. Ideally, there should be financial sanctions for service failure. What was more, I wanted improved complaints procedures and to ensure that members of the public got redress, an explanation, an apology or even compensation when things went wrong.

I set out these ideas in some detail in a speech to the Conservative Central Council on 23 March 1991. It was there that I used for the first time the phrase 'Citizen's Charter', and undertook that with it we would look systematically at every part of public service to see how higher standards could be achieved. I did not much like the name 'Citizen's Charter'; with its unconscious echo of revolutionary France, it had a faintly alien ring to it. At one point I thought of calling it 'the People's Charter', but such populism was thought to be risible, and likely to be taken as a gimmick. 'This is, after all,' said one civil servant, 'a serious policy.' So 'Citizen's Charter', more stuffy and formal, became its name.

The speech and the proposals in it stand up fairly well today. But at the time it was greeted with some disdain by a number of colleagues and commentators, who failed to see its relevance, and who completely underestimated my will to force it through. In late March I met senior colleagues for policy discussions at Chequers. We advanced privatisation by moving coal and rail off the backburners onto which departments had quietly slid them. It was clear to me that whatever the problems of improving rail standards and defining a model for introducing private ownership and competition – and they were immense – preserving the megalith of nationalisation was not the way to do it.

At Chequers that weekend we also decided to take a new look at the effectiveness of the utility regulators, to extend contracting-out, to deliver a fully independent Schools Inspectorate, to advance and simplify testing in schools, and to increase as fast as possible the number of grant-maintained schools. This fitted with my belief in devolved local management, and would shift the balance of power to head teachers and parents, and away from local bureaucracies. I also instructed the Department of Transport to prepare an action plan for measuring and publishing standards of performance and for improving the service provided by British Rail and London Underground, together with penalties for poor performance.

This was progress, but it was not enough. On the Monday morning, when I had returned to Number 10, I minuted all nineteen departmental ministers with public service responsibilities, explaining in clear terms what the Charter initiative was about. I asked them to submit, within one month, ideas for fitting into our plan of action. In order to allay Treasury concerns, it was made clear that the ideas should not involve any significant addition to public expenditure. The Treasury breathed a sigh of relief, but they did not really believe it.

The responses from most departments were slow in coming, and weak in genuine content. Some failed to address the key issues of service quality, real or surrogate competition, local delegation of power and improved accountability, and appeared to believe that institutional change within Whitehall would see me off. Wilfully or carelessly, the point was being missed. Sarah Hogg and Nick True in the Policy Unit were pushing as hard as they could, but it was soon clear that I needed to reinforce the Unit with strengthened official machinery if they were to be enabled to go as far as I wanted them to go.

I raised the problem with Sir Robin Butler, the Cabinet Secretary. Robin was quick to see the scope and importance of the initiative. He shared the acute disappointment that I and the Policy Unit felt at the poor quality of commitment seen so far, and welcomed the suggestion that we should at once set up a special *ad hoc* official committee in the Cabinet Office to work with the Unit and the Treasury in overseeing progress on the Charter. Such minutiae of government organisation may seem obscure, but Number 10 is a small place. I was not the first prime minister, nor will I be the last, to find the Cabinet Office, properly deployed, an effective weapon in asserting authority and calling Whitehall to order.

The new committee was chaired by a senior Cabinet Office official, Andrew Whetnall. He did a truly outstanding job. He not only pulled together the official strands, but showed an infinite capacity to absorb and translate into action a never-ending flow of minutes and ideas from Nick True and the Policy Unit. The committee comprised Andrew, Nick, two Treasury officials, Robin Fellgett and Kit Chivers, as well as another indefatigable Cabinet Office member, Diana Goldsworthy. Diana became one of the Charter's most ferocious advocates, I fear not always endearing herself to Whitehall colleagues as a result. Her eventual loss to the public service, which was partly born of frustration, was greatly to be deplored. Between them, in just three months, Andrew and Nick's group were, with Francis Maude, to distil or design the Charter programme and almost all that later flowed from it.

At this stage such an outcome seemed far from certain. So, in a speech in Scotland on 10 May 1991, I decided to up the ante by firmly promising a White Paper in the summer. As a further stimulus to action, I also agreed to a Policy Unit plea to bring together senior private-sector managers, forward-looking public-service figures, auditors, inspectors, regulators, consumer representatives and some of the pundits who had looked favourably on the idea. The aim would be to cross-check if we were on the right course, and to tease out further ideas for better customer service from some of those most actively involved. We set up a seminar at Chequers.

Before it met, there was one other key piece of the jigsaw to be put in place. The schizophrenia of the Treasury when presented with a scheme to improve public service was wonderful to behold. Some continued to fear that it was a deep-laid plot to raise spending. Others saw the opportunities presented by radical structural change to force greater efficiency out of the public sector. What the Treasury *was* keen on doing was pressing on with privatisation, contracting-out and competition policy. I too was all for this; indeed, I saw it as an intrinsic part of the Charter programme. So I sensed a chance to turn the fire of the Treasury away from the Charter and onto its opponents.

On 3 May Norman Lamont asked for my agreement to set up his Financial Secretary, Francis Maude, to run a series of head-to-head meetings, or bilaterals, with departmental ministers in which he would challenge them on their plans for privatisation, competition and contracting-out. I sent Sarah Hogg and Nick True to sound Francis out on whether he would respond seriously if we were to expand his round of talks to take in all the other planned aspects of the Charter. To have a Treasury minister at the heart of the operation would be the best way of nullifying, or at least limiting, any Treasury obstruction.

The runes were good. Francis was keen. With the Chancellor's agreement, I minuted Francis in mid-May to ask him to take on this task. He and his able Private Secretary, Philip Rutnam, took readily to the challenge. Over the summer, with the help of Nick True from the Policy Unit and the members of the official group, they conducted hearings with all the main service departments, calling some of them back more than once, and forced them to disgorge what was to be the meat of the Charter.

The process was a simple one. Nick True, in close consultation with me and with the help of Policy Unit colleagues, prepared a range of challenging questions to be put to departments on my behalf in bilaterals by Francis Maude, Andrew Whetnall and other members of the official group. Thereafter, one by one, the members of the Cabinet and their permanent secretaries were invited to explain what more they could offer up in the way of public service improvement. I asked Francis to bring a paper and, if possible, a draft White Paper to colleagues at the end of June.

We timed a Chequers seminar to take place before the final round of talks with departments, in order to provide the inquisitors with fresh ideas. It was held on 3 June. Among those invited were public sector managers such as Bob Reid of British Rail and Michael Bichard of the Benefits Agency, think-tank representatives such as David Willetts and Graham Mather, private sector figures such as Richard Greenbury of Marks & Spencer, regulators such as Bryan Carsberg, inspectors such as Stephen Tumim, the ombudsman Sir William Reid, and the most actively involved ministers, such as Francis Maude.

I still had doubts as to whether both outsiders and some inside practitioners would endorse the Charter approach. I was wrong. The discussions were keen and enthusiastic, and threw up many new ideas. Richard Greenbury was very encouraging; he said that once our ideas had been published he had no doubt many private firms would pick up on them. He was right – it was striking how after the Charter White Paper was put into the public domain, consumer-friendly packages were brought forward by many leading private sector firms.

Ideas from the seminar were fed into Francis's bilaterals. It would be otiose to describe the comings and goings in these, in which I was not in any case directly involved. Suffice it to say that some departments, notably Transport, the Home Office, Education and the DTI, needed to be led several times to the fence before being ready to jump. And then only reluctantly with the whip on their back.

The Department of Transport seemed to be in thrall to the most blinkered elements within BR management. It had been forced to agree to the principle of privatisation – although the details remained to be thrashed out later. But it recoiled from such revolutionary ideas as compensating passengers for poor performance, ensuring that staff could be identified, setting service standards, and giving passengers information on performance line by line. I finally managed to move them on all these points, but it was frustrating and hard pounding.

In our talks on education it had become clear that, while the department had agreed reluctantly to the publication of schools' examination results, there was strong official resistance to publishing these in a common, comparable format, accessible nationwide. It seemed to Nick True and John Mills in the Policy Unit, and to me, that we should insist on this further step. Ken Clarke readily agreed. Thus was born the now-popular idea of national performance tables, which would clearly have application to a wide range of public bodies and services. Bitterly opposed by a blinkered Labour Party then, and by the complacent ideologues of the education establishment then and since, they proved so popular that the new Labour government accepted them, and also implemented our plans for the publication of yet more data on the comparative performance of hospitals. This is only one of many policies they mocked in opposition, but were to adopt in government. This form of accountability and surrogate competition is a powerful force for good, and it is here to stay as a feature of public life.

The Home Office jibbed at publishing performance tables for the police service, although in the end they accepted them. It also initially resisted the inclusion of lay members in the Police Inspectorate. The Chequers seminar had strongly endorsed separating the function of checking on performance from that of service provision. Independent inspection, most notably perhaps in education, was to be one of the foremost features of the Charter. I was also keen to ensure that a lay element should, wherever possible, be included. Often providers and scrutineers came from the same charmed circle and shared the same unthinking professional assumptions. It was all too cosy. I believed that letting outside, indeed consumer, eyes into the process would illuminate musty corners and introduce fresh insights. I am convinced this approach was right.

The principle of independent inspection became widely accepted – although, in what I now regard as a mistake, I did not press more forcefully to introduce it to the field of social services. I had little doubt that there were weaknesses in many local social service departments. We saw the tragic results of slack standards, with children and other vulnerable members of society failing to receive the protection they needed. But I was not attracted to unthinking 'bash the social worker' views. Social work is a difficult and dedicated profession. We did strengthen the Social Services Inspectorate, but it was not enough. Throughout my time in Number 10 the Department of Health strongly resisted the idea of imposing inspection on the schools, prisons or police model, and in the White Paper we accepted the compromise principle of in-house 'arm's-length' inspection units. But, on reflection, I should have pushed further. Full external, independent inspection is needed.

The Department of Health was also difficult to persuade about the benefits of revealing public information and waiting times. It was as much in awe of the British Medical Association's sensibilities as the Department of Education was of the teaching unions'. So we had to settle for the publication of only partial service information – not yet including clinical areas, now rightly being opened up. However, I did, after a very hard struggle, succeed in securing commitments on the vexed question of often indefinite waits in hospital outpatients departments. I also insisted on pushing through the first national guarantee of maximum waiting times for operations, with specific undertakings for key treatments such as hip replacements, cataract removals, heart bypasses and hernia repairs. The number of heart bypasses increased by a third between 1991 and 1995, and the number of cataract operations by two-thirds. This was a significant reduction in unnecessary suffering, of which the NHS could be proud.

Overall, we offered a guarantee that no one would wait more than two years for treatment, a target the Health Secretary Virginia Bottomley was later able to reduce to eighteen months. This programme proved a significant success. In 1990 over 200,000 patients typically waited over a year for treatment. By 1996 this was down to fifteen thousand, just over one in a hundred of all patients waiting for admission. I regret very much that the present government's obsessive concentration on the far less significant indicator of overall waiting lists is predictably leading to distressingly long waits once more, as well as distorting the pattern of service provision in our hospitals. This is an area where the new government should have adopted our policy but did not.

The problem with the DTI, and associated with it the Department of Energy, was different again. For one thing, they were reluctant to accept my view that the formal powers of the various regulators to secure better service standards, to require more clarity about appointment times and to offer compensation, should be brought up to the level of the strongest. We did win agreement ultimately, but sadly, despite very many service improvements, the utilities have not succeeded in ironing out the irritations and indignities that their back offices still too often inflict on the customer. The concept of a timed appointment, common across the business world, remains a mirage for many utilities, whereas it should be standard practice.

At the time of the Charter we envisaged applying a regulatory goad to raise customer standards. Thereafter, over time, I anticipated formal regulation steadily withering away, as the effects of growing competition were felt. We now appear to have the worst of all worlds. There is increased competition, yes; but there are still weaknesses in customer service, on which too little pressure is applied, combined with intrusive and costly regulation of the financial policies of what are now private companies. A re-examination of the balance between competition and customer choice on the one hand, and fussy regulation and interference on the other, should be on the agenda of the next Conservative government.

The Post Office also remained in the category of uncompleted business. As I had indicated to the Policy Unit at the outset, I was always sceptical of the case for the full privatisation of the Royal Mail, but my doubts did not extend to all aspects of the Post Office. I was always aware that it needed to improve its general performance and to secure greater commercial freedom.

However, when it came to defining a policy there was pressure from all directions. The Treasury was keen on full privatisation; the DTI was more concerned to protect the Post Office's position; the Charter team were interested in securing guarantees of service standards; the advocates of privatisation were uneasy about agreeing any policy which might end short of privatisation. Finally a compromise was reached. The plan was to lift the Post Office monopoly on carrying items whose postage cost less than £1, to establish a new independent regulator and to have service standards set externally by the DTI. There would be better information rules and improved compensation where standards fell short. The Post Office was also to be required to allow bulk customers to pre-sort and trunk their own mail.

This package was the basis of our 1992 manifesto policy. It was always a compromise. I was not surprised when, after the election, both Michael Heseltine and Norman Lamont sought to re-examine the policy. In the end the Royal Mail proved to be one of those areas where, because of doubts within the parliamentary party, we were not able to reach satisfactory solutions. Doubters on both the left and right wings of the party ensured that we had no majority for Post Office privatisation – Conservatives as hawkish as Rhodes Boyson and Nick Winterton shrank from the policy.

Even a short account of some of the most contentious areas of the Charter gives a flavour of the broad range of the initiative. It also illustrates the scepticism, sometimes rank obstruction, which we faced. It would be wrong, though, to focus only on the difficulties. Thanks largely to Francis Maude, backed by my personal intervention where needed, and Whitehall battles fought by Sarah Hogg and Nick True, most of the major problems were overcome. We were able to take to Cabinet on 11 July 1991 a package whose scope and coherence seemed to impress even the most dubious of our colleagues. Such political opposites as Michael Heseltine and John Redwood were especially enthusiastic.

The official parliamentary and public launch of the White Paper took place on 22 July. Labour were hostile. They regarded the public sector as their preserve, and would have attacked anything we had done to improve it. Some commentators on the far right were characteristically shallow – they had no real interest in public services. But overall the reaction was positive. Frankly, though, I was not too concerned about the immediate, and often predictable, responses. I was concerned about what came next, about what the Charter was out to achieve – a transformation in the quality and standing of public services, to the benefit of the bulk of our citizens.

In order to keep up the momentum I formed a unit inside the Cabinet Office, but reporting to Francis Maude. I also appointed a panel of outside advisers, under the able chairmanship of James Blyth, the Chief Executive of Boots. Together these bodies were intended to help develop our thinking further. Both initiatives proved their value.

After the 1992 election I decided to formalise this structure further. I created a new department of state, the Office of Public Service Standards (OPSS), to ensure that the drive for higher standards was not sidelined, as has often tended to happen to new initiatives once, as is inevitable, a prime minister's eye is drawn elsewhere. I had hoped that Francis Maude would be able to lead this department in the Cabinet, as he had so richly deserved, but sadly he lost his seat in the 1992 election. His intended place was taken by William Waldegrave, who stepped into the job with characteristic intelligence.

What did it all amount to? What *does* it all amount to? For, after all, the Citizen's Charter is one of the few things left untouched by the obsessive, and somewhat disturbing, mania of the Blair government to rebrand and reinvent anything it did not create itself. I had always seen the Charter as a ten-year programme at the least. Six years on, despite all the sniping and difficulties, it has stood the test of events. Its emphasis on standard-setting and reporting was, as Rick Greenbury had forecast, imitated widely even in the private sector. The Citizen's Charter Unit, and later the OPSS, were visited by representatives of governments from around the world interested in learning how the toolkit we had put together could be applied to their own domestic problems. But the best and most important payback was at home. Over the years that followed July 1991 we steadily carried through the programme laid out in the White Paper and began, year by year, to ratchet up the standards we were setting for public service.

There was not an element in the programme that did not come into play. But I was quietly very satisfied by the way those who worked in the public service – if not always their trades union leaders – came to recognise the increased self-esteem that would follow providing better service to the public. Our innovation of the Charter Mark, a dedicated award held for three years by public service organisations who achieved set standards, soon became immensely popular, with many thousands of nominations each year, and widely recognised by service users. We kept the standards demanding; but within five years of the Charter White Paper almost 650 Charter Marks had been awarded, and a further 350 bodies highly commended. Raising the standing of public servants, as well as raising the standard of service, had always been my objective.

Some said the Charter was not radical. But it confirmed rail privatisation. It carried forward bus deregulation. It gave citizens the right to sue in cases of unlawful industrial action which was blocking public service. It promoted much more contracting-out and competitive tendering. This was not a programme without a sharp cutting edge.

Some scoffed at what they said was the pettiness of the programme. This was always nonsense. Laying one brick may be a trivial endeavour, but lay enough and you have built a mansion. It is true that we wanted to let people take weekend driving tests, book them by telephone and pay for them by credit card. True that we wanted to guarantee that all parents would receive an annual report on their children's progress at school (as, contrary to the belief of at least one former permanent secretary, hundreds of thousands never did). True that we wanted better treatment of witnesses and jurors in courts. True that we wanted to halve, as we did, the waiting time for a passport. Yes, true even that we wanted to put more service areas on our motorways.

It is the simplest thing in the world to belittle such improvements. However, the patient piling up of such bricks has brought benefits to countless people who may well never have realised that the Charter was responsible. And the Charter's impact helped to transform the great core services of health and education immeasurably for the better. There is always far to go, but without the change in attitudes and the new focus on standards and accountability the long march would not have begun.

Here was the true radicalism contained in the initiative: to break out of the old, stereotypical view that the only means of progress was through use of the government's (which means the taxpayer's) chequebook, and to show that in the raising of standards freedom of action by local management, balanced by public accountability, would be more effective than legislation, circulars and regulation. The bureaucrat will always dream up new rules; the politician should be concerned with end-results. It was those that the Charter was conceived to identify, to target, and to measure.

We followed up the publication of the original Charter with annual reports on progress, and set out new targets for improved performance. We also produced, sector by sector, specific documents which laid down the standards expected, guarantees offered and responsibilities undertaken by every significant public service. These papers were printed in plain language that all consumers could read and understand. By 1997, forty-two individual Charters had been published. Their elements were on display in public offices, airports, railway stations, hospitals and many other places right across the country. Copies of the main documents, such as the Parent's, Patient's and Tenant's Charters, were distributed directly to homes. These documents contained specific objectives. Revised when necessary to toughen the targets, they were among the key levers by which service standards could be raised.

Regretfully, I must admit to being convinced that names and hype do matter. The Citizen's Charter failed to catch the public imagination as it should have done with the sheer scale and breadth of its attack on old-fashioned working methods and poor public service. We were so quiet about our revolution that few noticed the wall being scaled. Even the similarity of the names of these separate Charters led some critics to allege that all the programme involved was publishing documents. The reality was, of course, very different. These short, focused individual documents were just part of the range of mechanisms by which our aims were put into action.

Among all the Charter's innovations, the setting publicly of standards of service and reporting on results, together with the publication of comparative league tables, has had the most far-reaching effects. Labour in government was forced by their popularity and practical value to abandon its opposition to league tables. We steadily rolled out the programme of league tables across the public services – not without resistance from the education unions, as I shall describe later. We were right to do so. It is surely sensible that standards should be publicly set and measured, that managers and providers should be challenged to do better and, above all, that the users of services should be able to compare their end-results. Few now would question that; before 1991, such a system was considered unthinkable.

We were also right to insist on the formal separation of powers between providers and those checking on them. The creation, or strengthening, of independent inspectorates was an essential component to lever up standards. When the plan to create a powerful Office of Standards in Education (OFSTED), statutorily independent of the Department of Education, was suggested (see page 397), it had few friends in government. I found support only from the Policy Unit, Ken Clarke and Michael Fallon, one of his junior ministers. Yet, once more, the received wisdom seemed to be profoundly wrong.

The arguments of Stephen Tumim at the Chequers seminar for fully independent inspection had backed my own strong instinct. Systems can become too comfortable if not exposed to outside challenge and stimulus. Circles of influence can become too mutually reassuring. I was determined to see that every school in the land was exposed to external inspection, so as to build up a base of knowledge, measured standards and information for parents on which we could truly build a renaissance of state education. Under Stewart Sutherland and Chris Woodhead, OFSTED began to do that job superbly. Independent inspection and audit is, and must remain, a key component in improving public service standards, whether in local authorities, schools, prisons, the police or social services. It may well have a place in the NHS. But it must resist the temptation to become over-bureaucratised. It must focus its resources on assisting the failures rather than taking the successes through the hoops of the rulebook. It must concentrate on securing good outcomes, not dictating specific approaches. And its independence from departmental influence should be entrenched. Whitehall has a tendency to lapse into cosy relationships with the representatives of public service providers. This is preferable to hostility, but it must not prevent rigorous scrutiny being advocated or upheld as it so often has in the past.

The changes we introduced were successful, and have been copied around the world. The information revolution empowered public service users as never before. It enabled them to know that higher standards could be achieved, and to press for them. Combined with our policies to increase choice, it brought competition into play. What was the value, for example, of parents having the right to choose a school for their children if they were not told what the standards were in the schools they were considering? Now they do know.

Competition and choice, directly exercised or imitated by proxy, were fundamental to the Charter approach. Along with them ran the setting of challenging targets for improvement, openness, accountability, convenience and consideration for the consumer, and the right to an explanation or compensation when things go wrong.

The Citizen's Charter was not a magic wand. I never claimed that it would be. It was the launch of a long, slow process of change. That change had to come for the good of our schools, hospitals, transport and other public services, and for the good of all those millions who depend on them. Now it is entrenched, it has to be carried further. In forty years of public service before the Citizen's Charter, too little progress had been made. In eight years since then, attitudes have changed, standards have risen and the esteem in which public service is held has, as I hoped, risen in many cases. It is not a process that can easily be defined, nor perhaps distilled in the headlines. Yet I am convinced that it was right, that its effects have been far-reaching and beneficial, and that it is here to stay.

# CHAPTER TWELVE

# *Maastricht*

'W̲E̲ K̲N̲O̲W̲ O̲U̲R̲ B̲O̲T̲T̲O̲M̲ L̲I̲N̲E̲. *I'm not shifting. The choice is theirs – we will say No if we have to.*'

I scribbled this rather aggressive note on a minute confirming that the six Christian Democrat leaders in the European Community had agreed that they would accept no outcome in the negotiations for a treaty on European union that 'puts in question the irreversibility of the democratic and federal developments of the future union'. They rubbed the point in by supporting the Social Chapter and demanding more powers for the European Parliament. It was an unwelcome message on the eve of my departure for Maastricht in Holland for the final treaty negotiations in December 1991.

Their views were interpreted as a warning to Britain. Since the Christian Democrat leaders were Chancellor Kohl and the prime ministers of Italy, Belgium, Greece and Luxembourg, as well as Prime Minister Ruud Lubbers of Holland, who would chair the meeting, it seemed we were in for a tough time. The Maastricht Treaty, as it was to become known, had loomed before me from the moment I became prime minister. The agenda for reaching economic and monetary union (EMU) had been set by the 1989 Delors Report, with political union added as a result of a bargain between Kohl and François Mitterrand. The summit threatened to be a divisive affair within the Conservative Party as well as with our partners. I thought it was a negotiation before its time, and was frustrated that a new treaty was still on the agenda.

The Single European Act in 1986 had created a single market for goods and services across Europe. This was excellent for trade, but it was also a motor for enhanced integration, and it whetted many an appetite to go further. Five years on, the single market was still not complete, since many of our partners were unreconciled to the implications of free trade and were resisting its introduction in key areas. Yet the mood to go forward was clear: our partners, pushed by the European Commission, were keen to supplement trade integration with monetary and political union, and were not prepared to be held back by the public's cautious attitude to 'more' Europe. The single European market needs a single European currency, was their cry. We should not have been surprised. It had been their ambition for a long time.

But their ambition was a problem for Britain. Any treaty pushing towards more power and influence for the Community was bound to be unpalatable in the UK, and the timing, so close to the end of the Parliament, could not have been worse. At the time, the direction of European policy was a pathological source of division within the Conservative Party. The wounds from Margaret Thatcher's departure were still fresh, and showed little sign of healing. Her most devoted supporters had convinced themselves that her policy of resisting European integration was the principal cause of her fall. They were sure to oppose any changes in that direction. Other Conservatives favoured a more cooperative attitude. These opposing views were not easy to reconcile at the best of times, but in the aftermath of Margaret's departure the task seemed impossible. She, meanwhile, was now unconstrained by office, and had become a figurehead for hostility to the sort of provisions our partners thought were essential.

I was a pragmatist about the European Community. I believed it was in our economic interests to be a member. I welcomed sensible cooperation. I had no hang-ups about Germany. I accepted that being one of a Community of fifteen meant that sometimes we had to reach a consensus that was not entirely to our taste. I was keen to rebuild shattered fences, to prevent Britain from being seen for ever as the odd man out to be excluded from the private consultations that so often foreshadowed new policy in Europe.

I had been shocked at my early European Councils to discover that Margaret's strength of will, so admired at home, was used against us abroad. It was the butt of sly little jokes. Most of the other leaders utterly disagreed with her. 'She is a unifying force,' I was told. 'She unites all of us against her.' After frosty exchanges our partners would restore good humour amongst themselves with a jest about the common enemy – Margaret.

Yet I shared many of her concerns. I recoiled at the prospect of a 'federal' Europe. I was deeply suspicious of political union. I did not wish to ditch sterling. I believed the conditions the Social Chapter sought to impose would add to employers' costs and push up unemployment. I did not wish to see a more powerful Commission. I did believe it was right to enlarge the Community and bring in the nation states of Central Europe. On that issue I was not alone, but on most others Britain was isolated. No one would join us, even when they thought we were right, because of our reputation as the in-house awkward squad.

We needed allies. Our power of veto enabled us to block unwelcome policies on matters of national interest, but it was a weapon that could only be used sparingly. One nation could not forever halt the ambitions of eleven others over policies to which the eleven were committed. I decided to get to know my fellow leaders. What made them tick? Why did they favour policies that we disliked so much? What were their priorities? What could they concede, and what was essential for them?

I soon found there was no institutional bias against Britain. Many of the other leaders were pro-British, but like us they were motivated first by the interests of their own countries. The three dominant policy-makers were Chancellor Kohl, President Mitterrand and Jacques Delors, President of the Commission.

Jacques Delors was a hate figure in the eyes of the British tabloids, but to those who knew him he was an able and sensitive man, if sometimes a little prickly. He spoke courteously, although his English often left his meaning unclear. At an early meeting with me he was lyrical about a European statesman called Du Glas. As he listed this man's virtues I began to be concerned. Why had I not been briefed better? Who was this paragon? It turned out to be *Dou-glas* Hurd.

European Councils have a standard format which includes an informal lunch for leaders at which the host nation lays on excellent food and exceptionally fine wine. At these lunches Delors was formidable – and dangerous. As the meal progressed, the summit chairman would invite him to raise pertinent matters, and Delors often took full advantage of the opportunity. If the topic was unappealing to the British his accent seemed to thicken, and vague generalities replaced the detail of which he was known to be a master. It was a trap for the unwary. I soon learned to forgo the wine, because a contentious proposition from Delors over lunch, if unchallenged at the time, would become a conclusion of the summit. I did not fancy telling the Commons that some dreadful proposal had slipped past me as I savoured an excellent glass of Puligny Montrachet.

I took to Helmut Kohl from the first, and we became firm friends and, on occasion, allies. We had much in common. He was the son of a minor official and had worked as a stonemason to get through school. Helmut was a sentimentalist, with the broad-brush instincts of a Willie Whitelaw and a distaste for detail. He had a ripe sense of humour and a deep interest in British politics. He admired Winston Churchill and often spoke of him with great warmth. All our meetings overran as we gossiped about the political intrigue of the day before turning to our agenda. Helmut was sharp and shrewd, and often trusted to instinct. As a student of German history, he never forgot his country's past, and his aim was to embed his nation securely in the Europe of the future.

He was full of banter about the ministerial red box carried by my Private Secretary. '*Ja – das ist*,' he would chortle, 'all the British government's secrets. How to overcome Europe in one box.' This became a running joke, often embellished over summit lunches, so, some years into our working relationship, I had a replica made for him. As Roderic Lyne, who succeeded Stephen Wall as my Private Secretary for Foreign Affairs, set it on the coffee table between us, Helmut began his usual banter. I told him, 'This one is different. It's full of German secrets,' and turned it around to reveal the German eagle and the words 'Herr-Bundeskanzler Helmut Kohl' stamped in gold on the front. Helmut's face lit up like a child's at Christmas. 'And next year,' I promised, 'you can have the key.'

Trivial exchanges, perhaps, but I believe such personal rapport can humanise diplomacy. With friendship and understanding can come a measure of trust that helps to make the world safer. It is cynical to believe that personal chemistry between leaders counts for nothing when the chips are down; only national interest counts. I don't agree. It is unwise to overvalue the coin of friendship in international affairs, but trust is not valueless. Reflect for a moment on how anger, petulance or misunderstanding can create difficulties.

François Mitterrand, like Helmut, also came from a modest background, but he was far more grand in manner. An erudite student of history, he had a formidable knowledge of Britain. Over lunch at Number 10, he asked me once who was the greatest of our kings. 'Henry II,' I teased him. 'Oh, really?' he said. 'That's interesting. Why him?' 'He conquered most of France and married the rest,' I replied. Mitterrand rallied: 'Myself, I think it was William I, who conquered all of England without marrying an Englishwoman.'

Mitterrand often looked waxen and sick at summits, as well he might, since he was suffering from the prostate cancer that would cause his death in January 1996. His courage in facing such an illness and remaining in office was remarkable. Sometimes, during boring speeches, he would write postcards. Then without warning he would come to life and dazzle the assembly with a pertinent analysis of the issue before us that invariably ended with a blunt assertion of France's position. If the Franco–German axis was united he would be gracious to Helmut Kohl; if it were not, he would pay him even more extravagant compliments. Helmut returned them: 'You must always bow three times to the Tricolour,' he told me. I soon realised that getting your own way in Europe was a specialised affair. It had its own natural rhythms. It was better to play by club rules. Britain needed to raise its voice from within the charmed circle.

In my first few days as prime minister the Gulf War, the Community Charge and the worsening economic situation dominated my attention. But Europe has a way of forcing itself onto the agenda, and it soon did so with the Rome summit in December 1990 and early meetings with fellow heads of government. I received a friendly greeting wherever I went, although I was surprised at the sour response in parts of Parliament and the press to my successful meetings with Helmut Kohl; both Euro-sceptics and the media would have preferred a row. Margaret Thatcher's decisions to accept the chairmanship of the Bruges Group (a ginger group hostile to many European developments) and the Conservative No Turning Back Group (a right-wing group also critical of the Community) provided a focus for battle lines to be drawn. She insisted that this had been far from her intention. Not for the first or last time, it was hard to know whether she was a great deal more, or somewhat less, naïve than she seemed.

As I sought to improve our profile in Europe I accepted an invitation, prompted by Sir Christopher Mallaby, our Ambassador to Bonn, to address the Konrad Adenauer Stiftung, a centre-right think-tank, in March 1991. Chris Patten and Sarah Hogg both urged me to accept, and contributed to my text. It was to prove fateful.

In the speech I said:

> My aim for Britain in the Community can be simply stated. I want us to be where we belong. At the very heart of Europe. Working with our partners in building the future.

I thought this was an unexceptional objective. I was wrong. Few sentiments in recent British political history have provoked such havoc or been so misrepresented. I did not see the danger at the time: I had used the phrase 'heart of Europe' before, during the election for leadership of the Conservative Party, in which many of those who were to become most anguished about it had voted for me. Moreover, in my speech in Bonn I made it clear also that I would bring forward our own proposals to the Inter-Governmental Conference at Maastricht, since I didn't like what was on offer. The essence of my message was perfectly clear, but the 'heart of Europe' ambition persuaded the Euro-fearful that I would accept federalism.

This was such copper-bottomed nonsense that I dismissed it as a serious criticism. Could anyone with a grain of sense wish us to be on the outskirts of Europe while others decided policy that affected Britain? I thought not. It seemed self-evident to me that if we were to stay in Europe, we had to be at the heart of it to protect our own interests. If we let others dominate the debate we would be forever on the back foot. This logic made no impact. The myth was created that I was too Euro-friendly, and my speech was used as a distorting mirror in which everyone could see what they wished to see. In the eye of the beholder, differing opinions focused and polarised.

And the beholder did not let go. In mid-June the *Daily Telegraph* gave prominent coverage to a Bruges Group pamphlet (written by a twenty-three-year-old) that accused me of favouring the federalist ideal in Europe, and Nick Ridley weighed in with trenchant comments. The combination of the Bruges Group and Nick convinced everyone that the pamphlet was a vehicle for the views of Margaret Thatcher. These eruptions began to widen divisions in the Conservative Party, and to create a belief that I had a private pro-federalist agenda. I did not appear hostile to Europe, therefore

I must be too accommodating towards it, was the facile reasoning. It did not seem to occur to my critics that root-and-branch opposition to everything European was an absurdity: it was poisoning the atmosphere and making it impossible for our case against federalism to be heard with any real chance of success. The Europeans read about our domestic debate and assumed that I argued against federalism merely to appease party opinion, and not out of conviction. So they listened politely and took no notice of what I was actually saying.

As the underlying divisions in the Conservative Party became more tense, the Dutch took over the presidency of the Community on 1 July 1991 and dropped a bombshell. They so disliked the draft of the Maastricht Treaty produced by Luxembourg, their predecessors in the presidency, that they scrapped it and produced their own. Their document was catastrophic. They seemed to have swept up the nightmares of every anti-European propagandist and put them into their text: new powers to decide foreign policy and home affairs at Community level; more authority for the European Court of Justice; power for the European Parliament to overrule decisions taken by sovereign governments; more majority voting to decide issues of social affairs, health and education. In short: a United States of Europe.

It was a profound misjudgement. If the Dutch believed that others would march to their drum, they were wrong. Such ambitious plans had no chance of winning support, even from strongly pro-European governments. President Mitterrand, for one, was affronted by the proposal that the decisions of sovereign governments might be vetoed, and told me so. His view, expressed to me privately, was that the European Parliament 'has no legitimacy and will not have for a hundred years'. He was not to say this publicly, but in the event he did not need to.

At a meeting of foreign ministers in late September the Dutch text was slaughtered. Jacques Poos, the Luxembourg Foreign Minister, was so incensed that his own draft had been torn up that he led the attack. The Dutch must have been astonished, since mild-mannered Monsieur Poos was usually a model of Euro-consensus. Not, however, over the destruction of his text; this was the hour of Poos.

And of Italy. Douglas Hurd had briefed Gianni di Michelis, the theatrical, disco-loving Italian Foreign Minister, and he too joined the opponents. The Danes, Irish and Portuguese then laid into the text; at the end of the debate it had but one friend, Belgium (and even that may have been merely due to Benelux solidarity). The final destruction of the Dutch draft came when the veteran Foreign Minister of Germany, Hans-Dietrich Genscher, a strong pro-European, conceded that the text would not pass muster, even though he agreed with it. Its demolition was reassuring, but the fact that the Dutch had floated it was not: it encouraged the suspicion among Euro-sceptics that there was a hidden agenda on European policy. This was impossible to refute since, in some cases, it was true.

As the final negotiations at Maastricht approached I met leaders across Europe to set out my concerns. I was determined to keep Britain free of harmful provisions. I began to lobby for allies and, to avoid any later charge of bad faith, I warned our partners early on that we could be forced to reject all or part of the treaty. I had already set up a Cabinet committee to examine the proposals likely to be put before us. Douglas Hurd chaired these meetings, except on a number of highly contentious issues where I presided myself to ensure that every Cabinet member was consulted and able to have a serious input into our deliberations. The Cabinet contained the same widely differing views that could be found among our back-benchers, and I needed all of them to be committed to my negotiating position.

The Dutch text had gone, but I was still dismayed by what stood before me. For years economic and monetary union had been an ambition of the Community. It had been implicitly endorsed in the 1957 Treaty of Rome, which Ted Heath signed up to when Britain entered the Common Market in 1973, and, more recently, by Margaret Thatcher in the preamble to the 1985 Single European Act. Now, following the Delors Report, it was no longer a vague ambition but an explicit proposition.

I did not wish to see a single currency. My objections were both economic and political. I could see the advantages of one large, powerful, anti-inflationary currency offering a strong bulwark against market turmoil, with Europe-wide low interest rates and transparency in pricing; the benefits of such a currency were obvious to anyone prepared to examine the matter dispassionately. But it was all too early. The nation states of Europe were far apart in economic efficiency and development. They needed to see how well and how swiftly they could converge economically before they considered a move to one pan-European currency. I had a second objection: enlarging the Community to include the Central and East European nations seemed to me to be a debt of honour. We had left them under Soviet dominion for fifty years, and an early move to monetary union would be likely to delay their entry as the Community concentrated on EMU. And, even when they joined, the new members would not be remotely ready to participate in the new currency.

Nor did I like the political implications of monetary union, which I believed would be untenable in the UK. A single central bank and a unified monetary policy would remove key economic policy options from the government and Parliament. It would give rise to demands for harmonisation of taxes (no doubt upwards) and destroy the UK's hard-won competitive advantage of low taxation. It would also lead to more power in Brussels, more regulation and, as Douglas Hurd put it, more interference in the 'nooks and crannies' of British life. Parliament would be weaker and democracy ill-served. None of this was remotely appealing, but I knew that if a single currency came into being it would present us with a difficult decision. From the outset, the ultimate choice was apparent: potential long-term economic advantages would have to be weighed against a weakening of our own sovereign responsibility for domestic decisions.

While my gut instincts were strongly opposed to a single currency, my assessment was that one day it would go ahead, and if it proved to be successful, an economic low-pressure system over the Continent would suck sterling into it. If our economic well-being demanded entry, as one day I thought it might, then in the end we would go in. That was my firm opinion.

It was with all those forebodings that I framed our policy to delay the single currency if we could, and to insert safeguards if we could not. In no circumstances should we commit sterling to enter, although if possible we should retain the right to negotiate how EMU progressed, with the option – without penalty – to enter if we chose, or to stay out if we preferred. It was not credible to believe that blocking the whole treaty would stop our partners – they would simply operate outside a treaty of the twelve, and Britain would have no influence at all over their plans.

Far from being a short-term expedient to postpone conflict, this policy was dictated by the long view. It was not influenced by the fundamental opposition to entry of Michael Howard, Peter Lilley, Michael Portillo and party elders like Norman Tebbit, Cecil Parkinson or Margaret Thatcher; nor was it decided by warm support for the principle from Ken Clarke,

Michael Heseltine, John Gummer and prominent figures like Ted Heath or Peter Carrington. I genuinely stood apart from both sides, and decided upon the policy I believed to be right; it was coincidental that it fell smack between the two.

But that was not how the decision was perceived. It was seen by commentators and observers as a whips' compromise, a piece of party management by a man without conviction or principle. The irony was that I was, in fact, procrastinating on principle, and on a principle deeply held. I have given up hope that this will ever be understood. I refused to commit myself until I could see what was right for Britain, and for my pains I was accused of all kinds of sins: of lack of leadership; of putting party unity before country; of dithering and weakness; of having no views at all; and much else. Those who allowed their emotions to gain sway over their judgement were united in criticism. I thought the expression of such simplistic views short-changed the British people over a complex issue that deserved to be treated more judiciously than it was. Emotion is all very well, but the emotion my critics brought to this issue was the sort that cried 'No Popery!' and burned witches. The country deserved better than that.

Nor was EMU the only problem that would have to be faced down at Maastricht. The proposals for a Social Chapter would reverse our domestic reforms to the labour market and push up unemployment. Conservative governments had spent years ending restrictive practices, promoting supply-side policies and forcing businesses to take decisions to promote their profitability. I did not wish to see all this wrecked by the job-destroying legislation that coalition governments across the Community had inflicted on their electorates. I was convinced we had to avoid such burdens being laid on British companies. I knew we would face accusations that we were in favour of 'low wages' and 'sweated labour', but since I had the old-fashioned notion that British workers were better off in jobs than on the dole, I was prepared to ignore these taunts. But they were to come – from the Labour Party, of course, and from President Mitterrand in some sharp clashes at European summits.

Other problems crowded in. We could not allow foreign or home affairs policy to come under the control of Brussels; or agree to a 'federal' destiny; or permit the Commission to have a role in defence policy. It was evident that we were bound to play the abominable no-men in the negotiations, and that we would face a domestic cacophony of conflicting advice.

Across Europe I argued our case, and tried to convince other leaders I was not bluffing. On the perils of a single currency I made no progress; it was a dialogue of the deaf. Some of our partners began grudgingly to accept that Britain would stay out, but many were not convinced: they had heard it all from British prime ministers before, and seen them sign up in the end. Patiently, and in detail, I set out our concerns, grinding out the same message: I was not bluffing, and I could not accept what our partners proposed.

Norman Tebbit offered frequent advice in public and with maximum publicity, and erupted in anger when I refused to rule out eventual British membership of a single currency. Every whisper from Margaret Thatcher was passed on to the waiting media, who fully reported her speeches and comments from lecture tours in the United States. She was invariably hostile to the single currency and the spectre of federalism, and her views continued to trigger a response from different factions in the party. All of this ensured that the debate continued to rage.

In view of the unpalatable choices facing us at Maastricht I decided to hold a Commons debate on 20 November 1991 to gain approval for our negotiating stance. Richard Ryder, the Chief Whip, was a strong supporter of this move. It was a risky strategy, but I wanted to flush out any parliamentary opposition. I had brought ministers along with me in Cabinet, now I needed the Commons as well. I was determined there should be no doubt about my bottom line: no commitment to join the single currency, and no Social Chapter membership. There was a danger that a Commons debate might box in my negotiating options, but I was prepared to take that risk. I knew that if the Commons backed my position it would add authority to my rejection of parts of the treaty.

The debate worked well. I set out our negotiating aims with great care. No federalism. No commitment to a single currency. No Social Chapter. No Community competence on foreign or home affairs or defence. Cooperation in these areas, yes; compulsion, no. It could not have been clearer. I set out too what we hoped to gain at Maastricht. More power for the European Parliament to control the Commission and investigate fraud. A more open Community that enlarged its borders to the east. Treaty acknowledgement of 'subsidiarity' – the principle that Europe should only do what the nation state could not do equally well – so that we could end the creep of increasing Commission power. I proposed power for the

European Court to impose a level playing field for industry to prevent abuse of the single market.

At the end of the debate I received a majority of 101, with only six Conservative MPs voting against. Teresa Gorman was one of several later rebels who supported my negotiating stance at Maastricht when they had the chance.

Margaret Thatcher spoke in the debate, in one of her rare interventions from the backbenches after her departure as prime minister. She advocated a referendum on the single currency. I saw the attraction of this idea, and could have been persuaded – although, since we had not spoken about it and I was unaware that she would raise it in the debate, Margaret did not know this. Her advocacy proved counter-productive. Ken Clarke, Douglas Hurd and Michael Portillo were among those in Cabinet strongly opposed to a referendum on constitutional grounds. Other ministers were unwilling to respond to what they felt was a populist ploy by the former prime minister.

But her argument demanded an answer; and it could only be no. Cabinet ministers reacted badly to Margaret's public advice, and would not budge. Francis Maude sought my instructions and, in winding up the debate, ruled out a referendum. Margaret went on television to accuse me of 'arrogance', blissfully unaware that her intervention had caused a hostile Cabinet reaction. It was the forerunner of many occasions when the tactics of the Euro-sceptics backfired because they made their demands in public without previously warning the government and giving us the chance, if we wished, to reply positively. I did eventually get approval for a referendum on the single currency late in 1995, but by then huge damage had been done as trench warfare split the party.

As the final negotiations approached, diplomatic manoeuvring increased. I had meetings with Helmut Kohl and Ruud Lubbers, who were key figures. The message I delivered was the same: I will not accept what is proposed, but I will agree a treaty if we obtain the concessions we seek. I was far from confident of success, and gloomily resigned to an ill-tempered outcome, with Britain blamed for wrecking an agreement all the other member nations were prepared to accept.

Politically the position I faced was dire. If I withheld agreement to the treaty, huge ill-will would be caused on the Continent, the Conservative Party would be split, and our opponents would claim that our once-internationalist party could no longer do business in Europe. If I reached an unsatisfactory deal I might earn goodwill on the Continent, but the Conservative Party would repudiate it, the Cabinet would split, and the agreement might fail in Parliament. We would then face a general election in the worst possible circumstances. Only if I obtained an agreement that met the objectives I had set out in the Commons could it be satisfactorily presented at home. Few believed that was possible. Audibly, knives were being sharpened.

Cabinet approved our final negotiating position on 5 December, although only after a great deal of private coaxing of Michael Howard and Peter Lilley, for which Douglas Hurd and I needed all our persuasive skills. Douglas and I set out for Cabinet all the areas of the draft treaty that were still in serious dispute: it was a long list.

We flew out to Maastricht on Sunday, 8 December. I was accompanied by Douglas Hurd and Norman Lamont, who had both been immersed for months in the political and economic aspects of the treaty. Tristan Garel-Jones, the Minister for Europe, was with us to handle the press during negotiations and firefight wherever necessary.

The British Civil Service is often derided by those who do not know it, but it has, at its senior levels, some of the best and most able men and women of their generation. I was fortunate in the team with me. Sir Nigel Wicks from the Treasury had done all the pre-Maastricht preparations on monetary union. He was in total command of his brief. Of medium height, open-faced, a little plump, often rumpled, suit pockets packed and over-flowing, he exuded the calm air of a college professor amiably dealing with the often misguided ambitions of his students. He had the draft of a British opt-out from EMU in his pocket.

Michael Jay from the Foreign Office also starred. One of the vastly capable and widespread Jay clan, who between them hold every respectable brand of political opinion, he was a master of the European scene. I once called European negotiations 'twelve-dimensional chess'. Michael could have played thirteen.

Also with us was the man Tristan called 'the cleverest man in the Western world' and I christened 'Machiavelli' – Sir John Kerr, our Ambassador to the European Union. Original, innovative, wholly familiar with the labyrinth of Europe, his advice would be crucial to our negotiating tactics.

Stephen Wall, my Foreign Affairs Private Secretary, and Sarah Hogg were indispensable. They knew my mind on every issue. Gus O'Donnell, my Press Secretary, had the almost impossible task of keeping up to date with rapidly-moving and complex negotiations and briefing a press corps avid for news or, in the absence of it, likely to go walkabout with sensational speculation.

As we arrived at Maastricht none of us was certain what to expect, but any tension was soothed away by the familiarity that exists between men and women who have an easy relationship through working closely together in a common cause. We knew the stakes were high.

That evening Douglas Hurd and I met Ruud Lubbers and his Foreign Minister Hans van den Broek to discuss the conduct of the meeting and to clarify the many areas of disagreement that were outstanding. Even as we spoke, bigger events were unfolding: the world did not stop to accommodate the Maastricht summit, even though there were, no doubt, those at the summit who would have wished it. Early that evening momentous news began to filter in: the Soviet Union was disintegrating.

President Yeltsin of Russia, together with President Kravchuk of the Ukraine and Mr Shushkevich, the leader of Byelorussia, had joined together to create a Commonwealth of Independent States (CIS), and declared in a statement: 'We note that the USSR ceases to exist.' The Soviet Union was dead – but what would follow it? No one could be sure. Nor did we know who would control the huge nuclear arsenal that had held the world in a Cold War for decades. Stephen Wall telephoned the White House to exchange the limited information available with Brent Scowcroft, National Security Adviser to President Bush. He then arranged for me to meet President Mitterrand the following morning to discuss the emerging situation. In truth we could be no more than onlookers. What was going on in that turbulent region? Would it be chaos at one end of the continent of Europe and stalemate at the other? I went to bed not knowing, and surprised that my mind was now focused on Russia and not on the negotiations that were about to begin.

Early the following morning our team met again for a final review of our line. The rumour mill that is an integral part of European summits was already in full flow, with the French said to be putting it about that Britain was prepared to sign up to a single European army. This was nonsense, and Gus O'Donnell was told to deny it vigorously. It was not to be the only trial balloon he would have to shoot down.

The conference began at the Provincienhuis in Maastricht on 9

December, with a brief speech from the President of the European Parliament. This was a traditional address to summits and, as was so often the case, it was listened to with only sufficient interest to avoid bad manners. Ruud Lubbers coaxed a few perfunctory questions from the taciturn heads of government before the President departed. The heads visibly perked up; battle was about to begin.

On the first day of European Councils everyone sets out their position at great length and explains what they can accept and what they will not. Overnight, the presidency considers all these contributions and produces a revised text which, in its view, has the best chance of securing agreement.

This text is usually circulated at around 6 o'clock on the second morning. Officials, some of whom may not have slept at all, then pore over the revisions and brief their ministers. Sometimes the text shows welcome improvement; often, for Britain, it contains very nasty passages that ministers must accept or remove. The second day is always tense, and can become very ill-tempered. The bargaining begins when everyone crawls through the overnight revisions attempting to tilt them in their own direction and deciding where to dig their toes in and where to concede. That lay ahead.

Ruud Lubbers introduced the agenda, and we began with economic and monetary union. Helmut Kohl spoke first. A single currency was crucial, he said, and must be irreversible; but the 'right economic conditions' were essential. We should be prepared for monetary union by 1996–97 if a 'critical mass' of states could meet the conditions. This was standard fare from Helmut, and the 1996–97 date was simply to frighten the laggards. The emphasis on economic preparedness was the authentic voice of the Bundesbank. Wilfried Martens of Belgium followed. He echoed Kohl: a single currency must be irreversible, and was the Community's most important decision since the Treaty of Rome.

With Norman Lamont beside me, I spoke next, before the tide of enthusiastic agreement rose too high. My remarks broke the consensus, but in a style I hoped was not confrontational. I made it clear that Britain was not ready to agree to enter a single currency, and set out the risks I saw of a two-tier Europe. The economic circumstances had to be right for monetary union to begin, and, in a pre-emptive dismissal of demands I knew were to come, I emphasised that there must be no suggestion of compelling unwilling countries to enter the new currency.

Felipe Gonzales, Prime Minister of Spain, a welcome companion away from the negotiating table, although an opponent around it, came in next to support Helmut Kohl and, by implication, oppose me. François Mitterrand followed him, and he too was hostile to the British position. The single currency must be irreversible, he told the meeting, and we must fix a date for it; he favoured early 1999. Any opt-outs – and here he was aiming directly at Britain – could not be indefinite in time or general in nature. The points that would cause trouble were becoming apparent as the speeches proceeded.

The divisions over economic and monetary union were not my main worry. Britain's determination to 'opt out' of the single currency had been well signalled in our pre-summit discussions, and was no surprise to anyone. Even so, much was at stake: the terms, the conditions, the price, if any, to be paid, and the influence we would retain in implementing future arrangements for the launch of the new currency.

We were well prepared. Since June the Treasury had been drafting an EMU opt-out tailored to our own needs; I intended to present it only when the European heads began to fear stalemate and failure, and would have less time or inclination to tear it to shreds. As the table circuit of speeches on monetary union came to an end, Ruud Lubbers invited Wim Kok, the Dutch Finance Minister, to chair a meeting of finance ministers to discuss the fallout of our discussion. Their main problem was the transition to the final stage of monetary union. I still held back the release of the draft of our Britain-specific opt-out, although, in meetings of officials, Nigel Wicks was coming under strong pressure to produce it. He stonewalled: 'I have no authority to do so yet.' His European colleagues gritted their teeth and waited, not always patiently.

The heads of government began to discuss foreign policy and defence, and Douglas Hurd joined me. Here again, controversy awaited us. Wilfried Martens demanded common defence provisions in the treaty; an end to decision-making by unanimous agreement, which effectively permitted a veto by one nation; and an end to unilateral action by nation states. I intervened to disagree, which promoted a spirited discussion that continued either side of an excellent lunch with Queen Beatrix of the Netherlands at the Château Nurcase. Queen Beatrix is a convinced enthusiast for European development. 'Are things going to be all right?' she enquired of me gently as she welcomed her guests. 'I hope so,' was all I could reply. But I was not sure they would be. At the time, I rather doubted it.

After lunch, we embarked on complex proposals to reform the institutions and powers of the Community, home affairs and immigration. I leavened our determination to keep foreign policy and home affairs for national decision-making in Britain by making a series of positive proposals on less emotive subjects such as the establishment of an ombudsman, the role of the European Parliament, the decision-making process, a Court of Auditors to improve financial control, and cooperation between governments on interior and justice matters. 'We can't accept the loss of the national veto,' I told the meeting, 'but the text before us is the basis of a deal.' This assertion brought a warm response from Lubbers – 'a good start' – and a boisterous table thump from Kohl – '*Ja. Ja.*'

In the general good humour I was able to re-emphasise our determination not to accept the goal of 'a federal vocation' in the treaty without drawing any open dissent, despite the known opposition of the Commission and every other head of government in the room. I sat back for a while as Douglas Hurd advanced our case on a subsidiarity clause, to ensure decisions were taken at Community level only when it was obviously beneficial to do so. Germany was as keen as we were on the principle of this clause, but wanted some changes in the details to reflect its own federal structure of government, and I intervened to support them. Douglas handled the discussion on allocating structural funds.

One bizarre series of exchanges illustrated how oddly, to British eyes at least, the European Council conducted its affairs. The finance ministers were not permitted to attend the heads of government meetings as a matter of right, even when financial or budgetary matters were being discussed. They wished to do so, and Wim Kok, the Chairman of ECOFIN, wrote to the summit to say so. Felipe Gonzales objected. Douglas Hurd observed mildly that the finance ministers had made their case for good reason and should not be brushed aside. Mitterrand bristled: 'Don't ask *my* finance minister,' he warned. '*I* make decisions here in the name of France.'

I reminded him that I, too, made decisions for Britain, but that it was important to be properly informed about the financial implications before one did so. This was too revolutionary a thought for Prime Minister Giulio Andreotti of Italy. 'The Community has always taken decisions without knowing how to finance them – and must be able to do so,' was the view he expressed. That explained rather a lot about the Community's finances, I thought. The ECOFIN proposal did not find favour. (Several years later,

Ken Clarke began to plonk himself down in the Chamber and defy anyone to remove him. No one did, and over time other finance ministers began to join him.)

As the first day of the summit ended, the problems had been thrown into focus and some of the solutions were taking shape. I briefed a crowded press conference in bullish fashion, but inwardly I was anxious: would our concerns be taken on board, or were our partners assuming we would give way at the end? I didn't know, and I thought the treaty could still fall because we would be unable sign it.

The early-morning news on Tuesday was not hopeful. Over a working breakfast made less than congenial by extracts of press reports from home, officials told me that many of the overnight revisions to the treaty were unsatisfactory, and that minor improvements to the social text had been made to help us, but did not do so. All the big issues remained unresolved. A long day was in prospect.

The presidency's amended draft was the basis of our renewed discussions. We soon turned to the hotly disputed issue of the Social Chapter, and Ruud Lubbers turned to me for a preliminary comment. I set out our position: the presidency proposal was fundamentally objectionable to us; it made small steps in our direction, but did not address our basic problems. I could not accept it.

Mitterrand made clear that he had reservations even about the small concessions offered to Britain by the Dutch presidency. 'There are too many matters of principle at stake,' he began. 'Watering down the text won't work.' He had reservations about the Dutch text too, but thought Europe must have a Social Chapter. He then spelled out his challenge: Europe must commit itself to it, or France would vote against the treaty. He would publicly oppose a sham charter, he warned. The gauntlet had been thrown down.

Felipe Gonzales was swift to agree. 'Is there anything to discuss?' he asked, looking in every direction but mine. 'There can be no political union without the social title. We must agree . . .'

Ruud Lubbers saw the danger. Britain would block the treaty if it had a Social Chapter, and France was threatening to do so if it did not. Others piled in. Wilfried Martens, like Mitterrand, could not agree to the treaty without the Social Chapter. Andreotti thought European public opinion would not understand if the Social Chapter was omitted from the treaty.

If anything, this attitude of follow-my-leader hardened my resolve. I was sure Mitterrand was bluffing, and I resented the implicit suggestion emerging around the table that the UK had inadequate social conditions. I set out our record, and said in unmistakable terms that I was not prepared to undermine the legislation the Conservative government had passed in the last decade. I pointed to the excellence of our record in job creation: we were creating more new employment in Britain than all our partners put together. I saw no purpose in adding Community programmes to our domestic effort. 'My position is no surprise to you,' I concluded, and added, referring directly to Mitterrand: 'Some colleagues won't sign without the Social Chapter; I won't sign with it.'

When I had finished there was a long silence. For the first time, I think, everyone realised the extent of the divide and that Britain was serious in her opposition and would not be budged.

'What shall we do?' queried Lubbers to no one in particular. Those who did not look at the ceiling looked at me to reply. 'Reflect,' I suggested, 'in bilateral discussions. The text is unacceptable. I will see if there is *anything* I can accept. I can't, of course, prevent others from agreeing to social policies for themselves.' This hint was not picked up.

Kohl acted as the voice of reason. 'We have overcome many difficult situations. Apart from the UK all are ready to accept. Put it in square brackets and return to it later.'

Lubbers agreed. Mitterrand protested: he didn't see what could be done. The UK couldn't accept, so we should look at the possibility of exemption for it. Delay would not help. Diplomacy must end. But he did not repeat his threat to block the treaty.

Lubbers tried to buy some time: the UK and Germany wanted delay, he ruled; we would re-examine the social issue later. Mitterrand persisted: 'I don't like it. The British Prime Minister was clear and is not afraid of his responsibility.' But Lubbers won – and we moved on. Norman Lamont and Douglas Hurd played musical chairs in joining me as, item by item, we began to advance through the text.

One odd facet of European Councils is that officials are not permitted to sit with heads of government and advise them. The heads are on their own. But messages need to be brought in – and sometimes sent out – from time to time, and a handful of treasured entry passes are available. One was in the hands of Sir John Kerr, who developed a gift for fast entry and slow exit, and crouched beside me at the table, staying as long as he could by trying to make himself as inconspicuous as possible. His advice at key moments was invaluable, but not sometimes without chaotic exchanges. John is a fine linguist, and so is Ruud Lubbers. Lubbers would often reply in the language most familiar to an individual head of government; this was no problem for the rest of us, as we received simultaneous translation through earpieces set at every place. John, crouched beneath the table, had no such advantage. He was comfortable with Russian, French, German and Italian, but Lubbers also spoke in his native language, Dutch. 'What did you make of that?' I whispered to him on one arcane point. He shifted his aching knees from crouching to kneeling. 'Dutch,' he hissed, 'Dutch. I don't bloody do Dutch.'

Meanwhile, there were dramas elsewhere. One iron rule of European Councils was that at some point the French would have a surprise proposal. They should never be underestimated or overlooked; they fight fiercely for their objectives, and are formidable in doing so. On the first day, at the finance ministers' lunch, they had a humdinger of a surprise: an Exocet that wrong-footed the Germans, unsettled the British, and was welcomed by Belgium and Italy.

The French proposed to write into the treaty a fixed date for the single currency to begin. The essence was that countries would commit themselves in the treaty to join at a later date when they met the agreed economic criteria. They proposed a contingent starting date of 1997, provided a majority of states were economically ready; or, if they were not, 1999, when those who did meet the criteria would enter even if they were a minority.

The effect of the French proposal was to turn a future option into a current commitment. Suddenly, the likelihood of the single currency loomed larger. Germany's Finance Minister Theo Waigel, taken aback, sucked his teeth and asked for time to consult: he agreed the following day. Norman Lamont was silent: as we were seeking an opt-out he decided not to say a word. Others agreed with the French, and over the finance ministers' lunch, monetary union became a much more likely prospect.

At lunchtime on Tuesday, after a lengthy bilateral with Ruud Lubbers on the social text in which we made no progress, I authorised Nigel Wicks to show our draft opt-out from monetary union to senior officials representing each government in a 'High Level' group chaired by Cees Maas, a distinguished Dutch official with bristling moustaches that would have been the envy of Hercule Poirot.

The High Level Group were astonished. They had expected a generalised form of words; instead they were given a long, detailed and precise document in full legal form that specified all the articles of the treaty that would not apply to the UK, and bolted the door on any alternative interpretations. The High Level Group bombarded Nigel with questions, notwithstanding his cheerful advice to them that 'It's not negotiable.'

Our opt-out, unchanged after the high-level officials had grilled Nigel Wicks, was referred by the summit for consideration to the finance ministers. Initially bored – and inclined simply to accept it – they then began to examine it in detail, and to pose significant questions. Norman Lamont, with Nigel Wicks beside him, knew our text was non-negotiable. But he had an excellent brief prepared by Mark Blyth, the lawyer who had drafted the document, and could have responded.

He chose not to do so. He became irritated at the questions and walked out, saying he must consult me. The French thought this was a theatrical gesture to raise the stakes, and rather admired it. Others were less charitable and did not admire it at all. It was an extraordinary way for Norman to behave. He could simply have asked for a recess. Instead, he just upped and went. Yet the opt-out we were seeking was part of the treaty, and every government would have to pass it in their domestic legislation. The other finance ministers were quite within their rights to query it, and reacted with irritation to Norman's departure. In any event, he was gone. He found me in the Chamber negotiating with the other heads of government, and in a state of high dudgeon told John Kerr that I must be asked to come out and see him. John protested, 'He can't come out, he's deep in negotiations,' and tried to cool Norman down.

Meanwhile, I was engaged in my own odyssey through the text of the treaty. Throughout the afternoon we had dealt with the enlargement of the Community, the problems of transition to Stage III of EMU, and Danish worries about a referendum to approve the treaty. At one point I remarked, 'We have no problems with referenda. It is for Parliament to decide. It's quite straightforward' – at which the Fates, knowing what lay ahead for me, must have chuckled. It had been a tiring but productive afternoon, although the big issues were still outstanding.

The meeting was moving very swiftly as weariness set in among the heads of government. Technical matters passed easily. I was working from a detailed brief – we called it a 'back-to-back' – which set out the import of every clause and our policy on it. I had briefed myself thoroughly, and my back-to-back was covered in my own handwritten notes to help me present my argument in the most compelling terms. After one break in proceedings I asked Stephen Wall for my back-to-back. It was gone. No one could find it. A frantic search took place as I returned to the negoti ations without it. Messages were sent in to me that it could not be found. The implications of losing the back-to-back began to sink in. Not only did I need it to negotiate, but even worse, if it had fallen into the hands of another delegation, all our bottom-line positions would have been revealed. Eventually Jeremy Heywood, Norman Lamont's able Private Secretary, let out a whoop of delight. He had discovered it amongst Norman's papers. Everyone breathed a sigh of relief. 'It was the worst moment of my professional career,' one diplomat told me later.

The hours moved on. The debate narrowed to the real points of sub stance still outstanding and the delegations concerned with them. Lubbers did not allow a break for food and drink, assuming, no doubt wisely, that privation would speed consent. Gradually the treaty provisions were put in place; in private discussions, many delegations urged us to compromise on the Social Chapter. There was no chance we would do so. Throughout the day Sarah Hogg had been in touch with Michael Howard, who provided useful ammunition against seductive offers. Michael, I think, feared we would reach an unsatisfactory fudge, but it was never likely: I disliked the Social Chapter intensely, and knew well enough the necessity of rejecting it if I wished to obtain approval in Parliament of the treaty as a whole.

As I returned to our delegation rooms, Tristan Garel-Jones bounded up to tell me that officials were wringing their hands in despair because 'the Chancellor's walked out of the finance ministers' meeting and the rest of them are discussing our opt-out. *Our* opt-out . . . and we're not there.'

In the break from negotiations, Ruud Lubbers had asked to see me to discuss the Social Chapter, and I asked for Norman to be found while I went to Lubbers's office with Stephen Wall. Helmut Kohl joined us there. Wim Kok appeared, obviously bursting to talk about Norman – unfavourably, I judged, from the expression on his face – but when he spotted me he merely chatted for a moment: 'There are difficulties. Ruud will tell you.' Lubbers turned to our opt-out first, and outlined some minor problems arising from the finance ministers' questions. They were swiftly solved as Norman Lamont joined us.

I explained to Lubbers and Kok that I had no room for manoeuvre on the EMU opt-out, but that provided I got it, I would not block their own ambitions. They were disappointed but matter-of-fact. After a little probing they conceded our opt-out within minutes – not least, I think, because their minds were fixed on the greater danger to the whole treaty from the impasse on the Social Chapter. Nor did they object to our future involvement in discussions on EMU, even though we would not be committed to it. They believed, I am sure, that they could finesse one such disagreement with the UK but not two. The opt-out was won. Our first main objective was in place.

I had expected to gain the opt-out, but to have got it without any onerous conditions attached was indeed a prize. The principle of economic and monetary union had often been discussed by finance ministers and by heads of government, but our opt-out had been obtained in the end without any real negotiation at all: it had been drafted in London, discussed in outline principle with other leaders in all my European bilaterals, presented at Maastricht, conceded to me by Lubbers and Kok, and as a result was now bound to be endorsed by the summit generally. The Treasury's work and preparation had borne fruit. Nigel Wicks was too modest ever to be flushed with triumph, but he was cheerful enough as he returned to the finance ministers' meeting and answered their questions. These came thick and fast, but there was no attempt now to keep our opt-out out of the treaty.

The EMU opt-out was a done deal, so Lubbers, Kohl and I turned to the Social Chapter, the last big item outstanding. The choice in my mind was simple: either we were accommodated on it or I would not sign the treaty. Gradually Lubbers began to accept that my position was not just a negotiating ploy. He dangled some tentative offers of watering down the social proposals, but there were none I could accept. He suggested amendments. I considered them, and said no. John Kerr was walking around with an 'upside down' Social Chapter we had had drafted, in which everything was agreed by unanimity except where specified to the contrary: this was such a watered-down proposition it was never likely to be acceptable to our partners. I preferred no Chapter at all. As Lubbers and I spoke, and failed to agree, a second opt-out or some other arrangement by the eleven that excluded the UK began to suggest itself.

But a second opt-out had obvious down-sides: it would mean that the

Social Chapter was in the treaty. I did not want that. Moreover, we had spent months perfecting the EMU opt-out, and I was not confident that, without a lot of care, we could draft a watertight provision on the Social Chapter that would protect us from a challenge in court. A botched provision would be very dangerous. I swallowed hard and rejected an opt-out: I told Lubbers I wanted *nothing* in the treaty.

Throughout these discussions, which must have been very tiresome for him, Ruud Lubbers behaved impeccably. He was well briefed, inventive and calm; at no time did tempers flare, although with more combustible natures they might well have done.

Lubbers, Kohl and I were alone. Once more we ran over the by now familiar differences. I suggested that they considered our watered-down Social Chapter simply to avoid seeming wholly intransigent, but I knew they could not accept it. Kohl disappeared briefly to discuss it with his officials, but it was soon ruled out. Finally, Lubbers suggested an agreement by the eleven *outside* the treaty. Kohl agreed. I accepted. Officials were invited back in and the deal was done. Union-wide, the Social Chapter was dead: it would apply only to the other eleven, and would be linked to the treaty by a protocol which spelled out the fact that it would not affect us. Kohl and Lubbers went to tell other delegations what had been going on. As I met our officials, I wondered if I had missed something. I had not. We had got our way, and it was now certain there would be agreement on the treaty.

The heads reassembled just after 9 p.m. There was a brief charade in which Lubbers, Kohl and I replayed our discussion and Kohl advocated a treaty of eleven and asked Lubbers to seek the agreement of every delegation. One by one – Mitterrand, Mitsotakis, Andreotti, Martens, Haughey, Santer, Schluter, Gonzales, Cavaco da Silva – they all fell in line.

Tired and weary, everyone pressed on with the clause-by-clause examination of the remaining provisions in the treaty. Only minor changes were made. Several hours passed. In the final table round, I rejected a proposal for research and development expenditure to be agreed by a majority rather than by unanimity. This was not bloody-mindedness on my part, but a hard-headed judgement that would give us continued leverage over how a great deal of money was spent. Lubbers said seductively, 'Eleven agree, can you?' 'Unanimity needs twelve,' I replied gently, 'not eleven.' No change was made. It was the last exchange. Kohl threw back his head and roared with laughter – at 1.30 a.m., negotiation of the Maastricht Treaty was over.

I warmly congratulated Lubbers on his chairmanship, and thanked Kohl personally. Their sensitivity to our concerns had made the negotiations far less traumatic than they might have been. I was very grateful to them. Wearily, everyone rose and headed off to prepare for the respective press conferences and interviews.

Gus O'Donnell briefed the press that 'The Social Chapter in the treaty has been dropped,' and 'There is a protocol of the eleven . . . in French on one side of paper.' He said firmly in answer to questions that 'We do not talk about victories,' but a member of his staff, delighted at the outcome, privately called it 'game, set and match'. This triumphalist crowing was attributed to me, and caused real anguish to Lubbers and Mitterrand, who thought it was graceless behaviour by the British. It should not have been said, and led a French spokesman to comment, 'We might regret Mrs Thatcher's departure,' and Jacques Delors to say in answer to a press question, 'I prefer the rules of football and perhaps your Prime Minister prefers the rules of rugby. Therefore it is difficult to assess the performance of your Prime Minister.' The bruises were showing.

Back at home, the press were ecstatic. 'Major wins all he asked for at Maastricht,' said *The Times* on Wednesday, and by the next day, as the outcome was examined, the response was even more positive. 'Tory MPs cheer Major's success at Maastricht,' trilled the front page of the *Daily Telegraph*, with 'Out of the summit and into the light' headlining its editorial comment. 'Job well done,' said *The Times*, commenting on an 'emphatic success for John Major'. It was, said the *Economist*, 'the deal Tory ministers and most backbenchers had been praying for'.

When I made a statement in the Commons on the outcome I was received with acclaim and the waving of order papers. In Cabinet all was sweetness and light, with Ken Baker particularly effusive. Douglas Hurd and Norman Lamont were received rapturously at meetings of Conservative backbenchers. It was the modern equivalent of a Roman triumph.

Soon, it would all be very different.

# CHAPTER THIRTEEN

*Winning a Mandate*

A FEW DAYS BEFORE the 1992 general election a hand reached out through the crowd. It was topped by a smiling face, and I grasped it warmly; but something was wrong.

I looked down and saw that my right hand and shirtsleeve were glistening with dirty black engine oil. Or was it ink? In the moments it took for me to comprehend what had happened, my assailant muttered a few words of abuse and slipped away into the crowd. It was a petty incident, and was not even, I think, reported at the time. But it disturbed me briefly that someone who did not know me could dislike me in this strangely personal way, and had stood waiting for his moment to strike. It was a silent and anonymous violation on the campaign trail.

This was not the only such incident. In Southampton an egg hit me high on the cheekbone with such force that it drew blood, and momentarily led me to think I had been shot. In Bolton a few days before there had been a near-riot. As the crowd jostled and yelled, Norma and I fought our way through the fracas, completing a full circuit of the square before returning to the safety of the battlebus with my protection officers.

It was their duty to keep us out of harm's way, of course. But in fact those moments gave me a zest for the streets and the crowds. Suddenly I was enjoying myself. The election came alive. The passion of the demonstrators showed what was at stake. I did not believe that any British prime minister should be forced off the streets by a rabble. I intended to stand up and openly speak to the crowds, and from that moment on I did so.

My decision on this was part instinct, part calculation. Neil Kinnock had been persuaded by Labour's strategists to fight an artfully arranged campaign, with crowds tucked behind barriers and with contrived photo-opportunities. He wanted to look like a prime minister. I *was* the prime minister, and I wanted a flesh-and-blood fight. I knew the cold fish-eye of the camera lens did me no favours. After the scenes in Bolton I insisted on more street campaigning, not less.

I soon had my chance when, some days later, I visited the Tory marginal of Luton South, where my old friend and PPS Graham Bright was our candidate. It was a quintessential key constituency – a seat Labour had to take if they were to have a hope of winning the election.

I was greeted by a large and lively crowd. Few people in it were neutral, and many were fiercely partisan. As the throng increased a wooden soapbox was hauled out of the boot of my car and I climbed on it to speak. This may have been a far cry from the conventional image of a prime minister on tour, but for me it worked to infinitely better effect than any toothpaste photo-opportunity could have done. The media latched onto it, some sneering and some approving. It certainly woke up any doubtful Conservatives in Luton. The soapbox became one of the icons of the election, much mocked, but whenever it appeared a sure crowd-puller.

This aspect of electioneering suited me well. I felt at ease hemmed in by a noisy mass of jostling humanity. The people were there because they chose to be. So was I. I liked the unpredictability and the dialogue with the crowds. I was invigorated when things went well, and shrugged off the few unpleasant moments. Mostly the reception was friendly, and often genuinely eager. There was a fizz about the impromptu soapbox meetings. Everyone enjoyed them, and they gave me more of a 'feel' for the electorate than any number of opinion polls, focus groups or position papers. When the crowds were roped off in the market square of one Pennines town I felt pinned back too.

The more I saw of the voters face to face, the more sure I was that we would win. I had an inner conviction about the result. I could not believe that I had come all the way from Coldharbour Lane to Downing Street to stay in office for only a few months. Thinking of this now, it seems an insubstantial reason for confidence, but it is an honest statement of how I felt at the time. I simply couldn't *see* Labour in government.

To some my confidence was puzzling, even laughable. Most of the fifty-seven national opinion polls conducted during the campaign pointed to a Labour government. Even in Number 10, where civil servants held a sweepstake on the outcome, most followed the polls and put their money on a Labour victory. Away from London, it felt to me as if there were two elections: the one I was part of each day, and the one I read about in the newspapers each morning. Many small incidents reinforced that feeling. In one town a tattooed skinhead pushed his way into my path. I tensed inwardly as I felt my protection officer thrust himself between us. The skinhead reached out to clutch my arm. ''Ere, John,' he cried out. 'Don't let Labour get away with it' and he shouted more encouragement as the crowd bore him away. The opinion polls never caught the views of people like him.

The uncelebrated success of the 1992 Conservative election campaign was winning in a recession, against the shadow of the Poll Tax, and with barely a mention of Europe. The electorate gave me – and the Conservative Party – the benefit of the doubt, unwilling as they were to elect Neil Kinnock and a Labour Party that still carried with it many socialist trappings. It was a huge satisfaction for me to win my own mandate. The general election had preyed on my mind from the moment I entered 10 Downing Street: I never forgot that it was the party's will to win, and the belief that Margaret Thatcher would lose, that had made me prime minister.

The interval between assuming that office and seeking my democratic mandate to keep it was not without a certain ambiguity. There was an administration to run, Margaret's legacy to build upon and in some respects to correct, ideas of my own to test and push forward – but always in the back of my mind was that huge and inescapable decision I would have to make: when to go to the country? Throughout that year and a half, I had the sneaking feeling that I was living in sin with the electorate. I wanted to change that. It took all my nerve to hold off calling the election until the Poll Tax had finally been buried and the Maastricht Treaty negotiations completed. What swayed me most, however, were my worries about an economy that stubbornly refused to improve.

There was a case for going to the polls in the spring of 1991, as soon as the Gulf War was over. This option had begun to be talked about even before the fighting had ended. I disliked the idea of a 'khaki election'. It struck me as cynical, and I thought that a victory won in the after-glow of Desert Storm would be a false one. Far from the Gulf War being a trigger for an early election, it became for me an argument against.

Chris Patten, as party chairman, was concerned that an election in the midsummer of 1991 would be too late for me to seize the initiative as newly appointed prime minister, and too early for the party to reap the benefits of any improvement in the economy that might occur. 'Go early or late' was his view. Conventional wisdom held that no government could win an election in a recession, but Treasury forecasts suggested that an upturn in the economy was at hand. A late election, therefore, became my preference.

Any lingering thoughts of the June 1991 date that Margaret Thatcher would almost certainly have chosen – she won her elections in four-year cycles – were ruled out by bad local election results in early May and the loss of the Monmouth by-election following the death of John Stradling Thomas, the sitting Conservative Member, a fortnight later. Labour ran a costly and manipulative campaign in Monmouth, spreading falsehoods and alarm about our plans for the NHS. It was a foretaste of their campaigns in both 1992 and 1997.

An autumn 1991 date remained a much-mooted possibility. The media were scratching at the idea, with rumours abroad that I would call the election in my speech to the Tory Conference at Blackpool in October. On Sunday, 29 September, just before the Labour Party Conference, Chris Patten and I considered the options: go for the autumn; postpone till 1992; or make no decision until after our conference.

Both Chris and I were against an early election. To wait until spring 1992, with the chance of better economic weather, looked sensible – with one caveat. The party conferences might just change things. So we decided to pause before making our decision. But this in itself posed a problem. If we said nothing, our conference was bound to be swamped by cries from the media of 'Will he . . . won't he name the day?' and jeers that a good Labour performance in Brighton the week before had scared me off. It therefore seemed right to reveal our thinking. We asked John Wakeham, a subtle and discreet operator, to talk to editors in the hope of toning down speculation.

This tactic backfired. Instead of the subject being dropped, there was a television splash that evening, and acres of newspaper coverage the next day unanimously assuring readers that there would be no autumn poll. The headlines were an embarrassment, but at least they did not remove the option I most favoured. I preferred a date in 1992 not least because, as 1991 came to a close, my thoughts became more and more focused on the Treaty on European Union to be negotiated at Maastricht in December. I remained nervous about Europe as an issue in the minds of voters – how unsettling would it prove, and how unpredictable would be its effects? – and preferred to go to the electorate with the negotiations concluded. In a foretaste of what I was to encounter in 1997, I also wanted to prevent my backbenchers from binding themselves to an anti-European posture that could either blow our election chances apart or, if we won, undermine my future negotiating strategy.

In January 1992 Chris Patten drew up a list of possible dates. Each had its disadvantages. By law, the election had to be held not later than July. I was sure the economy was about to improve; less certain that any improvement would reach voters' pockets by early summer. That pointed to a spring poll. One date shone out at me: 9 April. Politically, this looked good. We would have time for our budget, and our legislation abolishing the Poll Tax would be on the statute book. But I had another reason for choosing it: it was the anniversary of the day I met Norma. With this sentimental thought in mind, I made my decision: 9 April it would be.

Curiously, the next morning I received an unexpected telephone call in my study at Number 10. It was Lady 'Bubbles' Rothermere, the vivacious wife of the owner of the Mail group of newspapers. 'I want you to win the election,' she said. 'But you mustn't go in April – it will be unlucky.' I did not know Lady Rothermere, but I thanked her for her kindness and rang off. Was her call, I wondered, an omen? If so, I would disregard it.

The formal announcement of the election was not issued until 11 March, but the campaign effectively began a day earlier, when Norman Lamont unveiled his 'budget for recovery'. As a former chancellor I took a close interest in all Norman's budgets, but that of 1992 was the one most influenced by Number 10 during my time as prime minister. I involved myself so deeply in the making of it partly, I must admit, because I rather regretted that I was no longer chancellor myself. Although Norman had helped me win the leadership contest in 1990, our relationship was a working one which never ripened into personal friendship, affable in manner and engaging company though he was. Perhaps some of the grit that was to cause the ugly split between us after Black Wednesday was already present.

The 1992 budget was one of the most widely covered of my premiership, not just because it came immediately ahead of a knife-edge general election, but because it allowed us to set out our case for leading Britain out of recession. To do this was now essential. Tory hearts sank every time the economic news came on television. It had become received wisdom among commentators that we would lose if the recovery did not poke its nose around the corner before polling day.

At its worst as the election neared in the first half of 1991, the recession had led to a sort of grumpy stability (although when the Treasury revised its figures five years later, it concluded that by 1992 Britain's economy was on the mend after all). But recovery was imperceptible, and not enough to make things easier for electors dogged by debt or unemployment, or faced with an insecure future. Many home-owners who had bought in the inflated housing market of the boom years of the late eighties saw the value of their homes drop, and were trapped in negative equity. This became the first 'white collar' recession, and its worst effects were felt in the South and South-East, where Conservative support was traditionally strong.

The benefits of this painful period – and there *were* benefits, in the form of low inflation and raised productivity – were, as the election campaign began, nowhere to be seen. When Norman Lamont pointed to 'the green shoots of recovery', his words rang hollow. In my speech to the party conference in October 1991 I had tried to reflect the mood: 'I know times have been tough. Unemployment has risen. Many people have faced great difficulties. I know how you feel.' But I pointed to a better future: 'We can now see the way ahead out of recession.' I believed this when I said it, and events proved me right. But the voters' scepticism in the meantime was understandable.

Indeed, that period of early 1992 seemed like economic midwinter. Though inflation had fallen below 3 per cent, the jobless total had passed 2.5 million, seventy-five thousand people had lost their homes through repossession the previous year, and national output had fallen, while government borrowing had grown. This was reflected in the opinion polls, which put Labour four points ahead after a year in which Neil Kinnock had often found his party lagging behind the Conservatives.

Our response was forceful. In June 1991, Central Office had costed Labour's new spending promises at a monstrous £35 billion; if they did not abandon them, this burden would have to be borne by taxpayers, alongside the extra spending caused by the recession. It was an open goal, and on 6 January 1992 we unveiled a campaign, masterminded by Chris Patten, to highlight 'Labour's Tax Bombshell'. It had an immediate impact, and we followed it up with a new phrase for the dictionaries of English idioms: 'Labour's Double Whammy'. 'The price of Labour,' our simple message ran, 'is £1,250 per year for every family.' Until polling day, tax remained our strongest weapon.

For Labour, there was a sting in the tail of what was otherwise a necessarily cautious budget. We did not have the funds available for grand spending schemes, but we confounded expectations on one point. At the very end of his budget speech, Norman Lamont announced: 'I propose this year to cut the rate of income tax by 5p, to 20p, for the first £2,000 of taxable income.'

This move, which would benefit every taxpayer in the country, but would be of proportionately greater benefit to those on low incomes, destabilised the opposition. In his reply to the Budget Statement, Neil Kinnock committed his party to repealing the 20p band. Coming on the back of our 'tax bombshell' campaign, it put Labour on the back foot as the election began. Nevertheless, the new tax rate was more than a pre-election gimmick. It cut marginal tax rates for around four million lower-paid people, as well as being a decisive first step towards our long-term commitment to reduce the basic rate of income tax to 20 per cent. The idea originated within Number 10, where, with the Policy Unit's help, I had been looking at a dramatic move on income tax rates for some time. I was not content with the usual Treasury practice of lopping a penny or two off the basic rate. The move fed into Norman Lamont's pre-budget discussions and met with his approval. It certainly surprised the commentators.

Almost a week after the budget, the Labour Shadow Chancellor John Smith unveiled a 'shadow budget' with mock formality. His Edinburgh advocate's air of solidity masked the nature of his proposals: £38 billion of additional spending, paid for by more taxes for nearly everyone. He presented this nonsense skilfully, and for a few days, while our Treasury team prepared a detailed response, Labour preened themselves as a government-in-waiting. In a televised debate between Norman Lamont and John Smith, John won comfortably even though he knew his proposals were utterly unrealistic ('We won't introduce half of them anyway,' he privately told Labour's pollster Philip Gould). But his early triumph was short-lived. His proposals fell apart under examination.

Labour had moved the agenda onto our ground. 'Dogs bark, cats miaow, Labour puts up taxes,' as Chris Patten put it. This rang true. By contrast, no one doubted that I wished the tax burden to fall, and when I was challenged by the journalist Tony Bevins, I said so clearly at a morning press conference during the campaign.

My wish to cut income taxes – especially at the lower end – was genuine, and I believed it could be done. At the time, I answered Bevins, Treasury estimates suggested that the budget deficit would peak in 1993–94 at £32 billion and then fall away, allowing taxes to fall. In fact, after the election Treasury income fell, and the deficit reached £46 billion. In such circumstances either taxes had to rise, or spending would have to be slashed at a time of recession. That would have been calamitous for many in Britain, and indeed for the economy as a whole. So taxes rose. Labour then claimed that I had 'lied' about taxes during the election. I had done no such thing. I may have been proved wrong, but I did not lie.

On the morning of 11 March, with the budget announcement still ringing in my ears and Labour three points ahead in the latest opinion poll, I called the general election. Cabinet that morning was abuzz: everyone present believed we could win, but not everyone thought we would. Looking around the cabinet table, I could see some ministers wondering if they would sit around it again; others were already geared up by the adrenaline of the fight ahead.

After Cabinet I drove to Buckingham Palace for an audience with the Queen, to seek the formal dissolution of Parliament. We met briefly in Her Majesty's first-floor study. Three attendant corgis became the first outside Cabinet to know of my intention, and one of them amiably settled with his nose on my foot. As I idly stroked the back of his neck, I wondered if Neil Kinnock liked dogs.

Twenty-four hours later I was in the Commons for what many suspected would be my last occasion answering parliamentary questions as prime minister. Neil Kinnock made a bogus demand for a televised debate between the party leaders, which I easily batted away with a low blow: 'Paddy and I would never get a word in.' It was so true it killed the issue.

In Downing Street, Nick True and Ronnie Millar began work on a string of speeches for the campaign. The pair of them, political junkies both, were locked in for the duration, writing, speculating, observing, calculating and turning out top-notch texts day after day. Ronnie was fuelled by good whisky. 'My dear boy, yes,' he would say, 'perhaps just a little more. No, no water, thank you – it dilutes the inspiration.' When I returned to Number 10 late at night after a day's campaigning and they emerged from their eyrie I found the inspiration as undiluted as the whisky. They added colour and humour to the end of many a tough day.

Despite Nick and Ronnie's best efforts I was generally unwilling to attack our opponents personally; but Michael Heseltine, in prime form, pitched into them mercilessly. It was his natural style, and it allowed me the scope to take a more conciliatory line. Chris Patten, too, had a surprising gift for tough oratory that resonated to our advantage.

But sometimes the temptation was irresistible. Midway through the campaign I picked up and parodied a moving speech Neil Kinnock had given during the 1983 election. If Labour win, I said, '*I warn you not to be qualified. I warn you not to be successful. I warn you not to buy shares. I warn you not to be self-employed. I warn you not to accept promotion. I warn you not to save. I warn you not to buy a pension. I warn you not to own a home.*' It was a deadly line of attack. Labour had no answer to it. 'It'll work,' chuckled the authors, Nick and Ronnie. It did.

Another idea worked less well – the 'Meet John Major' open meetings at which I would speak briefly to groups of voters and then answer their questions. In the Gulf I had enjoyed addressing the troops massed around me. 'It's pure theatre,' I thought, and such events fitted well with my intention to take the election out of the television studios and live to the public.

Trial runs of the format long before the campaign went well, but then the rot set in. I had hoped to hold meetings in the open air, in market squares or shopping centres, and take questions from all comers. But the police took fright: it would be impossible to protect me. I might get shot. Central Office was even more jumpy: never mind me getting shot, the meetings might get disrupted. 'It'll be a playground for nutters – bad television,' was one of the more encouraging comments.

So the meetings were scaled back – to be held indoors, before a chosen audience. Hecklers and assassins were not invited. The questions remained spontaneous, but no one believed that they were. Worse, we foolishly held the first 'Meet John Major' in my own constituency of Huntingdon. This really killed the idea. The press had been promised a remarkable new election format, and all they saw was an amiable after-lunch discussion between the Prime Minister and a group of people many of whom he knew. It looked like a fix – which it was not, but it meant that the idea did not have a chance. Though I did three more 'Meet John Majors', none was widely noticed, and we abandoned the format. It was a pity. I enjoyed doing them, and there were no reportable gaffes – another reason, perhaps, for the press's disappointment.

I notice that Tony Blair's promised 'Meet the People' campaign after the 1997 election was soon quietly buried. Perhaps he discovered the same drawbacks as I had.

My election schedule, under the determined guidance of Shirley Stotter, had been agreed before the campaign began. The aim was to shuttle me around the country, travelling mostly on the party's battlebus, with the twin intentions of highlighting our predetermined themes and visiting constituencies across the country. The aim was to pull together image, word and action.

It did not turn out like that. The initial theme – lasting all of the first week – had been unveiled in what was known as the 'near term campaign' in January. It saw Chris Patten brilliantly push home our message on Labour's tax policies, catching Neil Kinnock off guard. But before long we could not hide our efforts to drag the media onto our chosen ground, and by the time the election was underway this had lost us the element of surprise.

Sometimes our themes fell out of step with the natural course of the election, which led to some silly scenes. One day I was touring a British Rail marshalling yard used by Pedigree Petfoods, with a hard-bitten press squad in tow, to illustrate some aspects of transport policy. Then events changed the agenda to the economy, while I was stuck in the sidings. It was not a public relations triumph.

There were more hiccups. Visiting Gravesham to highlight British exports I was herded into a huge warehouse full of shiny fresh apples – only to notice that they were South African imports, not Kentish exports. As my minders interposed themselves between the apples and the photographers, I was hustled outside. Every campaign has such moments of horror that linger in the memory.

Sometimes we ran hours late, lurching around narrow lanes while the press grumbled that they had missed their deadlines. Odd, therefore, that one evening – well past deadline time – when Norma and I were eating fish and chips on the battlebus at Cardiff Airport, the photographers grabbed their cameras and our late feast received wide coverage next morning. Evidently deadlines could be flexible when needed.

Out on the stump we were informal, travelling with a small team and insulated from the election being fought in the media, fuelled by – as it turned out – misleading opinion polls. Norma was with me throughout, easy-going and tremendously popular at every stop. The image of her as a shy, home-loving woman keen to shun the limelight is, at best, only a fragment of the truth. She fiercely wanted us to win, and carried with her the cheery aura of someone in no doubt about the result.

But I came down to earth every night with a bump when I arrived back at Number 10 to be confronted with the latest election news – often dismal, for bad news gets priority. Frequently, too, I would find that allies of my predecessor had been in touch with political and Policy Unit staff at Number 10 during the day, to warn me that our campaign was failing and that the party would lose the election because of it. It was confusing to spend all day with the public, who seemed so enthusiastic, and afterwards to return to this array of negative thoughts.

Most evenings Chris Patten was on hand, a rock of calm in a tempestuous sea. Chris bore up valiantly against his own worries. Tired out from shuttling between London and his Bath constituency by helicopter, he faced the inner turmoil of knowing that, while he might deliver an election win for me, he was unlikely to hold his own seat, where the impact of the Poll Tax had been particularly savage. He was a voice of reason when problems cropped up, as they did all the time, and had the endearing quality of admitting his mistakes when he believed he should take the blame. Confession, he said, is good for the soul. There spoke the convinced Catholic.

I woke each morning at about 6.30, usually to find an already alert Sarah Hogg waiting edgily for me to approve a statement for that morning's press conference. Then I would scan documents briefing me on the live issues of the day, gather up ministers due to appear with me, and head over to Central Office.

'I'm here to fall on my sword on your behalf, Prime Minister,' Chris Patten would say in private before the press conferences began. He meant that he would step in if the press questioning became troublesome – a gaffe from the party chairman is one thing; a glaring error by the prime minister quite another. I was well briefed, and we generally avoided the rocks. Chris chaired the press conferences with skill, smiled happily and hit hard. His virtuosity was an asset.

I unveiled our manifesto, *The Best Future for Britain*, a week into the campaign. Farcically, our launch came on the same day as Labour's. We had delayed things by a day, in order to prevent John Smith's shadow budget from obscuring what we had to say – little knowing that Smith had decided to advance his shadow budget so as to avoid our manifesto taking the spotlight away from his tax policies. I was genuinely enthusiastic about our manifesto proposals. 'It's all me,' I said at the launch. 'Every last word of it is me'– and, although I had not written it all, it did reflect what I stood for: effective policy, not ideological confrontation. The manifesto was detailed, with 350 policy pledges, including commitments to increase competition within public utilities, privatise British Rail and the coal industry, and work for the enlargement of the European Union. It was also radical.

The contents of our manifesto had been finalised in the inevitable last-minute scramble under the guidance of an exhausted Sarah Hogg, and finished only hours before it had to go to press. Manifesto writing is never easy, though the groundwork had been laid early, during meetings of senior ministers at Chequers in 1991, and carried forward in January 1992, when the 'A-team' of senior ministers and advisers had started work.

It did not take long for critics to decide that the manifesto lacked a new 'big idea'. Quite what they expected after thirteen years of Conservative government I am not sure. The party's manifestos in 1979 and 1983 had lacked any radical theme, yet Mrs Thatcher comfortably won both those elections, and revolutionised the country. In 1992 Labour had ditched their *old* big idea: the word 'socialism' did not appear once in their manifesto.

We crept into the second week of the campaign still behind in the opinion polls, and under fire. One of our core election messages – 'You can't trust Labour' – was being altered on posters all over the country to 'You can trust Labour'. Another, with the slogan 'Labour in – everybody out', inevitably had 'celebrating' tagged on the end. Good jokes, but I remained sure of what we were about. I did not believe that the country trusted Labour to take office, whatever electors were telling the opinion pollsters.

Two party election broadcasts, one from each major party, then came to grip the media's attention, if not the nation's. The first, 'The Journey', was made for the Conservative Party by the renowned film director John Schlesinger, and broadcast on the night of our manifesto launch. It focused on my leadership of the party and my upbringing in Brixton. I was famously reluctant to make the film, and to this day I remain embarrassed about it.

Others say it is a moving and effective portrayal of what I stand for and where I come from, but I have always felt uncomfortable about personalised politics, and disliked using my upbringing in an attempt to win votes.

Chris Patten had first suggested the film months before the election. He brought Schlesinger to see me, and I liked him, but still bridled at the idea that was outlined to me. It took a great deal of coaxing on Chris's part to get me to agree. Schlesinger wanted to take me to Brixton and guide viewers around places I had known in my childhood, but two of the curses of a prime minister's life – security worries and a lack of time – meant that I could only make a short visit, mostly by car. We stopped at Brixton market, which had changed little since I used to shop there in the 1960s, and then drove up Burton Road towards the old house I had lived in with my parents.

'Is it still there?' I asked as we came close – reasonably enough, since the road had been redeveloped. Then, in answer to my own question I exclaimed: 'It is, it is, it's still there. It's hardly changed!' I was genuinely surprised, but the media were, perhaps inevitably, cynical. Throughout the campaign, as the battlebus neared Central Office each night, tired journalists cried out mockingly: 'Is it still there? It is, it is.' Tim Collins, in charge of my press relations, was on the receiving end of these taunts, and on election night he took his revenge. 'Is he still there?' he claimed after I had been re-elected. 'He is, he is. He's still there!'

The other election broadcast which attracted attention came from the Labour Party, and led to one of those spats which seem vital at the time but silly in hindsight. The film featured two little girls, both in need of operations on their ears. One girl's family, it said, could pay for private treatment, and the other's could not – with the result that the child suffered. It was close to the mark of what is acceptable and what is not (as was a Labour poster which began: 'Georgina Norris died because the NHS is short of money'), but it would have passed without much notice had Labour not boasted that the story was based on a real case. After a complex series of leaks and counter-leaks, the press tracked down the family of the child whose treatment had been delayed. Insults were traded between the parties, and the whole thing became known as 'the war of Jennifer's ear'. Although Central Office played some role in identifying the family – after relatives of the girl had contacted us to complain about Labour's use of the story – I was uncomfortable with a dispute which moved the election focus onto the Health Service, which was very much Labour's ground. The only winners from this mess were the Liberal Democrats, who for a few days crept upwards in the polls, raising again the threat of a hung Parliament.

I was settled in my mind on what I would do if we did not win a majority. I could not have done a deal with Paddy Ashdown and the Liberal Democrats, and would have preferred opposition to his likely price of proportional representation. Nor were we personally compatible. I always felt there were two Paddy Ashdowns: the agreeable companion over dinner, and the rather pompous politician on public display. I had a low threshold for pomposity, whereas the public Paddy knew no ceiling to it. We could have dined together easily enough, but there was no prospect of a working relationship.

This meant that the only available coalition partners for us were the Official Ulster Unionists, under Jim Molyneaux. Jim would have been a perfectly amiable partner, but any coalition with his party would have condemned Northern Ireland to another five years of stalemate, since no nationalist group would have believed in our good faith so long as the Unionists had official status in the government. I could not accept that.

As it was, media attention began to turn to the chances of a deal being struck between Neil Kinnock and Paddy Ashdown. I was happy to see this story run, since it made the pair look like trimmers prepared to scrabble for whatever bit of power they could get. I was surprised, too, since Kinnock seemed to be coming close to winning power without the need for a partner, if you believed the election being reported on television and in the press.

On Wednesday, 1 April, as I boarded my plane to return to London after a rally in Bristol, I heard a voice shout out a question about the latest opinion polls. 'What was that?' I asked Norman Fowler as we took our seats. He brushed it aside, but I persisted. I was buoyant, and was waiting for the polls to move in our favour. They hadn't. With reluctance, Norman showed me three opinion polls that would be published the following morning. They gave Labour a lead of up to 8 per cent. I was shocked. A good day's campaigning, a huge degree of enthusiasm, a successful rally, and yet it seemed the public mood was moving against us. Was I wrong? Had we run out of road after thirteen years? Gloom swelled up inside me. 'They're only polls,' said Norman. 'Remember the crowds.'

'Isn't that *my* line?' I replied. It is not true that politicians ignore opinion polls. They study them avidly even if they distrust them, and these polls pointed unwaveringly to a Labour victory. When I returned to Downing Street that evening, Chris Patten and I sat in the flat and speculated on what was happening. I was puzzled. Chris was guarded. Perhaps these predictions would prove helpful to our cause, driving uncertain voters back into our fold. Over the next few days, as I talked to people throughout the country, the insistence of our supporters that we must win – 'We mustn't have Labour, you must stop them, John' – was sharper than ever.

This sentiment was strengthened by a celebratory rally held on 1 April by the Labour Party in Sheffield, marked by an over-enthusiastic display of premature triumphalism by Neil Kinnock. Confronted with the real prospect of a Labour government, many people in Britain made up their minds to support us once again.

I believe two other factors worked in our favour. Oddly, the recession helped us. The electorate believed we could steer through it more effectively than Labour. In the end they were proved right. In 1997 we handed over a sparkling economy, though the pain in achieving it cost us dear.

Voters also began to see the implications of a Labour victory for the constitution. This was something I had spoken about in February, during a visit to Scotland, and raised again at the start of the campaign. Labour's policy of devolution had hardly been debated outside Scotland; even north of the border many voters had given it little consideration. It troubled me deeply that the issue was receiving so little attention. Britain risked sleepwalking into an era of radical constitutional upheaval which threatened the very unity of the country.

During the election a casual remark by a press officer at Central Office was reported to me. He had said that my apparent interest in the Union was of little account, and that the *only* important message was tax. I was furious, and asked Nick True and Ronnie Millar to write a substantial speech on the constitution for a Scottish rally. It concluded on an emotional high. 'If I could summon up all the authority of this office, I would put it into this single warning – the United Kingdom is in danger. Wake up, my fellow countrymen. Wake up before it is too late!'

The effect in the hall was powerful, and I repeated the message with increasing urgency. It took root with the public, and people asked me about it when I went campaigning.

For whatever reason, in the last few days of the campaign the difference between the two main parties in the opinion polls closed to almost nothing, and the Liberal Democrats fell back. Late one evening, two days before the vote, Chris Patten and Tony Garrett, one of the most able people in Central Office, came to see me at Downing Street. We were joined by Sarah Hogg and Jonathan Hill. Tony had been speaking to candidates and party agents throughout the campaign, as well as running our private polling programme, and set out the result he expected. We would be the largest party in the new Parliament, he predicted, winning between 316 and 339 seats. (His guess was pretty good – we won 336 seats.)

Comforting though it was to be told we would win, I knew Tony's figures meant that many Conservative MPs would lose their seats. I asked for the names of some of those who might not make it. 'Francis Maude,' he said – the minister in charge of the Citizen's Charter. 'John Maples' – another rising star. 'Graham Bright' – my Parliamentary Private Secretary and an ally since 1979. 'And I am afraid, Prime Minister, that we will lose Bath' – Chris Patten's seat.

It was a bitter blow. Bath was a perpetual marginal, sometimes swaying towards Labour and sometimes towards the Liberals, but Chris was so good, and had such a high national profile that I did not think it would fall this time. But now it looked as if the Party Chairman would be defeated. 'Is that right, Chris?' I asked. 'Absolutely, Prime Minister,' he replied. I could say nothing. Graham Bright had already warned me that his seat was likely to be lost – 'You'll win the election, but I'll lose,' he had told me (in fact he held Luton South against the odds, with a majority of just 799; perhaps the massive coverage of the soapbox's first appearance helped). Now I was faced with the prospect of building a government for a fourth term without the help of some of the people who had brought me so close to victory. There was little I could do except hope Tony was wrong.

By the morning of the election, some opinion polls had us half a point in the lead. As the polls were at least a day out of date and the drift was in our favour, I assumed we were decently ahead when the polling booths opened. 'In any event,' I thought, 'we'll soon know.'

9 April was warm and sunny – as it usually is on polling day, at least in my memory. The papers mostly called on their readers to vote Conservative – though somewhat to my surprise the *Financial Times* came out for Labour. The *Sun* filled its front page with a cruel picture of Neil Kinnock superimposed on a lightbulb, and the headline: 'If Kinnock wins

today, would the last person in Britain please turn out the lights.' I threw it down on the kitchen table in front of Norma. She glanced at it quizzically. 'It might be you next time,' was her only comment.

I spent the day visiting the polling stations and Conservative committee rooms in my constituency. Everywhere I saw Tories with rosettes, and cheerful voters waving. Early in the evening I returned to Finings and awaited the verdict. A little before 10 o'clock I was telephoned privately and told the figures for ITN's exit poll. It pointed to a Conservative total of about 303 seats – too few to form even a minority government without a partner. I poured a large brandy and waited.

Norma and I were joined at Finings by Jonathan Hill, Sarah Hogg, Tim Collins and Edward Llewellyn – who had spent some of the election trying to block eggs thrown at me while I spoke from the soapbox. We were sitting in front of the television when the first result came through, from Sunderland South. Chris Mullin had held it for Labour with a very small increase in his vote; I knew it was not enough for Labour to win nationally. I was already thinking of victory when the scene at Basildon flashed on the screen. The seat was another key marginal, like Luton  one that Labour had to gain if it was to establish itself in power. As the candidates filed onto the platform, the cameras panned in on the face of the Conservative, David Amess. It was a mask of suppressed emotion. 'He's lost,' muttered someone. I looked at his wife. 'No, he hasn't. He's won. Look at her.' Moments later the result was announced and David's arms were aloft in triumph.

'That's it, we've won,' I remember saying, and going into the room where Elizabeth and James were watching the results coming through. 'If we've won Basildon we've won the election,' I told them. And we had.

Chris Patten did lose Bath, as Tony Garrett had predicted. I watched from Finings as the successful Liberals jeered and chanted when the result was announced. In London, though I did not know it, Margaret Thatcher's former Party Treasurer Alistair McAlpine and his election-night party guests cheered Chris's defeat too. 'Tory gain at Bath!' they mocked. Even though McAlpine was no longer in the inner circle of the party, and was increasingly disaffected over our European policy, it was a vindictive reaction to the defeat of the Conservative Party Chairman. My heart went out to Chris and his wife Lavender, drawn and pale by his side, as he battled to speak. Chris had lost his seat. I had lost my next chancellor of the exchequer.

But we began to hold marginal seats, and even made a gain in Scotland. Sure now that I would stay in office, Sarah Hogg opened the briefcase on her lap and told me, smiling, about the documents she had with her. They set out how I would have departed from Downing Street if I had lost. To the fury of some civil servants she had refused to discuss this with me unless it became necessary.

Nor was this the only spat. 'You have, of course, ordered a removal van?' one senior civil servant had said to Norma at the start of the election. She had not. She did pack a few books and other personal items, but more as a gesture than in the serious belief that we would lose. It was an odd question for an official to ask, almost implying that it might be hard to remove a defeated prime minister from Downing Street. Later we were given, in error, one of the briefing papers prepared in the event of a Labour victory. It offered Glenys Kinnock government money to redecorate the flat in Number 10. This rankled a little too, since we had been discouraged from redecorating when we arrived.

At the declaration of my result in Huntingdon, I got a massive majority, 36,230, far exceeding the predictions of my agent Peter Brown but reflecting the wonderful campaign he had run in the constituency. The atmosphere in the huge hall where the ballot papers had been counted was oddly subdued. Very few of my party supporters had been allowed in. Only the Monster Raving Loony Party's Screaming Lord Sutch and his rival fringe candidate, Lord Buckethead, added a spot of colour. 'I'm so glad you've won,' Sutch confided to me. I was able to repay the compliment by telling him he had been the most intelligent of my opponents. Since Lord Buckethead was in his full fig I couldn't hear his comment, but he seemed friendly enough.

At about half-past three in the morning, Norma and I sank back into the seats of the official armoured Daimler and sped towards London. We were so tired our mood was more one of satisfaction than triumph. 'It looks as though we've got another five years,' I remember saying to Norma as the car radio ground out late results. 'Good,' she replied. 'I can take it if you can.' I turned to reply, but she was asleep. I sat slumped in my seat thinking about what I would say on arrival at Central Office, and reached for a pad to make notes. There was a reshuffle to consider, and a new parliamentary programme.

Outside Central Office to greet me, in front of a deliriously excited crowd, was Chris Patten, no longer a member of the House of Commons. Muted by Chris's defeat, we went inside to join the celebrations. Despite his loss, and the traumatic scenes at his count, Chris joined in touring Central Office to thank all the staff who had worked so hard. I felt his loss keenly.

The following day, the full election result became clear. The Conservative Party had won 336 seats, Labour 271, the Liberal Democrats twenty, and the Scots and Welsh Nationalists seven between them. I was delighted to see that the former Sinn Fein MP, Gerry Adams, was not among the seventeen MPs elected in Northern Ireland. We had an overall majority of twenty-one. In the afterglow of victory it looked like plenty, but that was to prove a mistaken judgement. In the years ahead it would seem cursedly small, as it was slowly sliced away through by-election defeats and defections. With more seats, I would have had the ability to act with force against those in the party who chose to rebel. It was a luxury which Margaret Thatcher had had to the full, but one which I did not enjoy.

We were desperately unlucky not to have had a larger Commons majority, since we polled more votes than any party in British political history – 14,092,891. We won half a million more votes than Labour would in their landslide of 1997, and a third of a million more than Margaret Thatcher had managed in 1987. On an even national swing, our lead in terms of seats would have been over seventy. And when the parties' respective shares of the vote were calculated, the Conservatives received 42.8 per cent across Britain, against Labour's 35.2 per cent: a lead of over 7 per cent. It was one of the biggest leads in votes since 1945, but it yielded only a miserly majority of seats.

The electors had given a clear-cut verdict. Labour was stunned, their shock carved deep in the faces at their party headquarters when Neil Kinnock conceded defeat. I felt for him. Neil was a more forceful leader than the Tory Party or the press ever acknowledged, and he carried through immense changes in his party at a time when doing so was both brave and difficult. His leadership was the essential pre-condition for what would become New Labour.

I had given only preliminary thought to the reshuffle that had to follow the election, but the changes I would make now set the course for the next five years. Chris Patten's defeat blew a hole in my plans. He would have made an excellent chancellor, and had he been available I would have appointed him to that post and moved Norman Lamont to another senior job. As it was – much to his relief, since I learned from within the Treasury that he was desperately worried he would be moved – I left Norman in place. This was to prove a misfortune for us both. As chancellor Norman had to face the turmoil of Black Wednesday, followed by a series of personal difficulties that gradually undermined his credibility. But that story lies ahead.

I asked Kenneth Baker to leave the Home Office, and appointed Kenneth Clarke in his place. I offered Ken Baker the Welsh Office, but he viewed this as an attempt by me to avoid sacking him, and refused to take it. He had, I think, suspected what was coming, for he had his letter of resignation in his pocket, but did not hand it to me until he had heard what was on offer. I thought he was wrong to see the offer of Wales as a derisory gesture; it was certainly not meant as such. In the back of my mind was Peter Walker, who had been prominent in government as Welsh secretary in the late 1980s; within a few years, of course, two Conservative Welsh secretaries would run for the party leadership, one of them successfully.

Kenneth Clarke, the new Home Secretary, was a bruiser well able to meet the challenges of one of the toughest jobs in government. A liberal by instinct, he could be totally bloody-minded, which was ideal for the hard-headed reforms to the justice system that I wanted to implement. Beneath his often carefree air he was as impervious to criticism as any man I ever met.

Douglas Hurd remained at the Foreign Office. I had toyed with the idea of offering him a managerial 'Willie Whitelaw' role, but he was too good a foreign secretary to move. Norman Fowler, my boss when I was at Social Security, agreed to return to the front rank of politics and take on the troublesome task of party chairman. Michael Heseltine gained the job he had wanted in 1990, leading the Department of Trade and Industry. Peter Lilley moved to bring his radical thinking to bear at Social Security, and William Waldegrave, after a turbulent period in charge of Health, took command of the Citizen's Charter.

Other long-serving ministers – Tom King at Defence, David Waddington as Leader of the Lords, and Peter Brooke at Northern Ireland – stood down from office. That gave me the scope to bring forward some of those who had been waiting in the wings. I put my fellow Blue Chip Club member John Patten in charge of Education, where unfortunately he did not thrive.

With the promotion of Virginia Bottomley to Health and Gillian Shephard to Employment, both on merit, I was able to bring women into the Cabinet. Finally, Michael Portillo, who had the reputation of a hawk on public spending, took on my old slot as Chief Secretary to the Treasury.

I chewed my knuckles about bringing Michael into the Cabinet, but decided that his ability merited promotion. In the years ahead, I was never able to make up my mind about him. He was a curious mixture – proud and self-contained, rarely revealing his inner feelings, and with a capacity to surprise. Years later, he came to see me in my room at the Commons to admit that he was the source of some anonymous unflattering comments about me in a *Spectator* article. I told him not to be so foolish again, and sent him away. I thought it was admirable that he had come to me; others did not, although it was only when I was writing this book that I learned that Michael's identity as the author of the remarks had leaked, and that in seeing me he had forestalled the likelihood of my finding out from other sources. On another occasion, after I had promoted him to Defence Secretary in 1995, he made an ill-judged speech using the SAS to make political points, after which he endeared himself to the military by calling in the Chiefs of Defence Staff to apologise.

This capacity to execute a complete volte-face was also evident after the 1997 election, in which Michael lost his Enfield Southgate seat. In government, nobody presented more of a hatchet-face as a rigid, unbending, new Conservative; out of it, nobody was saying we had to listen and understand more speedily than the newly unelected Michael Portillo.

The morning after the election, Chris Patten and I met at Number 10 to talk things over, our minds already set on the prospects for the next five years. Neither of us thought a fifth straight election win was likely, and I believed we had stretched the democratic elastic as far as it would go. Labour were in disarray, and I suspected the media and our own backbenchers might prove to be the real opposition. This turned out to be all too true.

As we talked, I asked Chris about his future. He shook his head and said he didn't yet know. 'I want you back in public life,' I told him, and set out some possibilities: a peerage and a senior place in the Cabinet from the Lords; a return to the Commons via a by-election for which I would create the opportunity; or the governorship of Hong Kong until the colony's return to Chinese rule in 1997.

We talked these choices through. Chris thought he was too young to go to the Lords, and, with memories of the unpleasant Liberal Democrat behaviour at his count at Bath still fresh in his mind, was adamant he could not put his family through a by-election. I tried to persuade him, but to no avail.

'Will you think about Hong Kong?' I pressed. 'And I'll keep the other options open.' He promised to do so, and we finished our conversation and went out into Downing Street to greet the crowds who had gathered there.

So the election was done and dusted. The future looked encouraging, the economy was climbing towards recovery, and the opposition had been trounced. Though the Maastricht Treaty had been negotiated less than six months before, barely a squeak had been heard from the Conservative ranks about Europe during the election campaign. Whatever my own forebodings, Tory MPs could not conceal their unfeigned delight that their party had managed to win a fourth term in office.

A summer of calm satisfaction beckoned. Then the shells began to explode. The Danish rejection of Maastricht; Black Wednesday; David Mellor's resignation; the coalmine closure programme; Maastricht ratification – the list runs on. Suddenly 10 April 1992 did not look quite the glad, confident morning it had appeared at the time. In opposition, the Labour Party took stock and started to pick itself up all over again. Hesitantly under John Smith, then relentlessly under Tony Blair, Labour set about changing itself in preparation for victory. Meanwhile the Conservative Party began tearing itself to bits.

I sometimes wonder what would have happened if we had lost in 1992. Labour, not the Conservatives, would have had to face Black Wednesday, BSE, and a Euro-sceptic attitude as rife in its ranks as it was in our own. Faced with these troubles, Neil Kinnock would have been hard-pressed to keep the left wing of his party at bay.

On form, the Conservatives would have won any election that followed a one-term small-majority Labour government. Assuming this, some Tories have engaged in a neat bit of historical doublethink: 1992, they argue, was the election we should have lost. What the Tories needed was not another spell in power, but the cold, sharp shock of opposition, an ideological cleansing of the palate.

Despite our defeat in 1997, I disagree. The idea that a Labour government in 1992 would have been good for Britain is hardly worth even taking the trouble to dismiss. Our victory ensured that our reforms over the previous thirteen years were made permanent. After some turmoil, it locked into place a new economic regime. With it came the benefits of recovery without inflation, a tremendous strength for Britain. It protected the country from the folly of Labour's grandiose spending plans, which would have meant either vast tax rises or the abandonment of all Labour had stood for on polling day. In addition, it deferred the threats to our constitution. Above all, our victory in 1992 killed socialism in Britain. It also, I must conclude, made the world safe for Tony Blair. Our win meant that between 1992 and 1997 Labour had to change. No longer is Britain trapped in the old two-party tango, with one government neatly undoing everything its predecessor has created. Unquestionably, this is good for the country.

It was right for Britain that the Conservatives won the 1992 election. And had the party chosen to behave like a party of government in the five years after our victory, it would have been good for the Conservative Party, too.

# CHAPTER FOURTEEN

# Black Wednesday

BLACK WEDNESDAY – 16 September 1992, the day the pound toppled out of the ERM – was a political and economic calamity. It unleashed havoc in the Conservative Party and it changed the political landscape of Britain. On that day, a fifth consecutive Conservative election victory, which always looked unlikely unless the opposition were to self-destruct, became remote, if not impossible.

I was the chancellor of the exchequer who took sterling into the Exchange Rate Mechanism, and I was the prime minister when we were forced to leave it. It is right for me to accept responsibility for what happened, and I do so. But the political disaster of our exit was not the result of a simple miscalculation of the rate at which we entered. Ideologues so often reason as though random events have some kind of structural inevitability. This is not my experience. The rigidities of the Exchange Rate Mechanism were certainly bound to cause frictions, subterranean pressures and tremors, but there was no inevitability about the earthquake. It was precipitated by a combination – to a degree haphazard – of circumstances. I think we did perhaps underestimate the risk of a seismic seizure when we took sterling into the ERM, but I do not think we overlooked a certainty.

Sometimes in politics the choice is between bad and awful. It was so in June 1992. That month, the Treasury forecast that the trade deficit would widen, government borrowing would grow and unemployment would continue to rise; we were in for a long haul. My hopes of a growing economy to bring about a gentler Conservatism were gone. Instead, to correct the economy, we would have to take decisions that were bound to hurt those I most wished to help.

Still, I think we could have overcome this had we not been sideswiped from an unexpected direction. On 2 June I was attending a dinner at the

Carlton Club when a message was brought to me with the result of the referendum in Denmark on whether or not to adopt the Maastricht Treaty on European Union: unexpectedly, the Danes had said no.

The day following the Danish vote a further decision was taken, also outside the UK, that was to have a serious impact on the currency markets. President Mitterrand announced that France would also hold a referendum on the Maastricht Treaty. This was an unwelcome shock, and soon opinion polls were to indicate that the French too might reject the treaty. This would have killed it, and ended – perhaps for good, but certainly for a long time – any progress towards European integration. Confidence was badly damaged, and the markets began to take fright. The pound sank steadily, from DM2.91 in May to DM2.81 in July, and DM2.80 in August – perilously close to our ERM floor of 2.778.

The forces which caused this to happen came from many directions, not all of them easily predicted. In 1992, the dollar was weak because the US Federal Reserve Bank was lowering interest rates in order to increase the rate of economic growth in the United States. As a consequence, a sea of money sloshed from Wall Street to the Square Mile in search of better returns. Much of it was invested in deutschmarks, the anchor currency of the ERM. This drove up the value of the deutschmark and put great strain on its links within the ERM to other member currencies such as sterling, the French franc and the Italian lira.

Sterling had entered the ERM in October 1990 at a central rate of DM2.95, and with a commitment that its value would remain within a 6 per cent bracket between DM3.12 and DM2.778. But as we entered, across Europe the maintenance of the exchange rate was becoming a political virility symbol. As our partners became more committed to the goal of a single currency their policy became more inflexible, and the nature of the ERM changed. German monetary policy changed too, as it faced up to the problems of reunification. There were massive expenditures, inflation soared, and the Bundesbank stepped in. This was a crucial development.

In Germany, interest rates were decided by the Bundesbank, which was independent of the government. The Bundesbank was bound only to consider the well-being of Germany. This it did – and in the choice between the correct level of interest rates for Germany and the correct level for Europe, Germany won. Since the deutschmark was the benchmark of the whole ERM mechanism, this put upward stress on interest rates across the whole of Europe. From the beginning of 1991 – a matter of weeks after sterling entered the ERM – to July 1992 the German discount rate rose by 2.75 per cent. It was a rise neither the Treasury nor the City had anticipated when we entered the ERM. The Bundesbank is too formidable an institution not to grasp the effects of its decisions, but neither it nor the German government did more than express sympathy and understanding for the havoc its policy was causing elsewhere. Amidst such ritual hand-wringing, policy went awry as a rising level of unemployment across Europe testified that this was not simply a British problem.

In mid-June 1992 Norman Lamont told Conservative backbenchers attending the Finance Committee that there was no question of ditching our commitment to the ERM. We were determined to bring inflation down, and this was the mechanism for doing so. He reiterated our policy later that month, coupling a firm defence of the system with the warning that it was 'the only policy that could work'.

Even as he spoke, it was clear that the economic recovery was stalling as companies marked down their expectations of profit; together with a fear of a 'double dip' recession, this further depressed the foreign exchange markets. Two other unwelcome factors then arose. The Italian lira came under huge pressure, and there were fears it would devalue. If it did, we wondered, where would the market strike next? Would it be sterling? The dollar was also creating great difficulties for the pound. It was continuing to weaken following the reductions in US interest rates. This was important because, despite our membership of the ERM, the high level of trade and investment between Britain and the United States meant that the markets still paid great attention to the sterling–dollar rate. When the dollar fell, sterling was vulnerable too.

As the dollar sank, money continued to leave Wall Street, pushing the deutschmark up in value. It rose further when the Bundesbank increased interest rates on 16 July. Sterling was trapped in the dollar–deutschmark crossfire. Our domestic economy required lower interest rates, but the strengthening of the deutschmark prevented this. All Europe suffered and grumbled, but the Bundesbank offered no policy change. They let the markets know there was no possibility of a cut in German interest rates; indeed, they might rise further.

The French referendum on the Maastricht Treaty, which would take place on 20 September, was also casting its shadow as opinion polls suggested that it might be lost. A defeat in France would be far more serious than that in Denmark. France was pivotal to Maastricht. If she could not ratify the treaty, it would be dead. Every government in the Community would have egg on its face, the French government would have to resign, and so might President Mitterrand. The stakes were very high.

With hindsight, it is possible to see how the factors that precipitated Black Wednesday were coming together. Our own domestic economic weakness; market turbulence worsened by political uncertainty; the fear that the Maastricht Treaty would fall if the referendum in France was lost; a weak dollar dragging down the exchange value of the pound as a strong deutschmark held up interest rates across Europe, pushed up unemployment and slowed down growth. It was a witches' brew.

On 14 July I was sufficiently alarmed to write personally to Chancellor Kohl. I had good grounds for being irritated by German policy, though my attitude was far from hostile. I was not seeking a row. I liked Kohl well enough, but he was at sea, apparently unaware of the damage being done by the Bundesbank's policy. I wrote to him because I wanted my letter to alert the German bureaucracy to the dangers that lay ahead, and to ensure that they had to address them in Helmut's reply to me. I could have phoned Kohl, but he was not comfortable with economic detail and would, I knew, have talked only in generalities.

I wrote frankly to set out my worries:

> I am very concerned about the effect of any further increase in interest rates in Europe, both on our economies and politically. In Britain there have been signs of recovery, but if interest rates are forced up again that could falter. I believe the same is true in Europe.
>
> We are also encountering resistance to the plans for economic and monetary union. The current difficulties with interest rates are being blamed on the way the ERM works, and the decision to tie ourselves to the deutschmark is increasingly being questioned, even by our supporters.
>
> I am going to have a really hard time holding backbench support for the Maastricht Treaty.

I concluded with what was to become a familiar complaint about a practice that would have a deadly outcome:

There have been a number of reports emanating from the Bundesbank to the effect that, if other countries were unhappy with the effects of maintaining their parities against the deutschmark, they could always devalue.

As you are well aware, it is the declared policy of the UK, France and Italy to sustain the present parities. It is extremely damaging, therefore, to have Bundesbank officials speculating to the press in a way which questions that commitment. I believe this has contributed to the difficulties in the foreign exchange markets. I very much hope you could indicate [to Dr Schlesinger, the President of the Bundesbank] how damaging such stories are.

Helmut Kohl would not have enjoyed receiving this letter; nor did I enjoy having to write it. I received no immediate reply, and to this day I do not know if Kohl spoke to Schlesinger. If he did, it had little effect, because Schlesinger's answer came from the barrel of a gun: two days later, the Bundesbank raised its discount rate by 0.75 per cent to 8.75 per cent, and further damaging briefings continued at regular intervals.

Schlesinger was very much a man of the old school of the Bundesbank, and much less interested than Kohl in the human politics of Europe – the French called him 'spiked helmet' because of his rigid, Prussian-esque attitudes. At a press conference he argued that the increase in interest rates was only a German domestic measure, but this facile contention was undermined when Italy increased its discount rate, the Netherlands and Belgium put up their advances rates and the Greeks postponed an expected rate cut. If it was a German domestic measure, it had a wide-ranging impact in other countries.

In late July I had a private conversation about the sterling–deutschmark relationship that was to have significant ripple effects later. I was invited by Andrew Neil, then editor of the *Sunday Times*, to dine with him at his home with a number of his colleagues. I accepted and was accompanied by Gus O'Donnell. It was end of term, not long before the summer parliamentary recess. I was relaxed and, I thought, talking off the record. I was expansive about my hopes for the government and the economy. Given the state of the markets, sterling was in the forefront of my mind. I spoke of my loathing of inflation, the persistent decline in value of our currency, and why – and how – I wished to correct it. I outlined the merits of the ERM as an anti-inflationary discipline and was lyrical about the value of a strong currency. I said that, *over time*, if we followed anti-inflationary policies I saw no reason why the pound should not be as strong as, if not stronger than, the deutschmark. I made clear – or at least I thought I had made clear – that this was a long-term ambition. I set out my wish to maintain a tough monetary policy, because of the long-term gains I felt sure it would bring. It was a convivial evening, and neither Gus nor I sensed any danger when we left to return to Number 10.

I was, therefore, startled to see the prominence with which the *Sunday Times* reported my views the following weekend, focusing in particular on my long-term ambitions for sterling in relation to the deutschmark. It was an irritation, but not a serious one, and I soon put it out of my mind. Insofar as I thought of it at all, my concern was simply that they had not put my ambitions in the correct time-frame. Bad sub-editing, Gus thought.

A few weeks later, after sterling's devaluation, the same semi-accurate story was used against me to great effect by John Smith in his first speech since succeeding Neil Kinnock as leader of the opposition. When I left office in 1997, by which time sterling had become a strong currency, the ridiculing of my ambitions for it to become so had been forgotten.

Although I intensely disliked the idea, and wished to avoid it if I could, sterling's market difficulties against the buoyant deutschmark forced me to consider a devaluation within the ERM. As a contingency measure, I had reluctantly asked Sarah Hogg for a note on this possibility as far back as the autumn of 1991. I then put it aside (without discussing the matter with Norman Lamont) as Treasury forecasts suggested sterling could trade without difficulty at its existing level. But I did not forget the possibility.

In the late afternoon of Tuesday, 28 July, the Chancellor and two senior officials from the Treasury made the short journey up Whitehall to Number 10 for a secret 'seminar on the economy', a bland title which belied the importance of the gathering, called at my request.

'I'm not looking for a standard defence of policy,' I said as we sat down. 'We have to contemplate outrageous things.' Everyone present knew well enough what I meant: staring us in the face was a tempting volte-face – to devalue the pound, either within or outside the ERM. It was a dramatic option. If we left the system it would mean retreating from the fight for a strong and stable currency, but it might allow us to cut interest rates, although it was not certain. That would help people struggling to meet their mortgage payments, and bring some life back into the economy. But it was also the 'soft option' I had warned against in 1989 when, as chancellor, I took Britain into the ERM.

I was not stubbornly opposed to a change of course if that was demonstrably the best option. But as we talked it became clear that it was not. In the midst of many arguments about the impact of such a policy change, the crucial judgement was made that a substantial devaluation, voluntarily made, would be likely to result in higher, not lower, interest rates, because the markets would lose confidence in sterling.

We could not let the value of sterling drop too far. If we withdrew from the ERM and its fall threatened to re-ignite inflation, we would have to raise interest rates, whereas we wished to cut them. This scenario of rising rates would be all the more likely if we walked away from the system without doing everything possible to remain in it.

In our discussion, I acknowledged that there were short-term competitive gains for Britain from devaluation, and that if economic output continued to slide there might be no alternative. But there were hopes that both economic recovery and cuts in German rates might be near at hand. When the meeting broke up, options had been aired, but neither Norman Lamont nor I was convinced that it would be right to devalue or to leave the system. Nor was anyone else present that afternoon. We had looked over the precipice and decided against jumping.

The situation worsened during August as the looming French referendum on Maastricht took a higher profile. Shortly before I left for a holiday, Eddie George, the Deputy Governor of the Bank of England, rang to let me know of his concern and to ask if he had my permission to raise interest rates if it became necessary. I told him that, *in extremis*, I would accept a rate rise. While I was away, Sarah Hogg minuted me with three options in the event of a French 'no' vote: to raise our interest rates; to devalue; or to leave the ERM and let sterling fend for itself. There was no easy way out.

By 21 August Norman Lamont had become sufficiently alarmed to telephone me from his holiday in Tuscany. That day eighteen central banks had tried to prop up the US dollar by concerted intervention, and had failed. It was the first big victory for the markets, and gave them a taste for blood that left them on the prowl, hunting ailing victims into which they could sink their fangs.

Speaking to me, Norman felt that the odds were against avoiding an interest rate increase. His view was that he should return from his holiday to handle what could be a crisis. 'If we go up 1 per cent now,' he warned, 'it is likely the French will have to follow.' He was concerned that a rise in French rates would weaken the chance of a 'yes' vote in the referendum on the Maastricht Treaty.

I worried, too, that a rise would further slow down recovery in Britain and drive more Conservative backbenchers into the anti-Maastricht camp, which currently numbered thirty to forty irreconcilables. Norman and I reluctantly agreed that an increase in interest rates might be necessary, but because of our concern about the weakness of our domestic economy we put in hand an assessment of the likely impact on the weak housing and construction sector.

On the Sunday following this discussion, I telephoned Terry Burns at the Treasury. I still wished to defend the value of the pound if we could. 'We have invested a lot in the ERM,' I said. 'If we devalue the first time pressure emerges, our anti-inflation policy will lose all credibility. So we must convince the Germans that if they don't move their interest rates downward, we may have to move ours up, and others will have to follow.' I noted that this would have a malign effect on the ERM and on the likelihood of carrying the Maastricht Bill.

A rise in our interest rates was a probability. The pound was still caught between the strength of the mark and the weakness of the dollar. Uncertainty was made worse because no one could disentangle the market effects of a possible 'no' vote in the French referendum, the turbulence caused by German monetary policy, or the backwash of the flow of funds from the weak dollar to the mark.

Norman Lamont began to lobby other finance ministers to persuade the Bundesbank to cut rates. With my backing, he was to pursue this effort relentlessly. On 25 August we breakfasted at Number 10 with Terry Burns, Sarah Hogg and Alex Allan, who had succeeded Andrew Turnbull as my Principal Private Secretary, and who was to be a tremendous support throughout the remaining years of the Parliament. Intelligent and likeable, Alex was from the Treasury stable, but was by no means an identikit civil servant. A fan of the Grateful Dead rock band, he had once windsurfed down the Thames, and photographs of a younger Alex with shoulder-length hair were to be found in his office. He worked the most unbelievable hours, and was universally popular as well as effective. I was lucky to have him, and blessed the fact on many occasions.

The meeting was intended to take stock and prepare for the forthcoming G4 meeting of British, French, Italian and German finance ministers in Paris, at which Norman hoped to secure a consensus on interest rates to put pressure on Germany. Over breakfast we reviewed the risks before us. It seemed likely that interest rates would rise in the UK, and thereafter in France and Italy. The impact of this could be far-reaching. In France the referendum could be lost. In the UK economic and European policy could be blown apart. Europe could be facing its worst economic crisis for many years. We refined Norman's brief with these fears in mind.

At the G4 in Paris, Norman was to get his consensus but not his rate cut: the Bundesbank were isolated but immovable. It was at this meeting that we agreed we would not leave the ERM and would not realign the value of sterling unless Germany revalued. I spoke to Helmut Kohl, and told him that Europe needed an early cut in German interest rates. In two later conversations that day I pressed Giuliano Amato, the Italian Prime Minister, to give him the same message. He agreed. I followed up my conversation with Helmut with a further letter in which I invited him to put four points to the Bundesbank Council. First, I set out the problem:

> The collapse of the dollar has pushed the deutschmark to record highs and forced up other ERM currencies too. The pound has now reached $2, an absurd level. But since the main flight has been into the deutschmark, the ERM has become stretched, with the pound, the French franc and the lira all close to the bottom of their bands.

I warned Helmut of our view that UK interest rates, which were then at 10 per cent, might have to rise to 12 per cent if Germany did not act, and that the French and Italians would have to follow suit, with serious consequences across Europe. I urged him to tell the Bundesbank Council that higher interest rates risked turning the recession into a slump; that high exchange rates were making European exports uncompetitive and enabling the USA and Japan to steal our markets; and that the result of the French referendum was at risk. (That day one French opinion poll forecast 51 per cent against the treaty.) Finally, I wrote bluntly that the choice was between a cut in interest rates in Germany and an increase in rates across all Europe.

The following morning, in an attempt to curb further turbulence, Norman issued a statement to the foreign exchange markets that we were committed to the ERM and we would neither leave it nor devalue. 'It is,' he said, 'at the centre of our policy.' He made the statement, he said, 'just in case there is a scintilla of doubt'. If there was, he now removed it. The next day, in my absence as I was chairing a conference on Yugoslavia, Norman spoke to the French Prime Minister Pierre Bérégovoy, who reported that in a meeting with François Mitterrand, Helmut Kohl had made it clear that there was no prospect of a cut in German rates.

On 28 August, I had yet another early meeting with the Chancellor. The previous day the Bank of England had not intervened in the markets. Sterling had come through unscathed; a good sign. But our long-term position still depended on a German rate cut, and I wrote for a third time to Helmut:

> I must say frankly that German reunification is at the heart of these problems ... Britain strongly supported [this] but many in Britain believe they are now having to pay a high price for it ... Against this background the attitude adopted by the Bundesbank ... is difficult to understand.

Again, I sought German action to calm the markets. Again, they declined to take it.

By early September the high levels of interest rates in Germany and referendum fears in France had brought the European monetary system to boiling point. The Treasury by now had assessed the impact on Britain of a 1 per cent rise in base rates. Mortgage rates would rise, the housing market would slide further, house prices would fall and repossessions and mortgage arrears would rise. This was bad enough. But on top of this, an interest rate rise would threaten smaller banks and possibly send one or two major building societies into loss.

On 3 September I telephoned Giuliano Amato, the Italian Prime Minister. He too was a worried man. Italy was defending the lira daily, as we were sterling, and he had got nowhere with Helmut Kohl over the impact of German policy. Like me, Giuliano was also trying to persuade the French to put pressure on Kohl (often a productive route), but as yet without success. We promised to keep in touch and to concert action amongst finance ministers at the ECOFIN meeting Norman Lamont was to chair that weekend in Bath.

The next day Norman announced that we had taken a foreign currency loan of ten billion ecus (over £7 billion) to support sterling. The markets received this news very well, and the pound rose above DM2.80, giving us some relief from speculation. It was to be fleeting. Suddenly, all the news was awful: Kenneth Baker was calling for a realignment, the United States had just cut interest rates, and the Italians, in deep trouble, had just raised them.

I spoke to Terry Burns and we speculated on the result of the French referendum. By now my preference was for a 'no' vote. 'That,' I said to Terry for the first time 'is an attractive thought.'

The Bath ECOFIN met in crisis. The convivial atmosphere created by a dinner at the Royal Crescent Hotel did not long survive the opening of the conference. Around the table there was a strong belief that Germany should revalue the deutschmark or cut interest rates, and Norman Lamont had been encouraged by a number of delegations to achieve this outcome. I spoke to him early in the morning and told him to keep the meeting running as long as it took to reach an agreement. 'The choice is between a crisis now and a slow death later,' I said. 'My inclination is to have the row now.'

Norman put his case forcefully and repeatedly, but he got nowhere, and the Germans became increasingly irritated. I was at Lord's watching the NatWest cricket final when word reached me from Norman's private secretary, Jeremy Heywood, that things were going badly wrong in Bath. Italy had led the call for German action, and Norman had stepped up the pressure. Tempers had frayed. A worried Norman was anxious to talk. Alarm bells were ringing in the Treasury; Terry Burns had abandoned his game of golf and was on his way down to Bath by car. At Number 10, Alex Allan was trying to patch together a conference call with Norman, Terry, Gus and Sarah, who was in Scotland. This was testing the famous efficiency of the Downing Street switchboard, which was having difficulty securing clear lines.

For security reasons, Terry Burns kept on the move while using his mobile, but eventually communication got so bad that I ordered him into a lay-by off the M4. Sarah was out walking with a friend, Vivien Duffield, in the Scottish hills, and had even greater difficulty getting quickly to a secure phone. Eventually she found a police post in a pre-fab, set up to cover the Queen's imminent appearance at the Braemar games. She and

Vivien were greeted with understandable scepticism – a Downing Street pass cuts little ice in the Highlands – but the police were no match for that pair, and finally agreed to connect Sarah to Number 10. She was, however, obliged to conduct her part of the conversation cheek by jowl with two constables in charge of traffic management.

In the event, it hardly mattered, since all we could do was try to calm Norman, who was clearly having a difficult time. Once Terry got to Bath, he said, he would be able to provide back-up and keep me informed. Sarah, however, has a vivid recollection of her one contribution, because of the reaction it provoked back in Braemar. 'Prime Minister,' she bawled into the crackling police phone, 'I don't think we can rely on the Germans.' The two constables, who had no idea what she was talking about but knew what was what in world affairs, responded in chorus: 'Dead right.'

As the afternoon dragged on the governors of the European central banks drew up a draft communiqué containing weak words about there being 'no case' for further German interest rate increases. Tempers rose. At one point Dr Schlesinger muttered in Bavarian, 'I think we should go now' and had to be dissuaded from walking out. Theo Waigel, the German Finance Minister, was also irritated. 'Norman,' he said, 'we are not doing this ten times.' Still Norman pressed for something more definite. After further inconclusive discussion, he called for a recess for bilateral talks. Then an embarrassing hitch cropped up: the room had been booked at seven o'clock for a private dance.

The faces of the British officials who had organised the meeting were red: they would have been redder still had it not become clear that the session was drawing to a conclusion. Unfortunately for us, the Germans were not going to give way; their stance was all the more infuriating because in private conversation over dinner that night Dr Schlesinger was to comment casually that the Bundesbank might well cut rates after all – but only if a parallel realignment could be arranged. France, determined to keep the 'franc *fort*', showed no sign of agreeing to that.

In the face of Germany's refusal to change course, the choice was between having a meeting to plan an Italian devaluation the next day or coming to an agreement that night and taking a chance with the markets. Norman Lamont discussed the alternatives with the Italians, who decided to take their chance. It did not last – they had to devalue only days later.

I was upset that the opportunity offered by the Bath summit had been missed; all the more so the following night when I heard the views of the translators at a 'EuroProm' concert at the Royal Albert Hall. Arranged to mark the beginning of the British presidency of the European Union, the concert ended with Beethoven's 9th Symphony. The 'Ode to Joy' from the symphony's final movement has been adopted as the Union's anthem, but there was little joy for me at the reception afterwards. The Germans had obviously deeply resented Norman Lamont's style of chairmanship at the Bath summit. As one of the interpreters present shook hands with me, I remarked that she must have had a busy day. Instead of the casual reply I expected, she ripped into Norman's handling of the meeting. It was, she claimed, very bad, had raised tempers, and had seemed like special pleading by Britain poorly dressed up as concern for the French. I learned that after the ECOFIN meeting the interpreters had met and talked about the performance of the various participants as though they were at a post-match assessment after a crucial cup-tie.

The suggestion that Bath was somehow thrown away by Norman over-playing his hand has been widely peddled by some of the participants in the conference. I do not think this is fair. However clumsily the meeting had been handled, it was clear that the Germans were not prepared to give way on interest rates *without a realignment, and the French were not interested in that.* Norman may have irritated his colleagues, but I do not believe he threw away any opportunity.

As I had still not received a reply to my latest letter to Helmut Kohl, I instructed our Ambassador in Bonn, Sir Christopher Mallaby – an able and experienced diplomat, well established in Germany – to ask where it was. The response from Kohl's office was very cool: the Chancellor would reply, they conceded under pressure, but my third message was 'unusual and beyond normal practice', and the answer 'would take a bit longer than usual'.

This was nonsense. I had been blunt, but the circumstances merited it, and Helmut and I knew one another well enough not to mince words. The delay was not due to Helmut, but to bureaucratic pique in the Chancellery. The reply came the next day.

It did not get us very far. Helmut wrote: 'The Bundesbank does not intend to further increase interest rates' – which was welcome as far as it went, but ignored the reality that reductions were urgently needed. He was understanding about the growing anti-European sentiment in the UK, but added revealingly: 'It will not be easy in Germany, either, to obtain the approval of Parliament . . . for the [Maastricht] Treaty. The German public is concerned that the treaty's aim of ensuring stability might not be taken equally seriously by all member states.'

At this, my ears pricked up. This was not Helmut-speak, but the authentic voice of the Bundesbank. Britain was not the target of this jibe, but because of the special circumstances of sterling, we were likely to be a victim of it. The Bundesbank did not like the idea of a single currency but feared that the politicians might force it through. If they did, the Bundesbank wanted a disinflationary Europe in which the economies of member states had been bled dry of inflation. I did not like the implications of this message at all. Helmut ended with a vigorous denial that German reunification was at the core of the problem.

I imagine the Italians would not have liked the message either, because that day they raised their interest rates to 15 per cent. Norman Lamont minuted me that evening, noting presciently that 'We shall need to keep the Italian position under very close review, as the risk of them being forced to initiate even more radical action before 20 September can't be ruled out.'

By now the French referendum was only ten days away. There was every likelihood that tensions in the markets would ease if there were a 'yes' vote, although this was not certain, and opinion polls continued to suggest the possibility of defeat. We hoped, and believed, that sterling would hang on for those few days. We were helped by public support for our membership of the ERM from Howard Davies, the Director-General of the CBI, but not by further disparaging remarks attributed to the Bundesbank. I was outraged, and Norman Lamont wrote to Dr Schlesinger.

> I was very disturbed to learn that sources at the Bundesbank were reported as saying that a devaluation of sterling was inevitable. I very much appreciate the action you took in issuing a denial. Nevertheless the incident was damaging. Regrettably this kind of report has emerged from the Bundesbank on at least two previous occasions.

Norman thus echoed my request to Helmut Kohl that the Bundesbank should be more careful.

That evening I travelled to Glasgow for a long-scheduled speech to the

Scottish CBI, at which I could not credibly avoid referring to sterling. Sarah Hogg and I sat in my hotel room agonising over what I should say. If I did not strongly support our exchange rate within the ERM, the rumour mill would grind out the message that sterling was a political risk, and the pound would be likely to fall precipitously. If, however, I supported it strongly and it still fell, I would look very foolish.

Sarah, well aware of the fragility of sterling, and with my personal interests as her main concern, urged caution. I hesitated, but concluded that I had no choice but to robustly defend the exchange rate. I took the view that if sterling were devalued it would be catastrophic anyway, and a little more egg on my face would barely be noticed. So, to Sarah's dismay, I went for broke.

I reminded the assembled businessmen that commerce and industry had been demanding two benefits from government: a stable pound and lower inflation. Before we joined the ERM, I said, inflation was 10 per cent and rising – now it was 3.7 per cent and falling; furthermore, wage increases were moderating, and the growth in underlying earnings that had so often led to inflation was down to the lowest level for a quarter of a century. It would, I continued, be madness to let our competitors steal the edge on inflation; we needed our present policies whether or not we were in the ERM. To make my anti-inflationary ambition vivid and personal, I went on: 'The soft option, the devaluer's option, the inflationary option, would be a betrayal of our future; and it is not the government's policy.'

Events were making a dissembler of me. I had been discussing suspending our membership of the ERM, but to protect against market damage I was nailing my reputation firmly to staying within the mechanism. It was an irony not lost on me as I delivered the speech.

That Sunday, 13 September, Giuliano Amato, sounding sad and depressed, telephoned me at Balmoral where Norma and I were guests of the Queen. I took the call in my bedroom at 9.45 a.m., before the Queen and her guests left for the morning service at Crathie church. As we spoke, a piper was walking up and down the lawn outside the bedroom playing a lament. At one point I could only hear Giuliano by putting a finger to one ear while holding the phone to the other.

Giuliano wanted to talk to me about a planned devaluation of the lira and parallel cut in German interest rates. I commented that the rate cut was welcome, the more so since the Bundesbank increase of 16 July had helped to cause the recent problems. He sighed and agreed, and told me that the Germans were now convinced of the need to change policy. A bit late, I thought, but welcome nonetheless. On Friday, the Italians had been told that the Germans were ready to revalue the mark and that an emergency meeting of the Bundesbank Council would cut German interest rates. Helmut Kohl had sent a personal message to Giuliano saying he was pressing for this but needed an Italian devaluation in response. As Helmut had always told me that German interest rate policy was solely a matter for the Bundesbank, I smiled somewhat wryly at this development.

Giuliano asked hopefully if sterling would be devalued too, and was disappointed when I said no, unless there was a general devaluation against the deutschmark, including the franc. The French were not prepared to contemplate this. He was disappointed: a sterling devaluation would have given him political cover in Italy.

Was this a missed opportunity? Almost certainly not, I think. It was not national pride that kept me from devaluing the pound while the franc stayed strong, but a hunch that the markets would ignore such a half-cocked move. That is indeed what happened: Italy's lone devaluation drew the predators in for the kill, and within days the lira was outside the ERM.

Later that Sunday the devaluation of the Italian lira was announced, and it became known that the Bundesbank would cut German interest rates the following day. It did, but by the most miserly amount: the internationally significant Lombard Rate was cut by only 0.25 per cent, and the discount rate by 0.5 per cent. As the first reduction for five years, it was distressingly small. Even so, this scrap was seized upon across Europe as evidence that German policy was easing. Pierre Bérégovoy, with his eyes on every vote he could get for the referendum, only a week away, said grandly that 'the spirit of Maastricht had overcome purely national considerations'.

Le Monde also attributed the German decision to reduce rates to the imminence of the referendum in its headline: 'The Bundesbank votes Maastricht.' The paper declared that the Bundesbank had been obliged to show that the ERM was not just 'a dictatorship of the mark'. It was evident that frustration at German policy was widespread. I suspected that the French had finally persuaded the Germans that the French referendum was likely to be lost without a rate cut – and with it would go the whole European Union Treaty.

327

The Bundesbank's trailing the rate cut in advance was unprecedented, and led public opinion in Germany to believe that it had given in to political pressure. Kohl's message to Amato suggested this too. 'Not so,' said Dr Schlesinger, as he attributed the decision to 'foreign currency flows' forcing the Bundesbank to buy more foreign exchange, mostly lira, under the EMS obligation. This had undermined monetary policy, he explained, and the Bundesbank had asked the Federal German government on 11 September for a realignment. European partners, he said, meaning Italy, had asked for a rate cut.

This unconvincing explanation was poorly received in Germany. At his press conference Dr Schlesinger was greeted with: 'Would you consider resigning, as the reputation of the Bundesbank has suffered' – which was not the awed respect to which the President of the Bundesbank was accustomed. Whether this unsettled him I cannot say, but only a few days later reports of thoughtless remarks he made to a newspaper were to have a dramatic effect on sterling.

Norma and I left Balmoral early on the morning of Monday, 14 September, knowing that a testing few days lay ahead. I met Norman Lamont, Terry Burns and Sarah Hogg that evening to review policy after the events of the weekend. Norman spoke first, to say he was content with remaining in the ERM even if there was a 'no' vote in France. He pointed to the benefit of staying in – low inflation – and argued that we should fight to maintain our position even if it meant interest rates had to go up. But – for the first time – he admitted we might have to reconsider if we entered 1993 without signs of an economic upturn. 'A good deal sooner than that,' I told him.

I set out my worries. 'I'm prepared to put interest rates up,' I said, 'but they might flatten the economy, and it's not clear they would help the exchange rate.' I put before the meeting the gloomy alternatives: 'That leaves us with two options: devalue or leave the ERM.' I then said that if France voted 'no' in the referendum we must tell the Germans the Maastricht Treaty was dead. À propos a 'no' vote, I also mused on the effect of a 2 per cent hike in interest rates, a possible devaluation, or leaving the ERM.

Norman thought these options were not fanciful if the referendum was lost. 'But we have made a commitment,' he added. 'Interest rates are what is needed to sustain it.' He argued that we had to be prepared to increase rates by 4 per cent, despite any 'screaming in the papers': 'Surrendering without a whimper would be very difficult. We would have to jump through hoops of fire before exit,' he concluded.

Rereading notes of our discussion, it is evident that we were preparing for a crisis but were not yet convinced it would come. Norman set out his preferred line of defence: first we would put up rates, then try to win a realignment of the exchange rate of sterling within the exchange rate system. Then, he said, 'the unthinkable has to be considered' – exit. But he hoped that would only come after 'three or four months'.

'It would be political chaos,' I said, and then added, 'But we might have to review it, although I'm not looking for exit.'

On Tuesday afternoon I heard a rumour that a German newspaper, *Handelsblatt*, was trailing an interview to be published the next day, in which Dr Schlesinger was reported as saying that 'the tensions in the ERM are not over . . . further devaluations are not excluded. There may still be pressure on other currencies.' After the Italian devaluation, and with sterling in the firing line, such views from one of the most influential central bankers in the world sent out only one message to the markets: 'Sell sterling.'

A swift and authoritative rebuttal from the Bundesbank was essential. It did not come. After repeated pressure from the Bank of England, the Bundesbank issued a weak statement which merely said: 'The text was not authorised. He did not say that and it was not what he intended to say.'

This non-denial, confusing, lukewarm and late, was worse than nothing at all. Carnage began. In New York later that evening the pound fell below its ERM floor, leaving dealers who bought sterling in New York able to make easy profits selling to the Bank of England in London at the intervention rate the following morning. This greatly weakened efforts to protect the exchange rate and cost us dear.

That evening, as I attended a long-arranged reunion with old friends from my days on Lambeth Council, my mind kept turning to what would happen overnight on the exchange market in New York. Early the next morning I found out.

Alex Allan came up to my flat at 7 a.m. It had, he said, been 'very bad', despite the Bank of England's intervention, and sterling had been widely sold. My Political Secretary Jonathan Hill, too, was an early visitor that morning. 'It'll be an interesting day,' I told him. 'Stick with me and see what happens.'

I spoke to Norman Lamont just before 9 a.m., when the London markets got into their stride, and we agreed on a strategy of further intervention, knowing that it would have to be very heavy, and with increases in interest rates if they were needed. We feared they would be.

With one eye on the value of sterling, I chaired a meeting at Admiralty House on how to respond to the result of the French referendum, due that weekend. In attendance were Douglas Hurd, Kenneth Clarke, Michael Heseltine, Richard Ryder, John Kerr, Alex Allan, Stephen Wall and Gus O'Donnell. The outcome still looked too close to call. We knew a 'no' vote would up-end policy all over Europe, but my immediate concern was the markets. Bad news filtered in, and a note of gallows humour spread into our exchanges. Nevertheless we agreed that relevant ministers would meet on Sunday evening as the French results came in to fine-tune our response. If the French said 'no', we would drop the Bill to approve the Maastricht Treaty. It would be dead. If the vote was 'yes', we would honour a promise I had given to Neil Kinnock at Prime Minister's Questions of a one-day 'Paving Debate' before reintroducing the Bill to the Commons. No one imagined the long-running parliamentary battle that was to follow this decision.

This was the first of three meetings I had that day with senior colleagues, in addition to my discussions with Norman Lamont. Some ministers were later to protest that they had 'no idea' how bad our position in the ERM had become. I find this surprising: the story had led the newspapers day after day. Now, on Black Wednesday itself, I had taken steps to ensure that senior ministers were kept informed throughout the day.

The Bank of England raised interest rates by 2 per cent at 11 a.m., while our meeting on the referendum was in progress. Neither the rise, nor their intervention on a vast scale to buy sterling, had any discernible impact on the wave of selling of the pound. Norman issued a statement that 'The government is prepared to take whatever measures are necessary to maintain sterling's parity within the ERM.' The market read the statement and ignored it. The interest rate rise became a political sensation. Fleet Street's finest rushed from the torpor of Harrogate, where they had been attending the Liberal Democrats' annual conference, back to Westminster.

At 12.45, a white-faced Norman Lamont hurried to see me at Admiralty

House, accompanied by the Governor of the Bank of England, Robin Leigh-Pemberton, his deputy Eddie George, Terry Burns and Sarah Hogg. The news was awful. 'It hasn't worked,' said a downcast Norman, referring to the interest-rate rise and the purchase of sterling by the Bank. 'They're still selling,' added Terry.

It was evident that they had been discussing our options, and Norman set them out: to carry on intervening; to raise interest rates yet further; to realign; or to suspend our membership of the ERM. None was appealing.

Norman was now in favour of a temporary suspension of sterling's membership of the ERM. He was dubious about how effective further intervention in the market would be, and cautioned that even higher interest rates would have severe economic and, for that matter, political implications. He opposed a realignment as 'embarrassing and risky'. Suspension, he felt, was the least bad option, but he emphasised that 'We would need to stress this was temporary and it was our intention to rejoin very quickly.'

I did not believe this was possible. If we left the ERM, I did not see how we could regain credibility within the system. And if we could not, there was no point in returning. I did not dwell on these thoughts, but turned to questions. Would the Germans intervene more heavily on our behalf? No, I was told, only if we repaid them. How effective would further interest rate rises be? Not very, was the advice, since they would need to be very high to compensate for a possible devaluation within days. How much would sterling fall if we left the ERM? The guess was 20 per cent. 'Realignment would be devaluation,' I concluded. 'And I'm not sure there is a rate that could be sustained. If we suspend our membership the pound will fall heavily – and why should anyone [in the markets] believe what we say ever again?'

Currency crisis notwithstanding, normal political life carried on, and I had to meet backbenchers to discuss a string of issues that mattered to them. Just after 1 o'clock, Douglas Hurd, Michael Heseltine, Kenneth Clarke and Richard Ryder returned to Number 10. I had summoned these key ministers since decisions were needed speedily and there was no time to call a full Cabinet. I told them that neither the interest rate hike nor intervention had worked, and set out the choices I had discussed with Norman. We knew that history was in the making, and the atmosphere was sombre and calm. Occasionally a wry joke would force a smile. We had all worked together for a long time, and there were no histrionics, no recriminations. We knew we had no time for consultation or reflection, just swift contributions to the decisions that had to be taken.

We considered the options. Could we get a general suspension of the ERM until the result of the French referendum was known and digested? We thought not. Could we put up overnight interest rates very steeply, as the Swedes had recently done? No – that was impractical in the absence of exchange controls and given the structure of interest rates in the UK. Could we withdraw from the ERM while trading continued for the day? Not legally.

Overwhelmed by the morning's events, Norman argued that temporary suspension was the only option he could support. Kenneth Clarke disagreed. Suspension would be a huge political reverse, he argued. Letting the pound fall like a stone would do a good deal of damage; he wanted interest rates to go up again. Michael Heseltine backed him and called for an ERM realignment. Douglas Hurd also thought this was the best option. The pros and cons were debated, and I summed up the conclusions.

We needed time to bring pressure on Germany and France to step up intervention on our behalf or to take helpful policy measures. The London market closed in two hours. The Bank of England would announce immediately that interest rates would be raised by a further 3 per cent, to 15 per cent, with the proviso that the increase would be delayed until the next morning. Norman Lamont, Robin Leigh-Pemberton and I would speak to our counterparts in the Community to see what joint action could be taken. If the announcement of the further rate rise had no effect on sterling, we would suspend our membership of the ERM later that afternoon. By the time we reassembled at 5 p.m. the die was cast.

At 2.15 p.m. I spoke to Helmut Kohl on the telephone and told him the pound would have no choice but to leave the ERM unless the European central banks either began to intervene on their own account and buy sterling or delivered a reduction of interest rates across Europe. If the pound left the ERM, I added, the French franc could be next, and the system might soon collapse entirely. Helmut promised to consult urgently and come back, though events moved faster than he did.

I also spoke to Pierre Bérégovoy, the French Prime Minister and an old finance minister colleague, who was scathing about the Schlesinger interview in *Handelsblatt*. Pierre's main preoccupation was the French referendum, now four days away; he needed market stability. He proposed either a general realignment of currencies, which would have been welcome, or that sterling should temporarily leave the system. 'These are high stakes,' he added, and asked for time to reflect. When he phoned back he had spoken to Theo Waigel, the German Finance Minister (he could not get to Helmut Kohl), and had concluded that sterling should leave the ERM as the French could not accept a realignment 'this week' – by which he meant, I assumed, before the referendum. A suspension of sterling's membership was looking ever more likely.

At 4.40 p.m. Norman and I met once more at Admiralty House. Norman reported that the further interest rate rise had made no difference: the situation was now untenable. He had received commiserations from his fellow finance ministers, but Germany had flatly refused to help. He recommended that, as required by ERM rules, we should seek a meeting of the Monetary Committee in Brussels, to be attended by our representative, Sir Nigel Wicks. Robin Leigh-Pemberton reported that, astonishingly, Dr Schlesinger had been 'unavailable' to speak to him. Nonetheless, he was certain that it would be 'impossible to find realistic terms for a realignment'. 'I know that,' I answered him. 'Bérégovoy told me so.'

It was soon agreed that if Nigel Wicks could not get a general suspension of the ERM (and we thought he could not), we would suspend our membership unilaterally. Already I was aware that this was a change of course for the long term. 'I can't see that we will be able to go back in,' I said. 'It will not be politically achievable.'

A few minutes later we were joined by Kenneth Clarke, Michael Heseltine and Douglas Hurd. Norman Lamont and Eddie George explained the situation. 'It's a pistol to our head,' was Ken's view. 'And with higher interest rates and a lower exchange rate it is a double disaster.' But he agreed we had no choice but to suspend our membership. He wanted interest rates back down immediately to 10 per cent. Norman had already agreed to reverse the second rise of the day, to 12 per cent.

Michael Heseltine endorsed Ken's case: 'We have to get the economy right,' he said. 'That is not compatible with interest rates at 10 per cent' – let alone 12 per cent. Norman Lamont did not join this rush to cut rates; he was aware that the pound was still falling off a very steep cliff, and needed a parachute.

I was sure we had to return rates to 10 per cent, but did not wish to box Norman into a decision while colleagues were present. I set out the action Nigel Wicks should take in the Monetary Committee, and made it clear that we would have to reconsider our options after the French referendum. In the meantime we needed to brief both Cabinet and Parliament.

In the early evening I sat in the Cabinet Room and spoke by phone to the Queen. I told her that at Cabinet the next morning I would recommend the recall of Parliament, but that I did not expect the government to lose a confidence vote, which would precipitate a general election. I added that I expected the markets to remain turbulent until after the French referendum, the result of which was still in doubt: a private opinion poll that day still gave the 'nos' a lead. I was, as always, frank with the Queen, and set out the extent of the reversal for the government. 'With the markets as they were,' I said, 'we could not have gone on – it would have looked like King Canute.'

At 7.30 that evening Norman announced the suspension of our membership of the ERM in a brief statement outside the Treasury, and confirmed that the interest rate rise from 12 per cent to 15 per cent would not now be implemented. I wished to reverse the first rise, too.

I went to bed half-convinced my days as prime minister were drawing to a close, and spent a fitful night as the events of the day intruded. We had suffered a great defeat, and I was not sure whether Norman and I could reconstruct economic policy. After such a setback, was it even possible (or proper) for me to stay in office? If I resigned, what would be the effect? Some would praise me for accepting the blame, others condemn me for leaving the party in the lurch.

If I went, Norman would have little choice but to go too. What would be the result of losing both the First and Second Lords of the Treasury? Would the government itself survive? How could we rebuild our economic policy? It was clearly urgent that we do so, but if I announced my resignation I would plunge the party into a leadership vacuum at a time when decisions needed taking immediately. If, on the other hand, I announced that I would resign later, when economic policy had been redesigned, I would be a lame duck whose policy writ might not run. In any event my successor might not agree with my judgements. The decision about my future went far beyond my personal feelings. Yet my own instinct was clear: I should resign. I was not sure I could ever recover politically from the devaluation of the currency. The collapse of sterling was a catastrophic defeat, and one which I felt profoundly. It had been a traumatic day that would change the perception of the government: we were never again to enjoy the same confidence as before Black Wednesday.

At 7.30 on the morning of Thursday, 17 September, Alex Allan rang Terry Burns to tell him that I wanted interest rates back at 10 per cent in time for that day's Cabinet. Two hours later I began to set the course of our future policy in a meeting with Terry Burns. When Cabinet met, Tony Newton was in New Zealand, Ian Lang in the United States and Gillian Shephard in Russia, so three strong allies were absent. Even so, a sombre Cabinet was supportive, and readily confirmed the decisions I had fore-shadowed to the Queen the previous evening. Our gloom deepened with the unemployment figures released that morning: up forty-seven thousand to 2.8 million, with few signs of a swift downturn.

The press were demanding that Norman Lamont should resign. Max Hastings, the editor of the *Daily Telegraph*, was convinced he should go. I subsequently heard of an angry conversation which had taken place between them. Up until then, Hastings had been more supportive of our middle-of-the-road European policy than some of his Euro-sceptic fellow journalists on the *Telegraph*. Press gossip was that he was given a bad time by them when the ERM imploded, and the support he had given us left him feeling exposed. He was never to make that mistake again. I felt an obligation to support Norman, and scribbled him a note telling him not to resign. He had inherited my policy and supported it so loyally that I believed I should decide my future before his was called into question.

The question of resignation continued to nag away at me. Cabinet colleagues advised against, but was that out of loyalty or conviction? I sought a dispassionate view from Stephen Wall, whom I knew well and trusted. He acknowledged the case for going, but put the other side too. Was going into the ERM a personal idiosyncrasy of mine, he asked, or was there overwhelming demand for it? Did not the City, the TUC, the CBI, the Cabinet and the party all support it at the time? Were not the opposition Labour and Liberal parties taunting us about not entering it? Were not the press also in favour? Was not sterling in trouble outside the ERM? Were not interest rates at a premium because we were expected to enter and had not done so?

All this was true, but politics has its own rules, and I was still concerned that we had gone into the ERM with me as chancellor and been forced out with me as prime minister. Nor did it alter the fact that I had considered suspending our membership of the ERM, but had decided to take no action without first trying to persuade the Germans to cut their interest rates, in order to relieve market tensions so that sterling could remain in the ERM. They had not done so, and I had not suspended membership, and catastrophe had struck. I had gambled for good and sound reasons, but I had lost. I took a bleak view of that.

That evening my sister rang (as she and my brother often did in troubled times). After asking how I was, and some typical banter – 'You seem to have the economy under fingertip control. You've just made us more competitive' – she asked what I was going to do. I told her I thought I would resign.

'That's absurd,' she said. 'You can't. If you've made a mess, clear it up. That's why you were elected.' This was typical Pat. 'You do as you think,' she summed up. 'But you shouldn't run away. You've only just been elected. What about the people who voted for you? Are they asking you to go?'

No, they were not. Douglas Hurd's view was along similar lines: 'You've only just been elected, you can't go' – a generous statement, since he must have known that had I gone he might have been the safe pair of hands that succeeded me. Norman Fowler was blunter. 'Resign? Batty.' Sarah Hogg thought resignation would be self-indulgence.

I was still unpersuaded by all these arguments, and wrote a draft speech for a resignation press conference or broadcast. I asked Stephen Wall to read it. He refused. Only after I had left Number 10 did he tell me that had he agreed, he would have been drawn into textual analysis that would have reinforced the likelihood of my going.

The weight of pressure was to stay, not to depart. I was never certain then that it was right, nor am I now. But stay I did. Some felt I was wrong. For years afterwards Simon Heffer, a fanatically anti-European journalist, continued to say that I should have resigned, and my failure to do so seemed to be the justification for his outpourings. He never knew it, but on this point I had some sympathy for his view. Others were kinder. Alan Greenspan, Chairman of the US Federal Reserve, sent friendly messages through Sir Robin Renwick, our Ambassador to Washington. With the French referendum looming, the markets were able to make a one-way bet against a date certain, he told Robin.

In meetings with Douglas Hurd and Norman Lamont we began to put together a recovery strategy. Norman agreed that there had been good reasons for remaining within the ERM, but that having suspended membership, he now felt it would not be sensible to rejoin quickly. Douglas agreed. Not quickly, and probably not ever, remained my view.

Out of the debacle some good emerged. I had considered suspending membership to bring down interest rates. Now we could. We were, said Norman, overachieving on our inflation target. I suggested a 2 per cent reduction straight away, and settled with Norman on a 1 per cent reduction within a week and a further 1 per cent soon after.

A bizarre little spat followed with the Germans. Firstly, reports attributed to them suggested I had told Helmut Kohl we would rejoin the ERM speedily – this untruth we rebutted, and I wrote to Helmut to ensure there was no misunderstanding. In fact I had no intention of returning at all unless the ERM was radically reformed to prevent a similar episode in the future, and I did not see how it could be.

Neither Norman nor I hid our dismay at how the Bundesbank had behaved, and the Treasury compiled an extensive list of its misdemeanours. Later in the month the German Ambassador, Herr von Richthofen, called on David Gillmore, the Permanent Under-Secretary at the Foreign Office, with a point-by-point rebuttal of our criticisms of Dr Schlesinger and the Bundesbank. David Gillmore was unimpressed, and sharply reminded the Ambassador that on at least one occasion, at a conference I had called on Bosnia, he had been with me when unhelpful public remarks by Hans Tietmeyer, Schlesinger's deputy at the Bundesbank, had cast doubt on sterling's position in the ERM; it had, Gillmore told the Ambassador, been heavily sold on the markets as a result, and had lost value. He then listed other transgressions.

It was an unhappy episode that spilled over into sharp words between Helmut Kohl and myself and a crisp letter from the Governor of the Bank of England to Dr Schlesinger. In it Robin Leigh-Pemberton, no doubt recalling Dr Schlesinger's unavailability on Black Wednesday, dissected the Bundesbank's defence of its actions. It was not only Norman Lamont and I who were furious at its behaviour.

As we struggled with the aftermath of sterling's exit from the ERM we were still awaiting the result of the French referendum. If it was lost, the Maastricht Treaty was dead. If it was won, we would have to enact the treaty in a far worse parliamentary atmosphere than we could have anticipated. I arrived at Admiralty House on the Sunday evening in no doubt about the size of the stakes.

Everyone present munched gloomily on the snacks provided as the votes were added up. The result looked knife-edge all evening, but our contacts in Paris seemed sublimely confident of the outcome. French predictions of the result were relayed to us hours before the count was over – which raised eyebrows on this side of the Channel. How could they know? Osmosis, no doubt. In the end the referendum was carried by the slenderest possible margin. 'They found Cook County,' was the jaundiced comment of one observer, recalling the infamous result that gave Kennedy his victory over Nixon in the 1960 US presidential race.

Though I welcomed the result publicly, I had private misgivings. I believed I had negotiated the best possible outcome for us at Maastricht, but it was always too soon for British public opinion, always a treaty too early. Having accepted the agreement and the concessions we gained, I did not believe I could opportunistically dump it; but if it had been rejected in the French referendum, I could have borne its loss with fortitude. A few French votes had saved it, but I knew we now faced an intolerably difficult parliamentary passage for the Maastricht Bill, with no certainty of success.

First I had to attend the recall of Parliament on Thursday, 24 September to debate the devaluation of sterling. The House was packed, excited and hostile as I opened the debate and faced repeated interruptions from all sides. A sharp question from Nick Budgen reminded me that many Conservative colleagues remained unreconciled to our membership of the European Union. In an attempt to head off a full-scale flight to Euro-scepticism I set out the parameters of the sort of Europe I favoured.

'There are,' I said, 'broadly three schools of thought about our membership of the Community. The first – it is spread thinly across each political party – is that we should leave the Community; that we should never have joined. It is a minority view, often disguised by rhetoric affirming support for the principles of membership while actions speak the opposite. There are people who, in their hearts, would prefer it if we were not in the Community, who trade under false colours and who do not address their arguments to the implications of non-membership for jobs, prosperity and the future.

'The second school of thought is that European development is inevitable and goes inexorably in one direction: that sooner or later a centralised Europe is inevitable. Those who take that view are often the direct descendants of those who, twenty years ago, thought that socialism was inevitable, before it became completely discredited around the world.

'The third school of thought, the one for which I stand, is quite different. It is that it is in the interests of Britain – our interests, our objectives and our prosperity – for us to be part of the development of our continent. By part, I do not mean a walk-on part; I do not mean simply being a member. I mean playing a leading role in the European Community. I mean helping to determine the direction of policy, building the policies that we want and fighting those that we do not want. We will need to compromise on some matters, but so will every national state in Europe unless we return to tribalism right across the European Community.'

My words made little difference – but John Smith's response did. It was a brilliant debating performance on his first Commons outing as leader of the opposition. Presented with an open goal, he joyfully smashed the ball into the net. I admired his oratory almost as much as his brass neck; this was, after all, the same John Smith who had repeatedly lambasted us for *not* being in the ERM, and who, when we joined, supported the conditions of entry. Now his criticism was fierce, in a riot of freewheeling hypocrisy which gave me ample evidence that here was a man of flexible opinions who would be a formidable opponent. It was a nasty and uncomfortable parliamentary occasion, but given the disaster that had overtaken us, it was hardly surprising.

Some of the press comment *was* surprising. Simon Jenkins, then a columnist on *The Times*, wrote that I had 'wobbled' on Black Wednesday, losing my nerve, and that there were rumours of a 'missing two hours' in the day. Jenkins did not check his story with me, but he is a respected journalist, and would not have invented it: someone must have fed it to him, and he must have believed it was an authoritative source. In fact it was a malicious invention and wholly untrue.

One argument that the Euro-sceptics were quick to begin floating was that Margaret Thatcher had been dragged unwillingly into the ERM by her new chancellor. Norman Tebbit, for one, advanced this somewhat flattering notion. It was, of course, an absurd statement. Margaret Thatcher had agreed to go into the ERM because she was a political realist and knew that, in the circumstances of November 1990, there was no alternative. The government was already committed, in principle, to entry when I became chancellor. No one held a pistol to Margaret's head, and the suggestion that this formidable woman was a pushover in the hands of her new chancellor was unreal. This was certainly not to be the last occasion on which Margaret's admirers tried to rewrite history. Their theme was always the same: if things had gone well, it was a result of her iron resolve. If they did not, then she had been hoodwinked.

In the days after Black Wednesday the markets turned savagely on the French franc. The Germans supported the French, and fought the speculators in a way they had not done in the case of sterling. A combination of substantial interest rate increases in France, large-scale intervention by both France and Germany, and a joint Franco–German declaration that exchange rate changes were not justified, just held the speculation at bay. The selling subsided and the central rate of the franc remained unchanged.

But within days Spain, Portugal and Ireland all reintroduced temporary exchange controls, and the following month both the peseta and the escudo were devalued. Sweden and Norway soon severed their link with the ecu. In the early months of 1993 Ireland, Spain and Portugal all devalued their currencies. The storm was spent.

We entered the ERM to general applause, and left it to general abuse. Yet membership turned Britain into a low-inflation economy. For thirty years, under every prime minister from Harold Wilson to Margaret Thatcher, inflation had drained away at intervals, only to flood back like the tide. In the autumn of 1990, before we joined the ERM, inflation was into double figures. After a year of membership, retail price inflation was less than 5 per cent; by June 1992 it was heading down still further – 4 per cent that month, and 3.5 per cent in July. We entered the ERM to curb inflation, and had done so. I was certain that it was vital to Britain's long-term future that for once we did not let it creep back.

High interest rates and a weakening economy played a part in the fall of inflation, and would have done so had we been in or out of the system. But the ERM gave credibility that our policy would otherwise have lacked. Throughout the 1980s, even when inflation went down to low levels, earnings growth never fell below 7.5 per cent. It was only in the early 1990s, when the ERM imposed a squeeze, that it fell to much lower levels. This helped inflationary pressures remain muted even when the economy started to pick up again.

Neither was the ERM always a constraint on interest rates: at 15 per cent when we joined in November 1990, they fell consistently to 10 per cent within eighteen months. It is true that they remained high, but this was not just because of the ERM, but because German rates were high *and rising*. In or out, our rate movements would have been driven by Germany's. One measure of the impact of ERM membership on interest rates – as opposed to the effect of general economic conditions – is that the long-term interest rate differential between sterling and the deutschmark fell during this time.

The ERM was far from the suffocating economic blanket caricatured by those with a political axe to grind. As a book by the respected economist Christopher Dow argued in 1998, Britain's economic troubles in the early 1990s were a result not of the ERM but 'the rebound from the previous boom psychology'. He argues that the 'collective, manic, euphoria which pushed up prices and encouraged many to go into debt left the economy exhausted'.

Our trade performance was improving before 'White Wednesday' – as the Euro-sceptics dubbed it – provided an explanation useful to their cause. We were climbing out of recession. And although the pound would have been happier at a moderately lower rate against an abnormally buoyant deutschmark, those who argue it was grossly overvalued should look at its long-term rate after exit from the ERM. As I write, one pound sterling buys DM3.126, a fraction *above* our ERM ceiling.

After we left the ERM, what Norman Lamont called our 'overperformance' on inflation enabled us to cut interest rates speedily, and we were to enjoy seven years of growth without wage- or price-inflation difficulties. This was unprecedented in recent years, and the ERM deserves much of the credit. It hurt, but it worked.

The ERM was the medicine to cure the ailment, but it was not the ailment – and no amount of rewriting history can honestly make it so.

# CHAPTER FIFTEEN

# The 'Bastards'

L ATE ON THE AFTERNOON of Friday, 23 July 1993, I sat in the White Drawing Room on the first floor of 10 Downing Street, utterly exhausted and drained of all energy. I had barely slept since Tuesday night, and in the intervening sixty hours I had come through one of the most dramatic parliamentary episodes this century. At the end of it, the Maastricht Treaty had been ratified after a year of gruesome trench warfare in the Commons, but only by the narrowest and most nerve-shattering of margins.

The night before, two unruly parliamentary votes had taken the government to the brink of collapse. The first, on a Labour wrecking motion to block the treaty, had been tied, an unheard-of outcome on so vital an issue. The second brought an eight-vote defeat for the government, thus preventing us from ratifying a treaty which I had negotiated and which Parliament had previously agreed with massive majorities. It was an absurd situation, brought about by a large number of rebellious Tories, and to resolve it I had tabled an emergency Motion of Confidence in the government. I made it clear that if we were defeated through another rebellion, I would seek a dissolution of Parliament and an immediate general election. For any prime minister, it was the ultimate gamble.

I had been trapped by an unholy alliance of Conservatives determined to kill the agreement I had reached at Maastricht, and an opposition that had supported the negotiation but was keen to destroy the government. Throughout the long saga, Tory rebels had obtained the tolerance, and in some cases the active support, of their local constituencies by telling them that they were acting out of conviction and principle. I now offered them a new principle – to support the policy upon which they had been elected, or to defend their seats in a new election.

When the result of the Confidence vote was read out the next day by

Madam Speaker we had won by thirty-nine votes. The defeat of the day before had been reversed. After thirteen months, the battle of Maastricht was won – although the war over European policy was not over.

Elated at the outcome of the Confidence Motion, I gave back-to-back interviews to radio and television journalists in Number 10, the last of which was with the seasoned Political Editor of ITN, Michael Brunson. The interview over, we sat chatting whilst the technicians cleared away their equipment. The cameras were off, but a 'feed' cable which had carried an earlier interview I had given to the BBC was still switched on, although neither Brunson nor I was aware of this as we ruminated on the current state of the Conservative Party.

Brunson suggested to me that three Cabinet ministers had threatened to resign over our European policy. I said: 'Just think it through from my perspective. You are the prime minister, with a majority of eighteen, a party that is still harking back to the golden age that never was and is now invented. I could bring in other people. But where do you think most of this poison is coming from? From the dispossessed and the never-possessed. You and I can think of ex-ministers who are causing all sorts of trouble. Do we want three more of the bastards out there?'

All this was piped to studios in Millbank, near the Palace of Westminster, and was soon common knowledge. It was careless of me to have spoken to Brunson so freely. In response to his questions I should simply have told him, 'No one has threatened to resign,' and left it at that. But months of posturing and off-the-record briefing from the sceptics had built up a frustration that encouraged me to be too frank. Even a prime minister can only bite his lip for so long.

The media were swift to assert that the three Cabinet ministers to whom I had apparently referred were the Euro-sceptic trio of Peter Lilley, John Redwood and Michael Portillo. The fact that they did so unanimously suggested that they knew something of those ministers' intentions that I did not. It was an open secret that unnamed ministers, their 'friends' and their advisers talked to the media in private about their dislike of the Maastricht legislation, but no minister had come to me and threatened to resign over it. Rereading the exchange with Brunson, it is easy to see why it was assumed that I was referring to existing Cabinet ministers. In fact I was not. Exhausted as I was, my words and my meaning became disconnected. Insofar as I had anyone in mind, it was former ministers who had left the government and begun to create havoc with their anti-European activities, given free reign by their release from collective responsibility.

It was an unhappy episode, and fuelled the resentment of some of the sceptics over the loss of a battle that had brought them to the verge of triumph and then to a very public defeat. It switched attention away from their failure and towards my attitude to them, and it reduced the chances of a much-needed reconciliation across the party. I have only myself to blame for that. But in itself the comment was merely a slip, not a calamity. It was one of the hiccoughs of government that are soon forgotten, and this it would have remained had some of the rebels not chosen to take affront at my words to suit their own ends. They saw my criticism of their activities as a badge of courage, and as confirmation that for me the conflict was personal. It was not, but for some of them it soon became so.

What had brought us to this state? The trigger had been the legislation to enact the Treaty on European Union that I had agreed at Maastricht in December 1991. But the genesis of the divisions within the Conservative Party went back much further.

Some in the party had never been at ease with Europe. When the Common Market was founded in 1957, Tory imperial tradition ensured that we kept 'clear blue water' between Britain and our neighbours. We stayed out. Ted Heath led a partial change of mood in the 1960s, heading negotiations about entry, but de Gaulle's peremptory 'non' to the then Prime Minister, Harold Macmillan, in 1963 showed a hostility to our membership on the other side of the Channel that was mirrored at home by many Conservatives, whose allegiance lay across the Atlantic or with the Commonwealth.

Battle lines in the Conservative Party were drawn up as the Common Market grew. They deepened when Ted Heath negotiated our entry to it in 1971. Both major parties were split as the legislation made its painful way through Parliament, but although opposition to entry was widespread and led to much friction, there was little of the bitterness that was to so disfigure debate in the 1990s. It is an irony that many of those who would fight the Maastricht Treaty with an almost religious fervour had welcomed entry to the Community many years before. The Bunteresque Alistair McAlpine, by 1997 one of the godfathers of James Goldsmith's Referendum Party, wholly antagonistic to Europe, helped bring about the 'yes' vote in the 1975 referendum on membership (as did Goldsmith himself). John

Wilkinson, one of those backbenchers whose Euro-scepticism alone gave him parliamentary significance, was once a straight-down-the-line supporter of Edward Heath, convinced that our destiny lay in European integration. The historian and thinker, the late Max Beloff, who went so far as to publish a book denouncing Maastricht, had advocated a 'European Federal system' not two decades before in a different work. They were not alone in their startling about-turns.

Nor was this irony confined to minor figures. Far greater players were involved. Margaret Thatcher, whose later enmity towards all things European became astonishing to behold, unwittingly brought European union closer by her own actions as prime minister. In the 1980s she pushed for a truly free market for goods and services across Europe, a development which was keenly supported by European bureaucrats, but loathed by more protectionist voices across what was known at that time as the European Community. Undeterred, she pressed on with her unlikely allies, determined to win in what was a good cause. And win she did – at a price. For in the Single European Act of 1985 she conceded the most dramatic advance of decision-making by majority voting – in essence a partial surrender of our sovereignty of decision-making in return for a share of pooled sovereignty – that had been seen since the Community was launched. Returning from her negotiations, she commended the agreement she had reached in warm terms, and it passed through the Commons without difficulty and in only a few days. John Biffen, a long-standing opponent of the European Community but at that time in the Cabinet as leader of the House, introduced a 'guillotine' motion to restrict the time for debate and bring the legislation into law more speedily.

The Single European Act whetted the Continental appetite for communal decision-making and fed the ambitions of the Commission. It even contained the first formal treaty reference to economic and monetary union, gave force to the argument that a single currency was needed in the single market, and strengthened the case for the further harmonisation of policy. The wind was in the sails of the federalists. In later years, as she opposed the logical extension of the changes she had set in train, Margaret Thatcher must surely have often reflected in private how much her success over the single market had accelerated them.

This was the background to the Treaty of European Union, agreed at Maastricht and already far developed when I became prime minister (see

Chapter 12). The negotiation was tough, and many unappealing notions were beaten off. I expressly excluded Britain from a commitment to enter the single currency and from social agreements that, as a result, were excluded entirely from the treaty (though agreed by our partners outside it). This outcome was greeted with acclaim in Commons debates, above all by many Tory MPs who after the election voted against the treaty night after night. Only a small number of long-standing Euro-sceptics remained unimpressed and hostile. At the time they were barely noticed, and were dismissed as irrelevant even by those who would soon be their allies. The treaty was signed for Britain in February 1992 by Norman Lamont, the Chancellor, and Francis Maude, deputising for the Foreign Secretary. Both acclaimed the agreement. Francis would later produce the fountain pen he had signed it with and wave it aloft proudly.

Now began our tortured efforts to gain parliamentary approval for what I had negotiated. In January 1992 we were within three months of a general election and I decided to wait until it was over before introducing the legislation to bring the agreement into law. In retrospect, many were critical of this delay, although none expressed their misgivings at the time. Certainly trying to rush the Bill through Parliament might have avoided the worst excesses of what was to follow, but there were serious impediments to doing so. First, the legislation was not drafted. Second, introducing it early would have meant abandoning a score of other Bills nearing completion. Third, even if we had sacrificed other Bills, we could have run out of time and gone into the election with ratification unfinished, which would have meant starting again from scratch afterwards. Nor did there seem any particular need for haste. The negotiations had been so well received across the House that ratification after the election appeared to present few obstacles.

When the newly elected Parliament assembled in May 1992, that still seemed to be the case. The agreement commanded a great majority on all sides of the Commons, and within the parliamentary Conservative Party. Some MPs who later became rebels, such as the veteran Sir Trevor Skeet, had gone out of their way to praise the Maastricht Treaty in their election addresses. But an all-important change had taken place: the government's majority had fallen to twenty-one – and there were many more than twenty-one sceptics on the Tory benches.

I had realised the dangers. The warning signs had been there: in 1991

Norman Fowler had narrowly defeated Bill Cash, MP for Stafford and one of the most intemperate opponents of anything to do with Europe, for the chairmanship of the backbench European Committee. Cash received ninety votes. And before the election Richard Ryder and I had concluded that the fifty or so Members retiring from the House in 1992 were overwhelmingly loyalist or pro-European, whereas many of their younger successors in safe seats would take an opposite view. In fact the composition of the parliamentary party had changed between 1979 and 1992. The older county and aldermanic guard, steady under fire and largely without ministerial ambitions, were replaced by a breed of professional politicians who, as ideologues, did not seem to realise that the Tory Party's survival and success had always depended upon institutional self-discipline.

Most of the newcomers wanted, and in some cases expected, to become ministers within months of arriving at Westminster. Four of the 1992 intake met the Chief Whip in 1993 to ask when they would be made ministers – unthinkable behaviour in previous generations.

Faction, too, had been encouraged during the 1980s, and ministers were supported or destroyed by them. Backbench officers were elected by factions. Ministerial jobs were demanded by factions. The Tory Party had begun to imitate the structural defects of old Labour, and was to pay the ultimate political price for it.

> As we wax hot in faction,
> In battle we wax cold,
> Wherefore men fight not as they fought
> In the brave days of old.

Macaulay, of course: *Lays of Ancient Rome*. His words were to be apt as new Members soon made clear that they were prepared to oppose both the treaty and the prime minister who had agreed it. They were, as Alan Duncan, one of their number, put it, 'combat trained', and they began to exercise their martial pretensions soon enough.

Even so, soon after the election, the Maastricht Bill sailed comfortably through its first and second readings. Then all hell broke loose. In a referendum on 2 June 1992, the Danish electorate narrowly rejected their government's agreement at Maastricht. This meant that the treaty could not come into force anywhere in Europe unless either the Danes changed their minds, or fresh agreements were reached among other member states. Either or both of these eventualities were possible, and, as will be seen, our future policy would hinge on their likelihood.

The result of the Danish referendum was ill fortune with a double vengeance for me, since it came as Britain was about to undertake the presidency of the Council of Ministers of the European Community, and the problem of rescuing the treaty was dumped in my lap. In Parliament, the Bill enacting the legislation was due to enter detailed consideration in committee the very next day.

Not since the heyday of the Vikings had the Danes precipitated such disruption. At such moments, the ordered calm of international diplomacy falls apart. We needed to know the Danish government's intentions before we could decide how to proceed ourselves, but this proved impossible. We could not get hold of either the Danish prime minister or foreign minister; presumably they were coping with the aftermath too.

Douglas Hurd, together with Richard Ryder and several of his colleagues in the Whips' Office, joined me in a discussion about whether it would be wise to begin the committee stage the next morning. We decided that we should go ahead, but the mood was gloomy. 'We'll get the Bill if we push it hard,' said Richard Ryder in answer to my question. 'But there'll be blood all over the floor.' Douglas Hurd agreed to be interviewed early the next day on BBC Radio 4's *Today* programme to make our position clear.

The whips marched from Number 10 down the corridor to their lair at Number 12 Downing Street pondering this conclusion. On the way they passed Number 11, where (it was said later) Norman Lamont had reacted rather differently to the Danish rejection of Maastricht. The vote, he thought, was a 'much better' result than our election victory months before. Such qualms had not been on display when he sat beside me as we negotiated at Maastricht. Nor did he express that view at the time.

David Davis, the European Whip, sharp and combative, was keen to press on. So was Tristan Garel-Jones, the Minister for Europe at the Foreign Office. Richard Ryder and I were uneasy with this. We felt that the legislative programme would be clogged up as the Euro-sceptics were joined by other colleagues, unwilling to endure a long and aggressive fight on the floor of the Commons for the sake of a treaty that might be dropped completely if the Danes, or the French after their own referendum, could not ratify it.

Upon further consideration the whips came down against going ahead with the committee stage of the Bill. I was contacted, agreed with the reassessment, and asked the whips to inform the Cabinet of the decision. Douglas Hurd used his *Today* slot to announce that the committee stage would now be delayed until the Danish government's intentions were apparent.

Was this right? I shall never be certain – a strong case can be made either way. If we had ploughed ahead we might have got the legislation through, carried by the impetus of the first and second readings. But it would have been a risky undertaking, with the certainty that Labour would have used the Danish vote as an excuse for mischievous opposition. Had this proved the case – and their later behaviour suggests that it would have done – then the Bill could have been seriously delayed at best, or lost at worst. It is certainly true that I would have been able to get it through speedily only with Labour and Liberal Democrat support. I thought it right, therefore, not to enter into a battle which would be divisive and might prove unnecessary, but instead to wait until the Danish position was clearer. Moreover, I was conscious of the immense antagonisms in the party over Europe, and was keen not to reignite them prematurely. That could only have laid me open to a charge of provocation and been used to justify even more virulent opposition.

In any event, the decision to delay was taken, and with it the legislation was kicked into the long grass. It was not to be revived until the year was nearly out, and in the interim the virus of Euro-scepticism infected much fresh tissue. The symptoms were apparent. The day after the Danish referendum a former minister, Michael Spicer, the MP for Worcestershire East, sounded out a number of backbenchers, including new boys like Nirj Deva, John Whittingdale and Michael Fabricant, about an Early Day Motion calling, in effect, for a new approach to Europe. Michael Spicer then tabled it, and Bill Cash ranged around the Commons telling MPs, 'Number 10 wants you to sign this.' I cannot imagine why he would have thought this, but, perhaps in part believing that they were being helpful, sixty-nine MPs – more than a third of Conservative backbenchers – did so.

Early Day Motions are often the parliamentary equivalent of graffiti, and the whips are generally unmoved by them. But not by this one. They knew its capacity for damage the moment they saw it. 'Perhaps you ought to know I've just signed the EDM,' one up-and-coming MP cheerfully told his whip that day, no doubt expecting to be thanked for his support.

'Oh, really?' he was told acidly. 'You know what EDM stands for, don't you?'

'No,' said the MP.

The Whip answered his own question: 'Extremely Dim Members.' The MP retreated abashed.

In the division lobbies, the whips set to work to undo the harm. David Lightbown, burly and gruff, with an abrasive style that hid a gentle and kind nature, approached one new Member, still wet behind the ears as to parliamentary ways. 'Take your bloody name off the EDM!' he growled. 'You have just blown your career.' Old hands knew that this was just David's style – the new boys did not.

But a fierce tongue was not going to be of much help when it came to sorting out Maastricht. A short time before, only twenty-two Tories had voted against the second reading of the Bill; now sixty-nine had signed the EDM.

Another difference soon became clear. Previously, a handful of sceptics had opposed Margaret Thatcher, which had hardly dented her large majority. Now the newly-ennobled Baroness Thatcher was at their side, and so were other recently retired members of her government in both the Lords and the Commons. Norman (now Lord) Tebbit worked openly to stoke the flames of rebellion, and – ever-sensitive to a changing wind – Kenneth Baker, who had warmly supported the Maastricht outcome in Cabinet and Parliament, called from the backbenches for the government to 'think again', predicting that the Bill would be defeated.

Shortly after the Danish vote Margaret Thatcher began urging Conservative backbenchers to oppose the government and defeat the treaty. Gerald Howarth, a former Member who had served as Margaret's parliamentary private secretary and was still close to her, telephoned new Members on her behalf, inviting them to meet her so that she could persuade them to vote against Maastricht.

It was a unique occurrence in our party's history: a former prime minister openly encouraging backbenchers in her own party, many of whom revered her, to overturn the policy of her successor – a policy that had been a manifesto commitment in an election held less than six months before. It was Margaret's support for the defeat of the Maastricht legislation which helped to turn a difficult task for our whips into an almost impossible one. Beyond this, she began to cast around to see how the party could be moved to a more Euro-sceptic position. By the early autumn of 1993 she was telling friends that she hoped for a leadership contest a year before the next general election, and for Michael Portillo to win it.

At Prime Minister's Questions on 3 June Neil Kinnock asked me if I agreed 'that the House should debate a report [on the implications of the previous day's Danish referendum] before any further progress on the Bill is sought'? This led to what became known as a 'Paving Debate'. Though it was not strictly necessary according to parliamentary practice, I thought it right to offer an opportunity for legitimate concerns to be raised in Parliament. It would tug the starter cord and send the legislation chugging into life once more after a significant pause. I might not have made the offer had I known of the political and economic neutron bomb that was primed to explode in the shape of Black Wednesday.

In the late summer of 1992, 10 Downing Street was out of action, under repair after the IRA bomb the year before, so I met the whips responsible for recommencing consideration of the Bill in the Cobra Room, a cold, neon-lit briefing room under Downing Street. Both Richard Ryder and David Davis speculated on the merits of allowing a free vote on the legislation – that is, one not constrained by the party whip.

Although they were attracted to this idea, I disagreed. An unwhipped Bill would have maximised dissent in the Conservative Party, and encouraged doubters to crawl out of the woodwork; perhaps half the backbench parliamentary party would have been tempted to vote against. We would have been forced to rely on the doubtful support of the opposition to pass a vital piece of legislation. These were strong arguments, but the reason I rejected not whipping the legislation was on the point of principle that 'we agreed this as a government and we must deliver it as a government.' I wanted no backsliding. A Conservative government had agreed the treaty, after consulting the Commons about our negotiating posture, and had had their policy endorsed by the electorate. The Conservative Party in Parliament had an obligation to deliver it – or we had no place in government.

'What do you think about that?' David Davis asked James Arbuthnot, an assistant whip, as they left the meeting. They both knew that by whipping the Bill I was tying my fate to that of the legislation. If it fell, so would I.

'Impressive but terrifying,' James replied.

On Black Wednesday, 16 September 1992, the pound fell out of the

ERM in a very public catastrophe (see Chapter 14). From then on, disputes within the Conservative Party over Britain's role in Europe dominated the political agenda. The true opportunities and challenges offered by our membership of the European Union were never fairly reflected in the rage. Analysis was cast aside in favour of emotion. Europe was either 'good' or 'bad'. To be Euro-phobe or Euro-phile – 'one of us' or 'one of them' – became the ludicrous, oversimplified test. Divisions in the party were prised open; fissures became chasms; factions became entrenched.

Black Wednesday turned a quarter of a century of unease into a flat rejection of any wider involvement in Europe. Many Conservatives threw logic to one side; emotional rivers burst their banks. For a few of my parliamentary colleagues, Black Wednesday awoke the instincts that turn a profound love of one's own country into a nationalism or insularity that encompasses a distaste for any other. In short, a small minority became not only pro-British, but anti-foreign. For those like me who believed in a tolerant, pragmatic, outward-looking Conservatism, the transformation was deeply disturbing.

Most Conservative MPs thought likewise. The hard core of rebels barely reached forty, and there were just over fifty in all who spoke out – though many others wished them well but stayed silent. The tag 'Euro-sceptic' became common currency at this time, but it implies considerably more homogeneity than the rebels possessed. About fifty Members floated in and out of rebellion on different issues and at different times. Some voiced genuine fears about the Maastricht Treaty, others used it as a cover for their wider hostility to British membership of the Community. A few cared less about Europe than about removing me from office, and revelled in the publicity their rebellion gained them. Some were almost unbalanced on the subject of Europe, and saw it only as a threat. Many more felt deeply uneasy about the impact of what they were doing to the government and the party. A few of the sceptics were resentful that their talents had not been recognised – although in some cases one would have needed a long telescope. Others felt bitter about the way in which their ministerial careers had been brought to what they regarded as a premature close. But all the rebels were united by the fact that our diminutive parliamentary majority meant that, whatever they thought and whoever they were, they mattered when it came to getting legislation through the House. In effect they had an armlock on the government.

The rebels also had ample finance – much of it coming from the Euro-phobic billionaire Sir James Goldsmith, although other sources doubtless existed. Their headquarters in Great College Street, Westminster, was one of the homes of Alistair McAlpine, the former treasurer of the party who was now thoroughly alienated from it. To many who knew him McAlpine was a jovial, popular fellow, but in my presence he was taciturn and uncommunicative, and ultimately he became an adversary. His involvement with the sceptics was curious. In 1993 he was to be heard suggesting that Kenneth Clarke ought to be the party leader. In 1994, his affections had settled on Michael Heseltine. Both Ken and Michael were more enthusiastic about European integration than I was, but this did not stop McAlpine, before the 1997 election and with much trumpeting, leaving the Conservative fold for Goldsmith's ultra-sceptic Referendum Party.

In the engine room of parliamentary opposition to the treaty was Bill Cash, who voted against the government's three-line whip more times than any other sceptic, though this did not stop him assuring people that he was 'in constant touch' with both myself and the Foreign Secretary. From information filtering through to me, I gathered that he seemed to believe I wanted him to keep up the rebellion so that we could 'put pressure' on the European Union to change course. If he did think this, he was mistaken.

Cash did not seem to realise the damage he was doing, and did, I think, genuinely believe that all we had to do was cast ourselves in opposition to Europe for the country to rally behind us. A studious lawyer, and an obsessive on the subject of Europe, Cash could recite long passages from the Maastricht Treaty from memory. He was descended from the nineteenth-century English liberal radical John Bright, and was proud of this ancestry: he would often assert that he did not share the right-wing heritage of many other rebels.

In 1997, after it was all over, and we had lost the election, I came across Bill one night in the Commons and offered him a drink. He accepted, and had the grace to chuckle as I ordered him a 'double hemlock'. We went on to talk amiably enough about cricket; for this, if not for many other things, we had a shared enthusiasm.

Teresa Gorman was another high-profile rebel. I remember asking her to see me one evening before a tight vote in the Commons. She came in and sat down. 'Now, Teresa,' I began, 'you can do something for me you have rarely done before. It's not going to be too difficult – and you might even enjoy it.' Her eyes widened. 'You can vote for the government,' I finished.

But she didn't that night, just as she didn't on many other occasions. Warm, volatile, sharp-witted and attention-seeking, Teresa was unusual among the Euro-sceptics for not taking herself entirely seriously. She once enraged a taciturn whip, responsible for allocating Commons offices, by singing 'You're the Tops' down the phone to him after he had found her a well-situated office. She too would have liked to have been a minister, and was open about it – but she was too much of a maverick.

Teresa was no fool, and she could be perceptive. 'We all laugh, but she has a point,' I remember saying one evening, watching her in a television interview as she rattled on yet again about the 'British interest' in Europe. The trouble was that, like many sceptics, she did not realise that the public was less concerned about Europe than she was, and that the constant impression of division damaged us hugely.

The machinations of the rebels were managed by James Cran and Christopher Gill, who became the sceptics' 'whips'. Gill was a former meat dealer from Shropshire, who became an MP late-ish in life. With no hope of office, he was unbiddable, and the hardest of hard-liners over Europe. 'Don't ever underestimate him,' was one weary whip's view. 'He has the cunning of a fox.'

I was sorry to see Gill's fellow rebel 'whip', James Cran, engaged in the battle against the government. He was a talented newcomer, and capable, as some were not, of putting the whole subject in context. By the end of the rebellion he came round to supporting the government, on the sensible grounds that while Maastricht was worth a battle, it did not justify a war. He has, I hope, a good career ahead of him.

We were fortunate that neither Gill nor Cran had served in the Whips' Office, since, without the skills of true whips, they missed many opportunities to defeat us: the tactics of Labour and the Liberal Democrats in voting against their beliefs often left us in a minority, but we rarely lost votes. Where the sceptic whips were successful was in keeping the rebels together and 'recapturing' colleagues who showed signs of voting for the Bill.

Michael Spicer, the originator of the Early Day Motion the day after the Danish referendum vote, remained one of the guiding spirits behind the rebels – although he also kept cordial contacts with the government whips throughout. Nevertheless, being whips, as a precaution they took his words with a barrowload of salt. Michael was amiable whenever we met, but rumour in the parliamentary ether was that he was among the most hard-line of rebels. It had been a long journey from his early days as a member of Pressure for Economic and Social Toryism (PEST), the left-wing Tory pressure group.

Brutish and blond, Tony Marlow was one of the most aggressive of the sceptics, a bull-necked MP known to colleagues – and the press – as 'Tony Von Marloff'. He was cheerfully destructive, without malice, but completely careless of the consequences of his actions. When the treaty was finally ratified after six months of needless bloodletting, he smiled and shook the hand of David Davis, the government whip who had taken the Bill through. Doubtless he already had his mind on his next rebellion.

John Wilkinson, who shared Marlow's distaste for Europe, was a courteous, well-mannered ex-RAF officer, who spoke like the defence minister he had hoped to become. He too had travelled the long road from passionate European to intense sceptic and, more than many others, nursed a bitter belief that the Conservative Party had betrayed Britain's sovereignty.

The longer-serving, more thoughtful rebel MPs opposed the treaty for many different reasons. Richard Body was a Quaker from what in some ways was a liberal tradition. Quirky – an early environmentalist and 'small-is-beautiful' campaigner – Body despised office and distrusted the big battalions – Brussels being his particular shibboleth. When the Conservative whip was taken away from a number of rebels in November 1994, Body voluntarily joined them. A comment I made of him in an unguarded moment was to become celebrated – at the mention of his name, I said, 'I hear the sound of white coats flapping'. In fact I was referring to his idiosyncrasy, not questioning his sanity.

Richard Body once said publicly that he had been cajoled into supporting the government on a vote after a call from the Prime Minister. I was puzzled by this, since I had not made any such call. He had, we found out, been duped by the TV impressionist Rory Bremner. When Sir Robin Butler, the Cabinet Secretary, told Body he had been taken in he refused to believe it at first; but eventually he was forced to accept it. Other MPs were not fooled. John Carlisle, another anti-European who often caused trouble, had a similar phoney call, but he smelled a rat and spoke to the whips. Whether

Bremner was the only impersonator to trick MPs I do not know, but his antics confused my staff at the time.

Richard Shepherd was a parliamentary romantic and, like a curiously large number of sceptics, sat for a West Midlands seat. Intense, idealistic and emotional, he was perhaps the best of them all, a loner, a conviction politician and not a plotter. He took brave stands on many civil liberties issues, and opposed the European Union because he saw it as a threat to British rights. Shepherd spoke with emotion in the Commons, and there was often a break in his voice. Nor did he view pro-Europeans with suspicion. He was, for example, close to Robert Rhodes-James, a parliamentary neighbour whose views on Europe were far removed from his.

The former Cabinet minister John Biffen was also a long-serving West Midlands MP, and like Richard Shepherd he was noteworthy for much more than his hostility to the drawing together of Europe. Bookish, thoughtful and in some ways liberal-minded, Biffen was uncharacteristically tolerant for a sceptic, and had disappointed Margaret Thatcher by thinking for himself. He was a constitutionalist, not an ideologue, and not a natural joiner of gangs. He offered heavyweight support to the sceptic cause, and was joined in that by Peter Tapsell, a formidable parliamentarian who was, on most issues, to the left of the party. I was an admirer of Peter, who could have made an excellent minister but somehow failed to enjoy the high office his talents deserved. He had a lofty disdain for many of the rebels with whom he found himself associating. I tried to detach him from them, but he held his ground.

Enoch Powell's successor in Wolverhampton North-West was Nicholas Budgen, a dry, short and cheerfully miserly, holes-in-his-socks barrister, a specialist in mischief. Budgen was a keen rider to hounds and defender of English traditions. You never quite knew where you were with him. He adopted Wolverhampton right-wingery as a sort of Powellite intellectual challenge. Secretly tolerant, he affected to be cynical – as when he tried to make an issue of immigration shortly before the 1997 election, although it failed to save his seat.

Some of Budgen's traits could also be found in George Gardiner, a former chairman of the parliamentary 92 Group, which embraced a wide swathe of right-wing opinion. George always puzzled me – he was so convoluted he could have featured in a book of knots. He saw himself as a Thatcher loyalist, but he was one that Margaret was never keen to promote. When new Members arrived in the Commons he would test their ideological mettle and, if he deemed them sound, drag them into his cabals – for them an experience like a brush with the angel of death. He was an instinctive plotter, organising the 'ticket' of right-wing candidates before elections to backbench committees. He thrived on rebellion, and was very good at encouraging it. When he was elected to the chairmanship of the 92 Group he used his position for relentless self-promotion. He would write to me demanding meetings to present the views of the Group, which, when I heard them, bore a startling resemblance to those he held himself. These meetings were invariably preceded by briefings to the press that he was going to see the PM to 'express dissatisfaction', or 'press for a change of course', or 'call for leadership'. He was keen to tell me which ministers should be sacked as incompetent or ideologically unsound and, being well prepared, he naturally had suitable candidates in mind from the right wing of the party to replace them. Once he overreached his leaking to such an extent that I dismissed him from my office in thirty seconds, and had the press briefed about what had happened. Even his friends were delighted by the incident, one of George's better contributions to the joy of the Commons. Shortly before the 1997 election George's Reigate constituency party decided not to select him as their candidate. He resigned the Conservative whip, sat briefly as a Referendum Party MP, and unsuccessfully contested the election in that capacity. The Conservative Party was able to bear his departure with fortitude.

Teddy Taylor was a long-standing, convinced sceptic on the subject of Europe, a sparky Scot who had opposed Edward Heath when Britain went into the Community, and who in due course joined Margaret Thatcher's Shadow Cabinet. He was merciless in his opposition to Maastricht, and would happily admit to being a fanatic about Europe. He became a fixture on the media during the passage of the treaty legislation.

Teddy entered Parliament in 1964 as Member for Glasgow Cathcart, before losing his seat in 1979 and moving south in search of a safer constituency. I had once sat with him over breakfast, and he had told me that he'd received a pile of letters begging him to stand for Glasgow once more. 'Were they all from Southend?' I enquired. It was a playful tease, but a gossip who had been seated at the table retold the story, and Teddy was terribly upset when it became public. But not half as upset as he was to become about Maastricht.

The Wintertons – Nicholas and Ann – sat for adjoining seats in Cheshire. Nicholas, the more long-serving of the two, was noisy and persistent and ideologically all over the place. Good-hearted, conceited and pink-faced when he perorated, which was often, if Nick had formed a government on his own he would have had to splinter off as a maverick against himself. He was devoted to his constituency and was an excellent local Member, enjoying support even from those who disagreed with his views. He was an engaging companion and a thoroughgoing parliamentarian, and among the best of the populists in the party.

In 1992 all these veteran anti-Europeans were joined by many new Conservative MPs. Chief among the rebels in the '92 intake were two able Members, Iain Duncan Smith and Bernard Jenkin. Iain was Norman Tebbit's successor as MP for Chingford. He was sharp-toothed and bright-eyed, with a keen prosecuting intellect and a strong right-wing ideology. He was also fiercely ambitious, and a busy operator behind the scenes. With Bernard, he was active in putting pressure on new Members to vote against the government. The son of Patrick Jenkin, a respected former MP and Cabinet minister, Bernard Jenkin was just as ambitious as Iain Duncan Smith, and was an ally of Michael Portillo. Sometimes engaging – in private he was a skilled mimic of Margaret Thatcher and, I am told, of me – he was one of the sceptics who tumbled into the anti-European cause, rather than lived and breathed it. Had he been given a government job early on, he could equally have been a loyalist.

In their march to defeat the innocuously-named European Communities (Amendment) Bill, such rebels did not journey alone. Pursuing a campaign which had echoes of Lord Beaverbrook's call for 'Empire Free Trade' in the *Daily Express* before World War II, a number of newspapers cast objectivity aside and became active participants in the debate. Making the news displaced reporting it. Many of the opinion-formers in the media had been hostile to Europe for a long time. Others jumped on the bandwagon after the Danish vote and Black Wednesday. Almost all the Tory press was captured by the anti-European cause and, at the time of writing, have not freed themselves from it.

Two of the three main media proprietors, Rupert Murdoch and Conrad Black, neither of them a British citizen, had from the start been deeply sceptical about Britain's involvement in Europe, and had appointed editors of similar mind. Black's chosen protégé was Charles Moore, with whom I had clashed during the leadership election of 1990. Moore, a clever but foppish figure who edited first the *Spectator* and later the *Sunday* and then the *Daily Telegraph*, adored Margaret Thatcher and was heavily influenced by her. He was a convinced Euro-sceptic and threw the weight of the *Telegraph*, the premier Conservative journal, behind our rebels and against our policy. Peter Stothard, the editor of Rupert Murdoch's *Times*, was less partisan on the issue, though he shared Moore's hostility to Europe and gave substantial coverage to the sceptic cause. In both newspapers the main comment and leader writers weighed in heavily against the Maastricht Treaty they had once applauded.

Some of the tabloids were equally hostile. The *Daily Beast* of Evelyn Waugh's novel *Scoop*, it seemed, was alive and well. The *Beast* itself, Murdoch's *Sun*, became the house magazine of England-against-the-world under the editorship of Kelvin MacKenzie, an oddball and a bully with a streak of populist genius. MacKenzie's ambitions eventually outreached themselves, and he left Murdoch's News International. Under his successor, Stuart Higgins, the *Sun* retained its xenophobia, but shed much of its humour and occasional brilliance.

One root of the press hostility was a circulation war at a time when overall newspaper sales were falling by a million a year ('You don't have to sell newspapers, that's my problem,' Stothard once confided to a friend when challenged about his paper's hostility to the government). Across Fleet Street, sensational and exclusive stories sold extra copies – straight reporting did not. Accuracy suffered, squandered for something, anything, 'new'. Quotes were reconstructed, leaks and splashes abounded, confidentiality was not respected and reputations sacrificed for a few days' hysterical splash.

Political journalists and politicians have always dined from the same table, but from Black Wednesday on, the Conservative press enmeshed itself closely with the more active elements of the Euro-sceptic cause. 'Chance' meetings on the Commons terrace, at *Spectator* lunches and *Telegraph* dinners, in Wilton's restaurant or at Royal Ascot, in shooting lodges in Scotland and the BBC studios in Westminster – all these brought together a group in Parliament and in the media whose superficial gossip, intellectual posturing and flock mentality endlessly swung rebellion this way and that, behind one right-wing hustler for the leadership and then another, behind flashes of patronising loyalty to me and then outright defiance.

A posse of columnists, always critical, rarely creative, churned out rank propaganda. 'Mother speaks for England,' one of them would bluster when Margaret Thatcher's name was mentioned. He was not alone. All these commentators delighted in defending an unthinking, class-ridden England against any form of progress or tolerance. They never thought that my country and my hopes for it were more real to most people in Britain than their tweedy fantasies.

Fantasies all too often took the place of facts. Under the heading 'Can Major Take the Strain?' *The Times* reported in October 1992 that I was losing weight, giving up alcohol and tinting my hair grey – all of which was as false as it was silly. 'If I really were tinting my hair,' I said to Alex Allan, 'would I have chosen *this colour*?'

Such daily opposition ripped into my premiership, damaged the Conservative Party and came close to destroying the government. Some of those involved would protest their genuine horror at the effect of what they were doing. 'Those newspaper people are all small men and small women with large powers,' said Margaret Thatcher privately. But, alas, not publicly.

Columnists of long-standing who should have known better played along. William Rees-Mogg, a former editor of *The Times* and a Conservative peer despite his position on the crossbenches, was full of warnings about the end of the nation state. The pendulum-like journalist Paul Johnson, once far-left and now far-right, and who-knows-what in the future, ranted in the *Spectator* against the government. He eventually ditched the sceptics for a new friend in Tony Blair.

Not every writer, or every paper, behaved in this way. Many journalists did not turn their concerns into bile. Hugo Young at the *Guardian*, Andrew Marr at the *Independent*, Simon Jenkins at *The Times* and Bruce Anderson at the *Spectator*, among others, all questioned the direction and composition of the government to varying degrees, but within the bounds of fair journalism.

On 20 September 1992, four days after Black Wednesday, a French referendum scraped a bare majority to ratify the Treaty of European Union, thus removing the greatest single threat to the survival of the agreement reached at Maastricht. The result also left me, as President-in-office of the Community, with the responsibility of helping the Danes to ratify the treaty, as well as facing down its opponents in the UK.

These opponents were none too scrupulous as they bandied about an absurd caricature of the agreement. If a fraction of the ill-informed nonsense they were peddling had been true, I would have vetoed the treaty myself. To counteract the misrepresentation, I repeatedly set out the facts: Britain was not committed to the single currency. We were excluded from the Social Chapter. Immigration policy was not under Community control. The treaty ruled out Community interference in education. Defence was kept outside the treaty. British citizens would remain just that – not citizens of Europe.

It was to no avail. When the Conservatives met in Brighton in early October 1992 for the party conference, the remarkable election victory of six months earlier had been forgotten. Given the mood, an observer might have been forgiven for thinking we had lost. Norman Tebbit led the opposition, with a speech that was a shameless parody of our policy. No one listening to it could doubt that here was a man with a root-and-branch contempt for the European Community. As he spoke, I recalled the image of Norman lurking in the division lobbies as a member of Margaret Thatcher's government demanding loyalty be given to the then prime minister by voting in support of the Single European Act, and I marvelled at his revisionism over that and the ERM, of which he was an early supporter. He received a tumultuous reception, playing to the emotions of a patriotic throng. I sat beside Douglas Hurd on the platform, and scribbled him a note urging him not to hold back when it was his turn to speak:

> Douglas,
> Good luck. Give 'em hell and don't worry about causing offence.
> John

Douglas delivered his best-ever conference speech in an attempt to keep the party in line. 'Give this madness a miss,' he urged representatives.

Worse was to come. Two days later, on the penultimate day of the conference, Margaret Thatcher published an article in the *European*, a now-defunct newspaper, in which she claimed that 'Maastricht will hand over more power to unelected bureaucrats and erode the freedoms of ordinary men and women.' The sub-text was clear: she would not have agreed Maastricht, whereas I had. She would have protected 'the freedoms of ordinary men and women', whereas I had not.

Coming as it did on the eve of my own speech to the conference, the article was perfectly timed to inflame opinion and play to the Euro-sceptic gallery. It was also in stark contrast to how Margaret would have acted in office. She would have signed the Treaty of European Union had she still been prime minister, and every official and minister who had worked with her knew it.

But this did not diminish the significance of the Thatcher–Tebbit axis. Here were two great warriors, laden with honours, moving away from the pragmatic skills that had guided them in office to the gut instincts that previously they had kept for private display. This was deeply confusing to a party reared on loyalty: a deal fêted a few months earlier was now being denounced by political figures whom the faithful had long admired.

The Conservative Party is a curious institution: at grassroots level every constituency party is autonomous. It chooses its own parliamentary candidate and tends to be fiercely independent. When, at particularly difficult moments during this crisis, area chairmen tried to persuade constituencies to bring rebellious Members into line, many of them resisted. The message back was often the same: 'What is right for Margaret Thatcher is right for our Member.' Almost every rebel was endorsed by his constituency party on this basis, and under the Conservative constitution, Central Office was powerless.

Margaret Thatcher and Norman Tebbit knew precisely what they were doing at the conference. Their public move to the Euro-sceptic camp – and the timing of it – was pivotal. From then on, apart from words occasionally uttered for form's sake, no holds were barred, and their opposition would be relentless. The dispute and conflict that followed was to reach its inevitable conclusion four and half years later, in the general election of 1997.

I was determined to enact the treaty. I had given my word on behalf of Britain, and I had done so only after having my negotiating aims overwhelmingly endorsed by Parliament. Moreover, Parliament had supported, indeed acclaimed, the deal when it was laid before it. I did not see how we could honourably repudiate a treaty we had helped negotiate. The long-term damage to our national prestige would have been appalling, and it was astonishing that there were those who could not see what to me was quite obvious. If we acted in such a fashion, who would trust us in future?

Who would make concessions to us if they suspected we would simply pocket them and then walk away? Our reputation as an honest nation would have been lost. I was not prepared to rat on the deal I had done. This was not a matter of pride or stubbornness. It was simply that I had pledged Britain's word. If Parliament overruled me – as it had the power to do – then I do not believe I could credibly have represented Britain again, and I would have resigned.

Apart from anything else, I believed in the deal I had agreed. We had succeeded – where most had thought we would not – in securing an opt-out from the two most questionable aspects of the deal agreed at Maastricht, the single currency and the Social Chapter, but retained the right to accept either should circumstances and opinions as to their benefits change. The treaty clarified and constrained the powers of the European Commission, while enhancing those of the European Parliament. It responded to the very different demands of the post-Cold War era, opening up the prospect of including many former Eastern-bloc states in the Union. It kept foreign and security policy where it belonged, in NATO and with individual nation states. It did not contain a commitment to 'federalism'.

When I spoke to a party conference still reeling from the Thatcher and Tebbit dramas, I tried to still fears:

> Debates over our place in Europe have always touched raw nerves – in our party and in our country. I don't find that surprising. There are gut issues at stake. Opinions are passionately held. It is right to speak plainly and directly, even if for some it is uncomfortable . . .
>
> For many of you, the heart pulls in one direction and the head in another. There is nothing that can stir the heart like the history of this country. Change isn't just coming, it's here. I want Britain to mould that change, to lead that change in our own national interest . . .
>
> That's what I mean by being at the heart of Europe. Not turning a deaf ear to the heartbeat of Britain. But having the courage to stand up and do what we believe to be right . . .
>
> Let no one in this conference be in any doubt: this government will not accept a centralised Europe . . .
>
> Emotion must not govern policy. At the heart of our policy lies one objective and one only – a cold, clear-eyed calculation of the British national interest . . .

If I believed what some people said about the treaty I would
vote against it. But I don't. So I'm going to put the real treaty
– the one I negotiated – back to the House of Commons . . .

When I hear some of the criticisms of the treaty I think of
Don Quixote. He saw things that weren't there.

I was to elaborate on this argument for month upon month, but it seemed
that nothing would convince the doubters, or some former friends of the
agreement. Ken Baker, once so supportive, was so no longer. 'I'll vote
against Maastricht – I can do no other,' he told a fringe meeting at the
conference.

Soon after Parliament had reassembled, Graham Bright came to see
me. Chatting over drinks at Number 10, he was unusually preoccupied for
such a jovial man, and it was clear he had something on his mind. 'I don't
know how to say this,' he eventually burst out, 'but the mood is very ugly.
A lot of them' – he meant the anti-Europeans – 'have turned against you
very badly. They'll get you out if they can. They thought you were phobic
about Europe, and you're not. Some of them voted to get rid of Margaret
but now they feel nostalgic for her – worse, they feel guilty.'

Some of this feeling in the parliamentary party became apparent following an off-the-record briefing held before I left for Egypt to commemorate
the fiftieth anniversary of the battle of El Alamein later in October. Inevitably, I was asked about the Paving Debate that I had promised Neil
Kinnock would precede the committee stage of the Maastricht Bill. I said
something to the effect that 'it was ultimately a matter for the electorate'
– meaning that if they disagreed with what I had done, they could toss me
out at the next election. No one remarked upon this reply at the time, or
thought it exceptionable, or even followed it up; but a day or so later the
Sun carried an inside-page story saying that I was threatening to call a
general election if I lost the vote. That was not what I had said. Had I
done so, it would have been a front-page story in every paper. I did believe
that I would have to resign if the vote was lost, but I had not considered
extending this to a request for a dissolution of Parliament, as Douglas
Hurd and I were to confirm during the debate itself.

Still, this flyer by the Sun caused yet another stir. On the plane to
Egypt my Press Secretary, Gus O'Donnell, was questioned about it. It was
nonsense, and in calmer times Gus would simply have said so. But since
Black Wednesday we had received a bloody press. We did not wish to feed

an outlandish story that had attracted only minimal interest. 'Major Denies General Election Threat' would only have encouraged wavering rebels into the anti- camp. I told Gus to brush the questions aside. On reflection, I should have been more bullish, for the absence of a firm denial was construed as confirmation of my intention, and led to widespread reports that an election would follow if we were defeated in the vote. This falsehood ignited fury in the Commons and encouraged Labour to ally themselves with our rebels. Suddenly a routine debate became a matter of crucial significance, with the risk of a government defeat. The stakes were raised dramatically.

On 29 October 1992, four days after my return from Egypt, I tried to still some of the passions when I spoke to the 1922 Committee of Conservative backbenchers. I reassured a packed meeting that I examined all European changes before I recommended them, and that in that sense I was 'the greatest Euro-sceptic in the Cabinet' – a phrase much used out of context later on.

Our rebels were convinced that if they could win the Paving vote they would blow apart the treaty. Their unofficial whips' operation knuckled down to work. To their advantage was the fact that if the main opposition parties voted against us, we would have no majority for the Bill. Both Labour and the Liberal Democrats wanted the Bill to pass, but were determined to squeeze us for every political advantage they could get, and to try to force us to incorporate the Social Chapter. The Ulster Unionists, by contrast, opposed the Bill but did not wish to bring us down and usher in a Labour government.

Richard Ryder and the government whips began an intensive lobbying exercise. Senior ministers were drafted in to talk to any backbencher they could influence. 'The PM will fall if we lose this one,' whips and ministers warned MPs – but they did not peddle the untruth that I had said I would call a general election.

On the evening before the vote, 3 November, Richard Ryder came to warn me that we were likely to be defeated. As he was doing so, the hard-core rebels were meeting in the Commons to brace themselves for a collective show of strength. They were buoyed up by the support and encouragement they were receiving from many quarters, especially from Norman Tebbit and Margaret Thatcher, who continued to summon Conservative backbenchers to her room in the Lords, encouraging them to oppose us in the vote. If they agreed, they were warmly commended; if they did not, they were given a dressing down.

Stories of these meetings soon filtered into the Commons. John Whittingdale, Margaret's former Political Secretary at Number 10, was a sceptic, but told her he would be supporting the government. Whittingdale was a sensitive man, independent-minded but basically a loyalist. When he left Margaret's room he was deeply upset at being made to feel so divided from the ex-Prime Minister he had served faithfully. Others promised opposition, and bounced out elated by the encouragement they received.

On the morning of the vote, 4 November, our whips were still alarmed about our chances. Richard Ryder is a rugby fan, with fond memories of Willie John McBride, captain of the victorious 1974 British Lions team in South Africa. McBride had a code: when he called out 'Ninety-nine' to his forwards it meant, 'Go in hard, and get your retaliation in first.' Richard made sure the whips knew this code too, and on the morning of the vote he looked at his eighteen-stone fellow whip, David Lightbown, built to be a second-row forward, and said, 'Ninety-nine today, David.' It was set to be a long day.

I spoke first in the debate that afternoon, and before defending the treaty, put our membership of the Community in context. Our opponents had no alternative to it. They would not, in public, commit us to leave the Community. Nor did they want us to be more deeply involved in it. Improbable scenarios that had been suggested – like a trade alliance with the United States, or a purely free-trade area in Europe (something which was not on offer) – were unrealistic and unattractive. We could opt out of some unappealing European developments – and I had done so – but scowling on the sidelines was not a proper role for Britain.

Throughout the day, Norman Tebbit made regular trips from the House of Lords to lurk in the Members' Lobby outside the Whips' Office, urging dissent. Like the Ancient Mariner, he would stop one in three and tell them his appalling tale. Our whips responded by redoubling their efforts. 'If he sits down, arrest him,' muttered one when he saw Tebbit in the Members' Lobby, since, by convention, peers cannot sit in this meeting place just outside the Commons Chamber. He spoke only partly in jest.

That evening, in my room in the Commons, I saw potential rebels in an attempt to encourage them to return to the fold. When I broke for a few minutes at about 9.30, Michael Heseltine came to see me. 'I think we're still behind,' he said.

We went to see Richard Ryder, who confirmed this. 'Probably by one,' he said.

'Let me deal,' urged Michael. He thought he could persuade Michael Carttiss and Gerry Vaughan to support us, and hurried off to find them. He promised the pair that, since we would not resume consideration of the Bill until the Danish position was clear, it was right to vote in the government lobby.

As I went into the packed Chamber for the final minutes of the debate, certain small dramas were coming together. David Lightbown had worked so hard in the run-up to the vote that he was on the point of exhaustion when the division bell began to ring. Racing around the Commons to make sure MPs were ready to head into the lobby and vote, he bizarrely found himself locked in a washroom. After all his work, David missed the vote. Meanwhile, some wavering MPs walking into the Chamber found pink slips with telephone messages waiting for them on the Commons message board. The notes were from Margaret Thatcher's former aide Gerald Howarth, and urged them to vote against the government.

As I took my place on the Treasury Bench I still did not know whether we were about to win or lose the division. I did know that a defeat could not be brushed aside. If we had lost, I would have risen from my place and announced my resignation: the combination of Black Wednesday and the inability to proceed with the Maastricht Bill would have made my position untenable. I would not have gone on.

In a clamour of excitement, the first vote on a Labour amendment to delay the passage of the Bill until after the Edinburgh European summit in December was won by only six votes. The second – more crucial – vote was on the government's Paving Motion to resume consideration of the Bill immediately. It seemed innocuous, but if we lost it would have been very difficult, and may have proved impossible, to reintroduce the Bill at all without splitting our party irrevocably. As I rose to go through the Division Lobby I saw Michael Carttiss, still hesitating despite his conversation with Michael Heseltine. His instinct was to vote no, but he did not wish to defeat the government or to embarrass me.

I put my arm around his shoulder, 'Come on, Michael,' I said. 'We need you tonight.'

'But the Danes might vote "no" again.'

'Michael, we won't complete the Bill until we know their position,' I explained.

He looked relieved, and we walked together into the heaving lobby. Whips came in to report on large numbers of Conservatives voting with Labour, and others abstaining. But the Liberal Democrats had kept their word, and voted with us. It was clearly going to be very close. I voted and returned to the Chamber still unsure if we had won. Beside me sat Richard Ryder, tight-lipped. The atmosphere was electric, and Members crammed back onto the benches. The tellers showed the Speaker the result. Behind the Speaker's chair, David Davis gave the thumbs up, and blew out his cheeks, indicating how close it was.

Apparently at this point I leaned down and pulled up one of my socks. Some members of the press in the gallery above noticed this, and were informed by a guest who had once worked with me as a civil servant (I have been unable to discover his identity) that it was always a sure sign that I knew I had won. At tense moments, he told them, a prime ministerial sock-tug is an unwitting giveaway. I have absolutely no idea whether this alleged habit is accurate or not. But if it is, then the moment was right.

The whips lined up before the Speaker and announced the result. We had won by just three votes. Pandemonium broke out. The majority of my colleagues were waving their order papers, but there was grim silence from a phalanx of hard-line sceptics, which boded ill for the future. The next morning, Michael Carttiss revealed our pre-vote exchange, in which I told him that we wouldn't complete the Bill until the position of the Danes was certain. This was widely reported as a desperate last-minute bid by me to win the vote.

Up to a point this was true, but my action reflected reality. A Third Reading vote to finally approve the Bill with the Danish position still unclear would have risked a rerun of the drama we were living through, and that would have been foolish. Nevertheless, in the hectic hours before the vote, I had not discussed the likelihood of delay with Douglas Hurd, the Foreign Secretary, and I should have done so. Michael Heseltine, who spoke first to Carttiss and Gerry Vaughan, is sure he told Douglas what he was doing when they sat together on the front bench as the debate drew to a close. Douglas was preoccupied with the speech he was about to make, and did not perhaps take in what Michael told him; when the news became public via a backbencher whose vote it had changed, it did look like a last-ditch offer.

The battle of Maastricht now moved three hundred miles north, to Edinburgh, which hosted a European summit in mid-December. It was a make-or-break meeting for the treaty, and for Britain's six-month presidency of the Community, but in the wake of Black Wednesday, the rise of British Euro-scepticism and an earlier, inconclusive, summit in Birmingham, expectations could not have been lower. The press were sure the whole thing would be a write-off. So were several European leaders. Fortunately, that did not turn out to be the case.

There were a number of tasks ahead of us. The toughest and most vital was to find a deal which would overcome Denmark's rejection of Maastricht, while leaving the treaty itself intact. The second was to agree the outline Community budget for the years running up to the end of the decade. Finance is always a contentious issue in Europe – the wealthier contributor nations, led by Germany, hope to emerge from negotiations with their bills reduced, while the poorer countries, headed by Spain, want more cash dropped in their coffers. It was my job to balance the two demands and I knew that if agreement could not be reached, as looked likely, both sides would turn their hungry eyes on the British rebate negotiated by Margaret Thatcher in 1984.

On top of this there was the issue of Community enlargement to consider. Britain was keen that Sweden, Austria and Finland should join the Community, and if the summit went wrong, it was possible that they might not get the chance for many years. Germany wanted more seats in the European Parliament in recognition of its increased population after reunification, but other member states were unhappy about this. And we had to consider what the Community could do to help Europe's struggling economies and rocketing unemployment. I compared the task facing us to completing a Rubik's Cube blindfolded. This remark appealed to Gus O'Donnell, who gave it wide currency. Others suggested the summit would be more like twelve-handed ping-pong.

I arrived in Edinburgh sure I had the skills needed to emerge with an agreement, but did not know if I would get one. Our meetings took place in Holyrood House, the Queen's official residence in Scotland. The grandeur of the setting was self-evident, but our working conditions were more suited to the age of Elizabeth I than Elizabeth II. Douglas Hurd, Norman

Lamont and their respective officials fitted themselves into a bedroom dominated by a huge four-poster bed. The Treasury team worked on one side of the room and the Foreign Office on the other, with the bed between them. No one, however, had any time to sleep.

One obstacle was overcome with surprising ease. Helmut Kohl and I had had a troubled few months. My feeling that we had not been treated well by the Germans in the run-up to Black Wednesday had led to some angry words between our two governments. I knew that if Helmut refused to cooperate the summit would get nowhere. In Edinburgh, however, he went out of his way to be helpful, brushing aside Jacques Delors's criticism of the length of time Britain was taking to ratify Maastricht, and backing my efforts to achieve a respectable outcome on negotiations over the budget. After hours of tough haggling we reached a deal which saw the Community budget increased from £51 billion in 1992 to £64 billion in 1999, without taking account of inflation. The increase was far less than had been proposed by a number of member states, and one that affected Britain proportionately less than other nations. I also protected and extended our budgetary rebate, overcoming the view of others that it should go. In the wake of the Edinburgh summit, contributions to the Community budget reflected more closely the wealth of each member state. Britain fell in the league table of net contributors, paying less than half the sum per capita required of Germany and the Netherlands. From 1992 to 1996, Britain's contributions to the Union approximated 0.3 per cent of its gross domestic product, while Germany's varied between 0.6 and 0.8 per cent of a much larger total. The strongly pro-European Netherlands was deeply upset at this. I expected that these welcome changes would encourage contributor nations to join us more positively in the crackdown on fraud within the Community that we had long sought.

That was one potential difficulty out of the way. Another was removed when, after tortured legalistic wrangling, a solution was found to the Danish problem. After interminable meetings and discussions throughout our presidency, I nudged the Community towards a series of opt-outs which pulled the thorns that had goaded Danish voters to reject the treaty. In May 1993, Danish agreement to ratify Maastricht was carried by a healthy margin in a second referendum.

With these two successes under our belt, and against all predictions, we also settled details for negotiations on enlarging the Community and met Germany's demand for more MEPs, balancing the increase against a smaller one for other large member states. We also went some way to refute claims that Maastricht meant a federal Europe. 'National powers are the rule and not the exception,' Europe's leaders agreed.

It was, Maastricht aside, the most successful European summit I attended as prime minister, and I am proud to have been in the chair. 'Little Optimism for Edinburgh', sniffed the *Telegraph* a few days before the meeting began. 'Summit Earns Europe's Thanks for Major', it reported afterwards. It was an unaccustomed headline at the time, and very welcome.

With the future of the treaty secured, the committee stage of the Bill could begin. It was taken on the floor of the Commons (rather than in a separate committee, as is the case for most legislation), and it was to be a marathon: over two hundred hours of debate in twenty-three full sitting days, during which over six hundred amendments and new clauses were debated. The rebels wasted huge tracts of time on artificial debates designed, as John Biffen candidly admitted, 'to prolong the committee stage of the Bill and thereby demonstrate the intensity and success of British scepticism. It was hoped that this would influence the Danes to again vote "no" in the second referendum.' It did no such thing, but it did encourage a British electorate weary and frustrated at Tory in-fighting to vote 'no' to Conservative candidates in national and local elections across the country.

As part of their campaign to frustrate the Bill, the Conservative rebels repeatedly struck deals with the opposition front bench, and with other minority parties. James Cran and Christopher Gill, the sceptics' whips, could frequently be seen in the Members' Lobby swapping names and numbers with Don Dixon, the Labour Deputy Chief Whip, or his representative. Bill Cash was among those who had no inhibition in coordinating tactics with the government's opponents, while George Gardiner often drove into the Commons with Derek Foster, Labour's Chief Whip. Labour was naturally keen to accommodate the Tory rebels. Ahead of big votes, a Labour whip later explained, 'I had brief words, with Bill Cash and Tony Marlow for example, to see what they were likely to do. From our point of view as an opposition, the drama of that final hour when people are just wondering what's going to happen is just part of the tactics of putting the government on the spot.'

He was right. It did put us on the spot. But what was ridiculous about this cooperation was that while Labour were willing to draw out the pain for the government, they did not want the Bill to collapse. The sceptics' trickery threatened only the Conservative Party's continuation in office, and not the legislation they so objected to. Our rebels delighted in the thought that they were using Labour. They were wrong. Labour were using them.

The committee stage dragged on through February and March 1993, with our whips having to practise their political maths. As a rough guide they could count on twenty-five rebels voting against us, and another twenty-five or so abstaining. But as well as these fifty there would be an unknown number who went through the government lobby while telling the rebels privately that 'I'm with you in spirit.' Some of this group were ministers. Many secretly gave support to the rebels whilst remaining silent within the government about their views and actions. It was all very debilitating. After Edward Leigh had been sacked as a junior minister in May 1993 he claimed – and I have no reason to disbelieve him – that a number of ministers met regularly whilst in government who 'would have been prepared to resign if we could have stopped [the Bill]'. None did. Nor did anyone ever come to me and threaten to do so.

Only once did any of them come close to it. Michael Portillo, Eric Forth, Peter Lloyd and Edward Leigh were among colleagues who insisted on a meeting with either the Chief Whip or myself. It looked like a nascent rebellion, and could not be allowed within the government. Richard Ryder sent his deputy, David Davis, to see them with a prepared statement. 'I am authorised to tell you all,' he began, 'if you want or insist on a meeting with the Prime Minister you will get one, individually and it will be brief and to the point – and probably your last. Any questions?'

There were none.

The rebels' strategy was guerrilla warfare – ambush and retreat. They sought delay to the passage of the Bill in the hope that some event beyond our shores (like the Danish referendum) might cause the Maastricht Treaty to collapse. If that did not happen, they hoped to force a referendum in the United Kingdom to take the struggle beyond Parliament. This mode of opposition kept the agonies of our divisions in the forefront of the public gaze for month upon month, to the despair of our supporters and the delight of our opponents.

In this atmosphere, sustaining a parliamentary majority became a nightmare for the whips, particularly as the rebels began to use a procedural device to prolong debate further. My instinct was to drive the Bill through, sitting in debate both day and night until it was agreed. To do so I required the special agreement of the House of Commons – the so-called '10 o'clock motion'. But here I had a problem. In order to win the vote to implement continued discussion, I needed either the full support of the Conservative Party or votes from elsewhere. I did not have sufficient Conservative support. The Liberal Democrats were prepared to back a limited number of motions, but after a while they saw the party political advantage of not doing so. This meant we could rarely be certain that we could continue debate beyond 10 p.m. at night. The restricted debates offered the dedicated and organised opponents of the Bill every opportunity to delay progress. They took these opportunities, and the Bill proceeded at a snail's pace.

This point was crucial. We could never be sure what progress we could make. Decisions had to be taken on a daily, sometimes hourly, basis. Once again, by using this tactic, the rebels played into Labour's hands. The government was hamstrung, and the Labour Party chuckled with glee. It was utterly demoralising and deeply damaging.

Throughout the passage of the Bill Richard Ryder regularly met his Liberal Democrat counterpart, Archie Kirkwood, to see if the party was prepared to back the government in any of the forthcoming votes. Sometimes Archie said they were, and he always delivered on his promises. David Davis, the whip in charge of the Bill, saw Archie Kirkwood almost every morning during its protracted committee stage.

Despite their diversity, the rebels were cohesive. Our whips peeled people off, but the rebel whips often wooed them back. This solidarity was fostered by the rebels' regular Tuesday meetings, chaired by Michael Spicer. At least one MP had qualms about these sessions: notes of what was discussed were usually left on a desk in the government Whips' Office. We never found out the identity of our informant, but it had to be someone at the very centre of the sceptic camp.

On 8 March 1993 a Labour amendment on a relatively minor matter – the composition of a European Community Committee of the Regions – was won by twenty-two votes, to the enormous joy of the sceptics. Nearly fifty Conservative backbenchers voted against the government, or abstained, in my first Commons defeat as prime minister. The amendment was unimportant, but the defeat was significant because it ensured that there had to be a report stage for the Bill, thus further delaying it. 'This was an authoritarian proposal ... that is why I voted as I did – on principle,' said Bill Cash when challenged about our defeat. In fact the effect of the vote was to exclude businessmen and regional leaders from the committee. It was an odd principle for a Conservative to hold.

The fall-out from this vote worsened the antagonism in the parliamentary party. Terry Dicks, the MP for Hayes and Harlington, who had only won his seat by fifty-three votes and who attributed his success to me, had bravely left his sickbed to support us in the vote only days after having undergone an operation. 'I would walk through broken glass to support John Major,' he said. 'If we had lost by one vote I would never have forgiven myself.' 'The Euro-rebels are acting like robots out of control,' said Michael Fabricant, MP for Mid-Staffordshire and no Euro-enthusiast himself. 'I do not think they have any grasp of the damage they're doing.' Many others felt the same.

By this time, many of the most persistent rebels were becoming minor national celebrities, and few political programmes were complete without their contribution. They became fixtures on College Green, the piece of turf across the road from the Houses of Parliament used by television interviewers, and were as much fêted in the media for sticking to their principles as the government was damned for sticking to its own. Some, of course, believed passionately in what they were doing. Others had less admirable reasons for their opposition. Every minor success for them was a setback for the government. It was no wonder that whenever I passed a Labour whip in the Commons, he would greet me with the most cheery of smiles.

Labour scored a real bullseye with an amendment in the committee stage designed to incorporate the Social Chapter, which I had rejected at Maastricht. On legal advice, Tristan Garel-Jones – the Minister for Europe and on his feet in the Chamber for hour after hour during the Maastricht Bill's committee stage – told the Commons that the amendment would destroy the whole treaty. Under parliamentary procedure, this made the amendment inadmissible for debate. As soon as Tristan had announced this, voices within the Foreign Office began to query the legal advice Tristan had received. Quite rightly, Douglas Hurd insisted the advice be re-examined. Even as he did so, an angry reaction in the Commons to Tristan's initial announcement put us badly on the back foot. When, to our embarrassment, the legal advice changed, Douglas Hurd had the unenviable task of making this clear to an angry and suspicious Commons which thought we had been caught out in a piece of sharp practice. It certainly looked that way, but it was not.

Labour and the rebels were thus let loose to propose an amendment which tied ratification of the treaty to acceptance of the Social Chapter. This was a neat trick on the opposition's part, for it allowed them to protest their support for the treaty while binding it with conditions they knew I could never accept. In this the Labour Party were being consistent: they had supported the Social Chapter all along. The rebels, however, most of them on the right wing of the Conservative Party, were firm opponents of any extension of social legislation from Brussels. Now they became allies in Labour's socialist campaign to undo our opt-out. It was a mad-hatter coalition.

At first, Labour's redrafted amendment was ruled out of order by the Deputy Speaker, amidst unjust muttering from Dennis Skinner – the razor-tongued 'Beast of Bolsover' – that he 'smelt a rat' and that the Deputy Speaker had been 'nobbled' by the government. This was, of course, absurd. Skinner was no fan of the European Union, and relished the opportunity to voice sentiments from the left of the Labour Party and to embarrass the government at the same time.

When the Deputy Speaker finally indicated that a new clause could be debated, a gleeful Labour Party dubbed it 'the ticking time-bomb'. This was an accurate tag. Although the amendment would not prevent the Bill from becoming law, it did require a Commons vote on the Social Chapter before the treaty could be officially ratified and come into effect. It set up a patently absurd situation.

In late April the Bill completed its weary passage through the committee stage, surviving a late assault by Euro-sceptics eager to trigger a referendum on ratification of the treaty *as a whole*. This call for a referendum was a familiar one. I opposed it on principle. Parliament, I believed, had the constitutional authority to choose whether or not to ratify the treaty, and I thought it odd that the rebels, always the first to speak in reverent tones about parliamentary sovereignty, were quick to seek means to bypass the will of the House of Commons when this sovereignty clashed with their own beliefs. Fortunately, the Labour leader John Smith felt as strongly as I did about this, and his party voted with the government to ensure that there would be no referendum.

With the committee stage over, the Bill was almost certain to become law. I marked this quiet triumph with a speech, on 22 April 1993, to the Conservative Group for Europe. I thought it a progressive and bullish speech which clarified my approach to Europe as the government emerged from the quagmire of the committee stage. It was to become famous for something very different.

'Maastricht,' I said, 'has been used as a scapegoat for the varied and nameless fears about Europe, most of them wholly unrelated to the treaty. I have never pretended that Maastricht is perfect, but Maastricht makes Europe better. We Conservatives,' I went on, 'must have the confidence and the sharp-edged determination to stay in the heart of the European debate to win a Community of free, independent, members.' The sceptics, I argued, were motivated by 'frustration that we are no longer a world power . . . they practise a sort of phantom grandeur, a clanking of unusable suits of armour'.

The theme of the speech was forward-looking and optimistic. But little of it won much attention beyond my immediate audience. What stuck in the media mind was my closing passage. My intention was to remind listeners that Britain's involvement in Europe did not threaten our national distinctiveness. 'Fifty years from now,' I said, 'Britain will still be the country of long shadows on county grounds, warm beer, invincible green suburbs, dog lovers and – as George Orwell said – old maids bicycling to Holy Communion through the morning mist. And – if we get our way – Shake-speare will still be read – even in school. Britain will survive unamendable in all essentials.'

I was not rhapsodising about the sort of country I wanted to create. I was pointing out that European cooperation did not have to mean European harmonisation unless we chose it to do so. It is no doubt useless to protest about the way this passage became an established shorthand for a caricature of my political philosophy.

A month after the speech, the Maastricht legislation made its final Commons outing on 20 May, passing the third reading with its true parlia-mentary majority revealed – 180. It was an anti-climatic moment for me. Triumph was tempered by the fact that forty-six Tory MPs rebelled on the vote, the worst figure so far. Nevertheless, against the background of no Conservative majority for the Bill, the achievement in carrying it was the finest piece of whipping I ever saw. Richard Ryder and his colleagues, especially David Davis and, from April 1993, his successor Bob Hughes, together with Greg Knight, the pairing whip, performed heroically. Without their efforts the government might well have fallen.

The bitter battle over Maastricht in the Commons was peppered with other setbacks, and the tragedy of the death of Judith Chaplin, my former Political Secretary both at the Treasury and in Downing Street. She had left Number 10 shortly before the 1992 general election to pursue her own parliamentary candidacy at Newbury, and had only been in the House a short time when a routine operation went wrong and she was snatched away. Her death was a terrible shock. I heard of it while being driven home to my constituency one evening. I had been so preoccupied with the situation at Westminster that I did not even know she was in hospital, and she had not mentioned it the last time we spoke.

The resulting by-election on 6 May was calamitous: the Liberal Democrats won the seat with ease. The county council elections in England and Wales on the same day were a rout. The constituencies were in despair, as dispute after dispute hit the parliamentary party. Norman Lamont left the government in a reshuffle (see pages 679–80) – despite being offered an alternative Cabinet post – and, no longer burdened with responsibility, became an angry critic of much he had previously advocated. In the midst of all this Michael Heseltine had a heart attack in Venice, and I was uncertain whether he would ever be able to return to front-line politics. It was a miserable period, made immeasurably worse by our parliamentary travails. Fighting one's political opponents is the very stuff of politics. It quickens the blood. But fighting one's colleagues was immensely painful. It deadened the appetite.

One bright spot was the House of Lords, which strongly backed the treaty. Despite the counter-advocacy of the constitutional expert Lord Blake, peers rejected the rebels' demand for a referendum even more comprehensively than the Commons. After completing its passage through the Lords in twelve days, quicker even than we had hoped, the Bill received Royal Assent on 20 July 1993.

It still faced hurdles. On 19 July its vehement opponent the journalist William Rees-Mogg was given leave to apply to the High Court to question the ratification of the treaty by judicial review. This was an irritation rather than a serious threat. I thought Rees-Mogg's application, financed by James Goldsmith and thus not short of cash, was no more than a speculative

JOHN MAJOR

and publicity-seeking wrecking tactic, and when he withdrew it I felt my judgement had been validated.

More worrying was the parliamentary vote on Labour's 'ticking time-bomb', scheduled to take place in July. We had managed to stave off the vote during the committee stage. I had hoped that by waiting until the Bill was law I could inhibit Tory rebels from joining the opposition in the lobbies. Even the last-ditch sceptics would surely be ashamed of backing Labour on the Social Chapter, I thought. With the Bill on the statute book, it would be time for them to admit the game was up. They did not. It was clear that Labour would vote *en masse* to incorporate the Social Chapter into British law, and (in a change of tactics by Paddy Ashdown) so would the Liberal Democrats. With them were the Scottish National Party and Ian Paisley's Democratic Unionists. If our rebels mustered in force against us, we faced certain defeat.

I was shocked that, hoping to stymie legislation agreed by Parliament, some of our rebels were even prepared to vote for a Social Chapter that nearly every Conservative believed was the antithesis of everything the Thatcher revolution had stood for – and our rebels were fervent admirers of that revolution. Some of them did fear that such a shameless vote would arouse the ire of their constituents, and were deeply unhappy; but the hard-core sceptics were prepared to risk all. It was a game of bluff, and no one could know which side would bluff best.

The rebel Conservatives met to plan tactics and reassure themselves that they would be in significant company if they voted against the government. Richard Ryder, counting heads, predicted that we would lose the vote, even though some surprising malcontents, like the right-winger John Carlisle, seemed to be coming our way. I sat juggling the need to write a speech for the debate and also to chair a series of meetings with Richard Ryder, Douglas Hurd, Ken Clarke, and Tony Newton, the Leader of the House. It was obvious to us that there was no easy solution: yet again we either won the vote or we faced disaster.

On Tuesday, 20 July the whips' headcount was that we would lose by twenty-five, with fifteen colleagues voting against us and sixteen abstaining. There was no comfort for us from the minor parties. Jim Molyneaux was sympathetic and wished to keep the government in office, but other members of his Ulster Unionist Party such as John Taylor and David Trimble were believed to be in league with our rebels on all European policy.

The following morning I received a note from Douglas Hurd with some ideas of how we might react to a defeat. In essence he proposed we ratified the treaty after a Motion of Confidence in the Government, but in addition entered into a complex arrangement that would involve us asking the House whether any future measures under the Social Chapter should be negotiated at the European Council under the Social Agreement (excluding the UK) or the Treaty of Rome and Single European Act (including the UK). It was an ingenious plan, but events were moving on.

Murdo Maclean, the indispensable Private Secretary to the Chief Whip of governments since 1978, was examining other possible Confidence Motions, including one that would specifically approve our policy on the Social Chapter – an idea that came out of a conversation with Michael Howard – and, in so doing, overturn any defeat we suffered and permit us to ratify the Act.

On 21 July the House authorities confirmed that such a motion could bring the Act into force. I asked Tony Newton, the Leader of the House, to hold a meeting with colleagues to test their views. Ken Clarke was robustly in support of the high-risk option: 'If we don't believe we can get a majority on a Confidence Motion, what is the point of governing?' So was Nick Lyell, the Attorney General: 'We'll never get the rebels to move otherwise. We must face them down.' David Heathcoat Amory, speaking for Richard Ryder, forecast that the Liberal Democrats would not help us, and agreed. The Employment Secretary David Hunt was not confident we would win, but saw no better alternative. The Leader of the Lords, John Wakeham, reluctant initially, came on board too. As Tony Newton summed up, Douglas Hurd and Richard Ryder joined the meeting. Richard believed 'something must be done before the summer – or haemorrhage'. Douglas cautioned, 'We can't let this drag on, but don't let ourselves be boxed in.'

Alex Allan reported this outcome to me. It was what I had hoped for, since I had no doubt we had to force the matter to an early conclusion. If we lost the vote, I favoured a Confidence Motion as early as Friday. But we could not let our intention leak. I realised we would need a Cabinet meeting on Thursday evening – as close to the vote as possible – to obtain approval for a high-risk Confidence Motion the following morning, and asked Alex to make early preparations for this.

The rebels needed to be offered a ladder to climb down, in the hope that we could end the long battle with a united vote. I discussed the possibilities with Richard Ryder, and we decided to offer them an assurance that we would not re-enter the ERM during the lifetime of the present Parliament. This was something they desired, but the offer was cost-free to us, since an early re-entry was unlikely in the extreme. It was a fig-leaf if they wanted one; but they were too deeply entrenched, and refused it.

At Cabinet on the morning of the debate, 22 July 1993, I spoke bluntly. The whips' assessment, I said, was that we would lose the vote on the protocol on social policy. Some of my colleagues were shocked.

'If we lose,' I went on, 'Cabinet will meet again this evening. I will not drop a treaty for which there was a large majority in the House.'

Everyone present knew that if we had a second Cabinet that evening the choices before us would be unpleasant, but no one dissented from the course I had set out.

Shortly after lunch I saw James Molyneaux. His official Ulster Unionists had once been almost a part of the Conservative Party, but were now independent of us. Jim was a wise old bird, small, sometimes almost mono-syllabic, but a shrewd observer of the scene. He weighed his words carefully, and could be more Delphic than the Oracle itself. He had walked a delicate path in the minefield of Northern Irish politics, and was highly regarded far beyond his own party. He had been supportive of me personally from the moment I became prime minister, but, like his colleagues in the UUP, he did not like the Maastricht Treaty. I hoped only to persuade his party to abstain, but Jim had a pleasant surprise for me. He would, he said, deliver nine votes for the government.

'For us?' I queried. 'Not abstentions?'

'For you,' he confirmed. Sensing that I was waiting to see if there was a price for this bounty, he went on, 'I don't think we should enter into a sordid deal, do you? We're both doing what we think is best.' He smiled enigmatically.

'They'll *think* we've done a deal,' I replied. 'How shall I answer that question?'

Jim's smile broadened. 'Nothing was asked for and nothing was given,' he said. This was true, and when I was questioned in the Chamber, it was what I said.

These nine votes were an uncovenanted bonus, and were, I think, offered because the Unionists loathed the policies of Kevin McNamara, the Labour spokesman on Northern Ireland and once the author of a policy document with the provocative title *Towards a United Ireland*. Jim Moly-neaux did not want a Labour government, which could have been the outcome had we lost that day's vote. Silently, I toasted him – and McNam-ara. But even with the Unionists' vote it still looked as if we were about to lose as I headed for the Commons to open the debate.

The debate was a potent affair. The fate of the treaty was at stake, and, perhaps, much more. Norma and James sat anxiously in the Public Gallery, knowing – as the House did not – what my response would be if we lost.

I did not mince my words. I believed the treaty was the best obtainable, and that Britain could not stand aside from developments in the outside world: 'For the first time in twenty years we are beginning to see a material move in the European Community agenda in the direction that Britain has long sought. It would be absurd for us to throw away our influence in the Community at that moment.' Nor did I spare John Smith and Paddy Ashdown. I thought their party games with the amendment were unscrupulous, since their support for the substance of the treaty was well known. During my speech, Michael Lord, Conservative MP for Suffolk Central and a mild Euro-sceptic, intervened to say that he would support the government. So did John Carlisle. Nick Winterton also hinted as much. After these interventions I hoped for a stampede from the sceptics' camp back into ours, but it did not come. Teresa Gorman and Peter Tapsell hardened their opposition, and positions became more entrenched. I left the Chamber to meet the Chief Whip. 'We're still down,' he said.

By chance, that afternoon had been set aside for me to address the usual end-of-session meeting of Conservative backbenchers. Most of the dissidents stayed away, but the bulk of the parliamentary party gave me a rousing reception. Partly, I think, this was because my speech had gone well a few hours before, but they were also venting their frustration at those in the party who were undermining us. I spoke of the dramas of the day, and of the improving economy and our plans for the future. As we left, Graham Bright, who had a marginal seat, smiled and said, 'I was glad to hear you talk of the future.'

He got a grim reply. 'If we have one,' I muttered.

At seven o'clock that night, three hours before the vote, the Cabinet met once more. I told colleagues that the whips believed the government would still be defeated. 'We will probably defeat the opposition amend-ment,' I told them, 'but we are likely to lose the main motion.' This would stop the Act coming into force. 'If that happens,' I said, 'a Motion of Confidence in the government would be inevitable.'

I set out the options we had considered. We could table a general Motion of Confidence and follow it up with a motion enabling the treaty to be ratified, or we could table a specific Confidence Motion that included the Social Chapter in its terms. I made it clear that this was a much higher-risk strategy, but that it was the one I favoured. I invited Murdo Maclean to join us, to ensure that my proposals were within the rules of order before our discussion began.

Most colleagues supported the high-risk strategy. The Cabinet was aware that a Confidence Motion, if lost, could be a death warrant, but saw it as preferable to the European battle continuing unresolved over the summer. Only a tiny minority of three colleagues dissented. They spoke of the risk of losing a Confidence Motion that enabled us to ratify the Maastricht Treaty, and wished only for one to enable us to continue in government. As this would have left us exposed to months of uncertainty, no one else supported them.

I summed up, saying that I hoped we would win the division, but that if we did not, a clear majority of Cabinet agreed to a Motion of Confidence endorsing our rejection of the Social Chapter and permitting us to ratify the Act immediately. I added that if we lost we would have the debate the next morning, and that Tony Newton would put down an appropriate motion for debate before the House rose that night.

I saw Richard Ryder chuckling at the end of the table. 'Charge of the Light Brigade,' he said in response to a raised eyebrow, and explained: 'After Cardigan had led the Light Brigade into the guns, with massive casualties, the Sergeant-Major galloped up to him, saluted and said, "Same again, sir?" That's what we're going to do.'

The last couple of hours before the vote were frantic, as the whips combed the corridors for converts. I returned to the Chamber carrying in my pocket the statement I had decided to make if we lost. The House was noisy and aggressive, minds fixed and argument now superfluous. David Hunt wound up the debate with a robust speech as Members chattered and shouted, all awaiting the drama at the division. As David spoke, other Members, some gravely ill but summoned by the whips, were arriving to vote. Some remained in an ambulance in New Palace Yard to be 'nodded through' the Division Lobby without having to walk through in person.

The news came that Bill Walker, one of our backbenchers who had claimed to be seriously ill and in Scotland, had arrived without warning to vote against us. He had, we heard later, been kept out of sight in Bill Cash's flat. As with other rebels, his constituency party condoned his duplicity.

There were two votes that night. We could afford to lose neither of them. As the first division proceeded, our whips counted the number of Conservatives voting with Labour, and told me the result was on a knife-edge. Millions watched live on television as the result was announced: for the Labour amendment 317, against 317. It was a tie. By tradition, in such a rare event the Speaker votes with the government to maintain the *status quo*. We had just scraped through. The next morning an error came to light. There had been a miscount in the lobbies, for in the heat of the moment an opposition teller had noted the cry 'All-out,' which clears the lobby at the end of a vote, as the name of another MP filing past. As a result, it was declared that we had in fact won by one vote, and the Speaker's casting vote was not needed.

The second vote was always more dangerous, and the result of the previous tied vote left us almost certain we would lose it. In scenes of great excitement we duly did so, by eight votes. The effect of this was to block us from ratifying a treaty that Parliament had already approved with a huge majority. The House was in uproar, with cheers, counter-cheers and recriminations filling the air.

I rose immediately to announce a Motion of Confidence in the Government, to be debated the following morning – which many had expected – and also the terms of it – which no one outside the Cabinet and my family had anticipated. I said:

> The House has not come to a resolution. We clearly cannot leave the matter there. Tonight's debate has shown there is no majority . . . to join the Social Chapter . . . a majority . . . is in favour of ratifying the Maastricht Treaty . . . We must resolve this issue; it cannot be allowed to fester any longer. I therefore give notice that the government will invite the House to come to a resolution tomorrow by tabling a Motion of Confidence in the following terms:
> 'The House has confidence in the policy of Her Majesty's government on the adoption of the Protocol on Social Policy.'

This left Conservatives with a clear choice. To vote for us and against the Social Chapter, in which case we could ratify the treaty; or to vote against us, in which case I would seek a dissolution of Parliament and a general election. I instructed the Number 10 Press Office to make the message explicit, so that our constituencies in the country could be in no doubt what was at stake. I hoped and expected that they would put pressure on our rebels.

After the uproar in the Chamber had subsided, I returned to my room in the Commons for the third Cabinet meeting of the day – there was no time to summon everyone to the Cabinet Room in Downing Street. It was nearly 11 p.m., and the meeting was brief and sombre, as we assessed events and put in hand arrangements to persuade our rebels to swing their votes behind the government. I pencilled in early September for the general election, then returned to Number 10 to begin work on my speech for the following day.

The debate on the Confidence Motion was an anti-climax after the events of the previous day. I spoke poorly. John Smith did rather better. The real action took place outside the Chamber. Conservative constituencies were livid with the rebels for risking the government's survival in defence of a Labour policy, and by mid-morning it was evident that the miscreants were clambering back on board as fast as their dignity would permit. When Douglas Hurd closed the debate the House was subdued, and the Confidence vote was comfortably won, by thirty-eight votes. The Maastricht Treaty was now law, and we could ratify it. The longest white-knuckle ride in recent British politics was over.

Since then I have often thought over these events – by turns tense, knife-edge, dismal, exhilarating and depressing. You can read the foregoing as a blow-by-blow account of an unfolding drama which could at so many critical moments have gone differently. Or you can turn away from the whole story in despair, as I am inclined to do, and ask how it ever came to this. How had so much bad blood welled up so fast? How had members of what had so recently been a winning team turned against each other, plotted against each other, betrayed each other, careless of the opportunity this was building for their common enemy?

And I, of course, must ask – as I constantly do – how I might have turned the situation around. Was there something I could have said, some policy I could have adopted, someone I should have fired, someone I could have hired, a speech, a broadcast, an argument which might have begun my party's journey back to sanity? Could a different man have done it? If so, I am no closer in my mind now to answering these questions than I was when they tormented me at the time. It would be comforting to believe that there was nothing anyone could have done. If there was, the knowledge of what it might have been still eludes me.

# CHAPTER SIXTEEN

# *Back to Basics*

A BOVE ALL ELSE, the quality of life for the people amongst whom I grew up depended upon the provision of health and education, and the maintenance of law and order. It still does for their descendants. Each of these services is predominantly the responsibility of the state, and should remain so. Yet the state has a patchy record. When I became prime minister the performance figures – where they were available – were dismal. Every MP knew that. The public were unhappy. I wanted to improve these services.

On health, on education and on crime, no prime minister acts alone. They are served by three of the biggest departments in Whitehall and many autonomous organisations. It was my job to suggest, to push, to approve and to criticise: to shape policy, but not to write it. That was the task of successive secretaries of state and their officials, a task which was to bring with it a measure of political opprobrium even as the policies themselves brought sustained improvement. At Education, Ken Clarke, John Patten and then Gillian Shephard took forward the reforms of the 1980s against the opposition of a teaching establishment uncomfortable with change, though its instincts and ideologies had left Britain's children less well-educated than they deserved to be. At the Department of Health, William Waldegrave, Virginia Bottomley and Stephen Dorrell shook up and improved a service that was vital to our people's well-being. And at the Home Office Ken Baker, Ken Clarke and then Michael Howard steered law and order on a new compass-bearing, away from a tendency to see crime as inevitable, and towards one in which there could be no doubt that wrongdoers had to pay for their actions.

It worked. School results improved; in our hospitals and doctors' surgeries, more patients were treated, and treated more quickly, than ever before; and crime fell. With the clarity brought by the Citizen's Charter (see Chapter 11), people could tell for the first time which services were doing well and which were failing. They were able to demand better, and often they got it.

Not that this was always evident. Like getting the builders in, the immediate effect of our work was to bring noise, heat, sparks, and a good deal of shouting all round. But when the dust had settled the end result was rather impressive. Public services emerged strengthened, better-funded and more responsive – and those in the opposition who had wanted to do nothing, and had chided us when we did much, benefited more than most. We peeled back the layers of complacency in the system that had left the public expecting the worst from the services their taxes paid for. New Labour was to take office in time to win some of the plaudits.

Behind much of what I did, and what I encouraged my ministers to do, lay a principle which became famous for a very different reason: 'back to basics'. Elsewhere in this book (see Chapter 23), I have set out how it became a tool in the hands of newspaper critics. Though the phrase was hijacked as being a public statement about personal morality, I did not forget its real meaning. 'Back to basics' came from my innermost personal beliefs. It set out to confront and overturn a range of ideas that had led policy – in crime, health, schools, social work – down blind alleys. Professional wisdom had become divorced from public sentiment and from reality. I wanted to bring back politics on a human scale.

On crime, I had seen enough of life to know that it was selfish, hurt others, and ultimately hurt the perpetrator, too. The permissive approach to criminology that hid this is easy to caricature. For years the *Daily Telegraph*'s 'Peter Simple' column lampooned with cruel brilliance the imaginary 'progressive thinker' from Hampstead, Dr Heinz Kiosk, whose perpetual cry was 'We are all guilty!' This sort of idiocy was not absent from debate even in the 1990s, and it drives any Conservative wild with fury – and with anxiety – for the *victims* of crime.

But in our angry response to what we see as the pernicious undermining of a sense of personal responsibility, we Conservatives have sometimes adopted brutally simplistic language which, while appropriate for the hustings and the conference platform, does not do justice to the complexities of real life. So we could be portrayed as overlooking those personal, educational and social difficulties which are linked to crime.

I never overlooked them. How could anyone with a Brixton boyhood like mine do so? I knew very well the temptations which crowd the path of anyone whose life or prospects seem hopeless. I have seen how bad environments breed mischief, and mischief breeds bad environments; and how an upbringing can curse – or bless – a child for ever.

But I also know that in every walk of life and at every level of income, an individual is capable of living honestly; and the vast majority, even of the unlucky, do. It is an insult to them and to everyone who has ever struggled with and resisted the temptation to crime, to greet criminals with a cry of 'We are all guilty.' The *criminal* is guilty. We should never brush that aside. He, or she, must be treated with understanding and even with mercy, but never with a disregard for what has been done or for those who have been hurt. To ignore culpability is to affront the victim, to offer to other potential offenders a shrug of the shoulders, and to devalue the individual's own capacity for moral judgement and right behaviour. To know all is not to forgive all.

And with guilt must go punishment. As sure as I was that prison is not the appropriate punishment for all, or even most, lawbreaking, I never forgot – and never wanted my home secretaries to forget – that an organised system of incarceration is the foundation, the reserve currency, of any system of criminal justice. If other admonishments fail, and if the whole panoply of deterrence, 'restorative' justice and rehabilitation has no effect, prison must be there, a reassurance to the law-abiding and a deterrent to the lawbreaker, a resort of which ministers should not be ashamed, and which the British people wish them humanely but sternly to administer.

Conventional opinion in Britain has always been civilised and decent, but has sometimes failed to focus fully on the horror of crime for many people. The greatest cruelty is to be found in tower blocks and in 'sink' estates and high-density housing, hurting most those whose voice is hardly heard in the making of policy. They are the unluckiest people in the community, and yet crime smashes most often on their frail front doors.

The infamous sixties did have something to teach Britain about tolerance, about understanding, and about the conditions in which crime breeds. But the nineties, I believed, had something to teach about personal responsibility and individual values. These were my beliefs, and that is why I was content that our approach to these matters should be called 'back to basics', for that is precisely what I meant.

It was with 'back to basics' in mind, although unlabelled as such then, that I appointed Ken Clarke to the Home Office following the 1992 general election. It is a misreading of Ken to put him at the liberal-wet end of the Conservative Party: he is robust, and splendidly careless of received wisdom. When Ken moved to the Treasury in 1993 his successor was Michael Howard, a very different sort of home secretary from those the Home Office had grown accustomed to. Michael is clever and able – he had won a strong reputation at the bar as an advocate – but in private is a shy and charming man, with an unstuffy, self-deprecating manner. He was always at his best without an audience; in public he could not help stirring things up. Too many people saw the polished barrister on the surface, and took against what they saw. They missed the substance underneath.

For me, Michael's contrasting qualities made him the right candidate for the Home Office – an ambitious, able politician who knew his way around the criminal justice system and who relished an argument. With his distrust of orthodoxy he was happy with the idea that I expected him to work closely with me and with my Policy Unit to raise the profile of our fight against crime.

Both Ken and Michael continued the work of their Conservative predecessors. Police numbers were increased, their salaries raised, and more civilians recruited to take routine work off their shoulders. I was also keen to raise police efficiency – which was not always all that it might be – so police forces were brought into the ambit of the Citizen's Charter and given performance indicators. Despite a terrific rearguard action from the system we managed to strengthen the Police Inspectorate and bring a genuine independent element into its make-up.

By October 1993 Michael was able to use the party conference platform to signal a radical break with the past consensus on criminal justice. He set out twenty-seven new points of policy for criminal justice, at the heart of which was the controversial contention 'prison works'. The speech was an advertising hoarding for the Bills on criminal justice and police and magistrates' courts that were introduced shortly afterwards.

The passage through Parliament of the Criminal Justice and Public Order Bill in 1993–94 was smooth enough, although its provisions giving the police powers to tackle hunt saboteurs, raves and so-called 'New Age' travellers generated outrage from the civil liberties groups. The Bill's other main provisions were less noisily received: to create secure training centres for habitual young criminals and revised conditions surrounding the granting of bail. The Bill also removed the right to remain silent on arrest and have no inference drawn in court – something which, though controversial at its introduction, has improved the operation of the justice system without damaging basic rights. Labour opposed these changes in opposition, but wisely retained them in government.

In 1995 we created a new National Crime Prevention Agency. I supported the growth of local initiatives, such as the expansion of Neighbourhood Watch schemes. We devoted tens of millions of pounds to crime-deterring initiatives such as closed-circuit television cameras, better lighting and security barriers. CCTV was a remarkable success in both preventing crime and securing convictions. With crime – and education – in mind I bullied the Department of Education to take a much stronger line on truancy, and to publish truancy figures in national league tables. Outside school, I was keen to see a reduction in the over-use of cautioning young offenders, and wider use of the revived concept of curfew orders, which could be monitored electronically.

By the time we left office these measures were beginning to bite. The number of suspects refusing to answer questions almost halved. Recorded crime in 1996 was over 10 per cent down on 1992 levels, the biggest drop since records began, and the biggest drop (equal with one other country) in any of the eighteen OECD nations. In the same period recorded crime in Germany fell by only 1 per cent, and in America by 3 per cent.

'Back to basics' went further than crime. I also wanted a change of gear on health. To do this, we followed through Margaret Thatcher's reforms to break the monolithic structure of health-care provision that had endured for four decades, and put in its place a system of self-managing hospital trusts, encouraging – though not compelling – GPs to become fundholders, looking after their resources on behalf of their patients. A comprehensive Health Service, free at the point of delivery, was guaranteed everywhere, but attention turned to the wishes of the patient in a way that had not always happened before. Unlike the old, centrally-planned system which had allowed backlogs to build up, the reforms raised standards and allocated resources according to real lives, real experience and real needs on the ground.

It was an elegant approach, and it allowed the system to adapt to costly advanced treatments undreamed of when the old NHS had been set up.

In most respects, under new names and without the internal market, it has survived the change of government in May 1997, and though it was criticised by some doctors, it came to be accepted and even welcomed by most. In 1990 there were over 200,000 patients who had had to wait over a year for treatment. By 1997 this had been cut to just fifteen thousand. The average waiting time was halved between those years, and by 1997 most people put on a list for hospital treatment received it within six weeks, and the NHS was treating 133 patients for every hundred it had managed to treat before the reforms: some six thousand more treatments a day.

Introducing this internal market, however, was a noisy business. The British Medical Association – the doctors' trade union – defended the way things had always been done, without reference to the palpable failings of the system. And the Labour Party, inevitably, leapt in too. Always we were harried by the suggestion that the creation of the internal market was a covert step on a path to full privatisation of the NHS. It was not, but we had no answer to the charge other than simply to say that it was not. This scarcely convinced the doubters, for the NHS has always, unfairly, been a sort of political quicksand for the Conservative Party – a fact shamelessly exploited by the Labour Party, which has, in truth, provided the only governments which have ever cut NHS capital and revenue spending. Such are the ironies of life. The public were always doubtful that the Conservatives really believed in the NHS. In fact we do – I did, anyway. I used it myself, and so did my family. But my hopes of persuading people of our good faith were never great.

Still, I had a go. In my first party conference speech as leader, I made my position clear:

> We have all been brought up with the Health Service. We use it. We cherish it. We are proud of it. I know that for millions of people in this country the National Health Service means security. I understand that because I am – and always have been – one of those people. I know that when you are fit and well, the NHS brings peace of mind – just to know it's there. It is unthinkable that I, of all people, would take that security away.
>
> And so that no one can misunderstand the position – and I hope the whole country is listening – let me make it even clearer. There will be no charges for hospital treatment. No charges for visits to the doctor, no privatisation of health care, neither

piecemeal nor in part nor as a whole. Not today. Not tomorrow. Not after the next election. Not ever while I am prime minister.

To make it clear that the internal market was a help and not a threat to the NHS, I pushed through plans for a Patient's Charter which prescribed for the first time what the public could expect from the system. There was quite a squabble behind the scenes over this. The Health Secretary William Waldegrave was constrained by the fact that he did not have the resources to give patients in England the same promised level of service as was offered to those in Scotland, where, under a long-standing formula, the system was better funded. In the end it was agreed to differ. Patients in Scotland were guaranteed an operation, should they need one, in no more than eighteen months, while in England at first the figure was not more than two years. In both England and Scotland the times were later cut, to one year and eighteen months respectively. Just to write these figures is to illustrate why the reforms – and the Charter – were needed.

As well as the internal market, we promoted preventative care. I chaired a seminar on this at Chequers in April 1991 which evolved into a White Paper in 1992, setting out twenty-five targets for raising health standards by the year 2000. The paper was introduced by William Waldegrave's successor Virginia Bottomley, as trusty and capable a colleague as any prime minister could ask for; she protested, 'I'm not ready for Cabinet,' when I appointed her, but she was, and she cared very much about public services. Virginia brought to her job a steely grace, and took with good humour the patronising and mockery that attractive women in politics still, stupidly, attract. In the face of crass male colleagues she could summon up a weary smile when a knee in the groin might have been better deserved.

Cornered in the House – the fate of all health secretaries – Virginia reeled off facts and figures until even her bitterest critics simply gave up. She was relentless, courageous – and magnificent. She was also utterly loyal. (In opposition later she kept up her interest in and attendance at Health Questions, only to be taunted by her Labour successor – the beneficiary of all the necessary rationalisation that had been carried through by the Conservatives – as 'a dog returning to its own vomit'. It was a sneer that will not be forgotten by some of us.)

Virginia – and from 1995 Stephen Dorrell – suffered in particular from attacks on our plans to rationalise medical provision in London. It was something that had to be done – even doctors admitted it – but although everyone wanted better facilities for GPs, no one wished to surrender any money to help provide them. Our intention was better health-service provision overall, but the effect this had on institutions with famous names – and none more so than St Bartholomew's (Barts) Hospital in the City, which was threatened with closure – made it an argument which in public relations terms we could not win. We persevered, but so did our opponents, and the issue was, I think, to be a factor in our dismal 1997 general election showing in London.

Such noisy controversies, and the introduction of the internal market, disguised the fact that spending on the NHS rose steadily in the years in which I was to have a direct impact, with cash increases from £32.6 billion in 1991–92 to £42.6 billion in 1996–97. I was under constant pressure to provide more: the Health Service can, and does, always justify calls for more money. It is the unhappy role of ministers sometimes to have to say no.

In truth, what is spent is less relevant than how well it is spent. Judged by that criterion, the health reforms were a success. I remember the facts I had in mind during the 1997 general election campaign. Two and a quarter million more in-patient and day cases were treated in our hospitals each year than in 1990. The number of cataract operations had risen by sixty thousand in five years. The agony of long waits for surgical treatment was almost eliminated. In the Tory years as a whole the number of elderly people given a new lease of life by a hip replacement doubled; heart transplants became an almost daily event, as opposed to a national headline; nurses' pay rose by two-thirds, and the average doctor, even allowing for price rises, took home in earnings £175 for every £100 he or she had earned in 1979.

Reality, not rhetoric. The Pharisees in the socialist temple may have beat their breasts and hymned aloud their devotion to the Health Service and its workers, whose astonishing record of achievement they daily traduced. But let it not be said of we Conservatives that in the sight of the old or the sick we ever once passed by on the other side.

The area I most wanted to return to 'basics' was education. 'How many people in our country are fulfilled?' I asked myself. 'How many do the jobs of which they are capable? How many have their minds stretched?' Not enough, I answered, not by many hundreds of thousands. Many schools were excellent. Others were not. I wanted teaching in the worst schools to be levered up towards the level of the best.

I put education at the top of my personal agenda when I became prime minister: it was an old tradition in the party of Disraeli and Balfour and Butler. I had personal reasons, too. I had failed at school, and while I couldn't prevent others from doing so, I could prevent the system from failing them.

Bad schooling, unassessed and unreformed, can be overcome in homes with books, but even then not easily. But bad schooling falls heavily on youngsters who come from homes without a single book. If 'the classless society' was to mean anything, those youngsters needed a ladder to climb, and the first rung had to be better education. It was ironic that even as I planned education reforms, overgrown schoolboys in the media were engaged in a silly hunt to find out how many 'O' levels I had passed – as if, thirty years on, it mattered a jot.

On education, as on other subjects, I did not shoot from the lip. I took time to consult and to reflect on where we were going right and where we were going wrong. It often, I think, seems to the public that the process of modern government is one of moving from one day's headlines to the next. In reality, there is – or certainly there was before 1997 – a long-term will and a way behind it all; and the changes I had in mind were far-reaching and intended to put excellence and choice at the centre of the education system. I knew change would be hard-fought. I looked at the bright young faces I saw in primary schools, and then heard the angry, alienated voices of enough young people to fill Wembley Stadium leaving school each year without a single qualification.

I wanted nursery education to be available for all, as soon as was affordable. I wished to see basic grammar and spelling taught in primary schools. I intended to update the National Curriculum, which had been introduced by Ken Baker in 1988 but hijacked by devotees of progressive learning. I was determined to extend testing and make the results available to parents. I was not less bothered by *how* teachers taught than by *how well* they taught. Parents had a right to such information, and I believed that if it was made available, pressure would push up standards. Getting in place a framework of tests was vital, but it was often strongly resisted by the teaching profession.

So were plans to extend choice. In theory, open enrolment had been introduced to schools in 1990. In practice, it did not exist: the information upon which parents could exercise choice was not available, and even if it had been, local authorities ran a Byzantine system which kept the gates of popular schools shut to many children. I also had other options in mind to improve choice: to encourage the growth of grant-maintained (GM) schools, free of local authority control; and to expand the Assisted Places scheme to enable bright children from low-income families to attend good independent schools. More than once officials from the Department of Education proposed the abolition of this scheme to the Number 10 Policy Unit – a plea I rejected on each occasion – and the Labour Party's hostility to it was consistent. (By the time they abolished it following the 1997 election, over eighty-five thousand children had been helped, most of them finding a place at university, usually the first member of their families to do so. Abolition of the scheme was a vindictive political act.)

One of the many outrages of established educational practice was the lack of published data on school performance. I was astounded by how little was available, and introduced the publication of test results, firstly by local authority, then by individual school. I insisted on every parent receiving regular reports on their child's progress. But the most far-reaching change was to be the introduction, under the Citizen's Charter, of comparative performance tables for all schools – the so-called 'league tables'. Teachers' unions didn't like them, because they put pressure on their members; but they worked. From 1992 we published the results of all schools in public exams. I saw parental choice and the publication of results as a powerful force to improve standards.

To open up the system still further, I wanted a genuinely independent inspection system. We were so much in the dark about schools' standards that the country needed a Domesday Book of education, on which we could then build. The old inspectorate lacked rigour. It was an arm of the Department of Education, whereas logically a standard-setter and a standard-checker should be separate. The Audit Commission had shown in 1989 that many local education authorities (LEAs) were failing to fulfil their obligation to monitor school performance. Under the existing system it would have taken two centuries to have inspected all the country's twenty-four thousand schools, and then through a system that was compromised. I instructed the Policy Unit to work with Ken Clarke on a system of thorough and speedy inspection.

I have, of course, never had anything against individual teachers; only against the ethos within which some of them worked. Over the years teachers had been tossed back and forth on the waves of educational experiment, and their training had left them inadequately prepared for life in the classroom. As a result, a militant element had gained the upper hand in some of the main teaching unions, making them implacable opponents of change, of independent appraisal and of better rewards for the *best* lifelong classroom teachers – the very people I wanted to keep in the profession. I accepted that the teachers' task had not been made easier by the bureaucracy and paperwork flowing from the new regulations of the Department of Education and as the National Curriculum was introduced. Relations between the profession and the government had soured, and I hoped to mend this. But I knew it was not going to be easy against the background of some of the reforms we had to push through. So, sadly, it proved.

John Patten told me as he planned the 1994 Education Bill that reform had to begin with teacher training. I was sure that he was right, and that we needed to give teachers a better practical start, and to cut the time spent – frequently the majority of their courses – on theoretical, rather than classroom, training.

In 1944, Rab Butler had planned an education system which gave as much status to technical and vocational education as it did to academic courses. For forty years we had failed to give technical education the attention it needed, and I wanted to put this right – to bring academic and vocational education closer, without fusing them or diluting academic quality. My final objective was to make higher education available to more people. I wanted to raise the status of some of the better polytechnics, whose standards were at least as good as many universities. I set the target of ensuring that one student in three went on to higher education by the year 2000, and we succeeded in passing that target well ahead of time. It was a massive improvement in opportunity for future generations that will not, I think, be reversed, and it will help our country, as well as individuals, to equip themselves for success. To do all this, I was lucky to have Ken Clarke as a resolute education secretary from 1990 to 1992. He shared my ambitions to improve excellence, widen choice and minimise state control.

As one of my first aims was to raise the status of teachers, the confrontation between Ken and Norman Lamont over the 1991 pay increase for teachers was only likely to end one way: in the teachers' favour. But increases in pay, and the announcement that we planned to introduce a new independent School Teachers' Pay Review Body, did not ease relations with the profession; any support these measures received from teachers was swamped by the adverse reaction to our plans for formal, universal testing of children.

In spring 1991, the first round of National Curriculum testing of seven-year-olds in the basics of English and arithmetic began. These tests, though demonstrating, as had been feared, wide discrepancies in LEA performance, were not published school by school. That was to come later. I had some sympathy for the profession's complaints about the complexity of the tests, and promised to simplify them; but this did not mollify the more militant unions. They were aggrieved, too, at a Citizen's Charter White Paper which set out our intention to publish, school by school, information on public exams, truancy levels and test results.

In 1993, teachers began to boycott school tests. Ken Clarke's successor John Patten stepped in, bringing in Sir Ron Dearing, a true master of compromise, to head a new School Curriculum and Assessment Authority. He produced reports that unequivocally upheld the importance of the National Curriculum and testing but that, subject by subject, restructured and simplified it, to general applause. The testing boycott ended, and this painful step in education became established.

But as they became available, the test reports confirmed the importance of another track of policy – to reinforce the effectiveness of primary teaching. Successive reports revealed a rash of low expectations and children performing below their natural capabilities. Against that background, the creation of an Office of Standards in Education (OFSTED) was vital. From the outset I wished to set up a regular and fully independent inspection of schools. The idea had few friends in the education establishment, but Ken Clarke carried it into legislation in 1992. Under its early chief inspectors, Professor Stewart Sutherland and Chris Woodhead, OFSTED was quite fearless in condemning low standards and opening up information long hidden from parents.

John Patten had entered Parliament the same day as me in 1979, and had been the first of the new intake to become a junior minister. I remember many of his friends cheering him on his first Commons performance from the Dispatch Box. He was highly intelligent, but less self-assured than his

rather donnish demeanour suggested. As a junior minister he was outstanding – well prepared and effective in maintaining backbench support – and
when I appointed him to the Cabinet in April 1992 he had made his way
there on merit. But he faced a constant battle within his department and
with the teachers' unions, and was rather worn down by it. His health
suffered, and in 1994 I decided he needed a sabbatical to recover. If he had
maintained his interest he could – and would – have returned to high
office.

His successor, Gillian Shephard, concealed a sharp mind and business-
like political skill beneath a kindly, almost mumsie informality. A moderate
and a pragmatist by instinct, she was a natural member of my team, though
to dismiss her as a genial facilitator would be a mistake: Gillian was not
to be elbowed aside, and could be arch and acid with opponents. Labour
MPs soon learned that the chirrupy figure was more sparrowhawk than
sparrow. This was true in government too, where she scrapped without
fear or favour – even on occasion against me. But it never caused rancour
between us, and when times were troubled her attractive political personality made her a good ally.

In 1994 Gillian introduced the power to send 'hit squads' into failing
schools and, in the last resort, to take them over from local authorities.
The same year we legislated to introduce a new Teacher Training Agency,
and from 1997 a national curriculum for teacher training. In 1996 we gave
OFSTED powers to inspect LEAs. The effects of all these changes will –
if not watered down – bite over time. But we also wanted to sustain that
other great mechanism for promoting standards, namely parental choice.
Choice is at the heart of the Tory philosophy, and certainly of mine. That
was why I defended the Assisted Places scheme, and was such an enthusiast
for grant-maintained schools, which had been permitted under the 1988
Education Reform Act to opt out of an LEA that had failed them, after a
parental ballot. It was a strikingly simple concept, devolving power from
the centre to the schools, enabling them to make their own decisions on
how to use resources and improve their performance, motivating heads
and staff, and giving them freedom from sometimes hostile LEAs.

There were only a handful of GM schools in 1990, and I took huge
satisfaction in seeing them grow in number – usually in the teeth of opposition from local Labour, Liberal, and sometimes even, deplorably, Conservative councils. The hardest thing in politics, it seems, is to let power

go. GM schools had an indefatigable champion in Sir Bob Balchin, whose Grant-Maintained Schools Foundation time and again found itself faced with opposition from council- and trade union-funded propaganda against opting out. The heads, parents and staff of many schools showed enormous courage in the face of what frequently amounted to outright intimidation. I heard appalling stories of late-night phone calls, threats of sackings if ballots were lost, and petty boycotting of GM schoolchildren by local orchestras and sports competitions.

Despite this war against choice, over 1,100 schools opted out. Almost one and a half million parents had voted to go GM by the time Labour pledged to end GM status, and the pace of opting-out slowed as the 1997 election approached. Since May 1997 the Blair government, which has no love for individual choice, has overridden the brave battles fought by, and totally ignored the free choice of, those one and a half million parents. It is educational vandalism, and the next Conservative government must reassert the principle of choice for parents and local independence for schools.

As economic recovery gathered pace after 1992, I returned to the issue of nursery education. I wanted it available for all four-year-olds by 1997, and to extend it to three year olds thereafter. There was a ferocious battle in Whitehall when my intentions became clear. The Treasury was alarmed at the resource implications, and the Department of Education did not see nurseries as a central priority. Nonetheless, again to widen choice, I decided to go for an education voucher – a sum of money given directly to parents to help pay for a place for their children in nursery school. This voucher could be spent in either the public or the private sector, and would have equal value in each. Vouchers were introduced on a pilot basis in 1996 and nationally in 1997. Parents of nursery-age children were given £1,100, and an equivalent sum was deducted from the spending allocation of each education authority. Before the infant voucher system became accepted, the election was lost, and the new government strangled the scheme. There were few protests. Parents had not become used to the new system, LEAs were hostile even as they exploited it, and the private sector was slow to see the advantages it offered.

What has followed was all too predictable. LEAs took over nursery provision. Bureaucracy and regulation have redoubled. Many private and voluntary providers have simply withdrawn. OFSTED has found that standards in LEA reception classes are generally far lower than in the private and voluntary sectors. We have what I wanted – universal availability of nursery education. But it is not as I wanted it. Choice has been stifled. Regulation is rife. Standards are not what they should be.

But I am proud that we let some indestructible genies out of the bottle. We pushed through testing. We secured truly independent inspection. We published league tables of results. And, on the basis of proper information, we began to give parents real choice. Basic facts about education standards will never again be able to be suppressed. Armed with this knowledge, we should have the courage to let go of much of the detailed control that is still taken over education. Broad-brush directions may be necessary. But do we need to dictate? So long as results are achieved and children are taught knowledge, values, self-respect, confidence and courtesy, and earn the qualifications to succeed in life, why bother schools with fussy regulations?

If schools are delivering the goods, let them opt out. Let parents and teachers choose. Give parents the resources to provide their children with the education they want, where they want. Remove controls on the size of existing schools and the locality of new ones. Education should have no fear of freedom, and no fear of choice. The state must ensure that information and choice are free, and that the weaker schools are not permitted to fail their pupils. But I believe that true responsibility must go back where I always wanted it to go – to the individual school.

CHAPTER SEVENTEEN

# Protecting our Heritage

CULTURE PASSED ME BY as a boy, apart from a rough-and-ready understanding of music hall and theatre, learned at my father's knee. Sport filled much more of my life, and often the most enjoyable part.

When I was first at the Treasury, cricket was as likely to be on the agenda as economics. Nigel Lawson is a keen follower of Leicestershire, and Peter Brooke knows more about the history of the game than almost anyone I know. He has an encyclopaedic knowledge of which cricketing clergyman scored a hundred before lunch in Bangalore in the 1860s, and with Sir Michael Quinlan, Permanent Secretary at the Home Office, used to set a very stiff cricketing quiz for the *Spectator*. Peter and I have challenged one another with cricketing questions for twenty-five years, often to the bemusement of others.

Michael Heseltine was always baffled by this. Cricket is a mystery to Michael. After he became deputy prime minister he would sit beside me in Cabinet looking quizzical and puzzled as notes were brought in for me to read. I showed them first to Robin Butler, the Cabinet Secretary (grandson of Richard Daft, a great batsman in Victorian days) who sat on my other side, and then threw them across the table to Ken Clarke. Prime Minister, Cabinet Secretary, Chancellor: at first Michael assumed the markets were playing up. After a while I took mercy on his eagerness to know what was happening, and showed him one of the notes: it was the latest Test score. 'I don't believe it,' he muttered, shaking his head and pocketing the note 'for posterity'. He built up quite a collection of these notes, which will no doubt form part of the Heseltine Papers in due course. But I don't believe he ever came to know the game.

Some years ago Sir George Edwards, the aircraft designer who was to design the Valiant, the Viscount, the VC10 and the British half of Concorde, tried to discover how the great Surrey and England bowler Alec Bedser made the ball swing in the air. For months he took measurements and made calculations, but in the end he failed: it was, he concluded, 'something indefinable'. That is as good a definition of cricket as there is: 'something indefinable'.

And there is actually more to cricket than leather on willow. When Sir Barnes Wallis was testing the 'bouncing bomb' that was to be so successful in destroying German dams during the Second World War, he tried to make it skip across the water by imposing top-spin on it. At first he failed. The bomb bounced a few times, then sank. Wallis's experimental manager at Vickers was George Edwards, and he argued that back-spin would increase the number of bounces. At first Wallis was sceptical, but eventually he was persuaded. The bomb was redesigned – and it worked. The bombs skimmed along and took out the great German dams of the Ruhr valley with back-spin – something akin to a 'flipper' in cricket jargon.

Cricket has been an important part of my life since I was a boy. My affection for it pre-dates politics and will outlast it. Even during the busiest times in government I carved out time to watch the game; and every time I entered a cricket ground, especially The Oval and Lord's, my worries vanished. Even on the day I left Downing Street for the last time, a visit to The Oval reminded me that there is more to life than politics.

As I grew older, I learned to love music, painting and sculpture. I visited beautiful buildings and marvelled at the architecture. A visit to a great museum or a cinema would fill a wet day. Later, opera and ballet entered my life. I did not have a specialised interest in the arts, but I did enjoy them. They seemed to me to be an important part of our life and our national identity. I do not believe that man can live by GDP alone, and the pressure for economic well-being cannot crowd out the instinctive love of great art, in all its many forms, that can so often make us catch our breath in admiration.

In our material society, where success is measured in fame and fortune alone, we have undervalued the arts for too long. It is almost impossible to comprehend how we have done so when many millions of British citizens enjoy them – but we have. Somehow they have been regarded as an optional extra, rather than an integral part of life. This always seemed wrong to me. Participation in and enjoyment of the arts, heritage and sport helps build the sinews of society, in much the same way that voluntary and charitable work helps sustain it. I wished to encourage all these activities, because where interest and access to them is absent, the quality of life is diminished.

The ravaged economy and nanny-state mentality of the 1970s left the arts an ill-equipped prisoner of the state. The drive to restore economic well-being and self-dependence in the 1980s ensured that they remained a Cinderella with an absentee fairy godmother. Some ministers, such as Norman St John Stevas and Grey Gowrie, sought to raise their profile in government, but it was hard pounding for them; economic imperatives dominated, and ephemeral pleasures were regarded as not very serious matters.

Though Margaret Thatcher cared about the finer things of life – arts and heritage – she did so for reasons of national prestige. She campaigned actively, for example, to try to secure for Britain the magnificent Thyssen art collection. She did not share the prejudices of the Conservative Party's philistine persuasion that culture was 'fat Italians in tights'; but she was conservative with a small 'c' in her tastes. She had nothing whatsoever in common with the liberal-left arts establishment, other than a mutual disregard.

Nor was sport a guiding interest in her life, although Denis, a former rugby referee with a love of that sport and of golf, must surely have made her aware of its importance. She tried occasionally to show an interest, and dutifully turned up to watch great sporting events, but always looked rather out of place. She once attended a Scottish Cup Final, and at its conclusion held forth at length on the performance of a player who, although listed in the programme, had not in fact played on the day. Amid much embarrassed shuffling of feet and gazing at the ceiling, no one told her.

When I was appointed to the Cabinet with responsibility for the allocation of public spending, I began to consider what practical help I could offer the arts. I was not hostile to the idea of subsidy, because the arts brought pleasure to many who could not afford to pay a commercial price to enjoy them, and they did perform a socially useful purpose. I was convinced that more money for sport and the arts was justified. First, to widen access so that more and more people could become involved, contribute and have fun. Second, to nurture and encourage the huge talent we have in Britain, and give it opportunities to find expression. Third, to encourage experiment, the exploration of new territory, new repertoire and technique. This process is seldom profitable in cash terms, but it is essential for the vitality of both the commercial and the subsidised sectors, and the enormous cross-fertilisation between them. Whatever public tastes may be, the true creative artist is not inspired by the prospect of rehashing *The Mousetrap* for the umpteenth year.

From the vantage point of Chief Secretary, I looked across government and observed that responsibility for cultural interests was shared among various departments, and was important to none of them. Arts and Libraries, although a separate department, had no minister in the Cabinet. Sport was part of Education; film came under Trade and Industry; broadcasting under the Home Office; tourism under Employment; and heritage under the Department of the Environment. It was a mess.

In aggregate, expenditure on the arts and sport commanded a budget of around £1 billion a year, but in the annual scramble for fresh funds they had little chance of success when competing with the demands of education, defence or health. Every year small increases were allocated, but rarely sufficient for innovation and expansion. No one really fought for them. In the empires of Cabinet ministers they were regarded as lightweight responsibilities, and something of an irrelevant diversion.

They would gain attention only when there was a problem (an outbreak of football hooliganism, or the recurrent financial crises over the British Library); but there was no one individual who could articulate a more coherent and positive strategy. And yet they were important for millions of people. We were undervaluing a national asset, and missing a political opportunity.

I saw, also, that the system tended to favour the interests of the articulate and well-connected London-based arts lobby. I asked the Treasury for figures, and learned that throughout the 1980s the Arts Council spent twice as much in London and the South-East as in the whole of the rest of the country. To some extent this was inevitable – our great national institutions were a pinnacle of excellence, of which everyone had cause to be proud, and they tended to be in London. But that was an unsatisfactory position: there is a continuum from our national theatres and great symphony orchestras down to the efforts of amateur dramatic clubs and local brass bands. Yet there was an enormous gulf between them in the help that was offered. The arts are, or should be, as democratic a source of delight and education as any known to man, and yet they had become seen as elitist – often justifiably. What the 'elite' tended to forget was that unless they broadened the base of the arts' public support, and recognised that they were part of a tradition which begins in the school and the village hall, they risked undermining their own claim to public subsidy. The problem was how to stimulate wider enjoyment and involvement when sufficient taxpayers' money was never likely to be available to do so.

As Chancellor of the Exchequer, in 1989 I announced the first of a series of substantial increases in arts spending – 12.9 per cent for 1990–91, the first of three settlements which saw arts funding increase significantly above inflation. I also introduced more money for sport, by cutting football pools duty, so that the reduced taxation could be available to improve spectator safety at grounds, following the tragic loss of life at Hillsborough.

On becoming prime minister, I began to get to grips with giving culture and sport the higher profile they deserved. I was convinced this could only be done by establishing a new department of state to bring together all aspects of the arts, sport and heritage, under a minister of Cabinet rank who would have real political clout – especially with my backing. I intended the new department to have a powerful voice around the Cabinet table. And I knew just the minister for the job.

Money was needed as well if we were to make an impact. I thought I could raise it by establishing a national lottery, whose proceeds would be protected from the annual bunfight over public spending, and would be exclusively used to give a real boost to good causes that were never likely to fare well from the public purse. I identified these as sport, the arts, our national heritage, charities and a fund to commemorate the millennium.

Above all, I saw the proceeds from the lottery as a means to stimulate and nurture talent and involvement at the grassroots in every part of the country. Why should not the child from a low-income family have the same chance to participate in and enjoy the arts and sport as the one from a more privileged background? And should not that child be given a better opportunity to do so than his parents ever enjoyed? I thought so, and I believed the lottery could bring that about. I always envisaged that large projects for our major national institutions would be eligible for funding, and rightly so, but above all I wanted the lottery to be a process which worked from the grassroots up, in which new ideas and projects would come from local communities, and in which greater involvement, public access and education for everyone were clear and explicit objectives.

I wanted David Mellor to lead this new initiative. I had discussed my ideas with him before the 1992 election, so he probably guessed that he would be the first secretary of state of the new department if we won. Some thought David brash. I knew him to be a knowledgeable enthusiast of the arts, especially music, and a lover of sport. He had served briefly as Arts Minister under Margaret, and had seen the opportunities, as I had, from the vantage point of being chief secretary to the Treasury. David was custom-built for the job. He relished the prospect, and his remark shortly after his appointment that he thought his new position would be 'great fun' meant that the new Department of National Heritage soon became known as the 'Ministry of Fun'.

Unfortunately, as it turned out, David's definition of fun ran rather wider than his departmental responsibilities. Two months after his appointment, in July 1992, the press reported that he had been having an affair with an actress (see pages 551–3). The fuss rolled on, and the media were relentless. Eventually David had no alternative but to resign. In private, he was candid: 'I've been bloody stupid,' he said. And he had. He bore up well despite the awful hammering he received, and self-pity never touched him.

The loss of David's flamboyance was a blow to the government, but I was fortunate that the former Northern Ireland Secretary Peter Brooke, a civilised and cultivated man who knew his Picasso from his Lautrec, was prepared to be recalled to the colours. Peter soon settled in at the new department, and under his leadership it became an established part of the Whitehall landscape.

During the mid-1990s the public expenditure settlements were very tough for every department of state, but on more than one occasion I intervened to protect the arts and sport from the worst ravages. What was petty cash to the big departments was a large sum to the Department of National Heritage, and I wished it to be a success. This protection from the scale of cuts imposed elsewhere did not impress those determined to believe that the arts were unfairly treated, but it happens to be the truth. I was not bothered by the criticism, because the new source of regular and dependable funding that I had in mind would dwarf all previous assistance.

The idea of a national lottery was nothing new. They were an established fact of life in the rest of Europe and around the world. In England, the first national lottery had been set up in 1569 to refurbish the Cinque Ports, and a lottery provided the funds to build the British Museum. The last lottery closed down in 1826, after Treasury officials embezzled the funds. Since that time, interest in reviving the idea had been expressed periodically throughout the last hundred years. In 1978 a commission under Lord Rothschild recommended that there should be a single national lottery, with its proceeds going to the arts, sports and good causes. During the 1988 National Health Service review, the government briefly considered the idea of a national lottery to help fund the NHS. However, it was felt – rightly – that such a source of funding, which was by its nature voluntary, should not be used for mainstream expenditure.

When I first proposed the idea of a national lottery in 1991, I was astonished to find that apart from Sarah Hogg and Chris Patten, only Tim Renton, the Arts Minister, and Kenneth Baker, then at the Home Office, were enthusiastic. Many ministers and officials were uninterested and others were downright hostile. The Treasury was uncomfortable too. It disliked the idea that a big new revenue raiser would yield funds for special causes in addition to government funding, which I insisted would continue. More credibly, they were also worried about whether a successful lottery would adversely affect revenues from the football pools, which swelled the public coffers. To his credit, however, Norman Lamont did not share the official Treasury view, and was sufficiently enthusiastic at one point to wish to announce our intention to legislate for a national lottery in his budget speech of March 1992.

The lottery went ahead, of course, and the Treasury acquiesced, although from time to time the old Treasury instinct continued to surface. In a speech in July 1994, during discussions about the policy and financial directions under which the lottery distributors would operate, I said, 'There are some in Whitehall who find it hard to give up the degree of control they have traditionally exercised.' It was a warning shot at the Treasury. As if on cue, Michael Portillo, then Chief Secretary, wrote round Whitehall suggesting that all lottery projects over £10 million should be scrutinised and approved by the appropriate departments. Any such requirement would have provoked a spate of resignations among the lottery-distributing bodies, who fiercely guarded the arm's-length status from government the legislation had given them. It would also have been costly and bureaucratic. Michael's proposal, an odd one from such a firm advocate of small government, went into the bin.

I insisted that the lottery should be in our manifesto for the 1992 election, and after our victory I had no difficulty in ensuring that legislation to bring it into being found an early place in our plans. Peter Brooke took it through Parliament and it received royal assent in autumn 1993.

We invited bids to run the lottery, and after an exhaustive examination of them the licence was awarded to the Camelot Group, a consortium of mostly British companies, by Peter Davis, the Director-General of the National Lottery.

Within six months of the grant of the licence, faster than anyone had thought possible, Camelot had built up a huge enterprise, with ten thousand ticket-selling outlets open on the first day of trading, rising to forty thousand over the next few months. They had also trained thirty-five thousand staff and established a network of regional offices and helplines. It was a massive undertaking.

In November 1994 I launched the lottery at the Tower of London. I was asked to buy a ticket, and did so. Irrationally, given the odds, I was terrified that I might win. I knew I could not keep the money, but explaining to my family that I'd given away £8 million or so might have been embarrassing, even though they would have understood. I must have been the only lottery-ticket purchaser ever to hope not to win.

From the day the lottery was up and running, views were expressed about it by two different but parallel worlds which seemed to have little contact with one another. Up and down the country, thousands of village-hall committees, brass bands, small arts groups, local theatres, sports clubs and charities galvanised themselves to dream up imaginative projects in the hope of winning lottery funding. The local media recorded the pleasure and pride felt by their communities which were able to realise their dreams with lottery money. The high streets were packed with people, clutching their lottery tickets, looking forward to a bit of harmless fun and make-believe during the weekly draw. In other quarters, the lottery was less well received.

Concern about gambling was frequently voiced, both during the passage of the Bill and afterwards by some of the bishops. I thought these fears were misplaced. At odds of fourteen million to one against winning the jackpot, the lottery was unlikely to attract the serious gambler. It was and remains innocent fun. Once the Bill was in place, many churchmen took the opportunity to apply for lottery funds to renovate old church bells or

*Right* With HM the Queen at Balinoral: September 1991.

*Below* The First Waltz at the Civic Ball in the Wintergarden, Blackpool: Party Conference, October 1991.

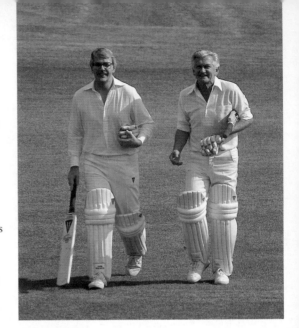

*Right* Returning to the pavilion after batting with Australian Prime Minister Bob Hawke at a charity cricket match in Harare during the Commonwealth Heads of Government Meeting in Zimbabwe: October 1991.

*Below* Opening Pandora's box: the Maastricht European summit, 10 December 1991. Tristan Garel-Jones is on my right and John Kerr, our EU Ambassador, on my left.

*Above* On the soapbox in Luton during the 1992 general election campaign. The Socialist Workers' Party were out in force but my PPS Graham Bright held his seat for the Conservatives.

*Left* Meeting the people of Tamworth during the 1992 general election campaign. Norman Fowler is behind me — not warding off evil spirits, but holding an umbrella.

With the Party Chairman, Chris Patten, at a Central Office morning press conference during the 1992 general election campaign.

*Above* Arriving at Conservative Central Office with Norma, Chris Patten, Elizabeth and James, in the early hours of 10 April 1992, having won the 1992 general election. Chris had lost his constituency of Bath to the Liberal Democrats.

*Left* With Norma and Chris Patten waving to supporters from inside Conservative Central Office on the morning of our election victory.

*Right* With Helmut Kohl at the Birmingham summit, October 1992. Helmut was in good humour: earlier that day angry miners had been chanting 'Coal for ever' outside the conference hall.

All smiles at Dublin Castle after a difficult day thrashing out the foundations of the Downing Street Declaration. Left to right: Paddy Mayhew, Douglas Hurd, self, Albert Reynolds and Dick Spring: 3 December 1993.

Following the Downing Street Declaration – with British troops at Gough Barracks, Armagh, during one of many visits to Northern Ireland: 22 December 1993.

*Above* Press conference with Bill Clinton at Chequers, following bilateral held between engagements commemorating the fiftieth anniversary of D-Day: 5 June 1994.

*Left* Two into one almost goes: taking the salute with Helmut Kohl.

Children from Birmingham Children's Hospital visit Number 10 to form a Junior Cabinet: 9 June 1994.

Whilst Parliament is in session, the Cabinet meets at 10.30 every Thursday morning. The boat-shaped Cabinet table was installed by Harold Macmillan, and allows the Prime Minister to make eye-contact with everyone around it: July 1994.

church roofs, and the criticism fell away. I was delighted, since old churches are an important part of our heritage, and one of the purposes of the lottery was to help preserve them.

The money raised for good causes exceeded everyone's wildest dreams, as over thirty million people began to play the lottery every week. It made a real difference to the quality of life in Britain. Between its launch in 1994 and July 1997, the lottery became the most successful innovation of any government for years, with over £3.5 billion raised for charities, sport, heritage, the arts and projects to mark the millennium. The lottery is now on course to raise £2 billion more than was originally expected by 2001.

It was an achievement of which the country should have been proud. Yet spates of bad publicity continued to overshadow it. I recall a mordant comment penned by a member of my Private Office at Number 10 on a press release giving details of new awards: 'A decent and populist selection which will receive no publicity.'

There was plenty of publicity for some of the criticisms of the lottery. Most of the abuse was directed at Camelot directors, as higher than expected proceeds from the sales of lottery tickets produced higher than expected profits. This triggered a row, stirred up by the Labour Party, about 'fat cats' and directors' bonuses. The critics overlooked the fact that the lottery could have failed, and that Camelot could have lost its investment altogether.

It was also forgotten that Camelot won the franchise on the basis of a bid which offered the maximum revenue for good causes, and retained the smallest percentage to cover costs and profit of any of the rival bidders. The Labour Party exploited the bad publicity by making a commitment to transfer the lottery to a not-for-profit operator, 'so that maximum funds go to good causes' – a non-sequitur, as they knew perfectly well. If any 'not-for-profit' operators harboured hopes of being awarded the lottery, they were to be disappointed. In office, the Labour government changed its mind.

In the early days of the lottery, Stephen Dorrell was Heritage Secretary. When I appointed him in July 1994 – it was his first Cabinet post – he seemed dismayed. It was not the job he had hoped for, and he was never at home in it. Stephen's boyish looks and languid manner concealed a keen ambition and an appetite for work. He had entered Parliament with me in 1979 (at twenty-seven he was the youngest Conservative in the intake), and had a leftish, pro-European reputation derived from his work for Peter Walker. But Stephen never joined the 'sulking tendency' among the 'wets', and, without compromising his beliefs, threw himself into the scramble for office, where his good brain and articulate manner served him well. He was mightily relieved to be moved from Heritage to Health after only a year.

Towards the end of Stephen's tenure, in May 1995, came the first in a series of rows about lottery grants, when the National Heritage Memorial Fund, the distributing body for heritage projects, announced a grant of £11 million to buy the Churchill papers owned by Sir Winston's grandson, Winston Churchill, the Conservative MP for Davyhulme. This row was rapidly followed by another, when the Arts Council announced an award of £55 million towards the redevelopment of the Royal Opera House. This was immediately seized upon as evidence that the lottery was being stitched up by toffs, for other toffs. It was being nabbed by the well-heeled London-based elite for their 'flagship' projects, whilst the provinces were left rattling their begging bowls for the leftovers.

The reality was that London, including its national assets like the Royal Opera House, received less per head in lottery grants than, for example, Manchester, Merseyside or Yorkshire. Indeed, in 1996 Lord Gowrie, by then no longer in government but presiding at the Arts Council, was complaining that too few grant applications were coming from London and the South-East. Moreover, large grants of over £1 million accounted for a minuscule 3 per cent of total awards. Nearly 80 per cent were for sums of less than £100,000. These facts were ignored, and all we seemed to hear was the brittle rasp of the critics' pens.

Sometimes our problems were worsened because the distributing bodies were careless in their handling of the media. The Charities Board seemed to specialise in sending out negative signals. A statement that medical charities would not be given priority in the first round of awards led to widespread complaints that medical charities would never be eligible for grants – an error which neither the Board nor ministers in the Home Office were able successfully to correct. Later on there were predictable complaints about other grants that did not conform to populist causes.

One of the most damaging allegations was that the lottery was reducing individual donations to charities, as it encouraged people to believe that by playing the lottery they were already giving their pennyworth to 'good causes'. This nonsense was stirred up by the National Council for Voluntary Organisations (NCVO), who claimed in 1995, on the basis of the flimsiest of evidence, that charities would lose £200 million a year from the lottery, while only gaining £150 million – a net loss of £50 million.

As even the NCVO's own figures suggested that charitable receipts from the lottery would be in the order of £300 million a year, the argument simply did not stand up, and the lottery provided a huge new source of income for charities, and continued to do so. Nor was there any real evidence that lotteries were having an adverse impact on charitable giving. The fact is that even before the lottery was launched there had been a long-term downward trend in charitable giving. Such evidence as there is suggests that the lottery made minimal impact on people's charitable consciences: an opinion poll conducted in 1995 revealed that just 2 per cent of people said they had reduced their charitable donations as a result of the lottery, while 4 per cent said they had increased them. The truth was that most people played the lottery for fun.

Our failure to rebut some of these criticisms was one of the factors which persuaded me in 1996 to shift responsibility for charities from the Home Office to the Department of National Heritage. It was a move which was broadly welcomed by charities and the voluntary sector, although for some reason the decision was to be partly reversed by the Labour government.

I had more sympathy with another criticism made of the lottery, which was that it took too little account of the need for revenue spending, with the attendant danger that we might end up paying for a herd of white elephants, beautiful empty buildings which no one could afford to use. This argument did have some force, although there were very good reasons why we decided to confine lottery funding mainly to capital projects in the first instance. The first was that, knowing the Treasury mind, I wanted to defend the lottery against Treasury pressure to use it as a source of revenue for mainstream public expenditure. The capital rule helped to ring-fence lottery funding, and to underline the principle that it would not be used to replace existing government spending. Second, I was very wary indeed of the lottery being sucked into a commitment to long-term revenue-funding. I was well aware that once you turn on the drip-feed of subsidy, the patient rapidly becomes dependent, and it can become impossible to turn it off again. I did not want resources pre-empted in this fashion, since the whole purpose of the lottery was to stimulate new projects, not merely to sustain existing schemes.

Nevertheless, I intended that once the lottery had dealt with the more pressing capital needs, it would be sensible to provide more leeway for everyday expenditure, and so, in 1996, Virginia Bottomley, by now Secretary of State at the Department of National Heritage, announced modifications to enable limited revenue-funding for the arts and sport, and for the preservation of heritage buildings.

If we had won the 1997 election, I would have permitted far more extensive revenue-spending on sport and the arts, to ensure that they benefited when the Millennium Fund was wound up. My preferred option was to pay for full-time sports teachers, and to put them back in state schools. Alas, that will not now happen, since the Labour government has snaffled the money for pet schemes of its own. This is a pity. Nurturing our young talent to give us the chance to beat the world at soccer, cricket and rugby would have done wonders for national morale.

My interest in promoting a renaissance in sport and the arts, and also in helping heritage and charities, was thought to be rather quirky by some of my colleagues. I disagreed with them then, and do now. Leisure, whether cultural or sporting, is immensely important, and so is encouragement for voluntary endeavour and the preservation of our architectural heritage. They enrich our lives. Too many politicians are keen to talk about duty and obligation, and forget about enjoyment – yet that is an important part of a rounded life too.

In 1994 I had appointed Iain Sproat as Minister of Sport with a brief to raise its profile. The following year we launched our 'Raising the Game' initiative, with the intention of putting sport back at the heart of weekly life in every school, and encouraging links between schools and sporting clubs. This had long been an ambition of mine. I believed it right to give every child the option of enjoying sport, and that over time the initiative would improve sporting excellence at national level.

Iain was as enthusiastic as I had hoped he would be. He was no respecter of seniority or bureaucracy, and trod on many toes, but he was very effective and knew he could rely on my full support. With the active involvement of my Policy Unit at Number 10 the initiatives rolled out: one hundred schools received lottery grants totalling £20 million within twelve months; a National Junior Sport Programme was launched by the Sports Council with both lottery and private-sector sponsorship; and Colin Cowdrey, one of England's greatest cricketers, chaired a committee of 'sporting ambassadors' to enthuse the young. We planned a British Academy of Sport, with regional academies to follow, and announced the building of a new English National Stadium at Wembley with £120 million of lottery money going towards the cost, and a further £60 million for a stadium in Manchester. Swimming benefited too, with £20 million for a new pool to enable Britain to host the 2002 Commonwealth Games. I willingly agreed to support the Football Association's bid to host the World Cup in 2006, and set up government and Football Association machinery to promote our cause. Sport is an important part of our national life, and I wished to support it.

After the 1997 election I watched warily to see what the new Labour government would do to the embryo Department of National Heritage and its responsibilities. I soon learned. They could not leave it be. They changed its name to the Department of Culture, Media and Sport, ditched some of my plans to help sport, and siphoned off some of the lottery money. This piece of larceny was ironic, since in opposition the Labour Party had been quick to pounce on any suggestion that the lottery was in danger of becoming a cash cow for the Treasury. But that is what it has now become. The new Labour government soon announced that after 2001, proceeds from the Millennium Fund would be used 'to provide direct support for a range of education, environment and public health projects'. I have no doubt that these will be worthy expenditures, but they are core government-spending programmes and should be funded by taxation.

So, while the arts world celebrated the election of the new Labour government, Labour succeeded where the Treasury had failed under the Conservatives: it looted the lottery. The door is now open for the government to treat the lottery as a guaranteed source of revenue, and to justify cutbacks in public expenditure in activities that benefit from it. This is precisely what I sought to avoid. If it happens, the lottery will lose its focus. This would be a pity: if the lottery rolls on unchanged for a decade or more, and is not plundered by the government, it will revolutionise sport, the arts and our built heritage.

The lottery has achieved so much in a very short period of time: arts centres here, new sports complexes there, restored churches, new village halls, festivals, new instruments for orchestras, cycleways, inner-city parks, and a thousand other benefits that give a new lease of life to all those

Burkean 'little platoons' who make our country what I believe it to be: the best place in the world in which to live.

In 1996, the National Heritage Select Committee said, 'It took vision to establish the lottery, to get it going and to make it the enormous success it has become.' I am proud that it was my vision. I hope that the lottery will continue to work its magic of turning dreams into reality, enriching us all.

# CHAPTER EIGHTEEN

## *The Union at Risk*

O N 1 MAY 1707, the Union between England and Scotland came into being. It had been opposed consistently and vehemently by the forerunners of the present Scottish Conservative Party. On 1 May 1997 – 290 years to the day – the Conservative Party, the only political party to defend the Union as a matter of policy, was swept out of every parliamentary seat it held in Scotland, in a disastrous election result. This outcome was Armageddon delayed. We had feared such a result in 1992, but our campaign for the Union had forced back the tide and we had made small gains. In 1997 the devolution bandwagon had five more years behind it, and the Conservative government had been weakened by five more years as the universal target of all the other Scottish political parties and the media.

Scotland mattered to me. From the moment I became prime minister I could see the danger of it sliding away to independence through the halfway house of devolution. I believed this would be damaging for the whole of the United Kingdom, and bad for Scotland.

I saw the UK without Scotland as a diminished power: less able to punch its weight at European Councils or in the world; without its place as one of the permanent members of the UN Security Council; perhaps excluded from the G7 Group of industrial nations. I foresaw Scotland and England not in harmony, but in competition, and I foresaw Scotland losing inward investment, losing political clout, facing higher taxation and pitted against an England in thrall to nationalism. My support for the Union was based on the political judgement that we should not break up a partnership that worked. But I knew that popular sentiment was moving slowly but inexorably towards devolution.

My instinct for the Union was not a personal aberration. It was shared by the majority of the Scottish Conservative Party. As Unionists, we defended it with conviction, even though it was not necessarily in the interests of the Conservative Party to do so. It was in the interests of the UK, and that, we believed, was sufficient.

Although for a period in the 1950s the Conservative Party held a majority of the vote and seats in Scotland, this was unusual. Throughout their long history north of the border the Conservatives had rarely been secure in the affections of the Scottish electorate. For most of the post-war period they had been faced with myths that were more compelling than the truth. Eighteen years in government since 1979 had added potency to these myths. This had helped lead to a divergence in electoral behaviour, with large Labour majorities in Scotland, and Conservative majorities in England. In the run-up to the 1997 election it was proclaimed by Labour, Liberals and Scottish Nationalists alike that Scotland was ignored and unfairly treated under the Tories; that the Conservatives were an English party; that industries had been wilfully closed; and that the Tories, for some unfathomable reason, never explained, were out to do Scotland down. It was nonsense, of course. But boredom after eighteen years of unchanged government lent an appearance of truth to every lie.

Scotland has always been a turbulent and restless neighbour to England. Scottish folk-heroes like William Wallace and Robert the Bruce owe their status to their hostility to the English. 'The Englishman sits apart, bursting with pride and ignorance,' wrote Robert Louis Stevenson. 'He figures among his vassals in the hour of peace with the same disdainful air that led him onto victory.' Little changes; national stereotypes are still as lopsided as ever.

It was the success of the changing Scottish economy, not its failure, that did the Conservatives most harm. Margaret Thatcher's economic medicine served Scotland well, and I carried it forward in the 1990s. Such changes are always painful. There were job losses in the shipyards on the Clyde, in the coalfields and, most symbolic of all, in the decline and closure of the steel plant at Ravenscraig. All were hurtful. And each one was presented as the result of an 'uncaring' English government.

Nevertheless, by 1997 Scotland was outperforming most of the rest of the UK on a wide range of economic indicators: productivity, inward investment, export growth and standards of living. It was a sea change from the 1970s, when Scotland's future seemed one of continual decline, palliated only by a drip-feed of subsidy. By 1997 there was a renewed sense of self-confidence, which led more Scots to believe that Scotland could go it alone. As they did so, the anti-Tory, even anti-English, sentiment grew and grew.

When I became prime minister in 1990, the prospects for the Conservative Party in Scotland and for the Union looked grim. In the 1987 election we had been reduced to only ten seats out of seventy-two in Scotland. In November 1991 this became nine when we lost a by-election at Kincardine and Deeside. As we approached the 1992 general election the opinion polls showed a surge in support for nationalism, and the desire for independence running at between a third and a half of the electorate. Ominously, enthusiasm for separation was strongest amongst younger voters.

There was widespread speculation that we were heading for a total wipe-out north of the border. I was deeply worried. Even if we won a majority across Britain, I did not know how we could continue to govern Scotland if we did not have sufficient Scottish MPs of good quality to man the Scottish Office. Devolution would have become inevitable, and I would have had to introduce it. The thought repelled me, and I determined to make the preservation of the Union a centrepiece of our appeal to Scotland in the general election to come.

By November 1990 Malcolm Rifkind, the Secretary of State for Scotland, was overdue for a move. I appointed him to Transport and brought Ian Lang into the Cabinet as his successor. It was vital to challenge some of the myths about our record and our concern for Scotland. I knew that Ian saw the problem as I did, as one for the whole party and the whole nation, and not just for the English bit of it. He was courteous, able and gentlemanly, and in 1990 his persuasive qualities were exactly what we needed to address the Scots' perception of the Tories as uncaring and extreme.

Ian soon faced a tricky problem caused by the end of the Cold War. The 'peace dividend', welcome as it was, merely added to our political troubles in Scotland. In July 1991 we proposed to reduce British Army personnel from 156,000 to 116,000, a reduction of 25 per cent, and to cut or amalgamate a number of famous regiments. There was fierce resistance throughout the country to the news that 'our' regiments were under threat. Nowhere was this stronger than in Scotland, where the Gordon Highlanders and the Royal Scots were among those facing the axe. All five Scottish Tory backbenchers lobbied hard to save the regiments, and Sir Hector Munro, the long-serving and widely liked Member for Dumfries, put the case to me, forcefully and personally, in Number 10.

As our problems across government multiplied, the press discerned – and magnified – the emergence of pro-devolution sentiment in a small part of the Scottish party. These Scottish Conservatives, who were very few in number, saw a commitment to a Scottish Parliament as the best way of heading off a possible constitutional crisis, and improving our chances at the next election. There was some force to this argument in party terms, but I believed it was fundamentally flawed: devolution, I was sure, would increase the likelihood of eventual independence. I thought it wrong tactically, too. Support for the Union in Scotland may have been confined to a minority (consistently around 26 per cent of the electorate), but it was a sizeable minority, and reason suggested that, against the prevailing prejudice, where there was a belief in the Union it tended to be strongly held. Most opinion polls also found that among Scots in general, constitutional issues were well down the list of their concerns. So I believed that many supporters of the Union would vote for a party which stood up for the Union, almost regardless of what they felt about its policies more generally. Indeed, lifelong socialists voted for us in Scotland on that very basis. It was 'niche' marketing, if you like.

Above all, the reason I would have no truck with devolution was out of principle, not pragmatism. I believed it would ultimately lead to the separation of England and Scotland. From the outset Ian Lang and I were at one in believing the Union was worth defending – even at considerable political risk to ourselves, even though it had precious few supporters in the Scottish media, and even though the opposition parties were, one way or another, committed to policies that were likely to bring about its end.

I was absolutely clear that the Labour Party's ideas for devolution to a new Scottish Parliament with tax-raising powers (ideas which they and the Liberal Democrats spelled out in detail shortly before the 1992 election) were a confidence trick. I believed that the establishment of a Parliament would create friction with Westminster without satisfying the demands of those who wanted independence for Scotland. The powers to raise income tax by 3p in the pound (which led Michael Forsyth to campaign later against what Ian Lang had christened the 'Tartan Tax') would bear heavily on many Scottish families and would, for the first time, create differential tax rates in the UK. Nevertheless, the money raised would represent just

3 per cent of total public spending in Scotland, a tiny proportion, and considerably less per head than is spent by the average Scottish local authority. The other 97 per cent would, as before, be dependent on decisions taken in Whitehall and Westminster. As, under the Treasury's arcane system of allocating funding, Scotland already received 25 per cent more per head than England in identifiable public spending, to spend as Scottish Office ministers thought fit, it was more or less inevitable that English MPs would over time seek to claw back some of the excess, leaving the Scottish Parliament to fill the gap with the proceeds of the 3p extra income tax. When this happened it would create bitterness and enable those with a separatist agenda to claim that the English were taking revenge for the establishment of the Scottish Parliament. It was all too predictable.

I feared also that by exposing the reality of the favourable spending treatment given to Scotland, devolution would stir up latent English nationalist resentment, leading to a backlash. I was already well aware that there was considerable discontent within English departments about Scottish money. Mostly this was confined to griping behind the scenes about the size of Scottish funding. Feeling was especially bitter among Members of Parliament with constituencies in English regions (such as the South-West, the North-East and many parts of London) which had social and economic problems every bit as serious as Scotland's, but which lost out badly in the annual public spending rounds, and lacked the economic clout exercised by the government agency Scottish Enterprise.

The unfairness was thrown into sharp relief once we began, through the Citizen's Charter, to measure and compare the performance of public services. As we set target waiting times for hospital appointments and operations, it became clear just how advantaged the Scots really were. As they raced ahead, cutting targets all round, English hospitals lagged well behind. I argued, not always convincingly even to myself, that this was a price worth paying to keep the Union and to restrain the Treasury's proposed butchery of Scotland's spending. Yet clearly there was a deep well of resentment in England that would surface if English tolerance was tested beyond reasonable limits.

Nor were these the only difficulties I foresaw. It was extraordinary that the English viewpoint was seldom thought to be a serious issue in the insular world of the Scottish left establishment. It was even argued that the threat of an English backlash was not a real one. Yet what the English were being asked to accept in principle was that, in addition to favourable treatment in the allocation of resources nationally, Scotland would be able to add to the disparity by raising extra resources of its own. This was patently absurd, unfair and bound to lead to trouble.

Nor was money the only issue that devolution would throw into sharp focus. Scotland had long been over-represented at Westminster, with seventy-two MPs, 10 per cent more than were justified by the size of its population. If anyone suffered a democratic deficit, it was the English. But not only did Labour have no proposals to address this problem, they would worsen it. Scottish MPs sitting at Westminster would have the right to vote on matters that affected England: health, education, local government, social work, housing, economic development, transport, law and order, the environment, sport and the arts; but in Scotland all of these areas would be dealt with in the Scottish Parliament, and English MPs would have no say whatsoever. It was an unbalanced bargain for the English. What possible justification was there for this? This in essence was the famous 'West Lothian Question', so called after the Labour MP for West Lothian, Tam Dalyell, who first raised it. By doing so, Dalyell, an honourable and long-standing opponent of devolution, has been rewarded with abuse, intimidation and threats from his fellow party members.

As I looked forward I saw a flight of jobs and investment to the south, escaping higher Scottish taxation. I could foresee that a Scottish Parliament, frustrated and resentful at its impotence to stop this, would institutionalise the prevailing Scottish gripe that they were being unfairly treated, and add to the feeling of alienation from the rest of the United Kingdom. All of this filled me with foreboding.

Ian Lang and I put these arguments before the Scottish people, but of course they were negative arguments, and easy to caricature as 'telling the Scots they can't govern themselves'. That wasn't the point: of course the Scots could govern themselves. The point was, how large an economic and political price would they be called upon to pay for it, and what would be the wider impact on the UK?

Part of the Conservatives' problem was that we had tended to defend the Union on the basis of past glories. These still had the power to inspire, and were central to the support for the Union in the Tory Party. In the years of empire, the advantages of the Union had been plain to hardheaded Scots who, as soldiers, entrepreneurs, administrators and missionaries were in the forefront of the British imperial advance. But as the imperial dream had faded, such arguments had little resonance with younger Scots. Moreover, they completely failed to incorporate an understanding of and sympathy for the Scottish desire for a separate identity, and the nation's pride in its own, separate history.

I felt that the case for the Union needed to be put in a way that would make it relevant to the future as well as the past, and would present it as the natural choice of those who were proud to call themselves Scottish. I determined to do this in three ways. First, by bringing the Union to Scotland, giving more practical demonstrations of its value in the modern world by staging national and international events there. Second, by listening to Scottish concerns and ensuring that where possible decisions about Scotland were taken in Scotland – 'bringing the Union alive', we called it. And third, by going to Scotland as often as I could to put the case myself to the Scottish people.

We advanced the argument, which I strongly endorse, that the Union still had enormous moral and political relevance in shaping our society. Moreover it was, and is, vital in enabling the United Kingdom to exert its full influence in world affairs. If the UK were to split into its component parts, it would not wield the same influence. Its voice would be fragmented and marginalised.

This is a national matter. My support for the Union has nothing whatever to do with advantage to the Conservative Party, and it was always rather a mystery that many Scots seemed to believe that our commitment was a selfish one. After all, with only nine out of seventy-two seats in Scotland, on the face of it separation would remove a major electoral handicap for the Conservatives, a point I made in a speech in Glasgow to Scottish parliamentary candidates on 22 February 1992:

> It is not the Conservative Party that gains, or has gained, from the ties between Scotland and England. And yet it is our party that supports the Union. Not because it has always been good to us, but because it has always seemed right to us. Not always in our political interest, but always in that of our kingdom and the countries within it.

From the start Ian Lang and I set out to illustrate the reality of the United Kingdom as a working partnership in Scotland itself. In May 1991

I chose Glasgow Cathedral as the venue for the national thanksgiving service for the successful conclusion to the Gulf War. On the whole this decision was well received, even though some of our political opponents voiced their approval through gritted teeth. Unfortunately the occasion was marred by a wholly characteristic and ridiculous row when it was discovered that the Very Reverend Dr William (Bill) Morris, the delightful minister in charge of the cathedral, had invited the Archbishop of York to give the sermon. Since this was a national occasion, it seemed reasonable to me to invite such a senior churchman from south of the border. Others disagreed. Why couldn't it have been the Moderator of the Church of Scotland, or even the Catholic Archbishop of Glasgow? Was it because they had opposed the war? asked the papers. Wasn't this yet another sign of English arrogance? The sad fact was that whenever there was a grievance to be found, the Scottish media and the opposition parties seized on it and turned it into evidence of the lack of understanding by the English for the Scots.

The Glasgow service was the first of a number of events in which the Union came to Scotland. In December 1992 we chose Edinburgh as the location for the European summit, partly to demonstrate the advantages to Scotland of retaining a united voice in Europe. EU environment ministers also met at Gleneagles. It was with the same basic intention, though with a less happy outcome, that I had chosen to make a major statement on my commitment to the Exchange Rate Mechanism to the Scottish CBI in Glasgow in September 1992, just a few days before the pound fell out of the ERM. The Union, warts and all, I suppose it might be called.

I wanted, too, to show that differences between Scotland and the rest of the United Kingdom could be accommodated within the Union. Defending Scotland's right to be different was not always easy. In education, in particular, it caused headaches. The grant-maintained movement, so successful and popular in England, simply did not fit into the quite different Scottish traditions and ethos. The scheme was, of course, discretionary, but over the years only one or two Scottish schools sought to opt out, usually for special reasons. As a result some of our key messages on education, major themes at our national party conferences, had little relevance in Scotland. Some of my advisers urged me to insist on a more active promotion of GM schools north of the border, but in the end I trusted the judgement of Scottish ministers that this would be seen as imposing English solutions on Scotland, and would be deeply resented. In this, as in many other areas with Scotland, I felt we were treading on eggshells.

Despite these frustrations, I did believe it was perfectly right and reasonable that, where possible, decisions about Scottish matters should be taken in Scotland. It was irritating that the term 'devolution' had been hijacked by people whose ultimate aim was separatism. I was always in favour of devolved government where it made sense for Scots to run their own show: to the Scottish Office, to local authorities, and direct to schools and hospitals, bypassing politicians. This last step was too radical for many devolutionists: they wanted Scottish *institutions* to have power, not Scottish *individuals*.

These then were the broad themes we developed before and after the general election of 1992. However, in the run-up to that election, things still looked pretty bleak. Ian Lang, with my support, had ruled out any steps towards a Scottish Parliament in a series of speeches, but we had not managed to get across the positive case for the Union. Ian was keen that ahead of the impending election I should go to Scotland and deliver a speech confined solely to the constitution. I was equally eager to do so

It was against the background of a surge in support for nationalism that on a foul, chilly morning on 22 February 1992 I flew up to Glasgow to speak to our Scottish candidates' conference. I went armed with a text which contained a more passionate defence of the Union than any speech made by any politician for many years, and I was apprehensive about how it would be received. Ian Lang met me at the airport, and we decided that in order to show we were listening, while ruling out a Scottish Parliament we would agree to 'take stock' of the government of Scotland within the Union to see how it could be improved and made more responsive to Scottish sentiment. I subsequently made this announcement during an interview with BBC Radio Scotland.

Though in many respects my Glasgow speech restated arguments I had often used before, the commentators saw it as 'seminal'. The truth was that the evident passion of my commitment to the Union took many by surprise. Some, for the first time, began seriously to examine what the Union really meant to Scotland and whether devolution was, as I claimed, a slippery slope, a Trojan horse for independence. What was more important from my point of view was the galvanising effect the speech had amongst our supporters in Scotland. 'I want the Scottish Conservative Party to do what no other party in Scotland is doing, to ensure that the case for maintaining our Union is placed before the people,' I said. They set off to campaign with united zeal.

We had not landed many punches on Labour and the Liberals' vague devolution plans, but our momentum was strengthened by the publication, shortly before the 1992 campaign started, of detailed plans for a Scottish Parliament set out by the Lib–Lab-inspired Constitutional Convention. Once it appeared, I felt instinctively that I was into a battle where I had a real chance to win hearts and minds and raise the level of debate above the petty political knockabout to a wholly different plane.

Originally, the party's election strategists at Central Office had not given high priority to the Union as an election theme. It was best played down, they thought. I felt they were wrong, and as the campaign got under way I decided, to their evident irritation, to make the defence of the Union the key theme of the election campaign. Ian Lang was already concentrating every speech, interview and press release on the constitutional issue; and Douglas Hurd made a number of typically thoughtful contributions to the campaign. At an election rally in Edinburgh on 26 March, I gave a ringing endorsement of the Union, and as I did so the hall came alive. As I looked round I could see the tears streaming. The Union was a theme that struck a deep and resonant chord, and I did not believe that the thousand or so people in the hall that evening were the only ones who could be moved by it.

I followed this up on 5 April, at an election rally in Wembley, with what turned out to be perhaps my most passionate plea for the Union of the whole campaign. It contained the almost apocalyptic warning: 'If I could summon up all the authority of this office, I would put it into a single warning: the United Kingdom is in danger. Wake up, my fellow countrymen. Wake up now before it is too late.'

I will never know quite how much my defence of the Union hardened support for the Conservative Party in Scotland during the election, or how it affected our support more widely. It is difficult to prove either way, but my instinctive feeling that it had had a significant effect was widely shared by many commentators at the time. There was anecdotal evidence that people decided to vote Conservative during the campaign simply because we were seen as 'more patriotic' than our opponents.

The result was that we confounded the obituary writers in 1992, increasing our vote in Scotland and our tally of seats, albeit only from nine to eleven. We held seats that Labour and the SNP had believed were theirs for the taking, including wafer-thin marginals like Stirling and Ayr. We also took back Kincardine and Deeside from the Liberals, who had a disastrous election in Scotland. The result was not a decisive reversal in the trend of decline in Tory support, but it did at least mark a temporary halt in the spiral, and gave us breathing space.

After the election, Ian Lang and I began to put some flesh on the bones of our commitment to 'take stock' of the constitutional links between England and Scotland. Over the ensuing months he and I held round after round of talks with leaders of opinion in Scotland to discuss the best way forward. The whole exercise showed that we were listening, and was well received. In a White Paper published in the spring of 1993, we set out proposals which fell short of a Scottish Parliament but gave Scotland more say over its own destiny. These included wider powers of debate and deliberation for the Scottish Grand Committee, which was composed only of Scottish MPs. They were to be given fresh powers to handle non-contentious legislation, to meet in towns and cities around Scotland, to hear statements from Scottish ministers and law officers and to cross-examine them, and to hold Scottish ministers to account during a new parliamentary question time. We devolved more functions to the Scottish Office, including responsibility for training, and announced the relocation of civil servants dealing with the regulation of North Sea oil from London to Aberdeen. We also revived the stalled Scottish Affairs Select Committee. Later, we demonstrated our sensitivity to Scottish opinion by rejecting proposals for full water privatisation, unlike in England.

In July 1995, after being re-elected leader of the Conservative Party, I appointed Ian Lang President of the Board of Trade and brought Michael Forsyth into the Cabinet as Scottish Secretary. Michael, a robust supporter of Thatcherite economic medicine, had been a controversial figure in Scotland (where he was dubbed 'the Demon King'), and his appointment raised many an eyebrow. Like Enoch Powell, he was a thinking-man's populist. Privately quite liberal, and by conviction something of a libertarian, he possessed a sharp-toothed feel for the saleable parts of his Thatcherite inheritance, particularly those saleable in Scotland. But he suffered from the fact that he always looked as if he was plotting, even when he was not.

Whether it was true or not that his daughter kept snakes, the story certainly amused the gossip-mongers. Michael was more attached to argument and creed than many of his blander contemporaries, and he was very ambitious. He had a way with words – he could rip into socialists with cruel skill – but he was no peacemaker, and a kind of anxiety, a vague sense of insecurity, always hung about him.

But Michael soon became as strong a defender of Scottish interests as his predecessors, undoubtedly Scotland's man in the Cabinet and not the Cabinet's man in Scotland. He was to prove more pragmatic and innovative than anyone expected, and he carried forward Ian's work. He proposed the widening of the role of the Scottish Grand Committee to include the opportunity to question *non*-Scottish Office ministers whose remit stretched to Scotland. This meant that the Grand Committee would have comparable powers to those promised by our opponents for the Scottish Parliament – except the power to impose more income taxes on Scotland.

But emotion as well as logic continued to drive the debate, and we were still facing daily accusations that we were un-Scottish and anti-Scottish. To passionate Scots in the Cabinet like Michael Forsyth, Malcolm Rifkind and Ian Lang – all Unionists who had fought for Scottish interests at Westminster – this was an especially aggravating charge.

In early 1996 Michael Forsyth proposed returning the Stone of Destiny to Scotland. I was non-committal. The Stone – for those who do not know its history – had sat for the best part of the last millennium in Westminster Abbey, under the Coronation Throne. But the origins of this block of pale yellow sandstone go back much further. The most romantic tale is that it was the stone pillow on which Jacob rested his head while dreaming of the ladder to Heaven. The Stone had once been kept at Scone Abbey in Perthshire, the coronation seat of Scottish kings, before being taken to Westminster as booty by Edward I in 1296. Thirty-two years later Edward III directed that the Stone be returned to Scotland, but a robust Abbot of Westminster refused to hand it over, and it remained beneath the Coronation Throne of Edward the Confessor.

Michael Forsyth was not put off by my initial reluctance, and events began to make his plan more attractive. The public records about the theft of the Stone in 1950 by Scottish nationalists were soon due for release. This raised the issue, which had been quiescent, and provided a focus for a nationalist grievance, whether we wished it or not. Moreover, as 1996 was the seven hundredth anniversary of the Stone's original removal from Scotland by Edward I, its profile would be raised even higher.

I began to consider Michael's plan for its return more carefully. I did not wish for another whipped-up dispute to inflame a grievance and fan pro-nationalist and anti-English sentiment. In law and logic I thought Scotland had a justifiable case for the return of the Stone. I asked James Mackay, the Lord Chancellor (and another Scot in the allegedly anti-Scottish Cabinet) for his view. He advised that the case for returning the Stone outweighed the disadvantages.

A further reason was then added to the case for transferring the Stone back home. The Crown, in the person of the Queen, was the legal owner of the Stone. If, as seemed inevitable, there was a row about the Stone, the Queen would be dragged into it. If ministers advised her not to return the Stone, controversy was inevitable. If it was returned after a row, the nationalists would claim the credit. None of this was appealing. I decided to forestall the fracas to come, and to let the Stone return.

Today, the Stone of Destiny is back where I came to believe it belongs, in the Treasury of Edinburgh Castle, beside the Scottish Crown Jewels. It returned on St Andrew's Day 1996, to a dignified reception from the Scottish establishment and a churlish one from those who doubted the government's motives.

None of this had any effect in satisfying Scottish demands for more autonomy. Nevertheless, Michael changed political perceptions about himself, if not the government. He managed the extraordinary feat of becoming quite popular with the Scottish media and with his opponents. In one respect, however, his success backfired. He proved so adept in exposing the logical flaws in Labour's plans for devolution that in 1996 Tony Blair, against the wishes of his party in Scotland, announced that before going ahead they would hold a referendum on the issue (having previously claimed it was unnecessary). Later he went further and announced that a Labour administration in Scotland would not levy the 'Tartan tax' in its first term. It was backtracking with a vengeance, and showed how poorly Labour had thought out its plans.

Even so, these commitments largely took the heat out of devolution as an election issue in 1997, as the Labour Party was able to claim that matters would be decided by the Scottish people later on, and that the full answers to all outstanding questions would be set out in a White Paper after the election. Sadly, when the White Paper, and later the legislation, came, no answers were forthcoming, and the issue of whether devolution will lead to separation will soon be tested by experience.

What really damaged our chances in the 1997 election was not the constitution, but the Conservative Party's problems generally. On Europe, the party was as split in Scotland as it was in England, and the repercussions of the BSE outbreak devastated our support in rural areas, where Scottish farmers, whose animals were generally grass-fed and were therefore largely unaffected by the disease, suffered badly as a result of the European beef ban imposed on the whole of the United Kingdom. In April 1995 we failed to take a single council in the Scottish local elections. A month later at the by-election in Perth and Kinross, following the death of the maverick Conservative MP Nicholas Fairbairn, we suffered a drubbing, losing to the SNP in one of Scotland's most prosperous constituencies. Once again, a handful of individual members of our party in Scotland began to raise the flag for a Scottish Parliament.

Things reached their nadir shortly before the election campaign began, when the 'sleaze' frenzy arrived in Scotland with a vengeance. First, Allan Stewart, the MP for Eastwood, and a former minister at the Scottish Office, stood down suddenly as a candidate following revelations about his private life. Then, on 29 March, I was stunned to be given the news that my friend Micky Hirst, the Chairman of the party in Scotland, had resigned, fearing the press were about to print rumours about his personal life. I was deeply upset. Micky's resignation was terrible news, not just politically, for Micky had always been a staunch ally, but personally. Of all the people I knew in politics, he was one of the most likeable and genuine. His humiliation and the suffering he and his family endured were deeply cruel, and totally unnecessary.

So began an utterly wretched election campaign in Scotland, in which no one was really interested in listening to any arguments at all. Labour fought a safe but dull campaign north of the border, concentrating on bread-and-butter issues and playing on our unpopularity after eighteen years in power. Not even ringing endorsements of the Union could save us from disaster.

In the midst of the election campaign I was in Gordon, supposedly a seat made safe for us by boundary changes, but the mood was flat and forced and felt all wrong. After a few minutes in the town I was certain we would not win there – and if not Gordon, what *would* be won in Scotland? My main hopes were that Ian Lang, Malcolm Rifkind and Michael Forsyth would win through force of personality, and that the great gentlemanly escapologist, Edinburgh West's James Douglas-Hamilton, would yet again emerge victorious. But I was not optimistic. In Gordon I saw defeat in Scotland and in the election as a whole.

Defeat duly came, and every Tory seat north of the border fell, though the swing against us was not as large as in Britain as a whole. We won just 17.3 per cent of the vote in Scotland.

What has happened since? The Scots decided in a referendum to approve the Labour government's proposals for a separate Parliament. The government, though, despite its pre-election promises, failed to address most of the unanswered questions. The Treasury Select Committee has suggested that Scottish spending should be brought more into line with England's. That means it will fall. English resentment is surfacing in Parliament, and more widely. Candidates campaigning to be the first directly elected mayor of London have argued that additional funds should be redirected to London from Scotland. In Scotland, the momentum towards full independence has gathered pace, and there is a greater expectation that it may happen. We are already on the downward slope I warned about.

None of this is surprising. What is extraordinary is the way in which the Labour Party convinced itself that the problem in Scotland was all to do with dislike of the Tories. They are now discovering that it is more deep-rooted than that, although I take no pleasure in seeing our prophesies fulfilled. The Labour Party always claimed that devolution to a Scottish Parliament would be compatible with the maintenance of the Union. Now they are not so sure. Their calculation that the creation of a Scottish Parliament would burst the bubble of nationalism has yet to be proved. Ironically, the speeches Tony Blair as prime minister began making in defence of the Union could have been made by me: 'Scotland and England and the rest of the UK: standing together, strong together, weaker apart. Better off together. Worse split apart.' His words, my message. The difference is that I spoke early, out of passionate conviction; he late, and out of fear that the legislation he introduced with such little thought may now tear the Union apart.

The Scottish Parliament has been opened with pageantry, and has been warmly welcomed in Scotland, but serious problems remain to be resolved.

Will Edinburgh or Westminster prevail when there are disputes? What happens if the Scottish Nationalists win a future election? How will the Scottish public react when their representation in the Commons is reduced and Exchequer funding of Scotland begins to fall? As the Scottish Parliament uses its tax-raising power, will it result in turning away inward investment in favour of the less highly taxed areas south of the border? How long will it be before the Scottish Parliament demands more power? Or direct representation in the European Union? Many questions must be faced in the months and years ahead.

Already the Labour government, and Tony Blair, find themselves victims of exactly the same sort of political abuse from the SNP that Margaret and I suffered over eighteen years. The SNP has been getting under Labour's skin by deriding it as a 'branch-office party' with policies 'made in London'. Tony Blair, they say, does not understand Scotland. It is the anti-English card in a new guise.

It may be Tony Blair's lasting memorial that he met the short-term wishes of the Scots but overlooked their long-term interests and those of the United Kingdom as a whole. He must now address the uncomfortable questions that arise from his actions, including rebalancing the constitution to take account of resentments south of the border. If he does not do so – and it will not be easy – then friction will arise that could lead ultimately to separation and an independent Scotland. That was always my fear. It still is.

Only the Conservative Party has consistently told the Scots the truth. It was not a popular message, but it was and is the truth, as time now shows. Labour never supported the Conservative Party when we stood alone for the Union. They used our unpopular, but accurate, message to hit us over the head. But we should not treat them in the same way. We are still the Unionist Party. If the Labour government fights to save the Union, it will have my full support.

# CHAPTER NINETEEN

# Into the Mists:
# Bright Hopes, Black Deeds

L ATE ON A GREY AND DISMAL February afternoon in 1993 a startling
message was brought in to me as I worked on some papers in the
Cabinet Room. It was from the leadership of the Provisionals, and had
come through an intelligence link which we and they maintained for private
communication. It read:

> The conflict is over but we need your advice on how to bring
> it to a close. We wish to have an unannounced ceasefire in order
> to hold a dialogue leading to peace. We cannot announce such
> a move as it will lead to confusion to the volunteers, because
> the press will misinterpret it as a surrender. We cannot meet
> the Secretary of State's public renunciation of violence, but it
> would be given privately as long as we were sure that we were
> not being tricked.

For many years successive British governments had rightly refused to
include the Provisionals in negotiations until terrorism ended. Now senior
figures in the Provisional Army Council appeared to be signalling that they
wanted to end the conflict in Northern Ireland. The message was dramatic,
but was it genuine? Was it believable? Were the Provisionals really ready
to end violence? Or was it just a ploy? Did they wish to suck the government
into negotiations in which they would demand unjustifiable concessions
in return for an end to their killing of the innocent? If that failed, would
they then blame us for the renewal of violence?

I knew that many of my colleagues would take a bleak view of the
message – with ample reason – and so would the Unionists in Northern
Ireland. I worried about being duped. The IRA were isolated from the
real world, steeped in bigotry and utterly ruthless. They were engaged in

cold-blooded murder, controlled their communities through fear and brutal intimidation, and thought nothing of terrorising pensioners or smashing the legs of teenagers with iron bars. They had tried to murder me in February 1991, when a mortar had landed on the Downing Street lawn during a Cabinet committee meeting. If it had been ten feet closer half the Cabinet could have been killed.

The Provisional movement as a whole was implicated in vicious terrorism. Many of its members knew no other way of living than through violence and criminality, and would never give it up voluntarily. They were blind to pity and deaf to reason. Loyalist paramilitaries on the other side could be just as bad, and this gave rise to another potential complication: would they respond too?

The Northern Ireland Secretary Patrick Mayhew and I were assured by Northern Ireland Office experts that the secret channel was reliable and the message was authentic; but it could still be a trap. The political risk should we proceed was high. Even entering into a preliminary dialogue with Sinn Fein was a dangerous political minefield. For uncertain gain we risked the alienation of the Unionist majority of the population in Northern Ireland, and outright opposition from many Unionist and Conservative Members of Parliament; it was not fanciful to reflect that if it went wrong, this could have ended both Paddy's and my careers. At best it was dicey. The chances of ultimate success were imponderable. Too many initiatives had failed in the past: the Whitelaw talks in 1972, Ted Heath's Sunningdale deal (1973), Jim Prior's Assembly (1982) and Margaret Thatcher's Anglo–Irish Agreement (1985) among them. Politically, it seemed to me to be all risk and no certain reward. When later in the year I gave John Smith a private briefing, he took a cheery and cynical view: he had no qualms about supporting us, he said, because no one would ever win votes in mainland Britain through Northern Ireland.

But the message raised other considerations. Suppose Republican leaders such as Gerry Adams and Martin McGuinness had finally recognised that the IRA could not win, that nearly twenty-five years of terrorism had brought them no closer to their objectives, and that the public mood was turning against them. What then? I was sceptical, but it was at least possible that we were beginning to see the fruits of our long-term policy of addressing legitimate Nationalist grievances, building support for the democratic process across the political spectrum inside and outside Northern Ireland,

and squeezing out terrorism by every means, persuasive as well as military.

The IRA leadership had their own perverted logic. For them, an offer of peace needed to be accompanied by violence, to show their volunteers that they were not surrendering. So, despite their secret message to us, the IRA's terrorism continued unabated. But while the timing and the stark language of the message were a surprise, it had not come entirely out of the blue: we had received intelligence reports that they were rethinking their approach.

The safe political response would have been to take no risks, and to invite the IRA to demonstrate their goodwill by calling a ceasefire. But I knew that those who had sent the message had themselves taken a risk; they would regard such a reply as a rejection, and we might have thrown away a golden chance for peace. The prize was too great to ignore: Paddy Mayhew and I soon agreed to go ahead.

We were well aware of the unlikelihood of success; but we felt we had a responsibility to find out whether this was a serious message, and to see if the leadership of the Provisionals, if offered fair and equal treatment, had the will and the ability to move away from terrorism. Early in my administration I had decided to make Northern Ireland one of my highest priorities. Now was not the time to step away.

When I became prime minister in December 1990 I knew very little of Northern Ireland, and had only once or twice visited any part of the island of Ireland. My previous political offices had not prepared me for the subject, and the conventional wisdom was that prime ministers were well advised to keep their distance. Margaret Thatcher's brief sally into Irish affairs – the 1985 Anglo–Irish Agreement – had cost her the resignation from the government of Ian Gow, one of her most loyal friends, and had provoked years of Unionist disenchantment for meagre benefits. Northern Ireland was generally regarded as an intractable issue best left to the security forces and the Northern Ireland Secretary, whose job was seen as worthy, necessary and thankless.

My lack of a track record in the Province's affairs had its advantages: my hands were clean; I came to it fresh. But I knew it would be fatal to step in without a thorough grounding. Ireland's politicians needed to escape from their history, but any outsider had to be sensitive to it. I had to learn to distinguish between Nationalist, or 'Green', language and Unionist, or 'Orange', language. I would have to confront political leaders who knew by heart every twist and turn of every past negotiation. I needed to know and to understand Northern Ireland's people; and, if I could, to win their trust.

My starting point was simple: to acquiesce in the abnormality of life in Northern Ireland and merely attempt to contain terrorism was no more acceptable to me than it would have been in my own county of Huntingdonshire. One corner of the realm could not be fenced off from the rest and treated differently. With no preconceptions about how to move forward, other than a belief in the politics of reason, I decided to get to know that corner, its people and its problems. I intended to see if direct, personal and consistent prime ministerial engagement, in close alliance with an equally committed ministerial team, could make a difference. To alter the old cliché, I put Northern Ireland onto the front burner.

It stayed there. In six and a half years I visited the Province far more often than any other part of the United Kingdom outside London, as well as holding countless meetings in Downing Street. Some of the most vivid memories of my premiership come from those visits – from the warmth of ordinary people in the streets, whether in Belfast or Londonderry, in Ian Paisley's Antrim constituency, the Republican stronghold of Newry or Jim Molyneaux's turf in Lagan Valley. Memories like that of a lady with tears in her eyes saying in the main street that meeting Norma was the happiest moment of her life. To recount such memories now sounds trite – but in Ireland things are so deeply felt that often English prose cannot capture it. The courage of voluntary workers and community groups was inspirational. I had an intensely moving discussion at Hillsborough Castle with the cross-community group FAIT (Families Against Intimidation and Terror) – brave Protestants and Catholics whose relatives had been murdered or maimed by paramilitaries, and who risked their own safety by campaigning for an end to violence. In good times or bad, visits to Northern Ireland were always emotional. My days there were long and tiring, but I never flew home without feeling uplifted by the bravery and resilience I found. Every visit recharged my determination to remove the stain of terrorism.

Three months after taking office, in late February 1991, I made my first visit to Northern Ireland as prime minister. By then I had taught myself much, helped by many policy discussions with the then Secretary of State, Peter Brooke, who had brought huge commitment and intellectual force to the job. With little public fanfare, steady progress had been made in the 1980s to address grievances which had fuelled the 'Troubles'. Rigorous legislation on fair employment for all religious groups had been introduced. Public services had been improved. Northern Ireland had some of the best state schools and public housing in the United Kingdom. The security situation had been contained. In many respects life was improving, but there had been no political progress towards bringing the violence to an end.

One depressing feature was the patchy calibre of political representation at all levels in the Province. There were some wise heads, but with many of the most senior figures having been in office for many years, thinking seemed to be stuck in grooves. For most of the younger generation, conventional politics held little appeal. Many bright youngsters were leaving the Province, and of those who stayed few wanted to enter local politics. Ancient feuds and fears had locked the political parties into entrenched and rigid reflexes. The chances of changing attitudes from within looked poor.

Peter Brooke was adamant that the status quo was unacceptable. In November 1990 he set out some cardinal points for the future, publicly declaring for the first time that the British government had 'no selfish strategic or economic interest in Northern Ireland . . . Britain's purpose is not to occupy, oppress or exploit.' This statement, unexceptional as it may sound, was to become deeply controversial, but it was a cornerstone of future policy. Peter was simply saying that we did not have a 'selfish' interest *separate from* the interests of the people of Northern Ireland. But his speech was misrepresented by Ian Paisley's hard-line Democratic Unionist Party (DUP), who wilfully overlooked the crucial word 'selfish', and misrepresented it as an expression of apathy – or even of willingness to sell Northern Ireland out. This was a perversion of the truth. We were prepared to accept the democratic wishes of the people of Northern Ireland, and we expected that Irish Nationalists, including the Irish government and Sinn Fein, should do likewise. If a clear majority of the people of Northern Ireland wished to leave the United Kingdom, we would not force them to remain, notwithstanding our deep attachment to the Union as a whole. But nor would we push them out. It was democracy at its purest: the people would decide.

This stance was essential if we were to act as an honest broker in negotiations to end violence. Ian Paisley may have been mischievous to represent it as subversive, but he was right to detect a new willingness to let the people of both the Protestant and the Catholic communities influence policy. Only if we were seen to deal in an even-handed way with both traditions, Unionist and Nationalist, would there be a chance of securing general support for any initiative. We needed also to demolish the false image purveyed by Republican propagandists of the British presence in Northern Ireland as an army of occupation. This charge had permeated ill-informed and often naïve public opinion in America, and was a recruiting sergeant for terrorism. Peter Brooke's statement was helpful to those moderate Nationalists in John Hume's Social Democratic and Labour Party (SDLP) who wish to achieve a united Ireland only by democratic means. They accepted the partition of Ireland as a fact of democratic life, and knew that many Roman Catholics did not wish to leave the United Kingdom and join the Irish Republic. Our impartiality did not mean indifference. Britain had shouldered a heavy burden to defend democracy and the rule of law in Northern Ireland. I had no intention of abandoning it.

Peter Brooke was exploring two parallel lines of movement. He was aware that since 1988 Gerry Adams, the leader of Sinn Fein, had been having private exchanges with John Hume; and we had evidence that a faction within the Provisional leadership was beginning to look for a way out of its unproductive 'armed struggle'. In 1990 Peter had authorised the reopening of the intelligence channel through which I was to receive the secret message from the Provisionals. At the same time, he was developing the outlines of a new political initiative.

It was from this base that Peter and I slowly built up our joint approach during my first year and a quarter in office. In March 1991 Peter publicly launched the initiative. With care and skill, he had persuaded the Irish government and the four 'constitutional' parties – Jim Molyneaux's Ulster Unionists, Ian Paisley's DUP, the SDLP under John Hume, and the Alliance Party led by John Alderdice – to take part in a new talks process.

To balance the different interests, Peter had devised a formula involving three 'strands'. The first strand covered the internal political development of Northern Ireland and focused on the desire of the Unionists to re-establish a Northern Ireland Assembly and a degree of self-government. As this was wholly an internal matter for the United Kingdom, the Irish government were not included in Strand One. But, since this was Northern Ireland, nothing was that simple. The Nationalists were only prepared to discuss an assembly if, in turn, the Unionists would agree to discuss closer links between Northern Ireland and the Republic, and accept some involvement in the overall process from the Irish government (whom the Nationalists saw as their protectors). The second strand addressed relations between the North and the South of Ireland, while in the third the two governments sought to develop a closer relationship between the United Kingdom and the Republic. A crucial feature was that the three strands interlocked. *Nothing* would be agreed until *everything* was agreed. This calmed Nationalist fears that the Unionists would win agreement on a new assembly, and then fail to deliver counter-balancing concessions on a closer North–South relationship.

Peter and I did not expect rapid progress in the talks. Just getting the parties around the table – in fact three tables – was an achievement. There was, at last, a process under way, where previously there had been a political doldrums. In the first three months the talks did cover useful ground; but in July 1991 they stalled, and we were not able to reconvene them until after the 1992 general election. The slow pace was frustrating. The Northern Ireland parties' mutual suspicions undermined all sense of urgency. They had dug themselves into deep trenches, and to budge them even an inch this way or that took a huge effort. Nevertheless, with his three-stranded formula, Peter Brooke had set the pattern for what, seven years later, under a different government, was to become the Good Friday Agreement.

When I called the 1992 general election, the talks were in a prolonged hiatus. Peter Brooke had put his all into the job, and needed a break. Two months earlier he had offered to resign after an incident in which he had been beguiled into singing 'Oh my Darling Clementine' on an Irish television chatshow a few hours after an IRA outrage. Though he stayed in the job, helped by strong support in the Commons, this had put him under a handicap. The Unionists had chosen to be deeply offended, and were in no hurry to forgive.

My choice as to his successor was never in doubt: I wanted Patrick Mayhew. This, too, was a happy appointment. Paddy, like Peter, committed himself utterly to the search for peace in Northern Ireland. Back in 1981 he had been my first boss in government when I served as his PPS, and he remained a close friend. The job needed a strong personality, and Paddy was a commanding figure and a man of unquestioned integrity.

Every politician has his detractors, and I knew that some Irishmen would call Paddy too patrician; but his fairness and honesty were never in doubt. Even his critics might have changed their view of him if they had been with me in his office at Stormont one day when we had a few minutes to spare before a press conference. Paddy decided to change his shirt. Then, wandering half-naked around the office, he decided to polish his shoes. Out came his old army shoe-kit, as we honed our lines for the inquisition that was to follow. There was no question of his asking anyone else in his establishment to do his shoes for him. Finally Her Majesty's (undressed) Secretary of State for Northern Ireland turned to his former parliamentary private secretary and said, with all humility: 'Prime Minister, can I do *your* shoes?' I can think of colleagues in whom that might have looked like servility – but never Patrick Mayhew. With Paddy we got two for the price of one, as his wife Jean joined him in throwing herself unsparingly into the job. She made their official residence at Hillsborough Castle a place of the warmest welcome. With no fuss or fanfare, she got out on the streets of Northern Ireland, charmed people, listened with sensitivity, and did an enormous amount to encourage different groups in the community. Her commitment and her antennae were invaluable.

The three-stranded process resumed soon after the 1992 election. At first it made good progress. In July we were able to hold formal talks at Lancaster House in London on the delicate second strand of relations between Northern Ireland and the Irish Republic. This was a breakthrough: the first time all the constitutional parties of Northern Ireland had sat around a table with the governments of the United Kingdom and the Irish Republic. By the summer break, many points of agreement had been reached. I was especially pleased that the Unionists had swallowed the painful medicine of accepting the involvement of the Irish government, although they remained acutely suspicious of its influence, and were unhappy at any suggestion of institutional links between North and South.

Dublin disappointed us by holding back from agreeing to amend Articles II and III of the Irish Constitution, which claimed the territory of Northern Ireland for the Republic – a position incompatible with allowing the people of the North to determine their own future. For the SDLP, John Hume insisted that a future assembly must be subject to six commissioners. He seemed loath to reciprocate Unionist concessions, and as time went on, to my surprise he appeared to lose interest in the process. By the autumn, the talks had stalled again.

It became clear that Hume's ambivalence stemmed from a preoccupation with his separate exchanges with the Provisionals. We, for our part, wanted progress in the constitutional talks because that would increase pressure on the Provisionals. At Coleraine in December 1992, Patrick Mayhew made it clear that we were prepared to treat all aspirations and viewpoints fairly, and were not shutting the door to anyone; but the Provisionals could only come into the talks if they renounced terrorism. We hoped to make them realise that if they excluded themselves by continuing violence, they would ultimately face marginalisation. I was puzzled that John Hume, whose desire for peace was not in doubt, seemed to reason differently. He appeared to want to wait until the Provisionals were ready to move forward. As far as I was concerned, this would have effectively put the gunmen in the driver's seat, with their hands on the brake lever: not a good negotiating position for any of us.

Another necessary link in the chain was to improve relations between London and Dublin, despite our sharply differing perspectives on the Hume–Adams approach. The Troubles in Northern Ireland had fanned old embers, and the relationship between the two governments had been sour and edgy. This was absurd. We were not only neighbours with a common language and intertwined economies and populations, but now fellow and equal members of the European Union. There is no doubt that our joint membership of the EU was helpful. Ministers met regularly on mutual ground and on non-Irish matters, and this familiarity eased disputes and bilateral tensions. Other developments helped too. The economy of the Republic was growing rapidly, reducing the disparity of economic well-being between the South and the more prosperous North.

If we were to progress towards a settlement, it was essential that Dublin and London worked in partnership. I wanted Dublin to exercise a constructive influence over the Nationalists in the North who needed reassurance that their interest would not be overlooked. At the same time it was essential to show the Ulster Unionists that Dublin acknowledged Northern Ireland's democratic right to self-determination. They had seen members of the IRA enjoy safe havens in the Republic for years (where they frequently lived, and where they stored and tested weapons). The Unionists also saw them receive funding from sympathisers in America. This was the oxygen of fear and resentment the Unionists breathed. To turn off the supply, I wanted both the Irish and the US governments to become active supporters of our drive for a just settlement.

In 1991 I had agreed with the Irish Taoiseach (Prime Minister), Charles Haughey, that we would meet every six months, but it was only when his successor, Albert Reynolds, took office in February 1992 that relationships really improved. Albert and I had met when I was chancellor. He was easy to get on with, naturally cheery and loquacious, and as keen as I was to see real progress in Northern Ireland. Over time, during and after his spell in office, Albert's tongue and his eagerness for a deal that would bring peace may have led him into the odd spot of embroidery; but his commitment was a plus. So was his love for a deal, born of making his fortune selling petfood and owning dance-halls; in his staff's words, 'Albert's a bottom-line man.' He was also an incessant 'spinner' to the press, and one of his own aides warned me that 'Albert never walked past an open microphone in his life.' There was never any malice in this. Albert pitched his line so as to ensure a good reception from his Nationalist audience, but unfortunately this invariably had the reverse effect on the Unionists. This nearly derailed the process on one or two occasions; but it was a price we were willing to pay for Albert's readiness to strike deals.

I liked Albert a lot, and I thought we could move things forward together. I invited him over for supper a fortnight after his election as Taoiseach. As Albert himself has recorded, 'the trust and understanding between us, that neither would sell the other short, was a very good starting point. We agreed at that first meeting to do everything possible not to condemn another generation in Northern Ireland to sectarian killing.' We met twice more in 1992. In November 1992, Albert was returned in a general election, with Dick Spring, leader of the Labour Party, as his Tanaiste (Deputy Prime Minister) and Foreign Minister in a coalition government. Though Albert was to enjoy less than two further years in office, much was to change in that time.

The 'peace process', as it became known, developed momentum in 1993, when different elements began to come together. There was no magic formula to turn the key for peace. We had to move forward on a wide front, and take account of the legitimate interests of all groups, not just one. That was particularly important for the British government as the constitutional authority for Northern Ireland. Other participants – the recognised parties, the Irish government – could take a partial view, as, in an extreme fashion, did the paramilitaries on both sides. We alone had to look at every aspect of the problem, and bear the responsibility for the decisions we took and any mistakes that resulted.

As 1993 unfolded, we found ourselves handling the incipient peace process through three, or arguably four, different channels – the three-stranded talks with the constitutional parties; the back channel to the leadership of the Provisionals; and the Joint Declaration Initiative, which had both John Hume and Albert Reynolds ferrying parallel, and often conflicting, messages to us.

In managing this multi-dimensional negotiation, it was essential for us to relay a single, consistent message to Gerry Adams, John Hume and Albert Reynolds on what the British government could and could not accept. There were, for me, a number of critical points which had to be respected. All parties coming to the table had to commit themselves exclusively to democratic and constitutional behaviour. Those who continued to use, or threaten, violence could not be admitted to substantive negotiations; we were not prepared to discuss Northern Ireland's future under duress, nor to ask others to do so. A clear renunciation of terrorism had to be part of the entry ticket to talks.

We insisted on a basis for negotiations which was fair to all sides, not one which tilted towards one result. The rules would not be written to favour one or other point of view; and the British government would not take sides. John Hume and Albert Reynolds pressured us to become a 'persuader' for the unification of Ireland, and argued that our role should be to 'deliver' the Unionists. I had no intention of doing so – the idea was unrealistic and undemocratic. After all, the Hume-Reynolds approach undermined the crucial importance of the principle of consent. The British government was prepared to be open-minded about Northern Ireland's future; but we insisted that the Province's status could only change with the clear consent of a majority of its people. The democratic right of self-determination had to remain *within* Northern Ireland. Any change to its status was not a decision to be taken over the heads of Northern Ireland's people by the government in London, still less by one in Dublin.

Quite apart from this important principle of democracy, a settlement which did not enjoy genuine consent would have stood no chance of working. The Unionist majority would have made Northern Ireland ungovernable; we would have replaced one problem with a far bigger one. We constantly had to remind Dublin and Washington that there were two sides to this conflict. In their eagerness to strike deals with the Provisionals, both sometimes seemed to overlook the existence of the Unionists. We knew that there could not be a lasting settlement without all-round acceptance of the consent principle; yet any settlement needed to include Sinn Fein and its military wing, the IRA, to whom the consent principle was anathema. This conundrum bedevilled all efforts to find a solution.

Of the different channels, the least productive during 1993 was the overt three-stranded talks process – the continuation of Peter Brooke's initiative. We could not persuade the parties to reconvene around the same negotiating table: they would talk to us, but not to each other. The Unionists were suspicious of John Hume's simultaneous dialogue with the Provisionals, whose terrorism showed no sign of abating. On the Nationalist side, the SDLP and the Irish government would not budge on the issues which had stalled the talks in 1992. To make matters worse, Dublin floated (or someone leaked) suggestions on joint sovereignty of Northern Ireland which were completely unacceptable to the Unionist majority, and made them ever more wary of a negotiating process involving the Irish government. It became obvious that Dublin's attention and that of John Hume did not lie mainly with the talks process, but were focused on the signals they – and we – were picking up from the leadership of the Provisionals.

I described at the beginning of this chapter the dramatic signal Patrick Mayhew passed to me from the Provisionals through the back channel in February 1993, and our decision to respond to it. This was a very different message from the few they had sent since Peter Brooke reopened the channel in 1990. Gerry Adams and Martin McGuinness appeared to be signalling that they wanted our help. Patrick Mayhew had tipped them off in advance about his Coleraine speech, promising a fair deal to all who abandoned terrorism. Their message, two months later, explicitly acknowledged his requirement for a renunciation of violence as a precondition for talks. This they were now offering – but not publicly.

To minimise the risk of leaks, Patrick Mayhew and I held the Provisionals' message within a very small circle of colleagues. In early March we agreed on a full but cautious reply from Patrick, saying that the government would agree to an 'exploratory dialogue' if there was 'a genuine and established ending of violence'. Future negotiations could not have a predetermined outcome, we stressed. We acknowledged that the eventual result of such a process *could* be a united Ireland – but *only* on the basis of consent to it by the people of Northern Ireland. We ended: 'It is important to establish whether this provides a basis for the way forward. We are ready to answer specific questions or to give further explanation.' The process was in train.

This reply became known as our 'nine-paragraph' message. It was firm on the consent principle, and it carried not the remotest suggestion that the British government would abandon its previous position and promote the unification of Ireland. The message emphasised that

> the British government does not have, and will not adopt, any prior objective of 'ending of partition'; and that 'unless the people of Northern Ireland come to express such a view [i.e. a desire for a united Ireland], the British government will continue to uphold the Union.

However, the key point first made in this message, and developed in subsequent back-channel communications, was the offer of an exploratory dialogue – 'talks about talks' – if we were assured that organised violence had been brought to an end. That offer was not, at this stage, in the public domain, though it was to become of central importance at the end of the year.

In the weeks following the sending of this message, our caution proved justified. There was no let-up in the IRA's terrorism. By a bitter irony, the IRA bombed the centre of Warrington in Cheshire, killing two young boys, Tim Parry and Jonathan Ball, on 20 March, the very day our message was delivered through intermediaries to Martin McGuinness. It was a sunny Saturday afternoon when I received a phone call at Finings to tell me of this horror; I despaired at such pointless brutality when moves towards peace had already begun. I wondered whether to go public on the process and denounce the IRA for their perfidy. Only the possibility that this was their usual tactic of trying to seem, as they saw it, 'strong' to enable them to negotiate, stopped me. But it was a close call. The murder of Tim and Jonathan nearly ended the process abruptly.

The following month, a huge bomb exploded in Bishopsgate in the City of London, causing one death and massive destruction. The bombers were working on the traditional IRA assumption (which twenty-four years of fruitless terrorism had not substantiated) that they could bomb their way to the conference table. I was not surprised when the Bishopsgate attack was followed by messages from Martin McGuinness in late April and on 10 May which offered not the unequivocal ending of violence we required, but a temporary ceasefire – in return for which he asked the government to fix a date and location for talks.

I thought it essential to show the Provisionals that these tactics would not wash. We would not enter even the most exploratory of talks under an active threat of violence. The onus was on them to convince us that they were genuinely heading in a different direction. I brought Douglas Hurd (who had long experience of Northern Ireland, from different angles), Kenneth Clarke (then Home Secretary) and the Attorney-General, Nick Lyell, into the discussion. We worked with Paddy Mayhew on a draft of a second substantive message, including a provision that Sinn Fein would not be able to join the political negotiations (the 'talks process') until it had 'sufficiently shown it genuinely does not espouse violence'. However, when the IRA followed up the Warrington and Bishopsgate bombings by setting off a large explosion in the centre of Belfast, we suspended work on the text. We were determined to make them realise that terrorism and talking were incompatible. I approved a holding message through the channel in July which repeated our insistence on a lasting end to violence. It began to seem we were in a blind alley.

The Provisionals renewed contact through the channel on 2 November. They were on the defensive. On 23 October a bungled IRA bombing in a fish shop in Belfast's Loyalist heartland of the Shankill Road had killed ten people, including the bomber. A week later, Loyalist gunmen retaliated with an equally horrific attack on a pub in the village of Greysteel, killing eight people and wounding nineteen, mostly Catholics. These outrages caused deep revulsion throughout both communities in Northern Ireland. Meanwhile, the Provisionals were worried about being outflanked. Their message complained that we could not solve the problem with Albert Reynolds and Dick Spring, and that we had rejected the Provisionals' request for talks in May. It suggested that our 'nine-paragraph' message and their 10 May reply could form the basis of an understanding. Most significantly, it asked when we would open dialogue 'in the event of a total end to hostilities'.

Like the February message, this appeared to be a sign that the leadership of the Provisionals was prepared to contemplate a permanent cessation of violence. The message did not try to set conditions. I convened a meeting which ran past midnight on the night of 3–4 November, and resumed twice the next day, with the new Home Secretary Michael Howard and Defence Secretary Malcolm Rifkind joining Paddy Mayhew, Douglas Hurd, Ken Clarke (now Chancellor), Michael Heseltine (now President of the Board of Trade) and me. We decided to spell out in detail what we would offer by way of exploratory dialogue, and what the Provisionals had to do to qualify for it.

We stressed that we would not make any secret agreement with them, and that dialogue could only follow a permanent end to violent activity. If we were assured unequivocally of that, and events on the ground matched the assurance, we said we were prepared to open exploratory dialogue 'within a week of Parliament's return in January'. We were looking for a public commitment, followed by about ten weeks of peace to back it up. We promised that the exploratory talks would look at what was needed for Sinn Fein to enter constitutional talks, and for them to play the same role in public life as other parties. They would also have to 'examine the practical consequences of the ending of violence', by which we meant removing the arsenals of illegal weaponry built up by the paramilitaries. I now know that the Irish government were making the same point through their secret channels to the Provisionals, but more explicitly and ahead of us. In a message of May 1993 Albert Reynolds had defined 'arms and equipment' as one of the issues to be dealt with expeditiously once public confidence in peace had been established.

We despatched our message on 5 November. It was the last substantive text to go by the private route to Adams and McGuinness and their colleagues. But then another of the leaks which at intervals so undermined the peace process occurred. In the second half of November rumours in Northern Ireland led to a story in the *Observer* that the British government had a channel of communication to the Provisionals. The source of the leak was never found.

As was presumably the intention of the anonymous leaker, the story sparked off recriminations against the government and put the peace process in jeopardy. Patrick Mayhew and I were accused of betraying our assurances that the government would not negotiate with Sinn Fein until there had been a cessation of violence. I had said in the House earlier in November, after the Shankill Road bombing, that it would 'turn my stomach' to sit down and talk with the Provisional IRA. I would not do it, because it would have conferred legitimacy on them. But it was necessary to have a link. This was very different from face-to-face negotiations.

Patrick and I decided to publish immediately the record of the government's exchanges with the Provisionals. This would show that we had used the channel to set out the government's known position, *had not held talks*, and had not struck any secret deals. Patrick did this through a statement to the House of Commons on 29 November. He was widely supported. However, it then transpired that, in their haste to transcribe the documents, Northern Ireland Office officials had made a series of typographical errors. This was deeply embarrassing to Patrick, who had to correct the record in Parliament and who, with characteristic honour, offered to resign. More seriously, these bureaucratic errors damaged the credibility of the government's account, as did the discovery that one of our intermediaries – without the authority of ministers – had had an unauthorised face-to-face discussion with Martin McGuinness.

These blunders allowed the Provisionals to put out a rival version of the back-channel exchanges, in which Martin McGuinness denied that he had sent the February message saying that the conflict was over: 'I don't believe there's a person in Ireland with a titter of wit,' he told a news conference, 'who would believe that I handed such a document or oral communication to the British government.' According to the Provisionals, we had told them in February 1993 that all that was required was a two-or three-week 'suspension' of violence, which would be followed by an intensive round of talks until decisions were reached. They claimed that we had offered to provide an aircraft to fly a Republican delegation to Scotland, Sweden, Norway, Denmark or the Isle of Man for negotiations with government representatives. They also claimed that the government's 'nine-paragraph' message of 19 March was followed only four days later by an oral message which effectively contradicted the written one. While our written message had required 'a genuine and established ending of violence', the Provisionals alleged that we then repeated a proposal for only a two-week suspension of violence, and said that 'the final solution is union. The historical train – Europe – determines that. We are committed to Europe. Unionists will have to change. This island will be as one.' This self-interested piece of Republican propaganda was a tissue of lies.

Sinn Fein and their apologists claim that Patrick Mayhew doctored the record, and changed, concealed or even forged messages. This is a slander which beggars belief. It is hardly surprising that the Provisionals put out a different version. Exposure of the channel by malign elements from one side or the other, or possibly both, had placed McGuinness and his colleagues in a dangerous situation. They needed to cover themselves. They, like us, had taken a considerable risk.

Subsequent events, however, were to prove our version to be the true one. *If* we had deceived Adams and McGuinness in the way they alleged, *if* we had made and then retracted an offer of direct and unconditional talks on a united Ireland, and *if* their intentions had been other than those they signalled to us through the back channel, the 1994 cessation of violence would not have happened. The messages we received from the Provisionals in February, May and November 1993, and our two substantive replies of 19 March and 5 November, helped to pave the way for the cessation of violence by spelling out clearly what was, and what was not, on offer – especially by defining the terms for 'exploratory dialogue'. I regretted the loss of the back channel. It gave us some difficult moments, but it played its part. Making peace is a tricky business.

The back channel collapsed just as another unannounced initiative – the 'Joint Declaration' – was about to move rapidly forward. The idea of a Joint Declaration had come from John Hume's talks with Gerry Adams, which had begun in 1988. Subsequently the Irish government had become involved. By 1991 Dublin was discussing a text with Adams. In December 1991, during our second meeting, the then Irish Prime Minister, Charles Haughey, first put to me a suggestion for a Joint Declaration between our two governments, designed to set out principles for an eventual settlement in a way which would attract the Provisionals. I reacted non-committally, but said I was prepared to look at the proposal's merits. A month later, in January 1992, Irish officials gave us a text for a declaration, the first I had seen. In February John Hume gave the Northern Ireland Office a different version, which seemed to have come from Sinn Fein.

It did not take us long to consider these texts. They were utterly one-sided, so heavily skewed towards the presumption of a united Ireland that they had no merit as a basis for negotiation. They were little more than an invitation to the British government to sell out the majority in the North, and the democratic principles we had always defended. An Irish official privately acknowledged that the Provisionals were not aiming at general acceptability. Their aim was to unite the Irish government and the SDLP in a pan-Nationalist front in order to negotiate Northern Ireland's future with the British government over the heads of the Unionists.

I was frankly surprised that John Hume and Charles Haughey, both very experienced politicians, should have lent themselves to such an unrealistic approach. They must have known that a settlement without the Unionists would be no solution. Nevertheless, the approach was interesting in one respect: with other intelligence, it suggested that some leading Provisionals were groping for a way out of terrorism and into talks.

By the spring of 1993, the Joint Declaration idea had been put aside for over a year. However, activity revived soon after the dramatic back-channel message from McGuinness. A Dublin newspaper publicised one of Hume's meetings in his Londonderry home with Adams. In late April Hume relayed a revised, though still unusable, declaration text to the Northern Ireland Office. Then, in June, Albert Reynolds, who had succeeded Haughey as Taoiseach early the previous year, came into the act with a flourish.

Albert had spent a year trying to shift the Provisionals into a realistic position. They had insisted on a timetable for Irish unification, but he had reportedly argued that this would contradict the consent principle, and could never be sold to the British or the Unionists; nor would we accept the role of 'persuaders' for unification. He had evidently not secured the changes to the declaration he knew were necessary. Nevertheless, he decided to put an unsatisfactory text to me to test the water. Whatever his inner misgivings, Albert presented it in effect on a 'take it or leave it' basis – this was his habitual style of negotiation. I deflected a bizarre suggestion that we should meet secretly somewhere in the United Kingdom. I did not want to have to give an instant reaction, and I thought a leak would be almost inevitable. Instead I asked the Cabinet Secretary, Sir Robin Butler, to go to Ireland to receive the letter, which the Taoiseach insisted on delivering personally.

Reynolds told Robin Butler that the draft declaration was a break-through, and a basis for 'a lasting cessation of violence'. He claimed that the Provisionals had accepted the consent principle and separate self-determination within Northern Ireland. Two days later, an irritated John Hume gave us a rival version of a declaration. He was annoyed with Reynolds, complaining that although he was Prime Minister of Ireland he did not understand the complexities of the text, and had given us an unsatisfactory draft.

We studied the rival texts carefully. Far from being a breakthrough, they still showed little comprehension of what might be acceptable to the British government, let alone to the Unionist majority – to whom they offered virtually nothing. The word 'consent' appeared, which was an advance, but inadequately. Crucially, Northern Ireland was *not* offered the right of self-determination. Instead there was to be 'self-determination by the people of Ireland as a whole' – a formula designed to secure Irish unity by swamping the Northerners with votes from the South. The text required the British government to persuade Northern Ireland's people to accept measures leading towards unification, and was hopelessly deficient in many other respects. It simply was not a starter. Albert Reynolds must surely have known that we would find it unacceptable – certainly his deputy, Dick Spring, did – even before this was confirmed by Sir Robin Butler.

Reynolds and Spring came to Number 10 in mid-June for a working supper. I took them through the many problems we had with the text of their draft declaration, and told them it was not a draft on which we could negotiate. The Taoiseach's main argument was that the draft showed movement on the part of the Provisionals. That was true; but it remained a Nationalist manifesto, not a potential agreement. An awful lot of movement was needed if the document was to have any value.

In September, Albert Reynolds sent me a secret and personal letter. In it, he made an anguished plea to me to negotiate on a text which had 'the backing of those who can produce peace on their [i.e. the IRA's] side at least'. He claimed that they were not necessarily seeking 'Irish unity or anything in that area within any limited timescale', and that the consent principle was fully accepted. This was Albert's seductive salesmanship at its best, but was not, it seemed to me, an accurate bill of goods. The text simply did not correspond with his description; and his officials told ours that there was little scope for amendment. John Hume came to see me with a parallel message. It was still take it or leave it, which didn't require much thought on our part.

The process was stuck, and its chances were then set further back. Against Reynolds's wishes, and to increase pressure on us both, Adams and Hume issued a joint statement on 25 September 1993 that they had made considerable progress, were forwarding a report to Dublin, and were suspending their dialogue pending 'wider consideration between the two governments'. The ball was placed publicly in our court; and yet the prospect of securing Unionist agreement to anything emanating from Adams and Hume was nil. Dublin did not even send the report to London.

We did receive a new Irish document, which was a little better. Albert had been active. Paddy Mayhew and I thought that if we could secure further improvements, and develop a text clearly separate from the one-sided Hume–Adams exercise, we might have a basis for negotiation. I convened the wider group of Cabinet ministers. We agreed on bottom-line negotiating objectives, but my senior colleagues were very sceptical of our chances of achieving them, and concerned at the risks of a failed negotiation. I also opened private consultation with the long-serving leader of the Ulster Unionists, James Molyneaux. To have any chance of gaining Unionist agreement, I thought it essential to take Jim into our confidence, listen to his views, and keep him briefed. Molyneaux is a wise man, canny and experienced, and widely liked and respected on the Conservative benches. His help would be invaluable, his opposition fatal.

Molyneaux was sceptical. He questioned the ability of the Provisional leadership to deliver a complete end to violence, without factions breaking away; and he pointed to elements of the text which were unbalanced and needed drastic alteration. After a further ministerial meeting, I sent Sir Robin Butler to Dublin with a deliberately discouraging message. I wanted Albert Reynolds to understand that the Joint Declaration, in its existing form, had no hope of winning British or Unionist acceptance, and suggested that we should look at other ways of moving forward.

For the next few weeks the process was on a knife-edge. I think it would have broken down had not the Shankill and Greysteel tragedies intervened. As Republican tradition dictated, Gerry Adams attended the funeral of Thomas Begley, the IRA bomber who had been killed in the Shankill Road explosion, and was pictured carrying his coffin. In the wave of revulsion that followed the Shankill bomb, the Irish government took a more critical attitude to the Hume–Adams process. In the Dáil, Dick Spring set out six principles, including a promise to re-examine Ireland's constitutional claim to the North and a strong affirmation of the consent principle. This was a helpful statement, noted carefully by Unionists. I then had a private meeting with Albert Reynolds during a European Council in Brussels. We agreed that the Hume–Adams process was so tainted as to be unusable;

the only way forward was for the two governments to take matters into their own hands. We said as much in a communiqué, to which Albert agreed with surprising ease: 'any initiative can only be taken by the two governments, and ... there could be no question of their adopting or endorsing the report of the dialogue that was recently given to the Taoiseach and which he had not passed on to the British government.'

The Brussels meeting and the statement by Dick Spring opened the road to a genuine negotiation and a much more balanced process, not one driven by Adams. This was not an easy step for Albert Reynolds – but Albert never lacked courage. John Hume raised the temperature by emerging from a meeting with me in Downing Street to tell the press that there would be 'peace within a week' if his proposals with Adams were endorsed, and his supporters gave Reynolds a torrid time at his party conference shortly afterwards. The Dublin government panicked under this intense pressure, and we had to endure a fraught two weeks of emotional phone calls, letters and threats of a breakdown before we could get back into sensible business. I tried to calm the atmosphere by stressing, at the Lord Mayor's Banquet in London on 15 November, that, if the IRA ended violence, Sinn Fein would be allowed after a suitable interval to enter the political arena as a democratic party. However, more fuel was then added to the fire by the leaking of an Irish government draft working paper which expressed the hope that the British government would endorse the goal of a unified Ireland, and then by a fresh joint statement from Hume and Adams.

Meanwhile, with a bilateral summit in Dublin scheduled for 3 December, we still had to decide whether, and how, to move forward with a Joint Declaration. We needed a different text, and I looked at two options with Cabinet colleagues on 23 November. One was to reshape the latest Reynolds text, which the Taoiseach said had been drafted with 'some input' from Hume. The other was to put forward a draft of our own. We decided on our own draft. We knew the Irish would not, indeed probably could not, accept an entirely new British draft; but it would demonstrate the width of the gap between us, and would help us to seek middle ground between the two positions. We had been working hard on that middle ground in private consultations with James Molyneaux and others; we sought advice also from the respected head of the Church of Ireland, Archbishop Robin Eames, and had a clear idea of where the document needed to end up.

The Taoiseach reacted to our draft as expected – first rejecting it, then threatening to publish his own text and call off the Dublin summit, then, after three days, offering important concessions and a deal to be agreed at the summit. In particular, in a telephone conversation with me on 29 November, he offered to drop a proposal for an 'Irish Convention', to which Molyneaux objected and which Archbishop Eames strongly advised against. Although there were still many points to be resolved, the prospects for the summit had dramatically improved – before taking a nosedive when our back channel to the Provisionals was exposed in the press on 28 November. Dublin accused us of double-dealing, and made a great show of indignation. This sat a little oddly with their own covert direct contacts with the Provisionals. Sauce for the goose was evidently not supposed to be sauce for the gander.

As a result, Albert Reynolds and I arrived at our summit in Dublin Castle, once the seat of British power in Ireland, with the Joint Declaration hanging in the balance under an accumulation of grievances and mistrust on each side. The summit was to be the defining moment in these long negotiations. Albert was steamed up over the back channel and the British draft declaration. I was angry over a series of Irish leaks, threats, and distorted press briefing (much of it coming from sources very close indeed to the Taoiseach).

We needed to re-establish trust. Albert readily accepted my suggestion that we should start the summit with an entirely private meeting. The two of us went into an ornate drawing room in the castle, leaving Paddy Mayhew, Dick Spring and two large delegations to talk elsewhere, and had the frankest and fiercest exchanges I had with any fellow leader in my six and a half years as prime minister. After half an hour alone, we brought in our two closest personal advisers, and continued the debate for another hour. Albert complained that the British government had been conducting a Dutch auction between the Joint Declaration and the back channel to the Provisionals. I took up the Irish government's deliberate foot-dragging over the three-stranded talks process, and finished up by laying down clearly the key points that had to be included in, and taken out of, the draft declaration.

The great point about my relationship with Albert Reynolds was that we liked one another, and could have a row without giving up on each other. The air was clearer when we left the room, and lunch was devoted to sporting banter, not politics. However, as we began the afternoon talks, now joined by our delegations, the survival of the declaration was still uncertain. We focused on a much-improved Irish draft which incorporated some language from Archbishop Eames, and for the first time we tabled our own amendments. Albert complained that these would 'up-end' the balance of the document, and one of his officials lost his temper and verged on the insulting. After a testing ninety minutes, Albert asked for a break and left the room with his team. We wondered if they were debating whether to call the whole thing off. Apparently they were speculating that we might walk out. After forty minutes the Irish team came back, looking far from happy. Albert resumed negotiating, but took a hard line. He insisted on retaining the 'Irish Convention', among five major points which we could not resolve; but we agreed to continue the negotiation through officials, and to meet again in Brussels a week later.

After months of fencing, we were at last in a real negotiation. From the Dublin summit onward, the cost of failure would be high to either side; but success was far from certain. It took two weeks of hard bargaining to pin down an agreement. Positions on my five points converged, but I had a difficult session with the Taoiseach in Brussels on 10 December. We reached a compromise acceptable to James Molyneaux on the 'Irish Convention', renamed the 'Forum for Peace and Reconciliation', it was seen by Unionists as a harmless talking shop, not a threatening new institution. I did not press Jim Molyneaux to commit himself explicitly to the text: like others, he had been sounded, but had not been a party to the negotiation. However, I established that he was not opposed, which was important to the document's chances of success.

On 14 December, Albert Reynolds and I resolved the final points in two telephone calls. We wanted to waste no time in launching the agreement. We expected Ian Paisley, among others, to denounce it (which he duly did, even before the text was given to him – 'It's like marriage with benefit of clergy,' one official remarked), and we needed to occupy the high ground. On the morning of 15 December, a mere sixteen hours after the deal was struck, Albert came to London to present the Downing Street Declaration with me in a joint press conference (which I followed with a parliamentary statement and my first ministerial broadcast since the Gulf War). It was the end of a marathon; but also no more than one stage in an even longer run.

'Peace within a week', or peace by Christmas, for which Albert had optimistically hoped, there was not. Nor did I have any reason to expect it. The Declaration was a statement of principles, not a deal negotiated with the paramilitaries on either side. It was greeted with huge cross-party support in the British and Irish parliaments, and near-euphoria in the media. The warmest of congratulations flooded in from around the world. Our problem was now in damping down hopes, because in the place that really counted – Northern Ireland – reactions were much more cautious.

Even moderate Unionists were suspicious of a declaration signed with an Irish prime minister, hailed in Dublin, and traceable back to the dialogue between John Hume and Gerry Adams. They could not find a sell-out in it, but its language was too 'Green' for their liking, and they feared a trap or the beginnings of a slippery slope. Jim Molyneaux bravely refrained from criticism and privately worked to get his UUP on board; but many of his members attacked the Declaration, while Ian Paisley and his hard-line Democratic Unionists were hell-bent on destroying it.

On the Nationalist side, though John Hume was disappointed that we had not gone further, the middle ground was with us, and Hume was supportive. The document placed the Provisionals in a dilemma. In the eyes of the Nationalist community, North and South, the two governments had left the Provisionals with no justification for terrorism. We were seen to have offered a fair entry to the political process for Sinn Fein if violence ended.

Historians like to identify turning points. Northern Ireland's history did not appear to turn on 15 December 1993; and when it did begin to turn, it was not solely as a result of the Downing Street Declaration. The Declaration itself had its origins in several sources and many hands. It was stimulated by the interest in negotiations shown by Gerry Adams and Martin McGuinness, through their talks with Hume and then with Dublin's secret emissaries and through their messages to us. It owed much to the vision and language of John Hume. It would not have happened without the drive and political courage of Albert Reynolds. Many of his ministerial colleagues were clearly sceptical (as was also the case in my government). On the Unionist side, Archbishop Robin Eames gave wise advice, and James Molyneaux, like Albert Reynolds, bravely went out on a limb. At the cost of much of his political ammunition, Molyneaux narrowly saved the UUP from the historic error of opposing the Declaration. Later in the process, not seeing the irony, Unionists were to quote its provisions endlessly in defence of their stance.

Was the Downing Street Declaration worth this Herculean effort? What did it signify? The Declaration was a powerful symbol. After twenty-four years of conflict and over seventy years of partition, it showed that there was a set of principles which the British and Irish governments could jointly accept. This had not happened before. And it had substance. Much of its language was convoluted and dense, because of the painfully negotiated balance. It would not have won an award for plain and unambiguous language. But, through the thicket, it guaranteed fair play. Unionists were assured that a united Ireland would not be imposed on them. Nationalists were assured that their traditions and aspirations would be respected. The paramilitaries were assured that they could enter political life if they accepted the rules of law and democracy and abandoned violence. The Declaration was not designed as a blueprint for a settlement, but it paved the way.

Gerry Adams's response to the Declaration was adroit. The pressure was on him. An opinion poll in the Irish Republic showed that 97 per cent of the population believed that the Provisionals should end violence at once. He didn't want to be seen to reject the Declaration, but his movement was divided, and he could not secure a consensus or an immediate end to violence. To buy time, he made an innocent-sounding demand for meetings with British representatives to 'clarify' the Declaration.

I was happy to give him as much time as he needed, and I set no deadline. The Declaration was not time-bound, and its worth did not depend on a reply from the Provisionals. But I was not going to get sucked into meetings to reinterpret or renegotiate our hard-won document under the guise of 'clarification'. That would have destroyed it. However long it took, the Provisionals had to be convinced that these principles were not negotiable.

My aim was to persuade the Provisionals to negotiate and give up violence. I wanted them to appreciate that they would never have a better opportunity for peace, and that they would forfeit support in Ireland and America if they spurned it. This, I felt, gave the best chance of an early breakthrough. Adams sought to deflect the pressure on him by dividing the British and Irish governments. Albert Reynolds reacted to rumours that the Provisionals would reject the initiative by lifting Dublin's twenty-year-old broadcasting ban on Sinn Fein, having his officials take the Provisionals through the text of the Declaration, and sending Adams a memorandum about it.

It was in the USA that Adams had a spectacular success. Up to then, Northern Ireland had barely featured on my agenda with Bill Clinton. In early 1993, at my request, he had dropped a campaign promise to appoint a peace envoy, which would have thoroughly alienated the Unionists. He had supported the Downing Street Declaration, and in November he had rejected a visa request by Gerry Adams on the grounds of the IRA's continuing violence. Adams applied again in January 1994, and on my instructions Rod Lyne, my Foreign Affairs Private Secretary, told the White House forcefully that we believed the offer of a visa should be held open until there was an end to violence. This would be helpful leverage, Rod told them. The US State Department and Justice Department, the FBI and the US Embassy in London gave similar advice, while the Irish-American lobby, including several heavyweight Democratic senators, applied intense pressure in the opposite direction. On White House instructions, Adams was asked by the US Consul in Belfast to state that he personally renounced violence and supported an end to the conflict on the basis of the Downing Street Declaration. Adams put out an equivocal statement which did not meet the US conditions; to my astonishment and annoyance, the White House gave him his visa.

Adams was fêted as a celebrity in New York. He skilfully milked the publicity, but, to the embarrassment of the White House, mounted hard-line attacks on the United Kingdom and the principle of agreement by consent. American hopes that the visit would lead to an early ceasefire were unfulfilled. The immediate effect of Adams's welcome in the United States was to shake the confidence of the Unionists, while bolstering the Provisionals against pressure to accept the Declaration. (When Adams applied for a further US visa in July, claiming that another visit was essential to the peace strategy, the White House turned him down – evidently without damaging the chances of a ceasefire.)

By Easter we were no further forward. Albert Reynolds's forecast in February of a cessation of violence 'sooner rather than later' had been dashed at Sinn Fein's Ard Fheis (party conference), when Adams had judged it politic to harden his stance. On 9 March the Provisional IRA had mounted an audacious mortar attack on Heathrow Airport. This did nothing for Adams's credibility in America, especially with his menacing comment that 'Every so often there will be something spectacular to remind the outside world.' Jim Molyneaux was under increasing pressure within the UUP to write the Declaration off, and Ian Paisley came to Downing Street to deliver one of his most histrionic performances, saying that the 'iniquitous' Declaration had been followed by seventy-four bombings, seventy-five shootings and nine murders. He and his deputy, Peter Robinson, ended an acrimonious meeting chanting in unison, 'The people of Northern Ireland alone,' to prevent me from speaking – a curious way for MPs to conduct a serious discussion, but passions were high. I had a better reception in Northern Ireland, where I was encouraged by universal support for the Declaration from the security forces, businessmen and community leaders. Seamus Mallon, John Hume's deputy, described it as 'the best step in Ireland for 150 years'.

To try to shift the stalemate, we then played two cards. Adams wrote to me twice, renewing the demand for meetings with the government. He published his letters. Downing Street's reply, also published, maintained our refusal to meet until there had been a cessation of violence. However, we amplified this by restating our detailed offer of an exploratory dialogue within three months of a cessation which we had first made through the back channel the previous November. We then moved to call Adams's bluff on the Declaration, quietly asking the Irish government to request him to define the points which, in his view, needed clarification. Adams sent Dublin a list of twenty questions. They proved our point. Only one, very simple question related to the clarification of the text. The other nineteen either raised extraneous matters or were self-evident attempts to reopen the Joint Declaration negotiations. We had no difficulty in providing factual answers based on our stated position, which we deliberately couched in non-confrontational language. The *Irish Times* commented that I had 'put the onus firmly on Sinn Fein to recognise the imperatives of constitutional politics and seek an end to violence'. That was the intention.

As we moved through June and July, evidence that the Provisionals were moving slowly towards a ceasefire began to mount. They enquired through the Irish government about our offer of exploratory dialogue. Sinn Fein's 'Peace Commission' showed considerable support for a cessation. We applied pressure through the White House. Reflecting RUC assessments, the Chief Constable, Sir Hugh Annesley, made cautiously optimistic comments. By early August our Ambassador in Dublin was reporting a growing feeling that there would be a ceasefire at the end of the month. When I returned from holiday on 25 August, I had firm advice from the Northern Ireland Office to expect this, though they forecast, accurately, that it would fall short of our request for a permanent renunciation of violence. I reflected this when I spoke to Albert Reynolds on 29 August. A buoyant Reynolds thought the Provisionals would 'go the distance', and said he was insisting on permanent cessation and a full commitment to the democratic process. Late on the same day, Number 10 quietly assented to an American request to let the IRA veteran Joe Cahill enter the United States to brief the associates of the Provisionals there. On Wednesday, 31 August 1994 the IRA declared that from midnight there would be a 'complete cessation of military operations'. They said:

> We believe that an opportunity to secure a just and lasting settlement has been created . . . we note that the Downing Street Declaration is not a solution, nor was it presented as such by its authors. A solution will only be found as a result of inclusive negotiations.

I replied:

> The IRA have declared a complete cessation of violence. I am greatly encouraged by this, but we need to be clear that this is indeed intended to be a permanent renunciation of violence, that is to say, for good. If it is, then many options are open. If they are genuinely and irrevocably committed to use only peaceful and democratic methods in the future, then we shall respond positively, as we said in the Joint Declaration. Let words now be reflected in deeds.

As soon as the IRA declared a halt to military operations, their supporters came out onto the streets to celebrate triumphantly. When you make a concession, it is smart politics to claim victory. The IRA were very smart, and their apparent delight demoralised the Unionists, who reasoned that they must have been sold out. The air was thick with rumours of secret deals, and we had to reassure Unionist leaders and Protestant churchmen that there was no covert pact – an assurance they relayed to their nervous followers. The IRA's cessation was a unilateral act in response to our public position, set out in the Downing Street Declaration and other statements.

Our problem was that the IRA's announcement fell short of a permanent renunciation of violence. Gerry Adams had *not* fulfilled a commitment to Albert Reynolds to declare that twenty-five years of conflict were over. John Hume had told me confidently in July that if there was a cessation for three months, the IRA would not be able to start up violence again; and he and Reynolds now interpreted the IRA statement as meaning that their violence was over for good. I hoped their confidence was justified, but I could not bank on it. The Provisionals had taken a huge step forward, and I wanted to encourage them to take further steps towards a lasting peace. But the security assessments I received showed that they were keeping open the option of terrorism. I decided that we needed more evidence before starting the timetable for exploratory dialogue.

The atmosphere in the North slowly calmed down. On 8 September the paramilitary Combined Loyalist Military Command indicated that they would also declare a ceasefire when they were convinced that the IRA meant what they said, and that there had been no secret deals. On 16 September, after over a fortnight without any IRA attacks, I thought the time was right for our first substantive response. On a visit to Belfast I announced a balanced package of measures. To reassure those who feared a sell-out, I committed the government to holding a referendum in Northern Ireland on any eventual outcome of constitutional talks. In response to the cessation, I lifted the ban on broadcasting the voices of spokesmen for the Provisionals and the paramilitaries (which had become farcically counter-productive, with actors reading their words) and, on the Chief Constable's advice, announced the relaxation of some security measures. The very positive reaction on all sides suggested that we had pitched this right.

Throughout September, Paddy Mayhew and his team were working hard on the next stages of the process. I held a planning meeting with them on 28 September. It was clear that the Provisionals were not going to make a clear verbal commitment to the permanent ending of violence. They had killed no one since 31 August, and internal support for the cessation was holding, for the time being; but the level of intimidation and vicious 'punishment' attacks had risen. To draw them towards a political process, we decided that at a certain point we would need to make a 'working assumption' that the ceasefire was intended to be permanent. I aimed to do this in the second half of October.

In early October we heard that the Loyalist paramilitaries were moving towards a ceasefire. In a conscious gamble, Paddy Mayhew allowed their representatives to consult their members in prison. This paid off. The Loyalists halted their campaign on 13 October, removing the risk that Loyalist attacks could spark an IRA resumption, and helping to clear the way for the next stage. Jim Molyneaux was among those who felt we should now 'drift into permanence'.

Like the first step on 16 September, my second package was designed to sustain momentum and to respond in a balanced way to concerns on both sides. I again took care to launch it in Northern Ireland rather than from Westminster. In a televised speech to the Northern Ireland Institute of Directors on 21 October, I unveiled fifteen new decisions and initiatives. I remained cautious about the permanence of the ceasefire, but said that on the basis of the actions of the Provisionals I was prepared to make a 'working assumption that the ceasefire is intended to be permanent'. I said we would convene exploratory talks before the end of the year. I announced that as a consequence of their ceasefire, the Loyalists would qualify for exploratory dialogue on the same terms as the Provisionals. The subjects to be covered included 'the practical consequences of ending the violence – most obviously how illegal weapons and explosives are going to be removed from life in Northern Ireland'. I foreshadowed a further relaxation of security measures. To maximise the benefits peace would bring, I promised that the government would convene an investment conference in Belfast, and anticipated an injection of new money from the European Union.

Throughout this period, we were under continuous pressure from Nationalists to accelerate Sinn Fein's entry into exploratory talks. Some of those who had confidently assured us that the cessation was irrevocable were, in almost no time, warning that it could break down unless we made rapid concessions to the Provisionals. As a confidence-booster for Sinn Fein, Albert Reynolds convened the first meeting of his 'Forum for Peace and Reconciliation' in late October, thus giving the Provisionals the cachet of participation in open debate with politicians from both the Republic and Northern Ireland (though not, of course, including the Unionists, who steered well clear).

On the opposite side, the Unionists were acutely nervous that principles would be abandoned under the duress of a threatened return to violence, and were extremely sceptical about the IRA's intentions. The security evidence showed that they had good reason for this view. Adams and many in the Provisional leadership seemed committed to a political process, but the IRA remained in full and active readiness. It was taking advantage of the ceasefire to recruit new volunteers and, at times openly, to reconnoitre targets. As ever, we did not have the luxury of taking a one-sided view. A settlement could not be achieved just by pandering to the IRA. Being criticised by both sides implied to me that our balance wasn't far out.

I was reinforced in this view by the way my second package of measures was received. Having made the speech, I flew to the border town of Newry, a bastion of hard-line Republicanism in an area scarred by the IRA. It had not previously been considered safe for a British prime minister to set foot in this corner of the United Kingdom. If we were thought to be handling the Republicans unfairly, I could have expected a hostile reception in Newry. Instead, the response there was astonishing. I was cheered in a crowded shopping centre, and people jostled to shake my hand and give me presents. I had an equally warm reception the next day from Unionists in Jim Molyneaux's Lagan Valley constituency.

After my 21 October speech, all eyes were on the opening of the exploratory dialogue. But first we had to surmount two more hurdles. Less than three weeks after my visit, armed Provisionals raided the Newry post office and shot a postman. This turned out to be botched criminality rather than a deliberate ceasefire breach, and the Provisionals indicated that no such actions would be sanctioned.

Then, on 17 November, domestic problems over a judicial case forced Albert Reynolds to resign as Taoiseach and leader of Fianna Fáil. I was sorry personally and dismayed politically to see him go, but I was to be lucky in his successor, John Bruton of Fine Gael. Dick Spring transferred the support of the minority Labour Party to Fine Gael, thereby retaining his own position as Tanaiste and Foreign Minister in the new coalition government.

Though Spring provided continuity, the change was disruptive. Albert Reynolds had been an erratic partner in our enterprise, but a courageous one whom I knew well and liked. He departed from the emerging peace process with much to his credit. John Bruton's style was very different – less nimble and voluble, and more straightforward. I had only met him on a couple of occasions, and initially he seemed daunted by what he had unexpectedly taken on. It took us time to read each other, but he too, despite the occasional row, became a friend – brave, decent and a trustworthy operator. In many ways he faced a trickier task than Albert Reynolds. His party was weaker and the coalition with Labour less cohesive – he and Dick Spring had had many a brush in the past. Above all, Bruton's conciliatory attitudes towards the Unionists and the United Kingdom had earned him the deep suspicion of Republicans and the unkind sobriquet 'Johnny Unionist'. I knew he would have to watch his back constantly, and would find it harder to make concessions to us than had Reynolds. But he too was committed to move forward.

1994, like 1993, ended on an upbeat note. On 9 December, a team of British officials sat openly across a table from a Sinn Fein delegation for the first time in a quarter of a century. The following week, a similar exercise began with the Loyalists. In between, peace-building took a step forward with the involvement of businessmen and government representatives from many countries in the investment conference which I opened on 13 December at the much-bombed, but splendidly repaired, Europa Hotel in Belfast. We entered 1995 conscious of a long and treacherous slope still to be climbed, but in a mood of rising optimism.

In parallel with the Downing Street Declaration, the Northern Ireland Office had been doggedly pursuing the three-stranded talks process with the four constitutional parties and the Irish government. Since 1992, we had been unable to get the parties together around the same table, although Patrick Mayhew and his Minister of State, Michael Ancram, had had sporadic bilateral contacts with them. The Northern Ireland Office had tried to persuade the Irish government to join us in working up papers on areas of agreement in the 1992 talks, and in January 1994 Paddy Mayhew proposed to Dick Spring that their officials should jointly broker 'an illustrative draft of a possible outcome of the process'. The Northern Ireland Office drafted an outline (quaintly titled the 'Notions Paper'), which Dublin opposed and which was leaked to the Irish press – and which the Unionists also opposed. The Unionists responded with a proposal for a Northern Ireland Assembly, relegating the idea of North/South cooperation. James Molyneaux, by now under fierce attack within his party for acquiescing in the Downing Street Declaration, was forced into a harder line. The earlier progress seemed to be unravelling.

However, at a meeting with Patrick Mayhew and me before an England–

Ireland rugby international early in 1994, Albert Reynolds and Dick Spring had agreed to recommit themselves to the talks process. By May, Northern Ireland Office officials were in negotiation with their Dublin counterparts on what were to become the 'Joint Framework Documents'.

The groundwork had been laid in the 1991–92 talks on Peter Brooke's three-stranded approach. It had not changed. Strand One proposed new arrangements for the internal government of Northern Ireland – a new assembly, executive and so on. It was, therefore, the sole responsibility of the government of the United Kingdom, to be brokered only with the parties and people of Northern Ireland. We firmly rejected requests by the Irish government to be consulted on the drafting of the paper setting out the arrangements for this. Its outlines had been established in the talks, but for us to be thought to be negotiating the *internal* constitution of Northern Ireland with Dublin would have destroyed the process.

Proposals on Strands Two and Three were to be set out in a second document. This did have to be negotiated with Dublin and presented jointly by the two governments, because Strand Two covered relations between Northern Ireland and the Republic, while Strand Three looked at the relationship between the United Kingdom as a whole and the Republic.

There was something in this complicated formula for everyone. Under direct rule from Westminster since 1972, local politicians in Northern Ireland had been denuded of power. The Unionists wanted to have more say in how they were governed, and to restore an assembly and an executive in which they were certain to have a majority. The Nationalists were prepared to tolerate the restoration of local democracy if it was balanced by a closer relationship with the Republic, and if measures were devised to allow the Dublin government to play a role as the protector of Nationalist interests in the North. To this the Unionists responded that they could only accept closer links with Dublin if they did not erode the United Kingdom's sovereignty over Northern Ireland or represent a step towards Irish unification. They could accept cooperation (reluctantly and within limits), but not the exercise of joint *authority* over Northern Ireland by the two governments. They wanted the Republic of Ireland to remove the claim to sovereignty over the whole island of Ireland which was asserted in the Irish Constitution.

All three strands had to interlock. No assembly for the Unionists without North/South institutions for the Nationalists; no Dublin involvement for the Nationalists without amendment of the Irish Constitution for the Unionists; and so on. The mantra of the talks remained, 'Nothing is agreed until everything is agreed.'

It took ten months, from May 1994 to February 1995, to finalise agreement with Dublin on the second Framework Document. During this period the Republican and Loyalist paramilitaries and their political wings were moving towards the cessation of violence and into exploratory dialogue with the British government, in the hope of then joining the constitutional talks. This shared ambition by the bitterest of opponents accentuated the importance of the Framework Documents as a set of proposals to focus the talks. However, our task was made harder by a struggle within the Ulster Unionist Party over the party's future direction. This conflict built up during 1994, as Jim Molyneaux came under attack from some of his colleagues. What the UUP might be persuaded to accept was one of the central issues in the Framework calculations. That was a hard judgement to make when the UUP was riven into factions, with its leader's authority constantly under threat.

The early negotiations on the Framework Documents were conducted primarily between officials haggling their way through acres of text. At intervals Albert Reynolds and I were engaged to try to resolve the most difficult issues: Dublin's reluctance to remove the claim to Northern Ireland from the Irish Constitution; Irish pressure for an ambitious range of North/South bodies, with extensive powers; an Irish demand that the intergovernmental conference should have power to intervene if the Northern Ireland parties did not respect the agreements – the so-called 'default mechanism' which, if granted, would have given Dublin the right to intervene in Northern Ireland's affairs. Nor did London and Dublin agree on the status of the Framework Documents. Our intention was to put a discussion paper to the parties. Dublin wanted a firm commitment by both governments to specific positions, thus allowing much less latitude for negotiation by the elected Northern Ireland representatives.

In between much detailed work by Patrick Mayhew, Dick Spring and their cohorts, Albert Reynolds and I hammered away at these points in meetings at Downing Street in May, Corfu (during a European Council) in June, Brussels in July (another European Council) and Chequers in October, interspersed with letters and telephone conversations. We were intensively involved at the same time in the separate issue of the cessation of violence and exploratory talks, but, inch by inch, we managed to narrow the gap on the Framework Document.

As ever, Albert Reynolds's unceasing dialogue with the Irish media made the Ulster Unionists increasingly suspicious and the negotiations more difficult. Before our Corfu meeting he raised expectations of a 'cross border Authority with executive powers'. James Molyneaux came in at once to warn me bluntly that this spectre made Unionist acceptance of any North/South institutions unlikely, and was putting at risk his own moderate position on the issue.

Between Corfu in June and Brussels in July, Albert conceded some ground – though not enough – on amending the constitutional claim, then asserted that he had gone to his 'outer limits'. Molyneaux insisted that we should not pay a high price for the removal of a claim which had no validity. Meanwhile, progress was steadily made on other issues. At Chequers in late October, Albert Reynolds and I agreed that the gap was bridgeable, and tentatively aimed at completion by Christmas. It was shortly afterwards, at the worst possible time, that Albert was unseated.

The transition to John Bruton in November put the Framework negotiations in balk for the better part of two months. As Bruton told me frankly at our first meeting in Downing Street just before Christmas, he could ill afford to make further concessions, irrespective of his own views. Albert Reynolds's party, Fianna Fáil, now in opposition under Bertie Ahern, was poised to accuse Bruton and Dick Spring of weakness or worse if they gave any ground to the British (even ground which Albert himself might have been preparing to give in a final push for a deal – as he had indicated in his last letter to me before leaving office).

During this hiatus, we lost the Ulster Unionists. James Molyneaux had bravely expended credit within his own party by quietly cooperating with us over the Downing Street Declaration. The high visibility of Gerry Adams throughout 1994 – visiting America, constantly on television, the focus of attention – had been hard for Unionists to stomach; and Molyneaux, a low-key operator who disliked the media, had not been able to counter this. Ian Paisley was working hard to attract Unionists into outright opposition, and derided Jim Molyneaux as 'Judas Iscariot'. Now the government was not only in a dialogue with the Provisionals, but was also developing a new accord with Dublin. Molyneaux's rivals for the UUP leadership exploited this, raising the spectre of a rerun of the 1985 Anglo–Irish

Agreement, for which the Unionists (not having been consulted) had never forgiven Margaret Thatcher.

I saw Jim Molyneaux on the same day I saw John Bruton, 20 December 1994. He was upset that, despite requests to the Northern Ireland Office since September, he had not been shown the draft of the Framework Document we were discussing with the Irish, but had merely been briefed in general terms. Now Albert Reynolds was quoting from it, and giving the impression that it would impose joint United Kingdom/Irish authority over Northern Ireland. I assured him that it would do no such thing, but he was unpersuaded, and his worries reverberated in the media and around the Commons. We had a further meeting on 24 January 1995, when Jim refused my offer to show him the text, but raised a series of objections to what he believed to be its key provisions. He did not wish to see the text because he did not want to be implicated in its provisions. I reassured him that we were only working on proposals. The Unionists could not be sold out, I told him, because the proposals would have to be agreed by the parties, by Parliament, and by Northern Ireland's people in a referendum – a triple lock. Nevertheless, he urged me to halt the exercise, citing the Irish government's extensive leaks as a reason. As pressure mounted on him, he expressed his concerns in public, making comparisons with 1985 and claiming that British and Irish civil servants had sabotaged the intention of the two prime ministers to issue a framework paper for public consultation.

In late January negotiations with Dublin resumed, and Paddy Mayhew obtained an acceptable commitment on changes to the Irish Constitution. However, any lingering hopes of securing a fair hearing from Unionists were then very deliberately torpedoed. Part of the text of the Framework Document was leaked to an ambitious young journalist on *The Times*. When we heard the story was coming, I asked my chief press officer to speak to the editor of *The Times*, and to point out that the story the paper was about to print was incorrect, and could damage the whole peace process. It was still printed, albeit with brief comments from us in an attempt to draw the poison from it. The leak was written up in an unbalanced way which asserted, without justification, that the Framework Document brought 'the prospect of a united Ireland closer than it has been at any time since Partition in 1920'.

To still the passions this would arouse in the Conservative parliamentary party I summoned a large number of my parliamentary colleagues to a late-night meeting in my room at the House. It was a tense occasion, but support for our position came from Robert Cranborne, the Leader of the Lords and a known supporter of the Unionist cause. This helped steady nerves. Paddy Mayhew spoke of 'black work at the crossroads', and I did all I could to limit the damage, making a broadcast to set out the facts, but to little avail. I would have liked to publish the full text of the draft documents, but they were still incomplete.

We could not turn back in the face of this malign behaviour. We redoubled our efforts to finish the exercise with Dublin, and I invited all the Northern Ireland parties to see me. Ian Paisley evaded me until the consultation period was past. Jim Molyneaux also did not come, but asked me to see the three of the mutineers within his party – Willie Ross, Martin Smyth and David Trimble. I spent two hours knocking down their fears that the documents were a 'Nationalist agenda'. Nonetheless, they wrote to me rejecting a text which they had seen only partially and in summary.

Having secured a final list of forty-three amendments from Dublin, I launched the two Joint Framework Documents with John Bruton at the Balmoral Conference Centre near Belfast on 22 February. The Ulster Unionists pre-empted this with a paper alleging that all-Ireland institutions with executive powers would be 'imposed by diktat', and that the Irish government was seeking to 'have Unionist politicians caged so that they may only function within tightly drawn parameters'. Though Sinn Fein would in reality have had great difficulty with the Framework Documents, Gerry Adams had the wit to welcome them, so as to drive deeper the wedge between Unionists and the government.

As we had promised, we put our proposals out for public consultation. The texts were published and distributed throughout Northern Ireland. The Ulster Unionists' response remained hostile. In Parliament they signalled their discontent by siding with the Labour Party in a finely-balanced EU vote on 1 March. A delegation of (Anglican) Church of Ireland bishops complained to me, while the Presbyterian Church warned that the documents were 'too Green'. Molyneaux's position was further weakened when a stalking-horse challenger to his leadership gained strong support at the UUP Conference at the end of March.

We did not rush the pace. The more the Unionists crawled through the documents, the more we hoped they would see that we had stood firmly by the Downing Street Declaration. They found few points of substance to justify claims that the Framework Documents had a 'Nationalist agenda'. Their objections – save those which were direct misrepresentation – were centred on the tone and the use of what they styled 'Green' language or 'Hume-speak'.

By April, however, it was clear that the UUP would not accept the Joint Framework Documents even as a basis for negotiation – or rather, that they could not be seen to be climbing down from their overstated opposition to them. In order to restart consultations, Patrick Mayhew abstracted key points from the texts, shorn of contentious prose, into a much shorter discussion document, the 'Issues Paper'. He broached this successfully with the UUP on 9 May. On 18 May, Patrick and I had a very friendly session jointly with the Ulster Unionists and the SDLP. Immediately afterwards relations went into reverse when the UUP reacted against Paddy Mayhew's first encounter with Gerry Adams, at an investment conference in Washington from which Jim Molyneaux was forced by his party to withdraw. Molyneaux was nearing the end of a long internal war of attrition.

In July 1995 David Trimble gained the high ground among disgruntled Unionists when he led an Orange Order protest at Drumcree, where a stand-off had developed after the police diverted a provocative Orange march from a Nationalist district of Portadown. At the end of August, Jim Molyneaux was ousted from the UUP leadership, and Trimble succeeded him as the popular choice of the membership of the party, although his fellow Ulster Unionist Members of Parliament told me that none of them voted for him. Jim had held the post for sixteen years, from the beginning of Margaret Thatcher's premiership until five years into mine. We had a warm valedictory lunch together at Chequers, at which, despite his legendary discretion, he was able to lift the veil on the machinations which undid him. At seventy-five, he had had a long innings and had fought hard for his people. He had sometimes made my life and Patrick's uncomfortable, but had done Northern Ireland a tremendous service in backing the Downing Street Declaration.

At the time of Jim Molyneaux's departure, the Joint Framework Documents appeared to have failed conclusively. In September 1995, a year into the ceasefire, the Provisionals and Loyalists were still far from participation in an 'inclusive' talks process; and the Framework Documents had not provided a focus for renewed constitutional negotiations with the four democratic parties. I blame myself for not injecting a wider political perspective into the drafting. I was heavily preoccupied in 1994 with the build-up to the ceasefire and the response to it. I did not focus adequately on the fine print and the tone of the draft texts until early 1995, by which time it was too late to reshape them fundamentally. Officials had done an expert job, but the end-product was not user-friendly. The texts were long and dense, with a mass of detail which offered many targets for attack by selective quotation. And the language *was* more 'Green' than the substance.

That said, the Framework Documents were undermined most by what was happening around them. They became a weapon in the hands of those who sought to wrest control of the UUP from Jim Molyneaux and take a tougher line against Nationalism and the government's conduct of the peace process. Not even the most perfect drafting would have kept our initiative out of the Unionist crossfire. My decision to go ahead with the documents certainly gave the lie to the thesis of Nationalist commentators who claimed that the Unionists had a stranglehold over the government because of our shrinking majority, although that canard was often used against us.

In a longer perspective, the documents appear in a more favourable light. They were a step along the road from Peter Brooke's initiation of the 'three-stranded' talks in March 1991 to the Good Friday Agreement of April 1998. The texts, having been taken apart and reassembled, became the basis for an agreement endorsed by many of those who had opposed the Framework three years before.

Throughout 1995 – the first year without terrorist killings in Northern Ireland in a quarter of a century, albeit not without violence – our aim was to make two separate negotiations converge. The talks with the four constitutional parties made faltering progress through the Joint Framework Documents. In the 'exploratory dialogue' from December 1994, we were trying to find an acceptable basis for Provisional Sinn Fein and the two small Loyalist parties, the Progressive Unionist Party (PUP) and the Ulster Democratic Party (UDP), to join the constitutional talks on an equal basis as democratic and law-abiding participants.

The talks with Sinn Fein immediately ran into difficulties over the IRA's

arsenal of guns and explosives – from the outset *the* fundamental obstacle
to the peace process. The point was simple but intractable. The Provisionals
had to choose whether to become a democratic political party, or to continue to be a movement backed by terrorism, and therefore outside the
law. They could not be both. Adams and McGuinness seemed ready to
make a commitment to exclusively democratic methods; but could they
carry the movement as a whole in the same direction?

It was always evident that the issue of paramilitary weapons would have
to be addressed. The Downing Street Declaration had required 'a permanent
end to the use of, or support for, paramilitary violence' and 'a commitment
to exclusively peaceful methods' – conditions self-evidently incompatible
with possession of an illegal arsenal. At this stage there was no daylight
between the British and Irish governments over illegal weaponry, and if
anything Albert Reynolds and Dick Spring made the running. Half a year
earlier, in a document he sent to Gerry Adams on steps to be taken after
a cessation of violence, Reynolds had specified that:

> Once public confidence in peace had been established, every
> effort would be made to deal expeditiously with issues such
> as long-standing prisoners, excepting cases of serious violence,
> particularly against the person; and arms and equipment, so
> that the legacy of the past twenty years and the cost could be
> put behind us as quickly as possible.

As early as September 1993 I had discussed the problem at Downing
Street with John Hume, who, like the Taoiseach, was in contact with Adams.
He too was clear that it would have to be tackled in the context of a
cessation of violence. In the following month, Patrick Mayhew said that
the IRA would have to make available its guns and explosives to show that
its violence was over. When the Downing Street Declaration was launched
on 15 December 1993, he repeated the point. So did Dick Spring, speaking
for the Irish government, when he told the Irish Parliament that:

> Questions were raised on how to determine a permanent cess-
> ation of violence. We are talking about the handing up of arms
> and are insisting that it would not be simply a temporary cess-
> ation of violence to see what the political process offers. There
> can be no equivocation in relation to the determination of both
> governments in that regard.

It could not have been more explicit.

When the Provisionals entered the exploratory dialogue a year and more after these statements by both governments, they knew what the dialogue would entail. Two months before their ceasefire, Dick Spring reminded them again:

> There will have to be a verification of the handing over of arms. As I said publicly on many occasions, there is little point in attempting to bring people into political dialogue if they are doing so on the basis of giving it a try and, if it does not work, returning to the bomb and the bullet. It has to be permanent and there must be evidence of it . . . There can be no participation by Sinn Fein/IRA in political discussions with either government until they have made a very firm commitment that the violence has ended.

So as to avoid any possibility of doubt, I reiterated the position when I opened the run-up to exploratory talks in my speech of 21 October 1994. I said the talks would cover

> the practical consequences of ending the violence – most obviously how illegal weapons and explosives are going to be removed from life in Northern Ireland. Peace cannot be assured finally until the paramilitaries on both sides hand in their weapons. This is a difficult issue but it cannot be ducked. We must consider therefore how guns and explosives can best be deposited and decommissioned. These weapons are both north and south of the border. So we shall be consulting the Irish government on a coordinated approach.

It was against this background that the Provisionals chose to seek entry to negotiations. At a later stage, to justify stonewalling over weapons, their propagandists were to claim that we had inserted decommissioning as a 'new' precondition after the ceasefire. That is patently false. Equally absurdly, they claimed that the British government was demanding the IRA's 'surrender'; we had, they said, made a grave mistake by failing to understand 'Republican psychology', or the Irish tradition of putting 'the pike in the thatch'. If so, the lack of understanding was manifestly shared by, among others, Albert Reynolds and, especially, Dick Spring – who can scarcely have been unaware of the Republican mindset – who made the toughest statements on disarmament. I was also careful *not* to demand surrender. Instead, with Paddy Mayhew, I set to work with Reynolds and Spring to find ways in which the paramilitaries could begin to take their weapons out of commission *without* their having to surrender them to us. With this in mind, we met at Chequers in October 1994 and set up a working group to develop a joint approach to decommissioning headed by Sir John Chilcot, Permanent Secretary at the Northern Ireland Office, and Tim Dalton, the Permanent Secretary at Ireland's Department of Justice.

A third, and more sophisticated, argument was advanced by Gerry Adams and others. Peace, they said, required total 'demilitarisation', or 'taking the gun out of Irish politics'. I agreed strongly with that view. Where I parted company with Adams was when he argued that weapons held, under the law, by the security forces should be taken out of commission in parallel. The army and the police could not be equated with terrorists: they did not bomb, murder or kneecap. Our position was simple and flexible. I was not prepared to negotiate the disposition of the security forces with the paramilitaries, but I was prepared to reduce security measures as soon as they were no longer needed. I looked forward to returning the RUC to normal civilian policing, and to letting the troops leave Northern Ireland for duties elsewhere. Moreover, I had demonstrated this by easing security measures in response to the ceasefire and, as peace took hold, reducing army patrolling and withdrawing troops. The signals of our good faith were unmistakable.

In the first round of exploratory talks on 9 December 1994, British officials made it clear to Sinn Fein that the retention of illegal weapons would be a barrier to their participation in political negotiations, and undertook to table a paper on the mechanics of decommissioning. Martin McGuinness countered by demanding 'demilitarisation' – by which he meant the British Army's withdrawal from Northern Ireland – and the speedy release of IRA prisoners. In the second meeting, on 19 December, Sinn Fein refused to enter into any discussion of decommissioning, or even to take delivery of the government's paper. McGuinness took up the farcical position that he did not represent the IRA, and had no control or influence over them. Whilst the Loyalists were engaging seriously in the parallel dialogue, Sinn Fein demanded to enter the all-party negotiations without further ado, and said it would be more realistic to deal with the arms problem in those talks.

At this juncture John Bruton paid his first visit to Downing Street since having succeeded Albert Reynolds as Prime Minister of Ireland. He was a very different personality to Albert, but was just as committed to a settlement. He gave his support to the peace process and endorsed the Chilcot/Dalton decommissioning exercises. It was important to make substantial progress on decommissioning, he told the press, and after our meeting I was confident we could carry the process forward.

Two further meetings with Sinn Fein were held in mid-January and early February 1995. Some progress was made on a range of issues, though the closest they came to the arms issue was an oblique reference to Sinn Fein possibly using their 'influence' over the Republican paramilitaries in a positive way. To avoid being drawn any further, they then stalled the talks and mounted a series of diversionary stunts. They demanded that the meetings should be raised to ministerial level, and warned that the ceasefire could break down, which struck oddly with the many Republican assurances of a complete cessation. On 9 February Sinn Fein walked out of the fifth exploratory meeting, claiming that there was a listening device in a Stormont ante-room. The room was then scanned in their presence. No bug was found.

On 28 February John Chilcot and Tim Dalton submitted their joint report, which saw it as realistic to get decommissioning under way, starting with 'a worthwhile quantity of arms'. This was to be encouraged by the prospect of parallel progress in other areas, such as security measures and the release of prisoners. Unfortunately the constructive thrust of this private report was offset when Dick Spring was quoted as saying in Washington that it would be a 'formula for disaster' to insist that nothing would happen before decommissioning. I was very sceptical when I was told what Spring had allegedly said, since it appeared to contradict his earlier firm stance, but once his comments were reported, they did damage. John Bruton tried to straighten things out, declaring that a way to decommission would have to be found before political talks could proceed: 'You won't see Ian Paisley or Jim Molyneaux sitting down with Gerry Adams until this issue is dealt with. If you are pursuing the democratic road you don't need arms. These arms are now redundant. It is a question now of how they are to be dealt with.' This was clear enough, but Dick Spring's alleged slip of the tongue was endlessly and selectively repeated, and lifted the pressure off Sinn Fein and the IRA.

So, on 9 March, did the announcement that Gerry Adams had been invited to President Clinton's St Patrick's Day Reception, and that the US ban on fund-raising for the Provisionals was being lifted. Other political leaders from the North and South were also invited in what the White House saw as an even-handed approach. In fact it was not, because the invitation to Adams encouraged the Provisionals to dig in to an increasingly hard-line position. It was all the more frustrating because Patrick Mayhew had been in Washington two days beforehand, and had told the White House that if any further concessions were made to the Provisionals, they should be contingent on serious discussion of decommissioning. The invitation to Adams undercut that. Paddy had set out publicly what we were seeking in what became known as the Washington conditions:

1. A willingness in principle to disarm progressively.
2. A common practical understanding of the modalities, that is to say what decommissioning would actually entail.
3. In order to test the practical arrangements and to demonstrate good faith, the actual decommissioning of some arms as a tangible confidence-building measure and to signal the start of a process.

These terms had been carefully constructed to be within what could be delivered by the Provisionals. They were merely being asked to decommission 'some arms' to show a commitment to the peace process before being admitted to full political negotiations on an equal basis with political parties with no arms whatsoever. It was an inherently reasonable proposition, representing, if anything, a softening of the government's position – and was attacked as such by Unionists, who said we were capitulating to the IRA.

The White House invitation followed exchanges in which Adams had told them he would 'discuss decommissioning seriously' if the exploratory dialogue was raised to ministerial level. This was not a new concession, as the White House apparently assumed; it merely repeated what he had already said to us. However, the lifting of the American fund-raising ban at a time when the IRA was still in the market for arms provoked justifiable anger in Northern Ireland. I warned the President in a letter of 10 March that, on Sinn Fein's track record, the Provisionals would pocket American concessions, play them against the British government, and fail to deliver anything in return. That turned out to be the case. As early as 13 March

Sinn Fein were denying the commitment the White House claimed it had secured, and Adams never made good on it. The Americans had been duped by Sinn Fein. They realised this, and swiftly sought to make amends. President Clinton telephoned and wrote to me, swearing that he would hold Adams to his commitment and would continue to say that Sinn Fein must address the hard questions of decommissioning – and start to discuss it now, not later.

I was dubious about whether the Provisionals would now move forward. We tested their commitment by proposing resumption of the exploratory dialogue, but raised to the level of Michael Ancram, Minister of State, on the basis of the Washington conditions. McGuinness agreed in writing to 'serious, substantive and constructive discussions' from which no issue, including the decommissioning of weapons, would be excluded. But when Michael Ancram proposed a detailed agenda to Sinn Fein, they procrastinated, demanding an additional item on 'demilitarisation'.

With Sinn Fein's promise to the White House unfulfilled, I visited Washington in early April. Over breakfast I briefed Vice-President Al Gore on the continuation of barbaric 'punishment beatings' by the paramilitaries, and on the definition by Sinn Fein Chairman Mitchel McLaughlin of 'demilitarisation' as meaning the removal of the British Army to barracks, pending their removal altogether from Northern Ireland. To demand that British troops should not be quartered in part of their own country was clearly a wrecking tactic. Gore, who had a good understanding of Northern Ireland, expressed his dismay, and asked how they should put things right. I suggested some points to him, and when President Clinton and I met later in the morning, he accepted all of them. He said at our joint press conference:

> I was very clear when the Adams visa was granted with permission to fund-raise that there must be an agreement – a commitment – in good faith to seriously and quickly discuss arms decommissioning. Without a serious approach to arms decommissioning, there will never be a resolution of this conflict. So I would hope there would be no difference in our position on that, because I think the Prime Minister is right about that: we have to deal with this arms decommissioning issue and I know that there is an attempt by the government to work with the paramilitaries on both sides to achieve that

objective and that is what I think should be done . . . The paramilitaries of both sides must get rid of their weapons for good
so that violence never returns to Northern Ireland.

This was a ringing endorsement of our position, albeit later than we
would have wished. Nevertheless, the Provisionals engaged in a further
month of hair-splitting correspondence before they met Michael Ancram
on 10 May. John Bruton did his best to help, proposing a further joint
exercise to plan for decommissioning and insisting that Adams should
discuss with Ancram how it could be brought about.

Michael Ancram became the first British minister openly to meet the
Provisionals, having by then held four meetings with the Loyalists. The
Provisionals quoted Dick Spring's reported description of decommissioning
as a formula for disaster, and demanded the withdrawal of the British Army
from Northern Ireland and the disbanding of the RUC. They said the IRA
would not give up weapons at that stage: the arms issue would be solved
in the context of a negotiated settlement – which, four years later, would
turn out to be yet another broken promise. The only small advance was
that McGuinness accepted a copy of the government's paper on modalities.
But overall Sinn Fein were still posturing and filibustering, and avoiding
genuine discussion.

Having achieved a meeting with Michael Ancram, the Provisionals now
demanded one with the Secretary of State. They expected a refusal, which
they would then have used to justify their own intransigence. To prevent this
coup for them, Patrick Mayhew met Gerry Adams during the Washington
investment conference on 24 May, when he underlined that there had to be
progress on decommissioning before Sinn Fein could enter the substantive
negotiations. President Clinton used the same event to appeal to the paramilitaries to 'take the next step: put aside the guns . . . decommission the
weapons'.

Martin McGuinness attended a second meeting with Ancram on 25
May, but offered no movement on decommissioning. Thereafter, having
come to only two meetings since February, and only six in all, it became
the Provisionals' tactic to avoid any further exploratory dialogue, and to
escape awkward questions about their armaments and the continuing violence being wreaked through 'punishment beatings'. The Loyalists, by contrast, had participated in twelve rounds of talks, including detailed
discussion of decommissioning. The Provisionals then launched their next

demand. Despite not having met the requirements we had defined, they now insisted on unconditional entry to full political negotiations, falling back on the traditional tactic of threatening a return to terrorism, as Adams warned in a *Sunday Telegraph* interview.

I reviewed the situation with John Bruton at a European summit in Cannes on 27 June. To help the Provisionals over the decommissioning hump, we decided to build on the idea, first floated by Ken Maginnis of the Ulster Unionist Party, of an international commission. Maginnis's proposal was significant, because international involvement had hitherto been anathema to the UUP. Now they were proposing it. The tireless workhorses Chilcot and Dalton were mandated to develop specific proposals. Following Cannes, the straight-talking US Ambassador in London, Admiral William Crowe, met Adams to protest about the Provisionals' refusal to move on decommissioning and their threats to return to violence, saying that President Clinton had taken risks, and 'you ain't given a goddam thing to him.'

July and August were tense months, running up to the first anniversary of the IRA ceasefire on 31 August. Nationalists reacted angrily to a recommendation in July by the independent and quasi-judicial Life Sentence Review Board that a British soldier, Private Lee Clegg, sentenced for shooting a Catholic girl in a car which had run an army roadblock, should be released from prison. The Provisionals exploited this opportunity to mount violent demonstrations, destroying property and burning vehicles. Within days militant Unionists and Loyalists countered with a protest of their own, confronting the RUC in the 'siege of Drumcree'. Ian Paisley moved centre stage to heat up the atmosphere, saying Drumcree was 'a matter of life or death . . . a matter of freedom or slavery'.

In the midst of these events, we pressed on with our efforts to persuade the Provisionals to move forward. I authorised three private ministerial meetings with Sinn Fein to try to break the impasse. The second of these meetings, between Patrick Mayhew, Michael Ancram, Gerry Adams and Martin McGuinness on church premises in Londonderry on 18 July, later became known about, and was predictably attacked by Unionists. In private, Adams and McGuinness were reasonable. They had boxed themselves in, and seemed to want help in getting out. Paddy Mayhew floated the 'twin-track' initiative he had been developing with the Irish since the Cannes meeting, based on parallel progress on decommissioning and political issues. Adams showed an interest, but wanted to link it to a high-profile meeting of all parties, including Sinn Fein. He took a similar line three days later with Bruton and Spring, and inclined towards our development of Ken Maginnis's idea of an international commission. John Hume added his weight to Adams's wish for a high-profile meeting, and suggested that the government should convene all-party talks in September – though he must have known that this was certain to be rejected by the Unionists. However, on 27 July, meeting Mayhew and Ancram again, to our frustration Adams went into reverse, standing pat on his counter-demand for the all-party conference he knew could not happen, and then opposing the international commission on decommissioning.

I assumed that the IRA had warned him off this latest UK–Irish proposal to find a way into the armaments issue. As the ceasefire anniversary approached, the Provisionals played on fragile nerves in Dublin, their threats of a breakdown provoking (as they had calculated) a torrent of requests to London for concessions and appeasement. Paddy Mayhew pre-empted the anniversary by bringing Northern Ireland prison sentence remission rates into line with those elsewhere in the UK. Despite forebodings from Dublin, 31 August passed without a breakdown.

I was determined not to let the Provisionals' opposition to an international commission drive the two governments off a promising idea. Since the Cannes meeting in June we had worked up the twin-track process, balancing political progress with an international commission on decommissioning. One idea, which was attractive to Unionists, was for an elected body to play a part in the negotiations. In July Patrick Mayhew sent a prospectus for the twin-track process to Dick Spring. John Bruton telephoned me to give his blessing, and we set 6 September as a target date jointly to launch the initiative in London.

As usual, the detail abounded with devils. The Irish were clearing every step they took with the Provisionals; and the Provisionals kept upping the ante. On 28 August John Bruton thought he had Sinn Fein on board. The next day the Irish backed away, after rough handling by the Provisionals. Gerry Adams and John Hume advanced a series of demands which had no hope of general acceptance – for an all-party convention to be held in September or October; for a fixed date for all-party political negotiations, not dependent on any progress in the interim; and for the proposed international commission to be replaced by a single arbiter, former US Senator

George Mitchell. They made no distinction between the legal arms of the security forces and the illegal weapons of the paramilitaries. No movement or concession by the Provisionals was offered or envisaged; Hume and Adams were asking the Unionists to turn up to negotiate with a fully-armed terrorist movement implicitly threatening a return to violence. It was not the most seductive of offers. Paddy Mayhew sniffed derisively, always a sign that this most reasonable of men thought someone was trying it on. And so they were.

On 1 September my office reached an agreement with the Taoiseach's on an announcement for the summit five days later. It would launch the 'International Decommissioning Commission', with the understanding that substantial progress had to be made on illegal weapons before all-party talks could begin. On the 'political' track, the governments proposed to meet the parties separately to prepare for all party talks. We declared an aim, but not a deadline, of convening such talks before the end of 1995, making it clear that this depended on creating the necessary conditions.

The Provisionals did all they could to block this agreement. We received reports that Irish officials were summoned to a meeting in Belfast with Provisional leaders at which they were threatened with a return to violence: if the twin-track process went ahead, they were reportedly told, there would be 'bodies in the streets', and they would be to blame. This blackmail shook the Irish government. John Bruton, to whom good faith was important, tried to hold the line, and we had a number of emotional and supportive telephone conversations. As late as the morning of 5 September Bruton said that he was sticking to the agreement. But John Hume, whose popularity across Ireland gave him great influence in Dublin, then weighed in decisively to support Adams's opposition to the twin-track agreement. This broke the nerve of the Irish government. A strained Bruton came out of a turbulent Cabinet meeting to explain the situation to me. During a chaotic afternoon the Irish position changed several times, with one set of Dublin officials withdrawing texts sent to us by another set. I had no choice but to postpone the following day's summit.

Most pundits assumed the twin-track process was now dead, especially with the election of David Trimble as UUP leader on 10 September, on a hard-line ticket. I did not agree – and in due course Trimble would surprise us. The idea was fundamentally sound, and had been seen as such by

my Irish counterpart. Nor was there any alternative. But after the intervention by Hume and Adams a crucial three months were lost to the peace
process.

The Americans made the first attempt to revive the initiative, during a
visit by Adams to Washington in mid-September. The summit postponement had dismayed the White House, as Bill Clinton was planning a
visit to Northern Ireland and the Republic before launching his re-election
campaign. But Adams rebuffed diplomacy by White House officials, and
hardened his stance.

A weekend get-together of EU leaders in Majorca gave me a chance to
talk entirely privately to John Bruton in the lush gardens of the Formentor
Hotel. He confirmed that he was as keen as I was to revive the twin-track
proposals – for an international commission on paramilitary weapons and
for political talks – and made a number of constructive suggestions. We
also had help from an unexpected direction. David Trimble made his first
policy speech as UUP leader while we were in Majorca, and surprised the
Taoiseach and me with a moderate proposal for an elected assembly, with
limited powers, as the route to all-party talks.

Another surprise, in late September, was a good-humoured and constructive encounter at Number 10 with Ian Paisley, who put forward his
own proposal for an elected negotiating assembly, in which he would be
prepared to sit with Sinn Fein. However, John Hume dismissed any form
of elected mechanism as a 'back-door Stormont'; nonetheless, John Bruton
agreed on the telephone that we should explore the assembly idea. He tried
it on Gerry Adams, and reported that he was less resistant than Hume,
conceding the possibility of a time-limited negotiating convention (though
he did not want it to be elected). Bruton also drew encouragement from
a conversation with David Trimble, who broke with recent Unionist tradition by going openly to Dublin on 2 October to meet him.

Trimble was proving a more flexible and adept leader than we had
imagined. Shy, and sometimes truculent, he was an articulate opponent of
the Downing Street Declaration and the Framework Documents, and of
Jim Molyneaux's ready acquiescence in our search for a settlement. His
relations with Paddy Mayhew were often scratchy – voices were raised and
papers thrown down as David proved his macho credentials. Yet, when he
succeeded Molyneaux, the reality of decision-making revealed a new and
more pragmatic Trimble, perfectly prepared to quote the Downing Street

Declaration to emphasise his argument. He grew visibly as a politician, and continued to do so after the 1997 general election when, at some risk to his own position, he worked closely with the new Labour government. He deserved the accolades that then came his way.

To focus the discussions, the Northern Ireland Office repackaged the twin-track proposals in a consultation document, the 'building-blocks' paper. It was to take tortuous negotiation through October and November to drive this through to a conclusion – essentially to get back to where we had been at the beginning of September.

The first complication was a visit by the US National Security Adviser, Tony Lake, and a Northern Ireland adviser, Nancy Soderberg; the *Irish Times* reported unhelpfully from Washington that they were going to bring new proposals and 'knock heads together'. It was a worthy objective, but their proposals (which they gave in advance to Adams through Hume) merely caused confusion, and Adams and McGuinness declined to come to London to meet them. The White House began to experience the problems we faced daily. Hume then administered a further snub by putting forward, in parallel with McGuinness, a counter-communiqué which Washington and Dublin had urged him not to table. It sought to render the commission impotent and to lay down an ultimatum for all-party talks in a way which, as John Bruton commented to me, had no hope of running. While some Sinn Fein members were privately showing interest in an elected body, John Hume remained implacable in his opposition.

A second hiccough occurred in early November. After a confrontational meeting with Michael Ancram, Sinn Fein told the press that the British government was insisting on surrender. To expose this falsehood the Northern Ireland Office published the 'building-blocks' paper. This alarmed John Bruton, who sent me some alternative proposals while we were in Jerusalem for the funeral of the assassinated Israeli Prime Minister Yitzhak Rabin. I had to go on to the Commonwealth Conference in New Zealand, where I received a worried letter from John. He was simultaneously under pressure from his coalition partners and Hume to take a more aggressive line against our ideas, and, ignoring American pleas, he let off steam in an uncharacteristic speech attacking British governments past and present and playing to his Nationalist audience. This provoked crisis headlines in the press. If the twin-track was going to work, I knew that the Irish government would have to take the Provisionals on, and ignore their objections. I understood

John Bruton's speech: he needed to buttress his support and show sympathy to hallowed Nationalist dogma. I regretted only that I was marooned in New Zealand and unable to help him out.

The final problem, inevitably, was the precise wording of the communiqué. I sent John Bruton a draft on 17 November, and we had intensive exchanges over the next eleven days. These focused on the terms of reference for the 'International Body' on decommissioning, and how to express the requirement for progress over the weapons issue before the paramilitaries could enter political negotiations.

This was less of a negotiation between London and Dublin than between the coalition partners in the Irish government. John Bruton was determined to get the initiative launched before the imminent visit by President Clinton. His deputy Dick Spring, the Labour leader, was not keen to make the necessary compromises. The tensions in Dublin led to some strange episodes. At one point the Taoiseach's senior aide came to London and reached agreement on most of the outstanding points. A posse of officials from other departments arrived in hot pursuit, and spent the next day unpicking all that had been agreed.

With Clinton due to land on the morning of 29 November, John Bruton came on the phone to me at 8 p.m. on the twenty-eighth to do the final deal. I was relaxed about the timing – getting the substance right was more important. But John was in a hurry; he had told the press he would be seeing me at 10 p.m., and my press office had heard that his plane was warming up on the runway in Dublin. He wanted a deal before Uncle Sam hit town. Moreover, after his bitter experience in September, he had to act fast to prevent the agreement being torpedoed again.

He accepted the points which mattered to me, and hopped on his plane. We met at Downing Street two hours later, with the press assembling in a hastily-prepared state dining room upstairs. But this was not quite the end of the story. Dick Spring had arrived in London simultaneously from Spain. The Taoiseach and his deputy asked if they could borrow a room while they met, so Paddy Mayhew and I waited downstairs in the Cabinet Room. At intervals I sent emissaries upstairs to see if the Irish were ready to meet us. Deadlines were passing, and we could not keep the press waiting indefinitely. The emissaries returned to report flushed countenances and requests for a few more minutes.

At last the Irish delegation trooped into the Cabinet Room. There was none of the air of celebration of the meeting in the same room two years before, when many of the same cast (swapping Reynolds for Bruton), had sealed the Downing Street Declaration. Bruton was tense and tight-lipped. Dick Spring was glowering. John Bruton sat beside me, but Spring walked all around the long Cabinet table so that he could sit alone, directly opposite the two prime ministers, who were flanked by Douglas Hurd and Paddy Mayhew. British and Irish officials hovered around the fringes, like spectators watching a street brawl.

An unhappy Spring began to interrogate me over the text. He didn't like our position on decommissioning (although it had once been his), and warned that differences between London and Dublin could lead to disaster. John Bruton's political difficulties were apparent. Government even by a single party is in a sense a coalition, but Bruton's experiences showed the downside of true coalition government. Spring, leading a minority party of modest size, had unmade the previous Irish government without an election, by transferring his allegiance; and that evening he looked ready to do the same to its successor.

With the clock ticking towards midnight (and Bill Clinton in the air, heading for London), John Bruton and I made our announcement in the State Dining Room at Number 10. Bruton gave a gutsy performance. He did not pretend that the International Body had the exact terms of reference he had wanted. However, he committed himself whole-heartedly to an initiative to induce the Provisionals to move forward on decommissioning, with help from George Mitchell; and also to accommodate all parties, Unionist, Nationalist and Republican, to the idea that they would need to begin talking seriously to each other. We asked Mitchell's International Body to report by mid-January 1996, and declared our 'firm aim' of achieving all-party talks by the end of February.

I had expected fierce arguments over the membership of the three-strong International Body, but this proved the easiest part of the negotiation. We agreed with the Irish that George Mitchell should head the body. The Unionists had never liked the idea of outside involvement in Northern Ireland, and were deeply suspicious of the Clinton administration, believing it to be susceptible to pressure from the Irish lobby in the Democratic Party. However, George Mitchell had begun to win them over in his role as the President's Special Adviser for Economic Initiatives in Ireland, and complaints about his appointment were relatively muted.

George Mitchell is a softly-spoken and patient man, widely respected in the US Senate. He was well placed to persuade the Provisionals to give up violence for good, and to commit themselves to the processes of democracy. The IRA had claimed that to make any concessions to us would be 'surrender', but they could hardly apply this to George Mitchell. His involvement would also serve notice to apologists for the IRA in America that a fair deal was on offer. When the two governments engaged him for six weeks, we had in mind that he could well play a role in the next stage – which we hoped would be refereeing the beginning of decommissioning. But I doubt if Mitchell, or his Canadian colleague General John de Chastelain, foresaw that this was the beginning of a new career, and that they would still be crucially involved four years later. They have shown admirable tenacity. De Chastelain came on board as the military expert. He had been educated in Britain before his parents moved to Canada, where he had risen to be Chief of the Defence Staff. His profile balanced Mitchell's, while the third appointee, Harri Holkeri, former Prime Minister of Finland, had an exquisitely neutral background.

Nine hours after I saw the Taoiseach off from the doorstep at Number 10, I welcomed Bill and Hillary Clinton at Westminster Abbey. The President and I wanted his visit to consolidate support for the peace process, and to give the twin-track initiative the chance of carrying us through to all-party talks. The Northern Ireland Office had worked hard to ensure that the President's programme during his visit to Northern Ireland was meticulously balanced, and could not be seen as favouring one or other side of the community.

During his three days in Britain and Ireland Bill Clinton did not put a foot wrong. He arrived from a gruelling battle over the US budget, and had barely slept. After a brief ceremony at the Abbey and a quarter-mile corridor of handshakes en route to Number 10, I took him alone into the Cabinet Room. Drawing on information which, for fear of leaks, I could share only with him, I briefed him on the IRA's active preparations for a return to terrorist operations, and on their continuing violence and intimidation within Catholic communities in the North. He was shocked to learn that, since the 1994 ceasefire, the Provisionals had carried out 148 vicious 'punishment' attacks, and the Loyalists seventy-five.

In Northern Ireland the next day, Clinton rammed home a powerful message, urging all parties to seize the opportunity of the twin-track initiative. He condemned punishment beatings, and was unequivocal about terrorism: 'You must stand firm against terror. You must say "no" to those who would still use violence for political objectives – you are the past: your day is over.' It was powerful stuff, and bang on target. The IRA's response, a week later, was a slap in the face: 'There is no question of the IRA meeting the ludicrous demand for a surrender of IRA weapons either through the front door or the back door.'

Just before Christmas, I made my thirteenth visit to Northern Ireland as prime minister. Norma and I started in the Protestant stronghold of Ballymena, where we were greeted warmly by Ian Paisley, his wife and a large crowd of his constituents who had waited in sleet and freezing rain. After a carol service and a visit to the predominantly Nationalist town of Downpatrick, we flew down to Dublin. I wanted a chance to relax with the Brutons after the tension of the twin-track negotiation, and to show my support for John. We had a short round of talks and a longer supper, dropping into a crowded pub on the way. We then caught the second half of a performance of Handel's *Messiah* at the National Concert Hall. To my astonishment, the audience rose in a standing ovation as we entered. They, and the cast, gave us a second ovation at the end, and cheered us through the foyer. As in Newry the previous year, the warmth of the Irish people was uplifting. British prime ministers don't expect to be cheered in Ballymena or in Dublin – let alone in both on the same day.

The elastic of the peace process was stretched tight as 1996 opened. We had had sixteen months of ceasefire, albeit not without violence. There had been nine deaths attributable to the 'Troubles' in 1995, compared to sixty-one in the previous year, and eighty-four in 1993. We had a target of the end of February for all-party talks, but no certainty of reaching it. The Unionists were not prepared to join political negotiations with Sinn Fein without some progress towards decommissioning illegal weapons.

The Provisionals, however, had dug in. As far as the IRA were concerned, not killing people for a while was the only concession they were prepared to make. They had not moved forward in any other respect since the ceasefire, but had used the opportunities it provided to recruit, to train, and to reconnoitre targets – even measuring mortar positions around Belfast's Aldergrove Airport and sitting cheekily outside army barracks, timing the electric gates. We knew the hard men were getting restive.

Setting a target date for all-party talks was a risk, because it could also be a target date for a return to bombing. As we were to discover, one IRA group was not going to wait even till then, but was already preparing to break the ceasefire.

George Mitchell delivered the International Body's report on 24 January. It noted 'nearly universal support . . . for the total and verifiable disarmament of all paramilitary organisations', which 'must continue to be a principal objective'. Straying beyond its brief, the body came up with six commitments to be made by the parties to a negotiation. They included 'the total disarmament of all paramilitary organisations', the use of exclusively peaceful means, and an end to 'punishment' killings and beatings. This was a firm stance, even though, in an attempt to keep the Provisionals on board, the principle of consent had been paraphrased and watered down from the statement in the Downing Street Declaration.

On the attitude of the paramilitaries, Senator Mitchell identified 'a clear commitment – to work constructively to achieve full and verifiable decommissioning as part of the process of all-party negotiations'. This was his most optimistic statement on the IRA's attitude, and seemed to offer a basis for moving forward. It was a generous assessment, as the Provisionals had shown little evidence of such a commitment – and it was not one which they were to fulfil when all-party negotiations eventually took place in 1998. Mitchell later explained that he was stretching a point for tactical reasons, and privately suspected that the IRA was on the verge of breaking its ceasefire. It was not the first or the last time that the pursuit of peace would require a nimble interpretation of the facts.

Mitchell concluded that 'the paramilitary organisations will not decommission any arms prior to all-party negotiations'. The body therefore recommended that the parties should sign up to the six principles, and that some decommissioning should take place *during the negotiations*, as a compromise. Picking up the reference in the twin-track communiqué to an elected body, Mitchell noted that 'an elective process could contribute to the building of confidence'.

The Mitchell report was a balanced and reasonable attempt to find a way through, and I accepted its recommendations in a statement to the House of Commons. But it did not solve all our problems. As I observed, Mitchell had not said that the IRA and other paramilitaries *could not* begin getting rid of their weapons, simply that they *would not*. Under those conditions – and with reason – the Unionists would not enter talks with them. The only possible way of getting the parties together was through an elected body. The Unionists were prepared to accept this, and at least one senior Sinn Fein spokesman, Mitchel McLaughlin, had promised to give 'very serious consideration' to taking part. But John Hume would not budge in his opposition, provoking the Ulster Unionist deputy leader John Taylor to label him 'the obstacle to the peace process rather than the one encouraging it along the road'. Such spats between senior Unionist and Republican figures repeatedly enlivened the process, but did not change Hume's view.

In the Commons, Hume bitterly attacked the election proposal, and accused the government of supporting it 'to try to buy votes to keep themselves in power'. I was astonished at his outburst. He knew that, notwithstanding our shrinking majority, the government had never traded the peace process for votes. Time and again we had knowingly put ourselves at odds with the Unionists, and they had withheld support in crucial votes. It was sad to see John Hume, who had given so much to Northern Ireland, taking a negative approach, with no rational explanation for his opposition to elections. I assumed he could not shed the ancient scars of Stormont.

With the Provisionals refusing even to contemplate putting their guns and bombs away, and the Unionists justifiably refusing to negotiate until they began doing so, an elective process appeared to be the only viable way forward. It was an option we had been discussing with Dublin for many months, and one in which the Taoiseach had shown interest. One of the most vociferous opponents turned out to be Dick Spring, who excoriated the British government and engaged in a war of words with Northern Ireland politicians. John Taylor then attacked him as 'the most detested politician in Northern Ireland'. These exchanges did not help the consultations. Even the moderate Alliance Party leader John Alderdice commented that Dick Spring was not prepared to listen to the Unionists.

Nonetheless, at a meeting with Patrick Mayhew on 7 February, Spring proposed that we should set up 'proximity talks' with all of the parties to agree a basis and timetable for constitutional negotiations. This was a variant of bringing the parties into proximity through an elected assembly. Meanwhile the target date for arranging all-party talks was only three weeks away.

Two days later, my worst fears were realised. Throughout the seventeen-month ceasefire, intelligence from all sources, overt and covert, had shown that much of the Provisional movement dissented from Adams's 'unarmed' strategy, and saw the ceasefire as no more than a tactic. Factions within the IRA did not want to be locked into the peaceful negotiations for which we were striving, and had been gearing up for a renewed campaign. Peace was a threat to those whose power stemmed from violent intimidation, and whose only skill was a capacity to murder and maim.

I was in my constituency on the evening of Friday, 9 February when I was told that the IRA had announced the end of its ceasefire. They declared: 'The blame for the failure thus far of the Irish peace process lies squarely with John Major and his government.' An hour later, a lorry packed with explosives detonated at Canary Wharf in London's Docklands, killing two people and injuring over a hundred.

I thought of all the hopes that had been invested in the peace process by the people of Northern Ireland, and my heart sank. Republican or Unionist, the overwhelming majority wanted a future free of violence, and now, with a lie on its lips, the Provisional movement had returned to bombing. Once more, innocent people had been murdered and maimed so that evil men could advance a political campaign. That evening I felt powerless: it seemed that the politics of reason and sanity had once more been cast aside.

In their traditional way, the Provisionals tried to blame the British government for their murderous act. An IRA spokesman said: 'The IRA leadership delivered a complete cessation of military operations on a clear, unambiguous and shared understanding that inclusive negotiations would rapidly commence to bring about political agreement and a peace settlement ... John Major reneged on these commitments.' John Bruton was also accused. The IRA said he had known 'the basis upon which we agreed to a complete cessation of military operations in August 1994. It was a quid pro quo understanding that all-party talks would commence rapidly ... which the previous Taoiseach was clear about and which John Bruton was informed of when he assumed office.' Both Bruton and Albert Reynolds denied that there had been any such deal, and I was certainly not party to one. It was a weak attempt at *ex post facto* justification by the IRA, made all the weaker by the fact that the British and Irish governments were working intensively to launch all-party talks by the end of February.

For all of us – for me, for Patrick Mayhew and his dedicated team, for the Irish government, for Bill Clinton so soon after his epic visit, but above all for the people of Northern Ireland – the Canary Wharf bombing (which we soon discovered had been planned for three months) was a massive setback. But was it the end of the road? I refused to accept this. It was not the time to abandon the course we had set, though there were those on the Conservative benches who urged me to do just that. Many had been sceptical of the policy, and Paddy Mayhew and I often felt there were few who agreed with the risks we were prepared to run for peace.

I could see two likely explanations for the IRA's behaviour. One was that it was instigated by hard-core Republicans who had never wanted the peace process to succeed, because it would mean giving up their way of life and, eventually, their weapons. The other was that it stemmed from the traditional IRA belief that bombs would soften the British position. In either case, sticking to our position was the right response. I said in the House of Commons that I was not slamming doors, since that would have played into the hands of opponents of the peace process. I added that we would continue the search for permanent peace and a comprehensive political settlement. We would work with all the democratic political parties and with the Irish government; but I said that British ministers would not meet Sinn Fein again until there was a genuine end to this renewed violence.

Privately, I had to reckon on a long haul. The Provisionals had paid a heavy price in lost support in Ireland and America for breaching the peace, and Gerry Adams's credibility had taken a huge knock. But it would take time for this to sink in, and for them to see that we were not reacting in the way they had anticipated. We were also entering an election year, which I knew would affect their calculations.

To follow up my Commons statement, I wanted to show rapidly that our efforts to arrange talks were going ahead – with or without Sinn Fein. Canary Wharf had brought London and Dublin closer together. In welcoming my statement, Dick Spring began to drop his opposition to an elected assembly. He said that 'imposed' elections would not work (I agreed: we had never suggested imposing an election), but that 'agreed elections on the right terms might'. John Bruton floated ideas for a combination of proximity talks and an election leading to all-party talks. The IRA had succeeded in getting the Irish government to embrace the electoral route.

By 28 February the two governments were able to launch a proposal for all-party talks to begin on 10 June. The format and structure would be prepared in proximity talks. Elections to the negotiating body would be held in May. All parties had to commit themselves to the principles of democracy and non-violence. The door was left open to Sinn Fein to take part if the IRA renewed its ceasefire. For Sinn Fein, Martin McGuinness called our proposals 'undemocratic', but he was at a loss to explain how the Docklands bomb was more democratic than an election. The IRA's campaign continued, ineptly. One bomb blew up its carrier in London's Aldwych. Others failed to go off.

Although the other parties had agreed to the package, the proximity talks – in the end not held in proximity at all – were tetchy and difficult. The Unionists thought we were making too many concessions to the Nationalists. The Nationalists were nervous that the elected negotiating forum would widen its remit and lead to the rebirth of the Unionist-dominated Stormont parliament; to allay such fears, we put an initial term on the forum of twelve months. The argument over decommissioning's place on the agenda rumbled on. We had decided to devise a very complicated electoral formula, guaranteeing a minimum of two seats to each of the successful parties, to ensure that a wide spread of viewpoints would be represented. With the end of the IRA ceasefire, Loyalist paramilitaries were straining at the leash; it was essential to have their political representatives at the table if we were to keep them on-side and off terrorism.

Confounding the sceptics, we were able to hold elections on 30 May. Having wavered over a boycott, Sinn Fein not only took part, but recorded its best-ever result, with over 15 per cent of the vote (against 24 per cent for Trimble's UUP, 21 per cent for Hume's SDLP and nearly 19 per cent for Paisley's DUP). Pundits were divided over whether Sinn Fein's vote was an endorsement of the IRA's bombing campaign or an encouragement for them to call another ceasefire and join the negotiating forum. The IRA gave their answer when they demolished the centre of Manchester with a massive bomb on 15 June, only days after the opening of the all-party talks under George Mitchell's chairmanship. They were evidently not applying for admission. John Bruton hardened his stance, and demanded an unconditional and irrevocable ceasefire before they could enter.

The Manchester bomb, deliberately placed in a crowded city centre, injured two hundred people and provoked deep revulsion. It confirmed that the IRA was stuck in a groove. Even more depressing in its political message was a reversion to wider sectarianism during the July–August marching season, despite the talks. As in 1995, Drumcree was again the flashpoint. To avoid clashes, the Chief Constable of the RUC Hugh Annesley routed an Orange Order march away from the Catholic Garvaghy Road. This decision provoked a risk of even greater violence, and had to be reversed. The reversal then triggered riots, and heightened tension between the two communities over several weeks.

Relations with Dublin deteriorated. John Bruton and Dick Spring fiercely attacked the British government for the Chief Constable's decision, even though not by a nudge or a wink did Paddy Mayhew or any British minister interfere in it. The decision was a serious defeat for law and order, but a victory for common sense. It saved lives. The Chief Constable knew that sixty thousand Orange marchers were assembling, that diggers to demolish the RUC's defences were en route to Drumcree, and that he had insufficient police and army manpower to guarantee safety in the area. He feared that violent groups would attach themselves to the march and torch the Garvaghy Road. Mr Annesley faced an impossible situation, and was courageous to change his decision in order to sidestep the danger to lives, rather than stubbornly maintain his position and see them lost. None of this restrained the criticism of the Chief Constable or of the British government.

The peace talks were suspended, and never regained momentum. As autumn passed into winter, attention shifted to the general election. Naturally enough, all the parties chose to wait and see who won, and to save their concessions for then. It was to be Labour, and Tony Blair picked up the baton with relish and energy.

The Northern Ireland initiative was, for me, a job uncompleted. It had its successes and its failures. As I write, two years on, it is still incomplete, though it has moved forward with the 1998 Good Friday Agreement. The paramilitaries have still not decommissioned a single weapon. Punishment attacks continue. This ceasefire has held longer than its predecessor, but is not yet permanent, and has been punctuated by eruptions from hard-liners – most horribly with the bombing of Omagh's town centre in August 1998, killing twenty-nine innocent people.

Working for a Northern Ireland settlement was the most difficult, frustrating and, from 1993, time-consuming problem of government during my premiership. It was also the most rewarding. I have never regretted my decision to get involved in such a direct way. I would have liked to have gone further. I wanted to reach the point where I could sit across the table from Gerry Adams (for all his murky background) and thrash out issues directly, as I did with Jim Molyneaux and David Trimble, John Hume, Ian Paisley, John Alderdice and, of course, Albert Reynolds and John Bruton. My successor as prime minister was right to do so, but in my time the process had simply not advanced far enough to allow me to engage personally with Sinn Fein.

The British government has no easy options in Northern Ireland. It cannot walk away from a part of its own country. It has a responsibility to look after all of its citizens fairly – both those who wish to remain part of the United Kingdom, and those who don't. It cannot impose a settlement: an imposed settlement would not work, and would not last. Likewise, emergency action to defeat terrorism would only guarantee that the problem would return at a later date, and in a more bitter form. The number of terrorists is relatively small, and many of them are known to the security forces. An all-out war against them could succeed in the short term, but it would widen the rift between the communities, create martyrs, and sow the seeds for another generation of violence.

So, a settlement has to be brokered with the parties representing both sides of the community, Unionist and Nationalist – or, in their more extreme forms, Loyalist and Republican. In most negotiations, the stronger side can afford to make some concessions. Northern Ireland is different. Each side has the mentality of a threatened minority: the Nationalists because they are a minority within Northern Ireland, and were an abused minority when the Unionists exploited their dominant position until the Stormont parliament was set aside by direct rule in 1972; and the Unionists because they are a minority in the island of Ireland, and fear that they will ultimately be sold out by Britain into subjugation in a united Ireland.

Persuading either side to give an inch was the hardest negotiating task I have ever faced. Each move had to be weighed and balanced minutely. The suspicions of each other, and of the British government, were intense. So were the emotions. If one side was happy, I knew I had probably got it wrong. If my proposals attracted no more than grumbling and grudging acquiescence from both sides, I was perhaps on the right track. The August 1994 IRA ceasefire was the most dramatic demonstration of this dual-minority psychosis. The Unionists did not rejoice at it, but were deeply troubled: because the Republicans had proclaimed it a victory and were celebrating, the other side felt it must be a defeat for Unionism.

The same phenomenon has afflicted the annual march of Orangemen to Drumcree for the past five years. If they march down the Catholic Garvaghy Road, it is a defeat for Nationalism. If they are rerouted, it is a defeat for Unionism. Neither side will give. Neither will allow common sense to prevail. Each will blame the Chief Constable of the RUC and the British government, whatever decisions they take. Each will accuse us of failing to understand 'Republican psychology' or 'Unionist psychology'. I learned a lot about conflicting psychologies over six and a half years: minority psychology, a deep-seated insecurity, is common to both communities in Northern Ireland, and is a considerable obstacle to all who try to make peace between them.

By the end of 1996, the logs were pretty well jammed. It needed the fresh spate of a general election to shift them. Only that could give the parties (and the two governments) a chance to adjust their own positions to a new situation. Had the Conservative Party been returned with a new mandate, I think we could have moved forward: the other players would have faced up to the reality of dealing with us for another five years. But a change of government made progress easier.

In opposition, Tony Blair had been totally supportive of the peace process: I could not have asked for more consistent and honest backing. Coming into government, he promised a continuity of approach, and he stood by all the agreements we had made. But he was also unencumbered by the baggage one collects in years of negotiation, and was therefore better able to show tactical flexibility. He has been unsparing in his efforts to pursue peace. When crises came, he involved himself fully in attempting to solve them. He and I would not have done everything the same way, or reached all the same judgements, but he has acted on every occasion in the way he thought likely to assist progress towards peace.

I have never believed there would be a single defining moment at which the Irish question would simply be 'settled'. The problem has too long and bitter a history. Attitudes and fears are too deeply ingrained. Sectarianism will take a very long time to erode. But Ireland, North and South, will not go back to how it was ten or more years ago, in the depths of the Troubles. We can be certain that there are further difficulties ahead. There may – for some years, perhaps – be sporadic episodes of terrorism. Wresting the ghettos out of the intimidatory grasp of ruthless paramilitary criminals will be no easy task. But the habits of peace and civilised behaviour will take root. I have no doubt that the peace process, from Peter Brooke's groundbreaking through the Downing Street Declaration to the unsparing efforts of Paddy Mayhew, and to the Good Friday Agreement and beyond, has pushed terrorism towards the margins. In time we shall push it off the page altogether.

This is an incremental process. Economic development, education and the advancement of human rights in Northern Ireland have played their part. So, too, has the modernisation of the economy and society of the Irish Republic. It is now much more widely accepted that Northern Ireland will remain a legitimate part of the United Kingdom for as long as its people so wish. Vastly improved relations between London and Dublin are making a major contribution.

Most important of all, the people of Northern Ireland have seen that there is an alternative to the mute acceptance of endless cycles of 'Troubles' and terrorism. Attitudes to violence have changed. There is less willingness to tolerate or endorse the destructive and mindless behaviour of the paramilitaries; more healthy anger against them. Whatever setbacks there may be, I do not believe that the clock can now be turned back fully.

# CHAPTER TWENTY

## The Wider World

I BECAME PRIME MINISTER at an optimistic moment in international affairs. The Cold War was ending, and a hesitant 'new world order' was being born. In November 1990, as I moved into Downing Street, communism was rotting. The Berlin Wall had fallen, and Germany was one country once more; Eastern Europe had been freed but was unstable; and the Soviet Union, in economic disarray, was soon to fall apart.

Beyond our continent, war in the Gulf looked unavoidable, and the Palestinian question was as potent as ever; Hong Kong, Britain's largest remaining colony, was preparing to return to Chinese rule amid the fallout from the 1989 massacre in Tiananmen Square; and South Africa was taking uncertain steps towards majority rule. The United Nations, held back for so long by disputes between members of the Security Council, was regaining its status.

It was an exhilarating time. A new round of trade liberalisation was being negotiated which, if successful, would boost economic growth. Technology was changing; satellite communication and the infant internet were opening up the dark corners of the world. There was a growing realisation that environmental issues, brushed aside for so much of the industrial era, could be ignored no longer. Nothing was settled. Everything was restless.

With the end of the Cold War, the old verities of foreign policy no longer applied: we needed a new compass. Over decades, Britain's influence had waned. By 1990 we had the lingering impulses of an imperial power, but no empire. Yet Britain still mattered. We were one of the five permanent members of the United Nations Security Council, and of the Group of Seven (G7) leading industrial nations. The disproportionate effectiveness of our armed forces, the special bonds of the Commonwealth, and our close links with the United States all ensured that our voice counted at the top table. I was determined that it should continue to do so.

In our own backyard of Western Europe we were a leading member of the European Community. Though Germany carried the greatest economic clout, Britain and France were the more significant international powers. I had no time for the facile Euro-phobic argument that we should 'choose' between our Atlantic alliance with the United States and our European partners in the Community. Our economic involvement with Europe was growing, but we retained substantial trade links with the United States, as well as a close military and security relationship. We needed to nurture both alliances. Ray Seitz, the engaging and Anglophile diplomat who served as United States Ambassador to Britain for much of my premiership, reinforced this view by telling me repeatedly that Britain's influence in America would grow as our role in Europe developed.

If the importance of the Anglo–American alliance needed any emphasis it was provided vividly by the Gulf War, an American-led operation that was the right war, fought for the right reasons and won with unexpected ease (see Chapter 10). Although the term 'special relationship' is often misused, there is a unique rapport between Britain and the United States. British politicians and the military do not have the reserve in dealing with their American counterparts that they show elsewhere, and confidences are shared as a matter of course. I saw this at first hand many times, and always marvelled that it happened so naturally. It is, I think, a product of history and the long relationship of trust between like-minded democracies with a common language and similar – but not identical – interests in the world.

I grew up with tales of America. My father retained an abiding affection for the great democracy where he had once lived, and I imbibed it at his knee. I have come to know the country, with its great wide-open spaces and its generous heart, and it has rarely disappointed me. My years at Number 10 coincided with two presidents of opposing philosophies, very different men in background and personality. But American interests did not shift with the change of presidency: both men were supporters of free trade, of NATO and of strong links with Europe. Both sometimes fretted to me about the introspective habits of Congress. Their instincts were different, but their political perceptions of America's responsibility to the world were much the same.

George Bush was the first president I came to know well. I have set out elsewhere our meetings over the Gulf conflict and the easy way in which we were able to work together. George was the pioneer of telephone diplomacy, and he kept his friendships around the world in good repair. At the presidential retreats of Camp David and Kennebunkport I saw the private man, different from the public one only in the fierceness of his competitive streak. In a speedboat he would derive enormous pleasure from outdistancing his protection team; but was patient enough to teach my son James to fish. At tennis and golf – even at pitching horse-shoes – he played for fun, but also to win.

George believed in public service and family values, and decency and moderation were automatic reflexes. He was a good friend and a poor hater – the very antithesis of the accepted caricature of politicians. His knowledge of the world was formidable, although his preoccupation with America's international obligations cost him dearly in the 1992 presidential election, with electors more concerned with domestic matters. Among his many legacies George handed over a strengthening economy, something that the American people came to see too late to do him any political good, but which was to endure.

When Bill Clinton was elected president in November 1992, many pundits forecast that my friendship with George Bush would disqualify me from forming an effective relationship with his successor. It was suggested, as if with inside knowledge, that there was some deep-seated animosity between us, and there was surprise in some quarters when our meetings went well. It is true, though, that at the time there were two issues on which Britain and America took different views: Bosnia and Northern Ireland.

When President Clinton entered the White House, the conflict in Bosnia was a preoccupation on both sides of the Atlantic. For two years it remained a running sore between us. The most strident criticism of our policy came from American Senate and Congressional hawks, who were both keen to dictate policy and unwilling to deploy American servicemen to Bosnia, where they would face the hazards that confronted European troops (see Chapter 22).

In the early days of the Clinton administration, more personal issues added a layer of frost to dealings between London and Washington. These were caused by reports that the Home Office had reviewed Bill Clinton's immigration file from the time when he was a student at Oxford, to search for ammunition with which to embarrass him in the presidential election. I was assured that this was nonsense, but it was widely believed to be true, and Clinton's staffers resented it and made no secret of their feelings.

Some of his entourage were also bitter that two junior Conservative Party officials had worked with the Republican campaign in 1992, albeit not with my knowledge nor at my bidding. Nevertheless, I was sanguine about this, since party interchanges between Britain and America were scarcely a novelty. In the run-up to the 1997 British general election, senior Labour politicians and their advisers crossed the Atlantic to receive coaching on how to defeat us from Democratic Party experts. Bill Clinton did not raise either of these earlier stories with me. It was a staffers' feud, and never an issue between the two of us.

Shortly after his inauguration in 1993 the new president invited me to meet him in Washington – the first foreign leader to do so – and he showed from the outset that he was keen for us to work together. He is also enormously hospitable. When he discovered that my father and grandfather had lived in Pittsburgh he arranged for us to visit the city together. We arrived on a freezing night to discover the street lined with demonstrators. On one side were IRA sympathisers, on the other domestic opponents of the President. We did a deal in the back of his limousine: he would shake hands with my opponents, while I shook hands with his.

Over supper at the Tin Angel restaurant we put official matters aside and talked instead of our childhoods, of the underclass in our societies, of how to improve the provision of education and health. Late that night we flew back to Washington, and after landing we transferred to the Marine One helicopter for the short journey to the White House. As we flew over Washington, the President asked the pilot to make a diversion, and pointed out the sites of his nation's capital from the air. Still on London time, my body clock insisted it was 5 a.m., and I knew we had an early start the next morning. But Bill Clinton's hospitality showed no sign of waning. After landing on the White House lawn we set off on a tour of the darkened mansion, examining his cherished book collection and the antique furniture in the rooms which he and Hillary had had restored. I slept, for what little remained of the night, in Mrs Abraham Lincoln's bed, in a suite once occupied by Winston Churchill during the war. Early the next morning I found the President in earnest conversation with my Private Secretary Rod Lyne, who had travelled with me, about the merits of toothpaste.

Bill Clinton is the most political head of government with whom I have ever done business. When we were in discussions together I could see, even feel, him calculating the political angle. I have seen him size up the people he is with, tune in to their wavelength and choose his approach. It is as instinctive to him as breathing. He never stops campaigning. Even in my Private Office at Number 10 he worked the room, shook hands, remembered names and drew people into his circle. That day he delivered a speech to both Houses of Parliament which was a masterpiece in delivery and content, and won over a sceptical audience.

Sometimes Bill Clinton's affinity for appeasing opinion at home made it difficult for his allies abroad to predict how his administration would behave – though it kept him well ahead in the domestic opinion polls. This was the biggest difference between his presidency and that of George Bush. At times in the early days of his presidency I found him alarmingly under-briefed, but when he turned his attention to an issue he would immerse himself completely in it. He once promised me that he was going to spend a long weekend swotting up the Uruguay round of the GATT (General Agreement on Tariffs and Trade) talks – a dry and difficult subject – and would persuade Congress to accept it. He kept his word.

During my time as prime minister the world's other superpower was ruled by two remarkable men, Mikhail Gorbachev and Boris Yeltsin. Gorbachev was a communist who believed communism could be reformed; Yeltsin was an anti-communist who believed it had to be destroyed. Both were reformers, and both changed the future of their country. When I entered Number 10, Mikhail Gorbachev was more popular outside the Soviet Union than within it. *Glasnost* (openness) had brought political liberty and ended the Cold War, but *perestroika* (reconstruction) had done little to overcome the Soviet economy's ruinous state, perhaps even worsening it. This problem was to bedevil everything Gorbachev – and, from 1992, his successor in Russia Boris Yeltsin – tried to do.

In July 1991 I chaired the G7 Conference of leading industrial nations in London, and extended it for a day so that Gorbachev could join us. When the work was done, over a late-night supper we talked of his hopes and fears for Russia. Gorbachev was schooled in tales of dark satanic mills, and expounded a very Victorian image of private ownership. His understanding of privatisation was negligible: he seemed to believe it was no more than a benevolent state selling a company to a profiteering private owner who would worsen the service and increase the price. He had no concept of the free market, and the merits of competition were alien to him. He simply could not understand how a company could be actively owned by many shareholders, who received a share of any profit and could make losses if the value of their shares fell. Nor did he appreciate that since they *owned* the shares, they had the right to sell them at any time. Gorbachev had changed the face of Russia, yet he was unable to grasp even the basic essentials of the free market into which he had released his country.

Gorbachev had a feisty, razor-sharp sense of humour, and made a number of playful comments that evening prefaced by 'When the people rise up against me . . .', an amusing expression from the leader of a self-declared revolutionary party. I am sure from his manner that he did not expect to be overthrown, but within a few weeks that was nearly his fate. On the morning of 19 August 1991 I was at Number 10 when news came through that communist hard-liners in the Soviet Union had launched a coup attempt and were holding Gorbachev hostage in his Black Sea *dacha*. All was confusion, but after conferring with my foreign policy adviser Percy Cradock I became the first Western leader to declare the coup unconstitutional. Other world leaders appeared to be waiting to see who would come out on top before they revealed their hand; I simply thought the coup illegal, and said so. I tried and failed to reach Gorbachev that day; the next afternoon, Number 10 managed to reach Boris Yeltsin, the Russian – as opposed to Soviet – leader on the telephone. Yeltsin was trapped in the Russian Parliament building, the White House, and was highly excited. I told him we were watching events with immense anxiety, and before I could say any more he burst out with an impassioned plea for support. Gorbachev was isolated, he said. There was a curfew in Moscow. Hundreds of thousands of demonstrators had taken to the streets to protest against the coup. Efforts were being made to capture the building from which he was speaking. Claims by the leaders of the coup that they were in control of the country were untrue.

As I was telling Yeltsin that I had publicly condemned the coup as illegal and unconstitutional, he interrupted me to say that tanks were heading towards the White House. 'I may have only a few minutes left,' he bellowed. He asked for the West to demand Gorbachev be freed, and gave me a list of actions he hoped I would discuss with President Bush and the leaders of the European Community. It was a highly dramatic outburst, and immediately afterwards, at an impromptu press conference on the steps of 10 Downing Street, I passed on Yeltsin's colourful message and repeated my support for reform in the Soviet Union.

The BBC World Service relayed my statement to Russia, and Mikhail Gorbachev subsequently told me had heard it in the Black Sea villa in which he was under guard. Over the next few days the coup fell apart and Gorbachev returned to Moscow. While Boris Yeltsin found both his status and his self-confidence enhanced by his stand against the plotters, Gorbachev never recovered his authority. Four months later, in December 1991, as I attended the European summit at Maastricht, the Soviet Union collapsed and Yeltsin emerged as the head of an independent Russia, within the newly-named Commonwealth of Independent States.

Yeltsin never forgot my opposition to the coup and my early support for him. His body language whenever we met made that clear, and so – my translators told me – did his use of affectionate pronouns. He was an emotional man, vulnerable and prone to mood swings, who welcomed support in his lonely role. His task of reforming Russia was near-impossible but he was a stronger man, and a better friend to the West, than was suggested by the caricature of the vodka-swilling, stumbling politician.

The most important relationship in Western Europe for Yeltsin was that with Germany. Gorbachev had been very far-sighted in 1989 when he began withdrawing troops from East Germany and enabled the country to be reunified. As Germany came together, the Soviet Union began to fall apart. Russia needed help, and Helmut Kohl and I discussed her plight whenever we met. Our views were very similar. The move to democracy and a free market in Russia was important far beyond its borders, and had to be encouraged. It would take years, perhaps decades, to establish such a massive change, but it was in the interests of the West to help Russia do so.

Russia needed – and received – a great deal of financial help, although talk of a 'Marshall Plan' was unrealistic and came to nothing. But her new role as a debtor nation was uncomfortable for a superpower and I believed she needed to be brought into the Western process of decision-making. To disregard Russia when she was weak might not be forgotten when she was strong once again.

Some of our European partners, for so long fearful of Russia, were less sensitive to her plight. When Boris Yeltsin dined with the leaders of the

G7 or the European Union he sometimes found himself interrogated on his progress in implementing economic reform by heads of government none of whom could have carried similar measures in their own democracies. It was, I felt, both bad policy and graceless behaviour.

Helmut Kohl shared my concern, and found an unconventional way of symbolising equality, by sharing a sauna with Yeltsin. I proposed the more mundane solution of bringing Russia into a political G8, meeting back-to-back with the G7 at its annual summit. This appealed to Helmut, who launched into a lengthy explanation of why it was psychologically right to help Yeltsin. 'I telephone Boris regularly,' he told me, and urged me to do the same. 'It may not necessarily solve all our problems, but it will mean a great deal to him.'

I saw this tactic in action during one visit to Bonn when, as Helmut and I were discussing Bosnia, reports came in about renewed Serb shelling of Sarajevo. The novel element was a rumour that the UN's headquarters there were being targeted, and had been hit. While officials were running around trying to get to the bottom of the story, Kohl suggested that we should telephone Yeltsin and encourage him to apply pressure to the Serbs. The switchboard operator found Yeltsin in Minsk, at a meeting with other leaders of the Commonwealth of Independent States. They had clearly enjoyed a very long and bibulous lunch. Interpreters were summoned, and we repaired to Kohl's office to take the call. It was a comic scene. Yeltsin didn't have the right sort of interpreters with him in Minsk, nor did Kohl have an interpreter who could manage English, German and Russian. So the phone would be passed from Kohl to a German–Russian interpreter, while my words went through a second interpreter into German and then into Russian, and Yeltsin's came back to me the same way. In practice the telephone was barely necessary, let alone the interpreters. In a voice that could have been heard in Minsk, Kohl bellowed '*Liebe Boris!*' while at the other end an unprepared Yeltsin tried to make sense of the situation before falling back on equally loud endearments of '*Dorogoi Helmut!*' and '*Dorogoi John!*' On the opposite side of Kohl's desk our foreign ministers, ambassadors and private secretaries sat in a line, attempting to conceal their professional horror. As an exercise in international crisis-management it was wholly ineffective; fortunately it turned out that there was no immediate crisis, as the story of the Sarajevo shelling – not for the first time – had been substantially exaggerated.

Germany was pivotal to Britain's European relations, and Helmut Kohl and I met often at seemingly endless sessions of the European Council. It was at informal meetings, however, that we really got to know each other. One took place at Bad Hofgastein, a small Austrian mountain resort where for many years Helmut had been taking a restorative Easter break in the same unpretentious hotel. In the spring of 1993 I joined him there for a walk and a chat rather than for official business. We met alone, except for Dorothea, his interpreter, with not an ambassador or a protocol officer for miles. Dorothea and I were served a lunch of several courses while Helmut looked on wistfully and drank only weak tea. 'I lose weight, of course, but I put that back on,' he told us. He tapped his head, 'But it clears the impurities up here.' After lunch he told a few lingering journalists that we were going to walk up the mountain. We walked only as far as his car, and drove up a winding road to a small café – Helmut's favourite – where I was offered cakes and he drank more tea. Then we returned to the car and drove back down the mountain. Somehow the walk was neglected.

I reciprocated by inviting Helmut to an informal day at Chequers. We each brought only one or two personal advisers, and sent them on a stroll around the grounds while we talked privately. Unfortunately the ever-vigilant Buckinghamshire police leapt out of the bushes, bearing sub-machine guns, and accosted Kohl's aides, both of ambassadorial rank. Kohl was highly amused when my Private Secretary Rod Lyne apologised for this accidental discourtesy, and it set the tone for a very amiable day. After we had disposed of foreign affairs business, undiplomatic anecdotes formed the bulk of our lunchtime conversation – made all the more amusing by the struggle of the highly professional Dorothea to keep a straight face. She failed.

In the European Union, I was keen to build up our relationship with France. This accelerated when, in May 1995, Jacques Chirac succeeded François Mitterrand at the Élysée Palace, initially forming the government with the support of his fellow right-wingers in the National Assembly. Jacques Chirac brought a populist touch and a much more flamboyant style than François Mitterrand to the job. Having studied in the United States he spoke good English, and he did not mince his words in any language. Within days of taking office he invited EU heads of government to a dinner at the Élysée so that he could get to know them before chairing formal meetings during France's EU presidency. He startled them by abandoning the customarily circumspect diplomatic language, and giving free reign to trenchant views on Europe's failings. This was good to see, but his views were not appreciated by the President of the Commission Jacques Delors or the Dutch Prime Minister Wim Kok – each of whom was given a blasting by Chirac. Kok was told that the Netherlands was a 'narco-state', and that the drugs freely available there were undermining the youth of France.

Chirac and I had met on many occasions before his election, and we had a broadly similar outlook. We set out to build up ties between our two countries – not to the exclusion of others, or in competition with the special relationship between France and Germany, but playing to the strengths and interests our countries had in common. Britain and France were the only nuclear powers in the Community, the only two countries in Western Europe with a genuinely global foreign policy, and the only two with permanent membership of the UN Security Council. We had by far the largest contingents in the UN Protection Force in Bosnia, and President Chirac and I gave instructions for much closer collaboration, including regular video-conferences, between the defence and security personnel responsible for our policy there. Likewise, we encouraged not only joint defence-industry projects (of which there were over twenty, some involving other countries), but also direct links between our armed forces. I was glad to see my successor continuing this approach, and also following up my efforts with Chirac to bury the damaging tradition of competitiveness between Britain and France in Africa.

To cement this renewed *entente*, I secured the Queen's agreement to a very early invitation to President Chirac to pay a state visit to Britain – the highest form of diplomatic compliment. There are normally only two or three such visits a year, and the invitation meant moving Chirac up the queue with unprecedented speed. To our puzzlement, the Élysée seemed embarrassed by the invitation, and were slow to reply. Enquiries were made, and an odd tale emerged. Our invitation had put the President in a quandary. One of his first acts as president had been to abolish some of the grandiose habits of his predecessor, including the practice of sweeping about Paris in motorcades with motorcycle outriders. Chirac was concerned that the traditional carriage ride up The Mall with the sovereign, amid a sea of uniforms, would not chime well with his desired image as the people's president. It took a fair amount of reassurance that state visits could include practical, down-to-earth events before he was content. Being no lover of formality myself, I sympathised with his qualms. The visit when it took place was a great success.

China and Russia both stepped out more into the Western world in the early 1990s. Each of them embarked on political and economic reform, although their chosen priorities were reversed. Russia began with political reform, intending economic reform to follow, whereas China took the path of economic reform, and used cruel force to suppress calls for political liberation. The Chinese leaders, often very elderly, were able and well-prepared, but from a political school which was unyielding. Their line was predetermined and inflexible.

My initial immersion in Sino–British relations came in 1991 when I made a controversial visit to Beijing, the first Western leader to do so after the massacre of student protesters in Tiananmen Square in June 1989. It would have been safer politically not to have gone, but I knew we would have to do business with China over Hong Kong, and I judged that an early visit would help me to do so. In China I raised the country's human rights record more sharply than the leadership expected. This was not simply a ritual purification of the democratic soul, but a message I hoped would be heard in my host country. I was encouraged that the young Chinese our embassy arranged for me to meet were eager for new ideas and seemed to share little of their forebears' communist dogma.

My dealings with China were dominated by one issue: Hong Kong, which was due to be handed back to China on 1 July 1997. In 1992 I appointed my former party chairman Chris Patten to be the colony's last governor, knowing him well enough to realise he would want to entrench the maximum amount of democracy in the territory before it returned to Chinese sovereignty. In Britain, the 'old China hands' argued forcefully against this policy. It would, they claimed, poison all our dealings with China, damage Britain's greater commercial and political interests, and disorder the system which had brought about the colony's fantastic economic success. They were not alone in their criticism, as British businessmen with contracts at stake (and some Conservative stalwarts) queued up to warn me that I should not alienate China.

Our policy towards Hong Kong was guided by the 1984 Joint Declaration, negotiated by Geoffrey Howe and Margaret Thatcher, which established the principle of 'one country, two systems' after the transfer of sovereignty in 1997. By the time I became prime minister, China itself had begun to embrace the free market, so it seemed that capitalism in Hong Kong had a future. Nevertheless, it was essential to ensure that the colony's successful political base should survive intact after handover – a policy which, in the way of these things, became known as the 'through train'. The greater the uncertainty as to whether the train would roll on beyond 1997, the greater the threat to Hong Kong's long-term health. Schemes begun under British rule, such as the Chek Lap Kok airport project, were at risk. One of the aims of my 1991 visit to Beijing was to impress upon the Chinese the importance of allowing these to proceed; but at the time they were unwilling to agree to do so. Only under Chris Patten's gubernatorial guidance was an agreement on the project reached.

Chris Patten arrived in Hong Kong as governor in July 1992, and from then on I supported his policy of political liberalisation in private as well as in public, together with the heavyweight support of Douglas Hurd. It was right that as Hong Kong changed, its constitution should change too. Throughout the 1960s and 1970s the colony had a low-cost manufacturing base, with no demand for political reform. By the 1990s it was a prosperous, educated financial centre of global importance, and expectations were far greater. The citizens of Hong Kong were now eager for political reform, and it would have been wrong to deny it, although the changes we implemented had to be within the terms of the Joint Declaration. I believed they were – although some in Britain and China argued otherwise.

I made two visits to the colony while I was prime minister. The first, in 1991, was a brief stop on my return from Beijing. The second, in March 1996, was more significant, the last by a British prime minister before the handover itself. As such, it was an opportunity for me to lay down principles for Britain's future dealings with the territory. 'If there were any suggestion of a breach of the Joint Declaration we would have a duty to pursue every legal and other means available to us,' I said in a speech to the Chamber of Commerce. 'Britain's commitment to Hong Kong will not end next summer.' To reinforce this, I announced that Hong Kong passport holders would continue to enjoy visa-free access to Britain after the handover to China.

I had good tidings, too, for twenty-nine war widows who lived in the colony. Their cause had been taken up by Jack Edwards, a British ex-serviceman who lived in Hong Kong. With a Union Jack in his hand, but without much hope, he had stood at the gates of Government House clutching a petition to plead their case. I asked for him to be invited to meet me, and told him we would restore British citizenship, and full pension rights, to the widows. His face brightened with surprise, and I reflected how rarely campaigners expect government to listen to their case, let alone respond positively to it.

One further loose end of empire remained to be tied up. There were five thousand or so people in Hong Kong whose roots lay in the Indian subcontinent, and whose future under Chinese rule was uncertain. Only a few had been granted British citizenship, but I made it clear during my visit that if they should come under pressure to leave the territory after 1997, Britain would offer them a home. It was a popular move in Hong Kong, but not so in parts of the Conservative Party or in sections of the British press. Nonetheless, on humanitarian grounds it was right.

In the early hours of 1 July 1997, Tung Chee-hua took office as the first chief executive of the new Special Administrative Region, as Hong Kong was now termed by the Chinese. Our former colony was in sparkling shape. Since 1992, investment in Hong Kong had grown by almost half, the gross domestic product had grown by a quarter, and exports by two-thirds. The people of Hong Kong had shown their appetite for the political rights granted by Chris Patten, voting heavily in favour of the United Democrats in elections in 1991 and 1995. Although the Chinese called Chris some colourful names – 'strutting prostitute', 'tango dancer', 'serpent' and 'Triple Violator' among them – from 1993, albeit haltingly, talks on Hong Kong's future proceeded. It is a tribute to their success that by 1997 the handover to China – seen a decade before as a terrible prospect and the cause of much emigration – passed with barely a murmur. Neither did Britain's wider relations with China break down during the years before the territory returned to Chinese rule. Between 1992 and 1997 Britain's exports to China doubled from around £2 billion to over £4 billion – hardly evidence of disastrous policy-making. As I write in 1999, essential political freedoms remain intact in Hong Kong, and the former colony's economy has escaped the worst effects of the Asian crisis.

Hong Kong was one legacy of Britain's imperial past. The Commonwealth was another, a curious and enchanting institution made up of large and small nations, held together by affection and a shared history. Superficially many of the Commonwealth members have little in common with each other. The United Kingdom, Canada, Australia and New Zealand are prosperous nations firmly cast, irrespective of location, in the Western system of democracy; Singapore and Malaysia are growing economic powers with a very different culture; South Africa and Nigeria have faced decades of civil unrest but have immense natural resources to build prosperity; whereas many of the small nations are dependent on aid and, in some cases, upon market demand for a single crop. In the Commonwealth all of them count, and they are bound together by ties that are invisible but effective. For many years dissent about South Africa's apartheid system divided the Commonwealth, but it did not break it. Now that South Africa is under majority rule, that pressure has gone.

The most potent force binding the Commonwealth together is the monarchy, and there is an abiding affection for the Queen among the member states. This is fully reciprocated by the Queen, who has an encyclopaedic knowledge of them. Often, if I mentioned a contemporary problem in the Commonwealth to Her Majesty, she would reply, 'I remember . . .' and reveal the roots of it, often going back many years. It was a sharp reminder that the Queen has been reading state papers since Winston Churchill's days as prime minister. 'I knew his father,' she would say of some political figure, and a vivid character sketch would follow. I hope Tony Blair seeks her advice and heeds her response. I found them invaluable on many occasions.

I had a particular affection for the Caribbean islands, and not only because, almost without exception, their leaders were cricket enthusiasts. Dame Eugenia Charles, Prime Minister of Dominica for fifteen years, was a forceful proponent of British values and the monarchy, and pleaded the cause of her country's banana industry with a passion that was irresistible. For such countries the Commonwealth is both a shield and a forum.

The Commonwealth was strengthened in 1994, when Nelson Mandela became President of South Africa, and the country rejoined after three decades of isolation. Britain had done everything it could to encourage the transition from minority rule, short of full sanctions, which successive Conservative governments believed would have utterly destroyed the South African economy and hurt most the very black South Africans it was meant to help. Others disagreed, but now the argument was over and everyone was keen to build for the future. More than any other country, Britain had an interest in South Africa: we were the largest overseas investor, and had more than a million British passport holders living there. The end of apartheid was a huge relief to us as well as to millions of South Africans. That it ended peacefully is thanks to the work of F.W. de Klerk, the last leader of white South Africa, and, above all, Nelson Mandela.

Nelson Mandela was released from prison in February 1990. I spoke to him often, but my most vivid recollection is of a visit he made to the United Kingdom after he became president of a multi-racial South Africa. His visit was unlike any other during my time as prime minister. Everyone who works in 10 Downing Street becomes used to celebrated visitors, and their arrival barely causes a stir. It was not so on this occasion. Nearly everyone in the building crowded into the corridor to greet the President. He shook everyone by the hand and said, 'Now I know why John is so successful – he has all these people working for him.'

Mandela was able to face down hard-liners in his own party, convince doubting whites, and bring South Africa back into the world community in a way no one else could have done. Part of his magic was the sheer moral force that clung to him as a result of all he had endured throughout his twenty-seven years of imprisonment. His response to South Africa's HIV crisis was a case in point: the African National Congress can be a very puritanical party, but Mandela brushed taboo aside, boldly wore an AIDS ribbon and talked openly about the disease in its social context. Only he could have done that.

I visited South Africa in September 1994, five months after the first fully democratic elections in the country's history, and addressed both Houses of Parliament. There was a limit to how much practical help Britain could give out of an overseas aid budget that is targeted at the very poorest nations, but I promised £100 million of assistance. Afterwards, at lunch – in the room in which, over thirty years earlier, Harold Macmillan had delivered his famous 'Wind of Change' speech – I saw something of the remarkable spirit that had taken the country into the new era. Former inmates of the notorious prison on Robben Island sat chatting with white MPs who had served in the previous National Party government.

That trip had many memories. After addressing the Parliament I flew to Johannesburg accompanied by British sports stars Alec Stewart, Judy Simpson, Rob Andrew and Bobby Charlton. Colin Cowdrey, who had brought the South African cricket administrator (and former Test captain)

Ali Bacher to see me in 1991 to seek to help readmit the South African team to international competition, was there to meet us. In Alexandria township I opened a new sports ground built with British funds whilst the British stars played pied piper to the children and began impromptu coaching sessions. In the nets, to my great satisfaction, I bowled out Steve Tshwete, the South African Sports Minister, with my first ball. It was one of the happiest of visits.

South Africa, Hong Kong, Japan, Russia and the United States were all well-trodden paths for British diplomacy, but in my time at Number 10 I put a tentative foot down some new routes. South America provided one. I became the first British prime minister for half a century to visit the continent when I flew to Colombia in June 1992, accompanied by Tristan Garel-Jones, then Minister of State at the Foreign Office. The centrepiece of our trip was an inspection of BP's oil installations deep in the rainforest. I flew in a noisy helicopter with Tristan and Gus O'Donnell. The press climbed aboard a separate helicopter, which arrived well before us, and as they waited at the airstrip they heard a rumour that the prime ministerial helicopter had crashed. Chris Moncrieff, the Press Association's veteran Westminster correspondent, contacted London and the news went out on the wires. Minutes later, when my helicopter landed, undamaged after all, Chris came up to me. 'Prime Minister,' he began, 'I must ask your reaction to reports of your death.' 'What happened to the pound?' I asked – and was encouraged to hear that it had fallen on the receipt of such news.

The Colombia trip was a foretaste of the central reason for my visit to South America, the Earth Summit held in Rio de Janeiro. I was the first head of a G7 government to announce that I would attend, an act which persuaded other leaders to come too. In all, delegates from nearly two hundred countries attended to look for ways of reconciling economic development with environmental protection. Global warming was a particular concern. I was not alone in seeing the irony of calling a vast international summit to discuss hot air, but concerted action was essential: it was little help overall if one country behaved well while others continued to pollute.

At the summit, two important conventions were agreed. One, on climate change, which committed us to cut the emission of 'greenhouse gases' to 1990 levels by the turn of the century, and the other on bio-diversity. In Rio I announced a 'Darwin' initiative to use British expertise to help developing countries that were rich in biodiversity but poor in financial resources.

Over eighty projects were later set up, ranging from the protection of mink, otters, species of oyster, insects and fungi to coral reefs and mangrove swamps. It has proved hugely successful. Michael Howard, then the Environment Secretary, showed a commitment to Rio that surprised those who knew the image of a dry-as-dust right-of-centre lawyer, but did not know the man. He was immensely energetic and supportive of the environmental case.

The 'Darwin' initiative was the brain-child of Sir Crispin Tickell, who was not only an expert on environmental policy, but also Britain's Ambassador to the United Nations. Crispin, a scholarly, tenacious diplomat, came to see me several times a year, and his tutorials were invaluable. As ideas were turned into policy, Britain started to shed its undeserved reputation as the 'dirty man of Europe', and became instead something of a front-runner.

In May 1993 John Gummer succeeded Michael Howard as Secretary of State for the Environment. John never holds any views half-heartedly, and was passionate about the environment ('He's a fully paid-up member of the green welly brigade,' was one colleague's comment after an erudite Gummer lecture to Cabinet on sustainable development). He built up an excellent reputation among lobby groups, and unfailingly challenged policies that had an environmental cost. He was the guiding force behind the White Paper on Sustainable Development we launched in January 1994, and lobbied energetically for me to include the subject in every speech I could to give it profile.

One spin-off from the White Paper was to establish a Panel on Sustainable Development under Crispin Tickell's guidance. The panel sought to bring environmental concerns into the everyday business of government, examining areas such as environmental pricing, education and the depletion of world fish stocks. It produced annual reports challenging the government to adapt policy to environmental concerns, and we responded with a paper outlining what we intended to do. It was not the stuff of headlines, but through such careful consideration our commitments at the Rio summit were turned into action. John Gummer kept a watchful eye on it all.

I often used overseas trips to combine foreign policy with British economic interest, and invited teams of senior businessmen to accompany me. My role was to open doors and facilitate meetings; theirs was to nail down contracts. We were usually accompanied by a press corps whose role was to generate sufficient stories to justify their air fares.

In January 1993 I led a trade mission to India at the suggestion of Narasimha Rao, the Prime Minister, who had invited me to be guest of honour on Republic Day, the country's most important celebration of the year. My party included the chairmen and chief executives of many blue-chip British companies, and for them the visit was a great success: British Gas clinched a £100 million contract on the first day. Many more contracts followed.

I flew from Bombay to Oman a few days later to meet Sultan Qaboos, the ruler, who was in the desert on his annual pilgrimage to meet nomadic tribes. The sight and sound as we landed at his encampment was of a welcome from an honour guard in kilts playing the bagpipes. It was all most incongruous. The Sultan was full of surprises. Lunch, under a canopy in the desert, was at a large and magnificently set table, while the nomads watched from a distance. Before the day was out I flew to Riyadh, the capital of Saudi Arabia, for dinner with King Fahd. A formal banquet finished just before midnight, but the King and I talked into the early hours – he was a late-night, not an early-morning, man – before he confirmed an order for forty-eight Tornado aircraft. The business component of the trip was an unqualified success, but the mood at home was becoming difficult for the government, and press coverage was sour. The travelling press corps were rarely interested in the successes of any visit – domestic dramas were far more entertaining for their readers.

In September 1993 I led a second group – arguably the most powerful delegation of British businessmen ever to fly out of the UK together – to Japan and Malaysia. £1 billion worth of business was sealed in the two countries, but the political climate at home was turbulent, and the large contingent of journalists travelling with us ignored the commercial success of the visit, which became known in Number 10 as 'the trip from hell'. In Britain, the now-annual speculation about a leadership challenge was in full swing. The media were looking for negative stories, and were none too scrupulous about how they were obtained.

An illustration of this was reported later by the *Independent on Sunday*. In London, Kenneth Clarke, responding to a question, said: 'Great attempts are being made . . . to arouse interest in a leadership challenge. I know of no person of real political judgement who could contemplate such a thing.'

In Tokyo, I was asked: 'Was it wise of Ken Clarke to pull a rabbit out of the hat about a leadership campaign?'

I replied: 'Heaven knows where these nonsenses come from.'

The *Daily Mail* wrote: 'Speculation was heightened by comments from ... Ken Clarke ... that there were factions canvassing ... to challenge the Premier.'

Perhaps this was just sloppy reporting, but it was by no means an isolated incident. At a reception in the garden of the British Embassy in Tokyo, I spoke to journalists about my frustration with the antics of my party critics. Such conversations are usually on a 'background-only' basis. On this occasion tape-recorded comments found their way into print, so that all Britain awoke to my views that some of my critics were 'barmy'.

The onslaught continued at press conferences in Japan, where the British media asked a barrage of hostile questions about our domestic politics, to the bewilderment of the Japanese, who listened in disbelief to the tenor of the exchanges.

*En route* home from Japan, a visit to Malaysia provided scant relief. Without warning, at a banquet the unpredictable Dr Mahathir, the Malaysian Prime Minister, launched into an ill-informed attack on our policy in Bosnia, which provoked some very tart exchanges between us over dinner. I didn't appreciate being a punchbag for his domestic audience, and told him so. Having secured his publicity, however, the cameras left and Mahathir oozed charm. The following evening he chortled and chuckled through a private dinner as Richard Needham, the Minister for Trade, entertained us with a stream of irreverent (and very funny) stories. With many contracts gained, the purpose of my trip was achieved; but the price in negative publicity was very high.

The benefits of international diplomacy are rarely quantifiable, but the Uruguay round of the GATT talks established a new, liberal order of world trade when, at last, it was completed in December 1993. The talks had been dragging on in a desultory way for years. Nearly every country paid lip-service to the benefits of freer trade to the world economy – but too many then sought to retain protection for their own interests. In the early 1990s the world economy needed growth, and it was clear to me that of all the actions governments could take, completing the GATT round was the one most likely to deliver it without the malevolent side-effects of inflation.

In 1990, 1991, 1992 and 1993 the G7 agreed to complete the GATT round by the end of the year. Each time they failed to do so. My involvement in overcoming this was twofold. As prime minister of a country with a significant voice in the European Union, I was able to draw together the strings of our partners' varied demands. France, in particular, was anxious to avoid including farm products in the final agreement, but without this it was unlikely that the United States would agree a settlement. Partly thanks to British pressure, the Community accepted the 'Blair House Agreement' (named after the Washington residence which houses foreign guests) in November 1992 – including farm products in the deal.

This put in place the foundations of a final conclusion to the Uruguay round, but it was not until negotiations at the 1993 Tokyo economic summit that the matter was settled. The main details were ironed out shortly before the end of the year. In 1994, the World Trade Organisation began work, policing the free-trade policies of the world's economic powers, opening new markets. This has been almost entirely to our benefit, since British markets were mostly open already. It is no coincidence (although other factors have, of course, been involved) that the GATT agreement has been followed by sustained economic growth in many of the world's largest trading nations.

Britain's global interests and the ever-more packed calendar of international events ensured that during the six and a half years I was in Number 10, I spent many months on journeys abroad. Every trip needed meticulous preparation by those inside Number 10 and across Whitehall, and before each visit I always faced a mountain of briefing notes compiled by the government machine. I tried to find out as much as I could about foreign heads of government before I met them, as familiarity is reassuring, and permits more productive exchanges. I took pains to study their body language, and asked interpreters whether their language was ambiguous, or whether it conveyed more than the words actually spoken. These insights were valuable, and were enhanced when the interpreters were familiar with the idiomatic use of their chosen language and had interpreted before for the head of government that I was meeting.

Relative novices in foreign affairs have become prime minister both before and after me, but in my case I was fortunate in the early years of my premiership in having Douglas Hurd as foreign secretary, and in having Malcolm Rifkind as his successor. Like Douglas, Malcolm was a foreign affairs specialist whose previous experience at the Foreign Office as a junior minister and later as defence secretary gave him a thorough grounding in all the issues he had to face. I knew from my own experience that he was a formidable negotiator, familiar with the art of brinkmanship, and a man with an ear forever alert for the emerging concerns of our party. He was also a fine orator – invariably without notes – with a mind well stocked with argument and invective.

At Number 10 I had a string of foreign affairs private secretaries, all of whom were of the highest calibre. Charles Powell, Stephen Wall, Rod Lyne and John Holmes were a remarkable quartet. Charles, sadly, left public service, but the others did not: Stephen became Ambassador to the European Union; Rod became Ambassador to Geneva, and is soon to be Ambassador to Moscow; and John is Ambassador to Lisbon. I was also served by Percy Cradock and Rodric Braithwaite, my foreign policy advisers, who supplemented the work of the Foreign Office. My experience at the Foreign Office and Number 10 left me with a profound admiration for the ability of the members of our diplomatic service. It is fashionable to denigrate them in some circles, but in my experience their skill and professionalism is the best the world has to offer, and should be treasured as a considerable national asset.

# CHAPTER TWENTY-ONE

# *At the Summit*

FOR A BRITISH PRIME MINISTER, international summits are a particular problem. We belong to more summit-holding clubs than almost any other nation: the European Union (two to four summits a year), the Group of Eight (once a year), the Commonwealth (every two years, for several days), NATO (roughly every two years), the Organisation for Security and Cooperation in Europe (every two years,) ASEM (a group of Asian and EU countries, which meets biennially), and of course the United Nations. On top of this the EU is getting into the habit of holding summits with other regional groups such as the Association of South-East Asian Nations (ASEAN) and the Latin Americans. Added to these are *ad hoc* summits and commemorative meetings.

Summit meetings can look glamorous from the outside, and tend to be held in exotic locations – Corfu, Cannes, Majorca, Naples. They used to be rare and significant events: the gold standard of international affairs. But over the last twenty years their currency has been debased in proportion to their alarming proliferation. Summitry exploded in the 1990s. Setting aside bilateral 'summits' – typically a half-day meeting and meal with the president of France, Russia, the United States or whomever – as prime minister I had to spend as much as three weeks a year travelling to multilateral events. Each required preparation, briefing, and perhaps a Parliamentary Statement afterwards. All too often they also obliged me to listen to interminable speeches before signing up to pre-cooked conclusions much longer on verbiage than on action.

These summits did provide opportunities for networking with other leaders in the margins and the corridors (the 'margin' or 'corridor' in question often being an over-ornate banquet, guest house or presidential hotel suite). Often this could have more value than the summit itself. But when you find yourself with many of the same leaders at several different summits in succession, the well of serious business can run dry.

If I sometimes became frustrated by the seemingly endless round of summits it was because, unlike most of his counterparts, the British prime minister has four distinct jobs: running the government, leading his party in Parliament, leading the national party, and being a constituency Member of Parliament. He neglects any one of these at his (or her) peril. By contrast, the president of the United States does not run large chunks of domestic policy (which are handled at state level or by officials such as the chairman of the Federal Reserve Board); rarely attends sittings of Congress; does not lead the national party; and can delegate to the vice-president. The French president has a prime minister below him, and a National Assembly in which he does not sit and to which he pays scant attention. Much of government in Germany is the responsibility of the prime ministers of the Länder, or regions, not of the federal chancellor; and so on down the list of those who sat with me around the summit tables. Bill Clinton's staff once proudly told mine that they were limiting him to a maximum of sixty hours' work a week. Mine would have been happy to limit me (and themselves) to a hundred. Over-frequent or over-long summit meetings were a treat I would have happily forgone.

By far the friendliest summits were those of the Commonwealth, once it was freed of the millstone of South African apartheid. The Commonwealth is more of a club than an organisation. It defies precise definition, but it has a common ethos and, crucially, a common language. Real debate is freer and easier when your tone and nuance are not filtered through interpretation, and you can chat without impediment to a neighbour over dinner or a drink.

Of all the summits and conferences I attended as prime minister, the 1991 Commonwealth Heads of Government Meeting at Harare, Zimbabwe, sticks in my mind as the happiest. It came after the release from prison of Nelson Mandela, and with that came a sense of wounds being healed. The substance of the meeting emerged as the Harare Declaration, which laid down the standard of good government expected of Commonwealth members. It was an important step, not least because it answered complaints that the Commonwealth harboured dictators. By 1997, almost every active member country had an elected government.

In Harare I took part in a cricket match at the leafy Wanderers ground.

Among those playing were Bob Hawke and Nawaz Sharif, prime ministers of Australia and Pakistan respectively, and Graeme Hick, the Zimbabwean-born English Test batsman. Hawke and I opened the batting, and at the end of each over he took a crafty single to steal the bowling. I was relaxed about this until, after a few overs, we were invited to retire and make way – as one umpire put it – for 'the real cricketers'. Hawke had known our tenure of the crease was limited, but somehow had forgotten to tell me: Australians always play hard.

Hawke's successor as Australian prime minister, Paul Keating, did so too, although rhetoric rather than cricket was his sport. In private I found Keating intelligent and often charming, and he did much to modernise his country's economy. But, by accident or design, he was apt to let his sharp tongue run away with him.

One such occasion was in the run-up to the November 1995 Commonwealth Heads of Government Conference in Auckland, New Zealand. At the time Australian public opinion was incensed by President Chirac's decision to hold a short series of underground nuclear tests at Mururoa Atoll in the Pacific. Paul Keating knew perfectly well that the tests were carefully controlled, and were a prelude to French accession to a complete ban on testing. More pertinently, he was also aware that the French test site was much further from Australia than Lop Nor, where the Chinese were continuing to explode far larger devices without international controls – and without a whimper from the Australian government, protective of its commercial and political interests in China. But Keating was running for re-election. To bash the French and the British in one go was irresistible, and he took a swipe at me in pretty unstatesmanlike language on a local Australian radio station. I wasn't bothered: the election was his problem, and the odd fleabite wasn't going to change my policy of supporting France over this issue. But the incident was, of course, manna to the British press. When Keating arrived in Auckland the hack pack pursued him in the hope of provoking a fresh outburst. Several of Fleet Street's finest jumped into a lift with him, and with his customary eloquence he invited them to 'Git out of here, you blowflies!' One tabloid man reportedly shot back: 'You know what attracts blowflies, Prime Minister?' before leaping for his life. When Keating came to see me for our bilateral in the margins of the conference he was cheery as could be, and anxious to make amends.

At the base of the brouhaha over nuclear testing was an issue of principle. I personally had doubts about the French decision; but they had valid scientific reasons for ensuring through low-yield tests that their nuclear deterrent was as safe and effective as possible before they signed up to a complete testing ban. It would have been hypocritical for Britain, a fellow nuclear power, to join the lowing herd by attacking the French. This was the route taken by many countries in Western Europe, as well as by Australia and New Zealand, which had been only too happy during the Cold War to shelter under the nuclear umbrella which safeguarded their existence. I was not minded to join them.

At the conference we wasted the first afternoon on the nuclear-testing issue. India and Pakistan, with their own covert nuclear programmes, were not keen to make too much of it, and the majority of Commonwealth members, from Africa and the Caribbean, saw it as remote from their concerns. Nor did they see much sense in kicking Britain for something done by France. Officials drafted a statement so that we could move on to the real agenda. It was somewhat mealy-mouthed, so I capped it by putting out a statement of my own. The French tests stopped soon afterwards.

The second and third days in Auckland showed the Commonwealth at its best. The question of what to do about General Sani Abacha's tyrannical regime in Nigeria loomed over the conference. Abacha had had the sense to stay away, and his Foreign Minister, Ikimi, made no friends in New Zealand with his bullying arrogance. On the second morning we awoke to the news that the Nigerian regime had hanged the writer and political dissident Ken Saro-Wiwa and other Ogoni activists who had been protesting against the environmental damage caused by oil drilling. I got my team together over breakfast to debate the Commonwealth's reaction. We were clear that Nigeria should be suspended from membership. We were less clear whether the other African nations would agree to this, and feared that if the proposal came from Britain, its chances would be diminished; but we could not keep silent at this outrageous affront to human rights and to the Commonwealth itself.

The question was answered for us by Nelson Mandela, at his first meeting as a Commonwealth head of government. President Mandela did not wait to sound out others. After his twenty-seven years in jail he was not interested in trimming on human rights, and he went on television to demand Nigeria's suspension from the Commonwealth. I made a statement in support, and Mandela and I then teamed up with New Zealand's Prime

Minister Jim Bolger on the plane down to the South Island for the conference's weekend retreat. By the following day we had Commonwealth agreement not only for the suspension of Nigeria from the Commonwealth, but for a package of measures to put Abacha's regime under increasing pressure to return to democratic rule. Four years on, it has been a pleasure to see Nigeria return to full Commonwealth membership after the election of President Olusegun Obasanjo.

The retreat – a weekend set aside following the conference for heads of government to take their discussions further in a more relaxed, informal setting – coincided with Remembrance Sunday in Britain. I was troubled to be missing the Cenotaph ceremony in London on the fiftieth anniversary of the end of World War II. The New Zealanders, whose young men travelled across the globe in two world wars to fight at our side with conspicuous gallantry, honour their war dead on a different date, ANZAC Day, in April, but they kindly laid on a special service at the war memorial outside Arrowtown. The memorial is an obelisk on a small hill at the foot of a valley, and New Zealand soldiers, including a Maori warrior, stood at each corner. On a bright spring morning, with snow still on the surrounding peaks, a choir sang, bugles played, and the hauntingly beautiful words of the ceremony of remembrance were uttered in this most appropriate place. Senior representatives of the British servicemen's associations had flown with me to the conference, where they had been royally looked after by their New Zealand comrades. They laid their wreaths, and we all recognised the special friendship between our two peoples – as distant geographically as it is possible to be, but at that moment also as close. As the last bugles sounded, the unmistakable drone of two Merlin engines floated up the valley. Two of the few extant Spitfires came thrillingly into view, then wheeled away in opposite directions, climbing over the mountain ridges. If we needed a reminder of what the Commonwealth was about, that was it. It was an intensely moving occasion.

Not to go to the UN 'Social Summit' in Copenhagen in March 1995 was one of my easiest decisions. The Foreign Office pleaded with me to change my mind, as did the Danes. I was told that sixty or seventy other leaders would be at this jamboree, including all the Europeans (though not President Clinton). If I didn't drop in to deliver the British speech, I was assured, it would look as if we didn't care about world poverty; and our relations with the host nation, Denmark, would suffer.

Instead I fulfilled a long-standing commitment to go to Israel, Jordan and Palestine. I cemented strong personal relationships with Israel's Prime Minister Yitzhak Rabin and King Hussein of Jordan, and was the first Western leader to visit Yasser Arafat in Gaza, in the newly-established Palestinian entity. I was able to give some modest help to the faltering Middle East peace process by brokering an agreement between Rabin and Arafat for monitors from the European Union to oversee the elections in Gaza. I like to think that I also did some practical good for world poverty, both by announcing a new aid package for impoverished Gaza and by encouraging my travelling party of senior British businessmen to think of investing and purchasing in Jordan and Palestine. Because of the Arab boycott of Israel they had never previously been able to fly from Israel to Jordan, and many of them had concentrated on the more profitable Israeli market.

Meanwhile, back in Copenhagen, the UN's summit was certainly a 'social' success. Days filled by predictable set-pieces were followed by nights of junketing. Wealthy nations flew in large delegations in presidential aircraft, burning up public money that could otherwise have helped the world's poor. Poor nations flew in large delegations in presidential aircraft, squandering scarce resources needed for development. Lynda Chalker, our Minister for Overseas Development, represented the United Kingdom with her customary expertise and aplomb (without needing a presidential aircraft and a retinue of courtiers). The UK's excellent relations with Denmark remained excellent. My absence made not a jot or a tittle of difference to the final outcome, any more than did the presence of the sixty or seventy world leaders.

The Social Summit lined the pockets of the prosperous hoteliers and restaurateurs of Copenhagen. Sadly, it did not make the world's poor a penny less poor. They needed the genuine economic development which flows above all from increased trade, investment and education – not a platitudinous document painstakingly drafted by diplomats in New York which none of them would even read.

European Union summits – the European Council – tended to be tense and exhausting ordeals, and (as I describe in Chapter 24) often rather undemocratic. I attended nearly twenty in all, and presided over two. They had the odd light moment, but I cannot pretend that I enjoyed them, or the shenanigans and horse-trading that was so often a feature.

Nonetheless, unsatisfactory though the process is, I do have a few fond memories of European Councils. The summit I chaired at Edinburgh in December 1992 (see pages 369–71) produced some of the best results of any European Council since Britain joined the Community, including an excellent budget settlement, retention of our rebate, and the decision to begin enlargement negotiations with Austria, Finland, Norway and Sweden.

The Council in Essen in December 1994 – which followed my veto of Jean-Luc Dehaene as President of the Commission at Corfu and an emergency Brussels summit to approve Jacques Santer (see pages 593–8) – was stage-managed by Helmut Kohl to smooth over those little differences and restore harmony. It was memorable for the private farewell speech delivered by Jacques Delors as he handed over the Commission presidency to Santer.

The day did not begin well. The protocol people had booked us into a gloomy hotel in the woods, and I awoke on a dank morning to find my ears blocked. I was about to go onto BBC Radio 4's *Today* programme, and I could scarcely hear a thing. Prime ministers used to travel with a doctor, but I only had my Private Secretary, Roderic Lyne. He rushed into the hotel kitchen and asked a startled chef to produce a bottle of olive oil and a spoon. Heating the oil with a match, he poured it into my ears, and I jumped up and down until my hearing was restored. Such are the qualities needed in modern British diplomats.

For once, I was glad to be able to hear Jacques Delors speak. Dinner was held in a pre-war baronial mansion built, I think, by the Krupp family. We had been warned to expect a manifesto for ever-closer European integration. Instead, after a day when Britain's economic strategy appeared to have become the conventional European wisdom, Delors surprised us all. He said, in effect, that his vision of Europe had been mistaken. The overriding priority should not be to bind yet more areas of domestic policy into centralised decision-making. We had to seize the opportunity to embrace the new democracies. Enlargement, to perhaps twenty-five nations, was necessary and inevitable, and it would make tight centralisation impossible.

Publication of Delors's last testament would have caused a minor sensation. It was a shame that it was given in private. Delors had owed his appointment to Margaret Thatcher, who preferred him to another Frenchman, Claude Cheysson. Though he had been cruelly attacked in the British press, he was not personally hostile to Britain. I disagreed with

Delors often, but I appreciated his honesty and decency. He went out on a good note.

Essen was mercifully free of the petty wrangles which so often disfigured European summits. For once the heads of government, stimulated by the thoughtful contribution from Delors, did what they ought to do. They looked at the big picture. They discussed the general heading of the European Union and how we could make our continent a better place. They even dared to ask themselves why unemployment was falling in Britain (and America) while it was continuing to rise towards post-war record levels in countries like Germany and Spain. I suggested that we should have more of this sort of discussion, and should devote a special brainstorming meeting to it.

So it was that in September 1995 we were invited by the Spanish presidency to an informal summit in Majorca, with no detailed agenda, conclusions or decisions. It was the most pleasant European summit I attended, and one of the most useful. Felipe Gonzales, our host, struck just the right note. We were secluded on the Formentor Peninsula, in a hotel which was not over-lavish but had a beautiful garden. The press were miles away, in the nearest town. The foreign ministers and most of the diplomats had stayed at home: each head of government was allowed only three aides inside the hotel perimeter. Felipe wanted us to meet entirely alone (bar interpreters) for free discussion, but this provoked a mutiny from Jacques Chirac, who declared that French presidents did not take their own notes. (In truth, Jacques, as a graduate of the prestigious French civil service college ENA, would have been better equipped to take his own notes than most of us.) But with only one diplomatic adviser each, we were able to preserve the relaxed atmosphere.

On the first afternoon we debated Europe's economic strategy. Confirming the message of Essen, high taxation and public spending, state regulation, central planning, protectionism and other socialist and corporatist mantras were suddenly unfashionable. I argued for flexible labour markets, to help create real jobs; for less red tape; for affordable social costs; and above all for making Europe a competitive, free-trading area if it were to remain prosperous and vibrant into the next century.

Then an unusual thing happened. In the privacy of that room, our European partners dared to be seen to be agreeing with the British Prime Minister. With the exception of Anibal Cavaco da Silva, the highly intelligent Portuguese Prime Minister, few of them had any technical understanding of economics. But they could all see that the old ways were not working. The case for change, as we had already changed in Britain, was unanswerable. Speaker after speaker, in breach of the deepest European conventions, opened his intervention by saying, 'I agree with John.' For a brief moment I knew what it must feel like to be Helmut Kohl.

At the end of the session Felipe Gonzales appealed for someone to lead off the following day's discussion on the prospects for Europe in foreign and security policy. He asked me, but as I had hogged the first afternoon and fancied a bit of relaxation, I proposed Kohl. I was outvoted, and given the assignment. We had no ready-prepared material with us, so my Private Secretary and I sacrificed a trip to the beach and scratched out a few thoughts on the changing security environment, from Russia and Eastern Europe through the arc of instability in the Middle East to the pressures from the African continent on our southern flank. This session, too, seemed to go down satisfactorily. The heads departed with what seemed close to a common vision of the medium term, pausing only to disappoint media hopes of a row. No row, no story; instead, a gathering which showed that European leaders could work together when they tried, even with a British viewpoint at the centre.

The annual economic summit of the leading industrialised nations was originally intended to be an informal brainstorming, rather like the EU's Formentor weekend. The first was convened without frills or bureaucracy by President Valéry Giscard d'Estaing of France at Rambouillet in 1975. To the original six members – France, Germany, Britain, Italy, the United States and Japan – President Ford added Canada in 1976. By July 1991, when, as the club's newest head of government, I found myself in the chair of the London summit, the 'G7' had become a grandiose and cumbersome, not to say expensive, exercise. It had been enlarged to include the President of the European Commission and the country holding the rotating Council presidency (making Luxembourg, with a population of under half a million, occasionally eligible for this top table). It had spawned tribes of 'Sherpas' and 'sous-Sherpas' who would spend months negotiating communiqués and declarations for the leaders to rubber-stamp; vast delegations; armies of security personnel; and a media pack which would fill a football stadium. Over-prepared discussions were squeezed in between photo-opportunities, banquets and protocol engagements. The original purpose of the event had all but disappeared from sight.

I made one change to the pre-set format for the London summit. I had been to Moscow three months before, and I knew that Mikhail Gorbachev was in a precarious position. To try to shore up the Russian reformers, I invited him to London – not as a member of the G7, but to meet the other leaders and receive backing from them. In the short term our support was patently not enough: the coup against Gorbachev would take place only a month later. However, we did sow the seeds of the closer relationship which saw the Russian Federation under President Yeltsin eventually become the eighth state in the club – G8.

The G7 summit in Munich in 1992 convinced me that we had to get back closer to the original concept. Behind a façade of pomp and circumstance, Munich achieved nothing: neither decisions (such as to unblock the Uruguay round GATT negotiations – see pages 513–14) nor useful discussion. I was not alone in questioning the value of such an event in an overcrowded international calendar. George Bush felt much the same.

After Munich I wrote to all the summit leaders urging the case for a much simpler style of conference, and franker discussion. I did so with the support of Whitehall officials, who thought, nonetheless, that I would cause offence with minimal chance of success. The 1993 Tokyo summit appeared to prove them right, but was in fact the turning point. The Japanese had spared no expense in their lavish hospitality. Twenty thousand soldiers and policemen had been drafted in to protect the eight leaders. Twelve thousand photographers, cameramen, sound engineers and journalists were accredited to record their every step and breath. When coffee was ordered for a meeting with four of my staff in my suite at the New Otani Hotel, it was served by no fewer than five dinner-jacketed waiters.

The meetings were held in the cavernous splendour of the Akasaka Palace. For our supposedly intimate discussions, the eight heads (one Sherpa, or senior official, as note-taker, discreetly seated behind each) were ranged around a table with a space the size of a badminton court in the middle. Mainly through the efforts of officials outside the room we managed to shift some of the roadblocks in the Uruguay round negotiations. Otherwise I remember a sumptuous Imperial banquet, but little of what we discussed. However, I found an ally for summit reform in Bill Clinton, who was attending his first G7 event, and who shared my frustration. We secured agreement that the next year's meeting would be scaled down.

In 1994 the Italians were the hosts. Silvio Berlusconi had become prime minister, which helped, because he was a businessman, used to moving briskly. We were bidden to Naples, where the heat in July was stifling. (A Foreign Office report on the summit described a fellow prime minister as 'sticking closely to his briefs', but I gather this was a typographical error rather than a reference to the heat.) When I arrived at the hotel it was plunged in darkness, with no lifts, air conditioning or fridges. Apparently the photocopiers and communications equipment imported by us and the Canadians had blown the local electricity substation. I went off to an official dinner, leaving my staff sweating over summit documents by the light of the streetlamps.

Although we met yet again in a palace (normally the city's art gallery), and had dinner and attended a short opera in another one (the magnificent Palace of Caserta, built by the King of Naples far enough inland to escape British naval bombardment), Berlusconi's masterstroke was to seat the summiteers elbow-to-elbow around a specially made small, circular table. Instead of making speeches at each other as usual, we chaffed and interrupted as if at a dinner party. The atmosphere and the value of the conversation were transformed. Boris Yeltsin joined us for the second day and, for the first time, was treated as a partner and friend, not a supplicant. That certainly registered with him.

One unprogrammed consequence of our free-ranging meeting was that we began to debate how to change the main international institutions to meet the challenges of the coming years. The United Nations, we all agreed, was in urgent need of reform and modernisation. The International Monetary Fund was struggling to cope with financial crises and to pre-empt emerging problems. As we began to sketch out some of the steps which were needed, news of our debate filtered out to the other rooms of the palace, where foreign and finance ministers were holding separate talks. G7 summits are run according to a curiously primitive system. Each head of government is allowed only one 'Sherpa' with him in the conference room. There is no voice relay to other rooms, and no verbatim record is kept. Instead the Sherpa – in my case my Principal Private Secretary, Alex Allan – sits behind his leader at a desk with a fax machine. He scribbles as fast and as legibly as he can, and feeds his notes by fax to his delegation, who are in a separate office. I am told that as our review of the future of the world took off, foreign ministers were seen pacing the corridors outside the conference room, looking ever paler and muttering that we were not briefed to discuss such matters. Some of us were departing from the party line. And it was certainly not the business of the G7 to lay down the law to the United Nations, even if four of the five permanent members of the Security Council were represented in the room.

After a stimulating discussion and a remarkable measure of agreement, we allowed the foreign ministers and their mandarins to tone down our conclusions for the official communiqué. However, we had started something useful. We were determined to have a deeper debate on the topic at the next summit, this time with proper briefing. That debate in turn became an impetus for serious reform of the United Nations.

The Canadians had once, famously, held a G7 summit in a log-cabin hotel at Montebello, with the press in a town an hour away. In 1995 Jean Chrétien decided to convene the summit in the small Atlantic port of Halifax, Nova Scotia. Halifax was ideal – a clean, unpretentious town not known for its palaces. The last big event there had been the explosion of an ammunition ship during the First World War.

Before the summit, the Canadian High Commissioner called at Number 10 with instructions to seek our priorities. My Private Secretary told him that the top priority was a small, round table. He offered the loan of one used at the 1991 London summit, which was in a meeting room in Downing Street, but advised the Canadians to copy Berlusconi's. I believe they borrowed it.

Landing at Halifax in mid-June, I was ferried from the airport in a small naval vessel. Street parties were being held in the town to celebrate the summit. The leaders met in a modest port-side office building which a firm of lawyers had been persuaded to vacate for the duration. From there I could take a ten-minute walk to my hotel. Everywhere we went, people welcomed us and shook our hands – a far cry from the understandable irritation usually caused to the local inhabitants by motorcades and special security. We lunched at the yacht club, dined in the simple house once used by the governor, and were entertained by a circus, not an opera. My parents, both circus performers, would have been delighted to see their son sitting in a tent with a group of presidents and prime ministers watching Canada's spellbinding (and animal-free) Cirque du Soleil.

It was at Halifax that one of my protection officers went jogging, by chance taking the same route as President Clinton. He was stopped by US

Secret Service agents and asked what he was up to. 'I'm the advance jogger for the Prime Minister,' he replied.

Halifax was the least stuffy of my six economic summits – during a mid-session break all the leaders signed a cricket bat for a charity auction. It was also one of the most productive. We got to grips with reform of the UN, the problems in Bosnia, the Mexican financial crisis and Russia. I talked to Bill Clinton about Northern Ireland, and how to make best use of his forthcoming visit. I also took advantage of the occasion to focus my mind on whether to call a leadership election in the Conservative Party (see Chapter 25).

In addition to the regular summits of one kind and another, a prime minister's diary also fills up with commemorative events which can turn into *ad hoc* summits. My term spanned all manner of fiftieth anniversaries, including D-Day, VE-Day, VJ-Day and the foundation of the United Nations. The electorate kindly spared me the millennium.

I felt that the fiftieth anniversary of D-Day, in June 1994, deserved commemorating in a spirit not of chauvinism but of reconciliation, recalling the extraordinary wartime alliance which gave peace and liberty to the Western world. The commemoration, masterminded by Robert Cranborne, began with President Clinton and me laying wreaths at the American war cemetery at Madingley, outside Cambridge, and concluded with the Royal Yacht *Britannia* ferrying fifteen heads of state or government at the head of an armada to France. It was dignified, moving, and a huge success.

Two months later I flew to Poland to commemorate the fiftieth anniversary of another wartime event, the ill-fated Warsaw Uprising. In August 1944 the Polish people had tried to pre-empt the approach of the Red Army by liberating their capital from Nazi occupation. The Western Allies attempted to help from long range, air-dropping supplies flown mainly from bases in Italy. Stalin stood by and watched in glee while the Nazis crushed the Poles with extreme savagery.

The Poles, now liberated from communist as well as Nazi occupation, were in an emotional mood for the commemoration. I met a small party of veterans from the airlift, one of whom had survived a fall into the Vistula from several thousand feet after his Liberator had been shot down and his parachute did not open. They told me that they had been fêted everywhere, not permitted to pay for anything, and treated with lavish hospitality. In the evening the Poles laid on a dramatic open-air re-enactment of the

Uprising. Germany's President Roman Herzog attended as a gesture of reconciliation, and expressed sincere and brave words of contrition. It was one of the hottest and most humid days on record – no matter how often we changed, our clothes were permanently drenched. Boy Scouts passed through the crowds handing out bottled water. As *the son et lumière* reached its climax, the heavens opened and, almost mercifully, we were drenched again.

My bedraggled party squelched back to the British Ambassador's leaking residence at midnight. As I began preparing for a mini-summit with the three Baltic states in Lithuania the next day, I felt ravenously hungry, having had no appetite in the heat of the day. My poor Private Secretary was despatched to the kitchen again, where he found some eggs and some bread, and produced more than passable scrambled eggs on toast. Getting a prime minister through summits requires more than just the ability to write the odd speech and to remember which leader belongs to which country.

After the Poles came the turn of the Germans. For nearly half a century, British, French and American troops had preserved West Berlin as an enclave of freedom. Now, with the Berlin Wall down and Germany reunited, their mission was complete, and Helmut Kohl wanted to thank them in style as they took their leave of the city. He also wished to make a special gesture to his friend François Mitterrand, who was seriously ill with cancer. He invited Mitterrand and me to the leave-taking in September 1994. Secretary of State Warren Christopher represented the United States.

It was another day charged with emotion. Kohl exuded *bonhomie* from every inch of his massive frame. There was a parade at the British barracks, a wreath-laying at the airlift memorial, and a splendid lunch. In the late afternoon we gathered at the concert hall. Schoolchildren sang, the Berlin Philharmonic played Beethoven; and then we spoke. These were not the usual official speeches. François Mitterrand had been out of the public eye for weeks, receiving medical treatment. He looked desperately frail, and his doctors hovered close by. It had taken a great effort of will for him to be there, but he spoke eloquently and without notes for some twenty minutes – a shade too long, but a performance of exceptional courage. I had a speech sensitively tailored for the occasion by Robert Cooper of our embassy in Bonn. Helmut Kohl, who had been dabbing his eyes throughout, came last, with an outpouring of gratitude to the adversaries-turned-allies who had protected his country throughout the Cold War.

When night fell, we were taken to temporary stands around the Pots-
damer Platz, facing the floodlit Brandenburg Gate. The square was lined
with troops from the three Allied powers. Beyond that, total darkness.
The setting was Wagnerian, and Wagner's swelling, powerful marches and
overtures thundered around the stands and stirred the crowd. Finally the
German army performed an evening ceremony handed down from the
time of Frederick the Great. To be in Berlin that evening was to feel the
weight of German culture and history.

Despite his illness, President Mitterrand was determined to see out his
term of office, which ended in May 1995. The fiftieth anniversary of VE-Day
was his farewell as a statesman. On the morning of Sunday, 7 May we held
a service of remembrance, thanksgiving and hope in St Paul's Cathedral,
led by the Queen and attended by the largest number of world leaders to
visit London since the Coronation in 1953. That evening I flew to Paris.
The noise all night at our embassy was deafening: close by, in the Place de
la Concorde, Jacques Chirac's supporters were hailing his victory with a
concert by Johnny Hallyday. On the Monday, President Mitterrand's
foreign guests joined him at a parade in the Champs Élysées and, for the
last time with him as host, for lunch in the Élysée Palace. That afternoon
I flew on to Berlin, where Helmut Kohl was holding a commemorative
event with Boris Yeltsin; then to Moscow, where I crawled into bed in the
not so early hours. Of all the Allies, the Russians had suffered by far the
heaviest losses in the Second World War, and however demanding the
itinerary, I needed to pay tribute by attending their fiftieth-anniversary
commemoration on Tuesday, 9 May. I had a private meeting with President
Yeltsin, whose appreciation of my attendance was evident. Flying home
after commemorations in four countries in three days prompted the reflection that, only one generation earlier, Harold Macmillan had been able to
take weeks off from Downing Street for a seaborne tour of Africa.

There are now 185 member states of the United Nations. Most of them
are small and poor, and few of their leaders can resist the lure of a summit
meeting, especially when it offers a chance to rub shoulders with the rich
and powerful, with guaranteed television exposure. The leaders of big countries are susceptible to the argument that they must not be stand-offish;
or that their country will lose trade opportunities in Asia or Latin America
or wherever if they do not show up. Nor are they immune to grandstanding
on the small screen, particularly in an election year.

I had to admire the way in which Bill Clinton, a master of television, worked the room at the 1994 NATO summit in Brussels. He delayed his entry until all the other fifteen leaders were at their seats in the circular chamber. (This meant winning a game of chicken with the *protocolaire* François Mitterrand. As a president of much longer standing, Mitterrand liked to exercise the right of coming in last.) It took Clinton seven and a half minutes to get from the door to his seat. He slowly circumnavigated the chamber, pausing to greet each leader in turn and engage in thirty seconds of animated conversation. His head was perfectly angled for the television crews tracking him from inside the doughnut of the round table. It was a personal gift to each NATO head. In fifteen nations the evening newscasts would show their leader deeply engaged with the President of the United States. And US television would have the President as the centrepiece of the event.

The goose that lays these golden photo-ops, however, cannot take much more fattening. The annual round of summits has got out of hand. It gobbles up millions of pounds' worth of taxpayers' money. It blocks pages of prime ministerial diaries. Some summits are justified by their results. Too many are not. In most cases foreign ministers or diplomats have already done the real business in advance, and the leaders are summoned for the pro-forma speech, the signing ceremony, the banquet – and the inevitable group photograph.

The devaluation of summits is a suitable case for British pragmatism. Between Munich in 1992 and Halifax in 1995 I believe that we helped prevent the G7 economic summit from sliding into irrelevance, and at Birmingham in 1998 Tony Blair continued the drive to bring it down to earth. In the Commonwealth, we pioneered a move for shorter and less formal meetings. This was agreed in Auckland in 1995, and took effect in Edinburgh in 1997. We should press the European Union to inject more small-scale Majorca-style discussions into the gigantism of the European Council. And we must team up with the other nations which fund the UN budget to contain the rash of enormous UN summits. The Earth Summit which I attended with over a hundred leaders in Rio in 1992 usefully awoke governments to the need for worldwide action on the environment; but events like the 1995 Copenhagen Social Summit, the UN fiftieth-anniversary celebration in the same year, and no doubt the 'Millennium Assembly' planned for autumn 2000, are gilt-edged boondoggles the world can ill afford.

# CHAPTER TWENTY-TWO

# Hell's Kitchen

T HE GULF CRISIS had faced the West squarely from the day I took office as prime minister: a first and obvious test. The conflict in Bosnia, however, crept up on us while our attention was on the turmoil in the Soviet Union, and took us almost unawares. It was as near impossible to deal with as any political problem could be. Its roots were bewildering, and the motives of the participants often far adrift from those expressed in public. James Baker, the US Secretary of State, emerged from a tortuous meeting in June 1991 saying, 'And I thought the Middle East was complicated.' 'What a people, what a country.' muttered the European Community's negotiator Hans van den Broek as he stormed out of another meeting a month later.

Lieutenant Colonel Bob Stewart of the Cheshire Regiment, on the ground at the time, recalled the situation in Bosnia as 'more complex than anyone dreams', with 'factions within groups and groups within fractions'. It was, he said, 'a situation as close to anarchy as any I have witnessed'.

From my perspective I could subscribe to all those comments.

The origins of this latest Balkan conflict lay in the stresses placed on the Federal Republic of Yugoslavia by the death of its post-war leader, Marshal Tito, in 1980 and by the collapse of communism across Europe in 1989. By then, Yugoslavia was dominated by the Serb leader, Slobodan Milosevic. He began to undermine the country's finely balanced system of regional autonomy, determined that a 'Greater Serbia' should rise from the ashes of Yugoslavia. The lever for this new state was the large Serb population in Croatia and Bosnia-Herzegovina, two of Yugoslavia's many republics. Milosevic's ambitions for Serbia led other republics to assert themselves: on the Austrian border, prosperous Slovenia prepared for independence; in Croatia, Milosevic was matched by the Croat leader Franjo

Tudjman, whose nationalism enraged the minority of Serbs in Krajina and eastern Slavonia. They in turn began to agitate for independence, and to look to Belgrade.

All sides exhumed memories from Yugoslavia's crypt of ethnic murder. When, in June 1991, Croatia followed Slovenia in declaring its independence, the Serbs in Croatia remembered their kin murdered by the country's fascist regime in World War II, and rebelled. Between July and August 1991, full-scale war broke out between Belgrade and Zagreb over the Serbian areas of Croatia. By November the Croatian city of Vukovar had fallen to the Serbs after the brutal shelling of its population.

The international community, fearful of violence on the borders of Western Europe, saw holding Yugoslavia together as the best chance of obtaining peace. The European Community appointed Lord Carrington, who had been Margaret Thatcher's first foreign secretary, as an intermediary, and the UN imposed an arms embargo. The Serbs blocked every idea Peter Carrington proposed. It became obvious that Tito's Yugoslavia, and its motto of 'brotherhood and unity', had gone for good.

Late on the evening of 16 December 1991 Douglas Hurd telephoned me at Finings to tell me that all the other eleven members of the European Community wanted to recognise Croatia's independence. Hans Dietrich Genscher, the veteran German Foreign Minister, was arguing that delay in recognition would encourage the Serbs to continue the war, and he made it clear that Germany would recognise Croatia unilaterally if the decision didn't go through. German public opinion, he had told his fellow foreign ministers, was outraged at Serbian atrocities. After agreement on minority rights was secured, the EC foreign ministers agreed to recognise Croatia. Peter Carrington was furious, arguing that the West had thrown away its only opportunity to oblige the Yugoslav republics to treat their minorities humanely and agree a settlement prior to independence. But Germany had prevailed.

A myth arose from this: that Britain capitulated on recognition of Croatia as a shady *quid pro quo* for German help over the negotiation of the Maastricht Treaty. This is a preposterous notion, and utterly untrue. It was given credence by Genscher's comment to the effect that 'We helped you on Maastricht, please listen to us on this one.' This was a personal plea made by him, not the opening sentence of a bargain to which we were committed. We got our way at Maastricht because I refused to sign the treaty unless we did. I did not owe the Germans any favours over Maastricht, and Douglas Hurd did not agree to recognise Croatia on that account.

The recognition of Croatia – and Slovenia – as independent states by the European Community in December 1991 set a precedent which led to the recognition of Bosnia in 1992, and is seen by some as the cause of the war in Yugoslavia. This is simply not so. The shelling of Vukovar and the expulsion of its Croatian population took place well before the recognition of the two republics: in Croatia, at least, the war was already underway when we recognised the country's independence. *If* there was a single cause of the war, it was the expansionist nationalism Milosevic employed to propel himself up the greasy pole of Serbian politics. Peter Carrington may be right to believe that by recognising the Yugoslav republics as independent states we surrendered a negotiating card too soon, but subsequent events do not suggest that withholding recognition would have prevented the evil that followed.

In February 1992 the former US Secretary of State Cyrus Vance, as the UN's representative, brokered the introduction of a UN Protection Force (UNPROFOR) into the Serbian areas of Croatia, and for three years UN troops successfully kept an uneasy peace there. This, however, was only the overture to Yugoslavia's misery. With the secession of Slovenia and Croatia, Bosnia was left dangerously exposed and with an unenviable choice: it could stay in a rump Yugoslavia dominated by Milosevic's Serbian nationalism, or it could take the risk of trying to leave. After a referendum, it chose the latter, and President Alija Izetbegovic's declaration of independence on 6 April 1992 brought a bitter war down upon Bosnia. Radovan Karadzic, leader of the Bosnian Serbs, responded by simultaneously declaring 'Republika Srpska', a Serb state within Bosnia, with Sarajevo as the capital 'currently under enemy occupation'. Fighting broke out, most viciously in eastern Bosnia. In May 1992 a Serb assault on Sarajevo led to a three-year siege of the city, and by the summer of 1992 the Bosnian Serbs, with aid from the by now largely Serbianised Yugoslav National Army, had over-run 70 per cent of Bosnia-Herzegovina. Vast columns of refugees – three-quarters of a million by June – fled as Serbian forces terrorised the civilian population. Ugly rumours circulated about 'ethnic cleansing' – the murder or compulsory expulsion of civilian members of different ethnic or religious groups; by August the existence of starving thousands in detention camps was revealed to the world. Hell's kitchen was cooking.

On 18 August 1992 I broke into my summer holiday and flew back to London for a six-hour emergency meeting in the Cobra Room beneath 10 Downing Street to consider what Britain could do to ease this terrible situation. I had asked the military chiefs of staff whether the three warring factions could be kept apart, and if so, how many troops would be needed to do the job. The answer was startling: 400,000 – nearly three times the size of the whole British Army. Moreover, any commitment of peacekeeping troops on the ground could be very long-term; it was not easy to imagine how troops, once in place, could be brought home. It was inconceivable that anything could be done without full-scale NATO involvement, and that was not forthcoming. Other countries too, no doubt, had made the same bleak military assessment.

In these circumstances our policy had to be dictated by two concerns: to save as many lives as we could while the slaughter continued, and to do all in our power to limit the conflict. At our meeting in the Cobra Room, the chiefs of staff told me that eight hundred men could successfully protect humanitarian convoys – which would get food to the refugees – and defend themselves, but if attacked, 1,800 men could defend themselves better, be more self-contained, and carry out more work. We decided to send 1,800 men. The French and the Canadians also sent troops.

At the time, many politicians and commentators argued that this decision was mistaken, that Britain had no strategic interest in the Balkans. I disagreed. I had no doubt that there were sound policy reasons to justify sending in our troops. Quite apart from humanitarian concerns, there were other flashpoints which an early international presence in Bosnia might subdue. Particularly worrying was Kosovo, a holy land for the Serbs but with a majority Albanian population and a militant minority of Serbs. I feared a full-blown Balkan war on the very borders of the European Union.

In the Commons, reaction to our decision to send troops to help the convoys was mixed, which strongly suggested to me that the old Cold War consistencies of British politics were breaking up. Tories robustly connected to the right wing and normally pro-military, like Sir Nicholas Bonsor, did not support action over Bosnia, while others in and beyond the Conservative Party were urging military adventures. Foreign policy had always contained a reliable left–right fracture. Now the fracture was along some more obscure axis, and within both the left and the right. An unlikely coalition against our policy was thrown together: left-wingers like Tony Benn, middle-ground pragmatists like Ted Heath, and right-wingers like George Gardiner.

No party was more split than the Conservatives, which was divided into four camps. Some argued that there was no British interest involved, and that we should have nothing to do with the war. Others thought we should try to deliver humanitarian aid, but not if our troops met opposition on the ground. Others urged us to bomb the Serb forces, and others still wanted both bombing and the deployment of ground troops. Overall, there was strong unease about growing British involvement in what were seen as treacherous conditions, with the risk of a military disaster.

These differing views were mirrored in the Cabinet. Even apart from questioning the cost of the operation, Ken Clarke and Michael Portillo were uneasy. Michael Heseltine was supportive but troubled about the policy, and Robert Cranborne and the Defence Secretary Malcolm Rifkind were equally dubious. Douglas Hurd and I, however, were completely committed to the use of troops to ease the plight of the civilian population in Bosnia. I was adamant that the danger of a trans-Balkan war meant that there *was* a British interest, and I also believed it would be immoral not to attempt to do something about such horrific and proximate suffering. In the face of reports that over a million Bosnians faced death from cold and hunger in the coming winter, I was compelled to send our troops to help ensure the delivery of food, medicine and blankets to the hungry, the sick and the cold. For all the bitter criticism we were to be subjected to as the horrific events in Bosnia unfolded, there was no clear consensus for an alternative policy, either in the Commons or in the country. At no point did the opposition call a division on the issue of Bosnia.

On 26 August 1992, a week after our decision to deploy troops, I jointly chaired a conference on Bosnia in London with the Secretary General of the UN, Boutros Boutros Ghali, in Britain's capacity as President of the European Union. Around thirty nations attended, together with representatives from all the warring parties. Rather embarrassingly, in one of those rare but not unheard-of diplomatic cock-ups, everybody forgot to invite the Russians. Moscow naturally thought this was no accident, and took umbrage. A hasty invitation was issued, and the Russian Foreign Minister Andrei Kozyrev joined the conference later. We were to have need of him.

Those who at the time were to brand the London Conference 'a triumph', and later 'a failure', were missing the point. It was never expected that it would 'solve' the Bosnian crisis. The conference was intended to provide a mechanism within which the political process could be taken forward, much as UN Resolution 242, which was passed over the Middle East in 1967, provided a framework that even today still governs mediation in that region. The process was merely intended to start at London.

The hope was that those participating in the conference would continue to meet. In September 1992 David Owen, who had been appointed the European Community's representative, and Cyrus Vance for the UN, set up a conference organisation in Geneva. Talks were to continue there between the Muslims, Croats and Serbs of Bosnia, and the Bosnian government. Our task that August was to make as auspicious a start as possible. In fact, merely holding the conference together was a struggle from start to finish. As it drew to a close the Dutch became very unhappy that it should end without our having formally admonished Serbia. Encouraged by Izetbegovic, the Dutch drew up a motion condemning the Serbs for their atrocities. The Serb delegation made it known that if the motion was tabled they would walk out. The Dutch said that if the motion was not tabled, *they* would walk out.

This impasse threatened to wreck the conference and give the Serbs an excuse for not getting around the table in future. I conferred with the other delegates, and Russia's Andrei Kozyrev was invaluable in bringing the Serb delegation around. A compromise was agreed: the Dutch motion would be tabled at the very last moment, and then the conference would be declared closed, with no time for discussion or a vote on it.

In my summing-up speech I duly handed the motions around the table, announced that everyone had read them, and closed the conference. Suddenly, the Albanian delegation made to address the conference, and were informed that it was too late. At that moment Milan Panic, the Yugoslav president who, in the pretence of hiding Greater Serbia behind 'Yugoslavia', Milosevic was allowing to represent the Serbian delegation rather than do so himself as the Serbian president, leapt to his feet on the other side of the conference room and pounded round to where I was sitting. He thanked me in a very demonstrative Balkan style for having rescued his delegation. It was not, of course, his delegation I was concerned about, but keeping dialogue in play.

At the conference, a revealing little farce had occurred. To Milosevic's fury, his placeman Panic turned out to be less pliant than he had expected him to be. Panic genuinely wanted to end the conflict, and kept making suggestions which I could see left Milosevic glowering in the second row. When Milosevic attempted to speak, Panic even passed him a piece of paper saying 'Shut up' in English. The two nearly came to blows in an adjoining room later. Milosevic soon moved to dispose of Panic. The very man who had negotiated the so-called 'Yugoslav' position with us at the conference found himself the subject of a no-confidence vote three days after he returned to Belgrade. It was just one instance of the long farce which characterised negotiations with the former Yugoslavia.

On paper a great deal of progress was made at the conference. The warring parties assented to the conference's demands: UN supervision of heavy weapons; an agreement to recognise the borders of Bosnia; and a 'no-fly zone' over its skies (though in the event this was not enforced against helicopters, for military reasons). They even agreed in principle to the return of the refugees and to setting up tribunals to investigate crimes against humanity. It looked like a decisive breakthrough.

We soon learned that an 'agreement' made with states of the former Yugoslavia is one of history's less useful pieces of paper. No side kept its promises. The Serb delegation never honoured any undertakings it made at all.

Our troops duly arrived on the ground in Bosnia in November 1992. The aid agencies were doing their best to relieve the suffering of the civilian population, which was on a scale unseen in Europe since the Second World War, but they needed protection if the convoys bearing food and medicines were to get through. Our troops were playing a part in providing that protection.

In December the Americans put forward a four-point plan to protect the aid convoys, including the enforcement of a ban on military flights over Bosnia-Herzegovina and a lifting of the UN arms embargo. Whilst we agreed with the objective, we had two worries: the US military did not seem to know *how* to enforce the flight ban, and the British troops deployed along a tenuous 150-mile-long axis were very vulnerable to the threatened retaliation of the Bosnian Serbs. The Americans soon saw this point.

Two days before Christmas I went to see the situation for myself. I flew to the Adriatic port of Split, then took a helicopter to a scrubby field on the Bosnian–Croatian border that had been secured by British infantrymen in blue UN helmets. I was met by Lieutenant Colonel Bob Stewart, commander of the 1st Battalion of the Cheshire Regiment, and taken to see the troops. As we climbed a hill the British base appeared before us. The troops had constructed a wooden stockade reminiscent of the Wild West to defend themselves. The Cheshire Regiment and Royal Engineers, operating from 'Fort Redoubt', as it was called, were making their presence felt in a harsh Bosnian winter, getting aid through and damping down the fighting where they could, in spite of the dangers they faced each day.

On the way back I visited the transport and engineer base at Tomaslavgrad. It was surrounded by huge UN lorries driven by female soldiers. We went into their barracks, and I was surprised to see that each of the drivers had a collection of teddy bears and soft toys on her pillow, one image which hitherto I had not associated with the army. The nearby village had a mosque and a Catholic church whose bell was ringing. Many of the houses had Christmas trees on their front porches. Peace on earth, but only to men of goodwill.

Early in the New Year, following attacks on British troops Malcolm Rifkind asked for reinforcements of key personnel and the deployment of an aircraft-carrier group to the Adriatic, equipped with an air group and light-gun battery. This was agreed. We also prepared for the deployment of heavy artillery and air support. Our concern that our commitment would grow was coming true sooner than we had imagined.

In February 1993 I met President Clinton at the White House. It was clear to me that he wished to do more to help our effort, but that he was hamstrung by US domestic opinion. David Owen and Cyrus Vance were developing a proposal to divide Bosnia between the warring parties. Troops would be needed to implement the plan and keep the sides apart, but the Americans simply weren't ready to provide them.

The President and I discussed the matter over a dinner also attended by Vice President Al Gore. George Bush had understood the importance to us of the safety of our troops when I had visited him in December 1992. Since then American opinion had become almost evangelical for the policy of 'lift and strike' – lifting the arms embargo and starting air strikes against the Bosnian Serbs – which greatly concerned us. In our discussions it became clear that there was an element of campaign rhetoric from the run-up to the presidential election of November 1992 in 'lift and strike', which the President was now content to re-evaluate. I left with the impression that, however close-run the decision might be, in the end, those in favour of 'lift and strike' would not carry the day.

While the troops tried to bring a semblance of normality to the war zone, the breathing space which they had created needed to be taken further, with a diplomatic settlement between the warring parties. But none seemed likely, and the Americans were making it clear that they were opposed to the proposed Vance–Owen peace plan. They did not approve of the way it cantonised the region, which they saw as a concession to the Serbs. As American opinion crystallised, policy disagreements over how to handle Bosnia were to widen into the most serious Anglo–American disagreement since the Suez Crisis over thirty years before.

I understood the American evaluation of the situation and their decision not to get involved on the ground; the American military was giving their government the same advice about the inadvisability of deploying troops as ours was. The memory of Vietnam was seared deep in the American mind. Politically as well, the Americans were inclined not to become engaged, not least because the crisis was in the EC's backyard at the moment that Europe was anxious to develop as a credible force internationally. Jacques Poos, Luxembourg's foreign minister, had famously declared, 'The age of Europe has dawned.' This, together with the recent débâcle over Somalia and the fact that the Americans had only just led the liberation of Kuwait, meant that the United States felt inclined to take a back seat over Bosnia.

This I accepted. More difficult to accept was that, having declined to put troops on the ground, some American politicians channelled the domestic protests against the conflict into demands that the administration implement the 'lift and strike' option. Gallingly, this approach avoided committing American troops, yet maintained a high moral tone and a strident appearance of engagement with the crisis. The neatness of the 'lift and strike' formula belied the fatal damage it would do to humanitarian operations; air strikes *on* former Yugoslavia were incompatible with neutral missions *within* former Yugoslavia to deliver humanitarian aid, and would put our troops on the ground at great risk. But public and political opinion put the US administration under great strain, and led to proposals we sometimes had to resist. It was a serious split.

Over the weekend of 19 April 1993 I spoke to Presidents Clinton and Mitterrand about Bosnia. President Clinton told me he did not have 'a settled policy', but was opposed to air strikes and leaning towards lifting the arms embargo on the Bosnian Muslims – although he said wryly that he was receiving differing advice on the subject. The Russians, too, were strongly opposed to lifting the embargo. President Mitterrand was blunt: he was *very* opposed to both air strikes *and* the provision of ground forces.

A week later I held a Cabinet committee meeting to discuss the options. We did not believe that lifting the arms embargo would give the Muslims the decisive advantage claimed for it, nor did we believe that air attacks would work. We did not lightly rule either out. I had asked the Chiefs of Staff about the feasibility of bombing to protect civilians. They advised that it would be almost impossible due to the meteorological and geographic features of Bosnia, and the highly confused situation on the ground.

Nor did they consider that air power alone was sufficient to end the conflict without ground troops. Even in the Gulf War it had not done so; and the flat terrain and favourable weather conditions in Iraq had provided optimal conditions for the use of air power. In Bosnia, the reverse position applied. The oft-present cloud cover in that mountainous region meant an aircraft typically had to fly under a blanket of cloud along a valley floor, at a low level which made it vulnerable to missile attack from the ground. In these conditions targets were visible only very fleetingly.

We had another concern. If we bombed, our soldiers would be at risk from reprisals. The Bosnian Serbs had repeatedly made clear that they would retaliate against UN troops from NATO countries on the ground (and indeed all UN and aid-agency workers), and in December 1992 I received a letter from the Bosnian serb leader Radovan Karadzic to this effect. This reinforced concerns the military had raised: protection from such threats was impossible in the conditions in which the troops were working without massive reinforcements.

Nor did we favour lifting the arms embargo, which had been put in place by the UN and the EC to prevent the war from intensifying and spreading. We felt that the likely result of lifting it would be the Serbs deciding to launch a full-scale war, to capture as much territory as possible before the new weapons came into the equation. The UN mission would be lost, as it could not stay amidst such a level of conflict – UNPROFOR was already working at the limit of the acceptable risk, and sometimes beyond it. The Croats might well decide that they couldn't afford to miss out on a final carve-up of territory, and rejoin the fighting. Bosnia would go under before the new weapons even arrived. If America, NATO and the UN wanted to avoid a humanitarian catastrophe they would have to fight a costly war to defend the Bosnian state. This was the key point: 'lift and strike' was founded on a wilful misreading of the realities. The persuasive moral case for lifting the embargo was only superficially compelling. To UN personnel on the ground, its presentation as a quick-fix solution was baffling and dangerous. They said forcibly that it was being demanded by those interested in attractive and fast solutions to the war, and those who wanted to use it as another stick with which to beat the UN.

Nonetheless, we did think long and hard about how justifiable the arms embargo was. It caused much heart-searching. The Bosnian Serbs had clear military superiority, especially in heavy weapons 'inherited' from the Yugoslav army, and there seemed a strong moral case to allow the Bosnian Muslims to even up the odds stacked against them. People's sense of justice was understandably offended by the embargo. The Bosnian Muslims presented the West's enforcement of it as a clear example of moral culpability for the suffering of the Bosnian people, an argument that made an impression amongst the Western public and in Washington, where the administration remained attached to 'lift and strike'. In May, Warren Christopher, the US Secretary of State, toured Europe to advocate the policy, but found no enthusiasm for it anywhere – although by then the Germans were flirting with lifting the embargo, but not with air strikes. There were other initiatives that came to nothing. The French proposed that they – together with the US, Russia and Britain – should put forces into Muslim towns at risk of attack, but this fell when the US barely entertained the idea.

In Bosnia our forces had settled down, but on the day of the Queen's Birthday parade Malcolm Rifkind was concerned about the possibility of reprisals against our troops after reports that a British UNPROFOR soldier had shot a Serb. Malcolm and I decided to speak to the local British commander. He was unfussed: 'No problem, Prime Minister. We've bagged quite a few snipers, but this was the only one the press saw. When they shoot at us, we shoot back. Those are the normal rules in the Balkans. They think it's fair enough. Still, we'll take care. I ought to tell the chaps to put on their helmets for a day or two.'

On Sunday, 25 July 1993 senior British and American officials met privately for three and a half hours at the Goring Hotel in London. The background was bleak. The viciousness of the fighting in Bosnia had meant that civilian supplies of food were breaking down, and the danger of starvation over the next winter was growing. The Serbs were strangling Sarajevo and blocking any constructive peace talks in Geneva. At the Goring Hotel it became clear that the US had decided to actively seek a 'realistic' settlement and help impose it. Worried at the prospective cry of 'Who lost Bosnia?' if the Serbs prevailed, and at the damage being done to the transatlantic relationship, they proposed to help implement and enforce an agreement between Serbs, Croats and Muslims under a credible threat of air strikes. Nor did they rule out US troops on the ground. They wanted a ceasefire and a sovereign Bosnia, but had no preconceptions about a final settlement. 'It is,' one US delegate said, 'the only chance to make lemonade out of lemons.' It was a pivotal change.

But a political settlement was not easily achievable, despite the constant search for one. None of the leaders of the warring groups showed an appetite for peaceful compromise despite the suffering of their peoples. By early 1994 the international community had not yet launched air strikes against the Serbs, but were on the verge of doing so. It was a gloomy time as the aid operation became more risky and a settlement seemed more distant. I was at home at Finings on Saturday, 5 February when I was told that a mortar bomb had been fired into an open-air market in Sarajevo, killing nearly seventy people and wounding over two hundred others. The obvious suspects were the Serbs – who vehemently denied responsibility – and later technical evidence suggested that the mortar came from a Bosnian position. No one was ever certain: both sides were capable of it. Nonetheless, it did not stop President Izetbegovic from saying pointedly, 'We feel condemned to death. Every government which supports the arms embargo against this country is an accomplice to acts of atrocity such as this.'

The Sarajevo mortar spurred diplomatic and military activity. Within days, in response to a request from the UN, NATO gave the Serbs ten days to withdraw from Sarajevo or place their heavy weapons under the control of UN forces. We instructed John Weston, our Ambassador to the UN, to agree that NATO should carry out air strikes in the event of further artillery or mortar attacks on Sarajevo. We also responded to a request from General Michael Rose, the commander of UNPROFOR, and dispatched a further battalion group to Bosnia. In March progress was made in withdrawing heavy weapons, and by the summer Warren Christopher was setting out aims for the Geneva peace conference that still included lifting the arms embargo.

To illustrate the folly of simply lifting the embargo, General Michael Rose took General John Galvin, President Clinton's special adviser, to see the Bosnian army in the field. As Galvin became familiar with the situation he accepted Rose's point that a flood of imported weapons would make little difference to it. The army's woeful lack of training and command disciplines were what hobbled it, and it was several years away from resolving these problems. The Bosnians demonstrated their failings time and again with ill-planned offensives which ended in disaster. The main factor preventing the defeat of the Bosnian Muslims and Bosnia was not the Bosnian army, with or without new weapons, but the presence of the UN troops, which almost alone gave the 'Bosnian state' meaningful territorial definition on the ground. The Americans finally began to revise the assumptions on which short-term solutions like 'lift and strike' were based. Later – in what was not perhaps a coincidence – President Izetbegovic announced that he was 'deferring' his request to lift the embargo for six months. Throughout the conflict 'lift and strike' had been the magic solution. Now, as it came to its climax, the beneficiary of 'lift' had asked for a deferral.

Soon the limitations of 'strike' also became evident when, after a series of air strikes in May 1995 to protect Sarajevo, the Bosnian Serbs duly took 250 UN personnel hostage, including thirty-three Royal Welch Fusiliers and an RAF officer acting as monitor. Most distressingly, they were used as human shields, being chained to heavy guns to ward off future NATO assaults. We held an emergency OPD meeting, at which the increasing gravity of the situation began to shake the confidence of many present as to the viability of the mission. Parliament was recalled in an emergency sitting to discuss the crisis on 31 May, and we warned the Bosnian Serbs of severe consequences if the hostages were harmed in any way. They were not, but the episode illustrated how dangerous it was for peacekeepers to be seen as war-fighters. The activities of the peacekeepers and convoy protectors had always been extremely hazardous, politically and physically. Both French and British peacekeepers were frequently the target of attempts to kill them from isolated and not-so-isolated elements of all three warring parties, who saw them either as enemies or as supporting the other side. It was evident that the peacekeepers and aid deliverers could only perform their functions so long as they were seen not to be favorably disposed towards any side. All this was foreseeable in 1992, and we had consistently argued so – to the accompaniment of much abuse from politicians and others who wished to grandstand from the safety of their armchairs, but had no responsibility for the lives of the peacekeepers on the ground.

The hostage crisis was far from the end of Serbian aggression. It flared up again in early July, with attacks on UN convoys and bases and assaults on Sarajevo, Srebrenica and other towns. When Srebrenica fell to the Serbs many of the inhabitants were slaughtered. There was an angry international demand – led by Paris and Washington – for a severe response, but without a full-scale land invasion, the question remained of what it could be. There was no agreement.

On Friday, 14 July 1995 I reconvened the London Conference for the following week, against disobliging noises from those who favoured action before consideration. I wished to see coordinated policy, not hot-headed action. The conference broke the stalemate. By the end of it the US had dropped their insistence on generalised bombing, and the French had set to one side some fairly hair-raising plans for the recapture of Srebrenica. We agreed to send an Anglo–French Rapid Reaction Force of 1,700 to Sarajevo, to defend the city against attack, and also that Bosnian Serb aggression would be met by disproportionate and punitive military attacks. This ultimatum was triggered by yet another mortar attack on Sarajevo market on 29 August, which killed thirty-seven people.

An air campaign then began. The technical problems remained, but all else had radically changed. The Bosnian Serbs had lost the political sponsorship of the Russians and, for their own cynical reasons, of Milosevic and his government in Belgrade; sanctions were beginning to bite, and Milosevic was concerned for his political position. The Americans were now diplomatically engaged in the conflict as never before. The Croats had built an army and armed it; they were defeating and ethnically cleansing Serbs in Croatia. The Croat Muslim Federation was attacking in western Bosnia. And the Bosnian Serbs faced a much stronger UN Rapid Reaction Force around Sarajevo, armed with mortars and heavy artillery. All these factors made air strikes credible, but even then they were not the decisive factor in rolling back the Serbian forces. A political settlement had also been tabled which was acceptable to the parties for the first time. None of this had applied when we said no to air strikes. Now it did.

The Dayton Peace Conference began on 31 October 1995 in Ohio. Sixty thousand NATO troops would oversee the implementation of the agreement, including, at last, the crucial American ground forces which the Vance–Owen plan had been denied. Despite Jacques Poos's premature declaration of Europe's influence, American involvement was, from the start, indispensable to a full and final settlement. It was a tragedy that it took three years before it was forthcoming. As the peace treaty was formally signed in Paris in December, the Western world looked on contentedly, wrongly thinking it had seen the last of the killing in the Balkans.

What is so striking, looking back, is the conspiracy of Yugoslavia's politicians, from all sides, willingly to start a war which brought so much death and destruction to their own towns and people, and to continue that war so unflinchingly. Ignoring the mediators, Slovenia decided that war – mercifully brief, as it turned out – was the best path to its independence and freedom. Serbia, and Croatia up until the eleventh hour, played with the Pandora's box of nationalism and proclaimed it to be a policy of national renewal. The Bosnian Muslim government was adamant that an early end to the fighting had to be avoided at all costs.

Yugoslavia could have gently gravitated from communism towards Western and Central Europe. Democracy and the development of the free market, trade and a rise in the standard of living were closer at hand there than in many other Eastern European states. Yet the old communist hands and the new nationalist leaders of emerging states alike calmly identified nationalism and war as the most rational policies to follow in the last decade of the twentieth century, and unhesitatingly prescribed them for their people.

This isn't to say that all were equally guilty. Milosevic was the driving force, and did most to trigger the war deliberately. Nevertheless, he did not act alone. Franjo Tudjman spoke nauseatingly of his 'destiny' to create an ethnically pure Croatian state larger than at any time in its history. Early in 1991 Tudjman and Milosevic began a series of meetings and worked out how both could simultaneously pursue their goals of nationalist expansion: by sharing the spoils in a division of Bosnia. This sort of treachery filtered down from the top. At no stage did any of the leaders stop and vote for peace, community and the lives of their miserable subjects. How were negotiators supposed to negotiate when the twisted logic and self-interest of Yugoslav leaders was in favour of bloodshed?

There are many villains in the sad tale of Bosnia, but there are unsung heroes too. I am not a starry-eyed supporter of the United Nations, but it was appalling the way the UN effort in Bosnia, and Britain's support for it, was traduced. It is bizarre that in the popular imagination British policy was seen as a callous washing of hands in the face of the nightly suffering of the innocent on the nation's television screens. Many countries did nothing to help the people of Bosnia. Britain wasn't one of them.

Our critics were numerous, and the constant drip-drip effect of their derision of our policy was very damaging. There was no shortage of crusaders demanding the impossible. Most of them ignored the infinite complexities of the Bosnian situation and wilfully brushed aside what the UN was able (and mandated) to do.

Many journalists, parachuted into Bosnia by their news organisations, and looking through those black-and-white eyes that make punchy stories, were drawn into the logic which dictated that the fruits of UN-brokered diplomatic and supply efforts be ignored. So the Western public rarely heard, for example, that for a long period during 1994 the utilities in Sarajevo were reconnected, trams were running, sniping ceased and consumer goods appeared in the shops. Meanwhile, as the Bosnian government railed at how useless the UN effort was, the Bosnian people, whose lives were incomparably better thanks to the presence of UNPROFOR, would thank UN soldiers in the streets, and say that as long as they were there they felt safe. Yet, outside Bosnia, the daily struggle and success of the UN mission passed so many people by. Its greatest triumphs were preventative, so its achievements tended to be ignored. 'Thousands of people saved from death in Bosnia' is not, unfortunately, newsworthy.

I saw for myself the simple truth of the impressive and unacknowledged impact that the presence of British troops had on the everyday lives of Sarajevans when I visited Sarajevo in March 1993 and toured it with General Michael Rose. We had got out of our car and were looking down a road known as 'sniper alley' in the centre of the city, along which two British soldiers were walking on patrol. I mentioned that I couldn't see any snipers, and General Rose pointed to one up ahead of us, a hundred yards away and within range. My protection officers went white, but the General was unconcerned. 'Look at those British soldiers patrolling,' he said. 'We control the ground here. Unlike everybody else, we have experience in Northern Ireland, which means that we can control these streets. They shoot at us, we kill them. They know that. They aren't going to shoot.'

We toured Sarajevo that afternoon, and I saw the extent of the British contribution. When we found a Russian armoured car allegedly guarding a bridge, General Rose banged on the side of the vehicle, to discover the Russian troops inside fast asleep. He was not impressed.

On the flight home, I was briefed in the cargo hold of a Hercules aircraft by a young pilot who flew in relief supplies. He told me that British aid aircraft had a radar system which chimed when missiles were fired at them, but that Russian aircraft did not. 'Isn't that nerve-racking?' I asked him. 'Why die knowing?' was his laconic response.

Lieutenant Colonel Bob Stewart, who like General Rose distinguished himself in Bosnia, was far from disillusioned with the UN mission, writing later:

> I believe the United Nations has achieved a great deal in Bosnia. We were sent there ... at a time when some people were fore-casting that hundreds of thousands of people were going to die in Central and Northern Bosnia that winter. Thanks to the collective efforts of UNHCR and UNPROFOR who worked closely together this did not happen ... Hunger and cold were the enemies we went into Bosnia to tackle, and I think we succeeded.

Were these achievements ignored because they were accomplished without fuss and ceremony, regarded as unremarkable because they were happening on a daily basis? I suspect the UN mission was the victim of its own success in turning the extraordinary into the mundane, and I was very much aware at the time how disgracefully the role played by British soldiers, and the UN effort in general, was traduced.

This is not a defence of all Western policy in Bosnia. As Douglas Hurd reflected later: 'Humility is in order among those of us who handled policy towards Bosnia. We were groping for a way to end a savage war which went on far too long.' This is true, and is deeply felt by everyone who had a responsi-bility for policy-making. For Britain's part, operating with the UN under constraints which drastically limited our options, I feel there was no alterna-tive policy which would have been better than the one that we followed. Had there been an alternative policy at any stage which was within our power and would have saved more lives, I would have taken it.

British soldiers (along with the French the largest in the UN contingent as a whole) often had to accept the bad to stave off the worse, sometimes the horrific to stave off the unthinkable. The UN never had sufficient troops to unilaterally impose itself, so it had to run on compromise and cooperation with the warring parties. That wasn't the UN's fault. Or Britain's. Or France's. The people of Bosnia were trapped in a vicious civil war in which the worst frequently happened to the most vulnerable. Too often – through lack of troops – the UN was obliged not to act in horrific circumstances it either could not see, had to ignore, was miles away from, or was powerless to stop. It is only fitting that this should be freely admitted, though it should be remembered that much of the most thorough ethnic cleansing took place in eastern Bosnia, where there was no UNPROFOR presence.

It was a tragedy for the people of Bosnia that the crisis occurred when it did, at a time when NATO, the EC and America were all unsure of their international roles, and the art of peacekeeping in the post-Cold War world was still unborn. As a leader of one member of the international community I accept the blame that must fall on all our shoulders for the inadequacy of the outside world's response to the crisis both then and in subsequent years. Yet it should be acknowledged that Britain did far more than most.

# CHAPTER TWENTY-THREE

# *Unparliamentary Behaviour*

THERE IS A GOOD CHANCE that, when many of the achievements of the last Conservative government this century have been forgotten, people will still remember one word: 'sleaze'. It was a charge hurled indiscriminately at the government as a whole because of the behaviour of a small number of individual Conservatives. It stuck because – even if the flames were fanned by the media and the opposition – the conduct of that handful genuinely dismayed a large number of people, including many Conservative supporters. The party paid a high price for the self-indulgence of that minority. 'Sleaze has been the dominant factor throughout,' said Labour during the 1997 general election, 'and sleaze has been the end issue. Nothing better encapsulates what people think of this government. Sleaze will be one of the things that brings this government down.'

And, in a way, it was. Not, as the opposition and some of the media liked to imply, because the charges against these individuals were all necessarily grave; mostly, they were not. Nor because these charges were all proven; often, they were not. But it fed the public belief that the Conservative Party as an institution had been in government for too long, and had got into bad habits. As the mood music to the final act, sleaze chimed with the times. The charges, endlessly repeated even when untrue, hurt us in the eyes of the electorate, and hurt our own self-belief. They hurt us still. Our critics chose the term shrewdly, and used it unscrupulously.

History will wonder why, when the behaviour of Conservative MPs in the 1990s was no more culpable – and often less so – than that of earlier generations of politicians, we suffered as they often had not. It will wonder too why the Labour government which took office on 2 May 1997 escaped the opprobrium heaped on our heads, despite revelations about the personal behaviour of senior members of the government and, on two occasions at least, changes in government policy that were convenient for large donors to Labour coffers.

The word 'sleaze' itself was a potent factor in the destructiveness of the issue. Its power lay in the fact that it was, at the same time, a very strong word and a very weak one. Strong in its ability to convey a generalised sense of decadence and wickedness. Strong in its catch-all ability to encompass everything from sexual sin to official malpractice. But weak in its capacity to identify with precision any actual misbehaviour. Under its broad branches gathered a huddle of tales: about 'cash for questions', some true, some serious; about 'arms-to-Iraq', all, in the end, disproved; and about personal shortcomings, in my view not significant to the conduct of government; all tales which had little in common bar the assertion, by those with a vested interest in saying so, that they were all 'sleaze', and all our fault.

I took a puritanical view of financial misbehaviour, a tolerant view of personal misdemeanours, and was frankly indignant and angry about the charges over Iraq. I was keen on openness – to correct the atmosphere which had grown up over cash for questions, to resist calls for the regulation of the press, and to remove the slurs over arms-to-Iraq. I sought to judge every allegation by reference to two points: whether it was true, and whether it constituted an abuse of public office. Nothing else, so far as I was concerned, was relevant.

I shared the public concern that some MPs were benefiting financially from improper behaviour, and reacted with speed to claims that ministers had acted dishonestly over defence exports to Iraq. In both cases I set up open and independent inquiries, even though I was accused of naïvety for doing so, because the issue then received prolonged coverage. I was unrepentant: such charges had to be proven or dismissed. My open approach also led me to respond with fury to the paper-thin claims that personal misdemeanours by a handful of Conservative MPs counted as sleaze *by the government*. In this regard we fell victim to an opposition without scruple and to a press without sympathy. The Conservative Party did not invent sin or sex, but it suffered from a great appetite to uncover – in some cases almost to initiate and to encourage – scandals about personal morality.

In July 1992 I was driving back to Finings after lunch with David and Carina Frost when my Cabinet colleague David Mellor phoned me in the car to tell me that a story was likely to appear in the *People* newspaper revealing that he had had an affair with an actress. He did not deny it, and broadly told me the details. I was sympathetic, concerned for the feelings of his wife Judith, and certain that the news did not affect his capacity to do his job as Minister for National Heritage. The story, however, proved to be the start of what became one of the silliest sagas in modern British politics: the hunt, using fair means or foul, by the tabloid press for gossip about the private lives of Tory Members of Parliament.

It soon became a routine. The phone would ring at Finings on Saturday, and I would be warned by my office that 'there could be a difficult story' the next day. I was never sure if the story would be printed, or what the details would be, or even whether it was true. Usually I knew it ought to have been beneath attention. Always, I knew it would cause a storm.

My instinct was to presume innocence unless and until shown otherwise, and in the interim to support the individual, not join the instant chorus of pretended outrage. I sacked ministers whose conduct in office breached the established rules of government, but I did not wish to dispose of people because of tittle-tattle, inconvenient to me, in the *News of the World*. Perhaps I should have been harder-hearted, for this inclination to fairness carried a political cost. I was seen as vacillating, the government as soiled, and if the minister resigned in the end, it was said I had caved in to press bombardment. I was prepared to put up with that for the sake of acting justly. I expected the climate to turn, and in any normal political cycle it would have done so. But with the Conservative Party mortally wounded over Europe, our blood was in the water and the media sharks circled until polling day. 'It just can't go on,' I would think each time another story broke. 'Surely there can't be any more.' But there always are if you look hard enough; and lots of people were looking.

In the absence of more substantial news stories, sex and sin sells newspapers. Once the public and media appetite for personal disgrace gains hold, any group of 650 men and women of any age will be able to supply examples of questionable behaviour. If the appetite is strong enough, the most trivial of misdemeanours will do. It is my belief that the level of sin in our political system holds fairly steady. It is the media appetite for reporting it which goes in waves.

'An affair with an actress?' the French politician Jack Lang exclaimed in amusement not long after the David Mellor story broke. 'Why else does one become minister of culture?' David had breached none of the guidelines for ministerial conduct, and any explanation was owed primarily to his wife and family. Early on the morning the story appeared I telephoned Robin Butler, the Cabinet Secretary, to discuss the matter. It was a simple conversation. Robin advised that there was no security aspect, and I therefore decided that David should not leave office.

And he did not. He survived the summer scandal, the victim of appalling innuendo and downright lies, remaining in office until September. He would have survived – as Robin Cook was to do six years later – somewhat tarnished, perhaps, if it had not been for fresh allegations that he had accepted a holiday in Spain from the daughter of the Treasurer of the Palestine Liberation Organisation. I spoke once again to Robin Butler. This time there was a question as to whether David's conduct was proper for a minister, even one with no involvement in overseas policy. I was inclined towards asking for David's resignation, but what finally led to it was the response of the backbench 1922 Committee, who were determined that David should go. The story developed as the government was assailed from other directions, by Black Wednesday and by the dispute over our plans to close much of the coalmining industry. None of this helped David.

I don't think my judgement on David Mellor was disturbed by all this, but it encouraged the party to feel that caution was best, and that he should depart. He made a wry resignation speech on 24 September 1992, blaming 'a constant barrage of stories about me in certain tabloid newspapers'. David behaved with good grace throughout, and came to see me several times afterwards to say how grateful he was for my support at the time. Thus the first scalp was taken.

It was a bleak period, and of all the high-profile issues facing the government, that relating to David Mellor was unquestionably the least substantial. I dismissed it as an unfortunate one-off, hardly suspecting that it was the first in a series of such difficulties. I had moved quickly, and according to my instinct about what was proper, both in July, when I made sure David did not resign, and in September, when fresh allegations meant that he had to do so.

Not many months later, in early 1993, I was compelled to take an action for libel against the *New Statesman & Society*, which had repeated crude and untrue claims (originally made in an ill-regarded and little-known satirical magazine) that I had had an affair with Clare Latimer, who ran a private catering company often used by Downing Street. Rumours had been swilling around Fleet Street for some time, I learned. They had no basis in truth. There being nothing to find, reporters found nothing, and only innuendo appeared in the mainstream press. Nevertheless, I gained the impression that it contributed to an insolent undercurrent in press reports.

To take legal action can give legs to a story which otherwise stands a good chance of dying within days; and it looks undignified – defensive, almost – for a prime minister to sue a penniless rag or a low-circulation, highbrow magazine over a bit of nonsense to which few serious people would have given any credence anyway. But a presumption has been growing in Britain in recent decades that 'no comment' means 'guilty'. A simple denial, followed by no action taken, encourages many these days to speculate that there may be something in a story. The press, though they often complain about the laws of defamation, are quick to raise an eyebrow and note pointedly that someone has not sued. Such was the atmosphere at the time that I judged that if I took no notice of the story it would echo around indefinitely, working its way from magazines to the serious pages of newspapers, and finally breaking cover in serious commentaries as an 'unanswered question'.

I was not prepared to put Norma, Clare Latimer, my children or myself at risk in this way, and decided to knock the story on the head. The matter was eventually settled out of court. I had no desire to go through a protracted legal procedure, nor to bankrupt the magazine; I simply wanted to ensure that no one else repeated a libel which by that time was generally recognised as such.

This did not, however, put paid to media muckraking. In October 1993 I made my annual speech to the Conservative Party Conference. It was a speech that was to be hung around my neck. 'The message from this conference is clear and simple,' I said.

> We must go back to basics. We want our children to be taught the best; our public service to give the best; our British industry to be the best. And the Conservative Party will lead the country back to these basics right across the board: sound money; free trade; traditional teaching; respect for the family and the law. And above all, lead a new campaign to defeat the cancer that is crime.

These sentiments seemed to me unexceptional. They expressed things I did (and do) believe, things that matter to me and ought to matter to any mainstream politician. I did not think of the speech as remotely controversial, though I did want our attention to these values to be expressed with emphasis, and to be noticed. Rereading the speech now I find it, if anything, somewhat trite; but that hardly distinguishes it from a score of other leaders' speeches at party conferences. At the time, this one seemed to go down rather well. The press liked it and picked up on it. 'Back to basics' might prove, I hoped, a keynote for the years ahead.

It certainly did, but not in the way I had wished.

In retrospect, it is easy to spot the dangers. Even before I spoke, a Central Office press officer, Tim Collins, now a Member of Parliament, had fielded a journalist's enquiry as to whether the 'basics' I had in mind included moral basics, and had confirmed that they did. It would have been eccentric for him to have answered otherwise; but I had, of course, no plan for a puritanical moral crusade – and had been faintly discomfited by some platform remarks by my Social Security Secretary, Peter Lilley, about moral values. John Redwood, too, had attacked parenthood outside marriage two months before the party conference, and was to do so again after it. But my 'back to basics' was not about bashing single mothers or preaching sexual fidelity at private citizens. I knew only too well the problems of single parenthood: both my sister and Norma's mother had brought up their children alone.

Some might have been led to believe that the comments by Peter Lilley and John Redwood were part of a campaign to suggest that a conservative moral revival was a government aim. It was not. I wanted nothing to do with a moral crusade under the title 'family policy'. I had always been extremely wary about politicians trespassing into the field of sexual morality, and hostile to any campaign which appeared to demonise any group.

On reflection, I should have seen the risk. The media interest was strong – the hounding of David Mellor bore testimony to that. Editors, ever hungry for human interest stories, still require a 'peg' on which to hang them, and one is the claim that the disclosures are being made 'in the public interest'. I, they decided, had now given them the opportunity to use this line of defence. From that day forward, any tittle-tattle about a parliamentary colleague could be published as a serious political news story, under the 'nose' (as I believe editors call it) of an opening paragraph along the lines of: 'Prime Minister John Major was last night severely embarrassed in his call for a return to moral basics by the shock disclosure that Mr X, now Junior Minister for Paper Clips, once spent a steamy night . . .' – and so on. I could write such stuff myself. Any fool could. Many fools did.

But that still lay ahead. I left Blackpool pleased to have made a solid speech which had been well-reported and well received by my party. I had no inkling how it would be perverted.

I soon learned that a junior minister, Tim Yeo, had fathered a child outside his marriage. The report reached my office in the late autumn; I did not see it as an automatic reason for him to resign, and after establishing the facts of the matter did nothing. He was good at his job, his wife had been forgiving, and he was providing for his child. But he was a minister, and therefore it was a story; outrage could be manufactured. Saving their cruelty until it would cause most pain to all involved, the *News of the World* published the tale on Boxing Day. I wanted Tim Yeo to stay in office, and made this clear. Likewise Richard Ryder, the Chief Whip, and Yeo's Secretary of State John Gummer thought he should stay. I assumed the prattle would die away, since Parliament was in recess. It was a total misreading of the situation. With no other news to print between Christmas and the New Year, other papers took it up. Members of Yeo's constituency began to express their doubts about his actions, and his situation became untenable. He resigned on 5 January 1994.

It was a second scalp for the media, and in the weeks that followed a stream of gossip was published, mostly remarkable only for its insignificance. The day after Tim's departure I restated what I meant by back to basics. 'It is not a crusade about personal morality and was never presented as such,' I said. 'It is about the policy issues of concern to everyone in the country.' But it was too late. Ministers, unpaid parliamentary private secretaries and even backbenchers fell victim to the Torquemadas of Fleet Street, just as the Royal Family had the year before. Much of what was printed was untrue, or only partly true, and all of it was sensationalised.

What stung me most was not the political cost of what was happening, but the personal impact on those involved. Sometimes that included me. One Saturday night in January 1994 I took a phone call at Finings. It was a deeply emotional Malcolm Caithness, our Transport minister in the Lords, with the shocking news that his wife had taken her own life. I tried to soothe him. It was heart-rending. The press soon reported that Malcolm's marriage had been in difficulty. I knew his subsequent resignation would be reported as 'sleaze', and so it was, though the story did not justify such pitiless attention.

Equally ghastly was an episode which followed soon afterwards. One afternoon in early February Alex Allan interrupted a meeting with the Chiefs of the Defence Staff and passed me a note: 'The police have found the body of one of your MPs. The circumstances are said to be upsetting.' That evening, as I attended the Conservative Winter Ball at the Grosvenor House Hotel, the news came out that Stephen Milligan, the young MP for Eastleigh, had died, on his own, in a bizarre ritual. Alex Allan confirmed the details when I returned to Number 10 later. It was a tragedy. I hardly knew Stephen, since he had only been elected in 1992, but he was widely liked and was said by the whips to be able and a likely candidate for promotion in the near future. Stephen's death only added to the belief that somehow the Conservative Party as a whole was guilty of sleaze.

If I was angered by the media's strutting over personal morality, nothing caused me more dismay and anxiety than the claims made about what became known as the arms-to-Iraq affair, which dragged on from the late 1980s to 1996. If these had been true it would indeed have been a very serious matter. But they were not.

The whole affair was deeply frustrating. First, the very title was a misnomer – Britain did *not* export arms to Iraq; the government never had any intention of doing so; indeed, it had imposed and enforced strict regulations on what could and could not be exported for most of the decade before I became prime minister, and had maintained them throughout my period in office, in contrast to the policy of most other nations. When United Nations troops went into combat in the Gulf War, they faced French aircraft, Russian tanks and Chinese missiles – but no significant British weaponry.

Second, the saga was triggered *before* I became either foreign secretary or chancellor, let alone prime minister. Two episodes were significant. One of them, the review of regulations governing the export of defence-related equipment to Iraq, took place in early 1989; and the other, the prosecution of the directors of the machine tools company Matrix Churchill for illegal exports to Iraq, related to actions which had taken place in 1988 and before.

Third, we suffered for our openness. The very existence of the inquiry I myself set up encouraged talk of Whitehall's supposed 'culture of secrecy';

encouraged rumours of corruption and malpractice; and encouraged the general assumption that there had to be much more to the affair than there seemed. This fallacious belief was fostered by the press, the opposition and, inadvertently, by the protracted nature of the inquiry itself, as conducted by Sir Richard Scott. Had I let slumbering dogs lie when questions had first been asked, there might have been no scandal, but government would have been less open.

As it was, the whole business enabled mud to be slung at us on an almost daily basis. The opposition enjoyed it to the full. Robin Cook, later Labour's Foreign Secretary, accused us of 'trying to cover up our role in arming Saddam Hussein'; John Prescott, later Deputy Prime Minister, suggested we were 'prepared to send innocent men to jail to cover our own backs'; and Tony Blair insisted the whole affair left the government 'knee-deep in dishonour'. In fact, as Sir Richard agreed at his report's publication, there had been no cover-up and no conspiracy. No minister had intentionally misled the House of Commons; there had been no action intended to lead to the conviction of innocent men; no encouragement of arms sales; and no arms sales. Blair's comment was at least general, but Cook and Prescott made specific charges that were groundless, and proven to be so. Neither ever apologised.

All political memoirs, I suppose, contain their share of special pleading, and if a self-justificatory tone creeps into these, readers will have their pinches of salt ready. But the Scott affair is rather different. I hope the serious reader will pause to study this account, for so assiduously did our opponents peddle the innuendo of serious scandal that doubts still remain to this day. Yet there was no scandal. The whole episode was grotesquely misrepresented.

The roots of the affair lie in the bloody and cruel war fought between Iran and Iraq for most of the 1980s. In late 1984 the British government imposed a unilateral restriction on the export of arms – or pretty much anything that might go towards the use of arms, such as computers, software, chemicals and radios – to Iraq. Any company which wanted to export such goods had to seek government approval, which, in significant cases, was unavailable. Some companies, frustrated at this, sought to conceal the nature of their exports, and the directors of one company suspected of doing this, Matrix Churchill, were brought to trial. Matrix Churchill was alleged to have shipped lathes to Iraq for use in its arms industry, having done so by claiming on documentation that they were for civilian use. The directors said that Alan Clark, a former Trade minister and minister of state at the Ministry of Defence, had been aware of this. Clark, always an engaging maverick and later a famous diarist, was interviewed by HM Customs and Excise, and told them he had not been.

In December 1990, long before the trial began, the *Sunday Times* alleged that Alan's claim that he had not been involved was misleading. In response, I called him in to Number 10 on the morning of 3 December, only days after I had become prime minister, to find out the truth. He assured Robin Butler and me that the paper's story was wrong, and that 'it was totally false to suggest he was advising the companies on how to prepare licence applications in such a way as to conceal their military use'. On the basis of this clear-cut reply, Tim Sainsbury, the Department of Trade minister responsible, spoke in the House that afternoon and dismissed the *Sunday Times*'s accusation. Alan sat next to him on the front bench as he did so.

The Matrix Churchill directors came to trial in November 1992. Questioned about his evidence, Alan Clark now changed his story. He told the court he had been 'economical . . . with the *acualité*' in his evidence to the prosecution – and, by implication, in his meeting with me. This has always seemed to me to be the nub of the 'arms-to-Iraq' issue.

The news that the Matrix Churchill trial had collapsed reached me on 9 November 1992, as I prepared to host a dinner for the Russian President Boris Yeltsin. My initial reaction (and it has never changed) was to doubt whether – whatever nod and wink Alan Clark may have given – there had been any other malpractice on the part of the government. Why did I feel that way? It was not only because I knew and trusted those ministers most closely involved. The main reason was that government simply does not work like that. The symbiotic relationship between ministers and civil servants, working along parallel lines of authority and accountability, does not permit such things to occur. If ministers had conspired to let innocent men go to prison the Whitehall machinery would have sounded the alarm, the Cabinet secretary would have been alerted, and he would have been in to see me immediately.

It was clear, though, that the matter had to be investigated. The opposition soon began to make the wildest allegations, which, *had they been true*, would have been shameful. In 1992, Robin Cook said: 'You cannot diminish the level of political scandal of a government that privately, covertly, without public statement, arms a brutal psychopath.' In 1993, he alleged: 'Ministers were prepared to see businessmen wrongly convicted rather than tell how much they knew about the arms trade with Iraq.' Such comments, repeatedly made and given wide currency, entered the public subconscious as if they were facts long before Sir Richard Scott's report showed them to be utterly untrue.

Whatever mistakes had been made (I was quite open to the possibility of mistakes), I wanted no cover-up. I saw Robin Butler and Alex Allan to discuss the format an inquiry might take and its terms of reference. We settled for the appointment of a senior judge, along the lines of the recent successful investigation into the collapse of the Bank of Credit and Commerce International. Lord Mackay, the Lord Chancellor, was consulted about who should take the role, and put the names of some senior judges to me, one of whom was Sir Richard Scott. 'Scott is an extremely liberal judge,' Mackay said. I was confident that there was nothing to hide, and Scott's independence of mind appealed to me. It would, I hoped, remove any suspicion that his inquiry was intended to be a whitewash. Likewise, I gave the inquiry very broad terms of reference. I announced Scott's appointment in the Commons the next day, 10 November.

This appointment, it soon emerged, was a mistake. Sir Richard was an honest, highly intelligent and committed inquiry chairman, and he produced a thorough report, but it became clear when he began work that he did not have the grasp of the workings of government necessary to put the issue at stake – the collapse of the Matrix Churchill trial – in context. I find it astounding that among the multiple volumes of his report he never deals with the misleading statement Tim Sainsbury unwittingly gave the House in 1990, the content of which allowed the Matrix Churchill trial to proceed. Instead he began a long and almost separate inquiry into the handling of guidelines surrounding exports to Iraq. Although the inquiry's terms of reference included this, so far as it affected the Matrix Churchill trial, Scott's prolonged investigation of it seems to me to be irrelevant, since the interpretation of the guidelines was not in question. If, from the start, Matrix Churchill had declared that its lathes were to be used to make Iraqi shells and rockets, ministers would have banned their export under *any* interpretation of the guidelines. Since the company did not declare this, HM Customs and Excise began a prosecution.

By extending his investigation into the technical handling of arms exports, Sir Richard delayed the publication of the report: it was not published until February 1996, almost two years late. Beyond this, many of those who appeared before Sir Richard and the Counsel to the Inquiry, Presiley Baxendale, were alarmed by the cross-examination they underwent. When I appeared before Scott on 17 January 1994 to discuss my limited involvement as foreign secretary and prime minister, I was treated with courtesy. I was concerned, however, that the inquiry was being run as if it were a court of law. Witnesses were not encouraged to bring their own lawyers to help them present their case, although Sir Richard did offer the courtesy of allowing individuals mentioned in the report to comment on his draft findings.

The investigation ambled through many parts of Whitehall, but only two significant issues seemed to concern Scott. The first revolved around the consideration, in early 1989, of the implications of the end of the Iran–Iraq war for exports to the region. The guidelines were not changed, and so no announcement was made to Parliament, but references to the conflict in the existing regulations became redundant. Even the most legalistic investigator, however, could find only one example where this inevitably more liberal gloss made any difference to an export licence. It did not affect Matrix Churchill.

Sir Richard was worried nonetheless that Parliament had been intentionally misled by written answers given on this matter, particularly by William Waldegrave, then a junior minister at the Foreign Office. William Waldegrave is a sensitive intellectual, and it was inconceivable to me that he would have been knowingly involved in sharp practice. He suffered terribly over the charges laid at his door.

The second issue which troubled Scott was more relevant: the handling of the Matrix Churchill trial, and in particular the use of Public Interest Immunity Certificates (PIIs) – technical notes, signed by ministers, which request that documents which otherwise might be exposed during a trial remain private for security reasons. Was their use in this case a sign that the trial had not been brought in good faith?

In fact, PIIs are not gagging orders (as the press and the opposition liked to describe them). It is for the trial judge to decide whether or not to send material subject to a PII forward as evidence, and in the case of the Matrix Churchill trial the judge decided the documents were needed.

They played a part in the cross-examination which led to Alan Clark's statement and the subsequent acquittal. Innocent men never risked imprisonment because of them.

The use of PIIs was the only significant element in the 'arms-to-Iraq' story which took place while I was at Number 10. Several ministers – I was not among them – had signed PIIs before the Matrix Churchill case, one of them, Michael Heseltine, only doing so when the Attorney General, Sir Nicholas Lyell, made it clear that it was his legal duty to do so. Nick Lyell is an honourable and correct man, a lawyer by nature and by profession; as with William Waldegrave, never for a moment did I doubt that he had behaved with total propriety.

Indeed, the advice he gave was correct – not surprisingly, since the Law Officers' department had researched the subject in detail two years before. Much of the criticism of the use of PIIs was politically-motivated bluster. In opposition, Robin Cook seized every opportunity to torment us over the issue; later, as foreign secretary, he signed one himself against a businessman involved in the arms-to-Iraq affair. In the two years after the 1997 general election, Labour ministers signed fifty PIIs – against thirty issued by the Conservative government in the two years before the election. Before the Matrix Churchill trial, it emerged, a particular effort had been made by Nick Lyell to ensure that the judge had read all the documents subject to the PII. Alan Clark, re-interviewed at Lyell's request on whether or not he had privately given a nod and a wink to the machine tools industry to export what they liked, insisted that he had not.

Both William Waldegrave in 1989 and Nick Lyell in 1992 had acted entirely properly. But in the time it took for this to emerge, our opponents had had a field day with their distorted picture. This was made worse because while the inquiry was underway all ministers exercised a 'self-denying ordinance', not speaking out to defend themselves. The temptation to do so was strong, not least when, in June 1995, early drafts of the report, containing criticism of William Waldegrave and Nicholas Lyell, were leaked to the BBC, ITN and the *Independent*. Sir Richard Scott refused William Waldegrave's request for him to seek an injunction to prevent the publication of the draft report, and instead allowed himself to be filmed cycling around the block by ITN for that night's *News at Ten*. They missed him the first time, so he obligingly did it again.

On 15 February 1996 the Scott report was finally published. Criticism leaked in the draft report was not present in the final version, and on the central questions ministers were acquitted of intentional improper behaviour. It fell to Ian Lang, the new President of the Board of Trade, to receive the report and present it to Parliament. It was a mighty job, with the burden of stopping and reversing in one day the tide of innuendo that had swamped us over the last three years. He knew that if he failed, at least two ministers, and perhaps the government itself, would fall.

Ian had begun preparing for the report's publication at the end of 1995 with an open mind. Like me, he had found suggestions that colleagues had conspired to send innocent men to jail hard to believe, but he was willing to accept that Scott might be able to prove it had taken place. Over two months he met officials and read all the back papers, but it was only days before its release that he was able to see the report itself. Opposition spokesmen found their access even more restricted: Robin Cook made great play of the fact that he only had three hours in which to digest the 1,800-page document, and perhaps we should have given him more time. We knew, however, that a debate would follow, and since Cook had attended the inquiry (and, as it happened, usually misrepresented it), we were not as sympathetic as we would have been to another Labour spokesman. We were also worried about premature leaks, which had damaged us often enough during the inquiry. In any event, Cook spent the first ten minutes of the time available to him to read the report speaking to the press in the street outside, so he could not have been too concerned.

With the backing of Cabinet, which met on the morning of 15 February, Ian Lang was at last able to rebut the serious charges that Cook and others had peddled for so long:

> For the past three years, week after week and month after month, the honourable gentleman has fed the House, the press and the public a sour stream of invective, innuendo and invention. It has been one of the most odious campaigns of manipulation and black propaganda that the House will be able to recall. Now the honourable Member for Livingston has been found out: it was all without foundation, and the Scott Report shows that. It was a cheap and nasty smear campaign, with his whole party joining in the chorus. Their behaviour was contemptible.

Ian's anger was plain to see, and I shared it. Robin Cook did not justify his earlier charges – indeed he could not, since Scott had dismissed them

– but he distorted and exaggerated less serious criticisms that Scott had made. It was a performance that won him plaudits, but left many Conservatives contemptuous of his behaviour.

Despite the sound and fury of the parliamentary exchanges, the Scott Report settled the substance of the issue. After it, though there was much huffing and puffing from the opposition and the press, the probity of ministerial conduct was not open to doubt, and the matter dragged on only as a vehicle for the opposition to mount attacks on the government. Eleven days after the publication of the report and the formal ministerial statement, the Commons debated the report. Labour hoped to use the debate to damage the government by forcing ministerial resignations. Since we had an unsteady majority, in single figures at the best of times, there was a good chance that their ploy would work.

Ian Lang made his second speech on the issue in this debate, on 26 February, adopting a more measured approach than he had a week before. Then, his aim had been to stop in its tracks the massive smear campaign that had built up. Now he sought to recognise that there were legitimate criticisms in the report, largely of an administrative nature and aimed at officials over many years. In particular, Scott criticised the handling by Customs and Excise of the evidence ahead of the Matrix Churchill case, suggesting in particular that inconsistencies in Alan Clark's evidence should have been uncovered earlier. He recommended substantial changes to the law relating to PIIs, strongly criticised the way Parliament had not been kept properly informed in the late 1980s, and called for a more open approach to ministerial statements.

The debate barely reflected these serious points. Crude political mathematics had taken over from rational consideration. On the night of the vote the Commons was packed: only a handful of MPs failed to attend. As the debate got underway William Waldegrave and Nick Lyell came to my rooms at the House. Though I was entirely satisfied that they were in the right, they knew that they would have to resign if we were defeated, and were reconciled to that. And although he did not tell me directly at the time, Ian Lang was considering whether he, too, would have to go if we lost. The resignation of three senior ministers over so serious an issue would have been a blow I doubt the government could have survived.

In the division lobbies Labour and the Liberal Democrats would be against us – that much was clear. So would some wavering Conservatives. Roger Freeman, Chancellor of the Duchy of Lancaster, set out to persuade Rupert Allason, the Tory MP for Torbay also known as the writer on espionage Nigel West, always unpredictable, and over Scott something of a self-taught crusader, to back the government. Eventually, Allason was won round. So was another doubter, John Marshall.

David Trimble, the leader of the Official Ulster Unionists, sought to maximise his negotiating position, seeking a deal on Northern Ireland in return for his MPs' support. I refused to contemplate this, since I knew it might compromise the peace process, even though when I turned down his offer it looked likely that the vote would be lost.

The debate was messy and unilluminating, and ended noisily. The division bell rang, the stampede for the lobbies began, and then, in the most tense atmosphere, the result was declared. Only Quentin Davies, the earnest and somewhat isolated Member for Stamford, had voted against the government from the Tory benches. We had crawled home by one vote, 320 to 319. William Waldegrave and Nick Lyell rightly kept their jobs.

The harsh charges laid against us over arms-to-Iraq were not sustained. But the Scott inquiry took place against another set of allegations about Conservative sleaze, which suggested that MPs were acting in Parliament on behalf of outside interests, without properly declaring the fact. I think much of this, too, was overblown. Again, ministers were not shown to have acted corruptly. Much of what was revealed was the result of the sudden spotlighting of a culture of contact between business and politics that had grown up in Parliament over the previous quarter of a century. But I do not deny that wrongdoing by Conservative politicians was also exposed.

The first incident was particularly puzzling. In May 1993, a story appeared in the press suggesting that Michael Mates, a minister of state at the Northern Ireland Office, had given a Cypriot businessman, Asil Nadir, an inexpensive watch engraved with the words 'Don't let the buggers get you down'. Nadir, once a darling of the stock market, had donated money to the Conservative Party when Mrs Thatcher was prime minister. Later, he had come under investigation by the Serious Fraud Office on suspicion of fraud and false accounting. There were some, and Michael Mates was not the only one, who felt that he was being unfairly targeted.

Michael had taken up Nadir's case – the businessman lived in his constituency – when he was a backbencher, and continued to take an interest in it after he joined the government. This was entirely legitimate and at no time was there a suggestion that he had made money out of his involvement. When the gift of the watch was first revealed, I told the Commons it had been 'a misjudgement', but was not 'a hanging offence'. It looked much worse when, subsequently, Nadir fled to northern Cyprus to avoid trial in this country, following which Michael behaved recklessly, dining with an aide to Nadir at the Reform Club. This was unwise, not corrupt, but the media exploded, and Michael resigned so as to avoid causing continuing embarrassment to the government.

This odd little episode put the issue of the probity of Conservative politicians back on the agenda. In its wake, John Smith, the Labour leader, lost no opportunity to draw attention to the links between the Tory Party and big business. He concentrated his fire on jobs taken by ministers after retiring, and on allegations of favouritism in public appointments. Though there were never any specific allegations of wrongdoing, and precious little evidence of any (one Labour Party list laughably included General Sir Peter de la Billière and the Duke of Kent on a list of Tory placemen), the campaign succeeded in sowing the seeds of doubt. No one then could have imagined Labour's tireless pursuit of business money in the run-up to the 1997 general election and beyond.

Attention moved to the behaviour of Members of Parliament themselves when, on 10 July 1994, the *Sunday Times* revealed that two of our MPs, Graham Riddick and David Tredinnick, had agreed to take payment from undercover reporters posing as businessmen, in return for asking questions in Parliament. I was in Naples at the G7 economic summit when I heard about the story, and was astounded by it. I could scarcely believe that anyone could have been so idiotic, but the facts seemed indisputable. I spoke to Richard Ryder by phone and agreed that the two should be immediately suspended from their (unpaid) jobs as parliamentary private secretaries, and ordered an immediate inquiry into what had gone on.

I was furious that the pair had been so foolish. There was no excuse for what Riddick and Tredinnick had done, but they were clots, not villains. How could they have behaved as they did? I thought long about this. My reaction was not the easy one of asserting that they were exceptions, and excluding them from the fold. My concern was for the long-term interests of Parliament, and whether the episode exposed something in our political culture which needed to be put right.

Many MPs were consultants to firms, known as such, and in this capacity asked questions in Parliament and sometimes lobbied on behalf of their employers. Their interest was declared in a public register. Ministers knew well enough when an MP had a stake in an issue that was raised in the House. But the fact that something had become established practice did not mean it was proper. I worried that the boundaries of parliamentary behaviour had become blurred, and the seeds of the inquiry I later asked Lord Nolan to carry out were planted in my mind.

Riddick and Tredinnick were reprimanded when a Commons All Party Committee agreed that their behaviour 'fell well below the standards which the House is entitled to expect from its Members' – though they themselves had suffered from devious tactics, for which the *Sunday Times* was rebuked by the Press Complaints Commission. But the two MPs' behaviour did expose how unclear the broader principle was. What, I wondered, was the difference *in principle* between being paid to put down questions on an *ad hoc* basis, and being retained to lobby and putting down questions as a result of that. There was not, it seemed to me, a difference in substance – only in openness.

The issue erupted three months later. On 20 October 1994 the *Guardian* published the allegation that two ministers, Tim Smith, the donnish Junior Minister for Northern Ireland, and Neil Hamilton, the bullish, right-wing Minister for Consumer and Corporate Affairs, had, *when backbenchers in the 1980s*, accepted money and gifts from the owner of Harrods, Mohammed Al Fayed, to act in Parliament on his behalf, without declaring so in the Register of Members' Interests. Prime Minister's Questions that afternoon was fraught. Tony Blair sought to exploit the matter to the full, claiming that the government I led was 'becoming tainted' – notwithstanding the fact that the events in question had been years earlier. His aim was to gain political advantage – the cynical duty of an opposition. Mine was to respond to the specific charges that had been made, albeit about events that took place before I became prime minister.

In doing so, I revealed that the *Guardian*'s story did not come as a surprise to me. 'The allegations were brought to me privately some three weeks ago,' I said, in answer to the first question of the afternoon. 'It was clear that the allegations reported to me originated, although they did not come to me directly, from Mr Al Fayed. I made it absolutely clear at the time that I was not prepared to come to any arrangement with Mr Al Fayed' – here I was interrupted by uproar from all sides – 'I immediately made it perfectly clear that those matters would be fully investigated and asked the Cabinet Secretary to undertake an independent and full investigation. He has been doing so and is continuing to do so.'

The episode had begun three weeks earlier. On the evening of 29 September I had been working in the Cabinet Room at Number 10 when my Press Secretary, Christopher Meyer, came in to tell me that Brian Hitchen, editor of the *Sunday Express*, wanted to discuss 'an urgent matter'. Chris had suggested that he see Hitchen on my behalf, but Hitchen would only speak to me. He came in, and Alex Allan joined us.

In the utmost confidence, Brian Hitchen described allegations about the conduct of four ministers – Michael Howard, Jonathan Aitken, Tim Smith and Neil Hamilton – and made it clear that he had been given his information by Fayed. He had been asked to act as an intermediary, and said that Fayed wanted to see me himself to ask for a report by the Department of Trade and Industry into his takeover of Harrods to be withdrawn or reviewed. Fayed was threatening to pass his allegations to the opposition. I responded that it would be impossible for me to see Fayed in such circumstances, and Hitchen went away.

I was incredulous at Fayed's approach, and was left with a dilemma. I was not inclined to believe Fayed's allegations, two of which – those against Jonathan Aitken and Michael Howard – were not new, and had previously appeared to be without foundation. The claims against Smith and Hamilton, however, were fresh. Having been presented with them, I had to act, and I asked the Cabinet Secretary, Robin Butler, to see if there was any truth in Fayed's statement.

Robin investigated the matter, calling in the two ministers. Tim Smith confessed. 'I did a very foolish thing,' he said. He admitted that in the mid-1980s, while a backbencher, he had asked questions in Parliament at Fayed's request, and had taken money for it. (During a later investigation, he confirmed that these payments had included cash in envelopes.)

It took Robin longer to reach Neil Hamilton – the party conference was underway – and when he did so, Hamilton strongly denied that he had taken money from Fayed, though he did admit to having received gifts and to having stayed at Fayed's Ritz Hotel in Paris. This presented a difficulty. Tim Smith had confirmed that Fayed's allegations against him were accurate. Circumstantially, this suggested that the charges against Neil Hamilton might well be correct too – but he had denied it.

Robin Butler reported to me on the course of his investigation on Monday, 17 October, after my return from the party conference. It was clear from what he said that Tim Smith would have to resign as a minister. But I wanted to make certain, too, that Neil Hamilton had not accepted money. I decided that Robin and the Chief Whip should talk to him once more, and decided to delay Smith's resignation until this had been done. As they were doing so, the *Guardian*, primed by Fayed, published the allegations against Smith and Hamilton.

At this, Tim Smith resigned immediately, accepting his fate without complaint. Neil Hamilton did not, since Robin Butler's investigation into his conduct was incomplete. All of this created the appearance of a great scandal, and the opposition milked it to the full. In fact, the only scandal that had been confirmed concerned Tim Smith's activities as a backbencher long before I had become prime minister. It irked me that the government I led was being blamed for this.

Robin Butler completed his report the following week, and I decided it should be published so as to demonstrate that there was no cover-up. It revealed, I told the House in a statement on 25 October, that in my meeting with Hitchen I had made it clear that 'if ministers had been guilty of wrongdoing . . . I was not going to make any sort of deal, regardless of the cost to the government's reputation'. That was my principle throughout. I wanted the truth to be known.

Robin Butler's report also made it clear that, as I said to the Commons, 'the Member for Tatton [Neil Hamilton] has rigorously rejected – both orally and in writing – the allegations of impropriety made against him.' That, however, was not quite the end of the matter so far as Neil Hamilton was concerned. He presented a particular problem in that he was the Minister for Corporate Affairs. The allegations against him, unless disproved, would prejudice his ability to do his job. Additionally, his conduct since the issue had first come to light had been insensitive and foolish: after visiting a school in his constituency he had marched out of it clutching a ginger biscuit. 'I must remember to declare this in the Register of Members' Interests,' he told the press. It was an ill-judged joke. On top of that, he compared his situation to mine over the Clare Latimer libel, which was both insulting and absurd.

I did not wish to sack him, thus giving the impression that there was validity in the charge against him, but I knew he could not remain in government. I hoped he would realise his predicament and would offer to step down – had he done so, he would have gained an enormous amount of parliamentary sympathy and ensured his return to government if the charges were dismissed. But he did not resign until he was confronted by the Chief Whip, who gave him little alternative but to go, and by Michael Heseltine, his Secretary of State, who explained why that needed to be so. Hamilton's supporters retaliated with claims that I had sacked him, but had been too lily-livered to do the job myself. In fact I had gone out of my way to help him leave office with as much dignity as possible.

Smith and Hamilton resigned as ministers within a week of the Fayed allegations becoming public. The position of the other two ministers accused in my meeting with Brian Hitchen, Michael Howard and Jonathan Aitken, was different. Robin Butler and I were confident that the claim that Michael Howard had accepted money was entirely without foundation, and no evidence has ever come to light which questions this judgement. Robin also doubted that there was anything to the second claim, that Jonathan Aitken, whom I had recently promoted to the Cabinet as Chief Secretary, had stayed at the Ritz Hotel in Paris as a guest of a Saudi Arabian business associate, while a junior minister, for the purpose of sharing very large commissions on Arab arms deals.

Robin had reached his opinion after having examined the matter, at Jonathan Aitken's request, some months earlier. Jonathan, who had been challenged on the point by the *Guardian*, had given Robin his word that he was in Paris for family reasons, and that the individual suspected of having paid his bill at the Ritz was an old family friend, godfather to his daughter, and not a business associate. Accordingly, Robin was satisfied that the ministerial rules had not been broken.

Aitken further sought to prove that he had paid his hotel bill himself, sending Robin a copy of it as proof. Robin and Alex Allan examined the document, and Alex noticed that the sum paid did not match the cost of the stay. Someone, presumably, had paid the difference. Jonathan began a convoluted and ultimately unsuccessful effort to prove that the missing sum had been paid by his wife. The *Guardian* challenged his story in print, and Jonathan Aitken resigned from the government in July 1995 in order to pursue a libel case against the paper. This collapsed in 1997, when it was demonstrated that he had deliberately misled the court. In 1999 he was convicted of perjury, and sentenced to eighteen months' imprisonment.

It was a sad and ignoble end. Jonathan Aitken was – is – a talented buccaneer, able politically, and with a fine pen – his biography of Nixon is an excellent book – and he had always been an ally in periods where I had faced difficulty. Perhaps I should have dug harder when the charges against him arose. But it is not in my character to act upon hearsay, and my instinct has always been to take a colleague's word until evidence appears which casts doubt upon it. Until the *Guardian* unearthed evidence which proved that Jonathan's wife had not been in Paris to pay the hotel bill – always a peripheral aspect of the allegations – there was no such evidence against him. My officials had been satisfied. I had been satisfied. And that seemed sufficient.

But why, some will ask, did I appoint a talented buccaneer in the first place? I like risk-takers, and you need them in government. Disraeli was a chancer. Jonathan was hardly in that league, but he was clever, quick, fluent, well-travelled, well-connected, and well-liked at home and abroad, where some of his government work had to be done. There may have been rumours about him, but that did not distinguish him from a score or more of high-calibre individuals on both sides of the House. Some such men and women go on to give distinguished service. If it is true that one or two people inside and outside the Conservative Party had whispered to me that there were question marks about Jonathan, it is as true that there were question marks about some of the whisperers, too. There's a great deal of whispering at Westminster, all the time, and a great many question marks too. In the end, you take a judgement. I took a judgement. It was wrong.

Ever since the Riddick and Tredinnick affair I had been giving serious thought to the idea of establishing some sort of independent committee to establish for everyone's benefit exactly what the rules on Members' outside interests should be. Since all the evidence suggested that the standing of MPs with the public was now at its lowest ebb, it would clearly not be enough simply to refer the matter to the House of Commons. Part of the problem was that there were grey areas – including the financial relationships between MPs and multi-client consultancy firms – and some MPs accused of misbehaviour had protested that they had not realised what the rules were. In the fevered atmosphere which followed the resignations of Tim Smith and Neil Hamilton I knew I had no choice but to act to restore public confidence by establishing such an inquiry.

Early on the Sunday morning after the *Guardian* had published its initial allegations about Smith and Hamilton, I rang Robin Butler to discuss the idea. It was the genesis of what became the Nolan inquiry. We acted fast: by the time I made my statement on 25 October, the details were settled. 'I have decided to establish a body with the following terms of reference,' I told the Commons. 'To examine current concerns about standards of conduct of all holders of public office, including arrangements relating to financial and commercial activities, and make recommendations as to any changes in present arrangements which might be required to ensure the highest standards of probity in public life.'

The announcement was well received in Parliament and outside. Nolan, as the committee became known, soon set about the task of taking evidence. Behind everything there was a fundamental issue of principle which touched on the character of our parliamentary democracy as it had developed over centuries; that was, whether MPs should be representative of the world outside politics, or whether they should be a cadre of high-minded political professionals. Some commentators seemed to imply that MPs should have no outside interests at all; others complained that there were too many MPs with little understanding of the 'real world'.

There were three urgent questions. First, was it right that MPs should have other sources of income beyond their parliamentary salaries? Second, should they be allowed to accept fees for services or advice which were only available by virtue of their status as MPs? Third, what should be the rules for declaring gifts, hospitality, and financial interests more generally?

I did have serious reservations about the relations between MPs and multi-client lobbying firms; I felt it was important that MPs should be in a position to know that the organisations with which they did business were reputable. But by the very nature of such arrangements, it was impossible to be sure.

On the issue of the declaration of earnings I was ambivalent. Provided it was clear that there were earnings, I remained to be convinced that the actual amount should be declared. Parliament had decreed that share-holders had the right to know what company directors were paid, so should not constituents know what their representatives in Parliament earned? However, shareholders owned the company which paid the directors. Constituents could be said to 'own' their MPs as MPs, and deserve to know – as they do – what they are paid for this work. But other remuneration was a grey area: sometimes relevant to an MP's work, sometimes private.

I set out my thoughts on this on 14 November 1994, in my annual speech at the Lord Mayor's Banquet in the City of London. 'I shrink from the notion of the wholly professional politician,' I said. 'It must be right for MPs to have other interests, but Parliament should not be, as frankly it sometimes has been, a way to other jobs. The Commons is an assembly, a forum, above all a legislature. It needs all trades but it should not be a hiring fair.'

As Nolan began hearing evidence, initial enthusiasm on our benches turned to resentment. From the first, it was clear that the opposition was not remotely interested in the issues, but was using Nolan as a handy cudgel with which to beat the Tories. Conservatives, hostile and apprehensive about what Nolan might recommend on MPs' business interests, began to accuse me of stirring up a constitutional hornets' nest. I remained confident that I had acted properly to protect the reputation of Parliament, and that this soreness was a sign that the committee was doing its job. It was remarked at the time – and it is true – that a prime minister has at least two rather separate roles: he is the chief of his party tribe, and he is the leader of a government of all the people. These roles sometimes clash, and never more so than when the financial interests of one's tribe are involved. Perhaps in my anxiety to do the right thing by the nation as a whole, I miscalculated the strength of tribal feeling.

Throughout all this, Lord Nolan and his committee – in great contrast to Scott – admirably refused to play to the gallery. They brushed away all requests to comment on particular allegations of sleaze and stuck heroically to their brief, which was to make recommendations about the rules and principles that should apply in public life.

The first Nolan Report was presented in May 1995, setting out recommendations covering the conduct of Members of Parliament, ministers and civil servants, quangos and NHS bodies. In relation to Members of

Parliament it recommended, most controversially, a ban on work for multi-client organisations, a new requirement to disclose earnings from outside consultancies, and the appointment of a new independent commissioner for standards. These recommendations were placed in the context of a report which declared that 'much of the public anxiety about standards of conduct in public life is based upon perceptions and beliefs which are not supported by the facts. We believe that the great majority of men and women in British public life are honest and hard-working and observe high ethical standards.' Thank God, I thought, for Nolan. Moreover, the report argued that Parliament would be less effective if all MPs were full-time politicians, and that MPs should not be prevented from having outside employment. It was a good report, thorough and convincing.

These points, it seemed to me, were vital statements of principle and deserved wide publicity. Unfortunately, by the time Nolan produced his report, all sense of proportion had been lost. Some of my colleagues had come to see the report as a slanderous attack on the integrity of MPs, a threat to parliamentary sovereignty and – though they did not express this so loudly – a threat to their freedom to engage in commercial activity. To the public, the reaction from the Conservative benches must have confirmed their worst fears. Not only did they succeed in giving the impression that Nolan had concluded that they were a bunch of crooks, which of course he had not, but they managed to suggest that there was some truth in the allegations by protesting too much. It was not a happy spectacle.

As Lord Nolan arrived to listen to the subsequent debate in the House, he was waylaid in front of the television cameras by Alan Duncan, the MP for Rutland, who accused him of wanting to obliterate the professional classes' representation in the House. The debate became ever more unreal. Ted Heath led the assault: 'We have now reached the stage where every man and woman in this House is an object of suspicion.' Ted was right, but that was not Nolan's fault. The debate showed the House of Commons at its worst, inward-looking, self-serving, pompously evoking ancient rights to cloak private interest. As the Leader of the House Tony Newton announced the proposal that a committee of senior backbenchers would be established to consider Nolan's proposals and make recommendations, the Chamber was almost empty.

It was in retrospect instructive that Tony Blair should press me on whether 'the government' would implement the whole of Nolan. He did not seem to understand the difference between the legislature and the executive. It had been my firm belief from the start that Parliament *itself* would have to consider and decide on Nolan's recommendations, and I had stated this at the outset. As it was, Labour and the Liberal Democrats sought to extract the maximum party political damage by threatening to boycott the All-Party Committee which we had announced would be appointed to consider Nolan.

The most important disagreement which the committee had to consider revolved around whether MPs who were also paid parliamentary consultants should be compelled to reveal not only this fact, but also how much they earned. The Nolan Report took the view that a ban on all paid advocacy was impracticable, but supported the declaration of income – both from advocacy and from second jobs outside politics. The Select Committee, under Tony Newton, took the opposite view, though not unanimously, when its report was published in late 1995.

Neither of these positions was absurd or indefensible, and both, I thought, were for the Commons to decide. I chose to put the issue to a free vote, with the indication that the Select Committee's proposals were our preferred option, and probably represented the majority view in the House. The majority of the Conservative Party strongly favoured the Select Committee's approach; their views on disclosure verged on the unprintable. Labour MPs received a three-line whip to vote in favour of Nolan, though many had private misgivings.

I was sanguine about the outcome. It seemed likely that there would be enough Tory defectors to deliver victory to the Nolan solution. Nonetheless, I tried to minimise Conservative dissent, though I knew that the vote might be lost. On 7 November 1995, twenty Conservative MPs voted with the opposition to defeat the Select Committee's proposals. Tactically, Tony Blair handled the debate to extract the maximum advantage for Labour.

The episode was followed by the defection to the Liberal Democrats of Emma Nicholson, the Conservative MP for Devon West and Torridge, apparently because of sleaze in the Conservative Party. Emma had wanted a job as a minister, and had approached the whips to promote her cause. The whips reported to me that she was unsuitable and unpopular, and I had dropped her from an earlier reshuffle. The appointment of two other

Conservative women, Angela Knight and Angela Browning, both junior in service to her, may have helped to convince Emma that her chances were few. She announced her defection on an evening news broadcast over Christmas. After the BBC reported it, I received a fax from her justifying what she had done. She had not previously approached me to discuss her intentions. Later, the Liberal Democrats nominated her as a life peer.

Emma will be forgotten. Nolan endures – and to our democracy's advantage, I believe. Though my party had preferred the Select Committee's approach to declaration, the Commons had chosen Nolan's, which was perfectly workable. After the vote we set about implementing it, along with his wider recommendations. In early 1996 Sir Gordon Downey was appointed as the first Parliamentary Commissioner for Standards. His investigations into many of the MPs criticised during the cash-for-questions affair was published after the general election the following year. Most were cleared. Neil Hamilton was among those who were not, though he has continued to assert his innocence.

Despite all the grief it caused me personally, and the difficulties it created for the government, I am proud to have brought Nolan into being. I would not have it any other way. But were I advising a prime minister concerned more with short-term advantage, I would suggest he play it differently. I was slow to accuse individuals or to accept accusation as fact, being instead determined to look carefully at the underlying problems, to inquire, and if necessary to reform – however awkward change might be for my own side. I was therefore damned by my opponents for giving accused colleagues time to answer charges and the benefit of the doubt while they did so, and damned by colleagues for the political risks inherent in the slower-burning inquiries I set up, one of which fingered their own interests.

Less scrupulous prime ministers might be advised to adopt the opposite philosophy: live by news-management rather than reason. 'Win' each morning's battle of the headlines by rushing to join the condemnation of whichever individual the lynch-mob is pursuing – but take very great care to have only internal inquiries, and avoid a more serious review which might raise uncomfortable or unpredictable questions later on. Never undermine the interests of your own tribe.

I persist in preferring the first approach. Implicit in such an approach is a measure of indifference as to whether one is given credit for it. What really counts if whether or not Parliament, as a whole, is better for Nolan. And it is.

# CHAPTER TWENTY-FOUR

## Faultline Europe

IN AUGUST 1993, Norma and I went on holiday to Portugal, staying at the house of friends, Ian and Cynthia Symington, in the Douro Valley. The weather was beautiful, the scenery spectacular, and the Douro wended its way placidly beneath our gaze. I sat in the sun and considered the dilemma of Europe.

Britain had been a member of the European Community for twenty years. Half our trade was with our immediate neighbours, and even though the rest was scattered around the world, our economic self-interest was inextricably linked to the Continent. We were no longer an imperial power, but a medium-sized nation that could 'punch above our weight' thanks to our historic legacy, our skilled diplomacy and the muscle of our armed forces.

We straddled the divide between the United States and Europe. We were the largest investor in the US, and the largest recipient of her investment. We were her closest ally in NATO. We shared a language. Our instincts and outlook were more often in tune with North America than with Western Europe. It was no wonder that many Conservatives hankered for an Anglo-Saxon alliance across the Atlantic, rather than a Continental alliance across the Channel. And yet, that could not really work. The US did not want a fifty-first state. As successive American ambassadors made clear to us, the United States wanted Britain to be a strong voice in Europe, as geography, economics and common values suggested we should be.

We had won many arguments with our European partners. The growth of free trade in the single market had been a British success, championed by Margaret Thatcher. Liberalisation of capital movement was an initiative led by Nigel Lawson. My contribution was the future financing arrangement settled at the Edinburgh summit in 1992: Europe was at last living within its means. All this moved in a British direction. So did the dramatic reduction of directives following the Maastricht agreement on subsidiarity. In 1993 sixty-five directives were adopted by the Council of Ministers. In 1994, in the wake of Maastricht, the figure fell to seventeen.

And yet Maastricht had been a fork in the road. Our partners wanted a single currency. We did not. They wanted a Social Chapter. We did not. They wanted more harmonisation of policy. We did not. They wanted more Community control of defence. We did not. Increasingly, they talked in private of a federal destination, even though in public they were reassuring about a Europe of nation states.

After nearly three years' experience at the European top table, my own views were evolving. When I had become prime minister, relations with our partners were in poor repair. I had no instinctive animosity towards the Community, nor was I a starry-eyed supporter of it. I was a friendly agnostic. I might have wished the European issue was not there, but it was. It could not be avoided.

By now I had got to know my fellow European heads of government. Helmut Kohl was the European Union's colossus, his uncertain start as Chancellor far behind him. He had driven through German reunification, including the controversial decision to exchange ostmarks for deutschmarks at par. Physically and politically, he towered above all other political figures in Germany, demonstrating in election after election his ability to absorb, guide and articulate the gut feelings of his voters. His ministers were deferential in his presence, and with few exceptions, other EU heads of government were also intimidated by him. Regardless of their own views, these heads would look to Kohl to show which way the wind was blowing: it was more than their economies' dependence on German largesse via the Community budget was worth to stand in the face of that wind. On all major international issues, German policy was made in the Federal Chancellery, largely irrespective of the views of the Foreign Ministry.

Helmut Kohl was a man for whom personal relationships and acts of friendship were hugely important. He could be ruthless when crossed, and was not averse to a spot of bullying in order to get his way; but he was also a warm, emotional and likeable individual with a strong sense of humour. For both of us, there was a political purpose to the friendship we formed. My predecessor's famously bad relationship with Kohl had self-evidently not helped British interests in Europe. Quite apart from their personal chemistry – akin to dropping magnesium into water – Kohl had been mortally offended by what he perceived as Margaret Thatcher's opposition to German reunification. While he made no secret of his cool relationship with Margaret, he was not anti-British. He was often puzzled by us, and hurt by xenophobic attacks in sections of our press. But he took an intense interest in Britain and British politics; his wife Hannelore spoke near-perfect English (Kohl, so far as I know, had no foreign languages), and his son Peter worked as a banker in the City of London. Above all, Kohl understood very well the importance to Europe of Britain – as one of the four large economies; as the country with the widest global interests and, arguably, influence; and as the most effective military power in postwar Western Europe. He of course yearned for us to become more 'European' in our outlook; but excluding Britain was not his aim. He was ready to be conciliatory.

There was an exceptional bond between Helmut Kohl and the French President, François Mitterrand. As sometimes happens, it was a bond between opposite types. Kohl was a conservative, a Christian Democrat, who liked a simple and unpretentious lifestyle; Mitterrand, nominally at least a socialist, relished the imperial trappings of the French presidency. Kohl was a rumbustious man of the people; Mitterrand an aloof intellectual. Kohl was a gourmand, fond of liverwurst and beer, and known on occasion to eat two full dinners in an evening; Mitterrand was very much the gourmet, who in his dying days ate the forbidden delicacy of the ortolan songbird at a last supper with his close friends.

I found Mitterrand invariably correct and courteous, but also formal and remote, standing on the dignity of his presidential office. There was no question of exchanging with him the sort of banter which was the stock in trade of my meetings with Kohl. In his closing years, with his health visibly deteriorating, and obliged by the defeat of his own party to cohabit with a prime minister and a government drawn from his political opponents, Mitterrand appeared semi-detached from day-to-day business. He was certainly not a man for detail. Discussions of the Bosnian conflict, for example, turned into seminars from Mitterrand on the Ottoman influence in south-eastern Europe since the late Middle Ages – an impressive display of learning, but of marginal relevance to the decisions in hand. He patently neither liked nor understood economics, and my questions on the economic consequences of the single currency simply passed him by.

My policy within Europe was to take the advantages that flowed from our membership. For me that meant consensus, yes; shared sovereignty where logic dictated it, yes. I was a convinced advocate of enlargement as a historic obligation to nations we had left on the wrong side of the Iron Curtain. But I did not relish changes that diminished the prerogative of the British Parliament. I knew that sometimes they would, and that we would have to swallow our pride, but I looked always for compensating advantages. I was a pragmatist, not an idealist, and a cautious pragmatist too. To me, the European Union was far more than a trading relationship, but I did not want to see it become a federation. This was then, and is now, I think, the mainstream view of the British people.

From the beginning of my premiership, I tried to maximise the advantages to Britain of our membership, and to minimise the concessions we had to make. I advanced our views in a softer tone of voice than my predecessor – though unaccompanied by any serious change of policy – and I sought a personal rapport with other heads of government. I went out of my way to work within the charmed circle rather than shouting from the terraces.

Up to a point, I succeeded. Old bruises faded. Britain's case was listened to. In the negotiations over the Maastricht Treaty I was offered cooperation and concessions that would not otherwise have been available. Maastricht had not disillusioned me, but the degree of self-interest across the Union in the run-up to and beyond Black Wednesday had begun to do so. The hypocrisy of the hectoring from the President of the Commission Jacques Delors and François Mitterrand over our delay in ratifying the treaty had hardened my heart further. Delors frequently inflamed more than the Euro-sceptics with ill-judged interventions, and Mitterrand utterly failed to understand the damage caused on the foreign-exchange markets by the French referendum to endorse the Maastricht agreement.

No other government in the European Union had faced Britain's difficulty in obtaining parliamentary approval for the Maastricht deal, yet I had honoured my word, even though the government had nearly fallen in doing so. As President of the Council of Ministers in the second half of 1992, I had fashioned the consensus that enabled Denmark to ratify the Maastricht Treaty, and so saved it. I resented the carping directed at me by those who had a cosy consensus in their own legislature, and whose parliaments lacked historical muscle.

I had now seen the Union in action from the inside. It was a dispiriting experience. Europe's heads of government met several times a year in the European Council. Always, there was a distinct hierarchy in these discussions. Delors, Kohl and Mitterrand mattered, and were referred to *ad nauseam* in other countries' contributions. 'I agree with Helmut' became an intensely irritating *leitmotif* in round-table discussions. Giulio Andreotti of Italy was an honorary additional member of this inner circle by virtue of his seniority. He often spoke for what I privately dubbed 'the old man's consensus'. In later years I would get on well with a succession of Italian prime ministers: Giuliano Amato, my guest at Chequers in 1993; Carlo Ciampi, whom I had known as a fine head of the Italian central bank; Silvio Berlusconi, the freewheeling businessman who was an excellent host and brisk chairman at the 1994 Naples G7 summit; and Lamberto Dini, a fellow member of the club of former finance ministers, who organised a memorable UK/Italian summit in the palaces of Florence (slightly marred by a lack of heating on a freezing day). My only problem was that as soon as I built up a personal relationship with an Italian counterpart he would be ousted, and I would have to start all over again.

Elsewhere in 'Club Med', Felipe Gonzalez of Spain had been a cult figure of the left, and was an unlikely soulmate for a British Conservative. Felipe was a young man in favour of consensus, although he would stand out against it if Spain's interests were threatened. He was then a dogged advocate until either he won his point, or so infuriated colleagues that he was taken aside by Kohl and told to compromise. Across in Greece was another socialist, but one who had seen better days, the seventy-six-year-old Andreas Papandreou. He carried on tenaciously while his body grew physically weaker, literally propped up at European summits by his young second wife and unable to sit through lengthy meetings.

To the north, Ruud Lubbers of the Netherlands tended to be among Britain's closest friends. He was prepared to ruffle feathers and did so, whilst avoiding slogans and remaining full of common sense. I often found him an ally, as, sometimes, was the likeable Anibal Cavaco Silva of Portugal, for whom I had a great deal of respect.

Discussion in the European Council also followed a somewhat weary pattern. Everyone around the table laid out their views in a set-piece speech that was frequently more for domestic consumption than a serious attempt to influence decisions. This was often because the decision had already been fashioned in private, and the discussion was merely the prelude to confirming it. Before every summit the Christian Democrat leaders met in caucus, and the French and Germans reached an agreed position if at all possible. The Commission was in touch with both groups.

Most decisions were proposed by the Commission, after negotiation with France, Germany and the country currently holding the Union presidency. The smaller nation-states, all of whom were net beneficiaries of the communal budget, often complained bitterly about this in private, but were consenting adults in public. Whenever I witnessed this phenomenon, Aneurin Bevan's famous explanation of how he persuaded reluctant doctors to join the NHS came unbidden into my mind: 'I stuffed their mouths with gold.' The glow of the precious metal beamed out from the silence of many of the heads of government. Their unwillingness to oppose a Franco–German consensus was striking, and, for Britain, highly irritating.

The Commission was rarely challenged; and when it was, there was often a cowardice to the criticism: any counter-proposal was preceded by a paean, together with the timid suggestion that, perhaps, just possibly, doubtless for the best of reasons, the Commission was wrong. Jacques Delors, confident in his position, brushed aside such half-hearted complaints easily, often with German or, more likely, French, support. Others rather smugly joined the consensus. Isolated, and made to feel they had behaved improperly, the critics conceded. It was cruel, and an absurd way to operate.

Only Britain was the grit in the oyster. I saw how and why Margaret Thatcher had become so unpopular among her fellow European heads of government. She was used to a democratic system in which criticism was harsh and often unfair, and where people spoke their mind. The pussyfooting of the European Council would not have been at all to her taste. Nor was it to mine. But when British ministers spoke the language of Westminster in Brussels it was like spitting in church. Others shied away from our 'non-consensual' approach, and the club closed ranks against us. Britain was isolated again. It was immensely frustrating.

From the moment I first crossed the threshold of Number 10 as prime minister I had dreaded the potential impact of Europe on the Conservative Party. In 1990 I sensed the depth of feeling over the issue. By 1993 I knew it all too well. Once the Maastricht Treaty had been ratified (see Chapter 12) I had hoped our European travails would be over. They were not. In the

Commons, a legacy of resentment lingered that flared up often enough to overshadow nearly everything the government tried to do. I began to suspect that a small minority were fanning these resentments; was their aim, I wondered, to force us into an ever-more sceptical posture, with their ultimate, though unstated, objective being a formal breach with our partners, and departure from the European Union? Europe had the capacity to split the Conservative Party and hurl it into the wilderness – or even, I feared, destroy it for good. The shadow of Sir Robert Peel never left my side.

The issue at stake touched the very core of Conservatism. Like all political parties, ours was a coalition. Here was an issue that ran along its faultline. One strand of our party saw further integration as inevitable, and believed we should embrace and lead it. Britain could no longer wield great influence in isolation, they argued, but as part of Europe it could not fail to do so. Narrow-minded nationalism should be cast aside; the Conservative Party was the party of Europe, and should remain so. This was the firm belief of the convinced Europeans.

But another strand of the Conservative Party also felt the tug of history and of instinct. Britain had always been a proud, self-governing nation with a strong Parliament, they pointed out. Our history in the twentieth century had been the polar opposite of our European neighbours: we had not been invaded, did not practise consensus politics, we traded around the world. We should not yield any more power from the British Parliament: it was against our national interest to do so. This was the firm belief of the sceptical Europeans.

The danger to the Conservative Party lay in the fervour with which both sides believed they were in tune with the party's history and instincts. Both believed they had the national interest at heart; both felt compromise would be a betrayal. Moreover, both had leaders able to convince them that theirs was the true faith. Edward Heath was a European; Margaret Thatcher was not. Geoffrey Howe was for the European adventure; Norman Tebbit was not.

My Cabinets included all shades of both views. Michael Heseltine, Douglas Hurd, Ken Clarke, John Gummer and David Hunt were for going forward. Michael Howard, John Redwood, Michael Portillo and Peter Lilley were for going back. The bulk of the Cabinet – colleagues such as Ian Lang, Gillian Shephard, Tony Newton and William Waldegrave – broadly favoured 'thus far and no further,' and only for that policy could a Cabinet majority be obtained. Within this middle group were many shades of opinion: some, like Malcolm Rifkind and Virginia Bottomley, favoured 'no further' for the time being, but later perhaps. Others would have accepted further movement, but believed it to be impossible politically in Britain. Others felt we were being dragged too far, but that we could not credibly resist, and that British isolationism from European advances was untenable.

Amongst so much conviction I remained a pragmatist. I did not like the drift towards a European federation, and did not believe we should join it. Nor did I believe the country would be prepared to do so. But neither did I like the increasing shrillness of the sceptics' case, in which the genuine patriotic conviction of some was buttressed by the paranoia and xenophobia of others. The expression of exaggerated fears was beginning to win the argument with the public, backed by lamentable misreporting of European issues by an increasingly Euro-sceptic press. The atmosphere was developing that would spawn the nakedly anti-European Referendum Party of Sir James Goldsmith.

My concern was twofold. First, what policy was right for Britain? Here I believed my policy of cautious engagement with Europe, but hostility to federalism, was the right approach. My second concern was whether this policy could unite the Conservative Party and prevent it from splintering.

The long-term well being of the Conservative Party mattered to me very much. I am, by instinct and conviction, a Conservative. I have an enduring affection for the way of life that Conservatism represents. In my view our country would be immeasurably poorer if it did not have a credible Conservative Party in government, or as a powerful opposition. I knew that if the warring factions within the party could not be stilled, I could not protect it from short-term tremors, and probably from political defeat. But with its long-term health in mind I was determined to shelter the party as far as I could from the detonation of the smoking bomb in its hands. I did not want the party to split, and I feared it might.

Nothing in politics is ever certain. With this in mind, I kept our options open on the single European currency. That was right for the country and, I believed, for the party. In 1993 the single currency was by no means certain to go ahead, and the economic and political implications of it were unclear. I wanted time for opinions to mature and a settled way ahead to become clear. Opinions change. It may not have been a heroic policy, but heroism, in the cause either of joining the currency or opposing it outright, could have smashed the party. In the long term, economic realities would determine whether or not we joined the single currency. Either way, Britain would still need a vibrant Conservative Party.

This party calculation was important to me, but was not my primary concern. For, as much as the party mattered to me, the long-term interest of my country mattered more. I was not prepared to sacrifice one for the other. The implications for the British economy of an early decision on the single currency were potentially severe. It would have been reckless to commit the country to enter on the back of the ERM debacle. Too many things remained to be clarified. When would the currency come into effect? What would the conditions of entry be? Would Europe's economies have converged? Would a single interest rate be appropriate for every country in the new currency? Where would it lead? What political changes would follow such economic change? Would other policies – such as tax – be harmonised? No one knew.

Above all, as I argued time and again, there was no need to take an early decision. I had negotiated the right at Maastricht to go in or stay out as we chose, when the new currency was launched. I was determined to decide only when it was clear that entry was or was not in our national interest, and in the meantime, since my instincts were against, to try to delay the project, point out the risks, and encourage our partners to concentrate on widening the Union to new members before integrating further.

My musing in the Douro Valley in the summer of 1993 led to an article I wrote for the *Economist* that autumn. In it, I argued that Europe should focus on what its people wanted, not the institutional reforms that so attracted its leaders. Peace, stability, growth, prosperity and employment should be our prime concerns. I challenged the prevailing view that we had to march forward to ever greater political and economic uniformity, and set out my own mantra:

> It is for nations to build Europe, not for Europe to attempt to supersede nations. I want to see the Community become a wide union, embracing the whole of democratic Europe, in a single market and with common security arrangements firmly linked to NATO. I want to see a competitive and confident Europe, generating jobs for its citizens and choice for its consumers. A Community which ceases to nibble at national freedoms, and so commands the enthusiasm of its member nations.

> Such a Community would be a more genuine and lasting Euro-
> pean Union than anything we have now. It offers peace. It pro-
> motes security. It widens free trade. It preserves and enhances
> infant democracies. It marches with the instincts of free people in
> free nations. It is an ambition for the new century that dwarfs the
> dreams of the founders of the Community. The Treaty of Rome
> is not a creed. It is an instrument. We must tune it to the times.

I caused a stir, but wasted my ink. Our partners did not shed their
ambitions, and in my party the Euro-sceptics redoubled their efforts. At
the party conference in October 1993, Norman Lamont broke cover, becoming the first serious Conservative to hint at withdrawal from the European
Union. I was surprised by the speed of his movement to the Euro-sceptics'
cause, since never in the years he had worked with me had he even hinted
at such a proposition. Now he openly spoke of it. Others were unsurprised,
which suggested that Norman had advanced views to them which he had
withheld from me. Bill Cash founded the 'European Foundation', which
was almost invariably hostile to the thrust of policy of the EU. It was to
become a running sore, though it did not approach the unthinking venom
of the Referendum Party founded by James Goldsmith.

The tenor of anti-European comment accelerated. Only the *Guardian*
and the *Independent* among the broadsheets provided any sort of balance
in press comment, despite the efforts of Christopher Meyer, who came to
Number 10 from the Foreign Office to succeed Gus O'Donnell as my Press
Secretary early in 1994 – 'Bernard Ingham with a posh accent', as one hack
described him. Chris was under no illusions about the enormous task he
faced. 'My adrenaline flows when there are problems,' he would say. It
must have flowed often. In February 1994, Michael Portillo, in unscripted
remarks, suggested that, unlike in Britain, qualifications in other European
countries could be purchased, and contracts won by bribery. He withdrew
the charges speedily, saying they had been made 'in the heat of the moment'.
It was a reckless comment which brought forth inevitable calls for him to
be sacked. He was too able to be dismissed for one piece of folly, and I
accepted his public retraction, which struck a chord with me: he had, he
explained, overreacted to unjustified attacks on the government over sleaze.
I sympathised with that, and took no action.

Michael's remarks were absurd, and he was wise to disown them without
delay, but this did not stop Hugh Dykes, the Conservative MP for Harrow

East and a fervent European supporter, to say unhelpfully that Michael had 'revealed the deep hatred of the EU felt by some extreme right-wing colleagues'. In this fashion, two reckless and ill-considered remarks damaged the Conservative Party and deepened the antipathy between its two wings. Events like this left me forever firefighting.

A worse problem was brewing that was to lead to one of the lowest points of my premiership. Many decisions in the EU were reached by what is known as a 'qualified majority'. Each country has a number of votes allocated to it. These ranged from Germany, France, Italy and Britain with ten votes each, to Denmark with three. Decisions could be blocked if a sizeable minority objected. The number of votes needed for a 'blocking minority' was twenty-three. In 1994 the Union was about to grow, as we planned the accession of Austria, Sweden, Finland and Norway (although in the event the people of Norway voted to stay out). Should the blocking minority be raised to take account of the new members? Logic said yes, but British self-interest said no. I wanted to retain our power to block unpalatable polices without having to assemble a large coalition of member states.

I was not alone in this, for at the outset we had powerful allies. France, Germany and Spain also opposed raising the blocking minority, and official advice to me was that this was a battle we could win. I brought the matter before Cabinet, and the conclusion was unanimous and clear: we should argue for the current blocking minority of twenty-three to be retained. Even the strongest pro-Europeans in the Cabinet spoke up for this policy. All were agreed. None dissented. No warnings of danger ahead were issued.

In the Commons and the press, as usual, the sceptics were setting out their demands and overplaying the importance of the issue. Tony Marlow and Bill Cash issued dire warnings that concessions would split the party – code, of course, to indicate that they would be as bloody-minded and as uncaring of Conservative Party unity as ever. This was unsurprising: their stance had become as one-eyed as a Cyclops, and neither rational argument nor party unity nor the damage to the government seemed to weigh with them.

Then the ground began to move beneath our feet. Germany and France, after private discussions, changed their minds and backed raising the blocking minority to twenty-seven. The Foreign Office began to fret, but did not change its view that we could still win. Spain seemed a reliable ally, and we stuck to our position. The stakes were raised, since in the prevailing political atmosphere in the Commons a retreat on this issue would have raised a storm. It would not have been seen as a pragmatic move away from a decision not worth a big argument, but as 'a further move towards federalism', 'a weak betrayal', and much else. Compromise would have been a calamity within the Conservative Party at that time. Even so, stepping back would have been the wisest course, and our decision in Cabinet not to do so was to bring humiliation. However, there was still a genuine prospect of winning if Spain stuck with us – two nations objecting could often ward off unhelpful changes.

When the matter was raised in Brussels in early March 1994, Douglas Hurd argued our case and the decision was postponed for a more significant European meeting of foreign ministers, to be held at Ioannina, in Greece, later that month. By now alarm bells were ringing as the issue grew in importance at home and our European partners began to dig in for the change. The Cabinet, including the pro-Europeans, remained firmly against a compromise. At Ioannina, Douglas found himself isolated as Spain too suddenly shifted its position. The choice was now stark: concede, and face uproar in the Commons; hold out, and block the accession of the new entrants to the Union; or seek a compromise. Douglas had no choice but to go for the third option.

Douglas's package, conceded only grudgingly by our partners, was to accept twenty-seven as the normal blocking minority, with a provision for those opposed to new legislation to hold it up for a reasonable, though unspecified, period provided twenty-three votes were cast against. It was a classic Euro-fudge.

I saw Douglas in Number 10 on his return from Greece. He had had a bad time with his European colleagues, and was unusually low. We had suffered a bad reverse and we both knew it. Ken Clarke joined us and predicted mayhem in the Commons, but was sure Douglas had been right to accept the fudge. I gained the impression that Douglas would leave the government if I rejected his compromise and continued to hold out for a blocking majority of twenty-three, although it was not his style to threaten resignation to force through a decision. The Cabinet hawks had become doves. Germany, France, Spain, the Foreign Office, Cabinet colleagues, had one by one nimbly moved away from our position. There was no choice. I accepted the deal.

It was a most humiliating retreat, and it hurt badly. I was deeply depressed by it, because it could have been avoided. I should have seen the danger. There were extenuating circumstances, of course, but no real excuses. The situation was made more painful by my ill-judged exchange in the Commons with John Smith before the Ioannina meeting when, at Prime Minister's Questions, I called him 'Monsieur Oui – the poodle of Brussels'. It was a gratuitous and graceless accusation, and I knew it as soon as the words left my lips in the heat of an exchange. When I was forced into defeat days later, this remark came back to haunt me. Tony Marlow – once again bidding to be the first rat off the ship – told me bluntly on the floor of the Commons to resign. He was at least honest in his view: others muttered the same in private, but did not say so publicly. The mood in the party was fierce. The press was hideous. It was an appalling time, made worse by the knowledge that the wound was self-inflicted.

The wound was also deep. The episode reawakened cocktail-party chatter and leadership speculation whenever journalists and politicians met. The stories whizzed around. A journalist, Simon Heffer, predicted: 'Peter Lilley might stand. Bill Cash is keen on the idea of Lilley and so is Peter Stothard [editor of *The Times*].' Andrew Neil, editor of the *Sunday Times*, had views too: 'I've always supported Heseltine and I'll be proved right. As to endorsing him, we shall see. I have to discuss that sort of thing with Rupert [Murdoch].' These views, whether true or not, were reported to me. Nor were the journalists alone. Soon after, I learned, Bill Cash told friends, 'We shall take our decision on whether there is to be a leadership challenge from our side of the party in the month between the European elections and the recess.' I was told that Margaret Thatcher was supportive, and dissented from all talk of a new leader: 'We've got to stop this ridiculous frenzy – everyone is being damaged by grapeshot.'

Labour loved it all. 'Why do the Tories keep banging on about Europe?' asked Peter Mandelson. 'We're divided too, but we keep it under our hats.'

Then, on 12 May 1994, John Smith died. I was in the middle of breakfast when Alex Allan came up to the flat to break the awful news. At first I could hardly believe it, but it was confirmed soon enough as I sat in the Cabinet Room. I asked for a few minutes on my own, and thought of the waste of John Smith's death. I wrote to his widow Elizabeth, and screwed up my first, inadequate note to her. I decided tribute should be paid in Parliament that day, and the House should then be suspended. I was joined by the private secretary who worked most closely with me for PMQs, and we began to draft a parliamentary tribute.

'John Smith was one of the outstanding parliamentarians of modern politics,' I began.

> He had no malice. There were things that he cared for passionately. He lived for them; he fought for them; he cared for them. But he carried his fight fairly, without malice, without nastiness. The bruises that existed soon faded after a dispute with John Smith.
>
> In our parliamentary democracy, it is the fate of party leaders to dispute, to scorn, to disagree. So it was in the nature of my political relationship with John Smith that we frequently clashed in public and in the House, yet afterwards, in private, we met often and amiably – again, no bruises. Inevitably, the prime minister and the leader of the opposition have to conduct business in private and on confidential matters. Whenever we did, I always found him courteous, fair minded and constructive, but also tough for what he was seeking and what he believed in. We would share a drink – sometimes tea, sometimes not tea – and our discussions on those occasions ranged far beyond the formal business that we were transacting. To the despair of my private office and, I suspect, sometimes of his, the meetings extended far beyond the time that was immediately scheduled for them.
>
> Political differences are not the be-all and end-all of relationships for members of the House. When I think of John Smith, I think of an opponent, not an enemy; and when I remember him, I shall do so with respect and affection.

John's death caused genuine grief in the Labour Party and far beyond it. In his mid-fifties, he was, in political terms, a young man. The expectation that he would one day be prime minister, and the belief that he had been cheated of this, was a potent boost to grief.

In the wake of John Smith's death, Margaret Beckett became temporary leader of a Labour Party that behaved superbly in the tragic circumstances. The party mourned in public, and the nation mourned with them. Parliamentary hostilities were suspended, and the aspirants for the Labour crown kept their ambitions out of the public gaze.

John Smith died in the middle of campaigning for elections to the European Parliament, due on 9 June. Many commentators, with glee, predicted a near wipe-out for the Conservative Party. Five parliamentary by-elections were held on the same day, and the results in these, declared first, were bad. Four formerly Labour-held seats returned the Labour candidates with vastly larger majorities, whilst at Eastleigh, where a by-election had been caused by the death of Stephen Milligan, our share of the vote fell by a quarter, and the Liberal Democrats gained the seat comfortably.

The results of the European elections were declared on Sunday – we lost fourteen of the thirty-two seats we had held, and won little more than 25 per cent of the national vote. It was an appalling performance, but nonetheless a much better outcome for the government than many had predicted. I was given credit for a good campaign, and my critics in the party scaled back their plans for a contest for the leadership. 'He's certainly safe until November, as we agreed at our Tuesday meeting,' Bill Cash observed grandly. David Evans, a member of the 1922 Committee executive, made it clear he was holding fire 'until after the reshuffle, but if he gets rid of Portillo, Redwood or Lilley, it's . . . war'.

The contest for the Labour leadership soon began. Margaret Beckett, the temporary leader, performed well enough in her role, but was never really a serious contender. Nor was John Prescott, although it would have suited me well to see him become leader. The shadow Chancellor Gordon Brown seemed a serious option, and one I would have welcomed. Although he was a fine parliamentary performer he carried with him an air of gloom and, in public at least, seemed to regard a smile as an optional extra. 'We won't pick Gordon,' a Labour whip told me. 'He's too like one of those undertakers in old western films that measure you for a coffin before the gunfight.'

That left the shadow Home Secretary Tony Blair, who was the press favourite from the outset. I knew almost nothing about him at first hand. His parliamentary career had never pitted him against me, although colleagues who had faced him reported that he was well briefed and able and, Michael Howard told me, 'uses the press well. He leaks a lot – and very effectively.' Tony Blair looked and sounded like a middle-of-the-road Tory, and was an attractive candidate, although very young and inexperienced. Nonetheless, I soon felt he was sure to win, and in one way I welcomed this: it would, so I thought, end the artificial difference between the two major parties, and stop the left–right pendulum by which each successive government repealed many of the measures of its predecessor. His persona, too, would minimise the class-based perceptions of Tory and Labour that were so damaging to intelligent political debate. I did not, at the time, appreciate the extent to which he would appropriate Conservative language and steal our policies. The attractive candidate was to turn out to be a political kleptomaniac.

Meanwhile, the Euro-sceptic mill ground on: the more difficult our political position became, the more the rebels turned the ratchet. They believed that showing hostility to Europe would restore the party's popularity. It did not. It simply convinced the electorate that we were more divided than ever. Our discordant notes dominated the airwaves, and a hostile press, much of it arm-in-arm with the sceptics, added to the din. Beyond our shores, our EU partners began to believe that every European position we took was determined by our internal rows, not our objective judgements. This was not true, but it appeared to be, and it weakened our case. A spat then arose that convinced our partners of it.

Jacques Delors was due to retire after two terms as President of the European Commission at the end of 1994, and two significant candidates to succeed him had emerged. Leon Brittan, the former Conservative Home Secretary and for five years a European Commissioner, sought my support as a candidate for the presidency. His ability was beyond question, and he believed he could attract votes from other governments. I doubted this, but was glad to back such an able British candidate. Ruud Lubbers, the Dutch Prime Minister, was widely expected to succeed Delors. He had strong credentials and, if Leon faltered, seemed to me to be an excellent candidate. I had no hesitation in deciding to support Lubbers as my second choice. A third candidate then emerged who was far less desirable from Britain's point of view. Jean-Luc Dehaene, the Prime Minister of Belgium, a firm ally of Kohl and Mitterrand, a convinced federalist, and keen to push the Union as fast as he could in the direction I least wanted it to go. He was emphatically not the candidate for me.

In April 1994 I had met Helmut Kohl and told him of my support for Leon Brittan. Helmut said he had not made up his mind. He did not mention Dehaene. I was alarmed, therefore, when I heard in May that Kohl and Mitterrand had struck a deal privately in a meeting at the French–German border town of Mulhouse to support Dehaene – not least since, like other European leaders, I had thought he was likely to support Lubbers (as, incidentally, did Lubbers). The Kohl–Mitterrand agreement seemed to me to be yet another attempt by the two leaders to bypass the normal decision-making structures of the Union. Soon we heard that one of Kohl's officials was acting as a *de facto* campaign manager for Dehaene and informing the smaller EU members, in none too delicate terms, how they were expected to vote. This led to considerable bad feeling around Europe. Lubbers had been Prime Minister of the Netherlands for a decade, and was widely respected. Many of his colleagues were not happy to see him being dumped unceremoniously in favour of one of the EU's newest and most junior premiers. Even the Belgians had reservations, as Dehaene was seen as one of the few people capable of holding his country together, and in the event of his retirement from the premiership he would be badly missed.

France and Germany's tactic was not a new one. For years past the two countries had pre-empted summit after summit with joint letters or statements that had influenced policy in their favour. I thought that if they now succeeded in inserting their own placeman as President of the European Commission, the rest of us might as well not even bother to turn up to meetings. I was clear about the course I should take. I liked Dehaene. He was easy company, with a passion for football and a strong sense of humour. Beneath a deceptively rough exterior, he had an acute mind. But politically he stood at the opposite end of the European spectrum to the British. Above all, the principle that Kohl should unmake Lubbers and decide, with Mitterrand alone, to foist the relatively obscure and much more pliable Dehaene upon their ten partners, was wrong. When we canvassed opinions, we found much private unhappiness among those partners, Belgium apart. Countries like Portugal could not afford openly to oppose the German–French *diktat*, but privately sympathised with our stance.

At the time, only Brittan and Lubbers were declared candidates. Nonetheless, in view of the Mulhouse rumours, I let the Belgians know that Dehaene would be unacceptable to us, and that I would veto him. I added that we were letting them know this privately, since I bore Dehaene no personal ill-will, and wished to avoid causing him public embarrassment. During this period I met Leon Brittan several times, and assured him of my support. He reported to me that he had toured European capitals and received a positive reception.

One week before the summit at Corfu on 25–26 June 1994, where the decision on Delors's successor was due to be made, and three weeks after the Franco–German meeting at Mulhouse, Dehaene's candidacy became official despite my private warnings to his office. Once more I told France,

Germany and Belgium that I would not accept him as President of the Commission. I also informed the Greek government, which would chair the Corfu summit. I did not want there to be any doubt about our position. At no time did anyone seek to dissuade us by advocating Dehaene's virtues. They simply took note of our position and assumed, no doubt, that if they had a majority for Dehaene I would cave in and accept him.

When our delegation arrived at Corfu it was clear that Dehaene was still a serious candidate. Our objections were known. There had been no consultation. And yet the Franco–German partnership still expected to prevail. It was a classic illustration of everything I least liked about the way the Union conducted its business.

On the first evening, the heads of government met for dinner at the splendid Achilleion Palace. We did so in the absence of both Lubbers and Dehaene, who were represented by their foreign ministers. Andreas Papandreou, the Greek Prime Minister, frail and ailing, was our host and chairman. Papandreou had no strong views about the presidency, and simply wished to see a decision made with a minimum of fuss and no row. He suggested Holland, Belgium and Britain each introduce their own candidate. Kohl objected. I suggested we discuss the merits of each candidate.

Albert Reynolds, the Prime Minister of Ireland, proposed a secret ballot, with each state noting its first and second preference. As several leaders did not want to reveal who they voted for (not wishing to alienate the eventual winner, or France and Germany), this was agreed. The ballot showed eight first-preference votes for Dehaene, three for Lubbers, and one – mine – for Leon Brittan. Lubbers received six second-preference votes. Though Dehaene was ahead, there was no consensus, and I said yet again in the meeting that he was unacceptable to Britain.

At this point, now after midnight, events became chaotic. Papandreou disappeared during a break in the discussion, and officials told us the meeting was over. He was old and ill, and we assumed he had been taken off to bed. No one was surprised, and everyone was sympathetic. Cars arrived and heads of government left. As this was happening, officials from Spain and Italy huddled in a corner and agreed, under pressure from France and Germany, to switch their votes from Lubbers to Dehaene 'in the interest of unity'. This, at such gatherings, was the traditional reason given for surrender after a certain amount of arm-twisting. As both countries needed support for large Union cash payments, it was not difficult to guess how this had come about.

At this point – fortunately I had not yet left – the meeting resumed. Other leaders were not so lucky. Several had to return from their hotels, and the Irish motorcade executed a U-turn on the highway and sped Albert Reynolds back to the palace. At the reconvened meeting in the early hours of the morning I maintained my opposition to Dehaene, and Wim Kok, the Dutch Foreign Minister, joined me in continuing to support his own Prime Minister, Ruud Lubbers. It was, I thought, intolerable to have a new president chosen in this manner. No progress was made, and we eventually wound up the meeting at around 2 a.m.

Back at my hotel I called Douglas Hurd and our officials together – it was now 3 a.m. – and set out the events of the evening. I hoped sense would prevail and Dehaene would withdraw the following morning. If not, I said, 'I intend to veto his appointment.' At this, there was a definite buzz – but no one attempted to dissuade me.

Later that morning a shock awaited me when I met Wim Kok. The Dutch had backed down. I asked why, but Kok had no real explanation. Leon Brittan had withdrawn, and I was prepared to support Lubbers, but the Dutch were not. I tried to persuade Kok to maintain his support for Lubbers, but it was clear he was not free to do so.

I returned to my delegation office. The Dutch had been put under great pressure, and their country's close relations with Belgium had weighed heavily with them. I was now alone in my opposition to Dehaene. In these circumstances, I was sure the French and Germans would continue to propose him, believing I had to accept since there were now no other candidates.

At Ioannina my allies had tiptoed away. Now it had happened again. But this time there was a difference: this time they did not have the leverage of holding back the enlargement of the Union. The decision on the presidency was taken 'by consensus'; it needed unanimity, and we did not have it. The absence of allies did not alter my own opposition to the Dehaene candidacy, since it had become for me a matter of principle. He was, I believed, the wrong man to be President of the Commission, and the Franco–German alliance was trying to bulldoze him through. On both counts I intended to stop him.

When the morning session began, Papandreou announced that Lubbers and Brittan had withdrawn. Tributes were paid to them. Only one candidate remained – Jean-Luc Dehaene. Papandreou looked around the room for a babble of consent and interventions in support of the only candidate. I pressed the button in front of me to indicate I wished to speak. There was utter silence. No mutters of either support or irritation. I reminded my colleagues of my position, and reiterated that I had made it clear from the outset and had not changed my mind. I then formally vetoed Jean-Luc Dehaene as president.

There was no row. No fuss. No one banged the table or expostulated. They knew my position and could not complain that my decision was a surprise. Some, I suspect, were secretly pleased to see the Franco–German candidate stopped, although no one, myself included, had any personal antipathy to Dehaene. Ruud Lubbers, I noticed, sat poker-faced with not even a twitch at the corners of his mouth. He would have made a fine president.

The meeting broke up. As it did so it became clear that the restraint of the heads of government in the European Council did not extend to their delegations, who briefed furiously against me. Jean-Luc Dehaene behaved with dignity. Others did not. EU officials predicted that Dehaene would be renominated, and Papandreou predicted a crisis unless Britain backed down. The French were outraged at my breach of propriety (pure humbug, since General de Gaulle had once paralysed European decision-making for six months). I remembered France's intransigence over the GATT round in 1993, and was unmoved by their criticism.

Back in Britain, Labour's acting leader Margaret Beckett claimed that I had vetoed Dehaene to appease the Euro-sceptic wing of my party, and Paddy Ashdown huffed and puffed to no effect. The Conservatives, for once, were delighted, my persistent critics full of praise. Leadership chatter vanished. I was astonished that one action, carried out for other reasons, could so transform opinions. Even at this distance in time I am sure my use of the veto was correct: it gave a necessary jolt to France and Germany, although sadly it did not encourage other countries to fight their own corners more robustly.

Speculation abounded as to what would happen. Rumour suggested another Belgian federalist would be proposed. Or Dehaene would be renominated. Peter Sutherland, Director-General of GATT – who would have been an excellent president – was mentioned, but the French threatened a veto. Two weeks later Helmut Kohl telephoned me to suggest Jacques Santer, the Christian Democrat Prime Minister of Luxembourg.

Santer had often been an ally on subsidiarity and cutting European expenditure, but he was not ideal, and I demurred. He was not the candidate I wanted: Ruud Lubbers was, on the assumption that Leon Brittan would not be appointed. It was clear, however, that every other member state had been consulted on this occasion and was content; a second British veto could not be so easily justified. Santer duly got the job, and was soon talked up by Kohl as being no different in outlook from Dehaene. Since Kohl had been instrumental in both candidacies, his opinion was unsurprising. It was wrong, though: Dehaene would have been much more dangerous from the British point of view. He was a more forceful character, less inclined to compromise, a socialist not a Christian Democrat, and a much more avid federaliser. Where Santer would be cautious, Dehaene would be bold, and such boldness would manifest itself in policies alien to the British interest. Although both candidates were approved by France and Germany, Santer's instincts were to encourage subsidiarity, whereas Dehaene's were to centralise; Santer favoured fewer European directives, Dehaene favoured more; Santer would try to hold the budget totals; Dehaene would seek to increase them. Both shared a similar vision for long-term European ambitions, but within that the differences were manifold.

At the time I referred to Santer as 'the right man in the right place at the right time'. This was, of course, in response to suggestions that he was indistinguishable from Jean-Luc Dehaene. 'The least unwelcome candidate available' would have been a more accurate reflection of my view, although to have expressed it would hardly have been tactful or helpful to Britain once Santer had been appointed. Nonetheless, my welcome to him was a comment I would live to regret – a salutory warning of the perils of diplomatic hyperbole.

There was an amusing sequel at the European summit convened in Brussels in July to endorse Santer. Behind the Council's closed doors, Mitterrand was taking the defeat of Dehaene much harder than Kohl, and made a long, abstruse intervention in which he argued *ex post facto* that there was no power of veto in the choice of Commission president. Not even Kohl offered support for this proposition. As we left the chamber, Mitterrand's Prime Minister, my old finance minister colleague Edouard Balladur, came gliding past, touched my elbow, and whispered: '*John – moi, j'aime le véto.*'

Europe cooled as an issue within the party for the rest of the summer, but it did not disappear completely. Simmering away, it was to boil over when the new session of Parliament began in November 1994.

At Edinburgh in late 1992 I had chaired the summit that agreed a five-year future financing deal for the European Union. It set the amount of money that each member state would contribute to – or receive from – the Union, and was an excellent deal for Britain, preserving our rebate and protecting us from any large increase in our contributions.

This outcome required legislation to bring it into force, and was included in the Queen's Speech setting out our programme for the next session of Parliament. The sceptics in my party began to growl; they would, they stated, oppose the legislation. I believed them, since at the time they were in a mood to oppose anything European, whether there was logic in their position or not. I discussed this dilemma separately with Richard Ryder, Douglas Hurd and Ken Clarke. It was evident to all of us that we could not afford a rerun of the lengthy dispute over the Maastricht Bill, yet it was more than likely that that would happen.

On Sunday, 13 November, three days before Parliament resumed, I met senior ministers over dinner at Number 10 to consider the session that lay ahead. Apart from Richard, Douglas and Ken, I invited Michael Howard, Michael Heseltine and Malcolm Rifkind. We assembled at 7.30 without Ken Clarke, who was running late, amid much joking that he had stopped off – as Richard Ryder put it – at the 'Dog and Trumpet'. This turned out to be the case: a relaxed Ken finally rolled up forty-five minutes later, full of bonhomie and apologies and talk of the watering-hole he had found on his journey into London.

It did not take long before our conversation turned to the big challenge ahead of us: the European Communities (Finance) Bill implementing the Edinburgh agreement. Douglas Hurd emphasised that the Bill was an international treaty obligation that could not be dropped without the government resigning (this view was later endorsed by Robin Butler at a meeting in the Cabinet Room). Malcolm Rifkind backed him. Ken Clarke was robust on dealing firmly with rebels, and Michael Heseltine also felt we should not give an inch. I made it clear that we had to enact the Bill, whatever the difficulties we faced.

As the discussion flowed it became evident that this was the overwhelming view. All the most senior members of the Cabinet were united in believing the Bill was a matter of confidence, and that to avoid any doubts, I should state that from the outset. Should we lose it, the government would resign and I would ask the Queen for a dissolution of Parliament.

Some will say this was provocative. I believe it was unavoidable. We were forced to enact the agreement by treaty obligation. Over Maastricht – after months of self-destruction – we were brought at the last to a Confidence vote. I did not wish to go through such protracted agony again. Richard Ryder agreed, but noted that this approach 'would have a knock-on effect on other votes'. In due course, it did.

I made our position clear on Wednesday, 16 November 1994 when I opened the debate on the Queen's Speech in the Commons: this Bill was 'inescapably a matter of confidence' I told the House. Our backbench dissidents affected shock, but had no reason to be surprised. Everyone in the Cabinet had been forewarned of our stand, and no one had come to me to protest.

A number of other minor explosions then took place, not all connected, but all contributing to another government 'crisis'. Some Central Office research, commissioned by a former minister, John Maples, was leaked to the *Financial Times*, revealing the public's unflattering view of the government. Nick Bonsor, the centre-right Member for Upminster, challenged Marcus Fox for the chairmanship of the 1922 Committee. I believe he would have challenged Marcus in any event, but it was interpreted as a warning shot against Marcus's support for the Confidence vote (fortunately Marcus survived, although not by many votes, or this story would have grown). A briefing to the press lobby by Ken Clarke then backfired. Listening to the gossip in the Tea Rooms, where he heard Euro-sceptic views that 'colleagues would stop my car going down The Mall' if I sought a dissolution of Parliament, Ken realised that the seriousness of our position had not registered with colleagues. He decided to make it clear. So, speaking off the record to journalists, he confirmed that senior ministers had met on Sunday evening to confirm that the Finance Bill would be a matter of confidence. (Our meeting had been written up as 'secret', and was therefore much more newsworthy.) Ken ridiculed suggestions that if the Bill was defeated I would resign and another Cabinet member would take over as prime minister. He knew that all Cabinet ministers had been informed of the decision, and was keen to imply agreement to it. It was, the press concluded from his briefing, a collective decision. This was taken as meaning that

*Above* HM Queen Elizabeth
the Queen Mother leading
the ceremony in Hyde Park
to commemorate the
fiftieth anniversary of
VE-Day, with HRH the
Princess Margaret and
Robert Cranborne:
6 May 1995.

*Left* Accompanying
HM the Queen during
commemorations of the
fiftieth anniversary of
VE- Day: 7 May 1995

*Above* Announcing my resignation as leader of the Conservative Party in the garden of Number 10: 22 June 1995.

*Left* The day after my resignation as party leader – a constituency day visit to Ailwyn Community School, Ramsey: 23 June 1995.

*Below* John Redwood (centre) declares his candidature for the leadership of the party, with his supporters (left to right) Tony Marlow, Teresa Gorman and Edward Leigh: 26 June 1995.

Restored to the leadership. Outside the campaign headquarters in Cowley Street, 4 July 1995. With Virginia Bottomley, Graham Bright, Norma and Michael Dobbs – the author and Deputy Chairman of the Conservative Party – in the background.

All in harmony: the Cabinet meets for the first time after the leadership election in the garden of 10 Downing Street, 6 July 1995. With John Gummer, Michael Heseltine, Gillian Shephard and Michael Portillo.

*Above* At Millwall
Football Club,
launching my
'Sport – Raising
the Game' policy:
14 July 1995.

*Right* Sharing a
story with Paddy
Ashdown and Tony
Blair before the
VJ-Day commemo-
ration on Horse-
guards Parade:
20 August 1995.

*Left* Norma and I
welcomed Bill and
Hillary Clinton to
Downing Street for an
official dinner in the
President's honour:
29 November 1995. The
staircase at Number 10
is lined with pictures of
all former prime
ministers.

Addressing British troops at their base in the Bosnian Serb town of Sipovo – fifty miles west of Sarajevo – on a one-day visit to Bosnia-Herzegovina: 24 May 1996.

A relaxed moment during lunch following the opening session of the G7 Summit in Lyon, France, 28 June 1996. Clockwise: Bill Clinton, interpreter, Ryutaro Hashimoto, Romano Prodi, Helmut Kohl and Jacques Chirac.

The Three Tenors (Placido Domingo, José Carreras and Luciano Pavarotti) visit Number 10 before their concert at Wembley Stadium: 4 July 1996.

*Above* Relaxing at Chequers: June 1996.

*Left* With Boris Yeltsin, at the conclusion of a press conference before his departure from RAF Brize Norton, following a two-day visit to Chequers: September 1996.

*Below* Trying to save the Union. In Scotland during the 1997 general election campaign with Ian Lang and Michael Forsyth.

*Above* Leaving Number 10 for the last time with Norma, Elizabeth, James and their partners: 2 May 1997.

*Right* The curtain falls: Concluding my final statement from Downing Street: 2 May 1997.

## LIFE OUT OF OFFICE

*Left* Supper with the Rolling Stones before their concert in Charlotte, North Carolina: October 1997.

*Right* An enduring special relationship – at Kennebunkport with George and Barbara Bush: September 1998.

*Left* One of my more friendly opponents: conversing with a cheetah in South Africa: November 1998.

Over two years of writing this book around the world and across continents: in a plane above the United States (1997) and cruising down the Nile (1999).

*every* Cabinet minister had agreed to the strategy – and reports soon made it clear that an indignant Michael Portillo had not, and that he, Peter Lilley and John Redwood had not been privy to the decision and had doubts about it. The pro- and anti-Europe camps were again at loggerheads.

This was a mess. Ken's lobby briefing, well-meant but, typically, done without consulting me or the Chief Whip, and the counter-briefing, fed the dispute. The Euro-sceptic media were on a perpetual lookout for such stories and were fed a diet of private briefings – often, it seemed, by special advisers or 'friends' of ministers – and it was never possible to identify the culprit. From my point of view it was disturbing to learn of the apparent unhappiness of Cabinet colleagues by way of third party press comment rather than in Cabinet or from the minister directly. It was a clear breach of collective responsibility, and it was tempting to sack the culpable minis-ter; but two factors militated against this. It would be a waste of ministers who, their behaviour on this issue apart, were able; and – more importantly – it would institutionalise and widen the European divisions in the party. The loser would be the Conservative Party. I put the thought to one side for further consideration in the summer reshuffle.

Nevertheless, it was time to knock heads together, and at Cabinet the following day I insisted on unanimous agreement that the Bill 'in all its essentials' *was* a matter of confidence. John Redwood said (much later) that he was 'close to resigning' over this. Perhaps so, but he kept his reservations to himself at the time, never voicing this view to me.

The turmoil grew when Bill Cash tabled amendments to the legislation, and Christopher Gill said at Prime Minister's Questions that he would resign the whip rather than vote for it. Norman Lamont, by now tuned only to habitual opposition on the backbenches, wrote that 'an unpopular government was threatening itself with extinction to increase the taxes we pay to Brussels'. 'No good came out of Maastricht or Edinburgh,' he told the ambassador of one of our European partners soon after. 'No good ever comes out of Europe,' he went on. It was hard to credit that this same Norman had welcomed the Edinburgh and Maastricht agreements as chan-cellor.

In the mayhem, the familiar whispers of leadership challenges to come were heard once more; gallons of ink were spilled in speculation. Such briefing from the Euro-sceptics was by now a familiar part of the landscape, and once again it came to nothing. The drama-a-day mentality of parts of the parliamentary party had colleagues huddling together to exchange gossip. Whenever a Cabinet minister was spied talking to sceptics, opinion was divided as to whether he was urging dissent or conformity. It was a madhouse. One BBC news cameraman who normally covered war zones was overheard during one of my photo-opportunities saying: 'Perhaps the Prime Minister should come and live with us, where we've only got bullets and staying alive to worry about.'

On 28 November, the second reading of the Finance Bill took place. Ken Clarke spoke for the government, giving rise to criticism that I should have done so as it was a matter of confidence. I had in fact discussed this with Ken, Douglas Hurd and Richard Ryder, and on balance we had decided that the Chancellor – whose business it was – would be better able to emphasise the Cabinet nature of our determination over the Bill and prevent a rerun of the Paving Vote drama, when I had been accused of petulantly threatening a dissolution of Parliament if we lost the division.

It was a hot-tempered debate. Ken told the House that the Bill would increase our net contribution to the European Union by £75 million within a year, and £250 million by 1999. This figure contrasted with earlier estimates by some of the Euro-sceptics of an increase ten times higher within the year, and up to a net £8 billion a year by 1996–97. Nick Budgen accused the government of 'blackmailing' backbenchers to force the Bill through. Norman Lamont – welcomed by cries of 'Stalking Norman' from a heckling Dennis Skinner – challenged the figures, as did Gordon Brown from the Labour front bench. John Wilkinson compared his fellow rebels to the anti-appeasers who opposed the Munich agreement – which was more enlightening about his agitated state of mind over the European Union than about the budgetary debate.

To maximise dissent on our benches, Labour had cleverly tabled an amendment which made the new budgetary contribution dependent on a reduction of fraud and a cut in the cost of the Common Agricultural Policy. This was simply a trouble-making device to engender a vote in which they could oppose a Bill they agreed with. And it worked, though the main Bill was approved with a majority of 285 votes, and Labour's amendment was defeated by twenty-seven votes, with our majority swollen by support from the Ulster Unionists. Eight Tories abstained on the amendment, notwithstanding the clear and consistent warning that they would lose the whip and that a general election would result if we were defeated. As agreed at the Sunday-evening dinner two weeks before, Richard Ryder withdrew the whip from all eight: Teddy Taylor, Teresa Gorman, Richard Shepherd, Christopher Gill, John Wilkinson, Tony Marlow, Nicholas Budgen and Michael Carttiss. Richard Body, their fellow in spirit over matters European, resigned the whip in protest and joined them.

It was a low moment on the fourth anniversary of my election as leader of the party. The rebellion over Maastricht had nearly brought us to defeat, and to avoid an encore we had exercised the strongest threat available. Now our colleagues' disregard of our warnings forced us to implement it. I had no compunction about doing so, but despaired that we had been driven to this, despite the fact that I am convinced we would have been defeated without a Confidence Motion.

The 'whipless nine' assumed the air of martyrs, and won the general applause of sceptic opinion. But I think that behind the scenes they were a little taken aback, although the whips had told them the implications of their declining to support us. They became a travelling circus, promoting Euro-scepticism wherever they went. Teresa Gorman and Christopher Gill wrote a pamphlet entitled *Not a Penny More*, which read like a manifesto for an alternative anti-European party. Gill suggested that the Cabinet was 'hell-bent' on sending more money to Europe, which sat oddly against the battle I had waged at Edinburgh to protect our rebate, hold down the growth in Community expenditure and reduce our relative net contribution to the overall budget. The real damage was done in Parliament. Without a majority, important votes were lost, and – on anything related to Europe – we could never be sure of getting the government's business through. One predictable and immediate consequence was a successful rebellion over the imposition of VAT on fuel and power, that meant Ken Clarke had to introduce a mini-budget to recoup lost revenue. It was a hideous situation.

In early January 1995, seven of the whipless rebels struck again, and we only narrowly won a vote on a fisheries policy in Europe. They sought the loosening of our ties with Europe, and the bumpy ride continued as, to great complaint from the right of the party, I refused to abandon my 'wait and see' approach to the single currency. It became fashionable to claim that I would have come out against it if I had not been restrained by the support of Michael Heseltine, Ken Clarke, John Gummer and others in the Cabinet for joining it. This is not so. I believed passionately that we should not commit ourselves to a decision until circumstances made it clear how our economic well-being would be affected by either joining or staying out. I had said so time after time. Moreover, the vast swathe of middle opinion in the party and the Cabinet supported this view, as, in polls, did public opinion as a whole. Nevertheless, those with fixed views – to go in or stay out – had the best lines, and often drowned out the pragmatic voices from the centre. The only policy movement I contemplated was a possible referendum prior to any decision to enter the single currency.

Ken Clarke, increasingly irritated by the sceptics, and unwilling to see policy tilted in their direction even to the extent of a referendum, stirred the pot further with a strongly pro-European speech to the European Movement on 9 February. When my Political Office in Number 10 saw a draft of this speech they were alarmed: Ken intended to say that it was possible to have monetary union *without* political union, which grandly swept aside the emotive issue of sovereignty. Not only did I disagree with this viewpoint, I knew it would cause a storm. My Political Secretary Howell James tried to get the offending words removed. He failed, and brought the problem to me while I was dressing for a black-tie dinner. I was alarmed, and sent a letter to Ken. But it was too late: the speech was delivered, and uproar followed. The fallout at Prime Minister's Questions and in the media was bloody, and I was unable to reply frankly to Tony Blair's questions about whether or not I agreed with my chancellor.

My working relationship with Ken was very close and, except in the matter of his more enthusiastic pro-Europeanism, we rarely disagreed. If I had fallen under a political bus I expected Ken to succeed me, and had told him so. Despite this knowledge, whenever I faced difficulties he was loud in my support and, except when he felt the Euro-sceptics were seeking to try to tug policy too far in their direction, he stuck to the agreed policy of the Cabinet. But under provocation Ken could be wilful. If his beliefs were biffed on the nose, he would biff back. The resultant flow of blood was satisfactory to both wings of the European argument, but not to me, who was left trying to mop it up.

In February I wearily instructed Cabinet once more to end the 'speculation and debate' over the single currency. In my heart, I knew my words would have little effect, and as expected, off-the-record briefing on the subject continued. Everyone, it seemed, had to scratch this obsessive itch.

It was worsened by a minority of 'advisers' to ministers who volubly fed their views to journalists under a cloak of anonymity over a good lunch. Ministers then protested their innocence to me – 'I've no idea where this came from ... I haven't seen [the journalist] for ages.' Moreover, the suggestion that it was their advisers who were to blame was robustly denied: 'No, he wouldn't do that.' This faction-fighting at second hand relegated the well-being of the government as a whole to a position far below the interests of individual ministers and their factions. It was almost impossible to deal with. Willie Whitelaw, a former chief whip as well as deputy prime minister, could not understand this at all 'Why do our people behave so badly?' he said to me. 'Do they understand nothing?'

In early March, Labour promoted a debate on our European policy. The Ulster Unionists voted against us, as did Norman Lamont, by now an angry voice. We won the division by only five votes, even though some of the whipless rebels supported us and others only abstained. This apparent softening of their antipathy was accompanied by pleas from their sympathisers on the right of the party that they should be given the whip once more. ('Nick would like to be back in the fold. Not all the group have the stomach for the fight,' one of the whipless nine was reported to me as saying.) Marcus Fox, Chairman of the 1922 Committee, also urged their return. Such messages to me or the whips, or to John Ward, who had succeeded Graham Bright as my PPS, became more frequent. Members of the 1922 Committee came to me to plead the outcasts' case, and Michael Spicer, the leader of the sceptics throughout the Maastricht rebellion, came as an intermediary to discuss the return of the whip. He spoke to Graham Bright and asked if I would see him. John Ward set up a meeting.

Michael was persuasive. He supported the views of the whipless rebels, but spoke disparagingly of their behaviour. 'We all want to win the election,' he told me, 'and they now wish to come back.' Nick Budgen had said as much to me in the Tea Room, but Michael insisted it was a general feeling.

'Will they toe the line?' I asked.

'Yes,' said Michael. 'I think they will, providing they don't lose face. I'll do my best to ensure they behave.'

Graham Bright was confident that Michael was genuinely attempting to end the impasse, and I formed the same view. I knew, of course, that the rebels were aware of his approach, and had held their own meetings about how to return to the fold. Michael had held the sceptics together in opposition to the Maastricht Bill, and it seemed likely he could hold them together in support of the government in the future. I gambled that he could, and spoke to Richard Ryder, who was far more dubious about readmitting the rebels, but agreed, albeit reluctantly, to do so. The whips were not pleased, but I judged that with the local elections pending, a show of party unity would be helpful to our candidates.

There were other factors as well. I was particularly struck by an article Nick Budgen had written in *The Times* in late January on why the rebels wished to rejoin the party. It was a seductive plea:

> This rift over Europe is ridiculous. Bad luck and mismanagement got us into this jam. Generosity and firm leadership will get us out of it. We eight or nine Tory so-called rebels have been given an importance in the eyes of the media which we never expected.
>
> A little generosity and a little good sense and we can then slip back into the no doubt well-deserved obscurity from which we came.

I decided to take Nick at his word and be generous and, to maximise goodwill, not to demand assurances of loyalty from colleagues who were, after all, in the same party and elected on the same manifesto. I did consider selectively offering the whip back – to Nick Budgen and Richard Shepherd first, and others later. I rejected this idea for two reasons: I did not believe that Budgen and Shepherd could (or would) separate themselves from their colleagues; and even if they did, it would worsen the bitterness and hostility of the others. So I decided that all must come back, and to trust that they would reciprocate the gesture of readmitting them without penalty by putting the party interest foremost. My trust was misplaced: Richard Ryder's suspicions proved all too accurate.

The whipless few rejoined the herd the next morning, but no sooner had they been readmitted than they held a cocky, unapologetic press conference before decamping to College Green for triumphal television interviews. They made no conciliatory noises, and refused to give any guarantees of party loyalty. Within days, Christopher Gill, speaking to the Anti-Common Market League, urged 'disentanglement from everything European, save the marketplace'.

Tony Blair made full use of the ammunition they handed him. 'I lead my party, [you] follow yours,' was his wounding jibe, the best one-liner he ever used against me. When I reflected on how, for the sake of the party, I had done everything possible – against the whips' advice – to avoid embarrassment to the rebels as they returned to the fold, I thought their behaviour was contemptible.

Some commentators, I think, were not surprised. A few days earlier the journalist Peter Riddell, always one of the more balanced observers, had written of the rebellious MPs:

> Some are motivated by hatred of John Major: some by their passionate opposition to the European Union.
>
> The main, or at least most vocal, critics of Mr Major are on the anti-Europe right. But there is a big gulf between the Cabinet right and their backbench allies. The Cabinet Euro-sceptics . . . will keep their dissent within limits. They will not capsize the ship as Tony Marlow, Teresa Gorman and a few others seem ready to contemplate.

I should have pressed for detailed promises of good behaviour, but had not done so because I believed that, since the whipless MPs apparently wished to return, they would both behave and be conciliatory. They did neither. The media accused me of a climbdown, and the loyalists in the party were angry – not without cause, as it turned out.

The run-up to the May local elections was woeful, and the results were appalling. We lost over two thousand seats, many of them held by long-serving councillors, loyal and able. But a plan to make a final, high-stakes bid to knock the party back into line was forming in my mind. The next few months were to see me carry it out.

# CHAPTER TWENTY-FIVE

## Put up or Shut up

O NE EVENING IN EARLY JUNE 1995 I saw Michael Heseltine at a 10 o'clock vote, and invited him to my room in the Commons for a drink. We discussed some matters concerning his department and then, inevitably, the disputes over Europe that were causing such havoc in the parliamentary party.

They were undermining everything we did. Nothing else was of interest to the media. Michael was keen to tackle the Euro-sceptics head-on. I too wished to isolate the ultra-sceptics, but could not see how we could separate them from the much larger band of colleagues who were not anti-European, but resented the manner in which the European Union was becoming more and more prescriptive and intrusive. I feared that Michael's head-on tactics might break things up altogether.

We drifted into a discussion of the forthcoming reshuffle. Michael was key to this. He was our best performer on the media, but he was constrained by his responsibilities at Trade and Industry. An obvious move would have been to make him party chairman, but I was sure he would not welcome such an offer. He enjoyed the DTI and policy-making too much.

Nor was I sure it would be right for him. Was he fit enough, after his heart attack in June 1993? Probably – but I was unwilling to take the risk. Michael would do the presentation brilliantly, but I did not want him to be bogged down with the administrative burdens which inevitably fall on the chairman, not to mention the countless speeches he would be called upon to make in the constituencies. The job of party chairman in the run-up to the election would be gruelling. I did not wish to risk him being ill.

I had been turning this conundrum over in my mind for some time. The only solution was a non-departmental job that would leave him free for the media appearances he did uniquely well. One by one I dismissed the alternatives. Leader of the House in a government with a small majority was for a conciliator-politician. Michael was a warrior-politician – quite wrong for the post. Chancellor of the Duchy of Lancaster, a non-departmental post, was a possibility, but did not reflect his seniority. Gradually, *faut de mieux*, the job of deputy prime minister forced itself into my mind. This would not be without problems either; many colleagues would dislike the appointment, and the post, which does not always exist, carried no clear responsibilities. But the potential gain was considerable. Michael on the media against opposition spokesmen could be a howitzer opposed by popguns.

That evening I probed Michael gently, and set out a range of possible options for the reshuffle. I made it clear that I had made no decisions yet, and would not do so for some weeks. Among the options was the deputy premiership – but any such offer would be dependent upon the as yet undecided structure of the reshuffle as a whole. Michael confirmed that he was attracted to the role – if it came about – but said he would want to talk to his wife Anne about it. There we left it. No deal was done. No firm offer made. No commitment entered into on either side. We did not return to the matter until the morning of 4 July.

Our conversation had taken place against the background of the fevered state of the Conservative Party in the spring and early summer of 1995. All the optimism, all the shine of 1992 had long gone; there was no feeling that people were marshalling strength for a general election which might come within a year; no sense of arming ourselves for the fight. Instead it was barely possible to turn on the radio or television without hearing someone discussing whether or not I would resign or be challenged for the leadership of the party.

The economy was coming out of recession, unemployment was falling and public services improving. We were helping to bring peace in Bosnia and Northern Ireland. The public finances were on the mend. Taxes would soon begin to fall. Interest rates and inflation were low. The opposition had no distinct alternative to offer. Yet Labour was winning twice the support of the government in opinion polls, and our position was dire.

I could take comfort from Chris Patten's maxim, 'There is no such thing as a voteless economic recovery.' Fate, however, did seem to be leaving it rather late. Confident as I was that the economy would come right, I was surprised that it was taking so long. What we needed was time and tranquillity. As Norman Blackwell, head of the Number 10 Policy Unit, had told a Political Cabinet meeting in April, 'We need to contrast what we stand for with what Labour would actually do. They have stolen our language so we need to expose their policy and the gulf between what they say and how they have voted.' We hoped the policy themes we had set out would establish clear ground between us and the opposition, but they were lost in the hubbub of our party squabbles. As Norman put it in a later Political Cabinet, 'To win the next election, the party has got to show unity of purpose.' This was not a startling insight. We all knew the truth. And yet, that same day, I read in *The Times*: 'Euro-sceptics want manifesto pledge to boycott single currency'. It was dissent first, and unity nowhere.

This in-fighting had to stop. The sane majority within the party was being constantly destabilised by a smaller but by no means negligible band. This band was less cohesive than the facile phrase 'Euro-sceptics' ever acknowledged. It included the disappointed and the disaffected, cemented together by shared hostility to Europe. Many of them wished to move the party further to the political right. This minority was joined by other, more moderate, parliamentary colleagues in an alliance of the obsessed, the worried and the well-meaning. On the other side there was a small tribe, at this stage not troublesome, of ardent Euro-supporters.

It was much the same in Cabinet. Most members shared my attitude to the single currency: we didn't much like it, but we knew that one day we might have to join it. A majority of colleagues, such as Douglas Hurd, Tony Newton, George Young, Virginia Bottomley, Patrick Mayhew and Ian Lang, shared this view and were never other than loyal. Michael Howard, Gillian Shephard and Robert Cranborne were cool towards a single currency but supportive of me personally. Peter Lilley, John Redwood and Michael Portillo were far more hostile to our European policy. Others like Ken Clarke, Michael Heseltine and John Gummer realised that their personal pro-European enthusiasms were impractical given the wary approach of the party as a whole.

The Euro-sceptics scratched at political sores in public, despite knowing full well that every time they did so they diminished still further our ability to regain lost ground against a Labour Party more federalist than any of us. In this they were encouraged by a few party elders, Margaret Thatcher and Norman Tebbit prominent among them, backed by a largely Euro-sceptical Tory press. Some of them believed Conservatism required an almost wholly hostile approach to Europe, and that anything short of that was to be opposed at almost any cost.

Most members of the public never shared this negative view. They weren't fond of Europe, which often irritated them – particularly by examples, real or invented, of petty intrusions into our day-to-day affairs – but nor were they obsessed by it. At Maastricht I had secured an opt-out from monetary union. I had made it clear that we were unlikely to join a single currency in the first wave, but I believed it would have been foolhardy to rule it out for the more distant future. To have done so would have denied us any serious influence over whether EMU went ahead, and if so, over the circumstances in which it did. Since at Maastricht we had secured a unique privilege – we could go in or not go in, entirely as we chose – it was absurd to give up our right to influence events in the meantime. To exert this influence without a commitment to join a single currency was a considerable luxury, and one which some of our EU partners deeply resented. Why surrender it? I was to note later how jealously my successor in Downing Street clung to the advantage I had left him – and he was absolutely right to do so.

Nothing in my stance on monetary union obliged the UK to join the single currency, and in the Commons I tried, as far as I felt able, to reassure the Euro-sceptical wing of the party on this point. 'I don't myself believe that the question of joining a single currency will in practice arise for some time . . . Arguably the circumstances may not ever be right,' I said at Prime Minister's Questions on 11 June 1995.

Further than this I was not willing to go. It would not have been right. I was determined not to cave in to the extreme anti-European views that were gaining ground. Though personally unenthusiastic, I knew a single currency might come about, and that if it did, and if it succeeded, our own economic interests might compel us to join. Politically, however, I thought that any government embarking on such a policy would be wise to obtain the emphatic and specific endorsement of the electorate, and for that reason I favoured a referendum on the question of entry. I had persuaded Douglas Hurd of the need for one before the European elections in 1994, but Kenneth Clarke, Michael Heseltine and John Gummer – and, for different reasons, Michael Portillo – were all opposed to it, and it was not until the end of 1995 that it became government policy. In retrospect it is a pity I did not force this through earlier. It was a mistake not to have done so.

But even if I had, there was a group in the party who would simply have upped their demands – a group whom nothing short of a fundamentally anti-European policy would have satisfied. Some of these people were obsessed with Europe to the exclusion of all other interests: Tony Marlow, Christopher Gill, Nicholas Budgen, Teresa Gorman and Bill Cash, for example. But some of those capable of the most damage were among my present or former ministers. Neil Hamilton, a former Minister for Corporate Affairs at the DTI, and Edward Leigh, soon an ally of John Redwood, were indefatigable in their cause, for example. Newer MPs such as Bernard Jenkin and Iain Duncan Smith were serious propagandists, too, and would work to a calculated line in the Members' Tea Room. They were strongly encouraged by wayward elders and lauded in the Euro-sceptical press. As spring turned to summer, their assaults became fiercer and those parts of the press in cahoots with them more difficult. Graham Bright, my former PPS, warned me not to underestimate this opposition: 'They'll unseat you if they can,' he told me bluntly.

The speculation about whether my leadership would be challenged was draining the government. It masked everything we did, and it was evident to me that we would not regain the political initiative unless we lanced the boil. I came to believe that if we delayed a leadership contest until the normal time of November, it would simply wipe out four months of the diminishing time we had left to put the government back on the rails before the general election. It would poison the summer reshuffle, allow havoc to continue through August and September, wreck the party conference in October and ensure a leadership challenge in November. Rumour, gossip, plot and counter-plot would obsess the media and set our cause even further back.

All of this pointed to a pre-emptive strike on my part: to force an early contest for the leadership, inviting my critics to 'put up or shut up'. I had thought of confronting them without warning in the past, and had discussed it with Sarah Hogg. I had also raised the idea with friends to test their reaction; but I had always decided against. It was a once-only option, and I had to be sure that I would be right to take the risk.

On top of this, leaks from Sir Richard Scott's inquiry into the arms-to-

Iraq affair whipped up a storm. *News at Ten* broadcast claims that the report would accuse three ministers – including William Waldegrave, a member of the Cabinet – of 'designedly' misleading Parliament. I was furious that someone was selectively passing on quotes from the unfinished report, presumably in the hope of blackening the government's name and destroying the careers of the three politicians. The smear was all the worse because the full report, when it was published in February 1996, did not charge them with this serious breach of parliamentary behaviour. Tony Blair turned the fire on me at Prime Minister's Questions the next day, and my refusal to commit myself to a course of action before I had considered what Sir Richard Scott actually said gave the press a second bite of the cherry. I was even more incensed soon after when sources close to the inquiry suggested we had leaked the story to draw the sting of the Scott Report ahead of its publication. We had not, and, as the full report showed, did not need to do so.

Soon afterwards, Margaret Thatcher weighed in, with the publication of the second volume of her memoirs, *The Path to Power*. Her descriptions of a Grantham childhood were harmless enough, but the book contained an epilogue, unrelated to the title or scope of the book itself, which could only be interpreted as an attack on my own policies. Certainly it was a good deal more publicity worthy than the rest of the volume. Such blows from my predecessor were impossible to disregard, since every interviewer raised them with me at every opportunity, as she must have known they would.

A subsequent television interview with Margaret herself made things worse. She talked of 'a thousand years of history wrecked by a single currency', which even to her supporters must have seemed a touch over the top. She attacked me for withdrawing the whip from the eight dissident MPs who had voted against the government on a matter of confidence (see pages 602–3). I knew, of course, that she was offering powerful support to the anti-European cause, but I did not expect her to flout traditional party discipline in a way so damaging to the government.

I remembered how she and Norman Tebbit had reacted to far milder criticism of the government during her premiership. I accepted entirely that she was entitled to her view, but as a former party leader she could have picked up the phone or come to see me about her concerns at any time. She never did so. She chose to speak out publicly or, at other times, to mutter privately. And when she muttered privately, her acolytes soon made sure her views became public.

Margaret, however, was only just getting into her stride. In a speech soon after, she called for a renegotiation of the Maastricht Treaty, asking me to 'do what [she] did between '79 and '90'. I thought back to the Single European Act, with its significant surrender of British sovereignty, and marvelled at her interpretation of history. To call for a renegotiation of the Maastricht Treaty, a treaty entered into and agreed four years previously, and approved with a huge majority by the House of Commons, was hardly credible. She must have known that to scrap Maastricht now was an absurd proposal. It accorded, however, with her own style in these matters: a variable approach to rules she herself found inconvenient, combined with severe criticism of those who, in her opinion, were not playing with a straight bat. If any British prime minister had returned to Europe and asked to renegotiate a treaty in which Britain had been accorded such a specially advantageous position, he or she would have received short shrift – and would have deserved it.

All this unhappiness could be strongly felt in the Commons; I sensed it whenever I entered the Chamber. Withdrawing the whip from the eight rebels had not worked. Perhaps dialogue would? I accepted an invitation to address the party's backbench 'Fresh Start' Group on 13 June. Broadly right-wing, it included MPs who had been helpful to me, as well as critics who had not. Michael Spicer, who chaired the meeting, told me that he hoped my presence might help to build bridges. In this he was proved wrong. The meeting was as rigged as a scaffold: some of the backbenchers present had rehearsed their attacks, and would have rounded on anyone who moved away from total hostility to all things European. An organised party campaign to change our European policy was under way, and in this cause I was disposable.

I had assumed that the meeting would be a civilised affair, in which I would set out my position on Europe, others would respond, and we would exchange views in a reasonable way. And that was how it began. I set out my position on the single currency to the fifty or so MPs present, as I had on many other occasions, telling them straight that I wasn't prepared to rule out entry, but also telling them why. 'We need to be involved in the negotiations, but if it is inappropriate we will not enter. We have the best of all worlds and it would be foolish to throw it away.'

All too soon it became evident that most of the MPs at the meeting did not agree with this. Their questioning became aggressive and hostile. Norman Lamont's intervention – the first time he had addressed a word to me since he left the government – was more a lance in the ribs than a hatchet to the neck, but the Member for Bridlington, John Townend, was intemperate to a degree: 'As far as most people in the party are concerned, Prime Minister, it is time for you to come off the fence.' With this blunt comment, the tone of the meeting plummeted. George Gardiner was oleaginous. Iain Duncan Smith raised some clever and intriguing points of detail, but failed to see how much we gained by keeping our options open. Bernard Jenkin could be heard muttering, 'No, no, no.' Bill Cash is never personally rude, but he is obsessive, driven, and, on Europe, frankly a bore. Discussing Europe with Bill is like spending an afternoon with the Ancient Mariner. Ivan Lawrence was emotive. He was not a hardline opponent: he was often on my side. But he did feel very strongly about this issue. His approach was to ask me if I would go in their direction, rather than to damn me for not doing so. In fact I had gone as far as I could without provoking similar but opposing dissent from elsewhere in the party.

In reply to suggestions that an anti-European stance would sweep the country in a general election, I told the meeting that the single currency did not obsess the public in the same way as it did the parliamentary party; that the whole of British politics should not be turned on the pinhead of ruling out – five years in advance – whether we should go into the single currency or not; and that it was absurd to believe that we had only to oppose all things European to become popular again.

The meeting was a disaster. Some were horrified by the tone of the exchanges. John Whittingdale, an MP and former adviser to Margaret Thatcher, sitting at the back between my advisers Norman Blackwell and Howell James, muttered: 'If he gives the right answers, OK; if not, deep trouble.' But *my* right answers were not what most of those in the room wanted to hear. Some of the hardline Euro-sceptics were beyond political argument, and regarded the destruction of our European policy as a crusade.

Afterwards, as I walked upstairs to my room in the Commons with John Ward, my PPS, I acknowledged that the exchanges had been damaging and would be big news. 'They'll be leaked,' John warned, 'with the usual colourful additions.' And so it proved. I partly blamed myself. I had believed that all my colleagues were open to argument, when some were not. As the questions became ill-humoured and intemperate I dug my heels in. Afterwards I wondered if I should have been more emollient, but I doubt it would have made any difference.

That meeting more or less made up my mind. We had to stop the rot, and now I felt I knew how to. A poll by the backbench Conservative European Affairs Committee showed that the bulk of the party, although silent, believed my 'wait and see' approach to monetary union to be right. I urged their leaders, such as Ray Whitney, not to speak out in public. To have one wing of the party up in arms was sufficient. Two would have been cataclysmic if I was to keep the party in one piece.

For me, the strain and frustration of trying to maintain a balance between the two sides was immense. I was no longer willing to endure the pain, and was prepared to put the leadership to hazard. I decided to give the parliamentary party the opportunity to replace me, taking from my shoulders the responsibility of keeping the Conservative Party together – or to re-endorse me, in which case I would be in a stronger position to do precisely that. I was, throughout, reconciled to either outcome. The situation as it stood was intolerable to me personally, and corrosive to the party.

There were moments when I became profoundly depressed about what was going on in the party. When that happened, I deliberately turned my mind to other things – to our economic success, and to things away from politics. Walking in the garden at Finings was always a great comfort. Nature tends to put things in perspective. It reminded me that politics was a very important part of my life, but not every part.

Before I could turn my mind fully to any contest, I had to fly to Nova Scotia in mid-June for the annual G7 heads of government summit in Halifax. This proved an ordeal. I had been working the usual seventeen-hour day in the run-up to the trip, and suffering throughout the period from very severe pain in my back and shoulder and in the base of my neck – a problem that had been recurring for years and was now getting worse.

We arrived in Halifax in the evening. The pain was aggravated by the long flight. That night I got no sleep at all, and the next night very little. Massage and acupuncture both eased the pain somewhat, but we could not allow the discomfort I was in to become more widely known, since in the prevailing atmosphere the headlines back in Britain would have written themselves: 'Major: A Pain in the Neck', or 'Desperate Major Seeks Alternative Medicine'. Chris Meyer, my Press Secretary, was hugely relieved that no hint of my trouble leaked out.

One evening, talking over a glass of wine with Helmut Kohl prior to a working dinner, I advanced my familiar theme that G7s would be more effective if they were smaller and less formal; we did not need the presence of vast numbers of ministers and officials. Helmut agreed, but pointed out that Germany had to bring both the head of government and the foreign minister because they belonged to different parties. 'I am in a coalition government of my own,' I replied.

It was a joke. But though there were no journalists with us in the garden, there were some about thirty yards away, and their microphones picked up the comment. It was reported in Britain, and caused further fuss in the papers about the party leadership. The next morning, when I left the hotel, I was asked the usual questions about splits over Europe, which were then distorted as a 'transatlantic' rebuke to backbenchers by the Prime Minister. In fact, I had simply stated the obvious – that there was no 'magic ingredient' certain to revive the party's political position. I had said: 'I have set the course. It is right, it is sensible, it is pragmatic.'

A further minor ripple was inadvertently caused by Kenneth Clarke. A last-minute press conference was called, from which Ken was missing – for the simple reason that, believing the formal part of the trip was over, he had packed and despatched his business suits, retaining only casual clothes for a spot of birdwatching before he left. Informed of the press conference, but judging it (correctly) to be less than crucial, he gave it a miss – for fear that his presence in twitcher's gear might raise eyebrows. His absence was misinterpreted. The media had played up my dismay at Tory disunity, and now my Chancellor had failed to join me for a final meeting! Thus are stories born.

On the flight home I talked again to Douglas Hurd about bringing the leadership contest forward. The present situation was untenable, I told him. I could resign from office and go; I could tough it out and face a contest for the leadership in the autumn; or I could take my critics by surprise. I told him that the third option – to resign and contest the ensuing leadership election – was the one I felt inclined to adopt.

I spoke to Ken along the same lines, but separately, because I wanted to get each man's opinion one to one. Both were reserved, though supportive. Both saw the logic of my plan, but neither was much attracted to it. However, by the time we landed at RAF Alconbury, the nearest airfield to Finings, they knew what I had in mind, and both of them kept it absolutely private.

I arrived home at about 2 o'clock on the morning of Sunday, 18 June, and went to bed. Later that day, as I always did when I had a difficult decision ahead, I walked round the garden, reflecting on the options and rehearsing the arguments in my mind. I talked to Norma, James and Elizabeth about my plan. All of them were enthusiastic. By chance that day there was an editorial in the *Sunday Times*, calling on me to 'put up or shut up'. They didn't remotely imagine I was going to do it, I guess. But the piece confirmed my serious reading of the situation. I was still worried that my decision might seem unwise, but by now I was committed to it.

As I walked in the garden the words of Montrose, which I have always admired, rang once more in my head:

> He either fears his fate too much,
> Or his deserts are small,
> That puts it not unto the touch,
> To win or lose it all.

Montrose, of course, was executed, but the principle seemed sound.

Meanwhile, things were getting worse in the party. An anonymous poll published in the *Daily Telegraph* on Monday, 19 June claimed that seventy Conservative MPs supported a leadership contest. The papers were full of talk about a 'Portillo–Heseltine dream ticket'. I didn't know whether this story was a press concoction or self-interested briefing, but 'dream ticket' seemed to me to be an odd description, given the difference on Europe between the two Michaels. If the right were not happy with me on Europe, goodness knows what they would have made of Michael Heseltine as prime minister.

I was also under attack for writing a foreword to an ardently pro-European pamphlet by Ray Whitney. This was a silly criticism. I would have offered a friendly but cautiously-worded paragraph or two to *any* important pamphlet by a large party group, right or left, which asked me to contribute. John Redwood would return to this when the leadership campaign was under way. It showed what an odd world he lived in. His objection was less to what I had written than to the fact that my having written anything at all showed that I was minded to maintain friendly relations with all responsible groups in the party I led. His obsession with Europe made it clear there was an element in the party for whom my goodwill would never be acceptable – unless accompanied by ill-will towards those with whom they disagreed.

On Tuesday morning, I asked Sarah Hogg to call at Number 10. It was a warm and sunny day and we sat in the garden. I told her what I had in mind and showed her two draft statements – one for the 1922 Committee Executive, the other for the press. I knew Sarah would rehearse the arguments against my plan, and I wanted her to use her formidable intellect to do so. That way, I could test whether I was making a bad judgement simply because I had lost all patience. But by now I had virtually made up my mind: unless some wholly unexpected obstacle stopped me, I was going to resign and fight. Sarah was quite strongly against this, but she had no knockdown argument, and as she left I think she knew what I was going to do.

I could not, however, be sure of the result of a leadership election, though I was on a better wicket than I realised. In the weeks before the contest a number of senior ministers, alarmed by the party's dissensions, had talked without my knowledge to Graham Bright, my former PPS. Some of them also attended a series of informal suppers held at Jonathan Aitken's house in Lord North Street. In conversation, ministers such as John Gummer, Jeremy Hanley, Robert Cranborne, Ian Lang, David Davis and Ann Widdecombe had been considering how to counter the internecine warfare and bring the party together. Sir Archie Hamilton, an old-school gentleman of the best sort, was a vital player. Unaware of my plans, they were nevertheless forming a campaign team for an election that looked likely to come sooner or later, whether I wanted it or not.

While he was my PPS Graham had built up a team of people whose function it was to keep in touch with party views and pass on intelligence. They met frequently, mainly in Graham's London flat. Members included Cranley Onslow, Peter Hordern, Archie Hamilton and Terence Higgins. Graham kept an up-to-date computer record of MPs' views, ready for any leadership election that might occur. To this end, three or four weeks before I announced the contest, he and his team had been carrying out a thorough canvass of the parliamentary party. Graham was no longer my PPS and was operating freelance, and at that stage did not know what I was contemplating. His was simply precautionary behaviour, the protective loyalty of a good friend increasingly worried that a challenge might come, presumably in the autumn. We had independently reached similar conclusions about this danger.

As a result, when the leadership election campaign did begin, he was able to predict that I would win. He had told me as much when I telephoned him at home on the Sunday evening after my return from Halifax, to tell him my thinking. 'You will win,' he said. 'I can guarantee you that. But I don't think you should go ahead.'

'I've thought about it,' I replied. 'I've told Norma and the family, and pretty much decided. We can't go on as we are.'

What neither Graham nor anyone else involved in my campaign knew was that I had discussed the result I wanted with Norma. Under the party rules, I needed only 165 votes (a majority of the parliamentary party) and a lead of 15 per cent over any other candidate to win. But I hoped for 230 votes or more, and had decided I would resign if I got 215 or fewer. I was not confident that I would reach this figure, but it seemed to me to be the minimum acceptable if I were to continue to lead the party. I wrote the figure on a scrap of paper and, rather theatrically, sealed it in an envelope.

Journalists who did not know me wrote that if I could keep clinging by my fingertips to the door of Number 10, I would. They were wrong. I knew before I called the contest that it could very possibly lead to my resignation as prime minister. If I had failed to win convincingly I would have shrugged my shoulders, said 'That's it,' and gone. I would not have obstructed my successor, because I would not have wished to damage the party's chances at the next election.

It seemed pointless to risk a public announcement before the last Prime Minister's Questions of the week, which took place after lunch on Thursday. Late on Thursday afternoon was the obvious moment. My opponents would be scattering for the weekend, and we would begin the battle by taking them by surprise. I knew who I wanted as my chiefs of staff, and my advisers drew up a note detailing what we had to do before the announcement. But in my hurry to set things moving, and with the prime minister's normal packed diary, I had little chance to work out exactly who needed to know what and when. Perhaps a bit more thought devoted to this might have made a difference. I shall never know.

On Wednesday afternoon John Redwood, the Welsh Secretary, came to see me at his own request with a series of representations about policy. Some of his ideas were clever, and others political non-starters. I would often have ministers in to talk about how they were doing, but this call, if not unprecedented, was certainly unusual. He had been badgering me for a meeting for some time, with an urgency that made me wonder whether, in the end, he said all he wanted to say.

Our conversation was also awkward. In the weeks before it, a number of senior ministers including Kenneth Clarke and Douglas Hurd had complained to me that John made a habit of not clearing his speeches before delivery, and that he trespassed upon the responsibilities of others. I had written him a sharp note about this when he had made a speech on health policy in Wales that had led to a spat with Virginia Bottomley, the Health Secretary, after an unhelpful article in the *Daily Mail*. 'Like you,' John wrote back to me, 'I was upset by the article in the *Mail*. I did not brief the press and following the article asked if anyone in the Welsh Office had briefed in such an unhelpful way . . . I took every step to kill the story.' Faced with John's categorical denial of briefing against Virginia, I let the matter drop.

A book published after the general election by John's adviser and confidant Hywel Williams makes it clear that such scruples did not always intrude. Apparently Mr Williams, disappointed that John Redwood's criticisms of our health policy were not receiving more prominence, decided to 'invite a small group of journalists [to] brief them in detail on the speech . . . the fuse had been lit and the result was the next day's "sensation"'. This behaviour was not unusual.

Others complained that reports of private meetings at which John Redwood was present tended to appear in the press. Fairly or unfairly, it was believed that he was either leaking them himself or talking to somebody in his entourage who was doing so. This meant that other ministers were unwilling to be frank when he was present.

He himself rarely intervened in Cabinet. Nor did he take to the Welsh people, or they to him. An obvious question mark hung over his future in the Cabinet, and when he called to see me I wondered whether he had heard gossip that there was a sporting chance that he might not survive the reshuffle planned for July. If so, it would have explained why, a few days later, he was bold enough to stand against me for the leadership. He had nothing to lose. But perhaps I am being unfair. Perhaps he really did have an urge to show support for a prime minister who, a few days later, he would seek to unseat.

If you are considering sacking someone you can't cosy up to them or take them into your confidence. So I didn't tell John what I had planned for the following day. Later he was to say this hurt him badly. It was uncomfortable for me too, but I had no alternative. It was vital to maintain the element of surprise.

To my delight, news of my plans did not leak out – a remarkable exception to the usual Westminster rule. On Wednesday evening I had a prearranged meeting at 6.30 p.m. in my private flat at Number 10 with Willie Whitelaw, Richard Ryder and Robert Cranborne. 'Things can't go on as they are,' Willie warned. After he had left I called Richard and Robert back and ran through my three options with them: resign, tough it out, or fight early. I told them I had already discussed these alternatives with Douglas Hurd, Ken Clarke and Tony Newton, the Leader of the House, and added: 'You're going to have to be pretty persuasive if you're to stop me going for the third.' They didn't try. Over several whiskies we talked. Robert, whom I appointed campaign manager, was extremely focused, and set out there and then what he wanted to happen. He then went to see Tony Newton. 'Oh, you've heard, then,' was Tony's greeting.

I woke on Thursday morning keyed-up, as I usually am when I get close to a battle. My mind was made up, and I knew we had ahead of us a *coup de théâtre*, if nothing else – a prospect I rather relished. I could recall no precedent for what I was about to do, and I was certain that I would catch most people by surprise. I felt confident that what I was doing was in the interests of the government and the Conservative Party.

In *The Times* that morning, there was a letter from the Northern Ireland Secretary Sir Patrick Mayhew, calling on 'colleagues to reflect on what they are doing'. 'Much damage has been done,' he said, 'but it can still be repaired. Any more of this commotion against the Prime Minister, however, and that may cease to be the case.' He hadn't known of my plans when he wrote the letter, and he did not tell me he had done so. It was typical Paddy – a supportive and honourable act. But it gave Tony Blair the chance to make a sharp point at Prime Minister's Questions later in the day.

That morning Robert Cranborne woke at dawn and telephoned Alex Allan, who was already in his office at Number 10. Five minutes later Robert was in the flat, where Howell James, my Political Secretary, was already talking to me. We agreed that Howell would be chief of staff in the leadership contest. Alastair Goodlad and Tony Newton were already signed up. I asked Ian Lang to come and see me in the Cabinet Room at 9 a.m. and he offered his support immediately. I wanted him to lead on the media, but in the event he did much more, and was a crucial figure. Later that day Michael Howard and Brian Mawhinney joined the team; two valuable recruits. Graham Bright was deputed to count heads with Sir Archie Hamilton, and to arrange funding for my campaign.

Robert was a supremely good organiser – the best we had. He had arranged the fiftieth-anniversary commemoration of the end of World War II with skill, and had the personal authority to organise a good team. He and I had joined the House on the same day in May 1979. Though we had been acquaintances rather than close friends, we had always had a very good relationship. I knew my campaign could not be in better hands. Robert's family, the Cecils, had been involved in the high intrigue of politics for more than four hundred years. It was in his blood. 'To know what Elizabeth I's great minister, Mr Secretary William Cecil, was like, just lunch with Robert,' I once said. 'There's no need to look in the history books.' His taste for intrigue was to emerge again, in spectacular circumstances, when my successor sacked him from the shadow Cabinet in 1998 for negotiating the reform of the House of Lords without authority to do so.

There was a Cabinet meeting that morning, and I gave Robert permission to miss it. There was a great deal to be done. He hurried off to brief Sir Marcus Fox, the wily Chairman of the 1922 Committee. With Richard Ryder in tow he passed a swarm of lobby correspondents heading for a post-Cabinet briefing. Odd – and fortunate – that none of them thought to ask why my Chief Whip and Leader of the Lords were not at Cabinet.

As ministers gathered for Cabinet I spoke to Michael Heseltine. He said he thought it a 'brave' decision, and that he would be 'supportive'. But there was no glib assurance that he was certain I would win. Frankly he was not. Michael told me he would not enter the contest while I remained in it, but that if I lost or withdrew, he had not abandoned his own ambitions. This was a decent response from a man who had always hoped to be prime minister. One or two of Michael's lieutenants, such as Richard Ottaway and Keith Hampson, put out feelers on his behalf during the campaign, but they must have been discouraged by Michael himself for there was no follow-through. He could, if he had chosen, have undermined my position, but he did not. He kept to his word – as he always did, in my experience.

Cabinet was surprisingly relaxed, given that some present were aware I was about to resign. It was a free-flowing discussion. I did not tell colleagues collectively what I proposed, as I did not wish to hear it reported on the one o'clock news. Telling politicians things one by one discourages leaks. Telling them in a large group guarantees them. Despite the dramas to come later in the day, I was fully focused on the Cabinet meeting, as indeed I should have been, for there was no certainty that I had many more to come.

After Cabinet I told Michael Portillo what I planned to do. He seemed surprised, but offered his support without hesitation. At the same time Ian Lang, with the help of Richard Ryder and Michael Howard, began to inform other ministers what was afoot. Stephen Dorrell heard at Lord's, where he was watching England's Test match against the West Indies; Malcolm Rifkind was briefed in Scotland; and William Waldegrave shortly before making a Commons statement. John Gummer was the last to know, as he was en route to New York. It was pure chance that John Redwood was among the last to be told, but the political tom-toms were soon beating to inform me of his fury that he had been kept in ignorance when he called on me the day before. It was careless of me not to have foreseen this, and not to have seen John personally to tell him of my decision, but at the time I knew of no reason to handle him with kid gloves.

I approached PMQs edgy that my plans might have leaked and that I would be asked about them, which would have put me on the defensive – but I wasn't. It was not a particularly sparkling Prime Minister's Questions. Labour had been attacking the government on 'sleaze', but it had emerged that members of Labour-controlled Monklands Council in Scotland had been giving plum jobs to members of their families. 'Their personnel department was more like their family planning department,' I told the House, to amusement on our side and smiles from some Labour Members.

At 4.15 p.m., the executive officers of the 1922 Committee gathered to see me in my room in the Commons. Sir Marcus Fox had told them nothing, and they had *no* idea what was coming. They strolled in expecting an innocuous meeting. I asked them to sit down, and they were served tea. I then spoke of the difficulties of recent months and said it was damaging to the government that uncertainty about my position was continuing. It had to be ended one way or another, I told them. They nodded sagely. I said then that I intended to resign as leader of the party, and would be announcing this in fifteen minutes' time at Number 10.

There was complete silence, followed by audible gasps. They were stunned. 'I intend to contest the election, and if win I expect the party to behave itself,' I said. 'If I lose, so be it. I will support my successor. Whatever happens, we cannot continue as we are if we are to win the general election.' I handed Sir Marcus my letter of resignation as leader of the Conservative Party and asked him to read it to backbench colleagues at the regular meeting of the 1922 Committee that was due to meet at 6 o'clock that evening.

Marcus then spoke, and was very staunch in my defence. So was Jill Knight, who twenty-five years before had helped me onto the candidates' list to find a parliamentary seat. So was Tony Grant, a parliamentary friend and neighbour in Cambridgeshire. I asked the gathering to say nothing until after the announcement had been made, then I left the room and returned to Number 10.

I intended to make my statement to the media in the garden of Number 10. When I arrived there, chairs and a lectern had been set out and the press were already assembled. We had summoned the lobby correspondents for 4.30 p.m., so as to ensure that my meeting with the 1922 Committee would not be reported. Chris Meyer, my Press Secretary, came into the Cabinet Room where I was watching the scene in the garden below, rubbing his hands with glee. 'They're in a state of fever pitch. *Fever* pitch,' he said. ' "What's going on?" they keep asking. I tell them, "I don't know." Anyway, when they came in I confiscated all their mobile phones, so they're absolutely incommunicado.'

'A pity we can't keep them like that for the rest of the year,' I replied.

I was ready to make the announcement, confident that I had a good text, which had been written overnight and polished during the day. I read it through, then at 5 o'clock I went into the garden. Norma, her secretary Lorne Roper-Caldbeck, Ian Lang, Brian Mawhinney, Howell James, Graham Bright, my personal assistant Arabella Warburton, my constituency secretary Gina Hearn, Norman Blackwell and others watched from the terrace. Ian McColl, my PPS in the Lords, stood behind me in the garden. I then said:

Let me just make a brief statement to you. I've been deeply involved in politics since I was sixteen. I see public service as a duty, and if you can serve, I believe you have an obligation to do so.

I've now been Prime Minister for nearly five years. In that time we've achieved a great deal, but for the last three years I've been opposed by a small minority in our party. During those three years there have been repeated threats of a leadership election. In each year, they turned out to be phoney threats. Now the same thing again is happening in 1995.

I believe it is in no one's interest that this continues right through until November. It undermines the government and it damages the Conservative Party. I am not prepared to see the party I care for laid out on the rack like this any longer.

To remove this uncertainty I have this afternoon tendered my resignation as leader of the Conservative Party to Sir Marcus Fox, the Chairman of the 1922 Committee, and requested him to set the machinery in motion for the election of a successor.

I have confirmed to Sir Marcus that I shall be a candidate in that election. If I win, I shall continue as prime minister and lead the party into and through the next election.

Should I be defeated, which I do not expect, I shall resign as prime minister and offer my successor my full support.

The Conservative Party must make its choice. Every leader is leader only with the support of his party. That is true of me as well.

That is why I am no longer prepared to tolerate the present situation. In short, it is time to put up or shut up. I have nothing more to say this afternoon. Thank you very much.

At Lord's, where England was in the process of beating the West Indies, they announced over the loudspeaker that I had resigned, but omitted to say that I was standing for re-election. Even some of the journalists who heard me in the garden of Number 10 misunderstood me at first.

My intention to force matters to head had not leaked. Everyone had thought the war of attrition within the parliamentary party would continue. No one had expected me to confront my critics. Journalists who wrote that I had 'gambled' everything misunderstood my intention: I wasn't gambling, I just needed a simple answer from my party. I hoped they would give me that: I would have preferred a clear 'no' to the disarray of the previous months. As I spoke I was aware that I might lose, especially if a heavyweight candidate came forward to oppose me. If my vote fell below the figure of 215 I had set myself as a minimum, I would resign. I was fatalistic about how the result would turn out, but it would be better to lose the premiership than to permit the disruption of previous months to continue. After I finished my statement I returned to the Cabinet Room. As the waiting press fled to file their story I re-emerged into the garden to give a string of television and radio interviews.

The surprise had been total, and for a while my opponents were non-plussed. Marcus Fox read my letter of resignation to the 1922 Committee. Nominations for the leadership contest would close in one week, on 29 June, and the ballot would be held on 4 July. Marcus made it clear that this would be the only leadership election this year, and almost certainly the last before the general election. He also announced – wrongly as it turned out – that all eighteen members of the 1922 Executive would sign my nomination papers. My critics could not come back in November: for them it was now or never.

For me it was business as usual, and I was driven home to Huntingdon, where I had a full day of long-arranged engagements on Friday. In the morning, with a boisterous media pack in tow, I visited Ailwyn Community School, a successful grant-maintained school in the north of my constituency. Sitting in its gardens I was photographed surrounded by hundreds of excited children – excited, I suspect, more by the chance to skip lessons than by a prime ministerial photo-opportunity. Still, fortuitously the visit made exactly the point I wanted to get across. Mainstream concerns, such as education, had been extinguished by chattering speculation about possible leadership challenges. I wanted to use this election to put them back on our agenda.

The next day's newspapers were far more encouraging than I had hoped. 'His stunning strike threw his enemies into confusion,' said *The Times*. 'A brilliant coup,' added the *Guardian*. 'It was a chance he had to take. Some will call it courageous. I think that it was right,' said Philip Stephens in the *Financial Times*. 'The best thing to happen to the Tory Party in a long time,' said Woodrow Wyatt in *The Times*.

But there was one question as yet unanswered. Would there be another candidate – and if so, who? The press's working assumption was that if no one else came forward, Norman Lamont would do so. I was sceptical about that, although at the time I did not know that Edward Leigh had offered to nominate him. I thought a candidacy by Norman would look too much like personal revenge, and I doubted that he would have much support among colleagues. I suspected also that his wife Rosemary would discourage him. For whatever reason, he did not stand. Built up as the great white hope of the Euro-sceptics on Friday, his star faded over the weekend.

Meanwhile, other potential candidates were in an agony of indecision. Michael Portillo, as he had promised me he would, issued a statement of support, perhaps not knowing that his friends were actively testing opinion among colleagues. David Hart, his special adviser, was telling all who asked that he was doubtful that Michael would enter the contest *on the first ballot*, but did not rule it out. George Gardiner was encouraging him to put his name forward. John Whittingdale was certain he would not. Trevor Kavanagh, political correspondent of the *Sun*, talked up the attractions of a Portillo candidacy. For a star of the right wing, Michael is surprisingly cautious. He is not reckless. He does not have spontaneity in his make-up. He carefully considers what has to be done, and then prepares himself for it.

John Redwood's adviser Hywel Williams sent out more hostile signals. Redwood had not yet issued a statement, and Williams was telling everyone who would listen that John had been poorly treated by me, and had gone to watch the Test match at Lord's to think things out. He would, said Williams, make his intentions plain on Monday. I did not think John would stand, because the signals were mixed. Only a few days before I had been told that he had strongly defended me at a lunch against hostile comments from the journalist Simon Heffer.

Uncertainty deepened as neither Michael Portillo nor John Redwood returned telephone calls from Robert Cranborne and others on his team. Robert enlisted the help of the Downing Street switchboard, who can locate people all over the world. But for all of Friday, Saturday and Sunday they were unable to locate the Secretaries of State for Employment and for Wales. If Michael and John were with me, this was puzzling. If they were keeping their options open, it made perfect sense. My assumption was that they were counting heads.

One other Cabinet minister's intentions were also unclear. The Social Security Secretary Peter Lilley did not issue an early declaration of support, and went to ground. My team found him unusually hard to get hold of. I was sorry about this, since although we were not philosophical soulmates I had a high regard for Peter's intellect, and he had been an early supporter in 1990. Though he subsequently said to the BBC that I had done the right thing, I learned that he had told at least one journalist that he had written a letter of resignation prior to announcing his candidacy, only to tear it up on the Sunday evening when he heard that John Redwood was going to stand.

On the Friday, though, I was still doubtful that a Cabinet minister would oppose me in the first round, and I said as much in an interview for the *Daily Express*. If the contest went to a second ballot, I knew that I would have left the fray by then: I would win by a knockout, or I would step down. Then it would be an open contest, and Michael Heseltine, Michael Portillo and Ken Clarke would all be free to pitch in. For the moment, my announcement had caught potential rivals by surprise. They had assumed that any contest would be in November. Now it was not, and they needed to make quick decisions.

The rumour mill was in overdrive. Norman Tebbit was predicting that there would be a rush of abstentions in the ballot. 'Friends' reported Michael Portillo's opinion as being in the same vein. Other messages too came from Michael's camp, which seemed to be very active. Bernard Jenkin was looking for pledges on his behalf, and we heard that Michael preferred the Isle of Wight backbencher Barry Field as a stalking horse rather than Norman Lamont. Barry had announced his availability for that role if no one else stood. Michael, we were told, wasn't sure what John Redwood was up to, but privately predicted that few colleagues who voted for him on the first round would stick with him thereafter. Hywel Williams, speaking for John, was worried that Michael might do a deal with Michael Heseltine.

Other colleagues made it clear that their constituency activists were backing me. David Willetts, though, thought I was losing the initiative. On Saturday I spoke at Central Office to a meeting of association chairmen and received a marvellous reception, which we exploited. The next day, the *Sunday Express* reported that they had polled 160 association chairmen, virtually all of whom backed me. Michael Mates, one of Michael Heseltine's lieutenants, was reported to be number-crunching with the psephologist David Butler.

Robert Cranborne put our campaign team into place with extraordinary efficiency. Howell James, effervescent as ever, was already in action as chief of staff, with Damian Green active in the press office and Tim Collins, professional and precise, as chief spinner. Tony Newton balanced his duties as Leader of the House with his wish to see me win. Brian Mawhinney was sharp, sometimes brusque, always to the point. Michael Howard – precise, incisive, sometimes pedantic but so right as to make his every word count. Archie Hamilton – bluff, overpowering during the campaign, trusting no one outside the inner circle (and not always them), checking and rechecking on colleagues' intentions. No one knew, or wished to know, how his intelligence network operated, but at least one of our moles was regularly reviled by our own supporters.

Then there was Graham Bright, dedication to the cause oozing from every pore. Alastair Goodlad – quiet, almost unnoticed, but one of the best lieutenants a Cecil ever had. Jonathan Hill had reappeared to help as if by magic, taking leave of absence from his job with the consultancy Lowe Bell the moment he heard what was planned. George Bridges and George Osborne did any job that came to hand. Debbie de Satgé ran the secretarial pool, and special advisers such as Rachael Whetstone, Gregor Mackay, Michael MacManus, Michael Simmonds and Sophie McEwan, who effectively took over the internal administration of the media exercise, all resigned their jobs to join the team.

A Steering Committee was formed that met at Alastair Goodlad's house at 8 o'clock each morning. Cecilia Goodlad served tea and coffee as they sat around a large dining table. I did not attend these meetings – Robert operated on a need-to-know basis, and I did not need to know – but my PPS John Ward kept me up to date with what was going on. Robert Cranborne chaired the meetings in his usual suave and good-natured manner. Cheryl Gillan, ever-present as his PPS, sat always at his side.

Ian Lang, the 'General in the Field', as Robert christened him, was in overall charge as well as running the Scottish Office. Quietly-spoken, firm, every move planned and implemented, his subtle masterminding of the press was one of the best-kept secrets of the campaign. He spent most of his time in the media hothouse of the basement and ground floor of the Goodlads' house, where up to twenty people at a time were working in very cramped conditions as the heatwave beat down outside. It was organised chaos as the team fielded bids from the media, chose and approached colleagues to do interviews, monitored and responded to news items and Redwood stories, planned and executed our own media campaign, wrote articles and tried to maintain initiative and morale. Ian did interview upon interview as the press laid siege to the house. Twice he had to arrange for more telephone lines to be installed. In the dining room Terence Higgins and others counted heads, cross-checked and collated intelligence. Penny Gummer turned up with home-baked cakes that were devoured on sight. We were gearing up.

If I won the contest I intended to appoint Alastair Goodlad chief whip in a reshuffle. I did not wish him to face the accusation that I was repaying him for letting us use his house as a headquarters, so I asked Graham Bright to find an alternative location. He returned with an offer from the former Conservative MP Sir Neil Thorne to lend us his house in Cowley Street, a short walk from the Houses of Parliament. British Telecom surveyed the house on Wednesday, and were installing lines as I announced the contest to the press. It was a splendid base, though Sir Neil's West Highland terrier, Zubin, did not take kindly to the invasion of his home, and voiced his protest, yapping at everybody throughout the campaign. As it happens, Alastair Goodlad's house was used discreetly as a secluded place to plan strategy. It was where most of the main decisions of the campaign were made. Alastair, of course, was unaware he would later become chief whip.

Graham Bright had set about raising money for the campaign. I instructed that there were to be no big donors lurking in the shadows. Much of the money was donated by parliamentary colleagues, though I was not to know this until later. The most anyone gave was £1,000, and the entire campaign cost only £12,000. This even included the cost of getting a plumber in to fix a lavatory which gave up midway through the campaign.

I owe the nature of the campaign to my team. Half of me would have preferred not to win at all than to win with the aid of salesmanship. It was they who insisted the campaign was proactive. I was at least half-inclined simply to say, 'I'm PM, they know me. Let them make up their minds.' Robert, Ian and the team strongly disagreed. They were right. 'Take no risks,' they said.

They practised as they preached. Two battered A4 ring-binders were filled with jotted notes on Tea Room gossip and snatched conversations, a page for each MP. 'Of course I've said I'll vote for Major, but I won't,' said one backbencher. 'Redwood's the man: Portillo's soft for not making up his mind,' said another. 'Wants to be bought off,' reported one of my team about a colleague. 'Wants to vote for the winner,' recorded another. Wavering backbenchers were put down for a 'Cabinet cuddle', and their concerns noted. Nothing was missed.

Douglas Hurd added to the drama. On Friday, he made public his decision to bring forward his retirement. First a prime minister had resigned as party leader, and now his foreign secretary was leaving the government. It looked sensational, but the explanation was less so. Douglas had wanted to resign the year before, and had only stayed on at my request. He made his move now to demonstrate that his decision was independent of the result of the leadership election – had he waited until the reshuffle that followed it, some might have assumed he had been sacked. I was sorry to see him go, and the timing was certainly unfortunate, but it did open up the chance for a bigger Cabinet reshuffle. Some on the right felt moved by the vacancy to support me, hoping one of their candidates would be appointed to fill Douglas's place. I didn't encourage this view, and no one on my campaign team did so with my permission.

On the Saturday following my announcement I was at Lord's, twenty-four hours after John Redwood had joined his PPS David Evans there, out of reach of the press and fellow Cabinet ministers trying to find out what he was up to. At one point when there was a lull in the play, the crowd began applauding and turning round in their seats. I wondered what the fuss was; then I realised that the TV cameras were trained on my box, and I was being shown on a giant video screen, watching the match. I was warmed and encouraged by this response, which matched the friendly reception I received around the country.

The next day, too, cricket whites made an appearance in the contest. This time they were worn by John Redwood, who spent the day taking part in a long-arranged match near his constituency. He was still not giving interviews, which may have been an error, since to fill their news-space the BBC used footage of John, as Welsh Secretary, inaccurately miming the Welsh national anthem.

Having a little trouble singing 'Hen Wlad fy Nhadu', however, was not going to be enough to stop him. As Sunday wore on it was clear that John was preparing the ground, searching out MPs likely to back him and sniffing around other potential runners to find out what they were up to. He did not want to challenge me if the result would be that he scraped in last, behind other challengers, with a handful of votes. On the BBC's *On the Record* programme I made it clear that the decision whether or not to stand was up to John, but I couldn't rule out the possibility that he might go for it.

In any event, I was relaxed as I travelled down to Kent to join Norma for a lunch, arranged some time before, with the Party Treasurer Phil Harris and his wife Pauline at High Quarry, their house near Edenbridge in Kent. It was a blazing June day and the house is beautifully situated. After lunch I walked round their garden with Phil and discussed my prospects. He was phlegmatic. 'Win or lose,' he said, 'there's a lot of life left. There's much more to it than politics.' These were my sentiments entirely. On the way back to London, listening to talk about the contest on the car radio, I was feeling positive, though the 'brave move' of Friday morning was now being reported as a 'gamble' which might not come off. The news obviously needed a new spin, while everyone waited to see if a challenger emerged.

By now I was certain that John Redwood would stand. I knew that if I was to have an opponent, he was the ideal one – beatable, Euro-sceptic, and a Cabinet colleague whose defeat would settle things beyond doubt. His adviser Hywel Williams was casting around all too obviously to find out if Michael Portillo had been in touch with Michael Heseltine (he hadn't), and was promising a statement the next day. Bill Cash was letting it be known that 'the die was cast', and that there would be a real candidate. It was not difficult to read the runes: John Redwood would stand.

On Monday morning the papers hurried to tell their readers everything about the previously inconspicuous Secretary of State for Wales. As I prepared to leave Downing Street for a ceremony to mark the UN's fiftieth anniversary and then a European summit in Cannes, Alex Allan called to let me know that John Redwood was finally on the line – on his mobile. It was a bizarre little conversation. He knew what he had to say, but not how to do it credibly, and in a rather curious way my heart warmed to him. He was not the sort of political rogue who could behave in a bare-faced manner. He had obviously made up his mind to resign as Welsh Secretary and stand against me the day before (a point made since in the book by Hywel Williams). I thought he was doing so because he saw the chance to outfox Michael Portillo and become the standard bearer of the Euro-sceptic right. My own predecessor had become leader of the party by daring to throw her hat into the ring while the heavyweights held back. And if John suspected that he might not survive in the Cabinet reshuffle he had nothing to lose. Naturally he said none of this. He told me he was only going to resign because I hadn't accepted his 'policy advice' the previous Wednesday, and because I had 'shocked him' by resigning. He seemed uncomfortable and embarrassed, and claimed later that he only made up his mind to resign during his conversation with me. This was certainly not true.

Later that morning John invited Michael Portillo to join his campaign. Michael declined – but made it clear that he would enter any second round, and would expect John Redwood to stand aside for him. John, in turn, declined to accept this condition. Their supporters began to snipe at one another.

Over the weekend some members of my campaign team had suggested I send Douglas Hurd on a valedictory trip to the European summit in Cannes in my place, and throw everything into electioneering in Westminster. They recalled the television pictures from November 1990 of Margaret Thatcher wining and dining in Paris while her job was being lost for the want of two votes in London. I disagreed with my advisers. I knew that I had to attend. I couldn't miss a European summit without everyone assuming I was panicking. And, as Ian Lang pointed out, it was no bad thing to give the Redwood campaign a chance to fizz and spit before our counter-attack took away some of its fire.

Installed in the Dirk Bogarde Suite at the Carlton Hotel in Cannes, I watched with Howell James as John Redwood's campaign was launched with a press conference on the television news. It was great entertainment, and did more to send wavering backbenchers into my camp than several days' hard campaigning on my part could ever have done. John had successfully attracted every oddball in the party, all of whom had dressed for the occasion. The candidate himself was lost in a mass of eccentric jackets and lime-green silk. Tony Marlow wore an amazing blazer which would have looked good on a cricket field in the 1890s. Following this extraordinary spectacle, I hoped they'd have three press conferences a day. 'If they do,' I thought, 'I can stay here and sun myself on the beach.'

The press conference provoked quite a reaction. Tim Collins called John's supporters 'the barmy army', a phrase which stuck. Many thought the event looked manic; but some, like Iain Duncan Smith, decided to lend John their support. One or two of the newspapers were angling for a Michael Heseltine–Michael Portillo contest, but in order to get that they needed to force my resignation. The battering ram with which they hoped to achieve this was to actively support John Redwood. Simon Heffer, though, thought Redwood had completely upstaged Portillo, and promised him a great run in the *Telegraph*.

Ken Clarke declared that the Conservatives 'would not win an election in a thousand years' if they adopted Redwood's 'right-wing programme', and Douglas Hurd was critical too. I agreed with them. But Robert Cranborne asked them to tone down their comments. He did not want attacks by pro-Europeans to herd back into the pen MPs deterred by John's bizarre launch. Later I learned that John himself had been dismayed by the spectacle his press conference had presented. It is possible to speculate that his campaign never recovered from its opening, and that without it it might have gained more momentum.

The European summit was uneventful and went well, with none of my fellow heads of government seeking any political capital from my difficulties at home. There were one or two scrappy arguments about arcane matters and, between myself and the French President Jacques Chirac, about the size of future European Development Funds to disburse overseas aid. But these were run-of-the-mill exchanges.

John Redwood released his policy statement the next day. It was an extraordinary mixture, parts of which were memorably described by one of my team as 'Neil Kinnock circa 1992'. As a Cabinet minister, John had signed up to most of the things that he was now disagreeing with. He called for 'low taxation' and spending cuts of £5 billion a year. None of us was against trimming spending or cutting tax; the question was how, when, and to what extent could this be done? In fact, John had *increased* spending in Wales while he was a member of the Cabinet. As for his call for an opt-out on the single currency, that already was our policy, which I had negotiated at Maastricht. He promised he would be tough on law and order. Tougher, I wondered, than Michael Howard? He wanted more spending on defence and local hospitals. But since he was also saying that I was a spendthrift and he wanted to cut taxes, that was an odd statement. Finally he declared: 'Tories keep royal yachts, not scrap them.'

Keep *Britannia*? Well, that was very much my position, though it wasn't the view of the whole Cabinet, since Ken Clarke was opposed, believing such expenditure would backfire and damage public support for the royal family. For that reason, the fate of the vessel remained unsettled. John Redwood, who was present when we discussed the issue, must have known this. His own rush of enthusiasm for royal yachts, moreover, hardly squared with his position on public spending. His headlong rush from dry and rather theoretical politics to tabloid populism was ungainly and, I suspect, painful for him. It was his second serious mistake in two days. Very few members of the Cabinet would have been prepared to serve under a prime minister who had concocted such a document.

Margaret Thatcher was not put off by any of these contradictions. On Tuesday she hinted at her support for John Redwood. Though she described both him and myself as 'good Conservatives', this was interpreted – correctly – as damning me with faint praise. Having sniggered at his campaign launch, the right-of-centre media now decided the Redwood challenge was a juicy story, and he began to receive a dream press. His campaign team robustly made it clear that they would not make way for Michael Portillo in a later ballot. Meanwhile David Hart, Portillo's adviser, was saying the party would soon get the contest it needed: Portillo against Heseltine.

I didn't wish to leave the press entirely to John Redwood while I was at the European summit, so I accepted an invitation to place an article in the London *Evening Standard*. It was a good shop-window because the paper is widely read in the Commons Tea Room by the electoral college of MPs. It would also provide copy for the media the following morning. Howell James and Norman Blackwell in Cannes and Jonathan Hill and Nick True in London worked on a text for me. It was based on the themes we wished to emphasise as we approached the general election, and reiterated my ambition to reduce public spending further and to cut capital taxes. The Treasury did not like the proposal on capital taxes at all, but the article achieved its purpose and received wide coverage.

I returned from Cannes on Tuesday night, heartened that the summit had gone well, to find Robert Cranborne and Ian Lang in a much less sunny mood. 'You've been away,' Robert told me forcefully. 'Now you've got to do some campaigning.'

This was first-class advice, but I was still prime minister, and had official duties which I was unwilling to turn into re-election stunts. The first of these was a press conference at the Foreign Office the following morning, on arrangements for the fiftieth-anniversary commemoration of VJ-Day. This was straightforward despite some tricky questions on Japan and war veterans. The press behaved impeccably, both at the press conference and at the brief doorstep interview on the election that I held in Downing Street.

That afternoon I made a statement in the Commons on the Cannes summit. I did not let the contest affect what I said, despite pressure from some in my campaign team to do so, but nor did I feel inclined to offer soft words to my opponents. When Bill Cash, a particular irritant, asked me a hostile question on the Commons floor, I told him he was 'talking through the back of his head'. Rude, perhaps, but deserved.

Early that evening the press told us that Michael Portillo's supporters were setting up a campaign HQ and installing telephone lines. This was confirmed when *Newsnight* showed coverage of telephone engineers putting in lines, and beds coming out of the house and being loaded into a removal van. As Michael had declared his support for me this caused a good deal of critical comment, especially from Redwood supporters. The next day's press covered this extensively, together with photographs of supporters of Michael going into the house. Michael's backers distanced him from the action, claiming it was 'private enterprise'.

Meanwhile, the contest was knocked off the front pages by events on the other side of the Atlantic. In California the British actor Hugh Grant was arrested and fined for 'lewd behaviour'. Over the next week, the press devoted more column inches to that spicy but ephemeral story than it did to the leadership contest. At the time commentators were combing almost every item of news for its possible effect on the leadership contest; none, so far as I know, managed to link Mr Grant's problems to those of either John Redwood or myself – a rare failure of imagination on their part.

Prime Minister's Questions on Thursday afternoon went particularly well. The House was packed and riotous and resembled a Roman arena. There was blood to be spilled – that was certain – but whose? Usually at the PMQ briefing we guessed at the topics Tony Blair would go for, and we had a high success rate. But on this occasion I thought he would steer clear of the leadership election, knowing that I would be prepared. He didn't. This became evident when Austin Mitchell, the first Labour questioner, asked me about it – a routine ploy by Labour whips to open a subject from the backbenches so that Tony Blair could follow it up.

Seeking to widen disagreement within the Conservative Party, Blair asked if John Redwood should have resigned earlier if he disagreed so strongly with government policy. His backbenchers roared their approval.

They assumed that I would either attack John, thus widening divisions between us and making them personal, or stonewall and look indecisive. Either way, the Labour benches were primed to jeer.

I was lucky. John's bogus reason for resigning gave me an open goal: 'I understand that he resigned from the Cabinet because he was devastated that I had resigned as leader of the Conservative Party,' I told Blair. He grinned, the tension vanished, and the mood of the House changed from that of a Roman circus to Sunday Night at the London Palladium.

The remainder of Prime Minister's Questions was in the same vein. The Labour MP George Foulkes, ever ripe for mischief, asked about Michael Portillo installing telephone lines in preparation for a second ballot. To general merriment, I brushed this aside with a tribute to the efficiency of a privatised British Telecom – a quip Ian Lang had suggested. When I left the Chamber it was to cries of 'More, more,' and the waving of Order Papers on every side of the House. Paddy Ashdown rushed to an interview to say that I had just saved my job. I was not so sure. But it did change the mood music, and it forced John Redwood onto the defensive.

Thursday was turning out to be a good day. Two polls, in *The Times* and the *Economist*, tipped a number of wavering MPs into my camp. The first suggested that only 29 per cent of voters put Europe among the most important issues facing Britain – which was what I had being saying all along. The second claimed that with John Redwood as leader the party would lose sixty-four more seats at the general election than if I remained. These findings put the loonies back in their box.

I sensed we were pulling further ahead and that the Redwood challenge, which had stumbled at the outset, then attracted more support, was hitting the rocks. David Evans, Redwood's former PPS, was a noted parliamentary character, whose trademark was as a plain-speaking man of the people quoting the pithy views of his wife – 'Janice says . . .'. Janice, as quoted, was often apposite and funny. David now went on the record to attack the 'nutty element' present at John's campaign launch. He, of course, had been there, and for this unconventional parliamentary performer to attack the 'nutty element' was amusing in itself, and certainly helpful to me. On Friday John's team put out a leaflet: 'No Change Equals No Chance. The choice is stark. To Save Your Seat, Your Party and Your Country, vote for John Redwood.' Its tone reinforced my case that a Redwood victory would be divisive, and would put off more potential supporters than it attracted.

Meanwhile, John failed to bounce me into holding a public debate, which I thought would advertise yet further the party's divisions over Europe. 'Dear John,' I replied to his invitation. 'I recall when I was a Tory candidate fighting a hopeless seat with no chance of winning. I was advised to challenge the incumbent MP to a debate. The gist of his reply was, "Nice try, but no." You may wish to know that he went on to win a handsome victory.' Nothing more was heard of this suggestion.

As the weekend approached I continued to meet colleagues to enlist their support. A meeting with the Positive European Group went particularly well. I saw many colleagues individually, but did not waste my time on the known lost causes. In response to an oft-repeated question I made it clear that I was not prepared to buy wavering votes by a change in policy on the single currency. Nor, in truth, could I. If I had done so the Cabinet would have broken apart and the solid centre in the party would have abandoned their support for me. In any event, the question did not arise. I believed it was right to maximise our negotiating influence by keeping our options open, and I was not prepared to change policy.

The media had no vote in our contest, but it did have a powerful voice, and the tone of it worsened amid rumours that the proprietors of three traditionally Conservative newspaper groups – Rupert Murdoch (News International), Vere Harmsworth (Associated Newspapers) and Conrad Black (Telegraph Group) – had met, armed with a black spot apiece. Whether this is true or false, it was widely believed to be credible, and spoke volumes for the extent to which it was presumed that the press was prepared to influence the domestic political process.

But the polls became progressively more encouraging even as press and public preference diverged. A poll in the *Sunday Times* showed 55 per cent of Conservative voters favouring me as leader, more than backed Heseltine, Portillo and Redwood put together. The *Sunday Express*'s poll of constituency chairmen gave me a landslide, with 96 per cent support, and MORI showed my approval rating sharply up. But the majority of the press were now committed to a change, and did all they could to engineer it. Most damaging was the *Telegraph*, the premier Conservative broadsheet.

The *Sunday Telegraph* supported John Redwood, while on Monday the *Daily Telegraph* printed an article by me which they had invited me to write, without disclosing that it would appear opposite a very hostile editorial. The *Independent* reported a few days later that the editor Max Hastings had been pressured by Conrad Black into supporting Redwood, but in any event he was consistent thereafter. Neither at the *Telegraph* nor, later, at the *Evening Standard*, was he ever again to be an ally. Mr Black, however, continued to assure me of the warm support of his papers whenever we met.

Gathering media support must in part explain the turnabout in John Redwood's fortunes after his dreadful start; but not wholly. His candidature never looked impressive, his style was never assured and his promises were seen to be absurd. So how did the impression grow of a rolling bandwagon? The press did not invent a hardening of his support among Conservative MPs. What happened, I suspect, once speculation about the identities and personalities of those who might challenge had died down, and rival affections for rival horses became irrelevant, was that the party was brought up hard against a simple choice. In this ballot it had to be me, or not me. And 'not me' had to be John Redwood, who, for whatever reason, had had the courage to stand. The support of all who disliked my leadership, or wanted to wrench the party in an anti-European direction, was now settling on his shoulders. It was considerable.

Meanwhile, Ian Lang, at Robert Cranborne's request, had prepared a strategy paper which was adopted as our plan for the second half of the campaign. It tried to weave together the growing support of colleagues; the powerful impact of constituency backing; and the negative issue of contemplating what might happen if I was not re-elected. It focused also on unrelenting attention to detail and the need to dominate the media up to and beyond the close of the poll.

An interview I gave to the *Financial Times* caused unease among my campaign team. In response to a direct question I refused to rule out resigning if I won a purely technical victory. This understandably upset colleagues who were working very hard for me.

Amidst all this came the news, on Monday, of the release of Private Lee Clegg, a soldier who had been convicted of murder after killing a joyrider while on active duty in Northern Ireland. If the decision looked like an attempt to appease MPs, many of whom had campaigned for his release, that was not how it had been intended. The timing, however, was unlucky, and the issue flared at PMQs the next day.

With rumours continuing to swirl around and estimates of the likely result being scrutinised and pored over, the campaign drew to a close. On the last evening both John Redwood and I appeared before a meeting of the 92 Group, which was packed with friends and foes. Some of my campaign team were worried that John's supporters would ask a string of questions intended to show that a vote for me would. mean continued disruption in the party. But they did not. If such a strategy had been planned, then the wrong questioners were called. The meeting passed off uneventfully, with few, if any, converts gained or lost by either John or me.

American Independence Day, Tuesday, 4 July, gave the party the opportunity, if it wanted, to be independent of me. It was another glorious summer day, but the final press throw was worse than I had feared. 'Time to Ditch the Captain' was the headline in the *Daily Mail*. 'Tories fear victory will be hollow,' said *The Times*. It was impossible to guess what effect this coverage would have on colleagues: they resented press interference, but they also knew that we had a general election to win, and that we needed to be able to present our policies and turn our fire on Labour with maximum effect.

Howell James came up to the flat in Number 10 early that morning. He was opaque about what our final canvass showed, but it became clear that it was in the region of 212 votes. I looked at the morning papers scattered on the floor, knowing that if that estimate was right and there was any more slippage of support away from me, I would announce my resignation as prime minister later that day.

I did not relish the thought of telling my team that those numbers were not sufficient for me to carry on with credibility. But the outcome was not certain, and in the meantime there was work to be done – and, if I won, an immediate and substantial reshuffle of the government to be undertaken. After the usual 9 a.m. gathering to take a preliminary look at PMQs for that afternoon, I asked Michael Heseltine to come and see me. We discussed the vote dispassionately and objectively. Neither of us was confident of the outcome. Michael agreed with me that a simple win by the rules would not be good enough, but did not indicate what he thought the minimum acceptable vote would be. We both knew that by tomorrow I might have resigned, and that if I had, he would be a candidate for the premiership.

The fact that Michael was at Number 10 for two and a half hours that morning gave rise to a totally untrue story that we had been engaged in a conspiracy, whereby he was negotiating a powerful job for himself in return for encouraging his supporters to vote for me. No job, no vote – and I would be out. That was the theory.

It was absolute nonsense. There was no deal. Michael was with me for a little less than an hour, during which time I referred to our conversation of three weeks earlier and offered him the post of First Secretary of State and Deputy Prime Minister, with a choice of responsibilities, were I to be re-elected as leader later that day. He could either remain at Trade and Industry with a second Cabinet minister in his department and add coordination and presentation of policy to his responsibilities; or he could go to the Cabinet Office, with responsibility for competitiveness and deregulation, as well as coordination and presentation of government policy. He chose the latter. I outlined what this would entail and the committees he would have to chair. I wanted him to use his skills on the media at every opportunity to boost presentation of our policies. He was keen to do this. At no time in our discussion did he bargain for preferment, or offer support only conditionally, or imply in any way that his promotion to deputy prime minister was necessary to ensure his support for my re-election.

Michael then left the Cabinet Room to go in search of an office suitable for his new job. His eyes lit mischievously on the Cabinet Secretary's room, but Robin Butler, the occupant, was having none of that. Within minutes Robin had identified an even more splendid conference room that could be adapted as an office. Michael returned to me, full of enthusiasm, to advocate the abolition of two departments of state: Employment and the Department of National Heritage. I told him I had decided to merge Employment with Education, but that the DNH was staying as it was.

In the Commons, the ballot box was filling up. Patrick Cormack and Peter Luff voted early for me, and Andrew Hargreaves for John Redwood. Teddy Taylor announced that he was still undecided. George Gardiner, to no one's surprise, declared himself for Redwood. No one really knew how the voting was going, but that did not stop people offering their views. Adam Boulton, the political editor of Sky News, thought there would be a second ballot, but Michael Brunson of ITN predicted that I would win. Andrew Marr of the *Independent* had been told things were going badly for me, with many abstentions. Trevor Kavanagh of the *Sun* was certain of it. He was predicting tactical voting to force another ballot with new candidates. The *Sun* wanted juicy news, and Heseltine versus Portillo looked just the ticket to them. Throughout the day these snippets were fed back to my campaign team.

After Prime Minister's Questions (which I came close to missing when my car was blocked in Downing Street by a builder's van) I returned to my room in the Commons to find Alastair Goodlad and Robert Cranborne waiting. Their body language made it clear they had a serious message to deliver. I knew what it would be. 'A win is a win,' they said. 'One is enough.' I must have my reshuffle and go on, they insisted. I disagreed. Unless I had a decent majority supporting me, I would have no true authority. Too many MPs would have openly shown their dissatisfaction. The party wouldn't bind. Better a new leader who might enjoy a fresh surge of goodwill and have no baggage from the recession or the disputes over Europe.

Alastair and Robert were unimpressed. 'No,' they said. I had a duty to go on. But I was adamant. The mood became grimmer as they began to accept that I was not prepared to be coerced. To avoid a row flaring, I asked, 'Do you really think the vote will be bad enough for this to be necessary?' They said they did not know what number of votes would be acceptable to me, but they thought I would win well. 'Then leave it,' I said. 'We'll know soon enough.'

John Ward came in to ask how the meeting had gone. 'Not easy,' I said. 'I'd like two minutes alone and a cup of tea.' I got the tea and John's advice as well. If I walked away I would have let down people who 'had worked their guts out eighteen hours a day'. History would not forgive me if I did that. He spoke his mind in my interest, and he did not mince his words.

Robert and Alastair may have been disgruntled when they left me, but within minutes they had moved into action. It was evident that they had made contingency arrangements to persuade me of their views if I showed signs of being stubborn. A letter had arrived already from the historian and constitutional authority Lord Blake, telling me I should remain if I won by the rules. I was touched by his thoughtfulness, until I noticed some words at the bottom of his letter – it had been copied to Robert Cranborne and, I have no doubt, solicited by him as well. I was glad Robert was on my side. Willie Whitelaw had earlier given the same message. No clue there, but I did wonder. Paddy Mayhew turned up at my office, full of confidence and positive vibes. So too did Malcolm Rifkind. There was a procession. Tom King brought in a note about the number of votes that would be acceptable, and then stayed ten minutes to talk. Other colleagues arrived. Robert knew how to impress. At 4.30 p.m. Jonathan Hill pointed out that the poll closed in thirty minutes, and I hadn't yet voted. I did so – one of the last seven MPs to vote – and returned to Number 10.

I had intended to hear the result alone with Norma, but Graham Bright was determined to be with me, and told Norma so. 'Are you the man in the grey suit?' she teased him, referring to the legendary senior Tories who are said to wait upon prime ministers to tell them it is time to go. When I arrived at Number 10 with John Ward, I found Douglas Hurd, Paddy Mayhew, Ian Lang, Brian Mawhinney, Alastair Goodlad and others standing self-consciously outside the Cabinet Room, having been gathered there by Robert to reinforce his view that I should stay come what might. I invited them all upstairs to join me for the result. I owed them all an enormous debt of gratitude, and welcomed their presence. 'If the result isn't good enough, I can tell them straight away,' I thought. We turned on the television in the flat to watch the carnival on College Green. It was packed with the media, MPs, peers and members of the public, all waiting for the result.

Initially, everyone stood around, watching the screen awkwardly. The atmosphere was tense. Then chairs were found and most colleagues were able to sit. I offered drinks – only to discover that all I had in the flat was some white wine that had not been chilled. We sent downstairs for cold wine and beer. I had a large brandy and nursed it pensively.

John Ward peeled off to the telephone in Norma's study, which Marcus Fox was primed to ring with early information about the result. Graham Bright joined him to discuss the likely total: Graham's prediction was 217. I stood with my back to the fireplace and with an arm around Norma. Douglas, characteristically with his left leg swinging, was draped over the arm of a chair, Brian by the window, Robert hunched near the television, Paddy prowled around restlessly, muttering, and Alex Allan, ever present when needed, stood beside me.

The phone rang. The result? Not quite. It was Elizabeth with a last-minute good-luck message. Then the phone in the study rang, and after what seemed an eternity, John Ward walked in, expressionless, and silently handed me a piece of paper with the result on it.

I looked at it, and showed Norma – the culmination of long months of disarray and despair, and a hard campaign. The sealed envelope with what I judged would be the minimum acceptable result was still in my pocket. I had planned to open it if I did not win enough votes, as evidence that I had thought the consequences out much earlier. Now I looked again at John's figures, and a moment later Norma said: 'Well, that's all right then,' and handed the piece of paper to John Ward to read out. It showed:

JOHN MAJOR 218
JOHN REDWOOD 89
ABSTENTIONS 8
SPOILED 12

It was three votes above the minimum I had set myself – less than I had hoped for, but more than I had feared. It was in the 'grey area', but the team cheered and applauded. There were kisses for Norma, hugs and handshakes. It was not really enough, but it was three votes too many to allow me to walk away.

Robert, Alastair and Ian Lang's master-stroke was yet to come. Within moments College Green was swamped with around forty senior colleagues, primed and victorious, giving interviews and proclaiming a famous victory. The same message echoed around the Commons, Millbank, Central Office and Cowley Street. Norman Fowler, Tom King, John MacGregor, Cranley Onslow and Jeffrey Archer were all prominent in disseminating it. The mood was set. Tony Marlow and Bill Cash appeared looking quizzical and then utterly morose. It was all over.

I felt deflated. There was no elation. The leadership had been settled for the present Parliament, but the size of John's vote meant that there were many storms ahead. Robert urged me into Downing Street to claim victory: 'Your crown is rolling in the gutter, Prime Minister. Go and pick it up.' I did so, taking the campaign team with me to provide a backcloth for the cameras. No one could have had better friends in a bleak time. Then Norma and I went off to Cowley Street to celebrate and express my thanks to many of our team who were gathered in the garden of Neil Thorne's house. Even Zubin seemed cheerful. Later more of our team arrived at Number 10, where the impromptu celebrations continued. The last guests left at 11.30, and as John Ward bade goodnight, Alex Allan and I sat down in the Cabinet Room to prepare for a government reshuffle the next day.

Michael Heseltine became deputy prime minister. Malcolm Rifkind moved from Defence to the Foreign Office, to be succeeded by a relieved Michael Portillo, who – after the episode with the telephones – had not been sure of his future. Ian Lang moved up to the Board of Trade, and Michael Forsyth joined the Cabinet as Scottish secretary. Other newcomers were Douglas Hogg at Agriculture and William Hague at Wales, who, replacing John Redwood, scurried off saying, 'Grand, I'll learn the Welsh national anthem straight away.' Roger Freeman became Chancellor of the Duchy of Lancaster, Brian Mawhinney was appointed party chairman, and Stephen Dorrell, Virginia Bottomley, William Waldegrave and George Young moved to new jobs. It was a big change, but even now the preferment of Michael Heseltine and Malcolm Rifkind caused anguish and dissent among those who wanted a harder line on Europe.

Had my strategy been successful? Would it make a genuine difference? Only the longer perspective of history can make a proper judgement on the unique episode of a prime minister voluntarily putting his job at risk. Tentative conclusions, however, can be drawn. My re-election ended the frenzy in the party, but not the conflict. The European dispute was too deep-seated to be cut off at its source, and in due course the bitterness engendered by it was a primary cause of our party's overwhelming defeat in the 1997 general election. Ultimately it did the damage I had always feared it would.

Was John Redwood right when he campaigned on 'No Change, No Chance'? The general election result might suggest that he was, but I am sure it is not so. The only change that could have made a decisive difference would have been a change in the mood of the party, bringing unity on Europe – and no such change was possible – or a change of heart amongst the electorate, who believed we had been in power too long.

If not John Redwood, then could another leader have changed the fortunes of the party? Neither the polls nor the feeling in the party at the time pointed to this. Nor do I think it would have done. In reaching this judgement, I am in no way underestimating the talents of potential successors. I simply believe that the public mood was set. Had the Archangel Gabriel been elected leader of the Conservative Party, I doubt whether he would have triumphed at the next general election.

The contest was beneficial in helping to clear the air. It was probably decisive in saving my leadership, for to have drifted on into the autumn, at the mercy of speculation about when my enemies would spring a contest on me (as opposed to my springing one on them), could hardly have added to the 218 votes I received in July. I firmly believe that my re-election as leader postponed – and, I hope, saved the party from – an irrevocable split over European policy. At the time, it would very likely have haemorrhaged if a leader had been chosen who gave unconditional backing to one side or the other in an argument so fundamental to the protagonists that none was prepared to concede.

The risk of a party split to the point of breakdown had been a nightmare for me since the day I first entered Downing Street as prime minister. It had been greatly increased by the manner of Margaret Thatcher's removal and the passions that action released. Those passions reverberated throughout my premiership, unleashing personal conflicts that deepened the divisions first opened on the black day when the labels 'wet' and 'dry' came into currency and came to be worn as battle honours. As the argument moved on from monetarism to Europe, from 'wets' and 'drys' to 'Euro-supporters' and 'Euro-sceptics', factions formed, the majority view became a target to tilt at, and belief in consensus – the acceptance of decisions arrived at by reason and compromise – was derided as lack of conviction and lack of leadership. Thus were logic and common sense ignored; and the electorate concluded we were so full of division that we should be ejected at the polls. In due course, we were.

# CHAPTER TWENTY-SIX

# Mad Cows and Europeans

I N THE EARLY AFTERNOON of Monday, 18 March 1996, I was in the Cabinet Room talking to the Party Chairman, Brian Mawhinney, when Michael Heseltine, Alex Allan and Norman Blackwell, head of the Policy Unit, walked in. Alex and Norman looked concerned, and Michael had that light in his eye and spring in his step which indicated serious trouble ahead.

Without any preamble, Michael said, 'Prime Minister, we have a real problem.' He told me that he had just seen a minute, written jointly that morning by Stephen Dorrell, the Minister for Health, and Douglas Hogg, the Minister for Agriculture. It was a short note explaining that the Spongiform Encephalopathy Advisory Committee (SEAC) – set up in 1990 to advise the government on the cattle disease Bovine Spongiform Encephalopathy (BSE) – was to meet later in the week, and was expected to announce new evidence of a linkage between BSE and a similar disease which affected the human brain, Creutzfeldt-Jakob Disease (CJD). This was dramatic news, since we had previously been advised that there was no link. The minute set out a number of options in response to this bleak possibility, ranging from the deboning of British beef to the horrifying prospect of the mass extermination of cattle herds. After some tough weeks, I had hoped we had just entered a period of political calm – and here it seemed, once more, was an unexpected event beyond our control which would blow everything apart.

We discussed the implications. Where was the proof of the link between BSE and CJD? Why had it suddenly become apparent? How great, in reality, was the risk to humans? What actions might the scientists recommend? No one knew the answers. We arranged an urgent meeting with Douglas Hogg, Stephen Dorrell and our chief adviser on BSE, Professor John Pattison, who set out the facts. All the scientists could say, however, was that there was a small, though *unproven*, risk that BSE *could* cause CJD, with the possible incidence of cases between two at best, and far more at worst. It was the worst sort of political problem: an unknown but potentially serious risk, and no scientific certainty of how to contain it.

The source of BSE was thought to be cattle-feed made from the carcasses of sheep, some of which had been contaminated by sheep suffering from scrapie, a brain disease which had been around for well over two hundred years. In 1988 the government had implemented a ban on this cattle-feed, and ordered that all cattle suffering from BSE be slaughtered. A year later, the government had decided to err on what was then seen as the side of caution and ban specified beef offal, including brain, spinal cord and intestines, from human consumption. In 1990 SEAC was appointed to investigate all aspects of the disease. Throughout this period, policy was handled routinely by successive agriculture ministers through relevant Cabinet committees. The general outline of the policy and the scientific advice on which it was based did not change significantly. The policy was agreed, and the important thing was to administer it effectively.

The BSE crisis was more serious than any previous health risk faced by a British government. Our strategy throughout was to rely on the available scientific advice, but therein lay a problem: the science was still developing, so the advice was provisional and kept changing. There were, and still are, a long list of unknowns. But at all stages the advice was, and still is, that the risk of transmission of BSE to humans was either non-existent or infinitesimal. We were caught between the Scylla of scientists, with their hypotheses, and the Charybdis of consumers, who demanded certainty.

By the time Michael Heseltine gave me the news in March 1996 that SEAC had established that there was a possible risk to human health, we had *already* acted to remove the likely sources of infection from the food chain. Only a few mavericks have ever suggested that there was a risk of infection from eating prime cuts of beef. Indeed, one of the great ironies was that at the time the cataclysm shook the industry there was, scientifically speaking, no longer a risk from eating British beef.

The following morning, Cabinet ministers, expecting a political discussion, instead found themselves exposed to a full discussion on BSE. Some of my colleagues questioned whether going public with such uncertain findings was the right thing to do; we did not, they pointed out, know enough about the disease to give any quantifiable view of the likely scale of the problem. Others, however, argued the consequences if we remained silent. We would be in no position to deny the truth of any reports of a link, and we would inevitably be accused of a cover up. The story had already begun to leak, and even if we had wished to remain silent until we were in possession of all the facts, it was not practical to do so.

It was agreed that Douglas Hogg would tell the House that afternoon that we would follow the SEAC advice requiring the deboning of meat from older animals, which were the most likely to develop BSE, and would also ban the use of meat and bonemeal as pig and poultry feed. These were precisely the kind of precautionary measures we had been taking, on scientific advice, since the existence of BSE had first come to light. As the new information raised a serious health issue, it was agreed that Stephen Dorrell should make a statement as well. This decision proved to be an error. Whereas the shadow Agriculture spokesman, Gavin Strang, was restrained in his reply to Douglas Hogg, Stephen Dorrell's statement gave Labour's Health spokesman Harriet Harman the chance to take to the Dispatch Box with an over-the-top performance that inflamed an already difficult situation.

Stephen was unable to answer in detail many of the questions raised in the House because the answers were simply not known. His protestations that British beef was safe, though valid, sat oddly with the action set in hand by Douglas Hogg. He was barracked and heckled throughout, amid suspicions that we were more certain of the health risk than in fact we were. It became open season for speculation. The *Daily Mirror*, for instance, told its readers: 'some experts fear we may already have consumed more than a million infected animals . . . and that as the incurable killer disease can take ten years or more to show up, some people are already living on borrowed time.' It went on to forecast: 'Sales of beef, pies, sausages, mince, joints and other products are expected to plummet.'

The *possible* link to the terrible illness of CJD was shocking, and public confidence in beef collapsed. In the ensuing panic, schools and restaurants – led by the burger chain McDonald's – immediately began taking British beef off their menus. Sales of beef plummeted by 90 per cent in one day, and workers were laid off across the industry. So began a sequence of events that would devastate one of Britain's most successful industries, cost the taxpayer billions of pounds in compensation to farmers, and sour our relations with the rest of Europe.

The reaction across the European Union to our initial announcement on BSE was hysterical, especially in Italy and Germany. On 25 March, with beef sales falling across Europe as a result of the British announcement, the European Union Standing Veterinary Committee imposed a temporary ban on the export of British beef products to the rest of the world. It was not banned for use in Britain, only everywhere else. The ban was implemented to protect beef farmers elsewhere in the EU, and to enable the rest of Europe to continue exporting. No EU official believed that British beef was dangerous following the measures already in place. They were responding to fear among their consumers after the hysterical press coverage. Moreover, action against only *British* beef carried the message that other beef – *their* beef – was safe.

The moment I heard of the ban – which we did not expect, after a less alarmist response by the EU scientists in Brussels a few days earlier – I telephoned the President of the Commission, Jacques Santer, and told him I was incensed by the decision. It was totally unjustified by the scientific evidence, a wholly disproportionate action which *would add to the fears in Britain and elsewhere*. I predicted that the cost would run into billions of pounds, with the virtual closure of much of the beef industry and the loss of many jobs. It was also bound to further inflame British opinion against the European Union. On my side, at least, it was a brisk and very heated exchange, and I left Santer in no doubt that I thought the Commission's decision would worsen the situation in Britain – and also damage confidence in the beef industry across Europe. Santer was taken aback, and had very little to say in response.

Three days after the imposition of the ban on British beef exports, I travelled to Turin for a European summit. My aim was to find a way to restore trust in the beef industry across Europe and to enable the ban to be lifted. Despite our earlier exchanges Jacques Santer was sympathetic, and expressed hopes that the Standing Veterinary Committee would recommend lifting the ban once measures acceptable to the EU had been agreed. I accepted that Britain must consider a massive culling programme, removing older cattle from the food chain. I was not convinced that this was necessary on scientific grounds, but I had to accept that it was essential if we were to restore faith in the safety of our beef.

The cull became even more frustrating when in April the European Union's Agriculture Commissioner, Franz Fischler of Germany, was asked directly whether he regarded British beef as unsafe. 'No,' he replied. 'If we had thought that, its sale would have to be banned in Britain as well as elsewhere.' When asked whether he himself would eat British beef, he replied, 'I would not hesitate to eat beef in England. I know no medical reason not to.'

As April wore on it was clear that 'the spirit of Turin', as I called it, counted for little. When I met my fellow European heads of government they were sympathetic, but their eyes slid away. Most of them knew that our public health precautions were more effective than their own. I was particularly affronted that the EU banned the sale of our beef *outside* Europe as well as within it. It was their legal right to do so, but it was unnecessary. It hit a raw nerve, although our European partners could not understand my frustration over it.

At the same time, EU member states continued to complain that we were not doing enough to persuade them to lift the export ban, while being unable to suggest what more we could do. In late April we submitted revised proposals to the Commission for the slaughter, and restrictions on the movement, of cattle thought to be most at risk of developing BSE, and began negotiating a timetable for lifting the export ban. A meeting of EU agriculture ministers agreed that measures we had put in hand would be 'part of a process which should allow the export ban to be progressively lifted on a step-by-step basis'.

The litmus test, so far as we were concerned, was the need for an immediate agreement to lift the ban imposed on three beef derivatives: gelatine, tallow and semen. There was no reason for a ban on these products; the World Health Organisation had advised in early April that they were safe if properly processed. On 8 May, the EU Commission argued in a recommendation to the Standing Veterinary Committee that once strict procedures for processing animal remains were in place, the ban on gelatine, tallow and semen should be lifted. In bilateral meetings with other EU governments Douglas Hogg and I were given clear and explicit assurances that our request to lift the ban on these derivatives would have their support.

As May wore on, we began to feel that progress was being made, and that the widespread and expensive slaughter of our cattle herds was restoring confidence and would lead to an early end to the ban. In Britain, however, the frustration over the ban became enmeshed in the hostility to European policy as a whole. Euro-sceptics were asking why the European Union had banned British beef around the world if it was considered safe to eat in Britain? Was this not a policy of self-interest? If so, should not Britain flex its muscles and respond? Was it not limp-wristed of the British government to try to negotiate its way out of the problem? Euro-sceptics advanced these arguments, but they had a resonance far beyond their circle.

Our European Union partners – admittedly themselves under heavy domestic pressure – seemed oblivious to these rising concerns in Britain. On 20 May a minority of member states on the EU's Standing Veterinary Committee, led by Germany, Austria and the Netherlands, blocked a majority vote in favour of the Commission's proposals for an eventual lifting of the ban on gelatine, tallow and semen.

This decision was yet another serious blow to the beef industry. Once again, it went against everything we had been led to expect, making our assurances at home look hollow and leading to charges that we had been 'humiliated'. I certainly felt misled. It seemed to confirm the most xenophobic claims that our European partners could not be trusted to keep their word. There was outrage in the Conservative Party, not just among the Euro-sceptics but among pro-Europeans, who up until this point had supported our approach of a targeted culling of cattle and of trying to negotiate an end to the ban. After the vets' decision I learned that individual members of the Veterinary Committee had been encouraged by their respective governments to vote to maintain the ban in order to pacify their own domestic opinion, rather than to take a decision based on scientific evidence alone.

I was as infuriated about this outcome as any Euro-sceptic. I had played by club rules, and the club had changed them. It persuaded me to take action which I disliked, and subsequently regretted, though with even pro-Europeans demanding retaliation, something of the sort was probably unavoidable. I decided that Britain would not cooperate with our partners if they would not cooperate with us. We would therefore withhold our consent from decisions that required unanimous approval until the rest of the Union seriously addressed the problem of British beef, stopped taking decisions that damaged our beef industry so as to appease their own domestic clamour, and agreed to discuss a framework under which the export ban would be lifted. On 21 May I announced to Parliament that on all EU measures requiring unanimity, British ministers would attend and use their veto. This was not the result of a uniquely British tantrum, but a variant of a tactic used previously by France, Italy and Spain. I told the Commons:

> A balanced proposal based on the best scientific advice has been ignored by a number of member states, in some cases despite prior assurances of support. I must tell the House that I regard such action as a wilful disregard of Britain's interests, and, in some cases, a breach of faith ... We cannot continue business as usual within Europe when we are faced with the clear disregard by some of our partners of reason, of common sense and of Britain's national interests. We continue to want to make progress through negotiation; but if that is not possible, we are bound to use the legal avenues open to us and the political means at our disposal.

The statement was greeted with rapture by many on the Conservative benches and by the Euro-sceptic press, who, I soon learned, saw it less as a tactic to force our partners to give priority to the scientific evidence over beef – and hence to agree how to lift the ban – than as a declaration of war on Europe. The Labour Party, which throughout the BSE crisis offered no alternative means of proceeding, sensed the prevailing opinion and supported the non-cooperation policy. Our action succeeded in its first aim, which was to force the issue of beef to the top of the agenda for the European summit at Florence scheduled for the end of June.

In preparation for the summit, I convened a special Cabinet committee under my chairmanship to put in place a clear eradication strategy on which we would negotiate a lifting of the ban. At the end of May, Jacques Santer called for unity and asked EU member states to back the Commission's proposal to lift the ban on the three derivatives. The ban on semen at least was subsequently lifted, and on 7 June Italian Prime Minister Romano Prodi, who would chair the Florence summit, pledged to secure the deal. As our partners seemed to become more positive, pro-Europeans in the government urged us to suspend our action even as the sceptics encouraged us to harden it.

By 17 June we had negotiated a draft agreement with the European

Commission setting out a framework for the progressive lifting of the beef ban. This included an extension of the culling programme, targeting sixty-seven thousand animals which might have been exposed to infection; the implementation of a cattle identification programme; the removal of meat and bonemeal from feedmills and farms; and tighter controls at slaughterhouses. All these measures would be subject to strict scrutiny. And, in what we believed to be a vital part of the package given the behaviour of the Standing Veterinary Committee, we secured a guarantee that in future, decisions of the committee would be taken '*only and exclusively on the basis of public health and objective scientific criteria*'.

Once we had reached this outline agreement, though there was no set timetable, I felt that it was probably as good a deal as we were likely to get. A sensible dialogue was in train, and we now knew what we had to do for the ban to be lifted. Once we had a timetable for doing it, we would be able to make progress. On that basis I was prepared to end the veto of EU business, and on 24 June, in my statement to Parliament following the Florence summit, I did so, setting November 1996 as our target date for the lifting of the ban. I expected that by then we would have met all the conditions necessary for the EU to lift the ban on meat from animals aged under thirty months. I told the Commons:

> In my statement on 21 May I shared with the House the government's frustration that two months after an unjustified ban on our beef exports had been imposed, some member states were still unwilling to address on a rational, scientific basis a clear path to lift the ban. I accordingly announced a policy of non-cooperation until two specific objectives had been achieved: the lifting of the ban on beef derivatives, and agreement on a clear framework leading to a lifting of the wider ban which was based closely on our proposals. In accordance with that policy, we subsequently blocked seventy-four decisions that required the unanimous approval of member states.
>
> The first objective was achieved on 10 June, when the ban on beef derivatives was lifted. That was followed on 19 June by unanimous approval of our Bovine Spongiform Encephalopathy eradication plan by the Standing Veterinary Committee. In Florence on 21 June, the second objective was achieved when the European Council unanimously accepted the framework and procedures put forward by the Commission for lifting of the

wider ban. The framework sets out steps for lifting the ban in stages. The Florence conclusions make it clear that decisions on each stage will be taken 'only and exclusively on the basis of public health and objective scientific criteria and of the judgement of the Commission'.

That is what we insisted upon above all. I was therefore able to lift our non-cooperation policy once the framework had been agreed. It is now up to us to meet the conditions for lifting the ban set out in the framework.

Even as I was speaking, Commission officials were giving off-the-record briefings that assurances that decisions would be reached only on the basis of scientific evidence were meaningless, since 'political decisions had never been a factor to begin with' – which was disingenuous, if not plainly untrue. Twisting the knife, they went on to suggest that the Florence agreement was 'just a piece of paper', offered as a sop to the UK to persuade us to back down on our policy of non-cooperation. It was a vintage bit of backstabbing by anonymous Commission officialdom, and inevitably led to claims in Britain that we had 'backed down'.

Within a few months, most of the commitments agreed at Florence were being implemented. But in September 1996 we shelved plans for a selective cull, *following fresh scientific advice that it would do nothing to further the eradication of BSE*, and that our existing scheme to slaughter cattle over thirty months old would suffice. But after our attempts to negotiate this with the EU got us nowhere – they saw the slaughter of our cattle as necessary to restore their consumers' confidence – we had no choice but to bite the bullet, and the selective cull began in early 1997.

The beef ban, however, remained in place. In September 1997, after the election, the European Union announced its willingness to lift the ban on the export of grass-fed cattle from Northern Ireland, but it was not until 1 August 1999 that the entire export ban was lifted, and even then Germany said it would not implement it immediately.

The whole episode was a terrible blow for the British beef industry, and deeply damaging to the government. The fact that we had invariably followed the scientific advice did not limit the political fallout. In November 1996 we scraped home by one vote on an opposition motion attacking our failure to get the ban lifted, with several Tory MPs demanding the reimposition of the non-cooperation policy. The flavour of the anger felt on the Conservative benches at the time was illustrated by two Euro-sceptics: John Townend – 'This country has been double-crossed by our European partners'; and Bill Cash – 'We must get an absolute guarantee that if we honour our side of the Florence agreement they will lift the ban. If not, there will be serious trouble from those on the Conservative benches.' From the pro-European wing of the party, Jim Spicer, the long-serving Member for Dorset West, said: 'I remember hearing the Italian Prime Minister saying [of the ban] "Absolutely ridiculous – it will not stand." Yet they went back, talked the matter over, and instructed their representatives on the scientific committee to vote to keep the ban in place.'

As Agriculture Minister, Douglas Hogg took a great deal of flak, and was brave and stubborn in turn, but remained phlegmatic. Early in 1997 he survived a Motion of Confidence moved against him by the opposition. As the purveyor of bad news, Douglas became a controversial figure in an age when 'shoot the messenger' was a commonplace cry. All the Hogg traits were on display during this crisis. A lawyer, who loves Parliament, Douglas is incapable of dissembling (which can be unnerving for someone expecting a swift answer, but who gets the unvarnished truth) or of making himself user-friendly. He took to wearing a hat that became a national object of ridicule. 'Douglas, the hat . . .' I began to say as he left one meeting at Number 10. 'It's a perfectly good hat, Prime Minister,' he replied, plonking it on his head and heading for the cameras waiting outside. The hat did not have a good beef war.

Douglas remained sanguine, despite continued sniping from within and without the party. After one bout of criticism I rang him to sympathise and, rushing to the telephone, he fell and broke his foot. He said nothing to me about it, and stoically carried on our conversation. Sympathy was in short supply – 'Hogg Breaks Trotter' headlined one report – but Douglas wouldn't have known what to do with sympathy anyway.

To raise an eyebrow at the way the European Union managed the politics of BSE is not, of course, to deny the seriousness of the issue itself. If BSE did cause CJD in humans it is terrifying, and an appalling tragedy for each of those who suffered and for their families. Whether BSE will have a large-scale impact on human health is not yet clear – and may not become so for many years. What is clear is that in the two years before the 1997 general election the UK beef market shrank by a third. By the time the export ban was lifted in August 1999, BSE had cost the taxpayer dearly, and vast numbers of cattle had been slaughtered. After the 1997 election, an inquiry began into the issue. It is still under way as I write.

# CHAPTER TWENTY-SEVEN

# The Economy: Rags to Riches

THE TRUE TALE of the British economy between 1990 and 1997 is so at odds with the contemporary perception that it must be set out with care. It is a story of an inherited recession; two chancellors with, as it turned out, widely differing views on Europe; an anti-inflationary policy that collapsed after succeeding in its aim; the building of a new and open economy; and a public-spending and tax rollercoaster. The outcome was a sparkling economy with secure growth, high employment, low inflation and low interest rates. This benevolent legacy was passed on to New Labour in May 1997.

There are leads and lags in economic cause and effect, and the actions taken in any one year must be set in the context of what went before. The economy Margaret Thatcher inherited in 1979 was a wreck, requiring complete renovation. Margaret and her Chancellor, Geoffrey Howe, began the job, but it was not until the drastic surgery of the widely reviled 1981 budget that the economy began to grow steadily.

Under the stewardship of Geoffrey Howe and his successor Nigel Lawson an air of economic confidence blew in. However, the economy continued to be subject to two persistent tensions that were to combine to undermine their achievements: an erratic exchange rate, and underlying inflationary pressure, with wages rising faster than in any competing economy. Throughout the 1980s, earnings never rose by less than 7.5 per cent a year. And sterling swung between a high of nearly five deutschmarks in 1987 and a low of near parity with the US dollar in 1985.

By 1986–87 the economy was beginning to grow swiftly – more swiftly, as it turned out, than was safe. A third successive Conservative election victory in June 1987 added to the air of confidence. But events were in train that would lead to disaster. On 19 October 1987 – 'Black Monday' –

stock values fell on Wall Street by nearly a quarter; similar falls followed in London. The *Economist* feared that the crash of 1987 would lead to the slump of 1988, and it was not alone. Labour called for interest-rate cuts to ward off economic downturn, and the then Chancellor Nigel Lawson, worried about recession, cut interest rates in October, November and December 1987. Politicians and economists focused on the fear of slowdown and not of boom, yet the world economy in fact picked up, further boosting our domestic growth. Nigel shadowed the deutschmark, which meant capping the rising value of the pound. In order to do this, he cut interest rates further. He abolished multiple mortgage tax relief for joint purchasers on the same property, but delayed the implementation of the measure. Purchasers piled in before the tax advantage was lost, accelerating the already steep rise in house prices. The 1988 budget cut taxes dramatically, further increasing purchasing power as wages rose and unemployment fell. The net result of all these separate events was to create a boom that could not last. This, in turn, led to the return of inflation in double figures and the need to introduce corrective policies.

After the 1987 general election I joined the Cabinet as Chief Secretary to the Treasury, and I must accept my share of the blame for the policy errors made after that date. So must every member of the Cabinet who worried about the Black Monday crash of 1987 and applauded the budget of 1988. It is neither fair nor credible to blame Nigel alone. No Cabinet minister, as I recall, opposed the tax cuts, or suggested that they would lead to excessive demand and price inflation. Nor did anyone forecast the fatal impact on house prices of the decision to delay the abolition of multiple-mortgage tax relief.

Nevertheless, the shared responsibility does not alter the central point: the recession was caused by the unwinding of the late 1980s boom, and not by our membership of the Exchange Rate Mechanism, which did not begin until October 1990. I am aware that this assertion upsets the rewriting of history by many convinced Euro-sceptics, but it happens to be true. The high interest rates which flung the housing market and many other sectors of the economy from boom to bust came in 1989. The impact of the ERM was not the cause of a recession that became inevitable long before our membership.

As soon as the scale of the boom became clear, Nigel took action to curb it, raising interest rates to 15 per cent. They were still at that level when I succeeded him as chancellor in October 1989. No one at that time, in the Treasury or, I think, beyond, envisaged the length or depth of the recession that lay in store, although it was evident that a prolonged period of painful deflation was unavoidable.

In the run-up to Britain's joining the ERM, during which I was chancellor (see pages 152–62), we were constrained in policy-making by growing inflation, which peaked only as I left the Treasury. Interest rates remained at 15 per cent, and I did not seriously contemplate reducing them until I obtained Margaret Thatcher's agreement to enter the ERM in October 1990, when she exacted a 1 per cent reduction as the price of entry. I wished later that we had cut them earlier, but none of the statistical information available to me justified doing so. Like Nigel Lawson before me, I had my eye on the wrong ball: the monetary statistics, and not the real economy. I have often reflected upon our caution at a time when economic activity was so weak. It was not that we were uninterested in the real economy, but that everyone – ministers, mandarins and the Bank of England – focused on rising prices, and was still scarred by the double-digit inflation of two decades before. No one wished to see a repeat of those humiliating days.

During 1990 the rate of inflation soared from 7.7 per cent in January to a peak of 10.9 per cent in the autumn, before the painful medicine of interest rates began to work. In November inflation began to turn around, and its subsequent collapse was accelerated by our membership of the ERM. If we had entered the ERM earlier I suspect we could have cut interest rates earlier; but we did not.

In November 1990, when I succeeded Margaret Thatcher as prime minister, Norman Lamont became Chancellor and David Mellor entered the Cabinet as chief secretary to the Treasury. A new team was now in place to confront the emerging problems. At that time the interests of the Conservative Party appeared to conflict with the long-term needs of the economy. We needed to get re-elected; the economy needed tough decisions. The conventional view was that these aims were incompatible, but I did not see things that way. I believed that if we attacked inflation – for so long the bugbear of our national well-being – we would benefit from it, and be given credit for our determination by the electorate. The battle to reduce inflation had to take priority, although, it must be said, the ever-rising total of jobless was a permanent tug in the direction of reflation.

Our policy was bound to be painful. When, as chancellor, I had warned in a speech, 'If it isn't hurting, it isn't working,' I spoke no more than the literal truth. I did not believe we could bring inflation down painlessly, since there was no way to do so. And yet it *had* to come down, or the currency would be debauched, savings would be devalued, and our economy would become uncompetitive. It was an acute political dilemma. In the virtuous cause of correcting the economy and ending inflation, our policy would add to unemployment in the pre-election period. This was not a recipe for popularity, but I knew that if we ducked the tough decisions, Britain would see higher unemployment in the long term. There was no choice: inflation to me was a social evil, and I did not think we should back away from confronting it, even if it carried a short-term political price.

The slowdown in the economy turned into a recession in the third quarter of 1990 – before we entered the ERM – a recession that deepened sharply until mid-1991 before languishing in the no-man's land of negligible growth. There were those who criticised us, with hindsight, for joining the ERM. We joined at the wrong time, some said. Or at the wrong rate. Or we shouldn't have joined at all. But few argued so at the time. The fact is that our monetary policy had lost credibility outside the ERM, and if we wished to lower interest rates – and keep them down – we had to be part of the Mechanism. Inside it, there was the chance that our monetary policy would be seen as credible again, and we could cut rates, as the ERM's discipline would prevent a collapse in the exchange rate, hold inflation in a vice and force it down.

And so it did, and interest rates fell. It is not the case, as some have argued, that the British economy was only freed after Black Wednesday. During our membership of the ERM interest rates were continually falling – from 15 per cent on 4 October 1990, the day before entry, to 14 per cent upon entry; 13.5 per cent and then 13 per cent in February 1991; 12.5 per cent in March; 12 per cent in April; 11.5 per cent in May; 11 per cent in July; 10.5 per cent in September; and 10 per cent in May 1992. It was a period of waiting for inflation to drop and easing monetary conditions whenever we were able to do so.

Was our ERM membership a constraint on the speed at which we could cut interest rates? In the first year, I do not believe so: the Bank of England was still very anxious about the underlying inflationary pressure, and would certainly have resisted rapid cuts. To begin with, membership clearly made cuts easier, since it reinforced our anti-inflationary credibility. It was only in the final few months of our membership that the tensions between domestic monetary policy and exchange-rate management became acute.

But the pain of disinflation was all too real. Unemployment rose from 1.75 million on the day I became prime minister to a peak of just under three million. This brought personal tragedy to those who lost their jobs, and led to the charge that the government was heartless. The recession had other victims too. Profits fell, bankruptcies rose, and negative equity trapped millions who had bought their homes in the sky-high price scramble of the boom years. In the search for scapegoats many fastened upon the ERM as the cause of our difficulties, and refused to accept that it was a part of the remedy.

Norman Lamont, the new Chancellor, was generally an ally in my aim of cutting interest rates, although, repeatedly, the official advice from the Bank of England and the Treasury was to delay reductions, often for several weeks: 'It's too early for the new Chancellor's credibility'; 'The Bundesbank have just increased their rates'; 'The markets will think it's a "political" cut'; 'We must look at external discipline first and the internal economy second.' These cautionary words were frustrating as the economy slowed, but they could not be ignored.

Norman and I worked closely together, and I grew to know him better. In private he was engaging, dry-humoured and fun, but curiously cautious about expressing his views unless we were on familiar territory. I had first met him in the 1970s when I was the prospective parliamentary candidate for Huntingdonshire. Norman's agent Peter Brown, an old friend of mine, arranged for me to meet him at the Commons to talk about life in the House, and I worked with him in government in the 1980s. We were never soulmates, but we got on well enough, although Norman would not have been human had he not been miffed at my promotion in 1987 to chief secretary of the Treasury while he remained in his post as financial secretary.

In the weeks leading up to Margaret Thatcher's July 1989 reshuffle it had generally been assumed that I would move on from the Treasury to head my own department. Nigel Lawson and I discussed my successor as Chief Secretary, and Norman was the obvious candidate. We believed he should either move upwards at the reshuffle or out of government altogether, since he could hardly be left in post again or be moved to a less senior one. I advocated Norman's promotion, and Nigel concurred. I certainly would not claim that I secured his move into the Cabinet, since although Nigel consulted me, he made up his own mind; but at the very least, I gave Norman's promotion a gentle push. What none of us knew then was that three months later Nigel would resign, and I would succeed him as chancellor. When I returned to the Treasury, Norman, the new Chief Secretary, and I were once more working together. Our relationship remained friendly but professional: neither of us sought out the company of the other, but on my side at least, I found him an amiable companion whenever we were thrown together.

When, in 1990, I contested the leadership of the party, Norman joined my group of backers and, as he worked with me at the Treasury, assumed the lead – not, I was told later, without some grumbling and dissent from others who had known me longer and were closer to me. At the conclusion of our successful campaign my original intention was to appoint him Trade and Industry secretary, but in order to ensure continuity of economic policy he became chancellor. Many thought his promotion was solely a reward for running my campaign, but in fact the reasons were both more substantial and more complex (see pages 205–6).

On 5 December 1990, at my first bilateral with Norman since I became prime minister, we looked gloomily at the economic indicators. Measures of output, unemployment and retail sales all pointed to a rapid slowdown in economic activity, though perversely there was a growth in credit. But wage settlements were not falling, and higher German interest rates inhibited immediate action on monetary policy. Public expenditure was a dilemma. The government's income was falling as the economy slowed, but spending was rising sharply as unavoidable social costs piled up, while the introduction of the Poll Tax had a disastrous effect on local government finance: local authorities needed extra support to hold down the level of the charge to local taxpayers. The unknown costs of the pending Gulf War added to the uncertainty.

The depth of the recession and its malign impact revealed themselves remorselessly. In 1991–92, public-sector borrowing to fill the gap between income and expenditure was forecast to be under £8 billion, but turned out to be nearly £14 billion; in 1992–93 the forecast of £28 billion became £36 billion. Disaggregating these figures is very difficult. They included rapidly falling income as the economic slowdown cut the tax yield; rising expenditure on unavoidable social costs such as unemployment benefit; some discretionary spending to protect people from the worst effects of the recession; and some unintended increases where inflation fell more rapidly than expected, leaving a bigger than planned growth in real expenditure.

The worsening situation became apparent in April 1991, when Norman Lamont and his deputy, Chief Secretary to the Treasury David Mellor, reported to me that spending was overrunning heavily, and that in the public spending round our colleagues had submitted bids that would increase spending by a further £15 billion in the next year (£700 million of which was to repay excessive spending by British Rail, which hardened my heart about privatising it).

David Mellor did his forceful best in the public expenditure negotiations, but it was still an expensive round, with £5.5 billion added to spending programmes. This was not profligacy intended to get us re-elected, since over £4 billion was required by increased social security costs. The one big area where we deliberately increased spending was health, which we awarded an extra £1.65 billion. Notwithstanding the growth in individual departments' budgets, the total of public spending as a proportion of national income remained well below the level reached during the recession of the early 1980s. It was certainly not a case of behaving irresponsibly, as some ill-informed comment would uncharitably suggest later.

The demand for increased public spending, however, did not abate. The following year, Norman Lamont and I were affronted by totally unrealistic bids from departments for a further £14 billion, though inflation was low and falling and the economy no longer in decline. It was evident that the system of bidding for public spending was breaking down. Moreover, even if we did not concede a penny of new money, the Treasury forecast that public borrowing would rise, since government income was below that expected. This was politically embarrassing, as both Norman and I had confidently forecast in the election campaign that our spending plans were sustainable. Now, only weeks into the new Parliament, we faced the age-old dilemma: cut spending, raise taxes, or borrow more.

Norman and Michael Portillo (who had become chief secretary following the election) advocated rigorous control of government expenditure. Inevitably, in the wake of the ending of the Cold War, the Treasury looked to defence for cuts, and Norman asked for a further full-scale defence review. I thought this was neither justifiable nor politically deliverable, but agreed to a smaller exercise which did later make a significant contribution to savings.

At a bilateral in mid-June 1992 Norman and I concluded that the rules of the public spending game had become too well known: every year each department took its existing level of spending as if it were an irreducible minimum, and put in a bid for additional money to accommodate inflation and new expenditure. Although the chief secretary minimised the bids in negotiation, the end result was invariably a further increase – lower than the department wanted, but more than the economy could afford.

I was clear that we needed a 'top–down' system, in which Cabinet agreed the maximum sum the economy could afford, and the public expenditure round allocated this sum between departments. Norman told me he was working on such a framework, that would 'restrain the growth of spending to within the growth of the economy'. It was a long-overdue reform. In July 1992, as the spending round began, Norman proposed that the remit should be to stick within the overall total agreed the previous year. He also proposed the introduction of a new Cabinet Committee, chaired by the chancellor, before which spending ministers would have to appear for interrogation by senior colleagues. 'EDX', as it became known, would replace bilateral bargaining. It was an excellent innovation – and since a member of my Policy Unit, usually Sarah Hogg, always attended as an observer, it also enabled me to keep an ear to the ground as negotiations went on. Sometimes they went on too long, amid loud complaints from Ken Clarke about endless sandwich lunches as he sat impatiently doodling bald heads on the pad before him.

This new system was seen by mandarins and ministers alike as rigging the rules so the Treasury could not lose. It was a culture shock for Whitehall, and at Cabinet it was agreed with long faces and tight lips. Norman urged me to enshrine the new process in legislation, but I did not think this was either necessary or sensible, as it would have been bound to be subject to pettifogging amendments. I was already beginning to realise that my small majority following the election could not be relied upon.

Curbing the appetite for high public spending was not the only economic distraction in the early months of the new Parliament. The long-awaited recovery was glimpsed, but then disappeared. During the brief post-election honeymoon all the key economic data was encouraging. Retail sales began to grow, production rose, and the monthly rise in unemployment began to fall. My optimism, expressed in the election as 'Vote Conservative on Thursday and the recovery starts Friday,' seemed spot-on. But growth faded, and any improvement was almost undetectable.

Norman did not confine himself to crisis management. He abolished NEDDY, the National Economic Development Council – 'the last vestiges of tripartite economic management' – and resisted pressure for public subsidy to the Canary Wharf development, which for a while looked as though it might fail. He and Michael Heseltine at the Department of Trade and Industry both advocated the privatisation of Royal Mail and Post Office Counters, despite early warnings from the whips that we might not be able to carry legislation to do so.

But the value of sterling was a persistent worry as it struggled within the Exchange Rate Mechanism. The stresses of the rising deutschmark, the falling dollar, our flat economy, the political uncertainties of European policy and the French referendum on the Maastricht Treaty combined to add to a general market turmoil across Europe that forced sterling out of the ERM on 16 September 1992 – Black Wednesday. That drama has been recounted in full in Chapter 14, but the reconstruction of economic policy that followed properly belongs here.

After Black Wednesday we could not return to the pre-ERM strategy of monetary targets and 'taking account' of the exchange rate; it was vital to develop a new strategy. I had a meeting with Sarah Hogg, Norman Lamont and Terry Burns from the Treasury on 22 September at which we discussed the options. Our objective was a low-inflation economy. Norman developed the theme in meetings at the Treasury, while Sarah fed in more ideas from Number 10 and liaised closely with Terry Burns and Treasury officials. Eddie George, the Governor of the Bank of England, which would have a more public role, was closely involved throughout. We agreed to set a target for the rate of inflation.

The target – an ambitious one – was not easily arrived at, and until it was completed the void was impossible to hide. In early October, on the first day of the Conservative Party Conference in Brighton, I had a further meeting with Norman, Terry Burns, Alan Budd (an economic adviser), Sarah Hogg and Alex Allan to finalise the strategy. We did so in somewhat bizarre circumstances. As we talked, our discussion was punctuated by competing demonstrations in the street outside – a kind of duet for trumpet and megaphone, with a Scottish orator bellowing a distinctly anti-government message at us. Demonstrators on a bus passing back and forth along the promenade chanted slogans, and as we considered the importance of building up credibility a loudspeaker van passed by, encouraging us to 'Rebuild Britain's economy.' As I was cautioning that it would be bad timing to cut interest rates in conference week, the loudspeaker urged us to 'Cut interest rates.' As I spoke of options to encourage enterprise, cries of 'End the recession; restore growth' cut into our debate. The demonstrators did not know it, but we were on the same wavelength, and the package we agreed proved hugely successful. It was far too detailed for Norman to announce in his conference speech, but he set it out in a letter to the Conservative MP John Watts, the Chairman of the Treasury and Civil Service Committee, and developed it further in the chancellor's annual set-piece speech at the Mansion House in London at the end of October.

The key ingredient was a specific inflation target of 1 to 4 per cent, with the aim of reducing it to 2.5 per cent – the lower half of the range – by the end of the Parliament. This was the first time we had so explicitly set out our inflation objective. Policy-making was also made more transparent. In future the Treasury would set out in detail the basic policy decisions after meetings between the chancellor and the governor of the Bank of England. As for the Bank, it would prepare an inflation report and assess the government's progress in meeting its target, while the Treasury would issue a monthly report detailing the movement of key economic indicators. Norman also appointed an independent group of non-Treasury advisers, inevitably dubbed 'the wise men'. The changes, taken further by Kenneth Clarke as chancellor with the publication of the minutes of his meetings with the governor of the Bank, were to endure.

In the throes of post-Black Wednesday turmoil, the government was fighting on every front. We then found ourselves in combat with the miners after a mistake that was to inflame public opinion more spontaneously than any other event in my years in Downing Street. Shortly before the 1992 Party Conference I heard from Michael Heseltine that British Coal was planning to announce the closure of thirty-one pits, with the loss of thirty thousand jobs – more than half the entire workforce. The market for deep-mined coal had been declining for decades. In 1947 there were 958 pits, supporting 718,000 coalminers. By 1992 there were fifty pits and only fifty-four thousand miners. The main customer was the electricity generating system, which was itching to replace coal with cheaper and cleaner gas power. An internal report by Rothschild's Bank, leaked two years previously, had set out the case for pit closures without one serious commentator or economist offering a practical alternative. In retrospect the lack of response to the Rothschild report was baffling; nevertheless, it was a contributory factor to the way in which we seriously misjudged the mood both of the miners and of the public.

We were far from unsympathetic to the miners, and the flavour of our internal debates was to get the uncertainty over speedily, so that we could begin to repair the communities that would suffer most from pit closures. With this in mind, over the summer Michael Heseltine and Tim Eggar, the minister responsible for the coal industry, had agreed a hard-fought deal with the Treasury, whereby the miners would get reasonably generous redundancy payments of £23,000 each, but as a *quid pro quo* would be made redundant in the 1992–93 financial year. The announcement was made on Tuesday, 13 October at two press conferences, one by British Coal (in which they blamed the government) and the other by Michael Heseltine, who to his surprise found himself facing a far more explosive response than he had anticipated. The prospect of whole mining communities being destroyed touched a raw nerve among the British people – including grassroots Conservatives, who understandably felt we had a moral obligation especially to the Nottinghamshire miners in the Union of Democratic Miners who had continued working throughout the long coal strike of 1984–85.

The Conservative benches were as angry as Labour's. Marcus Fox, Chairman of the 1922 Committee, called the closures 'unacceptable'. The press were uniformly hostile, expressing incredulity that we had so misread the public mood. As the storm raged I chaired a European summit in Birmingham. It was too good an opportunity for the miners to miss. They took to the streets to demonstrate against pit closures, and their chanting of 'Coal for ever!' drifted up to us. Blissfully unaware of the background, Helmut Kohl beamed happily and waved back to them.

Two factors that we should have foreseen made the public reaction to the closures worse. After Black Wednesday and its attendant dramas the government was a daily target for the media, and the timing of such a controversial announcement could scarcely have been worse. In addition, the decision on *immediate* redundancies was a big mistake. There are occasions when purely economic decisions have to be overridden, even if to do so has a financial cost in the short term, and this was one of them.

That I did not do so was a failure I came to regret – particularly since I had instinctively known how Michael's announcement would be received. But the Treasury favoured early closure, as did the DTI, and I was told that even the miners would rather have the £50 million a month we were wasting on subsidising the coalmines put into job-creation schemes. All the logical arguments were in favour of the decision we took, yet that decision was an absolute political disaster. And I knew it would be. My feelings were based on instinct, which is not easy to justify against the logical economic judgements when the economy is ailing, and your chancellor and your energy secretary are sure the policy will work. Nonetheless, I must accept ultimate responsibility for this.

I realised from the moment the storm broke that we would have to execute a swift and undignified partial U-turn, and saw Michael, Norman Lamont and a handful of other ministers at Number 10 on the evening of Sunday, 18 October to hammer out a solution. I did not want to back away from a policy that was unavoidable, but did want to mitigate its worst effects. We may have been maladroit in our handling of the situation, but not in our judgement that the market for coal had collapsed, and the government could not continue to subsidise, at the expense of the taxpayer, an industry for whose product there was no longer a demand. At Cabinet the next day we endorsed our decision not to deviate from our aim of putting the industry onto an economic footing, but agreed in the meantime to find an extra £165 million for the miners and to review the future of twenty-one of the pits scheduled for closure. Labour had tabled a motion for debate two days later, and the initial advice of the whips was that we might well lose the vote at the end of it. After I had made public our decision to change course, we were able to win the vote with a majority of thirteen.

In March 1993, our promised review of energy policy was published. Inevitably, it confirmed the unassailable economic case for a further run-down in coal output. Nevertheless, we brought in an extra subsidy to help British Coal seek customers as a short-term incentive to help the industry reduce costs, thereby improving prospects for at least some loss-making pits. We also announced £200 million in assistance for the areas affected by colliery closures. For its part, British Coal agreed not to close any pits without offering them for sale first to the private sector. After the events of 1992, the privatisation in 1994 of British collieries proceeded as smoothly as could be hoped. British Coal had succeeded in bringing coal prices down significantly, making the remaining pits an attractive prospect for investors; even the National Union of Mineworkers joined in one of the many bidding consortia. The coal industry returned to the private sector.

On 16 October 1992, as I had faced European leaders inside the Birmingham Conference Centre and miners demonstrated outside, another small drama had been unfolding in London. During September and October the onslaught on the government had been relentless. In the aftermath of our ejection from the ERM, Norman Lamont bore most of the criticism, and was under tremendous strain. As I chaired the summit I received an urgent message to telephone the Treasury *immediately*, and left the meeting in Douglas Hurd's hands to do so. Terry Burns informed me that there was a crisis – the Chancellor had apparently walked out of an EDX meeting after a row, and no one knew where he was.

EDX was, by definition, a forum for tough debate. When it failed, as it sometimes did, to iron out disputes over spending allocations, the disagreement was resolved in Cabinet. I knew that things were getting extremely difficult for Norman, whose authority amongst his colleagues had suffered from the events of Black Wednesday, and had asked Sarah Hogg to stay behind from the Birmingham summit to keep a watching brief. At EDX Norman met fierce resistance to the proposals he and Michael Portillo had put forward for holding down expenditure. Ken Clarke and Michael Heseltine agreed that reductions were necessary, but argued that they should come from current spending, and not from capital investment on the infrastructure. Norman, they thought, was cutting capital too much. It was a bee in both their bonnets, and they let it buzz.

The argument raged, with other spending ministers content to let Michael and Ken take the lead. Neither of them was defending his own departmental budgets – Michael's main concern was urban regeneration, and Ken's was hospitals and school buildings – but, as was so often the case, they reinforced each other's arguments. Moreover, as the dispute became more heated they dug in, particularly when Norman did not engage them on the merits of his proposals, but, arguing that 'We must have the political will to do things,' simply kept repeating the necessity for cuts.

Slowly he was losing control of the meeting. Ken, whose outgoing personality masks an insensitivity to other people's moods, banged on. The protagonists became more entrenched. Norman was inflexible; Ken and Michael immovable. Someone then suggested that if we weren't able to cut current spending, taxes should rise to protect capital spending. Norman flipped, stood up muttering, 'No political will ... it's a waste of time,' and strode out of the room.

His deputy, Michael Portillo, continued to manage the meeting well, but the situation was tense; no one knew whether the Chancellor was about to resign. Tony Newton, who is always able to see the other man's point of view, was aghast that Norman, Ken and Michael patently could not. 'It'll be a disaster if anyone finds out that the Chancellor's walked out,' was his gloomy contribution, and it was agreed to say nothing back at the departments, but to alert me as quickly as possible.

No one knew where Norman had gone, although within an hour his office had spoken to his wife Rosemary and found that he was at home, and had calmed down. Michael Portillo handled the situation loyally, telling Treasury officials that it was not as bad as it looked, and that it had been towards the end of the meeting. Other ministers' accounts were more vivid. In Birmingham, some of my colleagues were suggesting that Norman should be sacked, and from that day this view grew amongst Cabinet colleagues.

That afternoon Norman returned to the Treasury, and the full extent of his frustration became evident. He told officials he was fed up with being pushed about by everyone on interest-rate policy and public spending. He complained that EDX was not prepared to cut expenditure, and the remit could not be reached. His ministerial colleagues' attitude, he felt, was unreal. Much of this was a justified grievance, but it was hardly a novelty: such squabbles were commonplace in every public spending round, and Norman had been in government long enough to know that. It was worrying that he had so overreacted, but I remembered Maastricht, and recalled that this was not the first time he had walked out of a meeting that was not going his way.

We met two days later at Number 10 on the afternoon of Sunday, 18 October. Norman was rational and calm once more as we discussed options on spending, taxes and economic packages, although he did seem agitated that he was being undermined by the whips and some colleagues. I told him he was wrong: the whips were reporting backbench concern to me, but not in such a way as to undermine him. He did not seem convinced.

After Black Wednesday and the row over coal the government needed to move the agenda on, and there was a will among ministers to relax monetary policy now that all the indicators suggested it was safe to do so. Sarah Hogg had been arguing this case for weeks and, given the fall in inflation, I agreed. Our domestic economy was still flat, and our markets abroad were weak. But our problems, although severe, were not unique: the United States market was depressed, Germany was slowing down, Japan was in difficulty. In an attempt to regain the political initiative, I summoned economic journalists to my room in the Commons the following day and briefed them that we were looking at a growth strategy. I then took the same message to the airways in a series of television interviews. The Treasury had not yet worked up detailed plans, but I had no doubt it was the right policy both economically and politically.

In the parliamentary party, the atmosphere lightened in consequence, though the thorny dispute over public spending rumbled on. At lengthy Cabinet meetings in October an agreement was hammered out. It was not easy. Michael Howard and Michael Heseltine both produced their own packages; the case for tax increases and pay freezes was aired; worries about cuts in capital spending were widespread. One by one the hurdles to agreement were overcome, and the decision to expand the Private Finance Initiative (PFI), by which private money would help increase capital spending on the infrastructure, provided a way through the rift that had caused such a rumpus at EDX.

Norman announced the outcome in his Autumn Statement on 12 November 1992. Pay increases in the public sector were held to 1.5 per cent, but education and the NHS both benefited from large increases in funding. A range of measures was announced to stimulate the property market – £750 million was allocated to buy up empty properties that were holding down housing activity, and Norman relaxed the rules on housing authorities so as to stimulate extra spending of their capital receipts from the sale of council housing. He also cut interest rates to 7 per cent, meaning they had been reduced in total by 8 per cent from the pre-ERM level, making borrowing cheaper than it had been for nearly fifteen years.

Overall the Cabinet target of no increase in government spending for the following year was met, and for the three years of the spending survey as a whole, the growth of public spending was held below the growth of the economy. The new 'top–down' system was a success for which Norman Lamont deserves much of the credit.

One other issue that intruded into this crowded period was the thorny question of whether the Queen should pay tax. In the late eighties and early nineties there was growing criticism in the media that she did not, together with wildly inaccurate assessments of the wealth of the Royal Family. What the critics did not know, however, was that in 1991, on the initiative of the Queen, much thought was being given to this matter at Buckingham Palace and in the Treasury, where a working group had been set up to examine the issue.

The intention was to have a fully worked-out set of proposals by the end of 1992, but by the autumn the group had completed its review. In November, however, Windsor Castle was seriously damaged by fire, and there was a public outcry over the government's decision to pay for the restoration. In the circumstances I consulted with the Palace, and on 26 November I announced that the Queen had decided on her own initiative to pay tax in full on a voluntary basis, and to reimburse the cost of parliamentary annuities to most members of the Royal Family. The claims that this decision had been influenced by the outcry over the fire at Windsor were wrong. Only the timing was affected.

Another worthwhile reform soon came forward. Norman Lamont wished to introduce a 'unified' budget, with the intention of bringing together decisions on public spending and taxation. The attraction was self-evident: each autumn there was pressure for *more* spending irrespective of the tax implications, and the following spring there was pressure for tax cuts notwithstanding spending increases. The Treasury was dubious about bringing together these two landmarks of the fiscal year, not least because the suggested autumn date clashed with the party conference season and the annual IMF meetings, and it was wary of concentrating so much work in such a short period.

With my support, Norman persisted, and Terry Burns backed him. I was amused when Norman used the argument to the Treasury that budgets get padded out with trivial and expensive measures that could be dropped if tax and spending were brought together: it was a well-targeted niche argument. The Treasury accepted the force of it, and Norman's 1993 budget was the last one to be divorced from spending decisions. Ken Clarke delivered the first 'unified' budget in November 1993, on the date his predecessor had proposed to me ten months earlier.

Norman brought one other idea to me that autumn that was unwelcome: he wanted to grant independence to the Bank of England. I disliked this proposal on democratic grounds, believing that the person responsible for monetary policy should be answerable for it in the House of Commons. I also feared that the culture of an independent bank would ensure that interest rates went up rapidly but fell only slowly. Norman did not press his case very hard, but neither did he let it drop. It simmered on, unloved by me, unsupported by Terry Burns at the Treasury, but, not surprisingly, it received enthusiastic backing from the Bank itself.

In early January 1993 pre-budget discussion began in earnest, although Norman and I had discussed our objectives a month earlier. Without action the level of government borrowing would still be far too high at the end of the Parliament. Norman faced a difficult balance: to raise revenue in order to cut borrowing, but without stalling the embryonic recovery. We realised we would have to look at tax increases to bridge the gap.

Black Wednesday was still casting its shadow. I believed we could cut interest rates faster against the background of a subdued housing market and no sign of a re-emergence of inflation. Lower interest rates would help protect the recovery against the impact of tax increases. The counter view was that monetary policy had already fallen substantially since our exit from the ERM, and too rapid a further movement would adversely affect market confidence. Norman and I noted these points in December 1992 as we considered the judgement to come. It was to be the most difficult budget in which we were ever involved. To his credit, Norman argued that we needed to be bold, and he set out a strategy to deal with the budget deficit. Our agreement in principle on the objectives was the prelude to some often frosty meetings over what were the appropriate measures.

The Treasury set their sights on those areas which were zero-rated for VAT; increasing it would not only raise revenue, but would also widen the tax base for the future. The argument was seductive: our average VAT rate was 10.5 per cent, compared to the European average of 13 per cent. The gap between our zero rate and our top rate of 17.5 per cent was very wide. Why not a reduced rate of, say, 5 or 8 per cent for the zero-rated items?

It sounded reasonable, but since zero-rated areas included food, children's clothing, passenger transport, prescription drugs, books, newspapers, supplies to charities and domestic fuel and power, it was not an attractive option, and I ruled out a blanket extension. Not only did I disagree with imposing VAT in such areas, I saw no prospect of getting parliamentary approval for a widespread imposition.

Still ringing in my ears was Norman's budget speech before the election, in which he had said: 'I have a very important announcement to make, to which I hope the whole House will listen carefully. I have no need, no proposals and no plans either to raise or extend the scope of VAT.' I too used that mantra whenever I was questioned. We believed it to be true at the time we said it, but I doubted that that would protect us if taxes rose. The House would have listened only too carefully, and would have drawn the conclusion that we would not raise VAT in any circumstances. Now it was being proposed. How, I asked Norman, could such an apparent U-turn be presented?

In response he pointed to the changed fiscal circumstances, and argued that we had to cut the level of borrowing and that tax increases were unavoidable. If not VAT, then where? We looked at the options which were least likely to damage the shallow recovery, but Norman returned repeatedly to a hike in indirect taxes including VAT. We reached an uncomfortable compromise, and when Sarah Hogg raised a quizzical eyebrow at the agreement, I explained: 'I had no better hole to go to.'

Such compromises are commonplace between every prime minister and chancellor. Some of my exchanges with Norman, however, seemed to creep out into public view in a distorted fashion. There were press reports that I was not prepared to put up taxes, and had taken economic policy away from the Treasury. There were also leaks that I was pressing Norman on interest rates. I did, it is true, wish to see them as low as possible, but my frustration was with delays in implementing cuts that were there to be taken. I wanted to see the Bank and the Chancellor consider reductions, but if they had a credible case for not implementing them, I accepted that. The press reports, however, helped to create a certain suspicion between Norman and myself. It seemed that when he disagreed with me he demurred gently face to face but more robustly elsewhere. This then leaked. Disagreements in private are the everyday stuff of politics, but when they appear in public they cause unease.

In his 1993 budget, the sternest for a decade, Norman introduced staged tax rises over three years, totalling £10 billion, including our compromise solution: an initial imposition of 8 per cent VAT on domestic fuel. We had settled on this, and discarded all other VAT increases, believing we could equate our need to raise revenue with our environmental commitment at the Rio Earth Summit in June 1992. A further, admittedly marginal, consideration was that the Liberal Democrats had advocated taxing fuel for environmental reasons, and we hoped for their support. We were not, however, surprised that as opposition to it mounted, they deserted the environment and joined the swelling chorus of dissent.

The tax increases we had to impose in order to reduce the level of borrowing were very large, and hugely unpopular. The campaign against us was predictable: our opponents claimed that we should have known at the last election that borrowing would soar, and that we had therefore been deceitful. Since neither we nor the forecasters had anticipated the deterioration in the public accounts, this was far from the truth; but it was effective. 'A lie,' as Mark Twain once remarked, 'can be halfway round the world before truth has pulled its boots on.' The many positive aspects of the budget – measures for the unemployed, the go-ahead for construction schemes, an increase in the threshold for stamp duty to help the housing market, a freeze on business rates – were all swept aside. The reaction was made worse by the reluctance of the Treasury to agree – and announce – the precise levels of compensation that would be paid to pensioners to compensate for the VAT on fuel. As so often, this money-saving caution was to prove extremely expensive in the long run.

The tax increase we imposed to meet the unforeseen growth in borrowing *could* have been seen as fiscally responsible if that had been the mood of the moment, but it was not; instead it was regarded as breaking our word on taxes and wrecking the Conservatives' reputation as the low-tax party. The problem was that borrowing was reaching a level we never anticipated, and that could not be ignored. Four years later the tax increases announced in the 1993 budget would still damage us at the polls. Those of my colleagues who urged me to raise income taxes as well grossly underestimated the importance of our reputation as a low-tax party.

The slowdown in the economy that began in 1989 and lasted until 1993 had been brutal. Throughout those years tax receipts fell in real terms, while spending rose sharply. The difference in the borrowing requirement compared to the projections in 1989 was nearly £50 billion. There was

677

simplistic criticism that we had squandered money, but that was patently not so. The reality was far more complex – as Goldman Sachs had found in 1992: 'much of the deterioration in the fiscal position has been due to the automatic effects of the recession [but] there has also been an exogenous easing in fiscal policy amounting to about 1.5 per cent of GDP in 1991–92 and 1992–93 taken together.' They concluded that two-thirds of that easing resulted from lower tax receipts. It was this gap that Norman Lamont had begun to fill.

In April 1993, as the budget bedded down, it was possible to see a brighter economic future; the recession seemed, at last, to be in retreat. Inflation was well down, retail and car sales and manufacturing productivity had been recovering for a year, growth in the economy had resumed in the first quarter of the year, equities were at an all-time high, and the pound was strengthening. The long economic winter was ending, but during its chill the government had been badly damaged, and no individual more so than the Chancellor. For months the media had waged a relentless campaign to ridicule Norman Lamont, with nothing too trivial to be peddled in the cause.

The recession had bitten deeply, and the press needed a target: Norman fitted the bill as if born to the role. To begin with, he was simply unlucky. In early 1991 he had let the basement of his London house to a lady who used it, without his knowledge, to offer 'sex therapy' sessions – not, let it be said, to Norman. It was a glorious story, and the press hooted with laughter until it was reported that the Treasury had paid part of the bill for evicting her, which made the coverage turn censorious. That the report was untrue made no difference. The reality was that £5,000 had been paid to Norman's solicitors for responding to questions about his private life that would otherwise have been directed to the Treasury press office. The payment was approved by the Cabinet Secretary and the Permanent Head of the Treasury, and by me. None of this stopped the falsehood in its tracks.

There were also contrived stories about Norman not paying hotel bills after a party conference – entirely fanciful, since the bill was being forwarded to him. He was allegedly seen buying drinks and cigarettes at a store in a seedy part of Paddington. This proved to be pure invention on the part of a shop assistant aided and abetted by a tabloid journalist. The press then asserted that Norman's credit card payments were in arrears – which was true, but insignificant. It was all trivia, but the damage to Norman and the government was cumulative.

Some of his public remarks added to the embarrassment. 'Rising unemployment and the recession,' he said, 'was a price worth paying for getting inflation down.' This was hugely provocative, and outraged the unemployed. Other quotes – 'singing in the bath' after sterling was evicted from the ERM, and '*Je ne regrette rien*,' at the Newbury by-election in May 1993 – were wrenched horribly out of context. (Although in the former case he hardly went out of his way to correct the impression that he was relieved that we had left.)

Norman's credibility plummeted. The satirists piled in, and speculation about whether he could survive was constant. Central Office and constituency MPs reported that party opinion wished to see a change. This all had an effect: in interviews ministers were questioned about Norman, while Norman himself was asked about trivia, and no one wanted to know about economic policy. In Cabinet committees he began to need the reassurance of getting his own way, and proper debate was constrained. He had become a bird with a wing down. Ministerial colleagues, by raised eyebrow, rolling eyes and dismissive gestures, let it be known that his position was becoming untenable. Gradually he lost the confidence of industry, the City, the media and a large part, though not all, of the Cabinet and the parliamentary party. My sympathies were with him as a man more sinned against than sinning, but I had no choice but to make a change. As the reshuffle approached I consulted senior colleagues; they all believed Norman had to go.

I saw Norman at Number 10 early on the morning of 27 May, and told him I intended to make a change of chancellor. I had thought long and hard about what other jobs he might like, and concluded it had to be a major department; a non-departmental job would not be enough. I therefore urged him to stay in the Cabinet, offering him the post of Secretary of State for the Environment, with the sweetener that he could keep the chancellor's official country residence of Dorneywood. Pale-faced and tense, he refused. I pressed him. He refused again. I expressed my regrets. Still he refused. My offer was genuine. I wished him to stay in the Cabinet, but it seemed he could not bear to do so if he left the Treasury. It was a stilted series of exchanges that illustrated the chill that had descended upon our relationship and the depths of Norman's hurt. 'Yes, Prime Minister,' 'No thank you, Prime Minister,' 'I wish to leave the Cabinet' were the only words he spoke. He turned and left. We have never spoken since.

Later Norman was to complain that he had told me he would be willing to leave the Treasury in November, after three years as chancellor. I remember no such conversation. He was aggrieved, too, that I did not offer him a job he would have enjoyed, such as Leader of the House. I offered him Environment because I had been told, from within the Treasury, that he would only take a substantial departmental job. It is not the case that I offered him a second-rate choice knowing he would turn it down. Environment was the post Michael Heseltine accepted when he rejoined the Cabinet after I became prime minister, and it would later be held by John Prescott as Labour deputy prime minister. It was a serious and substantial appointment.

During his term as chancellor Norman Lamont had presided over many innovations. The new public spending system, the 'unified' budget, the new economic policy were all solid successes. He began the action to repair our national finances and bore the pain of many unpopular decisions. He had to go, but I was sad he went with such rancour, and was outraged at the cruel and triumphant press gloating at his departure.

Norman did not depart silently from government, and rumours soon abounded that he was bitter and angry. My instinct was to speak to him, since I had no wish for a personal rupture between us, but I was warned by the whips that this would be fruitless. In the lobbies of the Commons during votes, he turned away if I was near him. At lunchtime on 9 June, when I was due to speak in a Commons debate sponsored by the opposition on economic and social policy, I learned that Norman proposed, a little belatedly, to exercise his right to make a Resignation Statement. The analysis he gave of the recession was one I shared:

> This recession was not caused by Britain's membership of the Exchange Rate Mechanism. The recession began before we joined the ERM – incidentally, before I became chancellor – and a large part of the fall in output occurred in late 1990 and early 1991, far too soon to be influenced by our membership of the ERM. No, this recession has its origins in the boom of 1988 and 1989. That boom made the recession inevitable.

His speech was intended to deflect much of the unfair criticism he had faced. But, in the anguish of his departure he struck out at colleagues still in office, if only by innuendo. And his recollection of the part he had played in events did not accord with mine. He claimed that he had insisted on keeping the ERM out of the Maastricht Treaty, but it had never been likely that it would be included. It had not been raised with me by any head of government. I was puzzled when he said that before Black Wednesday he had raised with me the prospect of suspending our membership of the ERM, and told the House I had not wished to do so. Nor, of course, did he. Indeed, as far as I recall, Norman did not raise the issue with me himself until a couple of days before Black Wednesday, and even then only as a *possible* course of action for 1993 *if we were still in difficulty*. Memories of those at that meeting recall my instinctive response that it was an option we might need a good deal sooner than that. He also informed the House I had asked him not to resign after Black Wednesday, which was true, but he left the misleading impression that this was for my own protection. Nor did I recall him telling me he did not wish to remain chancellor for long.

Norman closed his statement with a soundbite which was, sadly, better than any he coined while in government: 'We give the impression of being in office but not in power.' We 'listened too much to pollsters and party managers', who were 'not even very good at politics'. That, ironically, had been precisely the party managers' greatest concern about Norman.

As Norman's successor I chose Kenneth Clarke. He accepted, commenting only that he would like to remain at the Treasury until the next general election. I hoped so too, as losing one chancellor was a desperate affair, and losing two would be above the normal ration. Ken was always a streetwise operator, and behind his bluff, no-nonsense, I-say-things-as-I-see-them persona, his sharp political intellect was shaped around long-held principles. I had worked closely with him since we had formed an alliance over the NHS reforms when I was chief secretary, and knew that we would be at ease with one another even when we disagreed.

Ken inherited a sunnier economic climate than Norman had done. As he went to the Treasury the recovery had begun, albeit cautiously, and interest rates had fallen to 6 per cent, with inflation below 2 per cent. It was an altogether more favourable scene than in 1990, when inflation had soared to double figures, with the danger that the value of money could be halved well within a decade.

Getting to this point and overcoming the recession had left scars. The task of regaining our economic reputation lay ahead. Norman had begun to correct our finances, but the task was unfinished. A new institutional framework for policy had been formulated, but it needed to be put into operation. Ken's objectives were to restore the public finances and prevent a resurgence of inflation. We must, he told everyone, at all costs avoid a return to 'boom and bust', and 'achieve sustainable growth with low inflation'. There was nothing new in this message, since it had been our consistent policy, but it was altogether better received as we emerged from recession than it had been when we were mired within it. It was all too easy before the recovery began to see our anti-inflation determination as a wilful refusal to help people in need. Ken developed a mantra that served him well, and he fell back upon it often: 'Good economics is good politics.' This was not, of course, always true, as some former chancellors could have told him, but with his cheery manner and breezy self-confidence it saw Ken safely through numerous rows and the imposition of many unpopular measures.

He settled in quickly as chancellor, and it was soon apparent that his style was vastly different from his predecessor's. Whereas Norman studied his papers and summoned officials to discuss, debate and delve, Ken glanced at the written advice and often took decisions without troubling the officials further. Where Norman agonised, self-doubt never crossed Ken's mind. Where Norman consulted, Ken put policy in train on the hoof. They were polar opposites, except for a shared passion for birdwatching.

Another shared attribute was controversy – but with a difference. Whereas it sought out Norman, Ken beckoned it in. He was at his happiest in the midst of a row. Within days of taking office he told me he supported raising the pensionable age for women from sixty to sixty-five, the same as for men. Like Norman, he favoured an independent Bank of England, but, cheerfully noting that there was 'not a snowball's chance in Hades' that I would agree, he merely chipped away at me by adding to the Bank's authority without conceding full independence. As part of a vigorous attack on the overall levels of spending, Defence caught his eye as an area ripe for savings.

Ken also took on the Treasury, determined to turn the Private Finance Initiative from an aspiration into a policy that delivered fresh investment into infrastructure schemes. He tackled this with enthusiasm, horrified that

Whitehall, in his view, regarded it as merely a way of getting spending off the balance sheet. He established a unit in the Treasury 'to kick PFI into life', instituted new rules about its use, and brought in senior figures from the private sector as advocates to bully unwilling departments across Whitehall. As the punches landed, new schemes began to come forward.

Ken took full advantage of his honeymoon as chancellor, cheerfully pointing up our difficulties in their most garish form in order to prepare opinion for his remedy. His first 'unified' budget in November 1993 made fierce cutbacks in projected spending and set the ambitious goal of eliminating government borrowing by the end of the decade. He froze personal tax allowances, reduced mortgage tax relief, cut the budgets for house-building, roads and defence and, in a reflection of the priorities he and I had discussed, raided the pockets of smokers and motorists to protect education, health and law and order. In the midst of these immediate decisions, he publicly announced our – by now agreed – long-term aim of raising the retirement age for women. He also took his first tentative step towards a 'welfare to work' policy by abolishing unemployment benefit and replacing it with an allowance for those seeking jobs. Later he would build on that.

This tough package was surprisingly well received and, together with Norman's March budget, set the public finances and the economy firmly back on the way to full recovery. It was a sure-footed start marred only by Ken's casual response to a skilful question from a Labour Member, Giles Radice, at the Treasury Select Committee, inviting him to agree that the cost of the budget measures for the three years was equal to an extra 7p on the standard rate of income tax. This was, of course, based on the aggregate of staged increases over three years in a growing economy, and hence very misleading, but as Ken happily conceded the point the myth took root that we had effectively raised taxes immediately by that amount. Labour added to this damaging direct hit with the charge that we must have foreseen the size of the borrowing gap, and the need for higher taxes, at the 1992 election. Ken, who knew we had not, was airily unconcerned by the fracas.

In 1994 the economy recovered sharply as investment rose, unemployment fell and inflation remained low. The pessimists, who didn't believe Britain could break out of its 'stop-go' cycle, were confounded as none of the adverse factors that had so often accompanied recovery showed themselves. Exports soared, the trade gap closed, and pay settlements remained low. I was delighted to welcome inflation-free growth, although, less happily for me, it would turn out to be a vote-free recovery as well.

The threat of a 'voteless recovery' had been identified by my Policy Unit at the first of the twice-yearly think-ins they held in 1993. The danger, Sarah Hogg argued, arose partly from our success in braking the inflationary momentum in our labour markets, which had so often in the past prevented us from sustaining the advantage of short-term success in the battle against inflation. Membership of the ERM helped change that psychology. Throughout my time in office, earnings never rose by more than half the lowest rate of increase experienced in the 1980s. This made us highly competitive, and prevented us from losing the benefit of the 1992 devaluation. But it also left us highly unpopular, since it allowed no scope for a 'feel-good' factor to develop amongst consumers.

In March 1994, Ken proposed the first of two measures to improve the openness of government and to enhance the transparency of policy-making. To end the criticism that interest-rate cuts were 'political', he announced that he would publish, six weeks in arrears, the minutes of the monthly monetary meeting with Eddie George, the Governor of the Bank of England. I was dubious at this small move in the direction of independence for the Bank, but backed the Chancellor's judgement. Cabinet, however, felt distinctly queasy about it, and it was probably fortunate that Ken had pre-empted their objections by making the announcement first. His second change, which I agreed was overdue and which I fully supported, was to enable the Bank to publish its regular inflation report without prior approval – which had often included changes to the text – by the Treasury. As a result of these innovations the Bank and the Governor moved a little more beyond the City and into the wider public gaze.

I saw the Chancellor each week, and his pivotal position in the government ensured that we discussed every issue and its financial implications. Although our views on the desirable depth of integration into the European Union often caused vigorous private debate between us, there were rarely other differences. Civil Service reform, the move towards universal free nursery education, public spending and budget decisions were all matters upon which we took a similar view. Our meetings were relaxed affairs heavily laden with political gossip and, if in the evening, rounded off with a drink.

Nor were our European differences that wide. Ken believed that the single currency would come into being, and that Britain should be part of it. I feared it would come too, and felt we might, one day, have to accept that joining it was in our national interests. Ken was enthusiastic. I was not. I had kept open the option of joining the single currency, and Ken supported me robustly against those wishing to rule it out. We both recognised that Britain's self-interest would be the determining factor in the decision upon membership, although I gave more weight than he did to the constitutional implications for our parliamentary system. Neither of us believed in entry unless the economic circumstances made it safe to do so. Until the spring of 1996 our differences were of degree only, and wafer-thin.

Notwithstanding the rapidly improving economy, the borrowing requirement, although declining, was still too high. The Chancellor ruled out tax cuts early, to prevent speculation that the improving circumstances would encourage tax-cutting in the November 1994 budget before the fiscal position was fully repaired. The most controversial measure in that budget, which was essentially a neutral package, was the second-stage increase of VAT on domestic fuel from 8 to 17.5 per cent, which yielded over £1 billion a year.

Although this was politically unattractive – and several Cabinet colleagues, including Ian Lang, John Redwood and the new Party Chairman, Jeremy Hanley, opposed it – we did not wish to abandon it. The Exchequer needed the revenue, and a retreat would prompt demands for the first tranche to be reversed. But it did restrict our options. Ideally, I would have liked to begin to ease inheritance tax (my old ambition to see wealth cascade down the generations), and to start the reform of capital gains tax so as to improve the efficiency of investment (too much capital being locked up to avoid triggering the taxation of gains). Although neither of these would have been an expensive move, Ken and I soon recognised – more to my sorrow than his – that they could not be contemplated at the same time as raising tax on a basic necessity such as fuel. Reluctantly I put the ideas aside for a later date, satisfied at least with some useful plans in the budget to elaborate on the theme of 'welfare to work'.

Past economic medicine was beginning to ease the pressure on government spending, and the Chancellor was able to reduce projected spending by £24 billion over the three years of the spending survey. The centrepiece of his announcement was to put in place incentives to encourage employers to offer starter jobs to the long-term unemployed. Ken was a hard-nosed politician for someone with a left-of-centre image, but he had a marshmallow streak for people genuinely in need of help, and was to return repeatedly to such reforms.

He was not alone. I was enthusiastic for such changes, and so was Peter Lilley, by now well settled in as Social Security Secretary. All of us were constantly harried by the indefatigable Ralph Howell, Conservative MP for North Norfolk, for whom work incentives had long been a personal crusade. Ralph favoured ambitious and expensive schemes; the Treasury costed them and said no. Now Ken was producing a variant of his own. It was ironic that, in the midst of so much humbug about sleaze and the self-interest of a handful of Conservative MPs, senior members of the government were concentrating on giving practical help to those who had little.

But it was the second-stage VAT increase that caught the public eye in the 1994 budget. Its fate was not helped by a row over the Bill amending contributions to the European budget as a result of the agreement I had reached at the Edinburgh summit in 1992. Eight of our colleagues voted against us on the very eve of the budget, and had the whip withdrawn. Feelings ran very high, and the VAT increase was the catalyst for the explosion. It soon became apparent that there would be a large backbench rebellion against the increase, and despite government assurances of help for pensioners to the tune of £100 million, it was rejected a week later by 319 votes to 311. The ill-feeling this caused was exacerbated by recriminations from our whips that some of our members had been less than frank about their voting intentions.

The VAT increase was a political millstone which cost us dearly. The Chancellor and I were adamant that we would have to recoup the £1 billion in lost revenue (we had agreed to do so before the defeat in the House), and in a mini-budget a few days later, drinkers, smokers and drivers paid the price for our internal dispute. It was a sour end to a miserable episode, and – since defeats on budgetary matters are very rare – prompted some early epitaphs for the government. The *Economist* was typical:

> Unlike a fish, which rots from its head, John Major's government is rotting from its tail. The stink pervades the corridors of Westminster as government ministers gloomily calculate the government's chance of survival ... The simple truth is that the Tory Party in its present state is ungovernable. After fifteen years in government, it appears to have grown tired of power.

This view was widespread, and so entered the political bloodstream that new and original policies and economic improvement alike were quite overlooked. It was galling that the ever-present rebellion of Conservative malcontents swept all else off the agenda as far as commentators and electors were concerned. And yet the economy – the traditional determinant of electoral well-being – was now on the mend, and beginning to outperform all our European competitors. Nevertheless, the 1995 budget was a restrained affair in which health and education received large spending increases, excise duties rose sharply, and the basic rate of income tax was cut by a penny to 24p.

By early in 1996 Britain had enjoyed the longest period of low inflation for half a century, and tax had been reduced to the lowest basic rate for thirty years. The real economy was powering ahead. Exports were at record levels, growth was healthy and, from the dreadful depths of nearly three million unemployed, more of our adult citizens were now in work and fewer unemployed than in any other major European economy. Ken Clarke's stewardship was paying dividends, and his refusal to levy taxes on business, pensions or savings had encouraged growth and, for millions, personal security as well.

We should have been popular. Economic buoyancy is the traditional recipe for political recovery. But it did not come in a climate in which there was no tolerance for our shortcomings. We had been in office, the public thought, for too long, and the accumulation of political debris over many years was a burden not even a strong economy could erase. Nor was our cause aided by continuing squabbles over Europe and, in particular, the single currency. The behaviour of a handful of colleagues was an advanced case of political suicide.

In 1994 I had persuaded an initially reluctant Douglas Hurd that if we decided to enter the single currency we should not do so without a specific national referendum to endorse the decision. My reasons were threefold. I believed that entering the single currency was a constitutional change of such magnitude that consent for it could not properly be obtained in the broad-brush decisions of a general election. Moreover, if we entered the single currency and, like the ERM, it went pear-shaped, the future of the party would be more secure if a specific mandate had been obtained. It must also be admitted that I hoped the decision would ease the tensions within my own party.

At the time I failed to persuade sufficient colleagues: both single-currency enthusiasts and doubters argued the constitutional case that referenda diminished the legitimate function of Parliament. In the course of a Cabinet discussion on 7 March 1996, the Agriculture Secretary Douglas Hogg unexpectedly raised the possibility of a referendum on the single currency. It was not part of the subject under discussion and I could have steered the meeting onto safer ground, but I refrained from doing so: I encouraged a round-table debate to weigh up emerging opinion. It was evident that there was an overwhelming majority for committing ourselves to a referendum. To avoid the familiar problem of a leak tilting the European discussion in one direction, thus provoking counter-briefing to tilt it in another, I announced that afternoon in Prime Minister's Questions that we were considering the circumstances in which a referendum would be appropriate.

Ken Clarke, Michael Heseltine and John Gummer were among Cabinet ministers who were irritated and felt bounced, even though they accepted the majority view. (Ken told me he thought I'd put Douglas Hogg up to it – which I hadn't.) They did not like referenda as an instrument, and feared we would be pulled further in an anti-single currency direction. In their view the anti-Europeans would never be satisfied, but would accept every movement in their direction and then demand more. 'You watch it,' they said. 'They'll just come back.' This of course was true, but it did not alter the fact that I had become convinced a referendum was necessary, and so were other pro-Europeans. It was for these reasons, after a series of meetings, that Ken, Michael and John accepted my commitment to a referendum, but thereafter they remained suspicious of further concessions to anti-European sentiment. In early April 1996, Cabinet endorsed the position that if we felt it was right to join the single currency in the next Parliament, a referendum would be held to obtain confirmation of entry. Cabinet held together – rather grudgingly – on this decision, but I knew no further movement in our policy on a single currency would be possible within the Parliament; fortunately I wished to make none.

During 1996 the general election began to loom large in our calculations. Despite the strong growth the economy had enjoyed since 1993, all the signs indicated that we would lose. The opinion polls were so bad we had little reason to expect victory. I was sure the true Labour vote was well below its poll rating, but there was too much corroborating evidence that our position was dire for me to be sanguine.

The economy remained our last, best hope, and the Chancellor was determined to take no risks with it. Interest rates fell gently in the first half of 1996, but edged back up a little in October to 6 per cent. The November budget tightened the fiscal stance by £1.75 billion, to minimise the risk of further interest-rate rises. It forecast further healthy growth, and cut the basic rate of income tax by a further penny to 23p, funded largely by indirect tax hikes. The budget disappointed those on our backbenches who were hoping for a pre-election bonanza, but it reinforced the healthy state of the economy. 'Good economics is good politics' remained the Chancellor's mantra.

In the last months of the Parliament the healthy economy was taken for granted as sleaze, Europe and short-term dramas took centre stage. It was ironic that in 1992 we had won an election in a recession, and were about to lose one in a glowing economic atmosphere. Somewhere the gods must have been chuckling. The iron law of politics that a good economy leads to a good election win was about to be broken.

Our election defeat duly arrived. If the new government was grateful for their legacy, they hid it. They accepted the buoyant economy as if it were their own creation and, without a blush, denounced its creators. They stuck to the public-spending figures they had previously denounced as 'cuts' and to the tax changes they had attacked. We should have been flattered by their adoption of our economic judgements, but from the first moment their eyes were fixed on the next general election, and our record was to be damned in every respect.

As I left office the figures told the story of the fall and rise of the economy. On the day I became prime minister the tax burden was 36.3 per cent. On 1 May 1997 it was 36.6 per cent, which, over the span, puts our tax record in a proper perspective. During my premiership interest rates fell from 14 per cent to 6 per cent; unemployment was at 1.75 million when I took office, and at 1.6 million and falling upon my departure; and the government's annual borrowing rose from £0.5 billion to nearly £46 billion at its peak before falling to £1 billion. The economy was growing by only around 0.5 per cent in 1990, shrinking by 1.5 per cent in 1991 before recovering to grow by 3.5 per cent in 1997. During the depths of the recession I inherited, all the economic indicators worsened, but they had all been corrected by May 1997. Above all, we had broken the inflationary psychology that had so bedevilled our economy. In November 1990, the rate of inflation was 9.7 per cent. In May 1997 it was 2.6 per cent. It was a fine legacy.

# CHAPTER TWENTY-EIGHT

## *The Curtain Falls*

'YOU NEVER STOOD A CHANCE.' 'It was always inevitable.' 'Nothing more you could have done.' After the election was over, these were common refrains. People believed that new Labour was bound to win before the campaign even started. They were right. I suspect most voters had made up their minds about how they were going to vote long before I asked the Queen for a dissolution of Parliament. We faced defeat, and we sensed it. But I knew that, even if we did not win, the outcome of the election could be improved by the conduct of the campaign. Although I was discouraged, I was determined not to let it show, and not to give up.

You may ask why. I often asked myself the same question. Where's the logic in cranking yourself up into a defiant display of optimism when in your bones you know the game is over? I would offer two reasons for the 'never-say-die' which was the unspoken watchword of the 1997 campaign.

First, in politics you can never be sure. On paper, there were solid reasons for believing the result might be a closer-run thing than our hunches told us. Theory might be right, our hunches wrong. For the record, it is worth reciting the very good paper arguments for believing – though I hardly did – that we were in with a chance. The economy was in fine shape, and was improving. The Labour Party and Tony Blair were deeply inexperienced; there was a real chance they would blunder in the heat of a campaign, and reawaken all the voters' suspicions about Labour that lay temporarily submerged. Nor was ill-chance – an unlucky stumble – all Labour had to fear. There was a vacuum at the centre of all their hype. Mr Blair's own political personality was strangely fluid, important elements of his party unconvinced of the need for change. The electorate needed to be warned – and they might listen. Although the opinion polls were dire, they showed a high quotient of 'don't knows', mostly voters who had ceased to back us, but who had found no new commitment. It was possible that they would wait until the last moment, before deciding to stick with what they knew – as they had done in 1992. As for the Referendum Party, which some polls were puffing up, when it came to the moment of decision, would the sane and sensible British waste their votes on empty xenophobia? I hoped not.

Second, the scale of the defeat – if defeat it was to be – mattered desperately. It mattered to marginal candidates, of course, but also to the sort of opposition the Conservative Party would be able to provide after the election.

Added to this was the matter of form. Politics was far more than a sport to me, but even in a game you play on until the final whistle blows, however unlikely it is that you will win. I owed every ounce of my campaigning energy to all those people who had fought for me, voted for me before, and placed their faith in me now; I owed it to my party and my country, and to the Conservatism I believe in; and I owed it to myself. To slink away into some token, half-hearted campaign would have been a disgraceful end to nearly seven years in which, with all their difficulties, we had achieved so much that would last.

So it was arguable that we might win, though I did not myself believe we could. No governing party had ever won a fifth successive election victory. I had long prepared myself for the probability of defeat – perhaps even a severe one. I did not expect the recession and Black Wednesday to be forgotten, and the perpetual civil war that had rent the Conservative Party was bound to repel many traditional supporters. Voters expect unity, and punish division. Since I was the focus of much of the division, I had discussed with Sarah Hogg as early as 1993 whether the party would fare better under a new leader who did not carry the baggage of Black Wednesday and the Maastricht negotiations. We decided then that it would not. There was no reason now to alter that view.

And now, even more than then, there were also defensive reasons for my leading this final charge. It was a fact that, placed plumb in the centre of the party so far as the European question was concerned, I stood a sporting chance of being able to hold it together for the duration. As a matter of fact, I did. This was by no means a foregone conclusion. Irreversible breakdown at the end – as at the beginning – of any premiership is always a possibility.

So I knew I must soldier on. Should I lose, I stood the best possible chance of delivering to my successor, as leader of the opposition, a party still in one piece: its internal contradictions unresolved, to be sure – but in one piece. That mattered to me, and matters still.

And should I succeed, and win? I knew that many of the things I had most wanted to do in government had not been completed in my time in Downing Street. I had been serious when I talked of a classless society; serious when I called for an education system that worked; serious when I argued for a compassionate Conservatism. I would dearly have loved to have been able to bring the Northern Ireland peace process to a successful conclusion. But many of these aims needed cash resources that we had mostly lacked, and a political coherence in the Conservative Party that had often been absent. Now, as the election loomed, the economy was strong. I would have liked the chance to use that strength to achieve the social aims I had set out before the 1992 election. It is vain to pretend that I thought that outcome likely; futile to pretend now that we ever got off the back foot long enough for me to inject that positive sense of future ambition into the campaign. But surely it was worth trying, worth one last push to achieve?

So much, then, for the reasons to fight. But why did the fight look (and feel) so much a struggle against the tide, even from the start?

There was deep national impatience with our party. We all felt it – much more, I think, than we sensed any surge of enthusiasm for the alternative. Labour did not win the election for themselves: they won because we started as losers. There was a feeling that the Conservatives had been in power too long, and that it was time to move on. A phrase I had used about our victory in 1992, that it 'stretched the elastic' of democracy too far, reflected this. The feeling was amplified many times by the bickering, squabbling and backstabbing that now afflicted Conservatism almost like a death-wish, and which did more damage to our prospects than Tony Blair could have dreamed of doing.

Reports of the behaviour of some Conservative MPs had disgusted the electorate. Tales of financial, sexual and personal misconduct had filled the press day after day. Although many of these stories were exaggerated, and some invented, they had enabled Labour to tie together 'Tory' and 'sleaze' as a daily mantra. Every peccadillo was attributed to the Conservative Party rather than the individual. It was perceived that Labour were above reproach, and the Conservatives beyond redemption. In politics, perception and timing are everything, and, catching the mood, Labour assumed an air of choirboy innocence and denounced us relentlessly.

It was, and I suppose still is, my complaint, tediously repeated, that this denunciation was a grotesque caricature of reality. Some – not all – of the 'sleaze' charges laid against us were true or partly true. The behaviour of those involved was wrong. But many of the offences were, however distasteful, commonplace – of a kind that afflict all governments: afflicted Margaret Thatcher's, Ted Heath's, Harold Wilson's and Harold Macmillan's before me, and have afflicted Tony Blair's since. Yet for a season these stories seemed all anybody could think about or notice. Start talking about real or potential Labour 'sleaze', and eyes went blank, attention wandered. Sin became a Tory prerogative. The level of corruption in British politics, modest by world standards but still too high for my taste, remains fairly constant. I suspect the national obsession with 'Tory sleaze' was as much a consequence as a cause of our fall from favour.

And the reason for this? Boredom had much to do with it: the irritation with the familiar and imperfect which can grow to fury as years pass. The longer you've been around, the longer the list of failures which attaches to you. With every reform, somebody had inevitably lost out. People had suffered high interest rates and the pain of the recession, and memories were fresh, personal financial difficulties still current. Voters did not balance the harsh decisions of earlier years against the buoyant economic conditions that were now all around them. All they heard was the daily message on sleaze and Europe. All they saw were the often exotic follies of a handful of MPs. And they knew that we had made our share of policy mistakes. It was not surprising that the anti-Conservative mood swelled, obliterating all else.

But in one respect Labour did indeed create their victory. The party managed not to seem frightening any more. For the first time in two decades many voters felt it was safe to abandon the Conservatives. Our successes had actually fed this mood. Dragons had been slain. The fears that had attracted voters to us in 1979, and kept them with us in 1983, 1987 and 1992, had receded. The Soviet bloc and communism had gone; the trade unions had exchanged militancy for moderation; and, more recently, inflation, unemployment and interest rates had started tumbling. Growing economic security made it possible for voters to vent their feelings without risk.

And Labour made it safer still by wearing a Conservative mask. They attacked our record, stole our policies, and parroted our philosophy. In a brilliant marketing strategy they shed their history to claim a future, and ditched their previous convictions to enhance their electability. They pronounced themselves 'new' Labour, and with that single word denied their past. Not unreasonably, the electorate rejoiced. Cloth caps were out, alongside CND badges and loony left councils. As a politician who had seen Labour at close quarters for nearly forty years and did not believe in miracles, all this seemed to me as unlikely as it was effective.

Effective it certainly was. It did us untold damage. The opposition's reincarnation as 'new' Labour robbed us of a familiar enemy. We faced a dilemma: was this makeover for real? If so, how could we attack a party that promised, 'We'll do what the Tories do, but better'? If it was fake, how could we expose it when the electorate, angry with us and egged on by a restless and impatient press, wished to believe it? This was a dilemma we never really solved; maybe have yet to solve. Even in my own mind I confronted two versions of Labour. One, the Labour of my Lambeth youth, was familiar to me in every crease and imperfection: I understood why I fought it, and I knew how to win against it – I had done so in 1992. But this new enemy, old Labour's devious offspring, born of Tony Blair, this Labour bewildered me; bewildered most of the Labour Party, too.

It was a particular problem for Brian Mawhinney, who had the unenviable task of being chairman of an unpopular party that had been in government for eighteen years. Every prime minister needs a party chairman who is tough as old boots and with a sharp intellect to kick things into shape for them. Brian, my constituency neighbour in Peterborough, did sterling work as a Downing Street henchman. Soft-spoken, with a slight Ulster accent and a hint of menace about him, he could be brutal with those he thought were wasting our time. There was a jaw-working impatience about him. He was just the man to get his teeth into the job, our opponents and – from time to time – colleagues as well, even though I occasionally had to smooth ruffled feathers.

We decided to counter-attack by pointing out the dangers in Labour's policies: 'New Labour: New Danger'. The first danger was rising unemployment. Labour's willingness to impose new burdens on business by agreeing to social legislation from Brussels was bound to increase the cost to employers of creating new jobs and, as a result, consign many of the unemployed to the dole for a long time. Elections always make politicians yap loudly at proposals from their rivals. At times this is cynical, with ritual denunciations of ideas that – off camera – are acknowledged to be sensible. (Throughout this period, for example, new Labour shouted that our spending plans were 'starving' public services of resources. In government they retained the very same plans.) But in this case I strongly believed what I was saying: the Social Chapter was bad for jobs and the economy. Now that its main provisions are in place, my view is unchanged.

We highlighted, too, the risk that Labour was prepared to be sucked further into a federal Europe. This too I genuinely believed, and again subsequent events have done nothing to alter my opinion.

In the summer of 1996 the Labour frontbencher Clare Short had spoken with contempt of the 'dark forces' surrounding Tony Blair and, with characteristic candour, had called 'new' Labour 'a lie – and dangerous'. Our advertisers Maurice and Charles Saatchi, who had done so much for the Conservative cause over the past twenty years, produced a one-off advertisement quoting her and depicting a manic-looking Blair in a devilish mask. Labour overreacted, and the 'Demon Eyes' poster, as it came to be called, received saturation coverage. One Labour insider has written of the image's effectiveness, and it won awards in the advertising industry. But I was not comfortable with it, and, with Brian Mawhinney's agreement, vetoed any repeats. Some colleagues disagreed, and tension among us on this issue was to re-emerge during the campaign itself. On what in a gentler age might have been called the etiquette of campaigning, I tied the hands of colleagues, staff and advertising agencies; I do not deny that.

With the election underway, I ruled out using a party political broadcast depicting Tony Blair entering into a Faustian pact with a devilish figure, selling his soul to a spin doctor. The video was said by those who saw it to be immensely powerful and compelling, and some on the election team, Robert Cranborne and Howell James among them, urged me to sanction its use. I declined to do so. Some election advertising is always negative – certainly Labour's had been – but I was anxious not to exacerbate this. I wanted to fight a campaign that would not give any credence to allegations that it had sunk into the mire. I had suffered enough personal attacks myself not to want to inflict them on other people. Perhaps I should have been less fastidious, but all my instincts were against it.

Added to this, I was not convinced that an overtly negative campaign would do us any good. New Labour was too fresh a product for such attacks to have much resonance with voters. The public's apparent willingness to vote Labour was based as much on hostility to the Conservatives as on any enthusiasm for the alternative: we had to win voters back to the fold, not try to scare them into it.

Despite the plausibility of our diagnosis, our 'New Labour: New Danger' approach did not work. Although I wanted to punch at the 'new', my fists were drawn by reflex towards the old: sometimes, I suspect, with the result that I missed both. It soon became clear that our campaign did not ring true on the doorstep. People believed that Labour had changed. Yes, they might be unprincipled and have ditched much they had once believed in, but three cheers to Mr Blair for making the Labour Party see sense. Of course some of their policies were woolly, and the Shadow Cabinet was inexperienced at government. But the voters were prepared to risk the unknown, rather than stay with the Conservative Party they did know. Quite simply, they had fallen out of love with us.

Nor was this our only difficulty. Conservatives made their own. I have already said a little about 'sleaze'; Europe, however, was to plague us even more mercilessly. It is worth recording just why the issue of Europe cost us so dear – not least because a determined effort to rewrite the history of this controversy is underway not just in Labour circles but, more perniciously, on the Conservative right. Falsehood, distortion and a sort of paranoid inventiveness have contrived to present a picture in which the Euro-sceptics are seen as men and women of untarnished honour, fighting to maintain a fixed and principled position against the aggressions of a provocative gang of starry-eyed 'Europeanists', ever ready to cheat, whose 'federal' aims betrayed their own country. In reality it was I who struggled – in large measure successfully – to hold a line against pressures from both sides, of which the so-called sceptics were the more numerous and subversive.

In the ruins of defeat, the reinvention of our past went further. Sceptics began to believe that pro-Europeans were not only the cause of our divisions, but the reason for our unpopularity. But for Europeanists tugging the tiller towards Brussels – it was said – the Conservative Party could have united against the single currency, establishing itself as wholly hostile to the European Union. This, argue some politicians and writers whose intellects should lead them to more honest and factual conclusions, would have won us the election.

'You need to explain why the distinctive right-of-centre Margaret Thatcher won three spanking election victories in succession, whereas when led by the middle-of-the-road Major, Clarke and Hurd and Heseltine, the party was smashed to pieces,' Michael Portillo, one of those smashed, asked after the election. This analysis does not survive examination. We lost, I hardly need to point out, to an explicitly middle-of-the-road Labour Party which proclaimed its enthusiasm for Europe, and we saw seats fall to the Liberal Democrats, a centrist third party unquestioningly committed to a federal destination. Against this, the right wing of the Conservative Party had (as the perceptive journalist Bruce Anderson noted) 'all the characteristics of populists save popularity'. Conservative candidates tarred with the Euro-sceptic brush did, by a fraction, less well at the polls than their colleagues. The anti-Europe Referendum Party was trounced. The 17.6 per cent swing against Teresa Gorman in Billericay and the crushing defeat of Norman Lamont in his newly-adopted Harrogate (for all his 'Vote Lamont to Save the Pound' banners) do not indicate, to me, a nation which shared their views. They suggest instead an electorate sick of division, from whatever source, and alarmed by the irrational isolationism of malcontents who could never accept that their obsessions and fears did not haunt the sleep of most people in Britain. Perhaps they should have – but that is a wholly different argument. The notion that Britain in 1997 was racked by anxiety over Europe is pure nonsense. Conservative politicians were. The electorate was not.

For the record, the position on Europe which I set out – and which was accepted, mostly with good grace, by all but the right and extreme left of the party – was one which I believe was shared by the vast majority of the British people. I was not an integrationist or a federalist. I did not favour the further large-scale transfer of powers from London to Brussels. I believed in a Europe of sovereign nation states. I was – unlike the opposition – prepared to be isolated in Europe on points of principle – over the Social Chapter, and over the choice of Jacques Delors's successor, for instance. I was not enthusiastic about the single currency, and had ensured that Britain was not committed to joining it. But these beliefs about what was best for our nation's future did not turn me against the European Union as a whole. I knew too, because I talked to them, that many of my hopes for Europe were also those of other European leaders. I was proud of the economic and social benefits Britain gained from membership, and aware how difficult our future would be should we decide to leave. Above all, I was not prepared to bury my head in the sand and rule out membership of the single currency for all time. I made my doubts about the project clear, guaranteed a referendum, but disagreed with the premature and narrow-minded certainty with which some in the Conservative Party sought to bind us.

But the squabbling went on. Spats over European policy, usually over the single currency, flared up time after time. These squalls distracted attention from good news on the economy. It did not seem to trouble the combatants that the more they debated the minutiae of our policy in public, the slimmer our chances of being in office to carry it out became. It reminded me, as it reminded many commentators, of the debilitating internal convulsions of the post-1979 Labour Party. There were too many petty little battles to relate all of them here; looking back, I am struck by the banality of so many. But it is worth relating one or two, to illustrate the mood.

Early in December 1996 the *Daily Telegraph* claimed that I was about to drop the government's 'negotiate and decide' stance on the single currency in favour of ruling it out for all of the next Parliament. Though I had recently talked to the paper's editor Charles Moore, a fervent Euro-sceptic, I do not believe I gave him any grounds to imagine that I planned to abandon a policy I thought right for the country. Perhaps someone else did; in any event, an alarmed Ken Clarke rightly described the story as 'preposterous' in an early-morning interview, and Michael Heseltine insisted that it was without any foundation.

But when, at the next Prime Minister's Questions, I announced truthfully that our policy was 'unchanged', this was written up emphatically to make it appear that Ken and Michael had 'blocked' a crucial policy shift by the Prime Minister. This was what the Euro-sceptic press wished to believe, and what Euro-sceptic ministers and MPs were telling them. It was part of the unceasing campaign to shift policy from the pragmatic centre-ground the Cabinet had settled on. The story had a cunning plausibility, as I doubt whether Ken and Michael would have accepted such a shift, had I had the least inclination to urge it. But I had not. Speaking to journalists off the record, several ministers did not hide their disappointment that I had upheld party policy rather than sack a successful chancellor and deputy prime minister weeks before an election.

This phantom story gathered pace when Ken Clarke and two BBC radio journalists lunched at a West End restaurant. Their conversation was private, but the Chancellor was spied by a Labour politician at another table. When, without quoting the source, one of the journalists broadcast some of Ken's alleged thoughts on the *Telegraph* story, including the suggestion that he would resign should I change party policy on the euro, gossip at Westminster soon put two and two together. The radio report claimed that Ken had accused advisers to Brian Mawhinney of feeding expectations that I would change tack. Ken's characteristically direct response to the Party Chairman was, 'Tell your kids to get their scooters off my lawn.'

The fallout from this wrecked any preparation for Prime Minister's Questions that day. The session went badly, and led to nasty exchanges at the 1922 Committee of backbench Tories. These leaked out and, of course, fed this non-story even further. In an unhealthy atmosphere fictions like this can scuttle around in a sort of loop, growing with each circuit.

I could not prevent ministers from holding differing opinions, but I did have the right to expect that they would uphold collective responsibility in public, and express their concerns only behind closed doors. But they did not: when Cabinet debated European policy, ample and accurate reports of who said what found their way into the morning papers with depressing regularity.

This pattern was consistent and intolerable, but it was never possible to identify the leakers. Euro-sceptic ministers tried repeatedly to tilt policy in their direction, and invariably drew a response from pro-Europeans which reopened the wounds. 'Friends' of ministers, always unnamed, stirred the pot repeatedly, often in a bizarre fashion. As Christmas neared, 'friends' of Michael Howard, a sceptic in the best and most honourable sense, provocatively suggested that he had 'no problem' with the idea of withdrawal from the European Union. Michael had never suggested this, but, as usual, others rushed to the microphones to put their own doctrines forward. None of this can be blamed on the opposition. We were doing it to ourselves.

By the New Year of 1997 there was, I think, no one in the Cabinet who truly believed we were likely to beat Tony Blair in the election. In private, Ken Clarke cheerily dismissed our chances of winning. Only Michael Heseltine retained any confidence, believing the strength of the economy would come to our aid. Confident we would lose, some ministers felt free to lapse into introspection. It was easier and took less energy than taking on 'new' Labour.

One effect of this bleak appraisal of our chances was particularly damaging. Senior ministers' actions and speeches were pored over by colleagues and the press for evidence that they were preparing themselves for the leadership contest that everyone expected to follow my resignation after the election. The most unlikely names were discussed as potential party leaders. Human nature being what it is, some of these speeches did carry a subliminal message about the leadership, but many were simply trying to bounce the party towards a particular position on Europe. One party strategist put it sharply: 'For most of the Parliament it has been backbenchers who made the headlines and let us down, but now it is Cabinet ministers who have their own agendas.'

In February 1997, with the dissolution of Parliament (as it was to turn out) but a month away, the Foreign Secretary Malcolm Rifkind made a speech in Bonn which edged him firmly towards the sceptical camp. He followed it up by telling an interviewer he was personally 'hostile to a single currency'. By a whisker, this was within party policy. But it upset Ken Clarke, who, confronted with the statement, described it as a 'slip of the tongue', adding, 'I firmly believe he is not hostile to the single currency, because he signed up to the policy.'

Malcolm, who was seeking to ease sceptic concern, should have forewarned Ken about his speech; Ken, concerned to prevent a Euro-sceptic ratchet shifting our policy, should have been more circumspect. The sight of the Foreign Secretary and the Chancellor seemingly at odds once more smothered our positive image.

The chatter always led back to one thing: Europe. The rewriting of history was already underway. Though poll after poll made it clear that the public's concerns lay elsewhere, many in the parliamentary party regarded it as an article of faith that hostility to the euro would guarantee a sweeping victory on polling day. As the pressure mounted for me to rule out membership of the single currency definitively, we were made to seem more extreme and out of touch. This was no way to go into a general election.

The decision not to dissolve Parliament in February meant that we had to fight an unwanted by-election in Wirral South, following the death of

Barry Porter. The fact that we conducted this by-election at all was an indication of how our position was unravelling. If we had been ahead in the polls, there would have been broad agreement that a by-election was pointless with a general election imminent. But we were so far adrift that postponement would have looked like panic; and, with our Commons majority gone, we were at the mercy of a vote in Parliament forcing the moving of the writ for the by-election. Defeat in Wirral South followed. The constituency was not marginal enough for us to dismiss the result as unremarkable, and even with a strong candidate, the loss was on a crushing scale, suggesting a Labour majority of around three hundred in a general election. The shock only served to increase the sense of defeatism among some colleagues.

The more our poll position remained dire, the more we needed credible, politically attractive ideas. But while Europe obsessed the Conservative Party, it did not, as I have said, and as our opponents were only too well aware, obsess voters. I had seen since the mid-term that we desperately needed to look up from our own disputes and address the cry of 'time for a change' – but I saw the need more clearly than I, or any but extremist colleagues, saw a solution. We had to burnish old values.

Work had begun on this shortly after Norman Blackwell succeeded Sarah Hogg as head of the Downing Street Policy Unit in early 1995. Replacing Sarah had not been easy, and I had interviewed a number of high-profile candidates. Norman appealed to me the moment we met: he had the gift of slow expression but profound analysis that characterises the thorough thinker. After he had settled in, the search for a fresh appeal had begun in earnest.

I had set up policy groups under Cabinet ministers and, in a series of meetings, sought the views of other ministers. All fed in new ideas, but most of the work was done in the Policy Unit under Norman's guidance. The themes that emerged after months of discussion and debate were protecting the Constitution, opportunity, enterprise, high-quality public services, and a safe and civil society. For each of these we looked at fresh policies. Norman 'market tested' our new ideas with frequent ministerial seminars. I also involved the party in the country, which prompted juvenile attacks that we were 'begging for ideas'; in reality we did so because our fractious, worried constituency party organisation needed to be involved.

Policy preparation was thorough and inclusive. Two big ideas emerged in the weeks before the election. We had faced much criticism that, in simplifying the tax system, we had tilted it too far against marriage. This had not been a deliberate policy, but was the outcome of incremental change over a decade or more. I wished to reverse this, and Norman Blackwell came up with the idea of permitting non-working wives to transfer their annual tax allowance to their husbands. I was enthusiastic, but Ken Clarke was not. He believed such benefits were outdated. Better, he thought, simply to lower taxes generally. Only after lengthy exchanges did he concede. 'I see the politics,' he said, and rowed in behind us. But he was not convinced.

The second idea came from Peter Lilley. He had been preparing a plan to reform pensions that would offer young people the opportunity to build a pension pot of their own, funded in part by a reduction in National Insurance contributions. I liked it. It was a good scheme: right in principle, far-reaching, and would help people to build up the long-term security in retirement that we wished to promote. There was a risk that the plan could be misrepresented as privatisation, but Peter and I thought a scare-story of this sort was unlikely, not least since we knew that the Labour social security expert, Frank Field, was working on similar ideas. There seemed to be a welcome consensus that long-term reform was necessary. I included Peter's last-minute plans in the election manifesto. In the event they were to cause the bitterest row of the campaign.

There are three tasks for any government seeking re-election: to defend its record, to set out new policies, and to expose the follies of its opponents. I knew that this election campaign, more than most, would be a battle for the agenda. Labour would attack Tory divisions on Europe, so-called 'sleaze', and our tax rises. The Liberal Democrats would echo them. We had to highlight the health of the economy, decreasing unemployment, lower interest rates and falling inflation. I wanted also to emphasise the freedoms we had extended to schools, to parents, and to doctors in the NHS. I believed this devolution of responsibility to the local level was a dynamic and beneficial change that would be at risk under a Labour government.

Norman Blackwell brought these ideas together in a first draft of the manifesto in the new year. In February David Willetts, the former head of the Centre for Policy Studies, George Bridges from the Political Office at Number 10, and Danny Finkelstein, director of the Conservative Research

Department, polished the text. Assembling a package that, while radical, did not underplay the achievements of the past eighteen years was a challenge. In truth, continued Conservative government was bound to look a static option to the electorate, although our ambitions were anything but stale.

By contrast, the opposition, which sold itself as a fresh choice, was in fact anything but that. I continued to be struck by the hollowness of 'new' Labour; there seemed a shallowness and fakery, a marketing-based superficiality and caution about it all. I was contemptuous of how they trawled the opinions of 'focus groups' and played back the results as their own convictions. I thought their dependence on endlessly repeated 'soundbites' trivial and cheapening to politics. Their jackdaw habit of policy theft was so blatant that I expected it to be ridiculed. But it was hardly ever commented upon.

Another opposition faced us in the form of the eccentric billionaire Sir James Goldsmith, who had founded the straightforwardly anti-European Referendum Party to contest the election. I barely knew Goldsmith, although he had once lunched informally with me at Number 10. I remember being astonished at the irrationality of his fears about Europe. Even so, I was surprised when he formed his party towards the end of 1995 and promised to back it with millions from his own fortune. I thought that his raw and unbalanced views were so out of the mainstream of politics that they would be seen as merely a distraction by politicians, pundits and the public. But it did seem likely – if he proceeded – that while he would be an outlandish irrelevance for the centre-left of politics, he could be a wrecker for the centre-right. In October 1995 I bumped into Goldsmith at Margaret Thatcher's birthday party at Claridge's. With Conservative Party Treasurer Charles Hambro, an old Etonian friend of Goldsmith, we agreed to meet.

We did so over dinner at Charles's flat, with Howell James, my Political Secretary, joining us. I outlined our policy, and urged Goldsmith to recognise the divisions in the Conservative Party, and to be patient while I moved to a policy of promising to hold a referendum on the single currency. He produced a paper that was a summary of the Referendum Party's position. At no time in our discussion was a full referendum on our membership of the single currency discussed – our talks never moved beyond the single currency and further integration. We parted amicably, and agreed to meet after the forthcoming Madrid summit. I did not know that Goldsmith was absolutely implacable: 'I vomit on the government,' was his colourful, if tasteless, remark to the columnist Hugo Young. He said nothing of that nature to me during our meeting.

Goldsmith pressed on with his creation of the Referendum Party, receiving a friendly response from the more overwhelmingly Euro-sceptic newspapers. Some Conservative backbenchers, sensing an ally for their own stance, began to support him, even though he was planning to fund candidates to contest the election expressly against sitting Conservative Members. It is possible some of my parliamentary colleagues felt that by offering support to Goldsmith they would ensure that they were not faced by a Referendum Party candidate. If so, they were badly mistaken.

Diary pressures and a certain caution over the drift of the Referendum Party's policy led me to delay my next meeting with Goldsmith. Charles Hambro began to pass on messages that Goldsmith was becoming restless; he also started to spend large sums of money advertising his party's aims. Charles gave me Goldsmith's telephone number at his ranch in Mexico and, during a low-key conversation, I outlined why I thought his expectations were unrealistic. I pointed out that the Conservative Party was itself now committed to a referendum before any move to join the single currency. I also reminded him once more of the damage his activities would do to his own cause if, by widening Conservative divisions, he increased the likelihood of a Labour victory. I followed up the conversation with a letter on 22 March 1996:

> Dear James,
>
> We both agree that Europe should be built around the nation state, not a federal agenda. Our IGC White Paper spells this out. Unlike Labour we have no intention of accepting further moves towards qualified majority voting, the erosion of the national role in Foreign and Security Policy, Justice and Home Affairs, inclusion in the Social Chapter or the extension of massive new powers for the European Parliament. In each of these areas, we have a similar approach.
>
> Your advertisement this week that we should consider a referendum on Maastricht is not something that either the Conservative Party or the House of Commons would welcome. However, I do believe that it is sensible now to be considering the circumstances in which a referendum around the decision on a single

currency might or might not be desirable. At present we are in the process of considering the conditions and mechanisms that would be necessary for this. For the moment, however, I am not sure that a meeting between us would serve a useful purpose.

Meanwhile, I trust that you will continue to weigh carefully the possible consequences of your actions for Britain's interests. The Labour Party's determination not to be isolated in Europe can mean only one thing for the United Kingdom. All of us who believe in a Europe of nation states should be working together at this crucial time to achieve just that, resisting the drive towards federalism and carrying forward our vision of a partnership of nations.

With warm regards,

John

Goldsmith unveiled his referendum question in November 1996: 'Do you want the United Kingdom to be part of a Federal Europe? Or do you want the UK to return to an association of sovereign nations that are part of a common trading market?' This was so ambiguous as to be meaningless. I was puzzled at the time, but as Goldsmith's agenda began to expand into a more widespread condemnation of the European Union I saw the virtue of his opaque approach, designed to catch each and every anti Europe breeze that might attract votes.

As the election drew nearer, Goldsmith decided he would personally oppose David Mellor in his Putney constituency, and a number of well-known figures, including the engaging actor Edward Fox and the bearded environmentalist David Bellamy, joined him as Referendum Party candidates. Bellamy stood against me in Huntingdon, although we did not meet until the night of the count itself. Neither he nor Fox was a narrow nationalist. They were driven not by a fear of foreigners but by a genuine feeling that something was happening to Britain which they did not like. In truth, they were unlikely footsoldiers in the Euro-phobic Goldsmith's army.

Nevertheless, it was evident that fear of European developments ran deep with many people in Britain, although I believed they would be deterred from voting for the Referendum Party by the paranoid nature of its policies. This did not put off some converts, including the former Conservative Party Treasurer Alistair McAlpine, who had done so much to encourage and support opposition to the Maastricht Treaty. Now ever-ready with a disobliging action, he signed up to a campaign to defeat Conservative candidates he had once supported. He became a fully-fledged anti-Conservative.

James Goldsmith achieved one coup which from my point of view was a blessing in disguise when he persuaded George Gardiner, Conservative MP for Reigate, to resign from the Conservative Party to become a Referendum Party MP and then candidate. Gardiner had once been a strong supporter of the Single European Act, but now his hostility to the European Union was deep-rooted. His opposition strengthened after his deselection as Conservative candidate by his constituency, his disloyalties apparently too much for them to stomach any more. He had been a viper slithering around in the parliamentary pit, and would have been so in the election. It was an embarrassment to have him stand against us, but a relief to know he would no longer be undermining us from within.

The question remained of when to call the election. One choice would have been to surprise our opponents (including those within the party) with an early poll. I had considered doing so, first with November 1996 in mind, then March 1997. March became an odds-on favourite, and over Christmas 1996 I talked with Robert Cranborne and Alastair Goodlad about going to the country in the early spring, and asked George Bridges to start work on speeches for the election trail. But in the end I reluctantly decided against both those dates – the rapidly improving economy and falling unemployment figures suggested it would be best to wait until the last moment. My senior colleagues agreed. Although the Cabinet has no formal role in settling on an election date, I discussed the matter with Brian Mawhinney, Michael Heseltine, Ken Clarke and Douglas Hurd, among others, and they agreed with my reasoning. An election in November 1996 would only have found favour had the opinion polls showed some sign of improvement; since they did not, the case for waiting was unanswerable. The same applied to March 1997, my preferred option until almost the last minute. Had circumstances looked at all propitious, I would have insisted on this date. But they did not, and it was clear from what Central Office was saying that the party in the country was not ready to go – and the Labour Party was.

Once the March option was gone, combining the general and local elections on 1 May became the only realistic choice. With hindsight, I do not think the result would have been any less terrible for the Conservatives had I called the election sooner; and an earlier date would have left us exposed to the taunt that we were cutting and running, opting to go early because we were privately aware that the economy was about to turn sour. Since Ken Clarke and I knew it was in fact going from strength to strength, it seemed wise to leave as much time as possible for this to be demonstrated.

On Monday, 17 March I made the journey from Number 10 to Buckingham Palace to ask the Queen for a dissolution of Parliament. It was a short meeting, and I suspected I was unlikely to be returning as prime minister after the election: the Conservatives were, on average, 22 per cent behind Labour in the opinion polls. That night I lay down to sleep with limited relish for our destination, but glad that the journey had started.

Opting for 1 May, I had set in train a long campaign of forty-five days. This was not an unheard-of length – the first three post-war elections were of similar duration. I also decided to prorogue Parliament as soon as possible. That meant that MPs would retain their jobs until dissolution after Easter, in early April, although the Commons would cease to sit. Some commentators complained about this – without much cause. It seemed to me self-evident that once an election campaign was in progress there was no useful business that could be done by the Commons, and that MPs would want to return to their constituencies for Easter, and to get their campaigns under way.

I wanted a drawn-out battle. I was sure the Labour strategy would be to duck policy discussions and highlight Tory weaknesses – this had, after all, been their policy since John Smith became leader, and it had proved very successful. The long campaign was an attempt to ensure that when 'sleaze' had run its course, there would be ample time to bring to the fore the economic and social issues that usually dominate elections; our best chance was to focus on the strong economic situation we had created.

Does this strategy sound naïve in hindsight? Perhaps. But it is easy to forget now that, in fact, it worked. Sleaze dominated the first fortnight of the election, as Labour pressed its advantage against us, but it moved from the front pages after that, just as I expected it would. For a few moments in the middle of the campaign it did look as though the election agenda was moving our way. Labour wriggled when pressed on its attitude to further privatisation, and a flurry of press headlines went in our favour ('New Labour Wobbles', said the *Independent*; 'Labour Lead in Freefall', exclaimed the *Telegraph*). But then the accursed issue of Europe reared up yet again within our own ranks and directed attention towards Conservative wounds. After that, the prospect of a heavy defeat became a certainty.

After announcing the date of the election, I made a clattering helicopter journey to Luton for my first engagement of the campaign. The visit symbolised my distaste for the clinical distance Labour maintained between itself and the electorate. I wanted to meet voters; Labour wanted to manipulate them. In 1992, Luton had greeted me with a near riot, and seen the launch of the celebrated soapbox. Now, five years later, in the midst of equally rowdy scenes, that venerable old platform made an early reappearance. Some people were aggressive, a few loyally supportive, and most simply excited by the unannounced prime ministerial visit. The *Socialist Worker* hecklers made an appearance, unchanged from the general election before. The crowds were so great it was a struggle even to get to the little square where the soapbox and a microphone had been set up, and I doubt if anyone could have heard what I said. But, as always, I was geed up by the heckling, handshaking, jostling and face-to-face contact, and returned to Number 10 in high humour.

My good mood soon evaporated. A few days earlier, Tony Blair had written an article about the single currency in the *Sun* that pandered crudely to that newspaper's prejudices. I suspected at the time that the article was intended as a catalyst for the *Sun* to switch its support to Labour, and when I returned from Luton to the Cabinet Room, I learned that my premonition was correct. On the next day's front page, the *Sun* would announce that it was backing Labour. Even though the signs had been obvious, I was still surprised at the sheer irrationality of this decision. It was evident that Labour were far more likely to take sterling into the single currency than the Conservatives, yet here was the *Sun*, the arch-nationalist, flag-waving *Sun*, supporting them on the flimsiest of pretexts.

I knew that the editor's mind had been made up for him by his proprietor. And just as I knew that, despite its claims, the *Sun* had not won the election for me in 1992, I was aware the *Sun* alone would not lose it in 1997. But it was an unhappy start to the campaign. My suspicions – then, as later – that Mr Blair's professed love for the pound might prove a shorter-lived crush than the *Sun* supposed, were strong, but unprovable.

As I pondered the *Sun*'s move, my mind turned to the rest of Fleet Street. I expected most of the papers to be uncertain allies at best. The

*Telegraph* and *Sunday Telegraph* would stick with us, but without enthusiasm, since their antipathy ran deep. The *Daily Mail* too would attack Labour, though their support for us would be half-hearted. So would the *Sunday Times*, the *Express* and the *Mail on Sunday*. *The Times*, I thought, would remain erratically Euro-sceptic (on the eve of polling day, it advised its readers to vote for a mix of right-wing Euro-sceptics and Old Labour diehards. Thankfully, most of them ignored this strange advice). The *Sun*, the *Mirror*, the *Guardian* and the *Observer*, I knew, would be out-and-out supporters of Labour. The *Independent* would be unhelpful at best, and I predicted that the London *Evening Standard*, under the editorship of the disaffected and unsympathetic Max Hastings, would be truly awful for us.

Before the election campaign began I had been urged to woo the newspaper proprietors. I was very reluctant. The media had been cavalier in their treatment of the government, and brutal to some of its members, myself included. I was contemptuous of the way Labour were flattering the egos of the proprietors, and did not wish to compete with them. During my time in Downing Street I had not used the honours system to reward journalists and newspaper proprietors; I owed them nothing, and did not wish to fall into debt now.

Even so, some weeks before the election was called I had invited Rupert Murdoch and his then wife Anna to dinner, for what was an amiable but unproductive evening. I have never found Murdoch an unpleasant man; in person he is reserved, almost shy, and far from the bullying press baron of legend. But in 1997 he made no offer of support, and I asked for none. Then, to my surprise, Lord Rothermere, the bewildering and inconstant owner of the *Daily Mail*, and his chief editor David English invited me to dine privately. They had both suggested tantalisingly that their papers could support Labour, but now they spoke of how 'we' could win the election, as though they were wholly on-side. Events were to prove otherwise.

One day into the election campaign, the shooting war began. But the first shot came from little more than a popgun. At Prime Minister's Questions the House was in end-of-term mood. Simon Hughes, the Liberal Democrat Member for Southwark and Bermondsey, rather muffed his question, and amidst sniggers and noisy barracking was upbraided by Madam Speaker: 'Come on Mr Hughes, spit it out.'

The burden of his question was to ask why I had dissolved Parliament early. He suggested that it was to prevent the publication of Sir Gordon

Downey's report on the 'cash for questions' affair. He was clearly trying to pull a fast one rather than make a serious point; I had been taunted almost daily by his party for not calling the election, and everyone knew that Sir Gordon's report had not been published because it was unfinished. In the event it was not published until 3 July, after the last possible date for an election, undermining claims that the matter could have been resolved in days.

I had no involvement in the timing of the report. I had promised a robust and independent inquiry, and that is what Sir Gordon conducted. (Indeed, had I, through private channels, pressured him to complete his investigation before the election was called, I would, rightly, have been criticised for compromising the inquiry's integrity.) Nonetheless, a day later, when a fall of sixty-eight thousand in the unemployment figures was announced, giving a real boost to our claim of an improving economy, this flawed demand for publication of the Downey Report was given wings by the Labour Party, and began to fly. It was a bogus demand, as Labour knew; they had not even thought of it in the first place, and had scoffed at Simon Hughes when he raised the matter. But the row erupted in the media. We were made to appear evasive and guilty of sharp practice, which we were not. It was a dispiriting little spat, and politics at its worst. The sixty-eight-thousand fall in the unemployed was forgotten.

As it happened, Sir Gordon did, on his own initiative, publish an interim report, clearing fifteen MPs (not all of them Conservative) of malpractice. He made it clear that his investigation into ten others would not be complete until after the general election, and denounced the leaking of sections of his draft report as 'against the interests of natural justice' – which it was. But the hare had been set running, and no amount of explanation from me was going to stop it.

At first, attention focused on those MPs not yet cleared or criticised by Downey; in particular, two former ministers, Tim Smith and Neil Hamilton. There was, I admit, a certain ambiguity about their status – were they, or were they not, guilty as charged by Labour and the *Guardian* newspaper? I did not know, but since Downey had not reported, I believed it only fair that they be allowed to stand as Conservative candidates once again, if that was what they and their constituency associations wanted. As Michael Heseltine tried to remind the media, 'A man is innocent until proven guilty.' I defended Hamilton's candidature until the end, because I believed it was morally right to do so; this despite his having conspired against my leadership of the party for much of the past few years

My support for Tim Smith soon proved unnecessary. Just over a week into the election, he resigned as a candidate, admitting that he had accepted £25,000 in cash from Mohammed al Fayed, the owner of Harrods; this relationship with Fayed had cost him both his ministerial and his parliamentary career. I was warned of Smith's decision in my car, on my way to a meeting. The press pack was waiting for me, primed with questions on the affair, and being almost wholly ignorant of what had happened, I had an uncomfortable few moments. So often in politics an instant response is demanded, despite a paucity of information. It provides excitement, but is not conducive to sane government.

Tim Smith's resignation was a double calamity for us, for it partly eclipsed Labour's embarrassment over its uncertain policy on the restoration of trade union rights. With Smith's departure, Conservative confusion deepened, and Labour's disappeared. Bad luck? To a degree, but I have to accept that by then the media were not remotely interested in anything other than bad news for the Conservative Party. This was not the result of any brilliance on Labour's part. From my own perspective – between the rock of an impatient electorate and the hard place of an approaching polling day – it seemed that what the parties' headquarters fed into the news media mattered less than the editorial process by which input was turned into output on the front pages.

In the midst of all this, Neil Hamilton remained determined to contest his Tatton constituency. He was supported by a majority of his local party's executive committee – not without some misgivings – and by his formidable wife Christine. Hamilton was the epicentre of the attacks on us for sleaze. He denied the charges against him, and insisted he was innocent of any wrongdoing (he continues to do so to this day). His decision to fight on was understandable, but it caused immense harm to the Conservative Party nationally, and certainly cost us seats. It made it look as though the party was arrogantly ignoring public concern about the issue of sleaze. In fact, it had been my concern about the serious allegations against MPs of all parties which had led to the setting up of Sir Gordon Downey's inquiry in the first place.

In the face of all this, I took the controversial decision not to turn against Hamilton. I did think then, and still think now, that he himself should have decided to withdraw from the contest, as Tim Smith had. It rapidly became clear that his candidature was bad for the Conservative cause. He knew this, but he chose to put his own interests first. I could have announced that I wanted him to withdraw, but under the traditional structure of local Conservative associations this would not have worked. I could have disowned his entire constituency party, but he would have remained a candidate, backed by a rebel association. This made me look powerless – and indeed, in this case, I was.

In a clever piece of politics, Labour and the Liberal Democrats persuaded their candidates in Tatton to withdraw in favour of a 'whiter than white' independent candidate, the respected BBC foreign correspondent Martin Bell, who campaigned against (and eventually beat) Neil Hamilton. It was the first indication of the extent to which the two parties were working together – sometimes wittingly, sometimes unwittingly – in an anti-Conservative alliance which would cruelly skew the election result against us and create such a huge majority for Labour. I do not believe Mr Bell was knowingly part of any such plot, but his election offered a luminous display of the potential power of a simple anti-Tory message.

In the face of Bell's candidature, it was certain that if the rules of the party had allowed me to drop Hamilton as a candidate and I had done so, it would have been assumed that I had judged him guilty, whatever disclaimers I may have offered. I am aware that my hands-off approach to the matter leaves me exposed to the charge that I worsened our election chances through a lack of leadership. But I felt it would have been morally wrong to destroy Hamilton's career when the evidence had not yet been heard. I knew that he had very many friends, particularly on the right of the party, who felt the same way. In retrospect, I still think I was right not to attempt to force him to resign his seat, and that he was wrong not to step down.

Labour and the press gave too much attention to Tim Smith and Neil Hamilton, but at least they had the justification that the charges against them were serious. This could not be said of the string of lesser stories which were raised during the election, though the personal cost to those caught up in them was at least as high. In any other circumstances, the episodes would not have been considered sleaze; they would have been thought beneath attention.

The first came before Easter. I watched in disbelief as Allan Stewart, the forthright and bewhiskered Member for Eastwood, our safest seat in Scotland, resigned as an election candidate following press allegations about his private life. I did not know Allan well – though he once beat me, by one vote, for the Conservative nomination for a council seat in Bromley – but I felt extremely sorry that his political career had been brought to an end in such a cruel way. His resignation eclipsed news of the best current account trading figures for over a decade. Once again, it was sin first, economy nowhere. By now, serious economic news stood no chance against sleaze for media attention.

Further blows followed. Piers Merchant, seeking re-election in Beckenham, a quiet enough place where I had once lived, was exposed in the *Sun* as having an affair with a seventeen-year-old Soho hostess. A photographer, handily placed behind a hedge, produced photographs as evidence. 'What on earth does he think he's doing?' I remarked when the news reached Downing Street. A few million other Britons, over their breakfast newspapers, must have been spluttering in similar vein.

Merchant's wife supported him, but Michael Heseltine came close to suggesting in public that his constituency association should drop him. I did not know that Michael was about to say this, and although, in terms of the Conservative Party's immediate needs, he was probably right, his call ignored the fact that local associations are loyal to a fault. A prime minister and his deputy can do many things, but sacking a Conservative candidate is not one of them – the same problem which faced us over Neil Hamilton. Following several days of unsavoury publicity Merchant was adopted by the Beckenham Association as their candidate for the election. After protesting his innocence and winning narrowly on polling day, he then returned to the hostess and did – at last – resign.

The worst shock for me came when Sir Michael – Micky – Hirst, our Party Chairman in Scotland, also resigned when he learned that a Scottish newspaper was about to publish claims about his private life. Michael was a decent man concerned to do the best for his country and his party. I cannot imagine him acting in anything other than an entirely straightforward way; certainly he behaved with complete honour and loyalty towards me. He resigned not because the allegations were grave, nor even necessarily true, but because he saw the damage sleaze was doing to the campaign, and hoped, by resigning, to avoid adding to the party's woes.

We certainly had enough to be woeful about. If the story of the first two weeks of the election was one of accusations about sleaze, and our difficulty in rebutting them, the final month rarely strayed from one topic: the canker within the Conservative Party over all things European. One after another, ministers and backbenchers published election addresses in which they professed their outright opposition to the single currency. One after another, the press reported this blatant rebellion. With Alastair Goodlad, the Chief Whip and a fellow moderate when it came to Europe, I managed, in a few cases, to talk individual MPs out of breaking ranks. Our argument against their doing so was a strong one, after all. We were not asking candidates to advocate something they objected to; merely requesting that they restrained outright opposition to the single currency until circumstances became clearer. But the imperative of party loyalty failed to sway most of the colleagues we spoke to, who seemed to believe that their anti-single currency stance would win them votes, even if it widened divisions in the party and unsettled our national election campaign. The damage that these deluded MPs, many of them senior and some of them members of the government, caused to the campaign was incalculable. It was hardly unreasonable of the news media to conclude that the party's leadership had lost authority.

Only the most naïve of my colleagues could have imagined that, a few weeks before an election, I would declare outright opposition to monetary union, when for years I had made it clear that it was not in the national interest to do so. Many of the Euro-sceptics accused me of weak leadership – because I would not change my mind and rip up a policy I had negotiated in 1991 and advocated ever since. I continued to believe our policy was right for Britain; in any event, an about-turn, had I wanted one, would have risked the resignation of many able and committed ministers, including Michael Heseltine and Ken Clarke, and split the party once and for all.

The sceptic wing of our party did not seem to understand that the pro-Europeans had principles as strong and as valid as their own. One evening in mid-campaign I returned to Number 10 following a public question-and-answer session in Westminster. Much election campaigning is artificial and contrived, but this meeting had been packed, the questions pertinent, and it had been fun. My spirits once again lifted after personal contact with electors, and I settled down with a decent-sized whisky to work on the official red boxes, unavoidable even during general elections.

Then a despairing Brian Mawhinney rang to tell me that two junior ministers, Jim Paice and John Horam (a man who managed the unusual transition from the Labour benches to ours via a spell in the SDP), had issued manifestos breaching our policy on the single currency. I was tempted to sack them immediately, and was urged to do so by senior colleagues. But I wanted no more martyrs to be lauded by the Euro-sceptic press, encouraging others to resign in their support. I knew, as few did, how close some had come to committing the same act of rebellion. Least said, soonest mended, I thought.

Sackings would have provoked uproar, and delayed any hope of moving to a positive agenda. I decided to note their behaviour for a post-election reshuffle (should there be one), dismiss their actions as idiotic, and move on as speedily as possible. Although this left me exposed to personal criticism, that was a lesser evil than provoking the catastrophic split I had tried so hard to avoid.

I went to bed spitting with anger at their foolishness, which forced me to ditch my plans to highlight falling unemployment at our press conference the following morning, and instead devote it to laying down the law on our European policy. The atmosphere of anticipation among the media as I rose to speak to them just after 9 a.m. in the confined room we used for briefings at Central Office was much as I imagine the crowd used to display at a long-awaited public hanging.

Unscripted and furious, I appealed over the heads of the party and the media directly to the electorate. It was, according to those who were watching me, a startling performance. I was utterly convinced of what I was saying, and for once this came across. For the umpteenth time I set out both the case for and the case against joining a single currency. This was no time, I insisted, to come down for ever on one side or the other. 'Like me or loathe,' I said, 'do not bind my hands when I am negotiating on behalf of the British nation.'

That press conference, fresh and unexpected, was the most charged of the election. Even Tony Blair described it as 'the defining moment of the election campaign' – though for him it defined his coming victory. It was the culmination of years of division and dissent in the Conservative Party. When it was over, those who opposed me knew they faced the starkest of choices: they could continue their dissent, costing us the election and many of them their seats. Or they could support my position, avoid fighting each other, and perhaps save their political skins. I went on that night, at Maurice

Saatchi's suggestion, to put the message directly to voters in a television address for our next party political broadcast, but by then the message had lost its immediacy.

The single currency issue calmed after this. But it was too late: the damage had been done. The party was seen as irredeemably split on the issue, considered as 'extreme' by some electors, as 'having lost its way' by others. It is ironic that, as I write, a Labour government and a Conservative opposition maintain a similar 'wait and see' approach (for varying lengths of time) to the one that earned me such hostility. Useless, no doubt, to complain, though Labour attacks on what they then called my indecision (but now portray as caution in the national interest) did much damage at the time.

My anger at what the European dispute cost us in terms of losing votes is underpinned by knowing also to what extent it prevented us from winning them. The story of the 1997 election was not just one of Conservative crisis and conflict – at least, not quite. Early in April we did make progress, digging into Labour's fragile support as the party stumbled. A fortnight later, with little more than a week to go before polling day, I learned to my delight of an ICM poll in the *Guardian* that suggested the gap between the two parties had closed dramatically. Labour's previously huge lead had been reduced to 5 per cent. Labour too heard about this poll before it was published, and tried several times to get details from the *Guardian*, which resolutely refused to give them. The poll, it turned out, was an aberration; Labour's lead had hardly been dented. But the dramatic figures had persuaded them that their lead was down to single figures, and they switched to Plan B.

Plan B was a straight piece of deception about Peter Lilley's pension plan. Gordon Brown and Tony Blair – who had made 'Trust me' the central plank of his appeal to voters – repeated the scare story that 'the Tories will abolish the state pension'. They must have known this was untrue, and that our plans, announced by Peter Lilley, guaranteed a state pension at the existing level, uprated for inflation. They knew our plans for reform would not affect anyone over twenty-five years of age, and yet they persisted in an untruth that frightened the most vulnerable members of our society.

This was deceitful beyond the usual parameters of an election campaign. It was claimed – absurdly – that the abolition of the state pension was a secret agenda of the right wing of our party. This was nonsense 'If anybody in my Cabinet actually prevailed in such an argument, I would not only leave Downing Street, I would leave politics,' I said. 'There is no question that any Conservative Cabinet would countenance proposals like this.'

Peter Lilley – undoubtedly from the right of our party – followed this up. Labour's 'wild accusations', he said, were 'simply bunkum'. But even after this categorical denial, Labour persisted, and reports came in from all over the country of their activists warning elderly voters that their pensions were at risk. Our private polling left us in no doubt that this attack worked.

The foregoing may read like the whine of the losing team, and certainly general elections are a rough old game, where gentlemanly rules do not apply. But the impression is sometimes given – and in the years since that election it has seemed to me to grow – that there are no rules at all. It is important to insist that there are – and were – and that this particular tactic, from an opposition which liked to bask in its claims to honesty, broke them. What I found extraordinary about this episode was Tony Blair's personal willingness – even after my flat rejection of his charges – to make accusations about our pension plans that he would have known were false. I had not expected such behaviour from him.

Blair's devious performance over pensions fed my belief that, head-to-head in fair debate, I could outperform him. This pointed to the possible advantage to be derived from a television debate between the party leaders. The idea was not new: I had rejected a debate with Neil Kinnock during the 1992 election, believing I had nothing to gain from it, and he had everything. But 1997 was different. We were wallowing far behind in the opinion polls. I was far better informed on policy than Blair, and convinced that if the debate was properly to cover the whole range of policy, he could not credibly survive on his soundbites and superficial knowledge.

But it was Labour which made the first move. In 1996 Peter Mandelson, one of Blair's closest henchmen and the mastermind of Labour's election strategy, had made the enticing offer that his leader would debate with me 'anytime, anywhere'. The idea grew on me as the election neared and the polls failed to improve. The broadcasters were keen, although the water was muddied by the wish of the Liberal Democrats to be involved. To entice Tony Blair into a debate, I agreed a role for Paddy Ashdown, even though his involvement would have been a distraction: the key point for me was a sufficiently lengthy one-on-one encounter to get beyond facile soundbites and focus on the economy and domestic and foreign affairs.

But it was not to be. 'Anytime, anywhere' became 'no time, nowhere' as Labour pulled the plug. In one sense, this was a comfortable outcome for me. I had accepted the challenge, but did not have to undergo the risk of carrying out my undertaking. I knew well enough that any slip-up on my part in live debate would turn the election spotlight entirely onto my leadership. But I wanted to take the risk, and to tell the British people directly why I wanted to win and why the opposition deserved to lose.

Labour did make mistakes during the campaign, but we failed to exploit them; and when we did exploit them, the press sometimes failed to report us. When it did report us, the news failed to chime with the popular mood. The life had gone out of our machine. Many people in the party, who had spent the last few years under a never-ending barrage of depressing publicity, and knew the result was more or less a foregone conclusion, merely went through the motions, and as polling day approached, became more concerned about their own futures than that of the party. The will to win, the fear of what Labour might do, the sense that a Conservative government would be the best future for Britain – these emotions, so abundant in 1992, were totally absent in 1997.

Was this my fault? I tried to engender spirit in the party, took the fight to my critics on Europe, and campaigned as hard as I ever had. Brian Mawhinney did all he could. Our daily press conferences usually went well. Some brave souls joined me. Michael Heseltine is a man who has never given up on anything, Ian Lang was a constant support, and many other MPs and ministers fought hard to the end. Robert Cranborne took on a difficult task as my chief of staff. Jonathan Hill gave up his job with Lowe Bell and returned to Number 10 to help the cause, managing my schedule of interviews with the help of Shana Hole. Charles Lewington did his best to put the party line across to the media. Maurice Saatchi, Tim Bell and Peter Gummer brought their great skills to bear on our publicity. Nick True and Ronnie Millar, a magnificent team of wordsmiths, worked on my speeches as they had in 1992; this time they were joined by George Bridges. I was grateful to them all.

But often they found themselves lone voices; team spirit was absent. Within the party, awareness of the impending cataclysm hampered our efforts to prevent it. I remember returning to Number 10, exhausted after long days of interviews and national tours, to find I had to choose between competing drafts of press releases, or rival bids for alterations to my campaigning schedule. It was no way to fight a war.

Election campaigns produce rich personal memories, some happy, some poignant, some sad. For some months Norma's mother, Dee, had been ill. In October 1996 she had been staying with us at Finings. Early one Saturday morning she beckoned me into her room. Tears spilled out of her eyes: 'I've got to tell someone,' she said, 'and I don't want to tell Norma. I've had tests, and I've got cancer.' I held her and spoke all the comforting words I could find: many cancers can be cured; many people recover; we'll be with you all the while. But she knew. 'I always wanted to know how I'd die,' she said. 'Now I do.'

By the time of the election, Dee had been treated for months with chemotherapy. She had borne bravely the dispiriting side-effects of treatment. Whether she was at her home in Beckenham or at Finings, where she often stayed, Norma would care for her. When the election began Dee was unwell, and Norma had left me to be with her while I campaigned. We had not made her illness public. It was a family matter, and she was entitled to the dignity of privacy as she faced the battle before her. But to *The Times*, Norma's departure from the election limelight was fair game. 'Norma Major's finely-honed "celebrity smile" vanished abruptly yesterday to reveal a persistently glum expression,' wrote their reporter. 'Whether she was suffering from first-day nerves or a wife's natural boredom . . . her gloomy countenance did little to lighten the Tory campaign mood.' It was churlish and cruel. Sheila Gunn, who had been seconded to me from the Press Office in Central Office for the duration of the campaign, was as outraged as I was, and took the reporter aside. He did not misreport again.

At the same time, Norma too discovered a mole on her back that we feared was malignant. She consulted Ian McColl, my Parliamentary Private Secretary in the House of Lords and an eminent surgeon, who thought it should be removed without delay. As Norma was reluctant to go into hospital during the campaign, when rumours would have been rife, Ian volunteered to remove the mole himself at Number 10. One evening, following a dinner in aid of the John Grooms Association, the only social event which remained in the Number 10 diary, because of its charitable status, Norma retreated to one of the bedrooms, where Ian and his wife Jean, also a doctor, were masked and gowned and waiting for her. Norma, in surgical drapes, lay on the bed. Ian lifted the knife. At that moment a Downing Street messenger opened the door, and saw a gowned surgeon, knife on high, about to operate on an unknown figure. He fled.

The following day, Norma insisted on joining me on tour. In a crowded market square she was clapped on the back by a friendly hand and nearly fainted with pain as the wound was reopened. She returned to the battle bus. This incident too was reported by the media as Norma losing interest in the campaign, and there were shots on the evening news of her looking out from the bus's window as I addressed the crowd. At that stage, we had yet to hear the results of the biopsy. A day or so later we did: the mole, thank goodness, was benign.

Throughout the campaign we kept up a punishing daily schedule. We travelled the country in a Boeing 737 jet loaned by Michael Bishop, chairman of British Midland, and a converted coach – our battle bus – that had a side section which, when lowered, became an improvised platform for speeches on the stump. I remember standing on it in Brecon and being heckled by a young man with his head shaved completely except for a Mohican coxcomb. I was calling for more youngsters to attend university when he shouted some complaint. 'I'm sorry you didn't quite make it,' I answered back.

'I did get in,' he yelled. 'You didn't.'

It was heckler 1, Prime Minister nil.

The atmosphere on our tours was buoyant despite the depressing daily news. Cut off from Westminster, with no time to watch television and hardly a chance to hear the radio or read the papers, I was insulated from the worst of what was happening. Howell James, my Political Secretary, is irrepressibly jolly, and John Ward, my Commons Parliamentary Private Secretary, a wry and amusing companion. Both accompanied me everywhere throughout the six exhausting weeks of full-blown campaigning. So did Sheila Gunn, who had to deal with the demands of the media, and Shirley Stotter, who fought with the logistics. Occasionally others like Robert Cranborne, Ian McColl and Norman Blackwell would abandon their central roles for a day to join us on the road.

It was all rather surreal. The tour continued. Speeches and interviews came and went. I visited market squares and factories in over fifty constituencies. And yet it was dead. The atmosphere was very different from 1992.

There was no hostility, and plenty of warmth. But it didn't feel right. People had turned off, made up their minds, and the campaign changed nothing. The players were acting out their roles, but the outcome was predetermined. All that was at stake was the scale of the defeat.

As we entered the final week, Tony Garrett at Central Office predicted that we would certainly lose by forty to sixty seats, and possibly by up to ninety. 'But,' he added, 'the unknown factor is the extent of tactical voting, which could make it worse.' I was not surprised by what he told me, since the nagging fear, ever present in my mind, was of an even worse outcome. I heeded Tony's prediction, because in 1992 Central Office – unlike most of the press – got the result right when they gave me their estimate.

But we fought hard to the end, nonetheless. Towards the end of the campaign I travelled to each corner of the UK to warn against devolution, toured marginal seats, and on the very last day ended as I began with rowdy crowd scenes – this time in Stevenage. My car picked me up at a lay-by outside the town, and I left the battle bus and bade farewell to my constant companions of the campaign. On a gloriously sunny afternoon I was driven home to Finings. That evening my family gathered, and I warned them of the result they should expect.

On polling day I woke early and sat in the garden. Peter Brown, my constituency agent, had assured me of a healthy majority in Huntingdon. I reflected on what was to come. I was reconciled to leaving Downing Street, and had made up my mind to resign as leader of the party. Robert Cranborne, who knew of this intention, had tried to dissuade me, but I thought it was the only possible course. After eighteen years, the Conservatives needed a new start, and I knew the baggage of my years in Downing Street would make an easy target for the new government. I had considered staying on for a while, but if I did, it was obvious that the party would be riven by the leadership campaigns of would-be successors, which would start immediately. It would be better to make a clean break.

There was one other factor in my decision. I was weary. The constant challenge of fourteen successive years as a minister, ten in Cabinet and nearly seven as prime minister had worn me down emotionally and physically – and I knew it. The lack of a secure majority in recent years, and the debilitating effort of battling almost daily with so many of my own colleagues as well as with the opposition, had led to mistakes being made.

I had no doubts and no illusions: if we lost heavily I should go immediately, and offer my full support to my successor.

As I ran through all this in my mind, Jeffrey Archer arrived, as he always did on polling day, to join me on my constituency tour. It was still early – a little after 8 a.m. – and we walked around the garden without talking politics at all.

A little later, Norma and I voted at the village hall in Great Stukeley, near our house. Foreseeing the shot the photographers had lined themselves up for, Norma warned, 'Don't pause by the exit sign.' Strange to think how such concerns had become second nature to us since 1990, and how very soon they would matter no more. Norma and my son James and his girlfriend Elaine left to tour part of my huge constituency, while John Bridge, my Association Chairman, joined Peter, Jeffrey and myself as we set off in the opposite direction.

The day passed pleasantly enough. Huntingdon turned out to vote for the Conservative Party, loyal as ever and apparently unswayed by the attractions of New Labour or the Referendum camp. But at around 5 p.m., Tony Garrett phoned me in the car from Central Office. 'Not good news, boss,' he said. 'The reports are very bad. Labour are right through the marginals, and are moving workers to safer seats. It looks worse than we thought.'

There was nothing to be done, and I returned to Finings, arriving there in the early evening. Ahead of me was a long and bloody night. Tony Garrett's call made it evident we had lost badly, although a faint hope lingered that the result might not be truly catastrophic.

I was sitting in the garden reflecting on this when Arabella Warburton arrived from London, cheerful and trailing balloons and bonhomie. Having bidden farewell to her colleagues in the Number 10 Private Office, she too knew the game was up, but was not going to admit it to me. I told her how bad I thought it would be, and, following the trail I had taken with Jeffrey early that morning, we wandered around a garden awash with evening shadows, talking only of inconsequential matters.

It was a beautiful spring evening, and I noted the work that needed to be done. The copper-beech hedge was growing well, but slowly. It was planted in a corner of the garden that was in turn either too damp or too dry, and this had retarded its progress. I looked at where we could plant more fruit trees by taking out the venerable old unpruned apples. A rambling rose was needed up against a wall, and there was space around the edge of the garden for more trees and new beds. The lime trees were in leaf, the Virginia creeper was opening, the wisteria was in bloom, the spring flowers were out and the election seemed far away.

We traipsed around two acres of unkempt land on my northern border that I would have liked to buy, although it was not for sale. I wanted it so that I could extend my garden and plant a large copse of hardwood trees – oak, chestnut and elm – to replace those destroyed by disease a few years earlier. There was ample space for a display of cherry blossom and lilac too. In my mind's eye I could see it all. My garden was a private refuge, a place of peace, as it had been so many times before. For a while that walk absorbed me utterly, and removed from my mind the prospect of what was to come. The sun had gone down. I was refreshed and ready for the slaughter.

At 10 p.m., ballot boxes all over Britain were sealed, and the television companies revealed the results of their exit polls. They warned us what the outcome would be. Then the results began coming in. Conservative seats tumbled, with little regard to the quality of the candidate or their views about the single currency or any other matter. I sat in the sitting room alone with Norma watching the results. We said little, except to express sadness at particular results. Arabella, Howell James and Norma's secretary Lorne Roper-Caldbeck sat in another room, while Sheila Gunn and Shirley Stotter based themselves in the kitchen. Elizabeth, James, and their partners Luke and Elaine mooched restlessly from room to room with consoling words.

At about 2 a.m. I asked Alex Allan to get Tony Blair on the telephone, so that I could congratulate him on his success. I spoke to the new prime minister from my study, with a gloomy Howell James at my side. I can remember little of what I said, I was so exhausted, but we were both friendly enough. There was much noise in the background in his constituency of Sedgefield – the beginning of celebrations, no doubt. Then I left for my own count.

It was a subdued affair. No one quite knew where to look or what to say when Norma and I arrived. Everyone seemed downcast, and even our opponents were not remotely triumphant. I saw how the count was progressing, chatted to the other candidates, and waited in an adjoining room, watching the election coverage on television. There were rumours that Michael Portillo had lost his seat, and pictures of Gillian Shephard at her count, sitting on an upturned box and shaking her head sadly. Thankfully, she won, but many others had not.

Tony Newton was gone, likewise Ian Lang and Malcolm Rifkind. So had Michael Forsyth, William Waldegrave and Roger Freeman, all members of the Cabinet. Robert Atkins and Graham Bright, friends for nearly forty years, were out. Scotland and Wales were looking like a whitewash, and the London results were gruesome. The Liberal Democrats stormed into the south-west of the country; Labour took most of the rest. David Mellor lost Putney; I was consoled only by the pitiful vote achieved by Sir James Goldsmith, who, like almost all the Referendum Party's candidates, comfortably lost his deposit. Across Britain, good people with much still to offer were replaced by unknown opposition candidates – some, no doubt of great ability and independence, but many, it has since proved, unable to discern the line between party loyalty and subservience.

I took no pleasure in the defeats suffered by those who had tormented the government from within the party. Norman Lamont lost badly in a seat he had expected to win, while Nicholas Budgen, Tony Marlow and Rupert Allason, all of whom had contributed to our present terrible situation, were not spared from the carnage. Michael Portillo's defeat at Enfield Southgate was confirmed. Candidates who had defied the party line fared as well – or as badly – as those who had abided by it.

In Huntingdon, I was re-elected with a majority of 18,140, and remembered in my acceptance speech – as I had not in 1992 – to express my gratitude to Norma. It was heartfelt. Such grace and charm through all the highs and lows of over a quarter of a century. I had always been proud of her. She had married a young local councillor, and fate had taken this shy woman into a public role she had never sought, but had carried out so well. As we left the count to return to London, we had to fight our way through a media crowd interested only in the next story to unfold: 'Will you resign?' they shouted. They would soon have their answer.

Norma, James and Elizabeth, Luke and Elaine followed us in a convoy of cars as we drove down a deserted A1 to London. Norma and I sat in the car listening to the dreary news, and then parked on the Embankment to allow the cars following us to catch up. As dawn broke, the sounds of revelry floated across the river from the Royal Festival Hall, where Labour was celebrating its triumph.

At Central Office we were met by Brian Mawhinney, newly elected in North-West Cambridgeshire, and Michael Portillo, whose loss of his seat had been the biggest shock of the election. As I put my arm around Michael and sympathised, I remembered Chris Patten's defeat at Bath five years earlier, and wondered if this would be another promising career cut short by untimely defeat. It was a bitter blow for one of my potential successors (and Euro-sceptic adversaries). In defeat, if not always in government, we were united.

Central Office was a mixture of long faces, etched with tiredness, and forced jollity. But they cheered and clapped and were wonderful. I thanked all the workers, made a brief speech from the stairs, shared a drink or two, and then, for the final time as prime minister, set off for the place that had been my home for the last few years, 10 Downing Street.

When I arrived in the early hours of the morning I found the flat above the official rooms largely empty; we had already packed and prepared to leave. Only a few people were still in the building. Alex Allan, who had run Number 10 with such spirit and professionalism for most of my time there, and was a friend as well as one of the best principal private secretaries any prime minister could hope to have, was solicitous with tea and comfort, but we both knew that he already had to begin the task of installing the new government. I lay on the bed for a few hours of fitful sleep before getting up in the early dawn to watch the election round-up on television. Then Brian Mawhinney, the Party Chairman, who had given his all despite an impossible task, arrived. When I left Number 10 I did so in his company.

Leaving was very painful. It is traditional for the Number 10 staff to line the long corridor behind the black door to 'clap out' a retiring prime minister, and to 'clap in' his successor. I knew our farewell would be a highly charged emotional moment, and I could not face it immediately before emerging to present a stoical face to the press assembled outside.

I asked Alex Allan to arrange for me to say farewell to the staff in the State Rooms on the first floor. Norma and I went in, tentatively and a little unsure of what to expect, to a welcome of immense warmth and kindness. Propinquity works. In six and a half years we had grown immensely fond of all these people. And it seemed that many of them felt the same way about us.

There were wet eyes all around the room – sometimes to my surprise. Norma and I spoke to everyone before I made a brief speech of thanks; then, hand in hand, we left the room. I went upstairs to the flat for one last gesture: I left a bottle of champagne for Tony and Cherie Blair with a brief note saying: 'It's a great job – enjoy it.' In such a mood I left Number 10. I will never go back. It is a building for government, not memories.

Outside, I expected some crowing from the media, but there was none, though they were excited and in carnival mood. It was a historic day. The Conservatives were out. Labour was in. New stories. New faces. They were all very jolly. But not even in the faces of my unkindest critics did I see glee – although some were not keen to catch my eye. I spoke outside Number 10 for the last time.

It has been an immense privilege to serve as Prime Minister over the past six and a half years. It is a privilege which comes to very few people, and is precious. As I leave Downing Street this morning, I can say with some accuracy that the country is in far better shape than when I entered it.

The economy is booming, interest rates and inflation are low and unemployment is falling. The growth pattern is well set, the health service is expanding, the education service is improving and the crime statistics are falling. The incoming government – to whom I repeat my warm congratulations upon their success – will inherit the most benevolent set of economic statistics since before the First World War. I hope very much in the interests of the whole British nation that they are successful.

I have been a Member of Parliament for eighteen years, of the government for fourteen years, of the Cabinet for ten years, and Prime Minister since 1990. When the curtain falls it is time to get off the stage, and that I propose to do. I shall advise my parliamentary colleagues to select a new leader of the Conservative Party.

I should like to add one final thought. During the six and a half years I have been in Downing Street there have been innumerable kindnesses from people, many of whom I have never met. I would like to extend my thanks to them and the millions of people in the British nation who have always given me their trust. I will say no more this morning. I have an appointment with Her Majesty the Queen in a few moments to tender my resignation so that a new government may be formally appointed. After that Norma and I will be able, with the children, to get to The Oval in time for lunch and for some cricket this afternoon.

I had thought about this speech over several months, and had prepared it, with some input from Nick True, earlier in the week. As I spoke, the words seemed familiar – almost as if I had delivered them before.

From Downing Street Norma and I travelled the short distance to Buckingham Palace. After taking my farewell of the Queen, where I formally relinquished the premiership, we drove to The Oval, where James, Elizabeth, Luke and Elaine joined us. We lunched among friends in the Committee Room and from the balcony watched the Combined Universities bat against Surrey, with some fine forcing strokes from a young batsman, Will House.

The scattering of spectators was very sympathetic. 'You had a rough decision, mate,' one called out jovially.

'Perhaps,' I replied. 'But the umpire's decision is final.'

We were home at Finings by early evening, with James, Elizabeth, Luke and Elaine on our heels. Moments later, Arabella arrived to spend the weekend with us, to fend off phone calls and cope with anything else that needed to be done. She had promised some weeks earlier that she would leave Number 10 with me and head my private office.

Arabella, James and Elaine brought in some food, and the seven of us spent the evening in the garden, in unseasonably balmy weather, enjoying a lengthy supper and several bottles of wine. There were no red boxes, no immediate crises. We reminisced about Number 10, the people we would miss, stories from overseas visits, the highs and lows of politics. I felt a huge surge of relief that my life was my own again, and that I could once again control it. I had not spent such an evening in the garden with my family for many years.

As the evening shadows fell, more and more flowers and messages arrived. Every few minutes one of the Cambridgeshire policemen who are part of our protection team appeared clutching the most beautiful arrangements and bouquets. Norma was in and out of her seat, finding vases and arranging the flowers in room after room around the house. It was all very moving, and, although it is perhaps extraordinary to relate of such a politically catastrophic day, that evening is one of the most vivid and treasured memories I have. Even though none of us had slept over the last thirty-six hours, it was very late when we went to bed.

Saturday was a lazy day. We all rose late – another novelty for me. Norma and I slept well, but the children slept longer. The police arrived with our mail – crates of it, literally hundreds of letters and messages, all of which must have been written immediately after the announcement of the result. Arabella sat in the sitting room opening them all and considering how we could reply – even on that first day, the sheer scale of correspondence was overwhelming. The British public is remarkable: even as they dismiss you from office, they write in support and to ease the bruises, for not all the letters were from Tory voters.

Buoyed up by this ocean of letters, I should have immediately set about writing to those many Conservative MPs who had lost their seats. I did not. This was unforgivable, but it was not an intended slight. I was exhausted, and with Number 10 now occupied by Tony Blair and Parliament in recess, I did not even have an office from which to work. When we moved into the leader of the opposition's office, events again overtook my best intentions. The letters went out in the end, but it took too long.

Radio and television were ignored throughout the weekend. I did not begrudge the Labour Party their triumph, but nor did I wish to observe it. Even the *Daily Telegraph* was dumped, unceremoniously and unopened, into the bin.

We were sitting around the kitchen table at the end of lunch on the Saturday after the election when the phone rang. The answerphone whirred into action, and a familiar voice rang out: 'Is that the lovely voice of Norma Major?' Actually, it was the lovely voice of Arabella, who had put the answerphone on to screen incoming calls. 'This is George Bush.'

Norma grabbed the phone and we both talked to George. 'I know what losing is like – I've been there,' he said. And on he went, warmly issuing invitations: 'Come to Kennebunkport. Bring the children. The blue fish are biting. Barbara sends her love.' It was a very cheerful and uplifting call. It was typical of George Bush, who is indeed a good friend. He was the first to call me when I became prime minister, and the first to call when I had lost.

Bill Clinton rang too, as easy and friendly as ever. So did Brian and Mila Mulroney from Canada, and many others. Amidst the battle of politics, courtesies exist too.

The press were posted outside our gates, with demands for photographs. Finally we agreed, and in they marched – bar one. Norma recognised an old foe who had harassed and pestered James, and she was not posing for him. He was ejected as she showed her steel. We are not public property now, was her view, and we would cooperate only on our own terms.

The weather was magnificent as Labour took up office and, at Finings, we considered the future. On Sunday we had planned a buffet lunch for some of our closest friends. It would be either a celebration or a wake, we had thought. It was a very jolly wake. There was no shifting of eyes, or mumbled 'sorrys' from our guests. Most knew us too well. There were hugs and a few tears, and much cheerfulness. Old and new friends came, including the group with whom we had spent New Year's Eve for years past, and others besides. We raided my best wines and sank the lot.

Lunch spread into supper as the party rolled on. The whole weekend was a mental windbreak: I went to bed thinking not of what had been, but of what was yet to come.

# AFTERMATH

SINCE THE 1997 GENERAL ELECTION, people have asked me why the way Britain changes its government has to be so brutal. Certainly it is not for the squeamish – one moment you are prime minister, the next you are out – but I accept the ritual. It is the purest expression of democracy. The people decide: off with the old, on with the new.

But it certainly gives you a jolt. Over the weekend after the election, Trevor Butler, the head of my Special Branch protection team, began escorting Tony Blair – his job was now to look after the new prime minister. A new team had been assigned to me. When, in the days after the election, 'switch' – the professional team who run the Number 10 switchboard – put telephone calls through, it was to 'Mr Major', not 'Prime Minister'. When friends rang, those formal enough to have called me 'Prime Minister' when I was in office reverted to 'John'. A page had been turned over in my life.

In the months after the election I received over 400,000 letters, all but a handful of them generous, though many people wrote to explain why they had not voted Conservative. We had 'been there too long' (a common theme), we were 'split on Europe', we needed 'a period in opposition to rethink'.

When I left Number 10, Arabella Warburton came with me. So too did Lorne Roper-Caldbeck, Norma's Assistant. During my short period as leader of the opposition, working from ill-equipped offices in the Commons only just vacated by Tony Blair, we were assisted by those who had worked in the Number 10 Political Office, a team led by the hugely efficient Judy Moorhouse. Slowly, working through long days and weekends, the backlog of letters was finally cleared. Throughout all these difficult days my Constituency Secretary Gina Hearn coped wonderfully with the huge flow of work from Huntingdon.

Though I had triggered a contest for the party leadership immediately after the election, I remained leader of the opposition until late June, when William Hague was elected, the youngest Tory leader since William Pitt.

The leader of the opposition has a tough job at any time, and never more so than after eighteen years of government and a severe election defeat. William has begun to think afresh, and he is right to do so, for the party must let go of its past in order to clear the way forward. The years of Conservative government were successful because our policies were right for the time; but we did not discover a political Holy Grail. We won in 1979 not *just* because of our strengths, but because the Labour Party was exhausted and discredited; we won again in 1983 and in 1987 not *just* because of Margaret Thatcher's leadership, but because the Labour Party was unelectable. We were able to move to the right and win elections because Labour had moved even further to the left. We won again in 1992 because we looked fresh, while Labour remained unreformed. We did not need to worry then that the opposition might try to capture the middle ground, since they had comprehensively lost it. That is no longer true, and the battle William faces is to make Conservatism appeal once more to mainstream voters. Elections cannot be won from the right if the centre is lost. William may have to make changes that will affront previous generations of Conservatives, and as he does so his predecessors must look on with tolerance and offer him the support he needs.

William has faced a difficult first two years with some courage. He is the parliamentary equal of anyone in the government, and amongst his depleted forces are some talented newcomers – Damian Green, Andrew Lansley, Theresa May, Caroline Spelman and Andrew Tyrie are among those who will join more seasoned colleagues in building enthusiasm for a new Conservative programme.

Conservatism is not an alarming philosophy. There is one way we could upset this, however: we could lose our sense of balance on Europe. William Hague has set out a firm and sensible line against joining the single currency in the short term, but he faces, just as I did, a cry from some in the party for a further hardening of hearts against the European Union. He is right to resist this cry. There are those on the Conservative benches in the House of Commons who want a commitment from the party to renegotiate our terms of membership of the EU, or to walk away from it altogether. Down this path lies madness and long-term opposition. A healthy scepticism is a tenable policy. Outright hostility is not. I believe the Conservative Party will return to government by defeating Labour in the centre of politics. The party must not turn in on itself or turn its back on Europe.

Labour has now been in government for over two years. It is difficult for a former prime minister to assess fairly the record of his successor in Number 10. When that successor has beaten him heavily at a general election, it becomes more difficult still. And when that successor has mocked and denigrated the record of those who went before, the temptation to lay objectivity aside and swipe back becomes almost impossible to resist.

In opposition, Tony Blair denounced Conservatism in extreme terms, even as he smoothly pocketed Conservative policies and attitudes. Labour sustained the pretence that sleaze was a uniquely Tory phenomenon, and launched hollow crusades on behalf of doctors, single parents, the poor and the elderly. Plans for privatisations that Labour would later attempt to engineer – of the Post Office, of the national air traffic control service, of London's Underground – were portrayed in the most apocalyptic terms when under consideration by the Conservative government. Labour fanned the flames of anti-Europeanism in the Tory Party without acknowledging the fact that the same fires burned strongly within its own ranks.

What Labour were so adept at distorting were often the everyday happenings of government: the choices, disappointments and mistakes that always take place. Since the election they have come to experience some of the necessary compromises of office. Election promises that have been kept are trumpeted; those which have been broken are brushed aside in the hope that no one will notice. Children from modest backgrounds who gained assisted places at private schools have lost out. So have grant-maintained schools. Taxes on business have been raised by stealth. The Labour Party's affection for the pound against the euro oscillates with the opinion polls. The Constitution has been knocked about with scarcely a thought for the long-term implications. The government machine in Whitehall has been politicised as never before. Parliament has been sidelined wherever possible. Image manipulation has been carried to new heights.

And sleaze did not die on 1 May 1997. Senior ministers have resigned in circumstances every bit as noteworthy as in earlier years. The Foreign Secretary has signed Public Interest Immunity Certificates – the very ones which he had previously denounced as 'gagging orders'. Labour Party funding has run into difficulties amid suspicions that government policy was being changed to accommodate the interests of generous donors. There has been no shortage of wrongdoing on the government side of the House since the election, and in time Labour's past and present eagerness to feed the media hunger for tales of Tory sleaze will rebound.

It is fair to say that in office Labour has been sanctimonious, arrogant, unjust, intolerant, spectacularly discourteous – and damn lucky. And if that were all there was to say, then I suppose that having got it off my chest I could now rule a line beneath this chapter and end my book.

But there is something more to say, and unless the Conservative Party in opposition – and that includes me – summons the grace to say it, then our own good faith will be diminished in the electorate's eyes. The right approach to this new Labour government is to be watchful, wary, alert and often deeply cynical – but at the same time to be ready to acknowledge personal, political and philosophical strengths where they have been proved in office.

Labour has left the Tory legacy largely undisturbed: our trade union legislation remains in place for the moment; not one of the many privatisations Labour consistently fought in opposition has been reversed; the government has retained, in a new guise, the devolved system of management we brought to the NHS; it has delighted in exploiting the performance targets and league tables the Citizen's Charter brought to public services; it has stuck by Michael Howard's determined approach to law and order; it has even retained the tax cuts of the Tory years. Perhaps when the legacy one leaves, the successes one achieved, remain essentially intact and are protected, imitated – even built upon – by one's successors, one should take it as a compliment (whatever political abuse accompanies it) and pay tribute to the good sense of those who have cherished their political inheritance in deed if not in word.

Nor should Conservatives notice only the preservation of some of our own achievements. Labour have had ideas of their own, some of them good. The 'New Deal' may be more hype than reality, but the government has been right to turn its attention to social exclusion. The abolition of the hereditary element in the House of Lords has been bungled, with serious consequences for our democracy, but like many Conservatives I accept the need for reform. The government may yet succeed in its aim of bringing Europe's defence and security policies closer together.

If, from the opposition benches, we recognise the government's strengths as well as its weaknesses and follies, our criticisms will carry more weight – and perhaps our positive advice will too. Elsewhere in this book

I have suggested that our political system, now free of socialism, has moved towards that found in the United States. There, Republicans and Democrats learn from one another and sometimes even agree with one another – and, of course, often strongly disagree, too. In this spirit, I continue to warn the government about the threat its treatment of Scotland and Wales poses to the United Kingdom. The dismemberment of Britain is in no one's interests, and must not be allowed to take place through inattention. I wholeheartedly back Tony Blair's efforts to sustain the Northern Ireland peace process, but question his government's continued willingness to take on trust the commitment of those responsible for the Province's difficulties in the first place. As one who has more experience than most of the effects of disunity within a political party, I am nonetheless certain that the determination of Tony Blair and his closest advisers to suppress criticism from his followers and to diminish and bypass the role of Parliament demeans the very core of our democratic system.

I acknowledge the brave common sense of the prime minister who preceded me, and the sometimes shrewd calculation of the prime minister who has succeeded me. Each of us has enjoyed the advantages and privileges of the office, and knows also the difficulties that must inevitably be associated with it. I make, in the end, no complaint about these, though I often muttered about them along the way. I loved Number 10 and the people within it, loved the job, loved the responsibility, loved – and will always love – the country I served. Now it is over, and life goes on.

# The Empty House

'WHY POLITICS?' I asked at the beginning of this memoir. The wider question at the end is – whither politics?

It is not easy to answer. After a long period of *relative* peace and prosperity, there is an anti-political mood in our country. People feel neither threatened nor afraid. Party allegiance has declined: no longer – in W. S. Gilbert's famous line – is every child either a little Liberal or else a little Conservative. The end of the Cold War and the defeat of socialism have broken the ideological bindings that held our political system rigid. The great giants – excessive trade union power, galloping inflation – have been slain.

At the same time a new consensus has been forged around a common acceptance of the market economy. The role of Parliament and government has declined. Parliament has shed too much power to retain its pre-eminence or its reputation. The Lords is in danger of becoming dominated by party nominees. The Commons has become a stage, not a forum. Cabinet government is falling into disarray, with ministers briefing against each other and often becoming less effective and influential than key advisers.

This dumbing-down of parliamentary government has added to disillusion with our political system. Too often we see judges in judicial reviews called upon to restrain the Executive, while at the same time the government thumbs its nose at a Parliament that is being bypassed, disregarded, treated as an irritation and 'modernised' out of effectiveness. Soon I will leave the Commons. I will miss it as it was, but less so as it is becoming.

Politics is rarely admired as a profession, and perhaps this is as it should be. We politicians set ourselves up to govern the affairs of our fellow citizens and, once elected, we direct their lives, tax their incomes and, in the end, are doomed to disappoint their expectations. It is unsurprising that politicians tend to languish at the bottom of public esteem, with their familiar companions journalists and estate agents.

This is not new. Politicians come and go and their days in the sun are transitory. But what is new is that Parliament itself is now being diminished as authority deserts it.

Some of the causes of this decline are long-term and unavoidable. Britain no longer rules a quarter of the world. The sun has set on the largest empire the world has ever known. The end of empire and of a dominating global role was bound to reduce the influence of the parliament which ran the affairs of so much of the world. In addition, the rise of collective government through bodies such as the United Nations, the Commonwealth and the European Union was bound to reduce Parliament's scope. All that would have been tolerable if Parliament had retained its internal authority. But, increasingly, this too is going. Parliament is losing control of events.

Some of the diminution of the power of Parliament has offsetting benefits – the EU is a case in point. Membership is, in essence, a trade-off: we surrender a portion of sovereignty over our own affairs, whilst gaining influence over the affairs of other nations. We gain economic benefit from membership and, in return, we pay a political price for it. This is a familiar, if controversial, equation that is perfectly defensible and is in our overall interest as a nation. Sir Nigel Broomfield, former Ambassador to Germany, has put the point well. He has said that the purpose of the European Union is to keep democracy *in*, nationalism *out* and barriers *down*.

Yet it must be acknowledged that collective decisions have reduced the unquestioned authority of Parliament. The trend of Parliament ceding domestic authority to the EU in return for wider influence has been remorseless – the Treaty of Rome (Heath), the Single European Act (Thatcher), the EU Treaty (Major) and the Amsterdam Treaty (Blair) have all done so. Few acknowledge the wider influence that has been gained; many regret the loss of parliamentary control. The growth of power of the European Commission may have been necessary to ensure European laws are obeyed, but because it is unelected it is not seen, in Britain at least, as democratically legitimate. Intrusive legislation imposed from Europe is deeply resented. Euro-scepticism has grown periodically and then fallen back – but each time leaving a higher residue of resentful and antagonistic feeling. The British press – overwhelmingly Euro-sceptic – has magnified real and imagined grievances whilst rarely reporting the beneficial effects of our membership. Its hostility has been a thorn in the flesh of successive governments.

Other blows to unfettered parliamentary authority come from market forces, and are unavoidable. Governments must roll with the punches and adjust their policies accordingly. They can no longer control markets: the bitter day on which currency flows swept sterling out of the ERM made that only too evident. They cannot control the internet or the availability of unsavoury, illegal, unpleasant or simply untrue information that flows along it. Nor can they control multi-national companies as they seek the most favourable terms for investment and the most attractive tax havens for domicile. Governments can cajole, entice or plead, but they can no longer control.

These external constraints on the untrammelled influence of Parliament have been accompanied by internal changes which have further weakened it. The most inexperienced government of modern times is tearing up a Constitution that has evolved over several centuries, and we have not yet begun to see the full ramifications in Parliament of these changes. The death of John Smith encouraged the then Labour opposition to honour their lost Scottish leader by elevating his unstructured enthusiasm for devolution into holy writ. Whether John Smith, a sharp-eyed lawyer, would ever have enacted such a mish-mash as the Act bringing devolution to Scotland will for ever be an open question, but his premature death closed down any serious debate about the most profound constitutional change to the UK for generations.

Perhaps some form of devolution was unavoidable; but the plans for Scottish home rule, in particular, were ill-thought-out and poorly examined. 'What can I do?' bewailed Tony Blair when the anti-devolutionist Labour MP Tam Dalyell pointed out their defects. There was much he could have done: for a start he could have examined their impact on the UK as a whole. But he did not. He let the devolution bandwagon take over: it was good for votes in Scotland, and the suspicion continues to linger that no deeper consideration was given to it. A referendum to approve the policy was held before the details of the legislation were available. The majority obtained in the referendum was then enlisted to rush ill-drafted legislation through Parliament. The government dispensed with the ancient tradition that constitutional change was debated fully on the floor of the Commons to enable every MP to contribute to debate; instead the Bill was sent upstairs to a committee. This cavalier disregard of the role of the Commons was in sharp contrast to the Devolution Bill in the 1974 Parliament, which was debated by MPs for forty-seven days, during which examination all sorts of defects emerged – most famously, as Enoch Powell dubbed it, the 'West Lothian question' first raised in those debates by Tam Dalyell, MP for that constituency. This question was – and still is – unanswerable: for how long would it be proper for an MP for a Scottish constituency such as West Lothian to vote, in the Westminster Parliament, on matters affecting English constituencies but not Scottish? This is not an arcane concern. Is it right, for example, for a Scottish MP, after devolution, to vote on English education policy when an English MP can no longer vote on Scottish education policy because it has been devolved? Is it right for a ban on hunting in England to be carried by Scottish MPs when such a measure would not affect Scotland?

Although that question is fundamental to Parliament, the government failed to address it in its legislation: it was brushed aside as being of no consequence. Nor, during the devolution debates, did the government consider related questions such as the imbalance of UK funding to Scotland by comparison, for example, to London. The government has taken insufficient action to reduce the long-standing anomaly of Scotland having far too many MPs in the House of Commons for its population. This imbalance helps Labour electorally, and the government seems in no hurry to entirely correct it. After devolution these anomolies are unsustainable and widely felt to be so, but, using its large parliamentary majority, Labour has ignored them.

There are unfortunate consequences of this: the power ceded to Scotland has reduced the influence of the Commons, whose writ no longer runs on significant issues; and the special financial and electoral advantages retained by the Scots fuel grievances against them felt by the English. The loss of parliamentary power to Scotland is mirrored to a lesser extent by devolution to Wales. In addition, a measure of self-government has been given to London, where, after a truly farcical campaign and a derisory turnout, with only one in three bothering to vote, Ken Livingstone was elected as the most famous mayor since Dick Whittington. Moreover, devolution to the English regions is a distinct possibility; this would turn the United Kingdom into a near-federal state.

The overall effect on the Westminster Parliament is to make it less relevant to the UK as a whole. The Scots and Welsh now look primarily to their own parliaments, and in due course Londoners will look to their mayor. Parliament is becoming part-redundant to millions of voters, and it must be likely that turnout in the general election of 2001 or 2002 will be sharply down, unless it is boosted by the prospect of a close result. But I doubt that this will happen: I suspect the greater likelihood, whatever the polls indicate, is a fall in turnout, quite possibly a sharp one.

The decline in the power and responsibility of the Commons is highlighted by the Blair government which, with its huge majority of new and compliant MPs, takes less note of parliamentary opinion than any government within memory. This disregard extends far beyond ignoring unwelcome views. In the government's first three years, policy initiatives were routinely announced by the chief press officer at Number 10 lobby briefings, or by ministers on the media, or at publicity-worthy events around the country – in any event, outside the Commons and sometimes outside the country: the Prime Minister even announced a proposal to fine hooligans on the spot at a conference in Germany. Parliament is bypassed. Statements to the Commons *follow* the public announcement, if they are made at all. The scale of this blatant disregard of Parliament, in particular of the House of Commons, is unprecedented, and makes Westminster seem impotent.

The first sign of New Labour's contempt for parliamentary niceties was the Prime Minister's unilateral decision to reduce his availability for questioning by the House of Commons from twice a week, on Tuesday and Thursday, to once only, on Wednesday. He neither discussed nor consulted upon this fundamental change in his accountability to the Commons with the leaders of other political parties. He simply informed the opposition of his intentions and imposed it. In doing so, he utterly ignored his responsibility, with an impregnable Commons majority, to make himself *more* available to the House and not *less*. Apparently he did not agree that, unless used with care, the power of a prime minister with a large majority can easily become too great, and needs to be restrained through accountability.

As a counter-balance the Prime Minister did increase Question Time from fifteen to thirty minutes for his one remaining appearance before the Commons, and this longer period has often seen him floundering against hard questioning. But once a week for thirty minutes is far less daunting a hurdle than two fifteen-minute sessions at which contemporary issues can be raised. The change has other undesirable side-effects: with PMQs ended by Wednesday afternoon, the Commons is often derelict on Thursday and Friday. The Smoking Room is empty. The Dining Room is empty. The Tea Room is empty and the Chamber of the Commons is empty. No government can be held to account in an empty House. The new arrangement for questioning the prime minister has instituted a three-day week without the excuse of a miners' strike. If this proposal had been subjected to parliamentary consultation and debate, as it should have been, such dangers would have been aired and the change might not have been approved.

Francis Pym once memorably pointed out that a huge majority for any party can have malign effects. That is certainly true of the present Parliament. Legislation is poorly scrutinised, arguments from the opposition are ignored and amendments defeated, often without debate under a guillotine motion. Criticism is treated with disdain or by abuse of the critic with no examination of the criticism. Only in the House of Lords is the outcome of argument and debate uncertain. What Quintin Hailsham once called an elective dictatorship is alive and flourishing upon its large majority.

The rise in central control by the party machines and the abuse of Parliament are opposite ends of the same seesaw. As opposition in Parliament has been sidelined by the absolute power of the government majority in the Commons, so parallel action by the Labour Party has further eroded the fragile public confidence in MPs, already damaged by the self-interested and unappealing behaviour of a minority over the preceding decade or more.

Labour has compounded this damage by undermining the political independence of Members. From the moment it took office in 1997, a 'line-to-take' on issues was fed out daily to Labour MPs on their pagers, with the result that the same, often rather silly, slogans were parroted again and again by Ministers and backbenchers alike. It was demeaning. MPs were made to look like ciphers, and the bracing views of those who were openly dissident were suppressed. Some were apparently threatened with deselection. New candidates were imposed from the centre and chosen for their biddability. The scale of party control far exceeded anything seen before. A party of elected politicians was treated like clones. I grew up with a healthy respect for the old Labour Party, even though I often disagreed with it. This belittling of elected MPs cannot last, I think, and backbench independence of spirit will grow in proportion to the inevitable decline in Labour's opinion-poll ratings. Nonetheless, although a timely vindication of Francis Pym, it has been a depressing experience to witness.

The constitutional tinkerers have not overlooked the House of Lords. The easy target was to abolish the hereditary peers and, although a stay of execution was granted to a minority of them, most have gone, accompanied by a volley of insults from senior Labour figures. The Leader of the Lords, Baroness Jay, said the chamber would be legitimate when the hereditaries were removed. They were, admittedly, an anomaly at the end of the twentieth century, although the best of them showed a welcome independence of mind. But they could not be saved even by their virtues: no pay, independence of the party whips, a wealth of experience and a tradition of public service which we can ill afford to lose.

Once the tumbrils bearing away the hereditary peers had departed, it seemed that Labour might have shot its own fox by increasing the legitimacy of the Lords. Certainly, their Lordships felt less inhibited in defeating government proposals. We do not yet know how the hereditaries will be replaced, and the fear remains that one way or another their successors will be yet more appointees at the whim of the prime minister and the party elites.

As Parliament has been dumbed down, there has been a danger of the Civil Service being politicised. An unwise step in that direction began with the appointment of Labour Party functionaries in Number 10 as effective head of the prime minister's private office (and thus the vital position of chief gatekeeper to the PM) and chief press officer. Other political appointments were made in the Number 10 Press Office. Across Whitehall, most of the Civil Service press officers were speedily culled, some rather messily. Number 10 filled up with political appointees as civil servants were relocated to make room for them: the number of 'special advisers' (all political appointments) went far beyond anything seen before, as did the taxpayer-borne cost of them. Some in the new administration saw Number 10 not only as the centre of government, but as the head office of the Labour Party.

The government press spokesman ceased to be a dispassionate civil servant, answerable for his straightforwardness and accuracy to the head of the home Civil Service, and instead became the partisan voice of the prime minister and the government (and, if he was forced to choose between them, of the prime minister). Previous press secretaries – Joe Haines and Bernard Ingham among them – had been fiercely loyal to their prime ministers – but nothing on this scale had been seen before. My own excellent press secretaries, Gus O'Donnell, Christopher Meyer and Jonathan Haslam, were all career civil servants. Their only similarity to the new chief press secretary was that the taxpayer funded their services too – although the political appointee was rewarded for his services far more lucratively than were his Civil Service predecessors. Even when, in mid-2000, the chief press secretary was replaced by a civil servant again – amid much 'spinning' that 'spinning' was ending – it turned out that this was merely *more* spin: he was simply being relocated to more effectively promote Labour Party interests as the election approached. He was, however, still to be paid by the taxpayer.

The politicisation of the Number 10 press interface with the public was an essential precondition for the successful 'spinning' of the government's tale. It became an obsession: spin and soundbite became more important than argument and fact – in the process, turning the public ratchet a little more towards cynicism. It is ironic that a party which, in opposition, demanded independent verification and supervision across a wide swathe of public life, removed the independent voice of the Civil Service from an important part of the very heart of government on its first day in office.

In the life-span of an over-mighty government the case for a free and vibrant media comes most into its own. Parliament, politics and politicians reach the British public largely through the media – and the public, though less trustful than in years past, still tend to believe much of what they hear or read. The media role, therefore, is a crucial part of our political scene. In recent years it has undergone many changes. The electronic media have exploded in size, with terrestrial, satellite, cable, national and local radio and television channels all demanding political news. Moreover, competition is such that they want this news immediately, and politicians on the stump are expected to respond to questions from journalists about events far away about which they have heard nothing and that they have not had time either to check or to think about. The dangers are obvious: a journalist is fed a question on his mobile, the context of which he may or may not understand. He asks it of a politician on the move, who is out of touch with events, but who unwisely answers. As a result, wholly distorted stories appear. Through error or mischief or carelessness, much damage can be done.

The written press has changed, too. *News*papers no longer exist in the true meaning of the word. The news is heard on the hour, via radio and television, and is stale by the following morning. As a result the written press is more likely to report what is expected to happen, and to favour comment as opposed to news. Direct reporting of Parliament is now rare, though some broadsheets have begun to reintroduce it.

With the fierce competition between newspapers, editors have become as disposable as football managers, and are as likely to be sacked in the washroom by their proprietor as ever they were. Their job security depends upon their circulation figures, which feeds an appetite that demands sensation. This applies to all news, but particularly to politics. Drama, personality conflicts, policy debate represented as dispute are all good copy: even more so if they are unearthed by 'leak' or private behind-the-hands briefing. The new breed of political advisers to ministers are a rich source of such information, and their indiscretions are often presented – sometimes correctly, sometimes not – as the views of their political bosses. Despite their individual virtues, political advisers as a class are a menace, and a wise government would cut their numbers significantly.

The dramatisation of events may be an entertaining sport for the media – and it does sell newspapers – but the backbiting and leaking that so often dominates the news is not an accurate picture of the routine worthiness of most political behaviour, and it misleads the public. In pursuit of news, politics is treated as soap opera, and the growth in political reporting is matched by a decline in its quality. In an ideal world a non-aligned media would report objectively and offer dispassionate and lofty comment: but the world is not ideal.

The present government observed the torrent of criticism suffered by its predecessor and set out to woo the media. Whilst in opposition, Mr Blair flew halfway around the world at the invitation of Mr Rupert Murdoch, who no doubt received him warmly. In government, the Prime Minister's awareness of the importance of the media was illustrated when, following critical comment in the *Sun*, he sent it a *handwritten* letter. Although this was surely a first for any prime minister the *Sun* was not impressed, and I doubt the voters were either.

None of this matters much, except in one respect: while politicians and media seek to ingratiate themselves with each other in the chattering world of Westminster, the real world outside is often ignored. Governments do become out of touch and, as the public sees this, the mood of cynicism grows: a feeble Parliament enables the electorate's drift of respect to accelerate.

The United Kingdom needs a strong Parliament to bolster a political system that has taken too many blows, and this offers a great opportunity to the Conservative Party. It is essential to restore the role of Parliament, especially the Commons, and much can be done to do so. Often enough in the past it has been the genius of the Conservative Party to synthesise change it didn't like and to make it work. It will have to do so once more.

This will not be easy. Devolution has cast a long shadow, and has set institutional conflict in train. The UK and Scottish parliaments are bound to clash, and unless wise counsel and policy prevail, Scotland may be irreversibly set towards becoming an independent country. The Conservative Party cannot unscramble devolution, but its deficiencies can be tackled. I see no choice but an English element to the Westminster Parliament to mirror devolved decision-making in Scotland and Wales. This would entail English Members alone deliberating and deciding certain policy issues relating only to England. Various models can achieve this, but none are without problems, especially if the scenario of a Conservative majority in England but a non-Conservative majority across the UK as a whole were to come about. It is messy, but these are the very problems thrown up by ill-considered devolution. They must be faced, and dealt with, or disillusion will grow. A *united* kingdom requires that they be dealt with speedily.

Other reforms are now necessary to counter-balance the surfeit of ill-thought-through changes that has been our diet in the present Parliament: we now need measures to enhance parliamentary control of the Executive and to reassure those concerned by assaults on the traditional role of Parliament.

When I was prime minister, I made it one of my central concerns to improve the performance of the public services. Many sophisticates scoffed at the Citizen's Charter because they did not understand it, but it has now been copied in many other countries, and has achieved a real and lasting improvement in performance in many public services. We now take it for granted, if we travel on the London Underground, that we know how long it will be before our train arrives. We take it for granted that railway companies will publish details of their punctuality record. We take it for granted that schools will publish details of their performance. We take it for granted that public bodies will be committed to performance standards. None of these things was taken for granted fifteen years ago, and their implementation has improved the accountability of public services to the public.

We must now improve the openness and accountability of the government to Parliament and people. We need, through the committee system, to make legislative procedure much more open, and to monitor the progress of legislation after it has reached the statute book, so that we can rapidly repeal legislation which is not achieving its effect. The accountability of the government will improve by making Parliament more efficient and more effective. A toothless Parliament goes with unaccountable government. Only a Parliament with teeth can yield genuine accountability.

It is not the purpose of this chapter to set out a full remedy, but the next Parliament must examine many ideas. In July 2000 Lord Norton of Louth published a report for William Hague proposing reforms. I encouraged William Hague to undertake such an examination, and I welcome the thrust of the report. I pause before elaborating upon this theme, conscious that I could have done more myself during my own years in Downing Street. Up to a point that is true, although much of what I now propose was not necessary then. Nor did I have a large enough majority to enact it. The fair-minded observer may note also that events dictated other priorities. However, what I did or did not do in office does not alter the underlying dilemma that the Executive is becoming stronger and Parliament weaker, and this should be reversed. This trend did not begin during the 1997 Parliament, but the style of the Blair government – and the size of its majority – have given a sharper focus to it.

Lord Norton's recommendations to William Hague cover the efficiency of Parliament as well as the accountability of the government. Among many proposals he advocates reforms to Prime Minister's Questions and enhancement of the Select Committee system to provide greater scrutiny of government actions. He proposes changes to the parliamentary year, the carry-over of legislation between parliamentary sessions, a reduction in the numbers of ministers and Members of Parliament and more legislation in draft form. Such changes are needed – and more besides.

The objective must be to strengthen Parliament so that it may check the Executive and thereby improve the quality of legislation. A reform not advocated by Norton would be for government to set out proposed legislation for longer than one parliamentary session, so that measures may be published in outline form, consulted upon and evidence taken in public upon their practicality. This would be a classic task for a pre-legislative Committee of Lords and Commons meeting together. It would enable the shortcomings of proposals to be identified before government was committed to them, and should ease the drafting of legislation and improve its quality. It is also a more democratic way of proceeding and, if carried out properly, would conclusively rebut concerns about electoral dictatorship.

Some legislation may be needed urgently and could be unsuitable for such a leisurely process but even in those circumstances a fast-track approach could be constructed. Such legislation would minimise the vast number of amendments that now accompany all Bills and clog up parliamentary time. It would give MPs time to focus more upon key issues. It would also expose unworkable ideas: neither the Poll Tax nor devolution would have emerged unscathed by such scrutiny.

As the system of cabinet government has declined, the power of the prime minister has increased. A prime minister may still have to face down colleagues in Cabinet, but more often these days he heads off unwelcome ideas long before they reach collective discussion and suggests to Cabinet colleagues, in one-to-one discussions, the proposals he wishes to see adopted. Most ministers comply – or they do not remain ministers. It is ironic that, in the age of careerist professional politicians, the Prime Minister's power of appointment and patronage has increased his influence and diminished that of parliamentarians.

In the present Parliament, the Prime Minister has increased the support structure he has at the centre of government. *Some* enhancement was necessary and is wise, although it would have been better if more of it had come from the Civil Service and less from political appointees. It cannot be argued that the new support at Number 10 has been used to good effect. The most startling aspect of Labour's first term is how little they have done with it given the sparkling economy they inherited, their unassailable majority in the Commons and the poodle performance of the Liberal Democrats. The comparison with those prime ministers who enjoyed similar majorities – the Attlee government of 1945–50 or the Thatcher term between 1983 and 1987 – is striking.

The counterpoint to growing prime ministerial power at the centre must be greater prime ministerial accountability in the Commons. The prime minister must not be able to hide behind his new appointees. Prime Minister's Questions should revert to its twice-weekly slot, and the convention that prime ministers do not attend Select Committees to be cross-examined should be revised. I wish I had done so myself. Indeed, I would now go further: I favour the proposal that the prime minister should regularly attend a meeting composed of all Select Committee chairmen to set out his policy objectives and be questioned upon them. Such exchanges would be far more revealing than Prime Minister's Questions, and should be of use to premier, Parliament and public. To ensure worthwhile exchanges the area of questioning should be notified in advance and the prime minister should be free, if he wishes, to be accompanied by the appropriate ministerial colleague.

One area of great controversy over recent years has been the enactment of treaties agreed by the government – most obviously, European treaties. A real dilemma exists: government puts its name to the international agreements that it negotiates and then asks Parliament, which has not been part of the negotiation, to agree the treaty unchanged and to legislate to bring it into force. This is – in strictly democratic terms – a very questionable procedure. I sought to overcome it with the Maastricht Treaty on European Union by setting out my negotiating position in detail in Parliament before the final negotiations, and sticking absolutely to the terms I had set out. Despite my hopes, it did not still the controversy.

Such problems will recur, especially upon European policy. For the future, I would advocate a Standing Committee of both Houses to take evidence in public upon such negotiations both before and after they are concluded. This would not drown out the voice of controversy, but it would be a great improvement on present circumstances. Moreover, the slow pace of the timetable for the preparation of European treaties and their subsequent enactment would enable such a procedure to operate. A similar innovation would be worthwhile where significant domestic constitutional reform was concerned. I have in mind such areas as devolution, changes to the electoral system, structural changes to the judiciary and local government reform. In each case the purpose would be the same: to allow consultation and representation; to expose and debate the implications and effects of such changes; and to permit fundamental reforms to sink into the consciousness of the electorate before they are enacted. The legislation that results could, of course, also be subject to examination by the pre-legislative committee when detailed proposals are drawn up in a parliamentary Bill.

The innovations I suggest would slow down our legislative process, and for fundamental changes that is no bad thing; but they would actively improve our democratic procedures and the quality of our legislation.

I agree with the Norton assessment that the House of Commons has become too big and unwieldy. The number of MPs could be reduced with advantage to no more than five hundred – perhaps, as Norton suggests, in staged reductions. The effect would be to increase the average electorate to the size of the larger seats – but, having had one of those for over twenty years, I know that is manageable. It would also enable the number of ministers to be reduced. We have far too many of them – often in the junior ranks – undertaking functions only because their time as ministers needs to be filled. A reduction of one-fifth to one-third in the number of ministers is quite possible, especially if ministers in the Commons were empowered to address and answer questions in the House of Lords on their responsibilities, and vice versa (without, of course, the right to vote other than in their own assembly). This would be novel, but has distinct advantages. It would remove the unsatisfactory situation of 'double bank-ing' ministers to accommodate each House, and would end the present procedure in which ministers in the Lords respond to debates upon matters with which they are not familiar and have no real day-to-day responsibility.

All this, if enacted, would further change Parliament but, contrary to recent changes, would strengthen the legislature and make the Executive more accountable. It would also improve the quality of legislation and the independence of MPs. This last point is a significant one. Too high a proportion of recent intakes to the Commons is narrow in experience and, because ambition quells conscience, often impotent to protest against wrong-headed policy. As we move towards an all-professional Commons we see more clearly the virtues of the amateur politician, for whom politics was merely a part of his life. They still exist, of course, but they are a dinosaur breed. It is a weakness in our system that the professional poli-tician too often believes he has the field-marshal's baton in his rucksack.

Parliament will change. It always has. The aftermath of devolution is going to throw up many ideas to improve the working of Parliament, and the above will be only a part of them. A stream of ideas exists already. But reform should be measured and its effects calculated carefully before it is enacted. For all the dissatisfaction it often creates, Parliament has been the guardian of our liberties for generations. It *can* regain much of the authority it has lost. It will be a worthy task for the ambitious and public-spirited men and women who wish to serve in it to see it do so, and if they can re-establish its moral and political authority, we will all be in their debt.

JOHN MAJOR
*July 2000*

APPENDIX A

# Brief Chronology

1943   29 March: John Major born, Worcester Park, London

1950   September: Enters Cheam Common Junior School

1954   September: Enters Rutlish Grammar School, Merton

1955   May: Family moves to Coldharbour Lane, Brixton

1959   JM leaves Rutlish Grammar School

1960   Family moves to Burton Road, Brixton

1962   27 March: JM's father, Tom, dies

1963   JM becomes Chairman of Brixton Young Conservatives

1964   May: Stands unsuccessfully for election to Lambeth Council, Larkhall ward

1966   December: Begins work for Standard Bank in Jos, Nigeria

1967   May: Returns to England from Nigeria after car accident

1968   May: Elected to Lambeth Council, Ferndale ward

1969   January: Becomes Vice-Chair of Housing, Lambeth Council

1970   June: Becomes Chairman of Housing, Lambeth Council
       17 September: JM's mother, Gwen, dies
       3 October: JM marries Norma Johnson

1971   May: Defeated in elections to Lambeth Council, Thornton ward
       November: Selected as prospective Conservative parliamentary
       candidate for St Pancras North; daughter Elizabeth born

1974   JM stands unsuccessfully as Member of Parliament for St Pancras
       North in general elections of February and October

1975   January: Son James born

1976   December: JM selected as prospective Conservative parliamentary
       candidate for Huntingdonshire

1979   May: General election: JM elected as Member of Parliament for
       Huntingdonshire with a majority of 21,563
       13 June: Makes maiden speech in House of Commons

**1981**   January: Appointed Parliamentary Private Secretary to Patrick Mayhew and Timothy Raison

**1983**   January: Appointed Assistant Whip
June: General election: JM re-elected for Huntingdon with a majority of 20,348

**1984**   October: Appointed Treasury Whip and Lord Commissioner

**1985**   September: Appointed Parliamentary Under-Secretary to Department of Social Security

**1986**   September: Appointed Minister of State at Department of Social Security

**1987**   June: General election: JM re-elected for Huntingdon with majority of 27,044; joins Cabinet as Chief Secretary to the Treasury; appointed Privy Councillor

**1989**   July: Appointed Foreign Secretary
October: Appointed Chancellor of the Exchequer

**1990**   March: Delivers budget in House of Commons
5 October: Britain enters the Exchange Rate Mechanism
27 November: JM replaces Margaret Thatcher as Prime Minister and leader of the Conservative Party after she resigns following leadership contest against Michael Heseltine
28 November: JM asked by HM the Queen to form a government

**1991**   January: Operation Desert Storm begins the liberation of Kuwait from Iraqi occupation
February: IRA mortar attack on Downing Street; ceasefire in the Gulf
March: Citizen's Charter unveiled
October: JM attends Commonwealth Heads of Government Meeting in Harare, Zimbabwe, which results in the Harare Declaration on good government
December: JM attends Maastricht Treaty negotiations

**1992**   April: General election: Conservative government re-elected with a parliamentary majority of twenty-one; JM re-elected for Huntingdon with majority of 36,230; fighting breaks out in Bosnia, former Yugoslavia
August: JM chairs London Conference on conflict in former Yugoslavia
16 September ('Black Wednesday'): Suspends Britain's membership of the Exchange Rate Mechanism
December: Chairs Edinburgh summit which sees negotiations to protect British rebate from the EU and to help Denmark ratify the Maastricht Treaty

**1993**  May: European Communities (Amendment) Bill – the Maastricht Treaty – completes Commons third reading; Cabinet reshuffle, Kenneth Clarke replaces Norman Lamont as Chancellor
23 July: Parliamentary vote on Social Chapter ratifies Maastricht Treaty, following tied Commons vote of confidence the previous day
October: JM's party conference speech launches 'Back to Basics'
December: Joint Declaration with the Irish Taoiseach, Albert Reynolds, lays groundwork for IRA ceasefire

**1994**  June: Belgian Prime Minister Jean-Luc Dehaene vetoed as President of the European Commission
July: Tony Blair becomes leader of the Labour Party
August: IRA announces ceasefire
September: JM visits South Africa and addresses South African parliament
October: Launches National Lottery

**1995**  February: Framework Document on future of Northern Ireland published
22 June: JM resigns leadership of the Conservative Party and challenges opponents to stand against him in the subsequent contest
4 July: Defeats John Redwood by 218 votes to 89 in leadership ballot
November: Dayton Accord ends conflict in Bosnia, following second London Conference in July

**1996**  February: Docklands bomb ends IRA ceasefire; Scott Report on so-called 'arms-to-Iraq' affair published
March: Commons statement suggests BSE in cattle may be dangerous to human health
May: Policy of non-cooperation with Europe – the 'beef war' – begins; continues until June
June: All-party talks begin in Northern Ireland

**1997**  March: JM announces general election will be held on 1 May
May: Labour win general election; Tony Blair becomes Prime Minister; JM re-elected for Huntingdon with a majority of 18,140; announces intention to stand down as leader of the Conservative Party
June: William Hague becomes Conservative leader

**1999**  January: JM awarded the Companion of Honour by HM the Queen

# The Cabinet, November 1990–May 1997

**Bold** indicates a minister moved in a reshuffle.
***Bold italics*** indicate a minister joining the Cabinet in a reshuffle.

In the reshuffle of 29–30 November 1990, Margaret Thatcher and Cecil Parkinson left the government.

### 30 November 1990–11 April 1992

| | |
|---|---|
| Prime Minister | **John Major** |
| Chancellor of the Exchequer | **Norman Lamont** |
| Foreign Secretary | Douglas Hurd |
| Home Secretary | **Kenneth Baker** |
| Lord Chancellor | Lord Mackay of Clashfern |
| Scotland | *Ian Lang* |
| Wales | David Hunt |
| Northern Ireland | Peter Brooke |
| Leader of the Commons | John MacGregor |
| Leader of the Lords | **Lord Waddington** |
| Trade and Industry | Peter Lilley |
| Defence | Tom King |
| Health | William Waldegrave |
| Social Security | Tony Newton |
| Environment | ***Michael Heseltine*** |
| Transport | **Malcolm Rifkind** |
| Employment | Michael Howard |
| Education and Science | Kenneth Clarke |
| Agriculture | John Gummer |
| Energy | John Wakeham |
| Duchy of Lancaster (Party Chairman) | **Chris Patten** |
| Chief Secretary to the Treasury | *David Mellor* |
| Chief Whip (non-Cabinet) | *Richard Ryder* |

## 11 April 1992–24 September 1992

Kenneth Baker, Lord Waddington, Tom King, Peter Brooke and Chris Patten left the government.

The Department of Energy was abolished and its functions subsumed in the DTI. A new Department of National Heritage was created. The Office of Public Service and Science was established. Chris Patten continued as Party Chairman until May 1992. Education changed title, losing Science to the OPSS, and Michael Heseltine sat in Cabinet as President of the Board of Trade.

| | |
|---|---|
| Prime Minister | John Major |
| Chancellor of the Exchequer | Norman Lamont |
| Foreign Secretary | Douglas Hurd |
| Home Secretary | **Kenneth Clarke** |
| Lord Chancellor | Lord Mackay of Clashfern |
| Scotland | Ian Lang |
| Wales | David Hunt |
| Northern Ireland | *Patrick Mayhew* |
| Leader of the Commons | **Tony Newton** |
| Leader of the Lords | **Lord Wakeham** |
| Board of Trade (DTI) | **Michael Heseltine** |
| Defence | **Malcolm Rifkind** |
| Health | *Virginia Bottomley* |
| Social Security | **Peter Lilley** |
| Environment | **Michael Howard** |
| Transport | **John MacGregor** |
| Employment | *Gillian Shephard* |
| Education | *John Patten* |
| Agriculture | John Gummer |
| National Heritage | **David Mellor** |
| Duchy of Lancaster (OPSS) | **William Waldegrave** |
| Chief Secretary to the Treasury | *Michael Portillo* |
| | |
| Party Chairman (non-Cabinet) | *Norman Fowler* |
| Chief Whip (non-Cabinet) | Richard Ryder |

## 25 September 1992–27 May 1993

David Mellor left the government.

| | |
|---|---|
| Prime Minister | John Major |
| Chancellor of the Exchequer | Norman Lamont |
| Foreign Secretary | Douglas Hurd |
| Home Secretary | Kenneth Clarke |
| Lord Chancellor | Lord Mackay of Clashfern |
| Scotland | Ian Lang |
| Wales | David Hunt |
| Northern Ireland | Patrick Mayhew |
| Leader of the Commons | Tony Newton |
| Leader of the Lords | Lord Wakeham |
| Board of Trade (DTI) | Michael Heseltine |
| Defence | Malcolm Rifkind |
| Health | Virginia Bottomley |
| Social Security | Peter Lilley |
| Environment | Michael Howard |
| Transport | John MacGregor |
| Employment | Gillian Shephard |
| Education | John Patten |
| Agriculture | John Gummer |
| National Heritage | *Peter Brooke* |
| Duchy of Lancaster (OPSS) | William Waldegrave |
| Chief Secretary to the Treasury | Michael Portillo |
| | |
| Party Chairman (non-Cabinet) | Norman Fowler |
| Chief Whip (non-Cabinet) | Richard Ryder |

## 27 May 1993–20 July 1994

Norman Lamont left the government.

| | |
|---|---|
| Prime Minister | John Major |
| Chancellor of the Exchequer | **Kenneth Clarke** |
| Foreign Secretary | Douglas Hurd |

| | |
|---|---|
| Home Secretary | **Michael Howard** |
| Lord Chancellor | Lord Mackay of Clashfern |
| Scotland | Ian Lang |
| Wales | *John Redwood* |
| Northern Ireland | Patrick Mayhew |
| Leader of the Commons | Tony Newton |
| Leader of the Lords | Lord Wakeham |
| Board of Trade (DTI) | Michael Heseltine |
| Defence | Malcolm Rifkind |
| Health | Virginia Bottomley |
| Social Security | Peter Lilley |
| Environment | **John Gummer** |
| Transport | John MacGregor |
| Employment | **David Hunt** |
| Education | John Patten |
| Agriculture | **Gillian Shephard** |
| National Heritage | Peter Brooke |
| Duchy of Lancaster (OPSS) | William Waldegrave |
| Chief Secretary to the Treasury | Michael Portillo |
| | |
| Party Chairman (non-Cabinet) | Norman Fowler |
| Chief Whip (non-Cabinet) | Richard Ryder |

## 21 July 1994–6 July 1995

Peter Brooke, John MacGregor, John Patten and Lord Wakeham left the government.

| | |
|---|---|
| Prime Minister | John Major |
| Chancellor of the Exchequer | Kenneth Clarke |
| Foreign Secretary | Douglas Hurd |
| Home Secretary | Michael Howard |
| Lord Chancellor | Lord Mackay of Clashfern |
| Scotland | Ian Lang |
| Wales | John Redwood |
| Northern Ireland | Patrick Mayhew |
| Leader of the Commons | Tony Newton |
| Leader of the Lords | *Lord Cranborne* |
| Board of Trade (DTI) | Michael Heseltine |

| | |
|---|---|
| Defence | Malcolm Rifkind |
| Health | Virginia Bottomley |
| Social Security | Peter Lilley |
| Environment | John Gummer |
| Transport | *Brian Mawhinney* |
| Employment | **Michael Portillo** |
| Education | **Gillian Shephard** |
| Agriculture | **William Waldegrave** |
| National Heritage | *Stephen Dorrell* |
| Duchy of Lancaster | **David Hunt** |
| Chief Secretary to the Treasury | *Jonathan Aitken* |
| Minister without Portfolio (Party Chairman) | *Jeremy Hanley* |
| | |
| Chief Whip (non-Cabinet) | Richard Ryder |

John Redwood resigned as Welsh Secretary on 26 June 1995. During the leadership election David Hunt was acting Welsh Secretary.

## 6 July 1995–2 May 1997

Douglas Hurd, David Hunt, Richard Ryder and Jonathan Aitken left the government, John Redwood already having resigned. Jeremy Hanley moved to a non-Cabinet post.

The Department of Employment was abolished and most of its functions taken over by the Department for Education. The office of Deputy Prime Minister and First Secretary of State was established.

| | |
|---|---|
| Prime Minister | John Major |
| Deputy Prime Minister | **Michael Heseltine** |
| Chancellor of the Exchequer | Kenneth Clarke |
| Foreign Secretary | **Malcolm Rifkind** |
| Home Secretary | Michael Howard |
| Lord Chancellor | Lord Mackay of Clashfern |
| Scotland | *Michael Forsyth* |
| Wales | *William Hague* |
| Northern Ireland | Patrick Mayhew |
| Leader of the Commons | Tony Newton |
| Leader of the Lords | Lord Cranborne |
| Board of Trade (DTI) | **Ian Lang** |

| | |
|---|---|
| Defence | **Michael Portillo** |
| Health | **Stephen Dorrell** |
| Social Security | Peter Lilley |
| Environment | John Gummer |
| Transport | *George Young* |
| Education and Employment | Gillian Shephard |
| Agriculture | *Douglas Hogg* |
| National Heritage | **Virginia Bottomley** |
| Duchy of Lancaster (OPSS) | *Roger Freeman* |
| Chief Secretary to the Treasury | **William Waldegrave** |
| Minister without Portfolio (Party Chairman) | **Brian Mawhinney** |
| | |
| Chief Whip (non-Cabinet) | **Alastair Goodlad** |

# INDEX

Abacha, Sani, 519–20
Acland, Anthony, 225
Acland, Jenny, 183, 225
Adams, Gerry: general election (1992), 307; Hume talks, 436, 447, 448, 449–51, 454; peace process, 441; ceasefire message question (1993), 432, 442; back-channel exchanges, 447; response to Downing Street Declaration, 455–6, 457; US visit (1994), 456, 465; IRA ceasefire (1994), 459; Joint Framework Documents, 467; Mayhew meetings, 468, 476, 477–8; arms decommissioning issue, 470, 472, 474–5; demands, 478–9; US visit (1995), 480; US National Security Adviser's visit, 481; loss of credibility, 489; JM's wish to meet, 492
African National Congress (ANC), 126, 509
Ahern, Bertie, 465
Ailwyn Community School, 627–8
Aitken, Jonathan, 23, 568, 570–1, 619
Alderdice, John, 436, 487
Aldwych, bomb (1996), 490
Allan, Alex: Principal Private Secretary to Prime Minister, 319–20, 360; sterling crisis, 322, 329, 330, 335; Confidence Motion, 379; G7 summits, 526; Stephen Milligan's death, 557; Scott Inquiry, 560; sleaze issues, 568, 571; John Smith's death, 590; leadership election (1995), 622, 633, 644, 645; inflation strategy, 667; BSE crisis, 648; election (1997), 723, 725
Allason, Rupert, 565, 724
Alliance Party, 436
Allnutt, Reg, 40
Amato, Giuliano, 320, 321, 326–8, 582
Amess, David, 305
Amory, David Heathcoat, 379
Ancram, Michael, 462, 475–6, 477, 481
Anderson, Bruce, 360, 697
Andreotti, Giulio, 280, 281, 287, 582
Andrew, Rob, 509

Annesley, Hugh, 457, 491
Anti-Common Market League, 606
Appleyard, Leonard, 221, 238
Arafat, Yasser, 75, 521
arap Moi, Daniel, 116
Arbuthnot, James, 351
Archer, Jeffrey, 61, 182, 184, 187, 645, 722
Arens, Moshe, 123–4
Argentina, relations after Falklands War, 118, 123
armed forces, reduction (1991), 417–18; see also Gulf crisis and war
arts: JM's interest in, 402–3; London lobby, 404; public spending, 403–4, 405; National Lottery funding, 405, 410–11
Arts Council, 404, 410
Ashdown, Paddy: Gulf War, 224, 236, 237, 238; JM's relationship with, 302; Social Chapter vote, 378, 381 European Commission presidency issue, 597; on Conservative leadership, 638; election campaign (1997), 717
Atkins, Dulcie, 121
Atkins, Humphrey, 77
Atkins, Robert: election (1979), 64; career, 66; relationship with JM, 121; leadership election (1990), 191; election defeat (1997), 724
Attali, Jacques, 149
Attlee, Clement, 13, 21, 748
Audit Commission, 110, 248, 395
Austria, EU membership, 369, 588
Aziz, Tariq, 123

Bacher, Ali, 510
'back to basics', 387, 389, 554–5
Baddeley, Eric, 62
Baddeley, Olive (Macaulay), 62, 186
Baker, James, 118–19, 223, 230, 532
Baker, Kenneth: quoted, 70; Education Secretary, 103, 394; relationship with Thatcher, 103, 171; Party Chairman, 111, 135; on ERM entry, 164; Poll Tax issue, 170, 171; Home Secretary, 208, 386, 407;

763